Biblical Apocrypha

THE DISPUTE
OF THE JUDEO-CHRISTIAN WORLD

Constantin Vaughn

Erebus Society

Erebus Society

All rights reserved; no part of this publication may be reproduced or transmitted by any means, electronic, mechanical, photocopying or otherwise, without the prior written permission of the publisher except for the use of brief quotations in a book review.

First published in Great Britain in 2019
by Erebus Society

1st Edition

ISBN: 978-1-912461-18-9

www.erebussociety.com

Table of Contents

About this Book

The word "Apocrypha" is commonly applied in Christian religious contexts involving certain disagreements about biblical canonicity. In other words, gospells, epistles, letters, and other texts that were selectively left out of the final version of what we know now as "The Bible".

The pre-Christian-era Jewish translation of holy scriptures, into Greek, known as the Septuagint included the writings in dispute. However, the Jewish canon was not finalized until at least 100–200 A.D., at which time considerations of Greek language and beginnings of Christian acceptance of the Septuagint weighed against some of the texts. Some were not accepted by the Jews as part of the Hebrew Bible canon. Over several centuries of consideration, the books of the Septuagint were finally accepted into the Christian Old Testament, by A.D. 405 in the west, and by the end of the fifth century in the east. The Christian canon thus established was retained for over 1,000 years, even after the 11th-century schism that separated the church into the branches known as the Roman Catholic and Eastern Orthodox churches.

Those canons were not challenged until the Protestant Reformation (16th century), when both the Roman Catholic and Eastern Orthodox Churches reaffirmed them. The reformers rejected the parts of the canon that were not part of the Hebrew Bible and established a revised Protestant canon. Thus, concerning the Old Testament books, what is thought of as the "Protestant canon" is actually the final Hebrew canon. The differences can be found by looking here or by comparing the contents of the "Protestant" and Catholic Bibles, and they represent the narrowest Christian application of the term Apocrypha.

Among some Protestants, apocryphal began to take on extra or altered connotations: not just of dubious authenticity, but having spurious or false content, not just obscure but having hidden or suspect motives, since the contents of these texts did not comply with their reformed beliefs. Protestants were (and are) not unanimous in adopting those meanings. The Church of England agreed, and that view continues today throughout the Lutheran

Church, the worldwide Anglican Communion, and many other denominations. Whichever implied meaning is intended, "Apocrypha" was (and is) used primarily by Protestants, in reference to the books of questioned canonicity. Catholics and Orthodox sometimes avoid using the term in contexts where it might be considered disputatious or be misconstrued as yielding on the point of canonicity. Very few Protestant published Bibles include the apocryphal books in a separate section (rather like an appendix), so as not to intermingle them with their canonical books.

Explaining the Eastern Orthodox Church's canon is made difficult because of differences of perspective with the Roman Catholic church in the interpretation of how it was done. Those differences (in matters of jurisdictional authority) were contributing factors in the separation of the Roman Catholics and Orthodox around 1054, but the formation of the canon was largely complete (fully complete in the Catholic view) by the fifth century, six centuries before the separation. In the eastern part of the church, it took much of the fifth century also to come to agreement, but in the end it was accomplished. The canonical books thus established by the undivided church became canon for what was later to become Roman Catholic and Eastern Orthodox alike. The East did already differ from the West in not considering every question of canon yet settled, and it subsequently adopted a few more books into its Old Testament. It also allowed consideration of yet a few more to continue not fully decided, which led in some cases to adoption in one or more jurisdictions, but not all. Thus, there are today a few remaining differences of canon among Orthodox, and all Orthodox accept a few more books than appear in the Catholic canon. Protestants accept none of these additional books as canon either, but see them having roughly the same status as the earlier Apocrypha. As Protestant awareness of the Eastern Orthodox increases in nations like the United States, interest in the full Orthodox canon might also increase enough for them to be published in the Apocrypha of some Protestant Bibles. ZS

Before the fifth century, the Christian writings that were then under discussion for inclusion in the canon but had not yet been accepted were classified in a group known as the ancient antilegomenae. These were all candidates for the New Testament and included several books which were eventually accepted, such as: The Epistle to the Hebrews, 2 Peter, 3 John and the Revelation of John (Apocalypse). None of those accepted books can be considered Apocryphal now, since all Christendom accepts them as canonical. Of the uncanonized ones, the Early Church considered some heretical but viewed others quite well. Some Christians, in an extension of the meaning, might also consider the non-heretical books to be "apocryphal" along the manner of Martin Luther: not canon, but useful to read. This category includes books such as the Epistle of Barnabas, the Didache, and The Shepherd of Hermas which are sometimes referred to as the Apostolic Fathers.

The Apocryphon of James

 ames writes to [...]: Peace be with you from Peace, love from Love, grace from Grace, faith from Faith, life from Holy Life!

Since you asked that I send you a secret book which was revealed to me and Peter by the Lord, I could not turn you away or gainsay (?) you; but I have written it in the Hebrew alphabet and sent it to you, and you alone. But since you are a minister of the salvation of the saints, endeavor earnestly and take care not to rehearse this text to many - this that the Savior did not wish to tell to all of us, his twelve disciples. But blessed will they be who will be saved through the faith of this discourse.

I also sent you, ten months ago, another secret book which the Savior had revealed to me. Under the circumstances, however, regard that one as revealed to me, James; but this one ... [untranslatable fragments]

... the twelve disciples were all sitting together and recalling what the Savior had said to each one of them, whether in secret or openly, and putting it in books - But I was writing that which was in my book - lo, the Savior appeared, after departing from us while we gazed after him. And five hundred and fifty days since he had risen from the dead, we said to him, "Have you departed and removed yourself from us?" But Jesus said, "No, but I shall go to the place from whence I came. If you wish to come with me, come!"

They all answered and said, "If you bid us, we come."

He said, "Verily I say unto you, no one will ever enter the kingdom of heaven at my bidding, but (only) because you yourselves are full. Leave James and Peter to me, that I may fill them." And having called these two, he drew them aside and bade the rest occupy themselves with that which they were about.

The Savior said, "You have received mercy ...

(7 lines missing)

Do you not, then, desire to be filled? And your heart is drunken; do you not, then, desire to be sober? Therefore, be ashamed! Henceforth, waking or sleeping, remember that you have seen the Son of Man, and spoken with him in person, and listened to him in person. Woe to those who have seen the Son of Man; blessed will they be who have not seen the man, and they who have not consorted with him, and they who have not spoken with him, and they who have not listened to anything from him; yours is life! Know, then, that he healed you when you were ill, that you might reign. Woe to those who have found relief from their illness, for they will relapse into illness. Blessed are they who have not been ill, and have known relief before falling ill; yours is the kingdom of God. Therefore, I say to you, 'Become full, and leave no space within you empty, for he who is coming can mock you."

Then Peter replied, "Lo, three times you have told us, 'Become full'; but we are full." The Savior answered and said, "For this cause I have said to you, 'Become full,' that you may not be in want. They who are in want, however, will not be saved. For it is good to be full, and bad to be in want. Hence, just as it is good that you be in want and, conversely, bad that you be full, so he who is full is in want, and he who is in want does not become full as he who is in want becomes full, and he who has been filled, in turn attains due perfection. Therefore, you must be in want while it is possible to fill you, and be full while it is possible for you to be in want, so that you may be able to fill yourselves the more. Hence, become full of the Spirit, but be in want of reason, for reason <belongs to> the soul; in turn, it is (of the nature of) soul."

But I answered and said to him, "Lord, we can obey you if you wish, for we have forsaken our fathers and our mothers and our villages, and followed you. Grant us, therefore, not to be tempted by the devil, the evil one."

The Lord answered and said, "What is your merit if you do the will of the Father and it is not given to you from him as a gift while you are tempted by Satan? But if you are oppressed by Satan, and persecuted, and you do his (i.e., the Father's) will, I say that he will love you, and make you equal with me, and reckon you to have become beloved through his providence by your own choice. So will you not cease loving the flesh and being afraid of sufferings? Or do you not know that you have yet to be abused and to be accused unjustly; and have yet to be shut up in prison, and condemned unlawfully, and crucified <without> reason, and buried as I myself, by the evil one? Do you dare to spare the flesh, you for whom the Spirit is an encircling wall? If you consider how long the world existed <before> you, and how long it will exist after you, you will find that your life is one single day, and your sufferings one single hour. For the good will not enter into the world. Scorn death, therefore, and take thought for life! Remember my cross and my death, and you will live!"

But I answered and said to him, "Lord, do not mention to us the cross and death, for they are far from you."

The Lord answered and said, "Verily, I say unto you, none will be saved unless they believe in my cross. But those who have believed in my cross, theirs is the kingdom of God. Therefore, become seekers for death, like the dead who seek for life; for that which they seek is revealed to them. And what is there to trouble them? As for you, when you examine death, it will teach you election. Verily, I say unto you, none of those who fear death will be saved; for the kingdom belongs to those who put themselves to death. Become better than I; make yourselves like the son of the Holy Spirit!"

Then I asked him, "Lord, how shall we be able to prophesy to those who request us to prophesy to them? For there are many who ask us, and look to us to hear an oracle from us." The Lord answered and said, "Do you not know that the head of prophecy was cut off with John?"

But I said, "Lord, can it be possible to remove the head of prophecy?"

The Lord said to me, "When you come to know what 'head' means, and that prophecy issues from the head, (then) understand the meaning of 'Its head was removed.' At first I spoke to you in parables, and you did not understand; now I speak to you openly, and you (still) do not perceive. Yet, it was you who served me as a parable in parables, and as that which is open in the (words) that are open.

"Hasten to be saved without being urged! Instead, be eager of your own accord, and, if possible, arrive even before me; for thus the Father will love you."

"Come to hate hypocrisy and the evil thought; for it is the thought that gives birth to hypocrisy; but hypocrisy is far from truth."

"Do not allow the kingdom of heaven to wither; for it is like a palm shoot whose fruit has dropped down around it. They (i.e., the fallen fruit) put forth leaves, and after they had sprouted, they caused their womb to dry up. So it is also with the fruit which had grown from this single root; when it had been picked (?), fruit was borne by many (?). It (the root) was certainly good, (and) if it were possible for you to produce the new plants now, <you> would find it."

"Since I have already been glorified in this fashion, why do you hold me back in my eagerness to go? For after the labor, you have compelled me to stay with you another eighteen days for the sake of the parables. It was enough for some <to listen> to the teaching and understand 'The Shepherds' and 'The Seed' and 'The Building' and 'The Lamps of the Virgins' and 'The Wage of the Workmen' and the 'Didrachmae' and 'The Woman.'"

"Become earnest about the word! For as to the word, its first part is faith; the second, love; the third, works; for from these comes life. For the word is like a grain of wheat; when someone had sown it, he had faith in it; and when it had sprouted, he loved it, because he had seen many grains in place of one. And when he had worked, he was saved, because he had prepared it for food, (and) again he left (some) to sow. So also can you yourselves receive the kingdom of heaven; unless you receive this through knowledge, you will not be able to find it."

"Therefore, I say to you, be sober; do not be deceived! And many times have I said to you all together, and also to you alone, James, have I said, 'Be saved!' And I have commanded you to follow me, and I have taught you what to say before the archons. Observe that I have descended and have spoken and undergone tribulation, and carried off my crown after saving you. For I came down to dwell with you, so that you in turn might dwell with me. And, finding your houses unceiled, I have made my abode in the houses that could receive me at the time of my descent."

"Therefore, trust in me, my brethren; understand what the great light is. The Father has no need of me, - for a father does not need a son, but it is the son who needs the father - though I go to him. For the Father of the Son has no need of you."

"Hearken to the word, understand knowledge, love life, and no one will persecute you, nor will anyone oppress you, other than you yourselves."

"O you wretches; O you unfortunates; O you pretenders to the truth; O you falsifiers of knowledge; O you sinners against the Spirit: can you still bear to listen, when it behooved you to speak from the first? Can you still bear to sleep, when it behooved you to be awake from the first, so that the kingdom of heaven might receive you? Verily, I say unto you, had I been sent to those who listen to me, and had I spoken with them, I would never have come down to earth. So, then, be ashamed for these things."

"Behold, I shall depart from you and go away, and do not wish to remain with you any longer, just as your yourselves have not wished it. Now, therefore, follow me quickly. This is why I say unto you, 'For your sakes I came down.' You are the beloved; you are they who will be the cause of life in many. Invoke the Father, implore God often, and he will give to you. Blessed is he who has seen you with Him when He was proclaimed among the angels, and glorified among the saints; yours is life. Rejoice, and be glad, as sons of God. Keep his will, that you may be saved; accept reproof from me and save yourselves. I intercede on your behalf with the Father, and he will forgive you much."

And when we had heard these words, we became glad, for we had been grieved at the words we have mentioned before. But when he saw us rejoicing, he said, "Woe to you who lack an advocate! Woe to you who stand in need of grace! Blessed will they be who have spoken out and obtained grace for themselves. Liken yourselves to foreigners; of what sort are they in the eyes of your city? Why are you disturbed when you cast yourselves away of your own accord and separate yourselves from your city? Why do you abandon your dwelling place of your own accord, making it ready for those who want to dwell in it? O you outcasts and fugitives, woe to you, for you will be caught! Or do you perhaps think that the Father is a lover of mankind, or that he is won over without prayers, or that he grants remission to one on another's behalf, or that he bears with one who asks? - For he knows the desire, and also what it is that the flesh needs! - (Or do you think) that it is not this (flesh) that desires the soul? For without the soul, the body does not sin, just as the soul is not saved without the spirit. But if the soul is saved (when it is) without evil, and the spirit is also saved, then the body becomes free from sin. For it is the spirit that raises the soul, but the body that kills it; that is, it is it (the soul) which kills itself. Verily, I say unto you, he will not forgive the soul the sin by any means, nor the flesh the guilt; for none of those who have worn the flesh will be saved. For do you think that many have found the kingdom of heaven? Blessed is he who has seen himself as a fourth one in heaven!"

When we heard these words, we were distressed. But when he saw that we were distressed, he said, "For this cause I tell you this, that you may know yourselves. For the kingdom of heaven is like an ear of grain after it had sprouted in a field. And when it had ripened, it scattered its fruit and again filled the field with ears for another year. You also, hasten to reap an ear of life for yourselves, that you may be filled with the kingdom!"

"And as long as I am with you, give heed to me, and obey me; but when I depart from you, remember me. And remember me because when I was with you, you did not know me. Blessed will they be who have known me; woe to those who have heard and have not believed! Blessed will they be who have not see, yet have believed!"

"And once more I prevail upon you, for I am revealed to you building a house which is of great value to you when you find shelter beneath it, just as it will be able to stand by your neighbors' house when it threatens to fall. Verily, I say unto you, woe to those for whose sakes I was sent down to this place; blessed will they be who ascend to the Father! Once more I reprove you, you who are; become like those who are not, that you may be with those who are not."

"Do not make the kingdom of heaven a desert within you. Do not be proud because of the light that illumines, but be to yourselves as I myself am to you. For your sakes I have placed myself under the curse, that you may be saved."

But Peter replied to these words and said, "Sometimes you urge us on to the kingdom of heaven, and then again you turn us back, Lord; sometimes you persuade and draw us to faith and promise us life, and then again you cast us forth from the kingdom of heaven."

But the Lord answered and said to us, "I have given you faith many times; moreover, I have revealed myself to you, James, and you (all) have not known me. Now again, I see you rejoicing many times; and when you are elated at the promise of life, are you yet sad, and do you grieve, when you are instructed in the kingdom? But you, through faith and knowledge, have received life. Therefore, disdain the rejection when you hear it, but when you hear the promise, rejoice the more. Verily, I say unto you, he who will receive life and believe in the kingdom will never leave it, not even if the Father wishes to banish him."

"These are the things that I shall tell you so far; now, however, I shall ascend to the place from whence I came. But you, when I was eager to go, have cast me out, and instead of accompanying me, you have pursued me. But pay heed to the glory that awaits me, and, having opened your heart, listen to the hymns that await me up in the heavens; for today I must take (my place at) the right hand of the Father. But I have said (my) last word to you, and I shall depart from you, for a chariot of spirit has borne me aloft, and from this moment on, I shall strip myself, that I may clothe myself. But give heed; blessed are they who have proclaimed the Son before his descent, that when I have come, I might ascend (again). Thrice blessed are they who were proclaimed by the Son before they came to be, that you might have a portion among them."

Having said these words, he departed. But we bent (our) knee(s), I and Peter, and gave thanks, and sent our heart(s) upwards to heaven. We heard with our ears, and saw with our eyes, the noise of wars, and a trumpet blare, and a great turmoil.

And when we had passed beyond that place, we sent our mind(s) farther upwards, and saw with our eyes and heard with our ears hymns, and angelic benedictions, and angelic rejoicing. And heavenly majesties were singing praise, and we, too, rejoiced.

After this again, we wished to send our spirit upward to the Majesty, and after ascending, we were not permitted to see or hear anything, for the other disciples called us and asked us, "What did you hear from the Master. And what has he said to you? And where did he go?"

But we answered them, "He has ascended, and has given us a pledge, and promised life to us all, and revealed to us children (?) who are to come after us, after bidding us love them, as we would be saved for their sakes."

And when they heard (this), they indeed believed the revelation, but were displeased about those to be born. And so, not wishing to give them offense, I sent each one to another place.

But I myself went up to Jerusalem, praying that I might obtain a portion among the beloved, who will be made manifest. And I pray that the beginning may come from you, for thus I shall be capable of salvation, since they will be enlightened through me, by my faith - and through another (faith) that is better than mine, for I would that mine be the lesser. Endeavor earnestly, then, to make yourself like them, and pray that you may obtain a portion with them. For because of what I have said, the Savior did not make the revelation to us for their sakes. We do, indeed, proclaim a portion with those for whom the proclamation was made - those whom the Lord has made his sons.

The Apocryphon of John

he teaching of the savior, and the revelation of the mysteries and the things hidden in silence, even thesethings which he taught John, his disciple.

And it happened one day, when John, the brother of James - who are the sons of Zebedee - had come up tothe temple, that a Pharisee named Arimanius approached him and said to him, "Where is your master whomyou followed?" And he said to him, "He has gone to the place from which he came." The Pharisee said tohim, "With deception did this Nazarene deceive you (pl.), and he filled your ears with lies, and closed yourhearts (and) turned you from the traditions of your fathers."

When I, John, heard these things I turned away from the temple to a desert place. And I grieved greatly in myheart, saying, "How then was the savior appointed, and why was he sent into the world by his Father, andwho is his Father who sent him, and of what sort is that aeon to which we shall go? For what did he meanwhen he said to us, 'This aeon to which you will go is of the type of the imperishable aeon, but he did notteach us concerning the latter, of what sort it is."

Straightway, while I was contemplating these things, behold, the heavens opened and the whole creationwhich is below heaven shone, and the world was shaken. I was afraid, and behold I saw in the light a youthwho stood by me. While I looked at him, he became like an old man. And he changed his likeness (again),becoming like a servant. There was not a plurality before me, but there was a likeness with multiple forms inthe light, and the likenesses appeared through each other, and the likeness had three forms.

He said to me, "John, John, why do you doubt, or why are you afraid? You are not unfamiliar with this image,are you? - that is, do not be timid! - I am the one who is with you (pl.) always.

I am the Father, I am the Mother, I am the Son. I am the undefiled and incorruptible one. Now I have come to teachyou what is and what was and what will come to pass, that you may know the things which are not revealedand those which are revealed, and to teach you concerning the unwavering race of the perfect Man. Now,therefore, lift up your face, that you may receive the things that I shall teach you today, and may tell them toyour fellow spirits who are from the unwavering race of the perfect Man."

And I asked to know it, and he said to me, "The Monad is a monarchy with nothing above it. It is he whoexists as God and Father of everything, the invisible One who is above everything, who exists as incorruption,which is in the pure light into which no eye can look.

"He is the invisible Spirit, of whom it is not right to think of him as a god, or something similar. For he is morethan a god, since there is nothing above him, for no one lords it over him. For he does not exist in somethinginferior to him, since everything exists in him. For it is he who establishes himself.

He is eternal, since he does not need anything. For he is total perfection. He did not lack anything, that hemight be completed by it; rather he is always completely perfect in light. He is illimitable, since there is no oneprior to him to set limits to him. He is unsearchable, since there exists no one prior to him to examine him. Heis immeasurable, since there was no one prior to him to measure him. He is invisible, since no one saw him.He is eternal, since he exists eternally. He is ineffable, since no one was able to comprehend him to speakabout him. He is unnameable, since there is no one prior to him to give him a name.

"He is immeasurable light, which is pure, holy (and) immaculate. He is ineffable, being perfect inincorruptibility. (He is) not in perfection, nor in blessedness, nor in divinity, but he is far superior. He is notcorporeal nor is he incorporeal. He is neither large nor is he small. There is no way to say, 'What is hisquantity?' or, 'What is his quality?', for no one can know him. He is not someone among (other) beings, ratherhe is far superior. Not that he is (simply) superior, but his essence does not partake in the aeons nor in time. For he who partakes in an aeon was prepared beforehand. Time was not apportioned to him, since he doesnot receive anything from another, for it would be received on loan. For he who precedes someone does notlack, that he may receive from him. For rather, it is the latter that looks expectantly at him in his light.

"For the perfection is majestic. He is pure, immeasurable mind. He is an aeon-giving aeon. He is life-givinglife. He is a blessedness-giving blessed one. He is knowledge-giving knowledge. He is goodness-givinggoodness. He is mercy and redemption-giving mercy. He is grace-giving grace, not because he possesses it,but because he gives the immeasurable, incomprehensible light.

"How am I to speak with you about him? His aeon is indestructible, at rest and existing in silence, reposing(and) being prior to everything. For he is the head of all the aeons, and it is he who gives them strength in hisgoodness. For we know not the ineffable things, and we do not understand what is immeasurable, except forhim who came forth from him, namely (from) the Father. For it is he who told it to us alone. For it is he wholooks at himself in his light which surrounds him, namely the spring of the water of life. And it is he who givesto all the aeons and in every way, (and) who gazes upon his image which he sees in the spring of the Spirit. Itis he who puts his desire in his water-light which is in the spring of the pure light-water which surrounds him.

"And his thought performed a deed and she came forth, namely she who had appeared before him in theshine of his light. This is the first power which was before all of them (and) which came forth from his mind,She is the forethought of the All - her light shines like his light - the perfect power which is the image of theinvisible, virginal Spirit who is perfect. The first power, the glory of Barbelo, the perfect glory in the aeons,the glory of the revelation, she glorified the virginal Spirit and it was she who praised him, because thanks tohim she had come forth. This is the first thought, his image; she became the womb of everything, for it is shewho is prior to them all, the Mother-Father, the first man, the holy Spirit, the thrice-male, the thrice-powerful,the thrice-named androgynous one, and the eternal aeon among the invisible ones, and the first to come forth.

"<She> requested from the invisible, virginal Spirit - that is Barbelo - to give her foreknowledge. And theSpirit consented. And when he had consented, the foreknowledge came forth, and it stood by theforethought; it originates from the thought of the invisible, virginal Spirit. It glorified him and his perfect power,Barbelo, for it was for her sake that it had come into being.

"And she requested again to grant her indestructibility, and he consented. When he had consented,indestructibility came forth, and it stood by the thought and the foreknowledge. It glorified the invisible Oneand Barbelo, the one for whose sake they had come into being.

"And Barbelo requested to grant her eternal life. And the invisible Spirit consented. And when he hadconsented, eternal life came forth, and they attended and glorified the invisible Spirit and Barbelo, the one forwhose sake they had come into being.

"And she requested again to grant her truth. And the invisible Spirit consented. And when he had consented,truth came forth, and they attended and glorified the invisible, excellent Spirit and his Barbelo, the one forwhose sake they had come into being.

"This is the pentad of the aeons of the Father, which is the first man, the image of the invisible Spirit; it is theforethought, which Barbelo, and the thought, and the foreknowledge, and the indestructibility, and the eternal-life, and the truth. This is the androgynous pentad of the aeons, which is the decad of the aeons, which is theFather.

"And he looked at Barbelo with the pure light which surrounds the invisible Spirit, and (with) his spark, andshe conceived from him. He begot a spark of light with a light resembling blessedness. But it does not equalhis greatness. This was an only-begotten child of the Mother-Father which had come forth; it is the onlyoffspring, the only-begotten one of the Father, the pure Light.

"And the invisible, virginal Spirit rejoiced over the light which came forth, that which was brought forth first bythe first power of his forethought, which is Barbelo. And he anointed it with his goodness until it becameperfect, not lacking in any goodness, because he had anointed it with the goodness of the invisible Spirit. Andit attended him as he poured upon it. And immediately when it had received from the Spirit, it glorified theholy Spirit and the perfect forethought, for whose sake it had come forth.

"And it requested to give it a fellow worker, which is the mind, and he consented gladly. And when theinvisible Spirit had consented, the mind came forth, and it attended Christ, glorifying him and Barbelo. And allthese came into being in silence.

"And the mind wanted to perform a deed through the word of the invisible Spirit. And his will became a deedand it appeared with the mind; and the light glorified it. And the word followed the will. For because of theword, Christ the divine Autogenes created everything. And the eternal life <and> his will and the mind andthe foreknowledge attended and glorified the invisible Spirit and Barbelo, for whose sake they had come intobeing.

"And the holy Spirit completed the divine Autogenes, his son, together with Barbelo, that he may attend themighty and invisible, virginal Spirit as the divine Autogenes, the Christ whom he had honored with a mightyvoice. He came forth through the forethought. And the invisible, virginal Spirit placed the divine Autogenes oftruth over everything. And he subjected to him every authority, and the truth which is in him, that he mayknow the All which had been called with a name exalted above every name. For that name will be mentionedto those who are worthy of it.

"For from the light, which is the Christ, and the indestructibility, through the gift of the Spirit the four lights(appeared) from the divine Autogenes. He expected that they might attend him. And the three (are) will,thought, and life. And the four powers (are) understanding, grace, perception, and prudence. And gracebelongs to the light-aeon Armozel, which is the first angel. And there are three other aeons with this aeon:grace, truth, and form. And the second light (is) Oriel, who has been placed over the second aeon. And thereare three other aeons with him: conception, perception, and memory. And the third light is Daveithai, who hasbeen placed over the third aeon.And there are three other aeons with him: understanding, love, and idea. And the fourth aeon was placedover the fourth light Eleleth. And there are three other aeons with him: perfection, peace, and wisdom. Theseare the four lights which attend the divine Autogenes, (and) these are the twelve aeons which attend the sonof the mighty one, the Autogenes, the Christ, through the will and the gift of the invisible Spirit. And the twelveaeons belong to the son of the Autogenes. And all things were established by the will of the holy Spiritthrough the Autogenes.

"And from the foreknowledge of the perfect mind, through the revelation of the will of the invisible Spirit andthe will of the Autogenes, <the> perfect Man (appeared), the first revelation, and the truth. It is he whom thevirginal Spirit called Pigera-Adamas, and he placed him over the first aeon with the mighty one, theAutogenes, the Christ, by the first light Armozel; and with him are his powers. And the invisible one gave hima spiritual, invincible power. And he spoke and glorified and praised the invisible Spirit, saying, 'It is for thysake that everything has come into being and everything will return to thee. I shall praise and glorify thee andthe Autogenes and the aeons, the three: the Father, the Mother, and the Son, the perfect power.'

"And he placed his son Seth over the second aeon in the presence of the second light Oriel. And in the thirdaeon the seed of Seth was placed over the third light Daveithai. And the souls of the saints were placed(there). And in the fourth aeon the souls were placed of those who do not know the Pleroma and who didnot repent at once, but who persisted for a while and repented afterwards; they are by the fourth light Eleleth.These are creatures which glorify the invisible Spirit.

"And the Sophia of the Epinoia, being an aeon, conceived a thought from herself and the conception of theinvisible Spirit and foreknowledge. She wanted to bring forth a likeness out of herself without the consent ofthe Spirit, - he had not approved - and without her consort, and without his consideration. And though theperson of her maleness had not approved, and she had not found her agreement, and she had thought withoutthe consent of the Spirit and the knowledge of her agreement, (yet) she brought forth. And because of theinvincible power which is in her, her thought did not remain idle, and something came out of her which wasimperfect and different from her appearance, because she had created it without her consort. And it was dissimilar to the likeness of its mother, for it has another form.

"And when she saw (the consequences of) her desire, it changed into a form of a lion-faced serpent. And itseyes were like lightning fires which flash. She cast it away from her, outside that place, that no one of theimmortal ones might see it, for she had created it in ignorance. And she surrounded it with a luminous cloud,and she placed a throne in the middle of the cloud that no one might see it except the holy Spirit who is calledthe mother of the living. And she called his name Yaltabaoth.

"This is the first archon who took a great power from his mother. And he removed himself from her andmoved away from the places in which he was born. He became strong and created for himself other aeonswith a flame of luminous fire which (still) exists now. And he joined with his arrogance which is in him andbegot authorities for himself. The name of the first one is Athoth, whom the generations call the reaper. Thesecond one is Harmas, who is the eye of envy. The third one is Kalila-Oumbri. The fourth one is Yabel. Thefifth one is Adonaiou, who is called Sabaoth. The sixth one is Cain, whom the generations of men call the sun.The seventh is Abel. The eighth is Abrisene. The ninth is Yobel. The tenth is Armoupieel. The eleventh is-Melceir-Adonein. The twelfth is Belias, it is he who is over the depth of Hades. And he placed seven kings -each corresponding to the firmaments of heaven - over the seven heavens, and five over the depth of theabyss, that they may reign. And he shared his fire with them, but he did not send forth from the power of thelight which he had taken from his mother, for he is ignorant darkness.

"And when the light had mixed with the darkness, it caused the darkness to shine. And when the darknesshad mixed with the light, it darkened the light and it became neither light nor dark, but it became dim.

"Now the archon who is weak has three names. The first name is Yaltabaoth, the second is Saklas, and thethird is Samael. And he is impious in his arrogance which is in him. For he said, 'I am God and there is noother God beside me,' for he is ignorant of his strength, the place from which he had come.

"And the archons created seven powers for themselves, and the powers created for themselves six angels foreach one until they became 365 angels. And these are the bodies belonging with the names: the first is Athoth,a he has a sheep's face; the second is Eloaiou, he has a donkey's face; the third is Astaphaios, he has ahyena's face; the fourth is Yao, he has a serpent's face with seven heads; the fifth is Sabaoth, he has adragon's face; the sixth is Adonin, he had a monkey's face; the seventh is Sabbede, he has a shining fire-face.This is the sevenness of the week.

"But Yaltabaoth had a multitude of faces, more than all of them, so that he could put a face before all of them,according to his desire, when he is in the midst of seraphs. He shared his fire with them; therefore he becamelord over them. Because of the power of the glory he possessed of his mother's light, he called himself God.And he did not obey the place from which he came. And he united the seven powers in his thought with theauthorities which were with him. And when he spoke it happened. And he named each power beginning withthe highest: the first is goodness with the first (authority), Athoth; the second is foreknowledge with thesecond one, Eloaio; and the third is divinity with the third one, Astraphaio); the fourth is lordship with thefourth one, Yao; the fifth is kingdom with the fifth one, Sabaoth; the sixth is envy with the sixth one, Adonein;the seventh is understanding with the seventh one, Sabbateon. And these have a firmament corresponding toeach aeon-heaven.They were given names according to the glory which belongs to heaven for the destruction of the powers.And in the names which were given to them by their Originator there was power. But the names which weregiven them according to the glory which belongs to heaven mean for them destruction and powerlessness.Thus they have two names.

"And having created [...] everything, he organized according to the model of the first aeons which had comeinto being, so that he might create them like the indestructible ones. Not because he had seen theindestructible ones, but the power in him, which he had taken from his mother, produced in him the likenessof the cosmos. And when he saw the creation which surrounds him, and the multitude of the angels aroundhim which had come forth from him, he said to them, 'I am a jealous God, and there is no other God be-sideme.' But by announcing this he indicated to the angels who attended him that there exists another God. For ifthere were no other one, of whom would he be jealous?

"Then the mother began to move to and fro. She became aware of the deficiency when the brightness of herlight diminished. And she became dark because her consort had not agreed with her."And I said, "Lord, what does it mean that she moved to and fro?" But he smiled and said, "Do not think it is,as Moses said, 'above the waters.' No, but when she had seen the wicked-ness which had happened, and thetheft which her son had committed, she repented. And she was overcome by forgetfulness in the darkness ofigno-rance and she began to be ashamed. And she did not dare to return, but she was moving about. And themoving is the going to and fro.

"And the arrogant one took a power from his mother. For he was ignorant, thinking that there existed noother except his mother alone. And when he saw the multitude of the angels which he had created, then heexalted himself above them.

"And when the mother recognized that the garment of darkness was imperfect, then she knew that herconsort had not agreed with her. She repented with much weeping. And the whole pleroma heard the prayerof her repentance, and they praised on her behalf the invisible, virginal Spirit. And he consented; and whenthe invisible Spirit had consented, the holy Spirit poured over her from their whole pleroma. For it was nother consort who came to her, but he came to her through the pleroma in order that he might correct herdeficiency. And she was taken up not to her own aeon but above her son, that she might be in the ninth untilshe has corrected her deficiency.

"And a voice came forth from the exalted aeon-heaven: 'The Man exists and the son of Man.' And the chiefarchon, Yaltabaoth, heard (it) and thought that the voice had come from his mother. And he did not knowfrom where it came. And he taught them, the holy and perfect Mother-Father, the complete foreknowledge,the image of the invisible one who is the Father of the all (and) through whom everything came into being, thefirst Man. For he revealed his likeness in a human form.

"And the whole aeon of the chief archon trembled, and the foundations of the abyss shook. And of the waterswhich are above matter, the underside was illuminated by the appearance of his image which had beenrevealed. And when all the authorities and the chief archon looked, they saw the whole region of theunderside which was illuminated. And through the light they saw the form of the image in the water.

"And he said to the authorities which attend him, 'Come, let us create a man according to the image of Godand according to our likeness, that his image may become a light for us.' And they created by means of theirrespective powers in correspondence with the characteristics which were given. And each authority supplieda characteristic in the form of the image which he had seen in its natural (form). He created a being accordingto the likeness of the first, perfect Man. And they said, 'Let us call him Adam, that his name may become apower of light for us.'

"And the powers began: the first one, goodness, created a bone-soul; and the second, foreknowledge,created a sinew-soul; the third, divinity, created a flesh-soul; and the fourth, the lordship, created amarrow-soul; the fifth, kingdom created a blood-soul; the sixth, envy, created a skin-soul; the seventh,understanding, created a hair-soul. And the multitude of the angels attended him and they received from thepowers the seven substances of the natural (form) in order to create the proportions of the limbs and theproportion of the rump and the proper working together of each of the parts.

"The first one began to create the head. Eteraphaope-Abron created his head; Meniggesstroeth created thebrain; Asterechme (created) the right eye; Thaspomocha, the left eye; Yeronumos, the right ear; Bissoum, theleft ear; Akioreim, the nose; Banen-Ephroum, the lips; Amen, the teeth; Ibikan, the molars; Basiliademe, thetonsils; Achcha, the uvula; Adaban, the neck; Chaaman, the vertebrae; Dearcho, the throat; Tebar, the rightshoulder; [...], the left shoulder; Mniarcon, the right elbow; [...], the left elbow; Abitrion, the right underarm;Evanthen, the left underarm; Krys, the right hand; Beluai, the left hand; Treneu, the fingers of the right hand;Balbel, the fingers of the left hand; Kriman, the nails of the hands;Astrops, the right breast; Barroph, the left breast; Baoum, the right shoulder joint; Ararim, the left shoulder-joint; Areche, the belly; Phthave, the navel; Senaphim, the abdomen; Arachethopi, the right ribs; Zabedo, theleft ribs; Barias, the right hip; Phnouth the left hip; Abenlenarchei, the marrow; Chnoumeninorin, the bones;Gesole, the stomach; Agromauna, the heart; Bano, the lungs; Sostrapal, the liver; Anesimalar, the spleen;Thopithro, the intestines; Biblo, the kidneys; Roeror, the sinews; Taphreo, the spine of the body;Ipouspoboba, the veins; Bineborin, the arteries; Atoimenpsephei, theirs are the breaths which are in all thelimbs; Entholleia, all the flesh; Bedouk, the right buttock (?); Arabeei, the left penis; Eilo, the testicles;Sorma, the genitals; Gorma-Kaiochlabar, the right thigh; Nebrith, the left thigh; Pserem, the kidneys of theright leg; Asaklas, the left kidney; Ormaoth, the right leg; Emenun, the left leg; Knyx, the right shin-bone;Tupelon, the left shin-bone; Achiel, the right knee; Phnene, the left knee; Phiouthrom, the right foot; Boabel,its toes; Trachoun, the left foot; Phikna, its toes; Miamai, the nails of the feet; Labernioum - .

"And those who were appointed over all of these are: Zathoth, Armas, Kalila, Jabel, (Sabaoth, Cain, Abel).And those who are particularly active in the limbs (are) the head Diolimodraza, the neck Yammeax, the rightshoulder Yakouib, the left shoulder Verton, the right hand Oudidi, the left one Arbao, the fingers of the righthand Lampno, the fingers of the left hand Leekaphar, the right breast Barbar, the left breast Imae, the chestPisandriaptes, the right shoulder joint Koade, the left shoulder joint Odeor, the right ribs Asphixix, the left ribsSynogchouta, the belly Arouph, the womb Sabalo, the right thigh Charcharb, the left thigh Chthaon, all thegenitals Bathinoth, the right leg Choux, the left leg Charcha, the right shin-bone Aroer, the left shin-bone-Toechtha, the right knee Aol, the left knee Charaner, the right foot Bastan, its toes Archentechtha, the leftfoot Marephnounth, its toes Abrana.

"Seven have power over all of these: Michael, Ouriel, Asmenedas, Saphasatoel, Aarmouriam, Richram,Amiorps. And the ones who are in charge over the senses (are) Archendekta; and he who is in charge overthe receptions (is) Deitharbathas; and he who is in charge over the imagination (is) Oummaa; and he who isover the composition Aachiaram, and he who is over the whole impulse Riaramnacho.

"And the origin of the demons which are in the whole body is determined to be four: heat, cold, wetness, anddryness. And the mother of all of them is matter. And he who reigns over the heat (is) Phloxopha; and hewho reigns over the cold is Oroorrothos; and he who reigns over what is dry (is) Erimacho; and he whoreigns over the wetness (is) Athuro. And the mother of all of these, Onorthochrasaei, stands in their midst,since she is illimitable, and she mixes with all of them. And she is truly matter, for they are nourished by her.

"The four chief demons are: Ephememphi, who belongs to pleasure, Yoko, who belongs to desire,Nenentophni, who belongs to grief, Blaomen, who belongs to fear. And the mother of them all isAesthesis-Ouch-Epi-Ptoe. And from the four demons passions came forth. And from grief (came) envy,jealousy, distress, trouble, pain, callousness, anxiety, mourning, etc. And from pleasure much wickednessarises, and empty pride, and similar things. And from desire (comes) anger, wrath, and bitterness, and bitterpassion, and unsatedness, and similar things. And from fear (comes) dread, fawning, agony, and shame. Allof these are like useful things as well as evil things. But the insight into their true (character) is Anaro, who isthe head of the material soul, for it belongs with the seven senses, Ouch-Epi-Ptoe.

"This is the number of the angels: together they are 365. They all worked on it until, limb for limb, the naturaland the material body was completed by them. Now there are other ones in charge over the remainingpassions whom I did not mention to you. But if you wish to know them, it is written in the book of Zoroaster.And all the angels and demons worked until they had constructed the natural body. And their product wascompletely inactive and motionless for a long time.

"And when the mother wanted to retrieve the power which she had given to the chief archon, she petitionedthe Mother-Father of the All, who is most merciful. He sent, by means of the holy decree, the five lights downupon the place of the angels of the chief archon. They advised him that they should bring forth the power ofthe mother. And they said to Yaltabaoth, 'Blow into his face something of your spirit and his body will arise.'And he blew into his face the spirit which is the power of his mother; he did not know (this), for he exists inignorance. And the power of the mother went out of Yaltabaoth into the natural body, which they hadfashioned after the image of the one who exists from the beginning. The body moved and gained strength, andit was luminous.

"And in that moment the rest of the powers became jealous, because he had come into being through all ofthem and they had given their power to the man, and his intelligence was greater than that of those who hadmade him, and greater than that of the chief archon. And when they recognized that he was luminous, and thathe could think better than they, and that he was free from wickedness, they took him and threw him into thelowest region of all matter.

"But the blessed One, the Mother-Father, the beneficent and merciful One, had mercy on the power of themother which had been brought forth out of the chief archon, for they (the archons) might gain power overthe natural and perceptible body. And he sent, through his beneficent Spirit and his great mercy, a helper toAdam, luminous Epinoia which comes out of him, who is called Life. And she assists the whole creature, bytoiling with him and by restoring him to his fullness and by teaching him about the descent of his seed (and) byteaching him about the way of ascent, (which is) the way he came down. And the luminous Epinoia washidden in Adam, in order that the archons might not know her, but that the Epinoia might be a correction ofthe deficiency of the mother.

"And the man came forth because of the shadow of the light which is in him. And his thinking was superior toall those who had made him. When they looked up, they saw that his thinking was superior. And they tookcounsel with the whole array of archons and angels. They took fire and earth and water and mixed themtogether with the four fiery winds. And they wrought them together and caused a great disturbance. And theybrought him (Adam) into the shadow of death, in order that they might form (him) again from earth and waterand fire and the spirit which originates in matter, which is the ignorance of darkness and desire, and theircounterfeit spirit. This is the tomb of the newly-formed body with which the robbers had clothed the man, the-bond of forgetfulness; and he became a mortal man. This is the first one who came down, and the firstseparation. But the Epinoia of the light which was in him, she is the one who was to awaken his thinking.

"And the archons took him and placed him in paradise. And they said to him, 'Eat, that is at leisure,' for theirluxury is bitter and their beauty is depraved. And their luxury is deception and their trees are godlessness andtheir fruit is deadly poison and their promise is death. And the tree of their life they had placed in the midst ofparadise.

"And I shall teach you (pl.) what is the mystery of their life, which is the plan which they made together, whichis the likeness of their spirit. The root of this (tree) is bitter and its branches are death, its shadow is hate anddeception is in its leaves, and its blossom is the ointment of evil, and its fruit is death and desire is its seed,and it sprouts in darkness. The dwelling place of those who taste from it is Hades, and the darkness is theirplace of rest.

"But what they call the tree of knowledge of good and evil, which is the Epinoia of the light, they stayed infront of it in order that he (Adam) might not look up to his fullness and recognize the nakedness of hisshamefulness. But it was I who brought about that they ate."And to I said to the savior,

"Lord, was it not the serpent that taught Adam to eat?" The savior smiled andsaid, "The serpent taught them to eat from wickedness of begetting, lust, (and) destruction, that he (Adam)might be useful to him. And he (Adam) knew that he was disobedient to him (the chief archon) due to light ofthe Epinoia which is in him, which made him more correct in his thinking than the chief archon. And (thelatter) wanted to bring about the power which he himself had given him. And he brought a forgetfulness overAdam."And I said to the savior, "What is the forgetfulness?" And he said "It is not the way Moses wrote (and) youheard. For he said in his first book, 'He put him to sleep' (Gn 2:21), but (it was) in his perception. For also hesaid through the prophet, 'I will make their hearts heavy, that they may not pay attention and may not see' (Is6:10).

"Then the Epinoia of the light hid herself in him (Adam). And the chief archon wanted to bring her out of hisrib. But the Epinoia of the light cannot be grasped. Although darkness pursued her, it did not catch her. Andhe brought a part of his power out of him. And he made another creature, in the form of a woman, accordingto the likeness of the Epinoia which had appeared to him. And he brought the part which he had taken fromthe power of the man into the female creature, and not as Moses said, 'his rib-bone.'

"And he (Adam) saw the woman beside him. And in that moment the luminous Epinoia appeared, and shelifted the veil which lay over his mind. And he became sober from the drunkenness of darkness. And herecognized his counter-image, and he said, 'This is indeed bone of my bones and flesh of my flesh.' Thereforethe man will leave his father and his mother, and he will cleave to his wife, and they will both be one flesh. Forthey will send him his consort, and he will leave his father and his mother ...

(3 lines unreadable)

"And our sister Sophia (is) she who came down in innocence in order to rectify her deficiency. Therefore shewas called Life, which is the mother of the living, by the foreknowledge of the sovereignty of heaven. Andthrough her they have tasted the perfect Knowledge. I appeared in the form of an eagle on the tree ofknowledge, which is the Epinoia from the foreknowledge of the pure light, that I might teach them andawaken them out of the depth of sleep. For they were both in a fallen state, and they recognized theirnakedness. The Epinoia appeared to them as a light; she awakened their thinking.

"And when Yaltabaoth noticed that they withdrew from him, he cursed his earth. He found the woman as shewas preparing herself for her husband. He was lord over her, though he did not know the mystery which hadcome to pass through the holy decree. And they were afraid to blame him. And he showed his angels hisignorance which is in him. And he cast them out of paradise and he clothed them in gloomy darkness. Andthe chief archon saw the virgin who stood by Adam, and that the luminous Epinoia of life had appeared inher. And Yaltabaoth was full of ignorance. And when the foreknowledge of the All noticed (it), she sent someand they snatched life out of Eve.

"And the chief archon seduced her and he begot in her two sons; the first and the second (are) Eloim andYave. Eloim has a bear-face and Yave has a cat-face. The one is righteous but the other is unrighteous.(Yave is righteous but Eloim is unrighteous.) Yave he set over the fire and the wind, and Eloim he set over thewater and the earth. And these he called with the names Cain and Abel with a view to deceive.

"Now up to the present day, sexual intercourse continued due to the chief archon. And he planted sexualdesire in her who belongs to Adam. And he produced through intercourse the copies of the bodies, and heinspired them with his counterfeit spirit.

"And the two archons he set over principalities, so that they might rule over the tomb. And when Adamrecognized the likeness of his own foreknowledge, he begot the likeness of the son of man. He called himSeth, according to the way of the race in the aeons. Likewise, the mother also sent down her spirit, which isin her likeness and a copy of those who are in the pleroma, for she will prepare a dwelling place for the aeonswhich will come down. And he made them drink water of forgetfulness, from the chief archon, in order thatthey might not know from where they came. Thus, the seed remained for a while assisting (him), in order that,when the Spirit comes forth from the holy aeons, he may raise up and heal him from the deficiency, that thewhole pleroma may (again) become holy and faultless."And I said to the savior,

"Lord, will all the souls then be brought safely into the pure light?" He answered andsaid to me,

"Great things have arisen in your mind, for it is difficult to explain them to others except to thosewho are from the immovable race. Those on whom the Spirit of life will descend and (with whom) he will bewith the power, they will be saved and become perfect and be worthy of the greatness and be purified in thatplace from all wickedness and the involvements in evil.Then they have no other care than the incorruption alone, to which they direct their attention from here on,without anger or envy or jealousy or desire and greed of anything. They are not affected by anything exceptthe state of being in the flesh alone, which they bear while looking expectantly for the time when they will bemet by the receivers (of the body). Such then are worthy of the imperishable, eternal life and the calling. Forthey endure everything and bear up under everything, that they may finish the good fight and inherit eternallife."I said to him, "Lord, the souls of those who did not do these works (but) on whom the power and Spiritdescended, (will they be rejected?" He answered and said to me, "If) the Spirit (descended upon them), theywill in any case be saved, and they will change (for the better). For the power will descend on every man, forwithout it no one can stand. And after they are born, then, when the Spirit of life increases and the powercomes and strengthens that soul, no one can lead it astray with works of evil. But those on whom thecounterfeit spirit descends are drawn by him and they go astray."

And I said, "Lord, where will the souls of these go when they have come out of their flesh?" And he smiledand said to me, "The soul in which the power will become stronger than the counterfeit spirit, is strong and itflees from evil and, through the intervention of the incorruptible one, it is saved, and it is taken up to the restof the aeons."

And I said, "Lord, those, however, who have not known to whom they belong, where will their souls be?"

And he said to me, "In those, the despicable spirit has gained strength when they went astray. And heburdens the soul and draws it to the works of evil, and he casts it down into forgetfulness. And after it comesout of (the body), it is handed over to the authorities, who came into being through the archon, and they bindit with chains and cast it into prison, and consort with it until it is liberated from the forgetfulness and acquiresknowledge. And if thus it becomes perfect, it is saved."

And I said, "Lord, how can the soul become smaller and return into the nature of its mother or into man?"Then he rejoiced when I asked him this, and he said to me, "Truly, you are blessed, for you have understood!That soul is made to follow another one (fem.), since the Spirit of life is in it. It is saved through him. It is notagain cast into another flesh."

And I said, "Lord, these also who did not know, but have turned away, where will their souls go?" Then hesaid to me, "To that place where the angels of poverty go they will be taken, the place where there is norepentance. And they will be kept for the day on which those who have blasphemed the spirit will betortured, and they will be punished with eternal punishment."

And I said, "Lord, from where did the counterfeit spirit come?" Then he said to me, "The Mother-Father,who is rich in mercy, the holy Spirit in every way, the One who is merciful and who sympathizes with you(pl.), i.e., the Epinoia of the foreknowledge of light, he raised up the offspring of the perfect race and itsthinking and the eternal light of man. When the chief archon realized that they were exalted above him in theheight - and they surpass him in thinking - then he wanted to seize their thought, not knowing that theysurpassed him in thinking, and that he will not be able to seize them.

"He made a plan with his authorities, which are his powers, and they committed together adultery withSophia, and bitter fate was begotten through them, which is the last of the changeable bonds. And it is of asort that is interchangeable. And it is harder and stronger than she with whom the gods united, and the angelsand the demons and all the generations until this day. For from that fate came forth every sin and injustice andblasphemy, and the chain of forgetfulness and ignorance and every severe command, and serious sins andgreat fears. And thus the whole creation was made blind, in order that they may not know God, who is aboveall of them. And because of the chain of forgetfulness, their sins were hidden. For they are bound withmeasures and times and moments, since it (fate) is lord over everything.

"And he (the chief archon) repented for everything which had come into being through him. This time heplanned to bring a flood upon the work of man. But the greatness of the light of the foreknowledge informedNoah, and he proclaimed (it) to all the offspring which are the sons of men. But those who were strangers tohim did not listen to him. It is not as Moses said, 'They hid themselves in an ark' (Gn 7: 7), but they hidthemselves in a place, not only Noah, but also many other people from the immovable race. They went into aplace and hid themselves in a luminous cloud. And he (Noah) recognized his authority, and she who belongsto the light was with him, having shone on them because he (the chief archon) had brought darkness upon thewhole earth.

"And he made a plan with his powers. He sent his angels to the daughters of men, that they might take someof them for themselves and raise offspring for their enjoyment. And at first they did not succeed. When theyhad no success, they gathered together again and they made a plan together.They created a counterfeit spirit, who resembles the Spirit who had descended, so as to pollute the soulsthrough it. And the angels changed themselves in their likeness into the likeness of their mates (the daughtersof men), filling them with the spirit of darkness, which they had mixed for them, and with evil. They broughtgold and silver and a gift and copper and iron and metal and all kinds of things. And they steered the peoplewho had followed them into great troubles, by leading them astray with many deceptions. They (the people)became old without having enjoyment. They died, not having found truth and without knowing the God oftruth. And thus the whole creation became enslaved forever, from the foundation of the world until now. Andthey took women and begot children out of the darkness according to the likeness of their spirit. And theyclosed their hearts, and they hardened themselves through the hardness of the counterfeit spirit until now.

"I, therefore, the perfect Pronoia of the all, changed myself into my seed, for I existed first, going on everyroad. For I am the richness of the light; I am the remembrance of the pleroma.

"And I went into the realm of darkness and I endured till I entered the middle of the prison. And thefoundations of chaos shook. And I hid myself from them because of their wickedness, and they did notrecognize me.

"Again I returned for the second time, and I went about. I came forth from those who belong to the light,which is I, the remembrance of the Pronoia. I entered into the midst of darkness and the inside of Hades,since I was seeking (to accomplish) my task. And the foundations of chaos shook, that they might fall downupon those who are in chaos and might destroy them. And again I ran up to my root of light, lest they bedestroyed before the time.

"Still for a third time I went - I am the light which exists in the light, I am the remembrance of the Pronoia -that I might enter into the midst of darkness and the inside of Hades. And I filled my face with the light of thecompletion of their aeon. And I entered into the midst of their prison, which is the prison of the body. And Isaid, 'He who hears, let him get up from the deep sleep.' And he wept and shed tears. Bitter tears he wipedfrom himself and he said, 'Who is it that calls my name, and from where has this hope come to me, while I amin the chains of the prison?' And I said, 'I am the Pronoia of the pure light; I am the thinking of the virginalSpirit, who raised you up to the honored place. Arise and remember that it is you who hearkened, and followyour root, which is I, the merciful one, and guard yourself against the angels of poverty and the demons ofchaos and all those who ensnare you, and beware of the deep sleep and the enclosure of the inside of Hades.

"And I raised him up, and sealed him in the light of the water with five seals, in order that death might nothave power over him from this time on.

"And behold, now I shall go up to the perfect aeon. I have completed everything for you in your hearing. AndI have said everything to you that you might write them down and give them secretly to your fellow spirits, forthis is the mystery of the immovable race."And the savior presented these things to him that he might write them down and keep them secure.And he said to him,

"Cursed be everyone who will exchange these things for a gift or for food or for drink orfor clothing or for any other such thing." And these things were presented to him in a mystery, andimmediately he disappeared from him. And he went to his fellow disciples and related to them what the saviorhad told him.Jesus Christ, Amen.

The Apocryphon According to John

THE APOSTLES' CREED

[It is affirmed by Ambrose, "that the twelve Apostles, as skilful artificers assembled together, and made a keyby their common advice, that is, the Creed; by which the darkness of the devil is disclosed, that the light ofChrist may appear." Others fable that every Apostle inserted an article, by which the creed is divided intotwelve articles; and a sermon, fathered upon St. Austin, and quoted by the Lord Chancellor King, fabricatesthat each particular article was thus inserted by each particular Apostle:-

Peter	1	I believe in God the Father Almighty
John	2	Maker of heaven and earth
James	3	And in Jesus Christ his only Son, our Lord
Andrew	4	Who was conceived by the Holy Ghost; born of the Virgin Mary
Philip	5	Suffered under Pontius Pilate, was crucified, dead and buried
Thomas	6	He descended into hell, the third day he rose again from the dead
Bartholomew	7	He ascended into heaven; sitteth at the right hand of God the Father Almighty
Matthew	8	From thence he shall come to judge the quick and the dead
James, the son of Alpheus	9	I believe In the Holy Ghost, the holy Catholic Church
Simon Zelotes	10	The communion of saints, the forgiveness of sins
Jude, the brother of James	11	The resurrection of the body
Matthias	12	Life everlasting. Amen

Archbishop Wake says: "With respect to the Apostles being the authors of this Creed, it is not my intention toenter on any particular examination of this matter, which has been so fully handled, not only by the late criticsof the

Church of Rome, Natalis Alexander, Du Pin, &c., but yet more especially by Archbishop Usher,Gerard Vossius,Suicer, Spanhemius, Tentzelius, and Sam.

Basnage, among the Protestants. It shall suffice to say, that as it is not likely, that had any such thing as thisbeen done by the Apostles, St. Luke would have passed it by, without taking the least notice of it: so thediversity of Creeds in the ancient Church, and that not only in expression, but in some whole Articles too,sufficiently shows, that the Creed which we call by that name, was not composed by the twelve Apostles,much less in the same form in which it now is."

Mr. Justice Bailey says: "It is not to be understood that this Creed was framed by the Apostles, or indeedthat it existed as a Creed in their time;" and after giving the Creed as it existed in the year 600, and which ishere copied from his Common Prayer Book, he says, "how long this form had existed before the year 600 isnot exactly known. The additions were probably made in opposition to particular heresies and errors.'

The most important "addition," since the year of Christ 600, is that which affirms, that Christdescended into hell. This has been proved not only to have been an invention after the Apostles' time, buteven after the time of Eusebius. Bishop Pearson says, that the descent into hell was not in the ancient creedsor rules of faith. "It is not to be found in the rules of faith delivered by Irenaeus," by Origen, or by Tertullian.

It is not expressed in those creeds which were made by the councils as larger explications of the Apostles'Creed; not in the Nicene, or Constantino-politan; not in those of Ephesus, or Chalcedon; not in thoseconfessions made at Sardica, Antioch, Selucia, Sirmium, &c. It is not mentioned in several con-fessions offaith delivered by particular persons; not in that of Eusebius Cae-sariensis, presented to the council of Nice;not in that of Marcellus, bishop of Ancyra, delivered to Pope Julius; not in that of Arius and Euzoius,presented to Constantine; not in that of Acacius, bishop of Caesarea, delivered into the synod of Selucia; notin that of Eustathius, Theophilus, and Sylvanus, sent to Liberius; there is no mention of it in the creed of St.Basil; in the creed of Epiphanus, Gelasius, Damascus, Macarius, &c.

It is not in the creed expounded by St. Cyril, though some have produced that creed to prove it.It is not in the creed expounded by St. Augustine; not in that other, attributed to St. Augustine in anotherplace; not in that expounded by Maximus Taurinensis; nor in that so often interpreted by Petrus Chryso-logus;nor in that of the church of Antioch, delivered by Cassianus; neither is it to be seen in the MS. creeds setforth by the learned Archbishop of Armagh. It is affirmed by Ruffinus, that in his time it was neither in theRoman nor the Oriental Creeds."

✝ The Apocryphon of John ✝

As it stood An. Dom. 600. Copied from Mr. Justice Baileey's Edition of the book of Common Prayer.

"Before the year 600, it was no more than this." -Mr. Justice Bailey.

1 I Believe in God the Father Almighty

2 And in Jesus Christ his only begotten Son, our Lord

3 Who was born of the Holy Ghost and Virgin Mary

4 And was crucified under Pontius Pilate, and was buried

5 And the third day rose again from the dead

6 Ascended into heaven, sitteth on the right hand of the Father

7 Whence he shall come to judge the quick and the dead

8 And in the Holy Ghost

9 The Holy Church

10 The remission of sins

11 And the resurrection of the flesh

As it stands in the book of Common Prayer of the United church of England and Ireland as by lawestablished.

1 I Believe in God the Father Almighty, maker of heaven and earth

2 And in Jesus Christ his only Son, our Lord

3 Who was conceived by the Holy Ghost, born of the Virgin Mary

4 Suffered under Pontius Pilate, was crucified, dead and buried

5 He descended into hell

6 The third day he rose again from the dead

7 He ascended into heaven, and sitteth on the right hand of God the Father Almighty

8 From thence he shall come to judge the quick and the dead

9 I believe in the Holy Ghost

10 The holy Catholic Church; the communion of saints

11 The forgiveness of sins

12 The resurrection of the body; and the life everlasting

Amen.

The Arabic Gospel of The Infancy of The Saviour

IN the name of the Father, and the Son, and the Holy Spirit, one God.

ith the help and favour of the Most High we begin to write a book of the miracles of our Lord and Masterand Saviour Jesus Christ, which is called the Gospel of the Infancy: in the peace of the Lord. Amen.

1. We find what follows in the book of Joseph the high priest, who lived in the time of Christ. Some saythat he is Caiaphas. He has said that Jesus spoke, and, indeed, when He was lying in His cradle said toMary His mother: I am Jesus, the Son of God, the Logos, whom thou hast brought forth, as the AngelGabriel announced to thee; and my Father has sent me for the salvation of the world.

2. In the three hundred and ninth year of the era of Alexander, Augustus put forth an edict, that every manshould be enrolled in his native place. Joseph therefore arose, and taking Mary his spouse, went away to Jerusalem, and came to Bethlehem, to be enrolled along with his family in his native city. And having come toa cave, Mary told Joseph that the time of the birth was at hand, and that she could not go into the city; but,said she, let us go into this cave. This took place at sunset. And Joseph went out in haste to go for a womanto be near her. When, therefore, he was busy about that, he saw an Hebrew old woman belonging toJerusalem, and said: Come hither, my good woman, and go into this cave, in which there is a woman near hertime.

3. Wherefore, after sunset, the old woman, and Joseph with her, came to the cave, and they both went in.And, behold, it was filled with lights more beautiful than the gleaming of lamps and candles, and moresplendid than the light of the sun. The child, enwrapped in swaddling clothes, was sucking the breast of theLady Mary His mother, being placed in a stall. And when both were wondering at this light, the old womanasks the Lady Mary: Art

thou the mother of this Child? And when the Lady Mary gave her assent, she says:Thou art not at all like the daughters of Eve. The Lady Mary said: As my son has no equal among children, sohis mother has no equal among women. The old woman replied: My mistress, I came to get payment; I havebeen for a long time affected with palsy. Our mistress the Lady Mary said to her: Place thy hands upon thechild. And the old woman did so, and was immediately cured. Then she went forth, saying: Henceforth I willbe the attendant and servant of this child all the days of my life.

4. Then came shepherds; and when they had lighted a fire, and were rejoicing greatly, there appeared to themthe hosts of heaven praising and celebrating God Most High. And while the shepherds were doing the same,the cave was at that time made like a temple of the upper world, since both heavenly and earthly voicesglorified and magnified God on account of the birth of the Lord Christ. And when that old Hebrew womansaw the manifestation of those miracles, she thanked God, saying: I give Thee thanks, O God, the God ofIsrael, because mine eyes have seen the birth of the Saviour of the world.

5. And the time of circumcision, that is, the eighth day, being at hand, the child was to be circumcisedaccording to the law. Wherefore they circumcised Him in the cave. And the old Hebrew woman took thepiece of skin; but some say that she took the navel-string, and laid it past in a jar of old oil of nard. And shehad a son, a dealer in unguents, and she gave it to him, saying: See that thou do not sell this jar of unguent ofnard, even although three hundred denarii should be offered thee for it. And this is that jar which Mary thesinner bought and poured upon the head and feet of our Lord Jesus Christ, which thereafter she wiped withthe hair of her head. Ten days after, they took Him to Jerusalem; and on the fortieth day after His birththey carried Him into the temple, and set Him before the Lord, and offered sacrifices for Him, according tothe command-meet of the law of Moses, which is: Every male that openeth the womb shall be called the holyof God.

6. Then old Simeon saw Him shining like a pillar of light, when the Lady Mary, His virgin mother, rejoicingover Him, was carrying Him in her arms. And angels, praising Him, stood round Him in a circle, like lifeguards standing by a king. Simeon therefore went up in haste to the Lady Mary, and, with hands stretchedout before her, said to the Lord Christ: Now, O my Lord, let Thy servant depart in peace, according to Thyword; for mine eyes have seen Thy compassion, which Thou hast prepared for the salvation of all peoples, alight to all nations, and glory to Thy people Israel. Hanna also, a prophetess, was present, and came up,giving thanks to God, and calling the Lady Mary blessed.

7. And it came to pass, when the Lord Jesus was born at Bethlehem of

Judaea, in the time of King Herod,behold, magi came from the east to Jerusalem, as Zeraduscht had predicted; and there were with themgifts, gold, and frankincense, and myrrh. And they adored Him, and presented to Him their gifts. Then theLady Mary took one of the swaddling-bands, and, on account of the smallness of her means, gave it to them;and they received it from her with the greatest marks of honour. And in the same hour there appeared tothem an angel in the form of that star which had before guided them on their journey; and they went away,following the guidance of its light, until they arrived in their own country.

8. And their kings and chief men came together to them, asking what they had seen or done, how they hadgone and come back, what they had brought with them. And they showed them that swathing-cloth which theLady Mary had given them. Wherefore they celebrated a feast, and, according to their custom, lighted a fireand worshipped it, and threw that swathing-cloth into it; and the fire laid hold of it, and enveloped it. Andwhen the fire had gone out, they took out the swathing-cloth exactly as it had been before, just as if the firehad not touched it. Wherefore they began to kiss it, and to put it on their heads and their eyes, saying: Thisverily is the truth without doubt. Assuredly it is a great thing that the fire was not able to burn or destroy it.Then they took it, and with the greatest honour laid it up among their treasures.

9. And when Herod saw that the magi had left him, and not come back to him, he summoned the priests andthe wise men, and said to them: Show me where Christ is to be born. And when they answered, InBethlehem of Judaea, he began to think of putting the Lord Jesus Christ to death. Then appeared an angel ofthe Lord to Joseph in his sleep, and said: Rise, take the boy and His mother, and go away into Egypt. Herose, therefore, towards cockcrow, and set out.

10. While he is reflecting how be is to set about his journey, morning came upon him after he had gone a verylittle way. And now he was approaching a great city, in which there was an idol, to which the other idols andgods of the Egyptians offered gifts and vows. And there stood before this idol a priest ministering to him,who, as often as Satan spoke from that idol, reported it to the inhabitants of Egypt and its territories. Thispriest had a son, three years old, beset by several demons; and he made many speeches and utterances; andwhen the demons seized him, he tore his clothes, and remained naked, and threw stones at the people. Andthere was a hospital in that city dedicated to that idol. And when Joseph and the Lady Mary had come to thecity, and had turned aside into that hospital, the citizens were very much afraid; and all the chief men and thepriests of the idols came together to that idol, and said to it: What agitation and commotion is this that hasarisen in our land?

The idol answered them: A God has come here in secret, who is God indeed; nor is anygod besides Him worthy of divine worship, because He is truly the Son of God. And when this land becameaware of His presence, it trembled at His arrival, and was moved and shaken; and we are exceedingly afraidfrom the greatness of His power. And in the same hour that idol fell down, and at its fall all, inhabitants ofEgypt and others, ran together.

11. And the son of the priest, his usual disease having come upon him, entered the hospital, and there cameupon Joseph and the Lady Mary, from whom all others had fled. The Lady Mary had washed the cloths ofthe Lord Christ, and had spread them over some wood. That demoniac boy, therefore, came and took oneof the cloths, and put it on his head. Then the demons, fleeing in the shape of ravens and serpents, began togo forth out of his mouth. The boy, being immediately healed at the command of the Lord Christ, began topraise God, and then to give thanks to the Lord who had healed him. And when his father saw him restoredto health, My son, said he, what has happened to thee? and by what means hast thou been healed? The sonanswered: When the demons had thrown me on the ground, I went into the hospital, and there I found anaugust woman with a boy, whose newly-washed cloths she had thrown upon some wood: one of these I tookup and put upon my head, and the demons left me and fled. At this the father rejoiced greatly, and said: Myson, it is possible that this boy is the Son of the living God who created the heavens and the earth: for whenhe came over to us, the idol was broken, and all the gods fell, and perished by the power of his magnificence.

12. Here was fulfilled the prophecy which says, Out of Egypt have I called my son. Joseph indeed, andMary, when they heard that that idol had fallen down and perished, trembled, and were afraid. Then theysaid: When we were in the land of Israel, Herod thought to put Jesus to death, and on that account slew allthe children of Bethlehem and its confines; and there is no doubt that the Egyptians, as soon as they haveheard that this idol has been broken, will burn us with fire.

13. Going out thence, they came to a place where there were robbers who had plundered several men oftheir baggage and clothes, and had bound them. Then the robbers heard a great noise, like the noise of amagnificent king going out of his city with his army, and his chariots and his drums; and at this the robberswere terrified, and left all their plunder. And their captives rose up, loosed each other's bonds, recoveredtheir baggage, and went away. And when they saw Joseph and Mary coming up to the place, they said tothem: Where is that king, at the hearing of the magnificent sound of whose approach the robbers have left us,so that we have escaped safe? Joseph an-

swered them: He will come behind us.

14. Thereafter they came into another city, where there was a demoniac woman whom Satan, accursed andrebellious, had beset, when on one occasion she had gone out by night for water. She could neither bearclothes, nor live in a house; and as often as they tied her up with chains and thongs, she broke them, and flednaked into waste places; and, standing in cross-roads and cemeteries, she kept throwing stones at people,and brought very heavy calamities upon her friends. And when the Lady Mary saw her, she pitied her; andupon this Satan immediately left her, and fled away in the form of a young man, saying: Woe to me from thee,Mary, and from thy son. So that woman was cured of her torment, and being restored to her senses, sheblushed on account of her nakedness; and shunning the sight of men, went home to her friends. And after sheput on her clothes, she gave an account of the matter to her father and her friends; and as they were the chiefmen of the city, they received the Lady Mary and Joseph with the greatest honour and hospitality.

15. On the day after, being supplied by them with provision for their journey, they went away, and on theevening of that day arrived at another town, in which they were celebrating a marriage; but, by the arts ofaccursed Satan and the work of enchanters, the bride had become dumb, and could not speak a word. Andafter the Lady Mary entered the town, carrying her son the Lord Christ, that dumb bride saw her, andstretched out her hands towards the Lord Christ, and drew Him to her, and took Him into her arms, and heldHim close and kissed Him, and leaned over Him, moving His body back and forwards. Immediately the knotof her tongue was loosened, and her ears were opened; and she gave thanks and praise to God, because Hehad restored her to health. And that night the inhabitants of that town exulted with joy, and thought that Godand His angels had come down to them.

16. There they remained three days, being held in great honour, and living splendidly. Thereafter, beingsupplied by them with provision for their journey, they went away and came to another city, in which,because it was very populous, they thought of passing the night. And there was in that city an excellentwoman: and once, when she had gone to the river to bathe, lo, accursed Satan, in the form of a serpent, hadleapt upon her, and twisted himself round her belly; and as often as night came on, he tyrannically tormentedher. This woman, seeing the mistress the Lady Mary, and the child, the Lord Christ, in her bosom, was struckwith a longing for Him, and said to the mistress the Lady Mary: O mistress, give me this child, that I maycarry him, and kiss him. She therefore gave Him to the woman; and when He was brought to her, Satan lether go, and fled and left her, nor did the woman ever

see him after that day. Wherefore all who were presentpraised God Most High, and that woman bestowed on them liberal gifts

17. On the day after, the same woman took scented water to wash the Lord Jesus; and after she had washedHim, she took the water with which she had done it, and poured part of it upon a girl who was living there,whose body was white with leprosy, and washed her with it. And as soon as this was done, the girl wascleansed from her leprosy. And the towns- people said: There is no doubt that Joseph and Mary and thatboy are gods, not men. And when they were getting ready to go away from them, the girl who had laboure-dunder the leprosy came up to them, and asked them to let her go with them.

18. When they had given her permission, she went with them. And after-wards they came to a city, in whichwas the castle of a most illustrious prince, who kept a house for the entertainment of strangers. They turnedinto this place; and the girl went away to the prince's wife; and she found her weeping and sorrowful, and sheasked why she was weeping. Do not be surprised, said she, at my tears; for I am overwhelmed by a greataffliction, which as yet I have not endured to tell to any one. Perhaps, said the girl, if you reveal it and discloseit to me, I may have a remedy for it. Hide this secret, then, replied the princess, and tell it to no one. I wasmarried to this prince, who is a king and ruler over many cities, and I lived long with him, but by me he hadno son. And when at length I produced him a son, he was leprous; and as soon as he saw him, he turnedaway with loathing, and said to me: Either kill him, or give him to the nurse to be brought up in some placefrom which we shall never hear of him more. After this I can have nothing to do with thee, and I will never seethee more. On this account I know not what to do, and I am overwhelmed with grief. Alas! my son. Alas! myhusband. Did I not say so? said the girl. I have found a cure for thy disease, and I shall tell it thee. For I toowas a leper; but I was cleansed by God, who is Jesus, the son of the Lady Mary. And the woman asking herwhere this God was whom she had spoken of, Here, with thee, said the girl; He is living in the same house.But how is this possible? said she. Where is he? There, said the girl, are Joseph and Mary; and the child whois with them is called Jesus; and He it is who cured me of my disease and my torment. But by what means,said she, wast thou cured of thy leprosy? Wilt thou not tell me that? Why not? said the girl. I got from His-mother the water in which He had been washed, and poured it over myself; and so I was cleansed from myleprosy. Then the princess rose up, and invit-ed them to avail themselves of her hospitality. And she prepareda splendid banquet for Joseph in a great assembly of the men of the place. And on the following day she tookscented water with which to wash the Lord Jesus, and thereafter poured the same water over her son, whomshe had taken with her;

and immediately her son was cleansed from his leprosy. Therefore, singing thanks andpraises to God, she said: Blessed is the mother who bore thee, O Jesus; dost thou so cleanse those whoshare the same nature with thee with the water in which thy body has been washed? Besides, she bestowedgreat gifts upon the mistress the Lady Mary, and sent her away with great honour.

19. Coming thereafter to another city, they wished to spend the night in it. They turned aside, therefore, to thehouse of a man newly married, but who, under the influence of witchcraft, was not able to enjoy his wife; andwhen they had spent that night with him, his bond was loosed. And at daybreak, when they were girdingthemselves for their journey, the bridegroom would not let them go, and prepared for them a great banquet.

20. They set out, therefore, on the following day; and as they came near another city, they saw three womenweeping as they came out of a cemetery. And when the Lady Mary beheld them, she said to the girl whoaccompanied her: Ask them what is the matter with them, or what calamity has befallen them. And to thegirl's questions they made no reply, but asked in their turn: Whence are you, and whither are you going? forthe day is already past, and night is coming on apace. We are travellers, said the girl, and are seeking a houseof entertainment in which we may pass the night. They said: Go with us, and spend the night with us. Theyfollowed them, therefore, and were brought into a new house with splendid decorations and furniture. Now itwas winter; and the girl, going into the chamber of these women, found them again weeping and lamenting.There stood beside them a mule, covered with housings of cloth of gold, and sesame was put before him; andthe women were kissing him, and giving him food. And the gift said: What is all the ado, my ladies, about thismule? They answered her with tears, and said: This mule, which thou seest, was our brother, born of thesame mother with ourselves. And when our father died, and left us great wealth, and this only brother, we didour best to get him married, and were preparing his nuptials for him, after the manner of men. But somewomen, moved by mutual jealousy, bewitched him unknown to us; and one night, a little before daybreak,when the door of our house was shut, we saw that this our brother had been turned into a mule, as thou nowbeholdest him. And we are sorrowful, as thou seest, hav ing no father to comfort us: there is no wise man, ormagician, or enchanter in the world that we have omitted to send for; but nothing has done us any good. Andas often as our hearts are overwhelmed with grief, we rise and go away with our mother here, and weep atour father's grave, and come back again.

21. And when the girl heard these things, Be of good courage, said she, and weep not: for the cure of yourcalamity is near; yea, it is beside you, and

in the middle of your own house. For I also was a leper; but when Isaw that woman, and along with her that young child, whose name is Jesus, I sprinkled my body with thewater with which His mother had washed Him, and I was cured. And I know that He can cure your afflictionalso. But rise, go to Mary my mistress; bring her into your house, and tell her your secret; and entreat andsupplicate her to have pity upon yon. After the woman had heard the girl's words, they went in haste to theLady Mary, and brought her into their chamber, and sat down before her weeping, and saying: O ourmistress, Lady Mary, have pity on thy hand-maidens; for no one older than ourselves, and no head of thefamily, is left- -neither father nor brother--to live with us; but this mule which thou seest was our brother, andwomen have made him such as thou seest by witchcraft. We beseech thee, therefore, to have pity upon us.Then, grieving at their lot, the Lady Mary took up the Lord Jesus, and put Him on the mule's back; and shewept as well as the women, and said to Jesus Christ: Alas! my son, heal this mule by Thy mighty power, andmake him a man endowed with reason as he was before. And when these words were uttered by the LadyMary, his form was changed, and the mule became a young man, free from every defect. Then he and hismother and his sisters adored the Lady Mary, and lifted the boy above their heads, and began to kiss Him,saying: Blessed is she that bore Thee, O Jesus, O Saviour of the world; blessed are the eyes which enjoy thefelicity of seeing Thee.

22. Moreover, both the sisters said to their mother: Our brother indeed, by the aid of the Lord Jesus Christ,and by the salutary intervention of this girl, who pointed out to us Mary and her son, has been raised tohuman form. Now, indeed, since our brother is unmarried, it would do very well for us to give him as his wifethis girl, their servant. And having asked the Lady Mary, and obtained her consent, they made a splendidwedding for the girl; and their sorrow being changed into joy, and the beating of their breasts into dancing,they began to be glad, to rejoice, to exult, and sing--adorned, on account of their great joy, in most splendidand gorgeous attire. Then they began to recite songs and praises, and to say: O Jesus, son of David, whoturnest sorrow into gladness, and lamentations into joy! And Joseph and Mary remained there ten clays.Thereafter they set out, treated with great honours by these people, who bade them farewell, and frombidding them farewell returned weeping, especially the girl.

23. And turning away from this place, they came to a desert; and hearing that it was infested by robbers,Joseph and the Lady Mary resolved to cross this region by night. But as they go along, behold, they see tworobbers lying in the way, and along with them a great number of robbers, who were their associates, sleeping.Now those two robbers, into whose hands they had

fallen, were Titus and Dumachus. Titus therefore said toDumachus: I beseech thee to let these persons go freely, and so that our comrades may not see them. And asDumachus refused, Titus said to him again: Take to thyself forty drachmas from me, and hold this as a pledge.At the same time he held out to him the belt which he had about his waist, to keep him from opening hismouth or speaking. And the Lady Mary, seeing that the robber had done them a kindness, said to him: TheLord God will sustain thee by His right hand, and will grant thee remission of thy sins. And the Lord Jesusanswered, and said to His mother: Thirty years hence, O my mother, the Jews will crucify me at Jerusalem,and these two robbers will be raised upon the cross along with me, Titus on my right hand and Dumachus onmy left; and after that day Titus shall go before me into Paradise. And she said: God keep this from thee, myson. And they went thence towards a city of idols, which, as they came near it, was changed into sand-hills.

24. Hence they turned aside to that sycamore which is now called Matarea, and the Lord Jesus broughtforth in Matarea a fountain in which the Lady Mary washed His shirt. And from the sweat of the Lord Jesuswhich she sprinkled there, balsam was produced in that region.

25. Thence they came down to Memphis, and saw Pharaoh, and remained three years in Egypt; and theLord Jesus did in Egypt very many miracles which are recorded neither in the Gospel of the Infancy nor in theperfect Gospel.

26. And at the end of the three years He came back out of Egypt, and returned. And when they had arrivedat Judaea, Joseph was afraid to enter it; but hearing that Herod was dead, and that Archelaus his son hadsucceeded him, he was afraid indeed, but he went into Judaea. And an angel of the Lord appeared to him,and said: O Joseph, go into the city of Nazareth, and there abide. Wonderful indeed, that the Lord of theworld should be thus borne and carried about through the world!

27. Thereafter, going into the city of Bethlehem, they saw there many and grievous diseases infesting the eyesof the children, who were dying in consequence. And a woman was there with a sick son, whom, now verynear death, she brought to the Lady Mary, who saw him as she was washing Jesus Christ. Then said thewoman to her: O my Lady Mary, look upon this son of mine, who is labouring under a grievous disease. Andthe Lady Mary listened to her, and said: Take a little of that water in which I have washed my son, andsprinkle him with it. She therefore took a little of the water, as the Lady Mary had told her, and sprinkled itover her son. And when this was done his illness abated; and after sleeping a little, he rose up from sleep safeand sound. His mother rejoicing at this, again took him to the Lady Mary. And she said

to her: Give thanks toGod, because He hath healed this thy son.

28. There was in the same place another woman, a neighbour of her whose son had lately been restored tohealth. And as her son was labouring under the same disease, and his eyes were now almost blinded, shewept night and day. And the mother of the child that had been cured said to her: Why dost thou not take thyson to the Lady Mary, as I did with mine when he was nearly dead? And he got well with that water withwhich the body of her son Jesus had been washed. And when the woman heard this from her, she too wentand got some of the same water, and washed her son with it, and his body and his eyes were instantly madewell. Her also, when she had brought her son to her, and disclosed to her all that had happened, the LadyMary ordered to give thanks to God for her son's restoration to health, and to tell nobody of this matter.

29. There were in the same city two women, wives of one man, each having a son ill with fever. The one wascalled Mary, and her son's name was Cleopas. She rose and took up her son, and went to the Lady Mary,the mother of Jesus, and offering her a beautiful mantle, said: O my Lady Mary, accept this mantle, and for itgive me one small bandage. Mary did so, and the mother of Cleopas went away, and made a shirt of it, andput it on her son. So he was cured of his disease; but the son of her rival died. Hence there sprung up hatredbetween them; and as they did the house-work week about, and as it was the turn of Mary the mother of Cleopas, she heated the oven to bake bread; and going away to bring the lump that she had kneaded, she lefther son Cleopas beside the oven. Her rival seeing him alone--and the oven was very hot with the fire blazingunder it--seized him and threw him into the oven, and took herself off. Mary coming back, and seeing her sonCleopas lying in the oven laughing, and the oven quite cold, as if no fire had ever come near it, knew that herrival had thrown him into the fire. She drew him out, therefore, and took him to the Lady Mary, and told herof what had happened to him. And she said: Keep silence, and tell nobody of the affair; for I am afraid foryou if you divulge it. After this her rival went to the well to draw water; and seeing Cleopas playing beside thewell, and nobody near, she seized him and threw him into the well, and went home herself. And some menwho had gone to the well for water saw the boy sitting on the surface of the water; and so they went downand drew him out. And they were seized with a great admiration of that boy, and praised God. Then came hismother, and took him up, and went weeping to the Lady Mary, and said: O my lady, see what my rival hasdone to my son, and how she has thrown him into the well; she will be sure to destroy him some day or other.The Lady Mary said to her: God will avenge thee upon her. Thereafter, when her rival went to the

well todraw water, her feet got entangled in the rope, and she fell into the well. Some men came to draw her out,but they found her skull fractured and her bones broken. Thus she died a miserable death, and in her came topass that saying: They have digged a well deep, but have fallen into the pit which they had prepared.

30. Another woman there had twin sons who had fallen into disease, and one of them died, and the other wasat his last breath. And his mother, weeping, lifted him up, and took him to the Lady Mary, and said: O mylady, aid me and succour me. For I had two sons, and I have just buried the one, and the other is at the pointof death. See how I am going to entreat and pray to God. And she began to say: O Lord, Thou artcompassionate, and merciful, and full of affection. Thou gavest me two sons, of whom Thou hast taken awaythe one: this one at least leave to me. Wherefore the Lady Mary, seeing the fervour of her weeping, hadcompassion on her, and said: Put thy son in my son's bed, and cover him with his clothes. And when she hadput him in the bed in which Christ was lying, he had already closed his eyes in death; but as soon as the smellof the clothes of the Lord Jesus Christ reached the boy, he opened his eyes, and, calling upon his mother witha loud voice, he asked for bread, and took it and sucked it. Then his mother said: O Lady Mary, now I knowthat the power of God dwelleth in thee, so that thy son heals those that partake of the same nature withhimself, as soon as they have touched his clothes. This boy that was healed is he who in the Gospel is calledBartholomew.

31. Moreover, there was there a leprous woman, and she went to the Lady Mary, the mother of Jesus, andsaid: My lady, help me. And the Lady Mary answered: What help dost thou seek? Is it gold or silver? or is itthat thy body be made clean from the leprosy? And that woman asked: Who can grant me this? And theLady Mary said to her: Wait a little, until I shall have washed my son Jesus, and put him to bed. The womanwaited, as Mary had told her; and when she had put Jesus to bed, she held out to the woman the water inwhich she had washed His body, and said: Take a little of this water, and pour it over thy body. And as soonas she had done so, she was cleansed, and gave praise and thanks to God.

32. Therefore, after staying with her three days, she went away; and coming to a city, saw there one of thechief men, who had married the daughter of another of the chief men. But when he saw the woman, he beheldbetween her eyes the mark of leprosy in the shape of a star; and so the marriage was dissolved, and becamenull and void. And when that woman saw them in this condition, weeping and overwhelmed with sorrow, sheasked the cause of their grief. But they said: Inquired not into our condition, for to no one living

can we tellour grief, and to none but ourselves can we disclose it. She urged them, however, and entreated them toentrust it to her, saying that she would perhaps be able to tell them of a remedy. And when they showed herthe girl, and the sign of leprosy which appeared between her eyes, as soon as she saw it, the woman said: Ialso, whom you see here, laboured under the same disease, when, upon some business which happened tocome in my way, I went to Bethlehem. There going into a cave, I saw a woman named Mary, whose son washe who was named Jesus; and when she saw that I was a leper. she took pity on me, and handed me thewater with which she had washed her son's body. With it I sprinkled my body, and came out clean. Then the-woman said to her: Wilt thou not, O lady, rise and go with us, and show us the Lady Mary? And sheassented; and they rose and went to the Lady Mary, carrying with them splendid gifts. And when they hadgone in, and presented to her the gifts, they showed her the leprous girl whom they had brought. The LadyMary therefore said: May the compassion of the Lord Jesus Christ descend upon you; and handling to themalso a little of the water in which she had washed the body of Jesus Christ, she ordered the wretched womanto be bathed in it. And when this had been done, she was immediately cured; and they, and all standing by,praised God. Joyfully therefore they returned to their own city, praising the Lord for what He had done. Andwhen the chief heard that his wife had been cured, he took her home, and made a second marriage, and gavethanks to God for the recovery of his wife's health.

33. There was there also a young woman afflicted by Satan; for that ac-cursed wretch repeatedly appeared toher in the form of a huge dragon, and prepared to swallow her. He also sucked out all her blood, so that shewas left like a corpse. As often as he came near her, she, with her hands clasped over her head, cried out,and said: Woe, woe's me, for nobody is near to free me from that accursed dragon. And her father andmother, and all who were about her or saw her, bewailed her lot; and men stood round her in a crowd, andall wept and lamented, especially when she wept, and said: Oh, my breth-ren and friends, is there no one tofree me from that murderer? And the daughter of the chief who had been healed of her leprosy, hearing thegirl's voice, went up to the roof of her castle, and saw her with her hands clasped over her head weeping, andall the crowds standing round her weeping as wall. She therefore asked the demoniac's husband whether hiswife's mother were alive. And when he answered that both her parents were living, she said: Send for hermother to come to me. And when she saw that he had sent for her, and she had come, she said: Is thatdistracted girl thy daughter? Yes, O lady, said that sorrowful and weeping woman, she is my daughter. Thechiefs daughter answered: Keep my secret, for I confess to thee that I was formerly

a leper; but now theLady Mary, the mother of Jesus Christ, has healed me. But if thou wishest thy daughter to be healed, take herto Bethlehem, and seek Mary the mother of Jesus, and believe that thy daughter will be healed; I indeedbelieve that thou wilt come back with joy, with thy daughter healed. As soon as the woman heard the wordsof the chief's daughter, she led away her daughter in haste; and going to the place indicated, she went to theLady Mary, and revealed to her the state of her daughter. And the Lady Mary hearing her words, gave her alittle of the water in which she had washed the body of her son Jesus, and ordered her to pour it on the bodyof her daughter. She gave her also from the clothes of the Lord Jesus a swathing-cloth, saying: Take thiscloth, and show it to thine enemy as often as thou shalt see him. And she saluted them, and sent them away.

34. When, therefore, they had gone away from her, and returned to their own district, and the time was athand at which Satan was wont to attack her, at this very time that accursed one appeared to her in the shapeof a huge dragon, and the girl was afraid at the sight of him. And her mother said to her: Fear not, mydaughter; allow him to come near thee, and then show him the cloth which the Lady Mary hath given us, andlet us see what will happen. Satan, therefore, having come near in the likeness of a terrible dragon, the bodyof the girl shuddered for fear of him; but as soon as she took out the cloth, and placed it on her head, andcovered her eyes with it, flames and live coals began to dart forth from it, and to be cast upon the dragon. Othe great miracle which was done as soon as the dragon saw the cloth of the Lord Jesus, from which the firedarted, and was cast upon his head and eyes! He cried out with a loud voice: What have I to do with thee, OJesus, son of Mary? Whither shall I fly from thee? And with great fear he turned his back and departed fromthe girl, and never afterwards appeared to her. And the girl now had rest from him, and gave praise andthanks to God, and along with her all who were present at that miracle.

35. Another woman was living in the same place, whose son was tormented by Satan. He, Judas by name, asoften as Satan seized him, used to bite all who came near him; and if he found no one near him, he used tobite his own hands and other limbs. The mother of this wretched creature, then, hearing the fame of the LadyMary and her son Jesus, rose up and brought her son Judas with her to the Lady Mary. In the meantime,James and Joses had taken the child the Lord Jesus with them to play with the other children; and they hadgone out of the house and sat down, and the Lord Jesus with them. And the demoniac Judas came up, andsat down at Jesus' right hand: then, being attacked by Satan in the same manner as usual, he wished to bitethe Lord Jesus, but was not able; nevertheless he struck Jesus on the right side,

whereupon He began toweep. And immediately Satan went forth out of that boy, fleeing like a mad dog. And this boy who struckJesus, and out of whom Satan went forth in the shape of a dog, was Judas Iscariot, who betrayed Him to theJews; and that same side on which Judas struck Him, the Jews transfixed with a lance.

36. Now, when the Lord Jesus had completed seven years from His birth, on a certain day He was occupiedwith boys of His own age. For they were playing among clay, from which they were making images of asses,oxen, birds, and other animals; and each one boasting of his skill, was praising his own work. Then the LordJesus said to the boys: The images that I have made I will order to walk. The boys asked Him whether thenhe were the son of the Creator; and the Lord Jesus bade them walk. And they immediately began to leap;and then, when He had given them leave, they again stood still. And He had made figures of birds andsparrows, which flew when He told them to fly, and stood still when He told them to stand, and ate anddrank when He handed them food and drink. After the boys had gone away and told this to their parents,their fathers said to them: My sons, take care not to keep company with him again, for he is a wizard: fleefrom him, therefore, and avoid him, and do not play with him again after this.

37. On a certain day the Lord Jesus, running about and playing with the boys, passed the shop of a dyer,whose name was Salem; and he had in his shop many pieces of cloth which he was to dye. The Lord Jesusthen, going into his shop, took up all the pieces of cloth, and threw them into a tub full of indigo. And whenSalem came and saw his cloths destroyed, he began to cry out with a loud voice, and to reproach Jesus,saying: Why hast thou done this to me, O son of Mary? Thou hast disgraced me before all my townsmen: for,seeing that every one wished the colour that suited himself, thou indeed hast come and destroyed them all.The Lord Jesus answered: I shall change for thee the colour of any piece of cloth which thou shalt wish to bechanged. And immediately He began to take the pieces of cloth out of the tub, each of them of that colourwhich the dyer wished, until He had taken them all out. When the Jews saw this miracle and prodigy, theypraised God.

38. And Joseph used to go about through the whole city, and take the Lord Jesus with him, when people sentfor him in the way of his trade to make for them doors, and milk-pails, and beds, and chests; and the LordJesus was with him wherever he went. As often, therefore, as Joseph had to make anything a cubit or a spanlonger or shorter, wider or narrower, the Lord Jesus stretched His hand towards it; and as soon as He didso, it became such as Joseph wished. Nor was it necessary for him to make anything with his own hand, forJoseph was not very skilful in carpentry.

39. Now, on a certain day, the king of Jerusalem sent for him, and said: I wish thee, Joseph, to make for mea throne to fit that place in which I usually sit. Joseph obeyed, and began the work immediately, and remainedin the palace two years, until he finished the work of that throne. And when he had it carried to its place, heperceived that each side wanted two spans of the prescribed measure. And the king, seeing this, was angrywith Joseph; and Joseph, being in great fear of the king, spent the night without supper, nor did he tasteanything at all. Then, being asked by the Lord Jesus why he was afraid, Joseph said: Because I have spoiledall the work that I have been two years at. And the Lord Jesus said to him: Fear not, and do not lose heart;but do thou take hold of one side of the throne; I shall take the other; and we shall put that to rights. AndJoseph, having done as the Lord Jesus had said and each having drawn by his own side, the throne was putto rights, and brought to the exact measure of the place. And those that stood by and saw this miracle werestruck with astonishment, and praised God. And the woods used in that throne were of those which arecelebrated in the time of Solomon the son of David; that is, woods of many and various kinds.

40. On another day the Lord Jesus went out into the road, and saw the boys that had come together to play,and followed them; but the boys hid themselves from Him. The Lord Jesus, therefore, having come to thedoor of a certain house, and seen some women standing there, asked them where the boys had gone; andwhen they answered that there was no one there, He said again: Who are these whom you see in thefurnace?' They replied that they were kids of three years old. And the Lord Jesus cried out, and said: Comeout hither, O kids, to your Shepherd. Then the boys, in the form of kids, came out, and began to dance roundHim; and the women, seeing this, were very much astonished, and were seized with trembling, and speedily,supplicated and adored the Lord Jesus, saying: O our Lord Jesus, son of Mary, Thou art of a truth that goodShepherd of Israel; have mercy on Thy handmaidens who stand before Thee, and who have never doubted:for Thou hast come, O our Lord, to heal, and not to destroy. And when the Lord Jesus answered that thesons of Israel were like the Ethiopians among the nations, the women said: Thou, O Lord, knowest all things,nor is anything hid from Thee; now, indeed, we beseech Thee, and ask Thee of Thy affection to restore theseboys Thy servants to their former condition. The Lord Jesus therefore said: Come, boys, let us go and play.And immediately, while these women were standing by, the kids were changed into boys.

41. Now in the month Adar, Jesus, after the manner of a king, assembled the boys together. They spreadtheir clothes on the ground, and He sat down upon them. Then they put on His head a crown made offlowers, and, like

chamber-servants, stood in His presence, on the right and on the left, as if He were a king. And whoever passed by that way was forcibly dragged by the boys, saying: Come hither, and adore the king; then go thy way.

42. In the meantime, while these things were going on, some men came up carrying a boy. For this boy hadgone into the mountain with those of his own age to seek wood, and there he found a partridge's nest; andwhen he stretched out his hand to take the eggs from it, a venomous serpent bit him from the middle of thenest, so that he called out for help. His comrades accordingly went to him with haste, and found him lying onthe ground like one dead. Then his relations came and took hun up to carry him back to the city. And afterthey had come to that place where the Lord Jesus was sitting like a king, and the rest of the boys standinground Him like His servants, the boys went hastily forward to meet him who had been bitten by the serpent,and said to his relations: Come and salute the king. Bat when they were unwilling to go, on account of thesorrow in I which they were, the boys dragged them by force against their will. And when they had come upto the Lord Jesus, He asked them why they were carrying the boy. And when they answered that a serpenthad bitten him, the Lord Jesus said to the boys: Let us go and kill that serpent. And the parents of the boyasked leave to go away, because their son was in the agony of death; but the boys answered them, saying:Did you not hear the king saying: Let us go kill the serpent? and will yon not obey him? And so, against theirwill the could was carried back. And when they came to the nest, the Lord Jesus said to the boys: Is this theserpent's place? They saint that it was; and the serpent, at the call of the Lord, came forth without delay, andsubmitted itself to Him. And He said to it: Go away, and suck out all the poison which thou hast infused intothis boy. And so the serpent crawled to the boy, and sucked out all its poison. Then the Lord Jesus cursed it,and immediately on this being done it burst asunder; and the Lord Jesus stroked the boy with his hand, andhe was healed. And he began to weep; but Jesus said: Do not weep, for by and by thou shalt be my disciple.And this is Simon the Cananite, of whom mention is made in the Gospel.

43. On another day, Joseph sent his son James to gather wood, and the Lord Jesus went with him as hiscompanion. And when they had come to the place where the wood was, and James had begun to gather it,behold, a venomous viper bit his band, so that he began to cry out and weep. The Lord Jesus then, seeinghim in this condition, went up to him, and blew upon the place where the viper had bitten him; and this beingdone, he was healed immediately.

44. One day, when the Lord Jesus was again with the boys playing on the roof of a house, one of the boysfell down from above, and immediately ex-

pired. And the rest of the boys fled in all directions, and the LordJesus was left alone on the roof. And the relations of the boy came up and said to the Lord Jesus: It was thouwho didst throw our son headlong from the roof. And when He denied it, they cried out, saying: Our son isdead, and here is he who has killed him. And the Lord Jesus said to them: Do not bring an evil report againstme; but if you do not believe me, come and let us ask the boy himself, that be may bring the truth to light.Then the Lord Jesus went down, and standing over the dead body, said, with a loud voice: Zeno, Zeno, whothrew thee down from the roof? Then the dead boy answered and said: My lord, it was not thou who didstthrow me down, but such a one cast me down from it. And when the Lord commanded those who werestanding by to attend to His words, all who were present praised God for this miracle.

45. Once upon a time the Lady Mary bad ordered the Lord Jesus to go and bring her water from the well.And when He had gone to get the water, the pitcher already full was knocked against something, and broken.And the Lord Jesus stretched out His handkerchief, and collected the water, and carried it to His mother; andshe was astonished at it. And she hid and preserved in her heart all that she saw.

46. Again, on another day, the Lord Jesus was with the boys at a stream of water, and they had again madelittle fish-ponds. And the Lord Jesus had made twelve sparrows, and had arranged them round Hisfish-pond, three on each side. And it was the Sabbath-day. Wherefore a Jew, the son of Hanan, coming up,and seeing them thus engaged, said in anger and great indignation: Do you make figures of clay on theSabbath-day? And he ran quickly, and destroyed their fish-ponds. But when the Lord Jesus clapped Hishands over the sparrows which He had made, they flew away chirping. Then the son of Hanan came up tothe fish-pond of Jesus also, and kicked it with his shoes, and the water of it vanished away. And the LordJesus said to him: As that water has vanished away, so thy life shall likewise vanish away. And immediatelythat boy dried up.

47. At another time, when the Lord Jesus was returning home with Joseph in the evening. He met a boy, whoran up against Him with so much force that He fell. And the Lord Jesus said to him: As thou hast thrown medown, so thou shall fall and not rise again. And the same hour the boy fell down, and expired.

48. There was, moreover, at Jerusalem, a certain man named Zacchaeus, who taught boys. He said toJoseph: Why, O Joseph, dost thou not bring Jesus to the to learn his letters? Joseph agreed to do so, andreported the matter to the Lady Mary. They therefore took Him to the master; and he, as soon as he sawHim, wrote out the alphabet for Him, and told Him to say Aleph. And

when He had said Aleph, the masterordered Him to pronounce Beth. And
the Lord Jesus said to him: Tell me first the meaning of the letter Aleph,and
then I shall pronounce Beth. And when the master threatened to flog Him,
the Lord Jesus explained tohim the meanings of the letters Aleph and Beth;
also which figures of the letter were straight, which crooked,which drawn
round into a spiral, which marked with points, which without them, why
one letter went beforeanother; and many other things He began to recount
and to elucidate which the master himself had nevereither heard or read in
any book. The Lord Jesus, moreover, said to the master: Listen, and I shall
say themto thee. And He began clearly and distinctly to repeat Aleph, Beth,
Gimel, Daleth, on to Tau. And the masterwas astonished, and said: I think
that this boy was born before Noah. And turning to Joseph, be said: Thou-
hast brought to me to be taught a boy more learned than all the masters. To
the Lady Mary also be said: Thisson of thine has no need of instruction.

49. Thereafter they took Him to another and a more learned master, who,
when be saw Him, said: SayAleph. And when He had said Aleph, the master
ordered him to pronounce Beth. And the Lord Jesusanswered him, and said:
First tell me the meaning of the letter Aleph, and then I shall pronounce
Beth. Andwhen the master hereupon raised his hand and flogged Him,
immediately his hand dried up, and he died. Thensaid Joseph, to the Lady
Mary: From this time we shall not let him go out of the house, since every
one whoopposes him is struck dead.

50. And when He was twelve years old, they took Him to Jerusalem to the
feast. And when the feast wasfinished, they indeed returned; but the Lord
Jesus remained in the temple among the teachers and elders andlearned men
of the sons of Israel, to whom He put various questions upon the sciences,
and gave answers inHis turn. For He said to them: Whose son is the Messias?
They answered Him: The son of David.Wherefore then, said He, does he in
the Spirit call him his lord, when he says, The Lord said to my lord, Sitat my
right hand, that I may put thine enemies under thy footsteps? Again the chief
of the teachers said toHim: Hast thou read the books? Both the books, said
the Lord Jesus, and the things contained in the books.And He explained the
books, and the law, and the precepts, and the statutes, and the mysteries,
which arecontained in the books of the prophets--things which the understanding of no creature attains to. That teachertherefore said: I hitherto have
neither attained to nor heard of such knowledge: Who, pray, do you think
thatboy will be?

51. And a philosopher who was there present, a skilful astronomer, asked
the Lord Jesus whether He hadstudied astronomy. And the Lord Jesus answered him, and explained the number of the spheres, and of theheavenly

bodies, their natures and operations; their opposition; their aspect, triangular, square, and sextile;their course, direct and retrograde; the twenty-fourths, and sixtieths of twenty-fourths; and other thingsbeyond the reach of reason.

52. There was also among those philosophers one very skilled in treating of natural science, and he asked theLord Jesus whether He had studied medicine. And He, in reply, explained to him physics and metaphysics,hyperphysics and hypophysics, the powers likewise and humours of the body, and the effects of the same;also the number of members and bones, of veins, arteries, and nerves; also the effect of heat and dryness, ofcold and moisture, and what these give rise to; what was the operation of the soul upon the body, and itsperceptions and powers; what was the operation of the faculty of speech, of anger, of desire; lastly, theirconjunction and disjunction, and other things beyond the reach of any created intellect. Then that philosopherrose up, and adored the Lord Jesus, and said: O Lord, from this time I will be thy disciple and slave.

53. While they were speaking to each other of these and other things, the Lady Mary came, after having goneabout seeking Him for three days along with Joseph. She therefore, seeing Him sitting among the teachersasking them questions, and answering in His turn, said to Him: My son, why hast thou treated us thus?Behold, thy father and I have sought thee with great trouble. But He said: Why do you seek me? Do you notknow that I ought to occupy myself in my Father's house? But they did not understand the words that Hespoke to them. Then those teachers asked Mary whether He were her son; and when she signified that Hewas, they said: Blessed art thou, O Mary, who hast brought forth such a son. And returning with them toNazareth, He obeyed them in all things. And His mother kept all these words of His in her heart. And theLord Jesus advanced in stature, and in wisdom, and in favour with God and man.

54. And from this day He began to hide His miracles and mysteries and secrets, and to give attention to thelaw, until He completed His thirtieth year, when His Father publicly declared Him at the Jordan by this voicesent down from heaven: This is my beloved Son, in whom I am well pleased; the Holy Spirit being present inthe form of a white dove.

55. This is He whom we adore with supplications, who hath given us being and life, and who hath brought usfrom our mothers' wombs; who for our sakes assumed a human body, and redeemed us, that He mightembrace us in eternal compassion, and show to us His mercy according to His liberality, and beneficence,and generosity, and benevolence. To Him is glory, and beneficence, and power, and dominion from this timeforth for evermore. Amen. Here endeth the whole Gospel of the Infancy, with the aid of God

Most High, according to what we have found in the original.

The Avenging of the Saviour

This version of the legend of Veronica is written in very barbarous Latin, probably of the seventh or eighth century. An Anglo-Saxon version, which Tischendorf concludes to be derived from the Latin, was edited and translated for the Cambridge Antiquarian Society, by C. W. Goodwin, in 1851. The Anglo-Saxon text is from a MS. in the Cambridge Library, one of a number presented to the Cathedral of Exeter by Bishop Leofric in the beginning of the eleventh century.

The reader will observe that there are in this document two distinct legends, somewhat clumsily joined together--that of Nathan's embassy, and that of Veronica.

HERE BEGINNETH THE AVENGING OF THE SAVIOUR

In the days of the Emperor Tiberius Caesar, when Herod was tetrarch, Christ was delivered under Pontius Pilate by the Jews, and revealed by Tiberius.

In those days Titus was a prince under Tiberius in the region of Equitania, in a city of Libia which is called Burgidalla. And Titus had a sore in his right nostril, on account of a cancer, and he bad his face torn even to the eye. There went forth a certain man from Judaea, by name Nathan the son of Nahum; for he was an Ishmaelite who went from land to land, and from sea to sea, and in all the ends of the earth. Now Nathan was sent from Judaea to the Emperor Tiberius, to carry their treaty to the city of Rome. And Tiberius was ill, and full of ulcers and fevers, and had nine kinds of leprosy. And Nathan wished to go to the city of Rome.

But the north wind blew and hindered his sailing, and carried him down to the harbour of a city of Libia. Now Titus, seeing the ship coming, knew that it was from Judaea; and they all wondered, and said that they had never seen any vessel so coming from that quarter. And Titus ordered the captain to come to him, and asked him who he was. And he said: I am Nathan the son of Nahum, of the race of the Ishmaelites, and I am a subject of Pontius Pilate in Judaea. And I have been sent to go to Tiberius the Roman emperor, to carry a treaty from Judaea. And a strong wind came down upon the sea, and has brought me to a country that I do not know.

And Titus says: If thou couldst at any time find anything either of cosmetics or herbs which could cure the wound that I have in my face, as thou seest, so that I should become whole, and regain my former health, I should bestow upon thee many good things. And Nathan said to him: I do not know, nor have I ever known, of such things as thou speakest to me about. But for all that, if thou hadst been some time ago in Jerusalem, there thou wouldst have found a choice prophet, whose name was Emanuel, for He will save His people from their sins.

And He, as His first miracle in Cana of Galilee, made wine from water; and by His word He cleansed lepers, He enlightened the eyes of one born blind, He healed paralytics, He made demons flee, He raised up three dead; a woman caught in adultery, and condemned by the Jews to be stoned, He set free; and another woman, mined Veronica, who suffered twelve years from an issue of blood, and came up to Him behind, and touched the fringe of His garment, He healed; and with five loaves and two fishes He satisfied five thousand men, to say nothing of little ones and women, and there remained of the fragments twelve baskets. All these things, and many others, were accomplished before His passion. After His resurrection we saw Him in the flesh as He had been before. And Titus said to Him: How did he rise again from the dead, seeing that he was dead? And Nathan answered 473 and said: He was manifestly dead, and hung up on the cross, and again taken down from the cross, and for three days He lay in the tomb: thereafter He rose again from the dead, and went down to Hades, and freed the patriarchs and the prophets, and the whole human race; thereafter He appeared to His disciples, and ate with them; thereafter they saw Him going up into heaven. And so it is the truth, all this that I tell you. For I saw it with my own eyes, and all the house of Israel. And Titus said in his own words: Woe to thee, O Emperor Tiberius, full of ulcers, and enveloped in leprosy, because such a scandal has been committed in thy kingdom; because thou hast made such laws in Judaea, in the land of the birth of our Lord Jesus Christ, and they have seized the King, and put to death the Ruler of the peoples; and they have not made Him come to us to cure thee of thy leprosy, and cleanse me from mine infirmity: on which account, if they had been before my face, with my own hands I should have slain the carcases of those Jews, and hung them up on the cruel tree, because they have destroyed my Lord, and mine eyes have not been worthy to see His face. And when he had thus spoken, immediately the wound fell from the face of Titus, and his flesh and his face were restored to health. And all the sick who were in the same place were made whole in that hour.

And Titus cried out, and all the rest with him, in a loud voice, saying: My King and my God, because I have never seen Thee, and Thou hast made me whole, bid me go with the ship over the waters to the land of Thy birth, to take vengeance on Thine enemies; and help me, O Lord, that I may be able to destroy them, and avenge Thy death: do Thou, Lord, deliver them into my hand. And having thus spoken, he ordered that he should be baptized. And he called Nathan to him, and said to him: How hast thou seen those baptized who believe in Christ? Come to me, and baptize me in the name of the Father, and of the Son, and of the Holy Ghost. Amen. For I also firmly believe in the Lord Jesus Christ with all my heart, and with all my soul; because nowhere in the whole world is there another who has created me, and made me whole from my wounds.

And having thus spoken, he sent messengers to Vespasian to come with all haste with his bravest men, so prepared as if for war.

Then Vespasian brought with him five thousand armed men, and they went to meet Titus. And when they had come to the city of Libia, he said to Titus: Why is it that thou hast made me come hither? And he said: Know that Jesus has come into this world, and has been born in Judaea, in a place which is called Bethlehem, and has been given up by the Jews, and scourged, and crucified on Mount Calvary, and has risen again from the dead on the third day. And His disciples have seen Him in the same flesh in which he was born, and He has shown Himself to His disciples, and they have believed in Him. And we indeed wish to become His disciples.

Now, let us go and destroy His enemies from the earth, that they may now know that there is none like the Lord our God on the face of the earth. With this design, then, they went forth from the city of Libia which is called Burgidalla, and went on board a ship, and proceeded to Jerusalem, and surrounded the kingdom of the Jews, and began to send them to destruction. And when the kings of the Jews heard of their doings, and the wasting of their land, fear came upon them, and they were in great perplexity.

Then Archelaus was perplexed in his words, and said to his son: My son, take my kingdom and judge it; and take counsel with the other kings who are in the land of Judah, that you may be able to escape from our enemies. And having thus said, he unsheathed his sword and leant upon it; and turned his sword, which was very sharp, and thrust it into his breast, and died. And his son allied himself with the other kings who were under him, and they took counsel among themselves, and went into Jerusalem with their chief men who were in their counsel, and stood in the same place seven years. And Titus and Vespasian took counsel to surround their city. And they did so. And the seven years being fulfilled, there was a very sore famine, and for want of bread they began to eat earth.

Then all the soldiers who were of the four kings took counsel among themselves, and said: Now we are sure to die: what will God do to us? or of what good is our life to us, because the Romans have come to take our place and nation? It is better for us to kill each other, than that the Romans should say that they have slain us, and gained the victory over us. And they drew their swords and smote themselves, and died, to the number of twelve thousand men of them. Then there was a great stench in that city from the corpses of those dead men. And their kings feared with a very great fear even unto death; and they could not bear the stench of them, nor bury them, nor throw them forth out of the city. And they 474 said to each other: What shall we do? We indeed gave up Christ to death, and now we given up to death ourselves. Let us bow our heads, and give up the keys of the city to the Romans, because God has already given us up to death. And immediately they went up upon the walls of the city, and all cried out with a loud voice, saying: Titus and Vespasian, take the keys of the city, which have been given to you by Messiah, who is called Christ.

Then they gave themselves up into the hands of Titus and Vespasian, and said: Judge us, seeing that we ought to die, because we judged Christ; and he was given up without cause. Titus and Vespasian seized them, and some they stoned, and some they hanged on a tree, feet up and head down, and struck them through with lances; and others they gave up to be sold, and others they divided among themselves, and made four parts of them, just as they had done of the garments of the Lord. And they said: They sold Christ for thirty pieces of silver, and we shall sell thirty of them for one denarius. And so they did. And having done so, they seized all the lands of Judaea and Jerusalem.

Then they made a search about the face or portrait of Jesus, how they might find it. And they found a woman named Veronica who had it. Then they seized Pilate, and sent him to prison, to be guarded by four quaternions of soldiers at the door of the prison. Then they forthwith sent their messengers to Tiberius, the emperor of the city of Rome, that he should send Velosianus to them. And he said to him: Take all that is necessary for thee in the sea, and go down into Judaea, and seek out one of the disciples of him who is called Christ and Lord, that he may come to me, and in the name of his God cure me of the leprosy and the infirmities by which I am daily exceedingly burdened, and of my wounds, because I am ill at ease. And send upon the kings of the Jews, who are subject to my authority, thy forces and terrible engines, because they have put to death Jesus Christ our Lord, and condemn them to death. And if thou shalt there find a man as may be able to free me from this infirmity of mine, I will believe in Christ the Son of God, and will baptize myself in his name. And Velosianus said: My lord emperor, if I find such a man as may be able to help and free us, what reward shall I promise him? Tiberius said to him: The half of my kingdom, without fail, to be in his hand.

Then Velosianus immediately went forth, and went on board the ship, and hoisted the sail in the vessel, and went on sailing through the sea. And he sailed a year and seven days, after which he arrived at Jerusalem. And immediately he ordered some of the Jews to come to his power, and began carefully to ask what had been the acts of Christ. Then Joseph, of the city of Arimathaea, and Nicodemus, came at the same time. And Nicodemus said: I saw Him, and I know indeed that He is the Saviour of the world. And Joseph said to him: And I took Him down from the cross, and laid Him in a new tomb, which had been cut out of the rock. And the Jews kept me shut up on the day of the preparation, at evening; and while I was standing in prayer on the Sabbath-day, the house was hung up by the four corners, and I saw the Lord Jesus Christ like a gleam of light, and for fear I fell to the ground. And He said to me, Look upon me, for I am Jesus, whose body thou buriedst in thy tomb. And I said to Him, Show me the sepulchre where I laid Thee. And Jesus, holding my hand in His right hand, led me to the place where I buried Him.

And there came also the woman named Veronica, and said to him: And I touched in the crowd the fringe of His garment, because for twelve years I had suffered from an issue of blood; and He immediately healed me. Then Velosianus said to Pilate: Thou, Pilate, impious and cruel, why hast thou slain the Son of God? And Pilate answered: His own nation, and the chief priests Annas and Caiaphas, gave him to me. Volosianus said: Impious and cruel, thou art worthy of death and cruel punishment. And he sent him back to prison. And Velosianus at last sought for the face or the countenance of the Lord. And all who were in that same place said: It is the woman called Veronica who has the portrait of the Lord in her house. And immediately he ordered her to be brought before his power. And he said to her: Hast thou the portrait of the Lord in thy house? But she said, No. Then Velosianus ordered her to be put to the torture, until she should give up the portrait of the Lord. And she was forced to say: I have it in clean linen, my lord, and I daily adore it. Velosianus said: Show it to me. Then she showed the portrait of the Lord.

When Velosianus saw it, he prostrated himself on the ground; and with a ready heart and true faith he took hold of it, and wrapped it in cloth of gold, and placed it in a casket, and sealed it with his ring. And he swore with an oath, and said: As the Lord God liveth, and by the health 475 of Caesar, no man shall any more see it upon the face of the earth, until I see the face of my lord Tiberius.

And when he had thus spoken, the princes, who were the chief men of Judaea, seized Pilate to take him to a seaport. And he took the portrait of the Lord, with all His disciples, and all in his pay, and they went on board the ship the same day. Then the woman Veronica, for the love of Christ, left all that she possessed, and followed Velosianus. And Velosianus said to her: What dost thou wish, woman, or what dost thou seek? And she answered: I am seeking the portrait of our Lord Jesus Christ, who enlightened me, not for my own merits, but through His own holy affection. Give back to me the portrait of my Lord Jesus Christ; for because of this I die with a righteous longing. But if thou do not give it back to me, I will not leave it until I see where thou wilt put it, because I, most miserable woman that I am, will serve Him all the days of my life; because I believe that He, my Redeemer, liveth for everlasting.

Then Velosianus ordered the woman Veronica to be taken down with him into the ship And the sails being hoisted. They began to go in the vessel in the name of the Lord, and they sailed through the sea. But Titus, along with Vespasian, went up into Judaea, avenging all nations upon their land. At the end of a year Velosianus came to the city of Rome, brought his vessel into the river which is called Tiberis, or Tiber, and entered the city which is called Rome. And he sent his messenger to his lord Tiberius the emperor in the Lateran about his prosperous arrival. Then Tiberius the emperor, when he heard the message of Velosianus, rejoiced greatly, and ordered him to come before his face. And when he had come, he called him, saying: Velosianus, how hast thou come, and what hast thou seen in the region of Judaea of Christ the Lord and his disciples? Tell me, I beseech thee, that he is going to cure me of mine infirmity, that I may be at once cleansed from that leprosy which I have over my body, and I give up my whole kingdom into thy power and his. And Velosianus said: My lord emperor, I found thy servants Titus and Vespasian in Judaea fearing the Lord, and they were cleansed from all their ulcers and sufferings. And I found that all the kings and rulers of Judaea have been hanged by Titus; Annas and Caiaphas have been stoned, Archelaus has killed himself with his own lance; and I have sent Pilate to Damascus in bonds, and kept him in prison under safe keeping. But I have also found out about Jesus, whom the Jews most wickedly attacked with swords, and staves, and weapons; and they crucified him who ought to have freed and enlightened us, and to have come to us, and they hanged him on a tree. And Joseph came from Arimathaea, and Nicodemus with him, bringing a mixture of myrrh and aloes, about a hundred pounds, to anoint the body of Jesus; and they took him down from the cross, and laid him in a new tomb. And on the third day he most assuredly rose again froth the dead, and showed himself to his disciples in the same flesh in which he had been born.

At length, after forty days, they saw him going up into heaven. Many, indeed, and other miracles did Jesus before his passion and after. First, of water he made wine; he raised the dead, he cleansed lepers, he enlightened the blind, he cured paralytics, he put demons to flight; he made the deaf hear, the dumb speak; Lazarus, when four days dead, he raised from the tomb; the woman Veronica, who suffered from an issue of blood twelve years, and touched the fringe of his garment, he made whole. Then it pleased the Lord in the heavens, that the Son of God, who, sent into this world as the first-created, had died upon earth, should send his angel; and he commanded Titus and Vespasian, whom I knew in that place where thy throne is. And it pleased God Almighty that they went into Judaea and Jerusalem, and seized thy subjects, and put them under that sentence, as it were, in the same manner as they did when thy subjects seized Jesus and bound him. And Vespasian afterwards said: What shall we do about those who shall remain? Titus answered: They hanged our Lord on a green tree, and struck him with a lance; now let us hang them on a dry tree, and pierce their bodies through and through with the lance. And they did so. And Vespasian said: What about those who are left? Titus answered: They seized the tunic of our Lord Jesus Christ, and of it made four parts; now let us seize them, and divide them into four parts,--to thee one, to me one, to thy men another, and to my servants the fourth part. And they did so. And Vespasian said: But what shall we do about those who are left? Titus answered him: The Jews sold our Lord for thirty pieces of silver: now let us sell thirty of them for one piece of silver. And they did so. And they seized Pilate, and gave him up to me, and I put him in prison, to be guarded by four quaternions of soldiers in Damascus.

Then they made a search with great diligence to seek the portrait of the Lord; and they found a woman named Veronica who had the portrait of the Lord. Then the 476 Emperor Tiberius said to Velosianus: How hast thou it? And he answered: I have it in clean cloth of gold, rolled up in a shawl. And the Emperor Tiberius said: Bring it to me, and spread it before my face, that I, falling to the ground and bending my knees, may adore it on the ground. Then Velosianus spread out his shawl with the cloth of gold on which the portrait of the Lord had been imprinted; and the Emperor Tiberius saw it. And he immediately adored the image of the Lord with a pure heart, and his flesh was cleansed as the flesh of a little child. And all the blind, the lepers, the lame, the dumb, the deaf, and those possessed by various diseases, who were there present, were healed, and cured, and cleansed. And the Emperor Tiberius bowed his head and bent his knees, considering that saying: Blessed is the womb which bore Thee, and the breasts which Thou hast sucked; and he groaned to the Lord, saying with tears: God of heaven and earth, do not permit me to sin, but confirm my soul and my body, and place me in Thy kingdom, because in Thy name do I trust always: free me from all evils, as Thou didst free the three children from the furnace of blazing fire. Then said the Emperor Tiberius to Velosianus: Velosianus, hast thou seen any of those men who saw Christ? Velosianus answered: I have. He said: Didst thou ask how they baptize those who believed in Christ? Velosianus said: Here, my Lord, we have one of the disciples of Christ himself.

Then he ordered Nathan to be summoned to come to him. Nathan therefore came and baptized him in the name of the Father, and of the Son, and of the Holy Ghost. Amen.

Immediately the Emperor Tiberius, made whole from all his diseases, ascended upon his throne, and said: Blessed art Thou, O Lord God Almighty, and worthy to be praised, who hast freed me from the snare of death, and cleansed me from all mine iniquities; because I have greatly sinned before Thee, O Lord my God, and I am not worthy to see Thy face.

And then the Emperor Tiberius was instructed in all the articles of the faith, fully, and with strong faith. May that same God Almighty, who is King of kings and Lord of lords, Himself shield us in His faith, and defend us, and deliver us from all danger and evil, and deign to bring us to life everlasting, when this life, which is temporary, shall fail; who is blessed for ever and ever. Amen.

The Book of James

or

Protevangelium

In the histories of the twelve tribes of Israel it is written that there was one Joachim, exceeding rich: and he offered his gifts twofold, saying: That which is of my superfluity shall be for the whole people, and that which is for my forgiveness shall be for tile Lord, for a propitiation unto me.

2. Now the great day of the Lord drew nigh and the children of Israel offered their gifts. And Reuben stood over against him saying: It is not lawful for thee to offer thy gifts first,-forasmuch as thou hast gotten no seed in Israel.

3. And Joachim was sore grieved, and went unto the record of the twelve tribes of the people, saying: I will look upon the record of the twelve tribes of Israel, whether I only have not gotten seed in Israel. And he searched, and found concerning all the righteous that they had raised up seed in Israel. And he remembered the patriarch Abraham, how in the last days God gave him a son, even Isaac.

4. And Joachim was sore grieved, and showed not himself to his wife, but betook himself into the wilderness, and pitched his tent there, and fasted forty days and forty nights, saying within himself: I will not go down either for meat or for drink until the Lord my God visit me, and my prayer shall be unto me meat and drink.

II

1. Now his wife Anna lamented with two lamentations, and bewailed

herself with two bewailings, saying: I will bewail my widowhood, and I will bewail my childlessness.

2. And the great day of the Lord drew nigh, and Judith her handmaid said unto her: How long humblest thou thy soul? The great day of the Lord hath come, and it is not lawful for thee to mourn: but take this headband, which the mistress of my work gave me, and it is not lawful for me to put it on, forasmuch as I am an handmaid, and it hath a mark of royalty. And Anna said: Get thee from me. Lo! I have done nothing (or I will not do so) and the Lord hath greatly humbled me: peradventure one gave it to thee in subtlety, and thou art come to make me partaker in thy sin. And Judith said: How shall I curse thee, seeing the Lord hath shut up thy womb, to give thee no fruit in Israel ?

3. And Anna was sore grieved [and mourned with a great mourning because she was reproached by all the tribes of Israel. And coming to herself she said: What shall I do ? I will pray with weeping unto the Lord my God that he visit me]. And she put off her mourning garments and cleansed (or adorned) her head and put on her bridal garments: and about the ninth hour she went down into the garden to walk there. And she saw a laurel-tree and sat down underneath it and besought the Lord saying: O God of our fathers, bless me, and hearken unto my prayer, as thou didst bless the womb of Sarah, and gavest her a son, even Isaac.

III

1. And looking up to the heaven she espied a nest of sparrows in the laurel-tree, and made a lamentation within herself, saying: Woe unto me, who begat me ? And what womb brought me forth for I am become a curse before the children of Israel, and I am reproached, and they have mocked me forth out of the temple of the Lord?

2. Woe unto me, unto what am I likened ? I am not likened unto the fowls of the heaven, for even the fowls of the heaven are fruitful before thee, O Lord. Woe unto me, unto what am I likened ? I am not likened unto the beasts of the earth, for even the beasts of the earth are fruitful before thee, O Lord. Woe unto me, unto what am I likened ? I am not likened unto these waters, for even these waters are fruitful before thee, O Lord.

3. Woe unto me, unto what am I likened ? I am not likened unto this earth, for even this earth bringeth forth her fruits in due season and blesseth thee, O Lord.

IV

1. And behold an angel of the Lord appeared, saying unto her: Anna, Anna, the Lord hath hearkened unto thy prayer, and thou shalt conceive and bear, and thy seed shall be spoken of in the whole world. And Anna said: As the Lord my God liveth, if I bring forth either male or female, I will bring it for a gift unto the Lord my God, and it shall be ministering unto him all the days of its life.

2. And behold there came two messengers saying unto her: Behold Joachim thy husband cometh with his flocks: for an angel of the Lord came down unto him saying: Joachim, Joachim, the Lord God hath hearkened unto thy prayer. Get thee down hence, for behold thy wife Anna hath conceived.

3. And Joachim sat him down and called his herdsmen saying: Bring me hither ten lambs without blemish and without spot, and they shall be for the Lord my God; and bring me twelve tender calves, and they shall be for the priests and for the assembly of the elders; and an hundred kids for the whole people.

4. And behold Joachim came with his flocks, and Anna stood at the gate and saw Joachim coming, and ran and hung upon his neck, saying: Now know I that the Lord God hath greatly blessed me: for behold the widow is no more a widow, and she that was childless shall conceive. And Joachim rested the first day in his house.

V

1. And on the morrow he offered his gifts, saying in himself: If the Lord God be reconciled unto me, the plate that is upon the forehead of the priest will make it manifest unto me. And Joachim offered his gifts and looked earnestly upon the plate of the priest when he went up unto the altar of tile Lord, and he saw no sin in himself. And Joachim said: Now know I that the Lord is become propitious unto me and hath forgiven all my sins. And he went down from the temple of the Lord justified, and went unto his house.

2. And her months were fulfilled, and in the ninth month Anna brought forth. And she said unto the midwife: what have I brought forth ? And she said: A female. And Anna said: My soul is magnified this day, and she laid herself down. And when the days were fulfilled, Anna purified herself and gave suck to the child and called her name Mary.

VI

1. And day by day the child waxed strong, and when she was six months old her mother stood her upon the ground to try if she would stand; and she walked seven steps and returned unto her bosom. And she caught her up, saying: As the Lord my God liveth, thou shalt walk no more upon this ground, until I bring thee into the temple of the Lord. And she made a sanctuary in her bed chamber and suffered nothing common or unclean to pass through it. And she called for the daughters of the Hebrews that were undefiled, and they carried her hither and thither.

2. And the first year of the child was fulfilled, and Joachim made a great feast and bade the priests and the scribes and the assembly of the elders and the whole people of Israel. And Joachim brought the child to the priests, and they blessed her, saying: O God of our fathers, bless this child and give her a name renowned for ever among all generations. And all the people said: So be it, so be it. Amen. And he brought her to the high priests, and they blessed her, saying: O God of the high places, look upon this child, and bless her with the last blessing which hath no successor.

3. And her mother caught her up into the sanctuary of her bed chamber and gave her suck. And Anna made a song unto the Lord God, saying: I will sing an hymn unto the Lord my God, because he hath visited me and taken away from me the reproach of mine enemies, and the Lord hath given me a fruit of his righteousness, single and manifold before him. Who shall declare unto the sons of Reuben that Anna giveth suck ? Hearken, hearken, ye twelve tribes of Israel, that Anna giveth suck. And she laid the child to rest in the bed chamber of her sanctuary, and went forth and ministered unto them. And when the feast was ended, they gat them down rejoicing, and glorifying the God of Israel.

VII

1. And unto the child her months were added: and the child became two years old. And Joachim said: Let us bring her up to the temple of the Lord that we may pay the promise which we promised; lest the Lord require it of us (lit. send unto us), and our gift become unacceptable. And Anna said: Let us wait until the third year, that the child may not long after her father or mother. And Joachim said: Let us wait.

2. And the child became three years old, and Joachim said: Call for the daughters of the Hebrews that are undefiled, and let them take every one a lamp, and let them be burning, that the child turn not backward and her

heart be taken captive away from the temple of the Lord. And they did so until they were gone up into the temple of the Lord. And the priest received her and kissed her and blessed her and said: The Lord hath magnified thy name among all generations: in thee in the latter days shall the Lord make manifest his redemption unto the children of Israel. And he made her to sit upon the third step of the altar. And the Lord put grace upon her and she danced with her feet and all tile house of Israel loved her.

VIII

1. And her parents gat them down marveling, and praising the Lord God because tile child was not turned away backward. And Mary was in the temple of the Lord as a dove that is nurtured: and she received food from the hand of an angel.

2. And when she was twelve years old, there was a council of the priests, saying: Behold Mary is become twelve years old in the temple of the Lord. What then shall we do with her ? lest she pollute the sanctuary of the Lord. And they said unto the high priest: Thou standest over the altar of the Lord. Enter in and pray concerning her: And whatsoever the Lord shall reveal to thee, that let us do.

3. And the high priest took the vestment with the twelve bells and went in unto the Holy of Holies and prayed concerning her. And lo, an angel of tile Lord appeared saying unto him: Zacharias, Zacharias~ go forth and assemble them that are widowers of the people, and let them bring every man a rod, and to whomsoever the Lord shall show a sign, his wife shall she be. And the heralds went forth over all the country round about Judaea, and the trumpet of the Lord sounded, and all men ran thereto.

IX

1. And Joseph cast down his adze (an ax-like tool for dressing wood) and ran to meet them, and when they were gathered together they went to the high priest and took their rods with them. And he took the rods of them all and went into the temple and prayed. And when he had finished the prayer he took the rods and went forth and gave them back to them: and there was no sign upon them. But Joseph received the last rod: and lo, a dove came forth of the rod and flew upon the bead of Joseph. And the priest said unto Joseph: Unto thee hath it fallen to take the virgin of the Lord and keep her for thyself.

2. And Joseph refused, saying: I have sons, and I am an old man, but she is

a girl: lest I became a laughing-stock to the children of Israel. And the priest said unto Joseph: Year the Lord thy God, and remember what things God did unto Dathan and Abiram and Korah, how the earth clave (opened) and they were swallowed up because of their gainsaying (contradiction). And now fear thou, Joseph, lest it be so in thine house. And Joseph was afraid, and took her to keep her for himself. And Joseph said unto Mary: Lo, I have received thee out of the temple of the Lord: and now do I leave thee in my house, and I go away to build my buildings and I will come again unto thee. The Lord shall watch over thee.

X

1. Now there was a council of the priests, and they said: Let us make a veil for the temple of the Lord. And the priest said: Call unto me pure virgins of the tribe of David. And the officers departed and sought and found seven virgins. And the priests called to mind the child Mary, that she was of the tribe of avid and was undefiled before God: and the officers went and fetched her. And they brought them into the temple of the Lord, and the priest said: Cast me lots, which of you shah weave the gold and the undefiled (the white) and tile fine linen and the silk and the hyacinthine, and the scarlet and the true purple. And the lot of the true purple and the scarlet fell unto Mary, and she took them and went unto her house. [And at that season Zacharias became dumb, and Samuel was in his stead until the time when Zacharias spake again.]But Mary took the scarlet and began to spin it.

XI

1. And she took the pitcher and went forth to fill it with water: and lo a voice saying: Hail, thou that art highly favoured; the Lord is with thee: bless-ed art thou among women. And she looked about her upon the right hand and upon the left, to see whence this voice should be: and being filled with trembling she~ went to her house and set down the pitcher, and took the purple and sat down upon her seat and drew out the thread.

2. And behold an angel of the Lord stood before her saying: Fear not, Mary, for thou hast found grace before the Lord of all things, and thou shalt conceive of his word. And she, when she heard it, questioned in herself, say-ing: Shall I verily conceive of the living God, and bring forth after the manner of all women ? And the angel of the Lord said: Not so, Mary, for a power of the Lord shall overshadow thee: wherefore also that holy thing which shall be born of thee shall be called the Son of the Highest. And thou shalt call

his name Jesus: for he shall save his people from their sins. And Mary said: Behold the handmaid of the Lord is before him: be it unto me according to thy word.

XII

1. And she made the purple and the scarlet and brought them unto the priest. And the priest blessed her and said: Mary, the Lord God hath magnified thy name, and thou shalt be blessed among all generations of the earth.

2. And Mary rejoiced and went away unto Elizabeth her kinswoman: and she knocked at the door. And Elizabeth when she heard it cast down the scarlet (al. the wool) and ran to the door and opened it, and when she saw Mary she blessed her and said: Whence is this to me that the mother of my Lord should come unto me ? for behold that which is in me leaped and blessed thee. And Mary forgat the mysteries which Gabriel the archangel had told her, and she looked up unto the heaven and said: Who am I, Lord, that all the generations of the earth do bless me?

3. And she abode three months with Elizabeth, and day by day her womb grew: and Mary was afraid and departed unto her house and hid herself from the children of Israel. Now she was sixteen years old when these mysteries came to pass.

XIII

1. Now it was the sixth month with her, and behold Joseph came from his building, and he entered into his house and found her great with child. And he smote his face, and cast himself down upon the ground on sackcloth and wept bitterly, saying: With what countenance shall I look unto the Lord my God ? and what prayer shall I make concerning this maiden? for I received her out of the temple of the Lord my God a virgin, and have not kept her safe. Who is he that hath ensnared me ? Who hath done this evil in mine house and hath defiled the virgin ? Is not the story of Adam repeated in me ? for as at the hour of his giving thanks the serpent came and found Eve alone and deceived her, so hath it befallen me also.

2. And Joseph arose from off the sackcloth and called Mary and said unto her O thou that wast cared for by God, why hast thou done this ? thou hast forgotten the Lord thy God. Why hast thou humbled thy soul, thou that wast nourished up in the Holy of Holies and didst receive food at the hand of an angel?

3. But she wept bitterly, saying: I am pure and I know not a man. And Jo-

seph said unto her: Whence then is that which is in thy womb ? and she said: As the Lord my God liveth, I know not whence it is come unto me.

XIV

1. And Joseph was sore afraid and ceased from speaking unto her (or left her alone), and pondered what he should do with her. And Joseph said: If I hide her sin, I shall be found fighting against the law of the Lord: and if I manifest her unto the children of Israel, I fear lest that which is in her be the seed of an angel, and I shall be found delivering up innocent blood to the judgement of death. What then shall I do ? I will let her go from me privily. And the night came upon him.

2. And behold an angel of the Lord appeared unto him in a dream, saying: Fear not this child, for that which is in her is of the Holy Ghost, and she shall bear a son and thou shalt call his name Jesus, for he shall save his people from their sins. And Joseph arose from sleep and glorified the God of Israel which had shown this favour unto her: and he watched over her.

XV

1. Now Annas the scribe came unto him and said to him: Wherefore didst thou not appear in our assembly ? and Joseph said unto him: I was weary with the journey, and I rested the first day. And Annas turned him about and saw Mary great with child.

2. And he went hastily to the priest and said unto him: Joseph, to whom thou bearest witness [that he is righteous] hath sinned grievously. And the priest said: Wherein ? And he said: The virgin whom he received out of the temple of the Lord, he hath defiled her, and married her by stealth (lit. stolen her marriage), and hath not declared it to the children of Israel. And the priest answered and said: Hath Joseph done this ? And Annas the scribe said: Send officers, and thou shalt find the virgin great with child. And the officers went and found as he had said, and they brought her together with Joseph unto the place of judgement.

3. And the priest said: Mary, wherefore hast thou done this, and wherefore hast thou humbled thy soul and forgotten the Lord thy God, thou that wast nurtured in the Holy of Holies and didst receive food at the hand of an angel and didst hear the hymns and didst dance before the Lord, wherefore hast thou done this ? But she wept bitterly, saying: As the Lord my God liveth I am pure before him and I know not a man.

4. And the priest said unto Joseph: Wherefore hast thou done this ? And

Joseph said: As the Lord my God liveth I am pure as concerning her. And the priest said: Bear no false witness but speak the truth: thou hast married her by stealth and hast not declared it unto the children of Israel, and hast not bowed thine head under the mighty hand that thy seed should be blessed. And Joseph held his peace.

XVI

1. And the priest said: Restore the virgin whom thou didst receive out of the temple of the Lord. And Joseph was full of weeping. And the priest said: I will give you to drink of the water of the conviction of the Lord, and it will make manifest your sins before your eyes.

2. And the priest took thereof and made Joseph drink and sent him into the hill-country. And he returned whole. He made Mary also drink and sent her into the hill-country. And she returned whole. And all the people marvelled, because sin appeared not in them.

3. And the priest said: If the Lord God hath not made your sin manifest, neither do I condemn you. And he let them go. And Joseph took Mary and departed unto his house rejoicing, and glorifying the God of Israel.

XVII

1. Now there went out a decree from Augustus the king that all that were in Bethlehem of Judaea should be recorded. And Joseph said: I will record my sons: but this child, what shall I do with her ? how shall I record her ? as my wife ? nay, I am ashamed. Or as my daughter? but all the children of Israel know that she is not my daughter. This day of the Lord shall do as the Lord willeth.

2. And he saddled the she-ass, and set her upon it, and his son led it and Joseph followed after. And they drew near (unto Bethlehem) within three miles: and Joseph turned himself about and saw her of a sad countenance and said within himself: Peradventure that which is within her paineth her. And again Joseph turned himself about and saw her laughing, and said unto her: Mary, what aileth thee that I see thy face at one time laughing and at another time sad ? And Mary said unto Joseph: It is because I behold two peoples with mine eyes, the one weeping and lamenting and the other rejoicing and exulting.

3. And they came to the midst of the way, and Mary said unto him: Take me down from the ass, for that which is within me presseth me, to come forth. And he took her down from the ass and said unto her: Whither shall I

take thee to hide thy shame ? for the place is desert.

XVIII

1. And he found a cave there and brought her into it, and set his sons by her: and he went forth and sought for a midwife of the Hebrews in the country of Bethlehem.

2. Now I Joseph was walking, and I walked not. And I looked up to the air and saw the air in amazement. And I looked up unto the pole of the heaven and saw it standing still, and the fowls of the heaven without motion. And I looked upon the earth and saw a dish set, and workmen lying by it, and their hands were in the dish: and they that were chewing chewed not, and they that were lifting the food lifted it not, and they that put it to their mouth put it not thereto, but the faces of all of them were looking upward. And behold there were sheep being driven, and they went not forward but stood still; and the shepherd lifted his hand to smite them with his staff, and his hand remained up. And I looked upon the stream of the river and saw the mouths of the kids upon the water and they drank not. And of a sudden all things moved onward in their course.

XIX

1. And behold a woman coming down from the hillcountry, and she said to me: Man, whither goest thou ? And I said: I seek a midwife of the Hebrews. And she answered and said unto me: Art thou of Israel ? And I said unto her: Yea. And she said: And who is she that bringeth forth in the cave? And I said: She that is betrothed unto me. And she said to me: Is she not thy wife? And I said to her: It is Mary that was nurtured up in the temple of the Lord: and I received her to wife by lot: and she is not my wife, but she hath conception by the Holy Ghost. And the midwife said unto him: Is this the truth? And Joseph said unto her: Come hither and see. And the midwife went with him.

2. And they stood in the place of the cave: and behold a bright cloud overshadowing the cave. And the midwife said: My soul is magnified this day, because mine eyes have seen marvellous things: for salvation is born unto Israel. And immediately the cloud withdrew itself out of the cave, and a great light appeared in the cave so that our eyes could not endure it. And by little and little that light withdrew itself until the young child appeared: and it went and took the breast of its mother Mary. And the midwife cried aloud and said: Great unto me to-day is this day, in that ! have seen this new sight.

3. And the midwife went forth of the cave and Salome met her. And she

said to her: Salome, Salome, a new sight have I to tell thee. A virgin hath brought forth, which her nature alloweth not. And Salome said: As the Lord my God liveth, if I make not trial and prove her nature I will not believe that a virgin hath brought forth.

XX

1. And the midwife went in and said unto Mary: Order thyself, for there is no small contention arisen concerning thee. Arid Salome made trial and cried out and said: Woe unto mine iniquity and mine unbelief, because I have tempted the living God, and lo, my hand falleth away from me in fire.

2. And she bowed her knees unto the Lord, saying: O God of my fathers, remember that I am the seed of Abraham and Isaac and Jacob: make me not a public example unto the children of Israel, but restore me unto the poor, for thou knowest, Lord, that in thy name did I perform my cures, and did receive my hire of thee.

3. And lo, an angel of the Lord appeared, saying unto her: Salome, Salome, the Lord hath hearkened to thee: bring thine hand near unto the young child and take him up, and there shall be unto thee salvation and joy.

4. And Salome came near and took him up, saying: I will do him worship, for a great king is born unto Israel. And behold immediately Salome was healed: and she went forth of the cave justified. And Io, a voice saying: Salome, Salome, tell none of the marvels which thou hast seen, until the child enter into Jerusalem.

XXI

1. And behold, Joseph made him ready to go forth into Judaea. And there came a great tumult in Bethlehem of Judaea; for there came wise men, saying: Where is he that is born king of the Jews ? For we have seen his star in the east and are come to worship him.

2. And when Herod heard it he was troubled and sent officers unto the wise men. And he sent for the high priests and examined them, saying: How is it written concerning the Christ, where he is born ? They say unto him: In Bethlehem of Judaea: for so it is written. And he let them go. And he examined the wise men, saying unto them: What sign saw ye concerning the king that is born ? And the wise men said: We saw a very great star shining among those stars and dimming them so that the stars appeared not: and thereby knew we that a king was born unto Israel, and we came to worship him. And Herod said: Go and seek for him, and if ye find him, tell me, that I also may

come and worship him.

3. And the wise men went forth. And lo, the star which they saw in the east went before them until they entered into the cave: and it stood over the head of the cave. And the wise men saw the young child with Mary, his mother: and they brought out of their scrip gifts, gold-and frankincense and myrrh.

4. And being warned by the angel that they should not enter into Judaea, they went into their own country by another way.

XXII

1. But when Herod perceived that he was mocked by the wise men, he was wroth, and sent murderers, saying unto them: Slay the children from two years old and under.

2. And when Mary heard that the children were being slain, she was afraid, and took the young child and wrapped in swaddling clothes and laid him in an ox-manger. Because there was no room for them in the inn.

3. But Elizabeth when she heard that they sought for her son John, took him and went up into the hill-country and looked about her where she should hide him: and there was no hiding-place. And Elizabeth groaned and said with a loud voice: O mountain of God, receive thou a mother with a child. For Elizabeth was not able to go up. And immediately the mountain clave asunder and took her in. And there was a light shining alway for them: for an angel of the Lord was with them, keeping watch over them.

XXIII

1. Now Herod sought for John, and sent officers to Zacharias, saying: Where hast thou hidden thy son? And he answered and said unto them: I am a minister of God and attend continually upon the temple of the Lord: I know not where my son is.

2. And the officers departed and told Herod all these things. And Herod was wroth and said: His son is to be king over Israel. And he sent unto him again, saying: Say the truth: where is thy son ? for thou knowest that thy blood is under my hand. And the officers departed and told him all these things.

3. And Zacharias said: I am a martyr of God if thou sheddest my blood: for my spirit the Lord shah receive, because thou sheddest innocent blood in the fore-court of the temple of the Lord. And about the dawning of the day Zacharias was slain. And the children of Israel knew not that he was slain.

XXIV

1. But the priests entered in at the hour of the salutation, and the blessing of Zacharias met them not according to the manner. And the priests stood waiting for Zacharias, to salute him with the prayer, and to glorify the Most High.

2. But as he delayed to come, they were all afraid: and one of them took courage and entered in: and he saw beside the altar congealed blood: and a voice saying: Zacharias hath been slain, and his blood shall not be wiped out until his avenger come. And when he heard that word he was afraid, and went forth and told the priests.

3. And they took courage and went in and saw that which was done: and the panels of the temple did wail: and they rent their clothes from the top to the bottom. And his body they found not, but his blood they found turned into stone. And they feared, and went forth and told all the people that Zacharias was slain.

4. And all the tribes of the people heard it, and they mourned for him and lamented him three days and three nights. And after the three days the priests took counsel whom they should set in his stead: and the lot came up upon Simon. Now he it was which was warned by the Holy Ghost that he should not see death until he should see the Christ in the flesh.

XXV

1. Now I, James, which wrote this history in Jerusalem, when there arose a tumult when Herod died, withdrew myself into the wilderness until the tumult ceased in Jerusalem. Glorifying the Lord God which gave me the gift, and the wisdom to write this history.

2. And grace shall be with those that fear our Lord Jesus Christ: to whom be glory for ever and ever. Amen.

The Book of Thomas the Contender

he secret words that the savior spoke to Judas Thomas which, I, even I, Mahaias, wrote down, while I was walking, listening to them speak with one another.

The savior said , "Brother Thomas while you have time in the world, listen to me, and I will reveal to you the things you have pondered in your mind," "Now since it has been said that you are my twin and true companion, examine yourself, and learn who you are, in what way you exist and how you will come to be.

Since you will be called my brother, it is not fitting that you be ignorant of yourself. And I know that you have understood because you had already understood that I am the knowledge of the truth. So while you accompany me, although you are uncomprehending, you have in fact already come to know, and you will be called "the one who knows himself". For he who has not known himself has known nothing, but he who has known himself has at the same time already achieved knowledge about the depth of the all. So then, you, my brother Thomas, have beheld what is obscure to men, that is, whatb they ignorantly stumble against." Now Thomas said to the lord, "Therefore I beg you to tell me what I ask you before your ascension, and when I hear from you about the hidden things, then I can speak about them. And it is obvious to me that the truth is difficult to perform before men." The savior answered, saying, "If the things that are visible to you are obscure to you, how can you hear about the things that are not visible? If the deeds of the truth that are visible in the world are difficult to you to perform, how indeed, then, shall you perform those that pertain to the exalted height and to the pleroma which are not visible? And how shall you be called "laborers" ? In this respect you are apprentices, and have not yet received the height of perfection."

Now Thomas answered and said to the savior, "Tell us about these things, that you say are not visible, but are hidden from us" The savior said, "All bodies [...] the beasts are begotten [...] it is evident like [...] [...] this, too, those that are above [...] things that are visible, but they are visible in their own root, and it is their fruit that nourishes them. But these visible bodies survive by devouring creatures similar to them with the result that the bodies change. Now that which changes will decay and perish, and has no hope of life from then on, since the body is bestial. So just as the body of the beasts perishes, so also will these formations perish. Do they not derive from intercourse like that of the beasts? If it, too derives from intercourse, how will it beget anything different from beasts? So, therefore, you are babes until you become perfect." And Thomas answered, "Therefore I say to you, lord, that those who speak about things that are invisible and difficult to explain are like those who shoot their arrows at a target at night. To be sure, they shoot arrows as anyone would - since they shoot at the target - but it is not visible. Yet when the light comes forth and hides the darkness, then the work of each will appear. And you, our light, enlighten, O lord." Jesus said, "It is in light that light exists."

Thomas, spoke, saying, "Lord, why does this visible light that shines on behalf of men rise and set?" The savior said, "O blessed Thomas, of course this visible light shines on your behalf - not in order that you remain here, but rather that you might come forth - and whenever all the elect abandon bestiality , then this light will withdraw up to its essence, and its essence will welcome it, since it is a good servant." Then the savior continued and said, "O unsearchable love of the light! O bitterness of the fire that blazes in the bodies of men and in their marrow, kindling in them night and day , and the burning the limbs of men and making their minds become drunk and their souls become deranged [...] them within males and females ...[...] night and moving them , ..[...] .. secretly and visibly. For the males [move... upon the females] and the females upon [males. Therefore it is] said, "everyone who seeks truth from true wisdom will make himself wings so as to fly, fleeing the lust that scorches the spirits of men. And he will make himself wings to flee every visible spirit." And Thomas answered, saying, "Lord, this is exactly what I am asking you about, since I have understood that you are the one who is beneficial to us, as you say." Again the savior answered and said, "Therefore it is necessary for us to speak to you, since this is the doctrine of the perfect. If, now, you desire to become perfect, you shall observe these things ; if not , your names is "ignorant", since it is impossible for an intelligent man to dwell with a fool, for the intelligent man is perfect in all wisdom. To the fool, however, the good and bad are the same - indeed the wise man will be nourished by the truth and (Ps. 1:3) "will be like a tree growing by the meandring stream" - seeing that there are some who, although having wings, rush upon the visible things, things that are far from the truth. For that which guides them, the fire, will give them the illusion of truth, and will shine on them with a perishable beauty, and it will imprison them in a dark sweetness and captivate them with fragrant pleasure. And it will blind them with insatiable lust and burn their souls and become for them like a stake stuck in their heart which they can never dislodge. And like a bit in the mouth, leads them according to its own desire. And it has fettered them with its chains and bound all their limbs with bitterness of the bondage of lust for those visible things that will decay and change and swerve by impulse.

They have alsways been attracted downwards ; as they are killed, they are assimilated to all the beasts of the perishable realm. Thomas answered and said, "It is obvious and has been said, [Many are .... those who do not know [...] ... soul"] And the savior answered, saying, "Blessed is the wise man who sought after the truth, and when he found it, he rested upon it forever and was unafraid of those who wanted to disturb him." Thomas answered and said, "It is beneficial for us, lord, to rest among our own?" The savior said, "Yes, it is useful. And it is good for you since things visible among men will dissolve - for the vessel of their flesh will dissolve, and when it is brought to naught it will come to be among visible thinsg, among things that are seen. And then the fire which they see gives them pain on account of love for the faith they formerly possessed. They will be gathered back to that which is visible. Moreover, those who have sight among things are not visible, without the first love they will persih in the concern for this life and the scorching of the fire. Only a little while longer, and that which is visible will dissolve ; then shapeless shades will emerge and in the midst of tombs they will forever dwell upon the corpses in pain and corruption of soul." Thomas answered and said , "What have we to say in the face of these things? What shall we say to blind men? What doctrine should we express to these miserable mortals who say, "we came to do good and not curse." and yet claim, "had we not been begotten in the flesh, we would not have known iniquity." The savior said, "Truly, as for those, do not esteem them as men but regard them as beasts, for just as beasts devour one another, so also men of this sort devour one another. On the contrary, they are deprived of the kingdom since they love the sweetness of the fire and are the servants of death and rush to the works of corruption. They fulfill the lust of the fathers. They will be thrown down to the abyss and be afflicted by the torment of the bitterness of their evil nature. For they will be scourged so as to make them rush backwards, whither they do not know, and they will recede from their limbs not patiently, but with despair. And they rejoice over [...] [...] madness and derangement .. They pursue this derangement without realizing their madness, thinking that they are wise. [They....] ... their body [...] Their mind is directed to their own selves, for their thought is occupied with their deeds. But it is the fire that will burn them." And Thomas answered and said, "Lord, what will the one thrown down to them do? For I am most anxious about them ; many are those who fight them." The savior answered and said , "Listen to what I am going to tell you and believe in the truth. That which sows and that which is sown will dissolve in the fire - within the fire and the water - and they will hide in tombs of darkness. And after a long time they shall show forth the fruit of the evil trees, being punished, being slain in the mouth of beasts and men at the instigation of the rains and winds and air and the light that shines above." Thomas replied, "You have certainly persuaded us, lord. We realize in our heart, and it is obvious, that this is so, and that your word is sufficient. But these words that you speak to us are ridiculous and contemptible to the world since they are misunderstood. So how can we preach them, since we are not esteemed in the world?" The savior answered and said, "Truly I tell you that he who will listen to you r word and turn away his face or sneer at it or smirk at these things, truly I tell you that he will be handed over to the ruler above who rules over all the powers as their king, and he will turn that one around and cast him from heaven down to the abyss, and he will be imprisoned in a narrow dark place. Moreover, he can neither turn nor move on account of the great depth of Tartaros and the heavy bitterness of Hades that is steadfast [...] [...] them to it.... [...] they will not forgive .... [...] pursue you. They will hand [...] over [to...] angel Tartarouchos [...] fire pursuing them [...] fiert scourges that cast a shower of sparks into the face of the one who is pursued. If he flees westward, he finds the fire. If he turns southward, he finds it there as well. If he turns northward, the threat of seething fire meets him again. Nor does he find the way to the east so as to flee there and be saved, for he did not find it in the day he was in the body, so that he might find it in the day of judgment." Then the savior continued, saying, "Woe to you, godless ones, who have no hope, who rely on things that will not happen!" "Woe to you because of the whell that turns in your minds! Woe to you within the grip of the burning, that is in you, for it will devour your flesh openly and rend your souls secretly, and prepare you for your companions! Woe to you, captives, for you are bound in caverns! You laugh! In mad laughter you rejoice! You neither realize your perdition, nor do you reflect on your circumstances, nor have you understood that you dwell in darkness and death! On the contrary, you are drunk with the fire and full of bitterness. Your mind is deranged on account of the burning that is in you, and sweet to you are the poison and the blows of your enemies! And the darkness rose for you like the light, for you surrendered for your freedom for servitude! You darkened your hearts and surrendered your thoughts to folly , and you filled your thoughts with the smoke of the fire that is in you! And your light has hidden in the cloud [or....] and the garment that is put upon you, you [...] [...] And you were seized by the hope that does not exist. And whom is it you have believed? Do you not know that you all dwell among those who that [...] [...] you as though you [...]. You baptized your souls in the water of darkness ! You walked by your own whims! Woe to you who dwell in error, heedless that the light of the sun which judges and looks down upon the all will circle around all things so as to enslave the enemies. You do not even notice the moon, how by night and day it looks down, looking at the bodies of your slaughters! Woe to you who love intimacy with womankind and polluted intercourse with them! Woe to you in the grip of the powers of your body, for they will afflict you!. Woe to you in the grip of the forces of evil demons! Woe to you who beguile your limbs with fire! Who is it that will rain a refreshing dew on you to extinguish the mass of fire from you along with your burning? Who is it that will cause the sn to shine upon you to disperse the darkness in you and hide the darkness and polluted water?" "The sun and the moon will give a fragrance to you together with the air and the spirit and the earth and the water. For if the sun does not shine upon these bodies, they will wither and perish just like weeds of grass. If the sun shines on them, they prevail and choke the grapevine; but if the grapevine prevails and shades those weeds and all the other brush growing alongside and spreads and flourishes, it alone inherits the land in which it grows; and every place it has shaded it dominates. And when it grows up, it dominates all the land and is bountiful for its master, and it pleases him even more , for he would have suffered great paints on account of these plants until he uprooted them. But the grapevine alone removed them and choked them, and they died and became like soil" Then Jesus continued and said to them , "Woe to you , for you did not receive the doctrine, and those who are [...] will labor at preaching [...]. And you are rushing into ... [...] [...] will send them down .... [...] you kill them daily in order that they might rise from death. Blessed are you who have (foreknowledge) prior knowledge of the stumbling blocks and who flee alien things. Blessed are you who are reviled and not esteemed on account of the love their lord has over them. Blessed are you who weep and are oppressed by those without hope, for you will be released from every bondage. Watch and pray that you not come to be in the flesh, but rather that you come forth from the bondage of bitterness of this life. And as you pray, you will find rest, for you have left behind the suffering and the disgrace. For when you come forth from the sufferings and passions of the body, you will receive rest from the good one , and you will reign with the king, you joined with him and he with you, from now on, for ever and ever, Amen." The Book of Thomas The Contender Writing To the Perfect . Remember me also, my brethren, in your prayers, Peace to the saints and those who are spiritual.

Clement of Rome Second Epistle

CHAPTER 1

That we ought to value our salvation; and to show that we do, by a sincere obedience.

1. Brethren, we ought so to think of Jesus Christ as of God as of the judge of the living and the dead; nor should we think any less of our salvation.

2. For if we think little things of him, we shall hope only to receive some small things from him.

3. And if we do so, we shall sin; not considering from where we have been called, and by whom, and to what place; and how much Jesus Christ condescended to suffer for our sakes.

4. What recompense then shall we render unto him? Or what fruit that may be worthy of what he has given to us?

5. For indeed, how great are those advantages which we owe to him in relation to our holiness? He has illuminated us; as a father, he has called us his children; he has saved us who were lost and undone.

6. What praise shall we give to him? Or what reward that may be answerable to those things which we have received?

7. We were defective in our understandings, worshipping stones and wood, gold, and silver, and brass, the works of men's hands; and our whole life was nothing else but death.

8. But being surrounded by darkness, and having such a mist before our eyes, we have looked up, and through his will have laid aside the cloud with which we were surrounded.

9. For he had compassion upon us, and being moved in his affection towards us, he saved us, having beheld in us much error and destruction, and

seen that we had no hope of salvation, but only through him.

10. For he called us who were not, and was pleased from nothing to give us being.

CHAPTER 2

1. That God had before prophesied by Isaiah that the Gentiles should be saved.

1b. That this ought to engage them especially to live well, without which they will still miscarry.

1c. Rejoice, you barren that bear not, break forth and cry you that travail not; for she that is desolate has many more children than she that has an husband. [Isa. 54:1]

2. In that he said, Rejoice you barren that bear not, he spoke of us: for our church was barren before children were given to it.

3. And again; when he said, Cry you that travail not; he implied thus much: That after the manner of women in travail, we should not cease to put up our prayers to God abundantly.

4. And for what follows, because she that is desolate has more children than she that has an husband: it was therefore added, because our people which seem to have been forsaken by God, now believing in him, are become more than they who seemed to have God.

5. And another Scripture saith, I came not to call the righteous but sinners. The meaning of which is this: that those who were lost must be saved. [Matt. 9:13]

6. For that is, indeed, truly great and wonderful, not to confirm those things that are yet standing, but those which are falling.

7. Even so did it seem good to Christ to save what was lost; and when he came into the world, he saved many, and called us who were already lost.

8. Seeing then he has showed so great mercy towards us; and chiefly for that, we who are alive, do now no longer sacrifice to dead gods, nor pay any worship to them, but have by him been brought to the knowledge of the Father of truth.

9. Whereby shall we show that we do indeed know him, but by not denying him by whom we have come to the knowledge of him?

10. For even he himself saith, Whosoever shall confess me before men, him will I confess before my Father [Matt. 10:32, 33]. This therefore is our reward if we shall confess him by whom we have been saved.

11. But, wherein must we confess him? Namely, in doing those things which he says, and not disobeying his commandments: by worshipping him

not with our lips only, but with all our heart, and with all our mind. For he says in Isaiah: This people honors me with their lips, but their heart is far from me. [Isa. 29:13]

12. Let us then not only call him Lord; for that will not save us. For he says: Not every one that says to me Lord, Lord, shall be saved, but he that does righteousness. [Matt. 7:21]

13. Wherefore, brethren, let us confess him by our works; by loving one another; in not committing adultery, not speaking evil against each other, not envying one another; but by being temperate, merciful, good.

14. Let us also have a mutual sense of one another's sufferings; and not be covetous of money: but let us by our good works confess God, and not by those that are otherwise.

15. Also let us not fear men, but rather God. Wherefore, if we should do such wicked things, the Lord has said: Though you should be joined to me, even in my very bosom, and not keep my commandments, I would cast you off, and say to you: Depart from me; I know not where you are, you workers of iniquity. [Matt. 7:23; Luke 13:26, 27]

CHAPTER 3

1. That while we secure the other world, we need not fear what can befall us in this.

1b. That if we follow the interests of this present world, we cannot escape the punishment of the other. Which ought to bring us to repentance and holiness, and that quickly: because in this world is the only time for repentance.

1c. Wherefore, brethren, leaving willingly for conscience sake our sojourning in this world, let us do the will of him who has called us, and not fear to depart out of this world.

2. For the Lord saith, You shall be as sheep in the midst of wolves [Matthew 10:16]. Peter answered and said, What if the wolves shall tear in pieces the sheep? Jesus said to Peter, Let not the sheep fear the wolves after death: also fear not those that kill you, and after that have no more that they can do to you; but fear him who after you are dead, has power to cast both soul and body into hell-fire. [Luke 12:4, 5]

3. For consider, brethren, that the sojourning of this flesh in the present world is but little, and of a short continuance, but the promise of Christ is great and wonderful, even the rest of the kingdom that is to come, and of eternal life.

4. What then must we do that we may attain to it? We must order our conversation holily and righteously, and look upon all the things of this world as

none of ours, and not desire them. For, if we desire to possess them we fall from the way of righteousness.

5. For thus says the Lord, No servant can serve two masters. If therefore we shall desire to serve God and Mammon it will be without profit to us [Luke 16:13]. For what will it profit, if one gain the whole world, and lose his own soul? [Matthew 16:26]

6. Now this world and that to come are two enemies. This speak of adultery and corruption, of covetousness and deceit; but renounces these things.

7. We cannot, therefore, be the friends of both; but we must resolve by forsaking the one, to enjoy the other. And we think it is better to hate the present things, as little, short- lived, and corruptible, and to love those which are to come, which are truly good and incorruptible.

8. For, if we do the will of Christ, we shall find rest: but if not, nothing shall deliver us from eternal punishment if we shall disobey his commands. For even thus says the Scripture in the prophet Ezekiel, If Noah, Job, and Daniel should rise up, they shall not deliver their children in captivity. [Ezekiel 14:14, 20]

9. Wherefore, if such righteous men are not able by their righteousness to deliver their children; how can we hope to enter into the kingdom of God, except we keep our baptism holy and undefiled? Or who shall be our advocate, unless we shall be found to have done what is holy and just?

10. Let us therefore, my brethren, contend with all earnestness, knowing that our combat is at hand; and that many go long voyages to encounter for a corruptible reward.

11. And yet all are not crowned, but they only that labor much, and strive gloriously. Let us, therefore, so contend that we may all be crowned. Let us run in the straight road, the race that is incorruptible: and let us in great numbers pass into it, and strive that we may receive the crown. But and if we cannot all be crowned, let us come as near to it as we are able.

12. Moreover, we must consider, that he who contends in a corruptible combat, if he be found doing anything that is not fair, is taken away and scourged, and cast out of the lists. What think ye then that he shall suffer, who does anything that is not fitting in the combat of immortality?

13. Thus speaks the prophet concerning those who keep not their seal; Their worm shall not die, and their fire shall not be quenched; and they shall be for a spectacle to all flesh. [Isaiah 66:24]

14. Let us therefore repent, while we are yet upon the earth: for we are as clay in the hand of the artificer. For as the potter, if he make a vessel, and it be turned amiss in his hands, or broken, again forms it anew; but if he has gone so far as to throw it into the furnace of fire, he cannot more bring any

remedy to it.

15. So we, while we are in this world, should repent with our whole heart for whatsoever evil we have done in the flesh; while we have yet the time of repentance, that we may be saved by the Lord.

16. For after we shall have departed out of this world, we shall no longer be able to confess our sins or repent in the other.

17. Wherefore, brethren, let us be doing the will of the Father, and keeping our flesh pure, and observing the commandments of the Lord, lay hold on eternal life: for the Lord saith in the gospel, If ye have not kept that which was little, who will give you that which is great? For I say to you, he that is faithful in that which is least, is faithful also in much. [Luke 16:10]

18. This, therefore, is what he is saying: keep your bodies pure, and your seal without spot, that you may receive eternal life.

CHAPTER 4

1. We shall rise, and be judged in our bodies; therefore we must live well in them, that we ought, for own interest, to live well; though few seem to mind what really is for their advantage, and not deceive ourselves: seeing God will certainly judge us, and render to all of us according to our works.

1b. And let not any one among you say, that this very flesh is not judged, neither raised up. Consider, in what were you saved; in what did you look up, if not while you were in this flesh.

2. We must, therefore, keep our flesh as the temple of God. For in like manner as ye were called in the flesh, ye shall also come to judgment in the flesh. Our one Lord Jesus Christ, who has saved us, being first a spirit, was made flesh, and so called us; even so we also shall in this flesh receive the reward.

3. Let us, therefore, love one another, that we may attain to the kingdom of God. While we have time to be healed, let us deliver up ourselves to God our physician, giving our reward to him.

4. And what reward shall we give? Repentance out of a pure heart. For he knows all things beforehand, and searches out our very hearts.

5. Let us, therefore, give praise to him, not only with our mouths, but with all our souls so he may receive us as children. For so the Lord has said: They are my brethren, who do the will of my Father. [Matthew 12:50]

6. Wherefore, my brethren, let us do the will of the Father, who has called us that we may live. Let us pursue virtue and forsake wickedness, which leads us into sins; and let us flee all ungodliness, so that evils overtake us not.

7. For if we shall do our diligence to live well, peace will follow us. And yet

how hard is it to find a man that does this? For almost all are led by human fears, choosing rather the present enjoyments than the future promise.

8. For they know not how great a torment the present enjoyments bring with them, nor what delights the future promise.

9. And if only they themselves did this, it might the more easily be endured; but now they go on to infect innocent souls with their evil doctrines, not knowing that both themselves and those that hear them will receive a double condemnation.

10. Let us, therefore, serve God with a pure heart, and we shall be righteous; but if we shall not serve him because we do not believe the promise of God, we shall be miserable.

11. For thus says the prophet: Miserable are the double-minded who doubt in their heart and say, These things we have heard even in the time of our fathers, but we have seen none of them, though we have expected them from day to day.

12. O ye fools! Compare yourselves to a tree; take the vine for an example. First it sheds its leaves, then it buds, then come the sour grapes, then the ripe fruit; even so my people have borne disorders and afflictions, but will hereafter receive good things.

13. Therefore my brethren, let us not doubt in our minds, but let us expect with hope, that we may receive our reward; for he is faithful, who has promised that he will render to every one a reward according to his works.

14. If, therefore, we shall do what is just in the sight of God, we shall enter into his kingdom and shall receive the promises: Which neither eye has seen, nor ear heard, nor have entered into the heart of man. [Isaiah 64:4; 1 Corinthians 2:9]

15. So let us every hour expect the kingdom of God in love and righteousness, because we know not the day of God's appearing.

CHAPTER 5 (A fragment)

Of the Lord's kingdom.

1. For the Lord himself, being asked by a certain person when his kingdom should come, answered, When two will be one, and that which is without as that which is within, and the male with the female is neither male nor female.

2. Now two are one, when we speak the truth to each other, and there is, without hypocrisy, one soul in two bodies:

3. And by that which is without as that which is within, he means this: he calls the soul that which is within, and the body that which is without. As

therefore your body appears, so let your soul be seen by its good works.

4. And by the male with the female is neither male nor female, he means this: he calls our anger the male and our concupiscence the female.

5. When therefore a man is come to such a pass that he is subject neither to the one nor the other of these (both of which, through the prevalence of custom, and an evil education, cloud and darken the reason,)

6. But rather, having dispelled the mist arising from them, and being full of shame, will by repentance have united both his soul and spirit in the obedience of reason; then, as Paul says, there is in us neither male nor female. [Galatians 3:28]

The Didache

"The Teaching of the Twelve Apostles" (Late first century)

CHAPTER 1
The Two Ways and the First Commandment

There are two ways, one of life and one of death, but a great difference between the two ways. The way of life, then, is this: First, you shall love God who made you; second, love your neighbor as yourself, and do not do to another what you would not want done to you. And of these sayings the teaching is this: Bless those who curse you, and pray for your enemies, and fast for those who persecute you. For what reward is there for loving those who love you? Do not the Gentiles do the same? But love those who hate you, and you shall not have an enemy. Abstain from fleshly and worldly lusts. If someone strikes your right cheek, turn to him the other also, and you shall be perfect. If someone impresses you for one mile, go with him two. If someone takes your cloak, give him also your coat. If someone takes from you what is yours, ask it not back, for indeed you are not able. Give to every one who asks you, and ask it not back; for the Father wills that to all should be given of our own blessings (free gifts). Happy is he who gives according to the commandment, for he is guiltless. Woe to him who receives; for if one receives who has need, he is guiltless; but he who receives not having need shall pay the penalty, why he received and for what. And coming into confinement, he shall be examined concerning the things which he has done, and he shall not escape from there until he pays back the last penny. And also concerning this, it has been said, Let your alms sweat in your hands, until you know to whom you should give.

CHAPTER 2
The Second Commandment: Grave Sin Forbidden

And the second commandment of the Teaching; You shall not commit murder, you shall not commit adultery, you shall not commit pederasty, you shall not commit fornication, you shall not steal, you shall not practice magic, you shall not practice witchcraft, you shall not murder a child by abortion nor kill that which is born. You shall not covet the things of your neighbor, you shall not swear, you shall not bear false witness, you shall not speak evil, you shall bear no grudge. You shall not be double-minded nor double-tongued, for to be double-tongued is a snare of death. Your speech shall not be false, nor empty, but fulfilled by deed. You shall not be covetous, nor rapacious, nor a hypocrite, nor evil disposed, nor haughty. You shall not take evil counsel against your neighbor. You shall not hate any man; but some you shall reprove, and concerning some you shall pray, and some you shall love more than your own life.

CHAPTER 3
Other Sins Forbidden

My child, flee from every evil thing, and from every likeness of it. Be not prone to anger, for anger leads to murder. Be neither jealous, nor quarrelsome, nor of hot temper, for out of all these murders are engendered. My child, be not a lustful one. for lust leads to fornication. Be neither a filthy talker, nor of lofty eye, for out of all these adulteries are engendered. My child, be not an observer of omens, since it leads to idolatry. Be neither an enchanter, nor an astrologer, nor a purifier, nor be willing to took at these things, for out of all these idolatry is engendered. My child, be not a liar, since a lie leads to theft. Be neither money-loving, nor vainglorious, for out of all these thefts are engendered. My child, be not a murmurer, since it leads the way to blasphemy. Be neither self-willed nor evil-minded, for out of all these blasphemies are engendered. Rather, be meek, since the meek shall inherit the earth. Be long-suffering and pitiful and guileless and gentle and good and always trembling at the words which you have heard. You shall not exalt yourself, nor give over-confidence to your soul. Your soul shall not be joined with lofty ones, but with just and lowly ones shall it have its intercourse. Accept whatever happens to you as good, knowing that apart from God nothing comes to pass.

CHAPTER 4
Various Precepts

My child, remember night and day him who speaks the word of God to you, and honor him as you do the Lord. For wherever the lordly rule is uttered, there is the Lord. And seek out day by day the faces of the saints, in order that you may rest upon their words. Do not long for division, but rather bring those who contend to peace. Judge righteously, and do not respect persons in reproving for transgressions. You shall not be undecided whether or not it shall be. Be not a stretcher forth of the hands to receive and a drawer of them back to give. If you have anything, through your hands you shall give ransom for your sins. Do not hesitate to give, nor complain when you give; for you shall know who is the good repayer of the hire. Do not turn away from him who is in want; rather, share all things with your brother, and do not say that they are your own. For if you are partakers in that which is immortal, how much more in things which are mortal? Do not remove your hand from your son or daughter; rather, teach them the fear of God from their youth. Do not enjoin anything in your bitterness upon your bondman or maidservant, who hope in the same God, lest ever they shall fear not God who is over both; for he comes not to call according to the outward appearance, but to them whom the Spirit has prepared. And you bondmen shall be subject to your masters as to a type of God, in modesty and fear. You shall hate all hypocrisy and everything which is not pleasing to the Lord. Do not in any way forsake the commandments of the Lord; but keep what you have received, neither adding thereto nor taking away therefrom. In the church you shall acknowledge your transgressions, and you shall not come near for your prayer with an evil conscience. This is the way of life.

CHAPTER 5
The Way of Death

And the way of death is this: First of all it is evil and accursed: murders, adultery, lust, fornication, thefts, idolatries, magic arts, witchcrafts, rape, false witness, hypocrisy, double-heartedness, deceit, haughtiness, depravity, self-will, greediness, filthy talking, jealousy, over-confidence, loftiness, boastfulness; persecutors of the good, hating truth, loving a lie, not knowing a reward for righteousness, not cleaving to good nor to righteous judgment, watching not for that which is good, but for that which is evil; from whom meekness and endurance are far, loving vanities, pursuing revenge, not pitying a poor man, not laboring for the afflicted, not knowing Him Who made them, murderers of children, destroyers of the handiwork of God, turning away from him who is in want, afflicting him who is distressed, advocates of the rich, lawless judges of the poor, utter sinners. Be delivered, children, from all these.

CHAPTER 6
Against False Teachers, and Food Offered to Idols

See that no one causes you to err from this way of the Teaching, since apart from God it teaches you. For if you are able to bear the entire yoke of the Lord, you will be perfect; but if you are not able to do this, do what you are able. And concerning food, bear what you are able; but against that which is sacrificed to idols be exceedingly careful; for it is the service of dead gods.

CHAPTER 7
Concerning Baptism

And concerning baptism, baptize this way: Having first said all these things, baptize into the name of the Father, and of the Son, and of the Holy Spirit, in living water. But if you have no living water, baptize into other water; and if you cannot do so in cold water, do so in warm. But if you have neither, pour out water three times upon the head into the name of Father and Son and Holy Spirit. But before the baptism let the baptizer fast, and the baptized, and whoever else can; but you shall order the baptized to fast one or two days before.

CHAPTER 8
Fasting and Prayer (the Lord's Prayer)

But let not your fasts be with the hypocrites, for they fast on the second and fifth day of the week. Rather, fast on the fourth day and the Preparation (Friday). Do not pray like the hypocrites, but rather as the Lord commanded in His Gospel, like this: Our Father who art in heaven, hallowed be Thy name. Thy kingdom come. Thy will be done on earth, as it is in heaven. Give us today our daily (needful) bread, and forgive us our debt as we also forgive our debtors. And bring us not into temptation, but deliver us from the evil one (or, evil); for Thine is the power and the glory for ever. Pray this three times each day.

CHAPTER 9
The Eucharist

Now concerning the Eucharist, give thanks this way. First, concerning the cup: We thank thee, our Father, for the holy vine of David Thy servant, which You madest known to us through Jesus Thy Servant; to Thee be the glory for ever. And concerning the broken bread: We thank Thee, our Father, for the life and knowledge which You madest known to us through Jesus Thy Servant; to Thee be the glory for ever. Even as this broken bread was scattered over the hills, and was gathered together and became one, so let Thy Church be gathered together from the ends of the earth into Thy kingdom; for Thine is the glory and the power through Jesus Christ for ever. But let no one eat or drink of your Eucharist, unless they have been baptized into the name of the Lord; for concerning this also the Lord has said, "Give not that which is holy to the dogs."

CHAPTER 10
Prayer after Communion

But after you are filled, give thanks this way: We thank Thee, holy Father, for Thy holy name which You didst cause to tabernacle in our hearts, and for the knowledge and faith and immortality, which You modest known to us through Jesus Thy Servant; to Thee be the glory for ever. Thou, Master almighty, didst create all things for Thy name's sake; Thou gavest food and drink to men for enjoyment, that they might give thanks to Thee; but to us You didst freely give spiritual food and drink and life eternal through Thy Servant. Before all things we thank Thee that You are mighty; to Thee be the glory for ever. Remember, Lord, Thy Church, to deliver it from all evil and to make it perfect in Thy love, and gather it from the four winds, sanctified for Thy kingdom which Thou have prepared for it; for Thine is the power and the glory for ever. Let grace come, and let this world pass away. Hosanna to the God of David! If any one is holy, let him come; if any one is not so, let him repent. Maranatha. Amen. But permit the prophets to make thanksgiving as much as they desire.

CHAPTER 11
Concerning Teachers, Apostles, and Prophets

Whosoever, therefore, comes and teaches you all these things that have been said before, receive him. But if the teacher himself turns and teaches another doctrine to the destruction of this, hear him not. But if he teaches so as to increase righteousness and the knowledge of the Lord, receive him as the Lord. But concerning the apostles and prophets, act according to the decree of the Gospel. Let every apostle who comes to you be received as the Lord. But he shall not remain more than one day; or two days, if there's a need. But if he remains three days, he is a false prophet. And when the apostle goes away, let him take nothing but bread until he lodges. If he asks for money, he is a false prophet. And every prophet who speaks in the Spirit you shall neither try nor judge; for every sin shall be forgiven, but this sin shall not be forgiven. But not every one who speaks in the Spirit is a prophet; but only if he holds the ways of the Lord. Therefore from their ways shall the false prophet and the prophet be known. And every prophet who orders a meal in the Spirit does not eat it, unless he is indeed a false prophet. And every prophet who teaches the truth, but does not do what he teaches, is a false prophet. And every prophet, proved true, working unto the mystery of the Church in the world, yet not teaching others to do what he himself does, shall not be judged among you, for with God he has his judgment; for so did also the ancient prophets. But whoever says in the Spirit, Give me money, or something else, you shall not listen to him. But if he tells you to give for others' sake who are in need, let no one judge him.

CHAPTER12
Reception of Christians

But receive everyone who comes in the name of the Lord, and prove and know him afterward; for you shall have understanding right and left. If he who comes is a wayfarer, assist him as far as you are able; but he shall not remain with you more than two or three days, if need be. But if he wants to stay with you, and is an artisan, let him work and eat. But if he has no trade, according to your understanding, see to it that, as a Christian, he shall not live with you idle. But if he wills not to do, he is a Christ-monger. Watch that you keep away from such.

CHAPTER 13
Support of Prophets

But every true prophet who wants to live among you is worthy of his support. So also a true teacher is himself worthy, as the workman, of his support. Every first-fruit, therefore, of the products of wine-press and threshing-floor, of oxen and of sheep, you shall take and give to the prophets, for they are your high priests. But if you have no prophet, give it to the poor. If you make a batch of dough, take the first-fruit and give according to the commandment. So also when you open a jar of wine or of oil, take the first-fruit and give it to the prophets; and of money (silver) and clothing and every possession, take the first-fruit, as it may seem good to you, and give according to the commandment.

CHAPTER 14
Christian Assembly on the Lord's Day

But every Lord's day gather yourselves together, and break bread, and give thanksgiving after having confessed your transgressions, that your sacrifice may be pure. But let no one who is at odds with his fellow come together with you, until they be reconciled, that your sacrifice may not be profaned. For this is that which was spoken by the Lord: "In every place and time offer to me a pure sacrifice; for I am a great King, says the Lord, and my name is wonderful among the nations."

CHAPTER 15
Bishops and Deacons; Christian Reproof

Appoint, therefore, for yourselves, bishops and deacons worthy of the Lord, men meek, and not lovers of money, and truthful and proved; for they also render to you the service of prophets and teachers. Therefore do not despise them, for they are your honored ones, together with the prophets and teachers. And reprove one another, not in anger, but in peace, as you have it in the Gospel. But to anyone that acts amiss against another, let no one speak, nor let him hear anything from you until he repents. But your prayers and alms and all your deeds so do, as you have it in the Gospel of our Lord.

CHAPTER 16
Watchfulness; the Coming of the Lord

Watch for your life's sake. Let not your lamps be quenched, nor your loins unloosed; but be ready, for you know not the hour in which our Lord will come. But come together often, seeking the things which are befitting to your souls: for the whole time of your faith will not profit you, if you are not made perfect in the last time. For in the last days false prophets and corrupters shall be multiplied, and the sheep shall be turned into wolves, and love shall be turned into hate; for when lawlessness increases, they shall hate and persecute and betray one another, and then shall appear the world-deceiver as Son of God, and shall do signs and wonders, and the earth shall be delivered into his hands, and he shall do iniquitous things which have never yet come to pass since the beginning. Then shall the creation of men come into the fire of trial, and many shall be made to stumble and shall perish; but those who endure in their faith shall be saved from under the curse itself. And then shall appear the signs of the truth: first, the sign of an outspreading in heaven, then the sign of the sound of the trumpet. And third, the resurrection of the dead -- yet not of all, but as it is said: "The Lord shall come and all His saints with Him." Then shall the world see the Lord coming upon the clouds of heaven.

The Epistle of Barnabas

CHAPTER I
After the Salutation, the Writer Declares that He Would Communicate to His Brethren Something of that Which He Had Himself Received

All hail, ye sons and daughters, in the name of our Lord Jesus Christ, who loved us in peace. Seeing that the divine fruits of righteousness abound among you, I rejoice exceedingly and above measure in your happy and honoured spirits, because ye have with such effect received the engrafted spiritual gift. Wherefore also I inwardly rejoice the more, hoping to be saved, because I truly perceive in you the Spirit poured forth from the rich Lord of love. Your greatly desired appearance has thus filled me with astonishment over you. I am therefore pursuaded of this, and fully convinced in my own mind, that since I began to speak among you I understand many things, because the Lord hath accompanied me in the way of righteousness. I am also on this account bound by the strictest obligation to love you above my own soul, because great are the faith and love dwelling in you, while you hope for the life which He has promised. Considering this, therefore, that if I should take the trouble to communicate to you some portion of what I have myself received, it will prove to me a sufficient reward that I minister to such spirits, I have hastened briefly to write unto you, in order that, along with your faith, ye might have perfect knowledge. The doctrines of the Lord, then, are three: the hope of life, the beginning and the completion of it. For the Lord hath made known to us by the prophets both the things which are past and present, giving us also the first-fruits of the knowledge of things to come, which things as we see accomplished, one by one, we ought with the greater richness of faith and elevation of spirit to draw near to Him with reverence. I then, not as your teacher, but as one of yourselves, will set forth a few things by which in present circumstances ye may be rendered the more joyful.

CHAPTER II
The Jewish Sacrifices are Now Abolished

Since, therefore, the days are evil, and Satan possesses the power of this world, we ought to give heed to ourselves, and diligently inquire into the ordinances of the Lord. Fear and patience, then, are helpers of our faith; and long-suffering and continence are things which fight on our side. While these remain pure in what respects the Lord, Wisdom, Understanding, Science, and Knowledge rejoice along with them. For He hath revealed to us by all the prophets that He needs neither sacrifices, nor burnt-offerings, nor oblations, saying thus, "What is the multitude of your sacrifices unto Me, saith the Lord? I am full of burnt-offerings, and desire not the fat of lambs, and the blood of bulls and goats, not when ye come to appear before Me: for who hath required these things at your hands? Tread no more My courts, not though ye bring with you fine flour. Incense is a vain abomination unto Me, and your new moons and sabbaths I cannot endure." He has therefore abolished these things, that the new law of our Lord Jesus Christ, which is without the yoke of necessity, might have a human oblation. And again He says to them, "Did I command your fathers, when they went out from the land of Egypt, to offer unto Me burnt-offerings and sacrifices? But this rather I commanded them, Let no one of you cherish any evil in his heart against his neighbour, and love not an oath of falsehood." We ought therefore, being possessed of understanding, to perceive the gracious intention of our Father; for He speaks to us, desirous that we, not going astray like them, should ask how we may approach Him. To us, then, He declares, "A sacrifice [pleasing] to God is a broken spirit; a smell of sweet savour to the Lord is a heart that glorifieth Him that made it." We ought therefore, brethren, carefully to inquire concerning our salvation, lest the wicked one, having made his entrance by deceit, should hurl us forth from our [true] life.

CHAPTER III
The Fasts of the Jews are Not True Fasts, Nor Acceptable to God

He says then to them again concerning these things, "Why do ye fast to Me as on this day, saith the Lord, that your voice should be heard with a cry? I have not chosen this fast, saith the Lord, that a man should humble his soul. Nor, though ye bend your neck like a ring, and put upon you sackcloth and ashes, will ye call it an acceptable fast." To us He saith, "Behold, this is the fast that I have chosen, saith the Lord, not that a man should humble his soul, but that he should loose every band of iniquity, untie the fastenings of harsh agreements, restore to liberty them that are bruised, tear in pieces every unjust engagement, feed the hungry with thy bread, clothe the naked when thou seest him, bring the homeless into thy house, not despise the humble if thou behold him, and not [turn away] from the members of thine own family. Then shall thy dawn break forth, and thy healing shall quickly spring up, and righteousness shall go forth before thee, and the glory of God shall encompass thee; and then thou shalt call, and God shall hear thee; whilst thou art yet speaking, He shall say, Behold, I am with thee; if thou take away from thee the chain [binding others], and the stretching forth of the hands [to sweat falsely], and words of murmuring, and give cheerfully thy bread to the hungry, and show compassion to the soul that has been humbled." To this end, therefore, brethren, He is long-suffering, foreseeing how the people whom He has prepared shall with guilelessness believe in His Beloved. For He revealed all these things to us beforehand, that we should not rush forward as rash acceptors of their laws.

CHAPTER IV
Antichrist is at Hand: Let Us Therefore Avoid Jewish Errors

It therefore behoves us, who inquire much concerning events at hand, to search diligently into those things which are able to save us. Let us then utterly flee from all the works of iniquity, lest these should take hold of us; and let us hate the error of the present time, that we may set our love on the world to come: let us not give loose reins to our soul, that it should have power to run with sinners and the wicked, lest we become like them. The final stumbling-block (or source of danger) approaches, concerning which it is written, as Enoch says, "For for this end the Lord has cut short the times and the days, that His Beloved may hasten; and He will come to the inheritance." And the prophet also speaks thus: "Ten kingdoms shall reign upon the earth, and a little king shall rise up after them, who shall subdue under one three of the kings. In like manner Daniel says concerning the same, "And I beheld the fourth beast, wicked and powerful, and more savage than all the beasts of the earth, and how from it sprang up ten horns, and out of them a little budding horn, and how it subdued under one three of the great horns." Ye ought therefore to understand. And this also I further beg of you, as being one of you, and loving you both individually and collectively more than my own soul, to take heed now to yourselves, and not to be like some, adding largely to your sins, and saying, "The covenant is both theirs and ours." But they thus finally lost it, after Moses had already received it. For the Scripture saith, "And Moses was fasting in the mount forty days and forty nights, and received the covenant from the Lord, tables of stone written with the finger of the hand of the Lord; " but turning away to idols, they lost it. For the Lord speaks thus to Moses: "Moses go down quickly; for the people whom thou hast brought out of the land of Egypt have transgressed." And Moses understood [the meaning of God], and cast the two tables out of his hands; and their covenant was broken, in order that the covenant of the beloved Jesus might be sealed upon our heart, in the hope which flows from believing in Him. Now, being desirous to write many things to you, not as your teacher, but as becometh one who loves you, I have taken care not to fail to write to you from what I myself possess, with a view to your purification. We take earnest heed in these last days; for the whole [past] time of your faith will profit you nothing, unless now in this wicked time we also withstand coming sources of danger, as becometh the sons of God. That the Black One may find no means of entrance, let us flee from every vanity, let us utterly hate the works of the way of wickedness. Do not, by retiring apart, live a solitary life, as if you were already [fully] justified; but coming together in one place, make common inquiry concerning what tends to your general welfare. For the Scripture saith, "Woe to them who are wise to themselves, and prudent in their own sight!" Let us be spiritually-minded: let us be a perfect temple to God. As much as in us lies, let us meditate upon the fear of God, and let us keep His commandments, that we may rejoice in His ordinances. The Lord will judge the world without respect of persons. Each will receive as he has done: if he is righteous, his righteousness will precede him; if he is wicked, the reward of wickedness is before him. Take heed, lest resting at our ease, as those who are the called [of God], we should fall asleep in our sins, and the wicked prince, acquiring power over us, should thrust us away from the kingdom of the Lord. And all the more attend to this, my brethren, when ye reflect and behold, that after so great signs and wonders were wrought in Israel, they were thus [at length] abandoned. Let us beware lest we be found [fulfilling that saying], as it is written, "Many are called, but few are chosen."

CHAPTER V
The New Covenant, Founded on the Sufferings of Christ, Tends to Our Salvation, But to the Jews' Destruction

For to this end the Lord endured to deliver up His flesh to corruption, that we might be sanctified through the remission of sins, which is effected by His blood of sprinkling. For it is written concerning Him, partly with reference to Israel, and partly to us; and [the Scripture] saith thus: "He was wounded for our transgressions, and braised for our iniquities: with His stripes we are healed. He was brought as a sheep to the slaughter, and as a lamb which is dumb before its shearer." Therefore we ought to be deeply grateful to the Lord, because He has both made known to us things that are past, and hath given us wisdom concerning things present, and hath not left us without understanding in regard to things which are to come. Now, the Scripture saith, "Not unjustly are nets spread out for birds." This means that the man perishes justly, who, having a knowledge of the way of righteousness, rushes off into the way of darkness. And further, my brethren: if the Lord endured to suffer for our soul, He being Lord of all the world, to whom God said at the foundation of the world, "Let us make man after our image, and after our likeness," understand how it was that He endured to suffer at the hand of men. The prophets, having obtained grace from Him, prophesied concerning Him. And He (since it behoved Him to appear in flesh), that He might abolish death, and reveal the resurrection from the dead, endured [what and as He did], in order that He might fulfill the promise made unto the fathers, and by preparing a new people for Himself, might show, while He dwelt on earth, that He, when He has raised mankind, will also judge them. Moreover, teaching Israel, and doing so great miracles and signs, He preached [the truth] to him, and greatly loved him. But when He chose His own apostles who where to preach His Gospel, [He did so from among those] who were sinners above all sin, that He might show He came "not to call the righteous, but sinners to repentance." Then He manifested Himself to be the Son of God. For if He had not come in the flesh, how could men have been saved by beholding Him? Since looking upon the sun which is to cease to exist, and is the work of His hands, their eyes are not able to bear his rays. The Son of God therefore came in the flesh with this view, that He might bring to a head the sum of their sins who had persecuted His prophets to the death. For this purpose, then, He endured. For God saith, "The stroke of his flesh is from them; " and "when I shall smite the Shepherd, then the sheep of the flock shall be scattered." He himself willed thus to suffer, for it was necessary that He should suffer on the tree. For says he who prophesies regarding Him, "Spare my soul from the sword, fasten my flesh with nails; for the assemblies of the wicked have risen up against me." And again he says, "Behold, I have given my back to scourges, and my cheeks to strokes, and I have set my countenance as a firm rock."

CHAPTER VI
The Sufferings of Christ, and the New Covenant, Were Announced by the Prophets

When, therefore, He has fulfilled the commandment, what saith He? "Who is he that will contend with Me? let him oppose Me: or who is he that will enter into judgment with Me? let him draw near to the servant of the Lord." "Woe unto you, for ye shall all wax old, like a garment, and the moth shall eat you up." And again the prophet says, "Since as a mighty stone He is laid for crushing, behold I cast down for the foundations of Zion a stone, precious, elect, a corner-stone, honourable." Next, what says He? "And he who shall trust in it shall live for ever." Is our hope, then, upon a stone? Far from it. But [the language is used] inasmuch as He laid his flesh [as a foundation] with power; for He says, "And He placed me as a firm rock." And the prophet says again, "The stone which the builders rejected, the same has become the head of the corner." And again he says, "This is the great and wonderful day which the Lord hath made. I write the more simply unto you, that ye may understand. I am the off-scouring of your love. What, then, again says the prophet? "The assembly of the wicked surrounded me; they encompassed me as bees do a honeycomb," and "upon my garment they cast lots." Since, therefore, He was about to be manifested and to suffer in the flesh, His suffering was foreshown. For the prophet speaks against Israel, "Woe to their soul, because they have counselled an evil counsel against themselves, saying, Let us bind the just one, because he is displeasing to us." And Moses also says to them, "Behold these things, saith the Lord God: Enter into the good land which the Lord swore [to give] to Abraham, and Isaac, and Jacob, and inherit ye it, a land flowing with milk and honey." What, then, says Knowledge? Learn: "Trust," she says, "in Him who is to be manifested to you in the flesh-that is, Jesus." For man is earth in a suffering state, for the formation of Adam was from the face of the earth. What, then, meaneth this: "into the good land, a land flowing with milk and honey? "Blessed be our Lord, who has placed in us wisdom and understanding of secret things. For the prophet says, "Who shall understand the parable of the Lord, except him who is wise and prudent, and who loves his Lord? " Since, therefore, having renewed us by the remission of our sins, He hath made us after another pattern, [it is His purpose] that we should possess the soul of children, inasmuch as He has created us anew by His Spirit. For the Scripture says concerning us, while He speaks to the Son, "Let Us make man after Our image, and after Our likeness; and let them have dominion over the beasts of the earth, and the fowls of heaven, and the fishes of the sea." And the Lord said, on beholding the fair creature man, "Increase, and multiply, and replenish the earth." These things [were spoken] to the Son. Again, I will show thee how, in respect to us, He has accomplished a second fashioning in these last days. The Lord says, "Behold, I will make the last like the first." In reference to this, then, the prophet proclaimed, "Enter ye into the land flowing with milk and honey, and have dominion over it." Behold, therefore, we have been refashioned, as again He says in another prophet, "Behold, saith the Lord, I will take away from these, that is, from those whom the Spirit of the Lord foresaw, their stony hearts, and I will put hearts of flesh within them," because He was to be manifested in flesh, and to sojourn among us. For, my brethren, the habitation of our heart is a holy temple to the Lord. For again saith the Lord, "And wherewith shall I appear before the Lord my God, and be glorified? " He says, "I will confess to thee in the Church in the midst of my brethren; and I will praise thee in the midst of the assembly of the saints." We, then, are they whom He has led into the good land. What, then, mean milk and honey? This, that as the infant is kept alive first by honey, and then by milk, so also we, being quickened and kept alive by the faith of the promise and by the word, shall live ruling over the earth. But He said above, "Let them increase, and rule over the fishes." Who then is able to govern the beasts, or the fishes, or the fowls of heaven? For we ought to perceive that to govern implies authority, so that one should command and rule. If, therefore, this does not exist at present, yet still He has promised it to us. When? When we ourselves also have been made perfect [so as] to become heirs of the covenant of the Lord.

CHAPTER VII
Fasting, and the Goat Sent Away, Were Types of Christ

Understand, then, ye children of gladness, that the good Lord has foreshown all things to us, that we might know to whom we ought for everything to render thanksgiving and praise. If therefore the Son of God, who is Lord [of all things], and who will judge the living and the dead, suffered, that His stroke might give us life, let us believe that the Son of God could not have suffered except for our sakes. Moreover, when fixed to the cross, He had given Him to drink vinegar and gall. Hearken how the priests of the people gave previous indications of this. His commandment having been written, the Lord enjoined, that whosoever did not keep the fast should be put to death, because He also Himself was to offer in sacrifice for our sins the vessel of the Spirit, in order that the type established in Isaac when he was offered upon the altar might be fully accomplished. What, then, says He in the prophet? "And let them eat of the goat which is offered, with fasting, for all their sins."

Attend carefully: "And let all the priests alone eat the inwards, unwashed with vinegar." Wherefore? Because to me, who am to offer my flesh for the sins of my new people, ye are to give gall with vinegar to drink: eat ye alone, while the people fast and mourn in sackcloth and ashes. [These things were done] that He might show that it was necessary for Him to suffer for them. How, then, ran the commandment? Give your attention. Take two goats of goodly aspect, and similar to each other, and offer them. And let the priest take one as a burnt-offering for sins. And what should they do with the other? "Accursed," says He, "is the one." Mark how the type of Jesus now comes out. "And all of you spit upon it, and pierce it, and encircle its head with scarlet wool, and thus let it be driven into the wilderness." And when all this has been done, he who bears the goat brings it into the desert, and takes the wool off from it, and places that upon a shrub which is called Rachia, of which also we are accustomed to eat the fruits when we find them in the field. Of this kind of shrub alone the fruits are sweet. Why then, again, is this? Give good heed. [You see] "one upon the altar, and the other accursed; "and why [do you behold] the one that is accursed crowned? Because they shall see Him then in that day having a scarlet robe about his body down to his feet; and they shall say, Is not this He whom we once despised, and pierced, and mocked, and crucified? Truly this is He who then declared Himself to be the Son of God. For how like is He to Him! With a view to this, [He required] the goats to be of goodly aspect, and similar, that, when they see Him then coming, they may be amazed by the likeness of the goat. Behold, then, the type of Jesus who was to suffer. But why is it that they place the wool in the midst of thorns? It is a type of Jesus set before the view of the Church. [They place the wool among thorns], that any one who wishes to bear it away may find it necessary to suffer much, because the thorn is formidable, and thus obtain it only as the result of suffering. Thus also, says He, "Those who wish to behold Me, and lay hold of My kingdom, must through tribulation and suffering obtain Me."

CHAPTER VIII
The Red Heifer a Type of Christ

Now what do you suppose this to be a type of, that a command was given to Israel, that men of the greatest wickedness should offer a heifer, and slay and burn it, and, that then boys should take the ashes, and put these into vessels, and bind round a stick purple wool along with hyssop, and that thus the boys should sprinkle the people, one by one, in order that they might be purified from their sins? Consider how He speaks to you with simplicity. The calf is Jesus: the sinful men offering it are those who led Him to the slaughter. But now the men are no longer guilty, are no longer regarded as sinners. And the boys that sprinkle are those that have proclaimed to us the remission of sins and purification of heart. To these He gave authority to preach the Gospel, being twelve in number, corresponding to the twelve tribes of Israel. But why are there three boys that sprinkle? To correspond to Abraham, and Isaac, and Jacob, because these were great with God. And why was the wool [placed] upon the wood? Because by wood Jesus holds His kingdom, so that [through the cross] those believing on Him shall live for ever. But why was hyssop joined with the wool? Because in His kingdom the days will be evil and polluted in which we shall be saved, [and] because he who suffers in body is cured through the cleansing efficacy of hyssop. And on this account the things which stand thus are clear to us, but obscure to them because they did not hear the voice of the Lord.

CHAPTER IX
The Spiritual Meaning of Circumcision

He speaks moreover concerning our ears, how He hath circumcised both them and our heart. The Lord saith in the prophet, "In the hearing of the ear they obeyed me." And again He saith, "By hearing, those shall hear who are afar off; they shall know what I have done." And, "Be ye circumcised in your hearts, saith the Lord." And again He says, "Hear, O Israel, for these things saith the Lord thy God." And once more the Spirit of the Lord proclaims, "Who is he that wishes to live for ever? By hearing let him hear the voice of my servant." And again He saith, "Hear, O heaven, and give ear, O earth, for God hath spoken." These are in proof. And again He saith, "Hear the word of the Lord, ye rulers of this people." And again He saith, "Hear, ye children, the voice of one crying in the wilderness." Therefore He hath circumcised our ears, that we might hear His word and believe, for the circumcision in which they trusted is abolished. For He declared that circumcision was not of the flesh, but they transgressed because an evil angel deluded them. He saith to them, "These things saith the Lord your God" (here I find a new commandment)-"Sow not among thorns, but circumcise yourselves to the Lord." And why speaks He thus: "Circumcise the stubbornness of your heart, and harden not your neck? " And again: "Behold, saith the Lord, all the nations are uncircumcised in the flesh, but this people are uncircumcised in heart." But thou wilt say, "Yea, verily the people are circumcised for a seal." But so also is every Syrian and Arab, and all the priests of idols: are these then also within the bond of His covenant? Yea, the Egyptians also practise circumcision.

Learn then, my children, concerning all things richly, that Abraham, the first who enjoined circumcision, looking forward in spirit to Jesus, practised that rite, having received the mysteries of the three letters. For [the Scripture] saith, "And Abraham circumcised ten, and eight, and three hundred men of his household." What, then, was the knowledge given to him in this? Learn the eighteen first, and then the three hundred. The ten and the eight are thus denoted-Ten by I, and Eight by H. You have [the initials of the, name of] Jesus. And because the cross was to express the grace [of our redemption] by the letter T, he says also, "Three Hundred." He signifies, therefore, Jesus by two letters, and the cross by one. He knows this, who has put within us the engrafted gift of His doctrine. No one has been admitted by me to a more excellent piece of knowledge than this, but I know that ye are worthy.

CHAPTER X
Spiritual Significance of the Precepts of Moses Respecting Different Kinds of Food

Now, wherefore did Moses say, "Thou shalt not eat the swine, nor the eagle, nor the hawk, nor the raven, nor any fish which is not possessed of scales? " He embraced three doctrines in his mind [in doing so]. Moreover, the Lord saith to them in Deuteronomy, "And I will establish my ordinances among this people." Is there then not a command of God they should not eat [these things]? There is, but Moses spoke with a spiritual reference. For this reason he named the swine, as much as to say, "Thou shalt not join thyself to men who resemble swine." For when they live in pleasure, they forget their Lord; but when they come to want, they acknowledge the Lord. And [in like manner] the swine, when it has eaten, does not recognize its master; but when hungry it cries out, and on receiving food is quiet again. "Neither shalt thou eat," says he "the eagle, nor the hawk, nor the kite, nor the raven." "Thou shalt not join thyself," he means, "to such men as know not how to procure food for themselves by labour and sweat, but seize on that of others in their iniquity, and although wearing an aspect of simplicity, are on the watch to plunder others." So these birds, while they sit idle, inquire how they may devour the flesh of others, proving themselves pests [to all] by their wickedness. "And thou shalt not eat," he says, "the lamprey, or the polypus, or the cuttlefish." He means, "Thou shalt not join thyself or be like to such men as are ungodly to the end, and are condemned to death." In like manner as those fishes, above accursed, float in the deep, not swimming [on the surface] like the rest, but make their abode in the mud which lies at the bottom. Moreover, "Thou shall not," he says, "eat the hare." Wherefore? "Thou shall not be a corrupter of boys, nor like unto such." Because the hare multiplies, year by year, the places of its conception; for as many years as it lives so many it has. Moreover, "Thou shall not eat the hyena." He means, "Thou shall not be an adulterer, nor a corrupter, nor be like to them that are such." Wherefore? Because that animal annually changes its sex, and is at one time male, and at another female. Moreover, he has rightly detested the weasel. For he means, "Thou shalt not be like to those whom we hear of as committing wickedness with the mouth, on account of their uncleanness; nor shall thou be joined to those impure women who commit iniquity with the mouth. For this animal conceives by the mouth." Moses then issued three doctrines concerning meats with a spiritual significance; but they received them according to fleshly desire, as if he had merely spoken of [literal] meats. David, however, comprehends the knowledge of the three doctrines, and speaks in like manner: "Blessed is the man who hath not walked in the counsel of the ungodly," even as the fishes [referred to] go in darkness to the depths [of the sea]; "and hath not stood in the way of sinners," even as those who profess to fear the Lord, but go astray like swine; "and hath not sat in the seat of scorners," even as those birds that lie in wait for prey. Take a full and firm grasp of this spiritual knowledge. But Moses says still further, "Ye shall eat every animal that is cloven-footed and ruminant." What does he mean? [The ruminant animal denotes him] who, on receiving food, recognizes Him that nourishes him, and being satisfied by Him, is visibly made glad. Well spake [Moses], having respect to the commandment. What, then, does he mean? That we ought to join ourselves to those that fear the Lord, those who meditate in their heart on the commandment which they have received, those who both utter the judgments of the Lord and observe them, those who know that meditation is a work of gladness, and who ruminate upon the word of the Lord. But what means the cloven-footed? That the righteous man also walks in this world, yet looks forward to the holy state [to come]. Behold how well Moses legislated. But how was it possible for them to understand or comprehend these things? We then, rightly understanding his commandments, explain them as the Lord intended. For this purpose He circumcised our ears and our hearts, that we might understand these things.

CHAPTER XI
Baptism and the Cross Prefigured in the Old Testament

Let us further inquire whether the Lord took any care to foreshadow the water [of baptism] and the cross. Concerning the water, indeed, it is written, in reference to the Israelites, that they should not receive that baptism which leads to the remission of sins, but should procure another for themselves. The prophet therefore declares, "Be astonished, O heaven, and let the earth tremble at this, because this people hath committed two great evils: they have forsaken Me, a living fountain, and have hewn out for themselves broken cisterns. Is my holy hill Zion a desolate rock? For ye shall be as the fledglings of a bird, which fly away when the nest is removed." And again saith the prophet, "I will go before thee and make level the mountains, and will break the brazen gates, and bruise in pieces the iron bars; and I will give thee the secret, hidden, invisible treasures, that they may know that I am the Lord God." And "He shall dwell in a lofty cave of the strong rock." Furthermore, what saith He in reference to the Son? "His water is sure; ye shall see the King in His glory, and your soul shall meditate on the fear of the Lord." And again He saith in another prophet, "The man who doeth these things shall be like a tree planted by the courses of waters, which shall yield its fruit in due season; and his leaf shall not fade, and all that he doeth shall prosper. Not so are the ungodly, not so, but even as chaff, which the wind sweeps away from the face of the earth. Therefore the ungodly shall not stand in judgment, nor sinners in the counsel of the just; for the Lord knoweth the way of the righteous, but the way of the ungodly shall perish." Mark how He has described at once both the water and the cross. For these words imply, Blessed are they who, placing their trust in the cross, have gone down into the water; for, says He, they shall receive their reward in due time: then He declares, I will recompense them. But now He saith, "Their leaves shall not fade." This meaneth, that every word which proceedeth out of your mouth in faith and love shall tend to bring conversion and hope to many. Again, another prophet saith, "And the land of Jacob shall be extolled above every land." This meaneth the vessel of His Spirit, which He shall glorify. Further, what says He? "And there was a river flowing on the right, and from it arose beautiful trees; and whosoever shall eat of them shall live for ever." This meaneth, that we indeed descend into the water full of sins and defilement, but come up, bearing fruit in our heart, having the fear [of God] and trust in Jesus in our spirit. "And whosoever shall eat of these shall live for ever," This meaneth: Whosoever, He declares, shall hear thee speaking, and believe, shall live for ever.

CHAPTER XII
The Cross of Christ Frequently Announced in the Old Testament

In like manner He points to the cross of Christ in another prophet, who saith, "And when shall these things be accomplished? And the Lord saith, When a tree shall be bent down, and again arise, and when blood shall flow out of wood." Here again you have an intimation concerning the cross, and Him who should be crucified. Yet again He speaks of this in Moses, when Israel was attacked by strangers. And that He might remind them, when assailed, that it was on account of their sins they were delivered to death, the Spirit speaks to the heart of Moses, that he should make a figure of the cross, and of Him about to suffer thereon; for unless they put their trust in Him, they shall be overcome for ever. Moses therefore placed one weapon above another in the midst of the hill, and standing upon it, so as to be higher than all the people, he stretched forth his hands, and thus again Israel acquired the mastery. But when again he let down his hands, they were again destroyed. For what reason? That they might know that they could not be saved unless they put their trust in Him. And in another prophet He declares, "All day long I have stretched forth My hands to an unbelieving people, and one that gainsays My righteous way." And again Moses makes a type of Jesus, [signifying] that it was necessary for Him to suffer, [and also] that He would be the author of life [to others], whom they believed to have destroyed on the cross when Israel was failing. For since transgression was committed by Eve through means of the serpent, [the Lord] brought it to pass that every [kind of] serpents bit them, and they died, that He might convince them, that on account of their transgression they were given over to the straits of death. Moreover Moses, when he commanded, "Ye shall not have any graven or molten [image] for your God," did so that he might reveal a type of Jesus. Moses then makes a brazen serpent, and places it upon a beam, and by proclamation assembles the people. When, therefore, they were come together, they besought Moses that he would offer sacrifice in their behalf, and pray for their recovery. And Moses spake unto them, saying, "When any one of you is bitten, let him come to the serpent placed on the pole; and let him hope and believe, that even though dead, it is able to give him life, and immediately he shall be restored." And they did so. Thou hast in this also [an indication of] the glory of Jesus; for in Him and to Him are all things. What, again, says Moses to Jesus (Joshua) the son of Nave, when he gave him this name, as being a prophet, with this view only, that all the people might hear that the Father would reveal all things concerning His Son Jesus to the son of Nave? This name then being given him when he sent him to spy out the land, he said, "Take a book into thy hands, and write what the Lord declares, that the Son of God will in the last days cut off from the roots all the house of Amalek." Behold again: Jesus who was manifested, both by type and in the flesh, is not the Son of man, but the Son of God. Since, therefore, they were to say that Christ was the son of David, fearing and understanding the error of the wicked, he saith, "The Lord said unto my Lord, Sit at My right hand, until I make Thine enemies Thy footstool." And again, thus saith Isaiah, "The Lord said to Christ, my Lord, whose right hand I have holden, that the nations should yield obedience before Him; and I will break in pieces the strength of kings." Behold how David calleth Him Lord and the Son of God.

CHAPTER XIII
Christians, and Not Jews, the Heirs of the Covenant

But let us see if this people is the heir, or the former, and if the covenant belongs to us or to them. Hear ye now what the Scripture saith concerning the people. Isaac prayed for Rebecca his wife, because she was barren; and she conceived. Furthermore also, Rebecca went forth to inquire of the Lord; and the Lord said to her, "Two nations are in thy womb, and two peoples in thy belly; and the one people shall surpass the other, and the elder shall serve the younger." You ought to understand who was Isaac, who Rebecca, and concerning what persons He declared that this people should be greater than that. And in another prophecy Jacob speaks more clearly to his son Joseph, saying, "Behold, the Lord hath not deprived me of thy presence; bring thy sons to me, that I may bless them." And he brought Manasseh and Ephraim, desiring that Manasseh should be blessed, because he was the elder. With this view Joseph led him to the right hand of his father Jacob. But Jacob saw in spirit the type of the people to arise afterwards. And what says [the Scripture]? And Jacob changed the direction of his bands, and laid his fight hand upon the head of Ephraim, the second and younger, and blessed him. And Joseph said to Jacob, "Transfer thy right hand to the head of Manasseh, for he is my first-born son." And Jacob said, "I know it, my son, I know it; but the elder shall serve the younger: yet he also shall be blessed." Ye see on whom he laid [his hands], that this people should be first, and heir of the covenant. If then, still further, the same thing was intimated through Abraham, we reach the perfection of our knowledge. What, then, says He to Abraham? "Because thou hast believed, it is imputed to thee for righteousness: behold, I have made thee the father of those nations who believe in the Lord while in [a state of] uncircumcision."

CHAPTER XIV
The Lord Hath Given Us the Testament Which Moses Received and Broke

Yes [it is even so]; but let us inquire if the Lord has really given that testament which He swore to the fathers that He would give to the people. He did give it; but they were not worthy to receive it, on account of their sins. For the prophet declares, "And Moses was fasting forty days and forty nights on Mount Sinai, that he might receive the testament of the Lord for the people." And he received from the Lord two tables, written in the spirit by the finger of the hand of the Lord. And Moses having received them, carried them down to give to the people. And the Lord said to Moses, "Moses, Moses, go down quickly; for thy people hath sinned, whom thou didst bring out of the land of Egypt." And Moses understood that they had again made molten images; and he threw the tables out of his hands, and the tables of the testament of the Lord were broken. Moses then received it, but they proved themselves unworthy. Learn now how we have received it. Moses, as a servant, received it; but the Lord himself, having suffered in our behalf, hath given it to us, that we should be the people of inheritance. But He was manifested, in order that they might be perfected in their iniquities, and that we, being constituted heirs through Him, might receive the testament of the Lord Jesus, who was prepared for this end, that by His personal manifestation, redeeming our hearts (which were already wasted by death, and given over to the iniquity of error) from darkness, He might by His word enter into a covenant with us. For it is written how the Father, about to redeem us from darkness, commanded Him to prepare a holy people for Himself. The prophet therefore declares, "I, the Lord Thy God, have called Thee in righteousness, and will hold Thy hand, and will strengthen Thee; and I have given Thee for a covenant to the people, for a light to the nations, to open the eyes of the blind, and to bring forth from fetters them that are bound, and those that sit in darkness out of the prison-house." Ye perceive, then, whence we have been redeemed. And again, the prophet says, "Behold, I have appointed Thee as a light to the nations, that Thou mightest be for salvation even to the ends of the earth, saith the Lord God that redeemeth thee." And again, the prophet saith, "The Spirit of the Lord is upon me; because He hath anointed me to preach the Gospel to the humble: He hath sent me to heal the broken-hearted, to proclaim deliverance to the captives, and recovery of sight to the blind; to announce the acceptable year of the Lord, and the day of recompense; to comfort all that mourn."

CHAPTER XV
The False and the True Sabbath

Further, also, it is written concerning the Sabbath in the Decalogue which [the Lord] spoke, face to face, to Moses on Mount Sinai, "And sanctify ye the Sabbath of the Lord with clean hands and a pure heart." And He says in another place, "If my sons keep the Sabbath, then will I cause my mercy to rest upon them." The Sabbath is mentioned at the beginning of the creation [thus]: "And God made in six days the works of His hands, and made an end on the seventh day, and rested on it, and sanctified it." Attend, my children, to the meaning of this expression, "He finished in six days." This implieth that the Lord will finish all things in six thousand years, for a day is with Him a thousand years. And He Himself testifieth, saying, "Behold, to-day will be as a thousand years." Therefore, my children, in six days, that is, in six thousand years, all things will be finished. "And He rested on the seventh day." This meaneth: when His Son, coming [again], shall destroy the time of the wicked man, and judge the ungodly, and change the-sun, and the moon, and the stars, then shall He truly rest on the seventh day. Moreover, He says, "Thou shalt sanctify it with pure hands and a pure heart." If, therefore, any one can now sanctify the day which God hath sanctified, except he is pure in heart in all things, we are deceived. Behold, therefore: certainly then one properly resting sanctifies it, when we ourselves, having received the promise, wickedness no longer existing, and all things having been made new by the Lord, shall be able to work righteousness. Then we shall be able to sanctify it, having been first sanctified ourselves. Further, He says to them, "Your new moons and your Sabbath I cannot endure." Ye perceive how He speaks: Your present Sabbaths are not acceptable to Me, but that is which I have made, [namely this,] when, giving rest to all things, I shall make a beginning of the eighth day, that is, a beginning of another world. Wherefore, also, we keep the eighth day with joyfulness, the day also on which Jesus rose again from the dead. And when He had manifested Himself, He ascended into the heavens.

CHAPTER XVI
The Spiritual Temple of God

Moreover, I will also tell you concerning the temple, how the wretched [Jews], wandering in error, trusted not in God Himself, but in the temple, as being the house of God. For almost after the manner of the Gentiles they worshipped Him in the temple. But learn how the Lord speaks, when abolishing it: "Who hath meted out heaven with a span, and the earth with his palm? Have not I? " "Thus saith the Lord, Heaven is My throne, and the earth My footstool: what kind of house will ye build to Me, or what is the place of My rest? " Ye perceive that their hope is vain. Moreover, He again says, "Behold, they who have cast down this temple, even they shall build it up again." It has so happened. For through their going to war, it was destroyed by their enemies; and now: they, as the servants of their enemies, shall rebuild it. Again, it was revealed that the city and the temple and the people of Israel were to be given up. For the Scripture saith, "And it shall come to pass in the last days, that the Lord will deliver up the sheep of His pasture, and their sheep-fold and tower, to destruction." And it so happened as the Lord had spoken. Let us inquire, then, if there still is a temple of God. There is-where He himself declared He would make and finish it. For it is written, "And it shall come to pass, when the week is completed, the temple of God shall be built in glory in the name of the Lord." I find, therefore, that a temple does exist. Learn, then, how it shall be built in the name of the Lord. Before we believed in God, the habitation of our heart was corrupt and weak, as being indeed like a temple made with hands. For it was full of idolatry, and was a habitation of demons, through our doing such things as were opposed to [the will of] God. But it shall be built, observe ye, in the name of the Lord, in order that the temple of the Lord may be built in glory. How? Learn [as follows]. Having received the forgiveness of sins, and placed our trust in the name of the Lord, we have become new creatures, formed again from the beginning. Wherefore in our habitation God truly dwells in us. How? His word of faith; His calling of promise; the wisdom of the statutes; the commands of the doctrine; He himself prophesying in us; He himself dwelling in us; opening to us who were enslaved by death the doors of the temple, that is, the mouth; and by giving us repentance introduced us into the incorruptible temple. He then, who wishes to be saved, looks not to man, but to Him who dwelleth in him, and speaketh in him, amazed at never having either heard him utter such words with his mouth, nor himself having ever desired to hear them. This is the spiritual temple built for the Lord.

CHAPTER XVII
Conclusionof the First Part of the Epistle

As far as was possible, and could be done with perspicuity, I cherish the hope that, according to my desire, I have omitted none of those things at present [demanding consideration], which bear upon your salvation. For if I should write to you about things future, ye would not understand, because such knowledge is hid in parables. These things then are so.

CHAPTER XVIII
Second Part of the Epistle

The Two Ways. But let us now pass to another sort of knowledge and doctrine. There are two ways of doctrine and authority, the one of light, and the other of darkness. But there is a great difference between these two ways. For over one are stationed the light-bringing angels of God, but over the other the angels of Satan. And He indeed (i.e., God) is Lord for ever and ever, but he (i.e., Satan) is prince of the time of iniquity.

CHAPTER XIX
The Way of Light

The way of light, then, is as follows. If any one desires to travel to the appointed place, he must be zealous in his works. The knowledge, therefore, which is given to us for the purpose of walking in this way, is the following. Thou shalt love Him that created thee: thou shalt glorify Him that redeemed thee from death. Thou shalt be simple in heart, and rich in spirit. Thou shalt not join thyself to those who walk in the way of death. Thou shalt hate doing what is unpleasing to God: thou shalt hate all hypocrisy. Thou shalt not forsake the commandments of the Lord. Thou shalt not exalt thyself, but shalt be of a lowly mind. Thou shalt not take glory to thyself. Thou shalt not take evil counsel against thy neighbour. Thou shalt not allow over-boldness to enter into thy soul. Thou shalt not commit fornication: thou shalt not commit adultery: thou shalt not be a corrupter of youth. Thou shalt not let the word of God issue from thy lips with any kind of impurity. Thou shalt not accept persons when thou reprovest any one for transgression. Thou shalt be meek: thou shalt be peaceable. Thou shalt tremble at the words which thou hearest. Thou shalt not be mindful of evil against thy brother. Thou shalt not be of doubtful mind as to whether a thing shall be or not. Thou shalt not take the name of the Lord in vain. Thou shalt love thy neighbour more than thine own soul. Thou shalt not slay the child by procuring abortion; nor, again, shalt thou destroy it after it is born. Thou shalt not withdraw thy hand from thy son, or from thy daughter, but from their infancy thou shalt teach them the fear of the Lord. Thou shalt not covet what is thy neighbour's, nor shalt thou be avaricious. Thou shalt not be joined in soul with the haughty, but thou shalt be reckoned with the righteous and lowly. Receive thou as good things the trials which come upon thee. Thou shalt not be of double mind or of double tongue, for a double tongue is a snare of death. Thou shalt be subject to the Lord, and to [other] masters as the image of God, with modesty and fear. Thou shalt not issue orders with bitterness to thy maidservant or thy man-servant, who trust in the same [God], lest thou shouldst not reverence that God who is above both; for He came to call men not according to their outward appearance, but according as the Spirit had prepared them. Thou shalt communicate in all things with thy neighbour; thou shalt not call things thine own; for if ye are partakers in common of things which are incorruptible, how much more [should you be] of those things which are corruptible! Thou shalt not be hasty with thy tongue, for the mouth is a snare of death. As far as possible, thou shalt be pure in thy soul. Do not be ready to stretch forth thy hands to take, whilst thou contractest them to give. Thou shalt love, as the apple of thine eye, every one that speaketh to thee the word of the Lord. Thou shalt remember the day of judgment, night and day. Thou shalt seek out every day the faces of the saints, either by word examining them, and going to exhort them, and meditating how to save a soul by the word, or by thy hands thou shalt labour for the redemption of thy sins. Thou shalt not hesitate to give, nor murmur when thou givest. "Give to every one that asketh thee," and thou shalt know who is the good Recompenser of the reward. Thou shalt preserve what thou hast received [in charge], neither adding to it nor taking from it. To the last thou shalt hate the wicked [one]. Thou shalt judge righteously. Thou shalt not make a schism, but thou shalt pacify those that contend by bringing them together. Thou shalt confess thy sins. Thou shalt not go to prayer with an evil conscience. This is the way of light.

CHAPTER XX
The Way of Darkness

But the way of darkness is crooked, and full of cursing; for it is the way of eternal death with punishment, in which way are the things that destroy the soul, viz., idolatry, over-confidence, the arrogance of power, hypocrisy, double-heartedness, adultery, murder, rapine, haughtiness, transgression, deceit, malice, self-sufficiency, poisoning, magic, avarice, want of the fear of God. [In this way, too,] are those who persecute the good, those who hate truth, those who love falsehood, those who know not the reward of righteousness, those who cleave not to that which is good, those who attend not with just judgment to the widow and orphan, those who watch not to the fear of God, [but incline] to wickedness, from whom meekness and patience are far off; persons who love vanity, follow after a reward, pity not the needy, labour not in aid of him who is overcome with toil; who are prone to evil-speaking, who know not Him that made them, who are murderers of children, destroyers of the workmanship of God; who turn away him that is in want, who oppress the afflicted, who are advocates of the rich, who are unjust judges of the poor, and who are in every respect transgressors.

CHAPTER XXI
Conclusion

It is well, therefore, that he who has learned the judgments of the Lord, as many as have been written, should walk in them. For he who keepeth these shall be glorified in the kingdom of God; but he who chooseth other things shall be destroyed with his works. On this account there will be a resurrection, on this account a retribution. I beseech you who are superiors, if you will receive any counsel of my good-will, have among yourselves those to whom you may show kindness: do not forsake them. For the day is at hand on which all things shall perish with the evil [one]. The Lord is near, and His reward. Again, and yet again, I beseech you: be good lawgivers to one another; continue faithful counsellors of one another; take away from among you all hypocrisy. And may God, who ruleth over all the world, give to you wisdom, intelligence, understanding, knowledge of His judgments, with patience. And be ye taught of God, inquiring diligently what the Lord asks from you; and do it that ye maybe safe in the day of judgment. And if you have any remembrance of what is good, be mindful of me, meditating on these things, in order that both my desire and watchfulness may result in some good. I beseech you, entreating this as a favour. While yet you are in this fair vessel, do not fail in any one of those things, but unceasingly seek after them, and fulfil every commandment; for these things are worthy. Wherefore I have been the more earnest to write to you, as my ability served, that I might cheer you. Farewell, ye children of love and peace. The Lord of glory and of all grace be with your spirit. Amen.

Epistle of Ignatius To Polycarp

CHAPTER 1
Commendation And Exhortation

Having obtained good proof that thy mind is fixed in God as upon an immoveable rock, I loudly glorify[His name] that I have been thought worthy to behold thy blameless face, which may I ever enjoy in God! I entreat thee, by the grace with which thou art clothed, to press forward in thy course, and to exhort all that they may be saved. Maintain thy position with all care, both in the flesh and spirit. Have a regard to preserve unity, than which nothing is better. Bear with all even as the Lord does with thee. Support all in love, as also thou doest. Give thyself to prayer Without ceasing. Implore additional understanding to what thou already hast. Be watchful, possessing a sleepless spirit. Speak to every man separately, as God enables thee. Bear the infirmities of all, as being a perfect athlete[in the Christian life], even as does the Lord of all. For says[the Scripture], "He Himself took our infirmities, and bare our sicknesses." Where the labour is great, the gain is all the more.

CHAPTER 2
Exhortations

[A] If thou lovest the good disciples, no thanks are due to thee on that account; but rather seek by meekness to subdue the more troublesome. Every kind of wound is not healed with the same plaster. Mitigate violent ... [B] If thou lovest the good disciples, no thanks are due to thee on that account; but rather seek by meekness to subdue the more troublesome. Every kind of wound is not healed with the same plaster. Mitigate violent attacks[of disease] by gentle applications. Be in all things "wise as a serpent, and harmless always as a ... [A] ... attacks[of disease] by gentle applications. Be in all things "wise as a serpent, and harmless as a dove." For this purpose thou art composed of both flesh and spirit, that thou mayest deal tenderly with those[evils] that present themselves visibly before thee. And as respects those that are not seen, pray that[God] would reveal them unto thee, in order that thou mayest be wanting in nothing, but mayest abound in every gift. The times call for thee, as pilots do for the winds, and as on tossed with tempest seeks for the haven, so that both thou[and those under thy care] may attain to God. Be sober as an athlete of God: the prize set before thee is immortality and eternal life, of which thou art also persuaded. In all things may my soul be for thing, and my bonds also, which thou hast loved. [B] ... dove." For this purpose thou art composed of both soul and body, art both fleshly and spiritual, that thou mayest correct those[evils] that present themselves visibly before thee; and as respects those that are not seen, mayest pray that these should be revealed to thee, so that thou mayest be wanting in nothing, but mayest abound in every gift. The times call upon thee to pray. For as the wind aids the pilot of a ship, and as havens are advantageous for safety to a tempest-tossed vessel, so is also prayer to thee, in order that thou mayest attain to God. Be sober as an athlete of God, whose will is immortality and eternal life; of which thou art also persuaded. In all things may my soul be for thine, and my bonds also, which thou hast loved.

CHAPTER 3
Exhortations

Let not those who seem worthy of credit, but teach strange doctrines, fill thee with apprehension. Stand firm, as does an anvil which is beaten. It is the part of a noble athlete to be wounded, and yet to conquer. And especially we ought to bear all things for the sake of God, that He also may bear with us, and bring us into His kingdom. Add more and more to thy diligence; run thy race with increasing energy; weigh carefully the times. Whilst thou art here, be a conqueror; for here is the course, and there are the crowns, Look for Christ, the Son of God; who was before time, yet appeared in time; who was invisible by nature, yet visible in the flesh; who was impalpable, and could not be touched, as being without a body, but for our sakes became such, might be touched and handled in the body; who was impassible as God, but became passible for our sakes as man; and who in every kind of way suffered for our sakes.

CHAPTER 4
Exhortations

Let not the widows be neglected. Be thou, after the Lord, their protector and friend. Let nothing be done without thy consent; neither do thou anything without the approval of God, which indeed thou doest not. Be thou stedfast. Let your assembling together be of frequent occurrence: seek after all by name. Do not despise either male or female slaves, yet neither let them be puffed up with conceit, but rather let them submit themselves the more, for the glory of God, that they may obtain from God a better liberty. Let them not wish to be set free[from slavery] at the public expense, that they be not found slaves to their own desires. ... submit themselves the more, for the glory of God, that they my obtain from God a better liberty. Let them not long to be set free[from slavery] at the public expense, that they be not found slaves to their own desires.

CHAPTER 5
The Duties Of Husbands And Wives

Flee evil arts; but all the more discourse in public regarding them. Speak to my sisters, that they love the Lord, and be satisfied with their husbands both in the flesh and spirit. In like manner also, exhort my brethren, in the name of Jesus Christ, that they love their wives, even as the Lord the Church. If any one can continue in a state of purity, to the honour of the flesh of the Lord, let him so remain without boasting. If he shall boast, he is undone; and if he seeks to be more prominent than the bishop, he is ruined. But it becomes both men and women who marry, to form their union with the approval of the bishop, that their marriage may be according to the Lord, and not after their own lust. Let all things be done to the honour of God.

CHAPTER 6
The Duties Of The Christian Flock

Give ye heed to the bishop, that God also may give heed to you. My soul be for theirs that are submissive to the bishop, to the presbytery, and to the deacons: may I have my portion with them from God! Labour together with one another; strive in company together; run together; suffer together; sleep together; and awake together, as the stewards, and associates, and servants of God. Please ye Him under whom ye fight, and from whom ye shall receive your wages. Let none of you be found a deserter. Let your baptism endure as your arms; your faith as your helmet; your love as your spear; your patience as a complete panoply. Let your works be the charge assigned to you, that you may obtain for them a most worthy recompense. Be long-suffering, therefore, with one another, in meekness, and God shall be so with you. May I have joy of you for ever!

CHAPTER 7
Request That Polycarp Would Send A Messenger To Antioch

Seeing that the Church which is at Antioch in Syria is, as report has informed me, at peace, through your prayers, I also am the more encouraged, resting without anxiety in God, if indeed by means of suffering I may attain to God, so that, through your prayers, I may be found a disciple[of Christ]. It is fitting, O Polycarp, most blessed in God, to assemble a very solemn council, and to elect one whom you greatly love, and know to be a man of activity, who may be designated the messenger of God; and to bestow on him the honour of going into Syria, so that, going into Syria, he may glorify your ever active love to the praise of God. A Christian has not power over himself, but must always be ready for the service of God. Now, this work is both God's and yours, when ye shall have completed it. For I trust that, through grace, ye are prepared for every good work pertaining to God. Knowing your energetic love of the truth, I have exhorted you by this brief Epistle.

CHAPTER 8
Let Other Churches Also Send To Antioch

Inasmuch, therefore, as I have not been able to write to all Churches, because I must suddenly sail from Troas to Neapolis, as the will [of the emperor] enjoins, [I beg that] thou, as being acquainted with the purpose s of God, wilt write to the adjacent Churches, that they also may act in like manner, such as are able to do so sending messenger, and the others transmitting letters through those persons who are sent by thee, that thou mayest be glorified by a work which shall be remembered for ever, as indeed thou art worthy to be. I salute all by name, and in particular the wife of Epitropus, with all her house and children. I salute Attalus, my beloved. I salute him who shall be deemed worthy to go[from you] into Syria. Grace shall be with him for ever, and with Polycarp that sends him. I pray for your happiness for ever in our God, Jesus Christ, by whom continue ye in the unity and under the protection of God. I salute Alce, my dearly beloved. Amen. Grace [be with you]. Fare ye well in the Lord.

Epistle of Ignatius to the Ephesians

CHAPTER 1
Praise Of The Ephesians

I have become acquainted with your greatly-desired name in God, which ye have acquired by the habit of rightcousness, according to the faith and love in Christ Jesus our Saviour. Being the followers of the love of God towards man, and stirring up s yourselves by the blood of Christ, you have perfectly accomplished the work which was beseeming to you. For, on hearing that I came bound from Syria for the sake of Christ, our common hope, trusting through your prayers to be permitted to fight with beasts at Rome, that so by martyrdom I may indeed become the disciple of Him "who gave Himself for us, an offering and a sacrifice to God," [ye hastened to see me]. I have therefore received your whole multitude in the name of God, through Onesimus, a man of inexpressible love, and who is your bishop, whom I pray you by Jesus Christ to love, and that you would all seek to be like him. Blessed be God, who has granted unto you, who are yourselves so excellent, to obtain such an excellent bishop.

CHAPTER 2
Congratulations And Entreaties

As to our fellow-servant Burrhus, your deacon in regard to God and blessed in all things, I pray that he may continue blameless for the honour of the Church, and of your most blessed bishop. Crocus also, worthy both of God and you, whom we have received as the manifestation of your love to us, hath in all things refreshed me, and "hath not been ashamed of my chain," as the Father of our Lord Jesus Christ will also refresh him; together with Onesimus, and Burrhus, and Euplus, and Fronto, by means of whom I have, as to love, beheld all of you. May I always have joy of you, if indeed I be worthy of it. It is therefore befitting that you should in every way glorify Jesus Christ, who hath glorified you, that by a unanimous obedience "ye may be perfectly joined together in the same mind and in the same judgment, and may all speak the same thing concerning the same thing," and that, being subject to the bishop and the presbytery, ye may in all respects be sanctified.

CHAPTER 3
Exhortations To Unity

I do not issue orders to you, as if I were some great person. For though I am bound for His name, I am not yet perfect in Jesus Christ. For now I begin to be a disciple, and I speak to you as my fellow-servants. For it was needful for me to have been admonished by you in faith, exhortation, patience, and long-suffering. But inasmuch as love suffers me not to be silent in regard to you, I have therefore taken upon me first to exhort you that ye would run together in accordance with the will of God. For even Jesus Christ does all things according to the will of the Father, as He Himself declares in a certain place, "I do always those things that please Him." Wherefore it behoves us also to live according to the will of God in Christ, and to imitate Him as Paul did. For, says he, "Be ye followers of me, even as I also am of Christ."

CHAPTER 4
The Same Continued

Therefore in your Wherefore it is fitting that ye also should run together in accordance with the will of the bishop who by God's appointment rules over you. Which thing ye indeed of yourselves do, being instructed by the Spirit. For your justly-renowned presbytery, being worthy of God, is fitted as exactly to the bishop as the strings are to the harp. Thus, being joined together in concord and harmonious concord and harmonious love, Jesus Christ is sung. And do ye, man by man, become a choir, that being harmonious in love, and taking up the song of God in unison, ye may with one voice sing to the Father through Jesus Christ, so that He may both hear you, and perceive by your works that ye are indeed the members of His Son. It is profitable, therefore, that you should live in an unblameable unity, that thus ye may always enjoy communion with God. love, of which Jesus Christ is the Captain and Guardian, do ye, man by man, become but one choir; so that, agreeing together in concord, and obtaining a perfect unity with God, ye may indeed be one in harmonious feeling with God the Father, and His beloved Son Jesus Christ our Lord. For, says He, "Grant unto them, Holy Father, that as I and Thou are one, they also may be one in us." It is therefore profitable that you, being joined together with God in an unblameable unity, should be the followers of the example of Christ, of whom also ye are members.

CHAPTER 5
The Praise Of Unity

For if I, in this brief space of time, have enjoyed such fellowship with your bishop--I mean not of a mere human, but of a spiritual nature--how much more do I reckon you happy, who so depend on him as the Church does on the Lord Jesus, and the Lord does on God and His Father, that so all things may agree in unity! Let no man deceive himself: if any one be not within the altar, he is deprived of the bread of God. For if the prayer of one or two possesses such power that Christ stands in the midst of them, how much more will the prayer of the bishop and of the whole Church, ascending up in harmony to God, prevail for the granting of all their petitions in Christ ! He, therefore, that separates himself from such, and does not meet in the society where sacrifices are offered, and with "the Church of the first-born whose names are written in heaven," is a wolf in sheep's clothing, while he presents a mild outward appearance. Do ye, beloved, be careful to be subject to the bishop, and the presbyters and the deacons. For he that is subject to these is obedient to Christ, who has appointed them; but he that is disobedient to these is disobedient to Christ Jesus. And "he that obeyeth not the Son shall not see life, but the wrath of God abideth on him." For he that yields not obedience to his superiors is self-confident, quarrelsome, and proud. But" God," says [the Scripture] "resisteth the proud, but giveth grace to the humble ;" and, "The proud have greatly transgressed." The Lord also says to the priests, "He that heareth you, heareth Me; and he that heareth Me, heareth the Father that sent Me. He that despiseth you, despiseth Me; and he that despiseth Me, despiseth Him that sent Me."

CHAPTER 6
Have Respect To The Bishop As To Christ Himself

The more, therefore, you see the bishop silent, the more do you reverence him. For we ought to receive every one whom the Master of the house sends to be over His household, as we would do Him that sent him. It is manifest, therefore, that we should look upon the bishop even as we would look upon the Lord Himself, standing, as he does, before the Lord. For "it behoves the man who looks carefully about him, and is active in his business, to stand before kings, and not to stand before Lord Himself. And indeed Onesimus himself greatly commends your good order in God, that ye all live according to the truth, and that no sect has any dwelling-place among you. Nor, indeed, do ye hearken to any one rather than to Jesus Christ speaking in truth. slothful men." And indeed Onesimus himself greatly commends your good order in God, that ye all live according to the truth, and that no sect 'has any dwelling-place among you. Nor indeed do ye hearken to any one rather than to Jesus Christ, the true Shepherd and Teacher. And ye are, as Paul wrote to you, "one body and one spirit, because ye have also been called in one hope of the faith. Since also "there is one Lord, one faith, one baptism, one God and Father of all, who is over all, and through all, and in all." Such, then, are ye, having been taught by such instructors, Paul the Christ-bearer, and Timothy the most faithful.

CHAPTER 7
Beware Of False Teachers

But some most worthless persons are in the habit of carrying about the name[of Jesus Christ] in wicked guile, while yet they practise things unworthy of God, and hold opinions contrary to the doctrine of Christ, to their own destruction, and that of those who give credit to them, whom you must avoid as ye would wild beasts. For "the righteous man who avoids them is saved for ever; but the destruction of the ungodly is sudden, and a subject of rejoicing." For "they are dumb dogs, that cannot bark," raving mad, and biting secretly, against whom ye must be on your guard, since they labour under an incurable disease. But our Physician is the only true God, the unbegotten and unapproachable, the Lord of all, the Father and Begetter of the only-begotten Son. We have also as a Physician the Lord our God, Jesus the Christ, the only-begotten Son and Word, before time began, but who afterwards became also man, of Mary the virgin. For "the Word was made flesh." Being incorporeal, He was in the body; being impassible, He was in a passible body; being immortal, He was in a mortal body; being life, He became subject to corruption, that He might free our souls from death and corruption, and heal them, and might restore them to health, when they were diseased with ungodliness and wicked lusts.

CHAPTER 8
Renewed Praise Of The Ephesians

Let not then any one deceive you, as indeed ye are not deceived; for ye are wholly devoted to God. For when there is no evil desire within you, which might defile and torment you, then do ye live in accordance with the will of God, and are[the servants] of Christ. Cast ye out that which defiles[you, who are of the most holy Church of the Ephesians, which is so famous and celebrated throughout the world. They that are carnal cannot do those things which are spiritual, nor they that are spiritual the things which are carnal; even as faith cannot do the works of unbelief, nor unbelief the works of faith. But ye, being full of the Holy Spirit, do nothing according to the flesh, but all things according to the Spirit. Ye are complete in Christ Jesus, "who is the Saviour of all men, specially of them that believe." belief, nor unbelief the works of faith. But even those things which ye do according to the flesh are spiritual; for ye do all things in Jesus Christ.

CHAPTER 9
Ye Have Given No Heed To False Teachers

Nevertheless, I have heard of some who have passed in among you, holding the wicked doctrine of the strange and evil spirit; to whom ye did not allow entrance to sow their tares, but stopped your ears that ye might not receive that error which was proclaimed by them, as being persuaded that that spirit which deceives the people does not speak the things of Christ, but his own, for he is a lying spirit. But the Holy Spirit does not speak His own things, but those of Christ, and that not from himself, but from the Lord; even as the Lord also announced to us the things that He received from the Father. For, says He, "the word which ye hear is not Mine, but the Father's, who sent Me." And says He of the Holy Spirit, "He shall not speak of Himself, but whatsoever things He shall hear from Me." And He says of Himself to the Father, "I have," says He, "glorified Thee upon the earth ; I have finished the work which, Thou gavest Me; I have manifested Thy name to men." And of the Holy Ghost, "He shall glorify Me, for He receives of Mine." But the spirit of deceit preaches himself, and speaks his own things, for he seeks to please himself. He glorifies himself, for he is full of arrogance. He is lying, fraudulent, soothing, flattering, treacherous, rhapsodical, trifling, inharmonious, verbose, sordid, and timorous. From his power Jesus Christ will deliver you, who has founded you upon the rock, as being chosen stones, well fitted for the divine edifice of the Father, and who are raised up on high by Christ, who was crucified for you, making use of the Holy Spirit as a rope, and being borne up by faith, while exalted by love from earth to heaven, walking in company with those that are undefiled. For, says[the Scripture], "Blessed are the undefiled in the way, who walk in the law of the Lord." Now the way is unerring, namely, Jesus Christ. For, says He, "I am the way and the life." And this way leads to the Father. For "no man," says He, "cometh to the Father but by Me." Blessed, then, are ye who are God-bearers, spirit-bearers, temple-bearers, bearers of holiness, adorned in all respects with the commandments of Jesus Christ, being "a royal priesthood, a holy nation, a peculiar people," on whose account I rejoice exceedingly, and have had the privilege, by this Epistle, of conversing with "the saints which are at Ephesus, the faithful in Christ Jesus." I rejoice, therefore, over you, that ye do not give heed to vanity, and love nothing according to the flesh, but according to God.

CHAPTER 10
Exhortations To Prayer, Humility, Etc.

And pray ye without ceasing in behalf of other men; for there is hope of the repentance, that they may attain to God. For "cannot he that falls arise again, and he may attain to God. See, then, that they be instructed by your works, if in no other way. Be ye meek in response to their wrath, humble in opposition to their boasting: to their blasphemies return your prayers; in contrast to their error, be ye stedfast in the faith; and for their cruelty, manifest your gentleness. While we take care not to imitate their conduct, let us be found their brethren in all true kindness; and let us seek to be followers of the Lord(who ever more unjustly treated, more destitute, more condemned?), that so no plant of the devil may be found in you, but ye may remain in all holiness and sobriety in Jesus Christ, both with respect to the flesh and spirit. That goes astray return ?" Permit them, then, to be in structed by you. Be ye therefore the ministers of God, and the mouth of Christ. For thus saith the Lord, "If ye take forth the precious from the vile, ye shall be as my mouth." Be ye humble in response to their wrath; oppose to their blasphemies your earnest prayers; while they go astray, stand ye stedfast in the faith. Conquer ye their harsh temper by gentleness, their passion by meekness. For "blessed are the meek ;" and Moses was meek above all men; and David was exceeding meek. Wherefore Paul exhorts as follows: "The servant of the Lord must not strive, but be gentle towards all men, apt to teach, patient, in meekness instructing those that oppose themselves." Do not seek to avert e ourselves on those that injure you, for says[the Scripture], If I have returned evil to those who returned evil to me." Let us make them brethren by our kindness. For say ye to those that hate you, Ye are our brethren, that the name of the Lord may be glorified. And let us imitate the Lord, "who, when He was reviled, reviled not again ;" when He was crucified, He answered not; "when He suffered, He threatened not ;" but prayed for His enemies, "Father, forgive them; they know not what they do." If any one, the more he is injured, displays the more patience, blessed is he. If any one is defrauded, if any one is despised, for the name of the Lord, he truly is the servant of Christ. Take heed that no plant of the devil be found among you, for such a plant is bitter and salt. "Watch ye, and be ye sober," in Christ Jesus.

CHAPTER 11
An Exhortation To Fear God, Etc.

The last times are come upon us. Let us therefore be of a reverent spirit, and fear the long-suffering of God, lest we despise the riches of His goodness and forbearance. For let us either fear the wrath to come, or let us love the present joy in the life that now is; and let our present and true joy be only this, to be found in Christ Jesus, that we may truly live. Do not at any time desire so much as even to breathe apart from Him. For He is my hope; He is my boast; He is my never-failing riches, on whose account I bear about with me these bonds from Syria to Rome, these spiritual jewels, in which may I be perfected through your prayers, and become a partaker of the sufferings of Christ, and have fellowship with Him in His death, His resurrection from the dead, and His everlasting life. May I attain to this, so that I may be found in the lot of the Christians of Ephesus, who have always had intercourse with the apostles by the power of Jesus Christ, with Paul, and John, and Timothy the most faithful.

CHAPTER 12
Praise of the Ephesians

I know both who I am, and to whom I write. I am the very insignificant Ignatius, who have my lot with those who are exposed to danger and condemnation. ... mercy; I am subject to danger, ye are established in safety. Ye are the persons through whom those pass that are cut off for the sake of God. Ye are initiated into the mysteries of the Gospel with Paul, the holy, the martyred, the deservedly most happy, at whose feet may I be found, when I shall attain to God; who in all his Epistles makes mention of you in Christ Jesus. But ye have been the objects of mercy, and are established in Christ. I am one delivered over [to death], but the least of all those that have been cut off for the sake of Christ, "from the blood of righteous Abel" to the blood of Ignatius. Ye are initiated into the mysteries of the Gospel with Paul, the holy, the martyred, inasmuch as he was "a chosen vessel;" at whose feet may I be found, and at the feet of the rest of the saints, when I shall attain to Jesus Christ, who is always mindful of you in His prayers.

CHAPTER 13
Exhortation To Meet Together Frequently For The Worship Of God

Take heed, then, often to come together to give thanks to God, and show forth His praise. For when ye come frequently together in the same place, the powers of Satan are destroyed, and his "fiery darts" urging to sin fall back ineffectual. For your concord and harmonious faith prove his destruction, and the torment of his assistants. Nothing is better than that peace which is according to Christ, by which all war, both of a rial and terrestrial spirits, is brought to an end. "For we wrestle not against blood and flesh, but against principalities and powers, and against the rulers of the darkness of this world, against spiritual wickedness in heavenly places."

CHAPTER 14
Exhortations To Faith And Love

Wherefore none of the devices of the devil shall be hidden from you, if, like Paul, ye perfectly possess that faith and love towards Christ which are the beginning and the end of life. The beginning of life is faith, and the end is love. And these two being inseparably connected together, do perfect the man of God; while all other things which are requisite to a holy life follow after them. No man making a profession of faith ought to sin, nor one possessed of love to hate his brother. For He that said, "Thou shalt love the Lord thy God," said also, "and thy neighbour as thyself." Those that profess themselves to be Christ's are known not only by what they say, but by what they practise. "For the tree is known by its fruit."

CHAPTER 15
Exhortation To Confess Christ By Silence As Well As Speech

It is better for a man to be silent and be [a Christian], than to talk and not to be one. "The kingdom of God is not in word, but in power." Men "believe with the heart, and confess with the mouth," the one "unto righteousness," the other "unto salvation." It is good to teach, if he who speaks also acts. For he who shall both "do and teach, the same shall be great in the kingdom." the Father. He who possesses the word of Jesus, is truly able to hear even His very silence, that he may be perfect, and may both act as he speaks, and be recognised by his silence. There is nothing which is hid from God, but our very secrets are near to Him. Let us therefore do all things as those who have Him dwelling in us, that we may be His temples, and He may be in us as our God, which indeed He is, and will manifest Himself before our faces. Wherefore we justly love Him. Our Lord and God, Jesus Christ, the Son of the living God, first did and then taught, as Luke testifies, "whose praise is in the Gospel through all the Churches." There is nothing which is hid from the Lord, but our very secrets are near to Him. Let us therefore do all things as those who have Him dwelling in us, that we may be His temples, and He may be in us as God. Let Christ speak in us, even as He did in Paul. Let the Holy Spirit teach us to speak the things of Christ in like manner as He did.

CHAPTER 16
The Fate Of False Teachers

Do not err, my brethren. Those that corrupt families shall not inherit the kingdom of God. And if those that corrupt mere human families are condemned to death, how much more shall those suffer everlasting punishment who endeavour to corrupt the Church of Christ, for which the Lord Jesus, the only-begotten Son of God, endured the cross, and submitted to death! Whosoever, "being waxen fat," and "become gross," sets at nought His doctrine, shall go into hell. In like manner, every one that has received from God the power of distinguishing, and yet follows an unskilful shepherd, and receives a false opinion for the truth, shall be punished. "What communion hath light with darkness? or Christ with Belial? Or what portion hath he that believeth with an infidel? or the temple of God with idols?" And in like manner say I, what communion hath truth with falsehood? or righteousness with unrighteousness? or true doctrine with that which is false?

CHAPTER 17
Beware Of False Doctrines

For this end did the Lord suffer the ointment to be poured upon His head, that His Church might breathe forth immortality. For saith [the Scripture], "Thy name is as ointment poured forth; therefore have the virgins loved

Thee; they have drawn Thee; at the odour of Thine ointments we will run after Thee." Let no one be anointed with the bad odour of the doctrine of [the prince of] this world; let not the holy Church of God be led captive by his subtlety, as was the first woman. Why do we not, as gifted with reason, act wisely? When we had received from Christ, and had grafted in us the faculty of judging concerning God, why do we fall headlong into ignorance? and why, through a careless neglect of acknowledging the gift which we have received, do we foolishly perish?

CHAPTER 18
The Glory Of The Cross

Let my sprat be courted as nothing for the sake of the cross, which is a stumbling-block" to those that do not believe, but to us salvation and the cross of Christ is indeed a stumbling-block to those that do not believe, but to the believing it is salvation and life eternal. "Where is the wise man? where the disputer?" Where is the boasting of those who life eternal. "Where is the wise man? where the disputer?" Where is the boasting of those who are styled prudent? For our God, Jesus Christ, was, according to the appointment of God, conceived in the womb by Mary, of the seed of David, but by the Holy Ghost. He was born and baptized, that by His passion He might purify the water. are called mighty? For the Son of God, who was begotten before time began, and established all things according to the will of the Father, He was conceived in the womb of Mary, according to the appointment of God, of the seed of David, and by the Holy Ghost. For says [the Scripture], "Behold, a virgin shall be with child, and shall bring forth a son, and He shall be called Immanuel." He was born and was baptized by John, that He might ratify the institution committed to that prophet.

CHAPTER 19
Three Celebrated Mysteries

Now the virginity of Mary was hidden from the prince of this world, as was also her offspring, and the death of the Lord; three mysteries of renown, which were wrought in silence, but have been revealed to us. A star shone forth in heaven above all that were before it, and its light was inexpressible, while its novelty struck men with astonishment. And all the rest of the stars, with the sun and moon, formed a chorus to this star. It far exceeded them all in brightness, and agitation was felt as to whence this new spectacle [proceeded]. Hence worldly wisdom became folly; conjuration was seen to be mere trifling; and magic became utterly ridiculous. Every law of wickedness vanished away; the darkness of ignorance was dispersed; and tyrannical authority was destroyed, God being manifested as a man, and man displaying power as God. But neither was the former a mere imagination, nor did the second imply a bare humanity; but the one was absolutely true," and the other an economical arrangement. Now that received a beginning which was perfected by God. Henceforth all things were in a state of tumult, because He meditated the abolition of death.

CHAPTER 20
Promise Of Another Letter

If Jesus Christ shall graciously permit me through your prayers, and if it be His will, I shall, in a second little work which I will write to you, make further manifest to you [the nature of] the dispensation of which I have begun [to treat], with respect to the new man, Jesus Christ, in His faith and in His love, in His suffering and in His resurrection. Especially [will I do this if the Lord make known to me that ye come together

CHAPTER 20b
Exhortations To Stedfastness

And Unity Stand fast, brethren, in the faith of Jesus Christ, and in His love, in His passion, and in His resurrection. Do ye all come together in common, and individually, through grace, in one faith of God the Father, and of Jesus Christ His only-begotten Son, and "the first-born of every creature," but of the seed of David according to the flesh, being under the guidance of the Comforter, in obedience to the bishop and the presbytery with an undivided mind, breaking one and the same bread, which is the medicine of immortality, and the antidote which prevents us from dying, but a cleansing remedy driving away evil, [which causes] that we should live in God through Jesus Christ.

CHAPTER 21
Conclusion

My soul be for yours and theirs whom, for the honour of God, ye have sent to Smyrna; whence also I write to you, giving thanks to the Lord, and loving Polycarp even as I do you. Remember me, as Jesus Christ also remembers you, who is blessed for evermore. Pray ye for the Church of Antioch

which is in Syria, whence I am led bound to Rome, being the last of the faithful that are there, who yet have been thought worthy to carry these chains to
the honour of God. Fare ye well in God the Father, and the Lord Jesus Christ,
our common hope, and in the Holy Ghost. Fare ye well. Amen. Grace [be
with you]. Epistle of Ignatius to the

Epistle of Ignatius to the Magnesians

CHAPTER 1
Reason Of Writing The Epistle

Having been informed of your godly love, so well-ordered, I rejoiced greatly, and determined to commune with you in the faith of Jesus Christ. For as one who has been thought worthy of a divine and desirable name, in those bonds which I bear about, I commend the Churches, in which I pray for a union both of the flesh and spirit of Jesus Christ, "who is the Saviour of all men, but specially of them that believe;" by whose blood ye were redeemed; by whom ye have known God, or rather have been known by Him; in whom enduring, ye shall escape all the assaults of this world: for "He is faithful, who will not suffer you to be tempted above that which ye are able."

CHAPTER 2
Rejoice In Your Messengers

Since, then, I have had the privilege of seeing you, through Damas your most worthy bishop, and through your worthy presbyters Bassus and Apollonius, and through my fellow-servant the deacon Sotio, whose friendship may I ever enjoy, inasmuch as he, by the grace of God, is subject to the bishop and presbytery, in the law of Jesus Christ, [I now write to you].

CHAPTER 3
Honor Your Youthful Bishop

Now it becomes you also not to despise the age of your bishop, but to yield him all reverence, according to the will of God the Father, as I have known even holy presbyters do, not having regard to the manifest youth [of their bishop], but to his knowledge in God; inasmuch as "not the ancient are [necessarily] wise, nor do the aged understand prudence; but there is a spirit in men." For Daniel the wise, at twelve years of age, became possessed of the divine Spirit, and convicted the elders, who in vain carried their grey hairs, of being false accusers, and of lusting after the beauty of another man's wife. Samuel also, when he was but a little child, reproved Eli, who was ninety years old, for giving honour to his sons rather than to God. In like manner, Jeremiah also received this message from God, "Say not, I am a child." Solomon too, and Josiah, [exemplified the same thing.] The former, being made king at twelve years of age, gave that terrible and difficult judgment in the case of the two women concerning their children. The latter, coming to the throne when eight years old cast down the altars and temples [of the idols], and burned down the groves, for they were dedicated to demons, and not to God. And he slew the false priests, as the corrupters and deceivers of men, and not the worshippers of the Deity. Wherefore youth is not to be despised when it is devoted to God. But he is to be despised who is of a wicked mind, although he be old, and full of wicked days. Timothy the Christ-bearer was young, but hear what his teacher writes to him: "Let no man despise try youth, but be thou an example of the believers in word and in conduct." It is becoming, therefore, that ye also should be obedient to your bishop, and contradict him in nothing; for it is a fearful thing to contradict any such person. For no one does [by such conduct] deceive him that is visible, but does [in reality] seek to mock Him that is invisible, who, however, cannot be mocked by any one. And every such act has respect not to man, but to God. For God says to Samuel, "They have not mocked thee, but Me." And Moses declares, "For their murmuring is not against us, but against the Lord God." No one of those has, [in fact,] remained unpunished, who rose up against their superiors. For Dathan and Abiram did not speak against the law, but against Moses, and were cast down alive into Hades. Korah also, and the two hundred and fifty who conspired with him against Aaron, were destroyed by fire. Absalom, again, who had slain his brother, became suspended on a tree, and had his evil-designing heart thrust through with darts. In like manner was Abeddadan beheaded for the same reason. Uzziah, when he presumed to oppose the priests and the priesthood, was smitten with leprosy. Saul also was dishonoured, because he did not wait for Samuel the high priest. It behoves you, therefore, also to reverence your superiors.

CHAPTER 4
Some Wickedly Act Independently Of The Bishop

It is fitting, then, not only to be called Christians, but to be so in reality. For it is not the being called so, but the being really so, that renders a man blessed. To those who indeed talk of the bishop, but do all things without him, will He who is the true and first Bishop, and the only High Priest by nature, declare, "Why call ye Me Lord, and do not the things which I say ?" For such persons seem to me not possessed of a good conscience, but to be simply dissemblers and hypocrites.

CHAPTER 5
Death Is The Fate Of All Such

Seeing, then, all things have an end, and there is set before us life upon our observance[of God's precepts], but death as the result of disobedience, and every one, according to the choice he makes, shall go to his own place, let us flee from death, and make choice of life. For I remark, that two different characters are found among men--the one true coin, the other spurious. The truly devout man is the right kind of coin, stamped by God Himself. The ungodly man, again, is false coin, unlawful, spurious, counterfeit, wrought not by God, but by the devil. I do not mean to say that there are two different human natures, but that there is one humanity, sometimes belonging to God, and sometimes to the devil. If any one is truly religious, he is a man of God; but if he is irreligious, he is a man of the devil, made such, not by nature, but by his own choice. The unbelieving bear the image of the prince of wickedness. The believing possess the image of their Prince, God the Father, and Jesus Christ, through whom, if we are not in readiness to die for the truth into His passion, His life is not in us.

CHAPTER 6
Preserve Harmony

Since therefore I have, in the persons before mentioned, beheld the whole multitude of you in faith and love, I exhort you to study to do all things with a divine harmony, while your bishop presides in the place of God, and your presbyters in the place of the assembly of the apostles, along with your deacons, who are most dear to me, and are entrusted with the ministry of Jesus Christ. He, being begotten by the Father before the beginning of time, was God the Word, the only-begotten Son, and remains the same for ever; for "of His kingdom there shall be no end," says Daniel the prophet. Let us all therefore love one another in harmony, and let no one look upon his neighbour according to the flesh, but in Christ Jesus. Let nothing exist among you which may divide you; but be ye united with your bishop, being through him subject to God in Christ.

CHAPTER 7

Do Nothing Without The Bishop And Presbyters

As therefore the Lord does nothing without the Father, for says He, "I can of mine own self do nothing," so do ye, neither presbyter, nor deacon, nor layman, do anything without the bishop. Nor let anything appear commendable to you which is destitute of his approval. For every such thing is sinful, and opposed[to the will of] God. Do ye all come together into the same place for prayer. Let there be one common supplication, one mind, one hope, with faith unblameable in Christ Jesus, than which nothing is more excellent. Do ye all, as one man, run together into the temple of God, as unto one altar, to one Jesus Christ, the High Priest of the unbegotten God.

CHAPTER 8
Caution Against False Doctrines

Be not deceived with strange doctrines, "nor give heed to fables and endless genealogies," and things in which the Jews make their boast. "Old things are passed away: behold, all things have become new." For if we still live according to the Jewish law, and the circumcision of the flesh, we deny that we have received grace. For the divinest prophets lived according to Jesus Christ. On this account also they were persecuted, being inspired by grace to fully convince the unbelieving that there is one God, the Almighty, who has manifested Himself by Jesus Christ His Son, who is His Word, not spoken, but essential. For He is not the voice of an articulate utterance, but a substance begotten by divine power, who has in all things pleased Him that sent Him.

CHAPTER 9
Let Us Live With Christ

If, then, those who were conversant with the ancient Scriptures came to newness of hope, expecting the coming of Christ, as the Lord teaches us when He says, "If ye had believed Moses, ye would have believed Me, for he wrote of Me;" and again, "Your father Abraham rejoiced to see My day, and he saw it, and was glad; for before Abraham was, I am; "how shall we be able to live without Him? The prophets were His servants, and foresaw Him by the Spirit, and waited for Him as their Teacher, and expected Him as their Lord and Saviour, saying, "He will come and save us."Let us therefore no longer keep the Sabbath after the Jewish manner, and rejoice in days of idleness; for "he that does not work, let him not eat."For say the[holy] oracles, "In the sweat of thy face shalt thou eat thy bread."But let every one of you keep the Sabbath after a spiritual manner, rejoicing in meditation on the law, not in relaxation of the body, admiring the worksmanship of God, and not eating things prepared the day before, nor using lukewarm drinks, and walking within a prescribed space, nor finding delight in dancing and plaudits which have no sense in them. And after the observance of the Sabbath, let every friend of Christ keep the Lord's Day as a festival, the resurrection-day, the queen and chief of all the days[of the week]. Looking forward to this, the prophet declared, "To the end, for the eighth day," on which our life both sprang up again, and the victory over death was obtained in Christ, whom the children of perdition, the enemies of the Saviour, deny, "whose god is their belly, who mind earthly things," who are "lovers of pleasure, and not lovers of God, having a form of godliness, but denying the power thereof." These make merchandise of Christ, corrupting His word, and giving up Jesus to sale: they are corrupters of women, and covetous of other men's possessions, swallowing up wealth insatiably; from whom may ye be delivered by the mercy of God through our Lord Jesus Christ!

CHAPTER10
Beware Of Judaizing

Let us not, therefore, be insensible to His kindness. For were He to reward us according to our works, we should cease to be. For "if Thou, Lord, shalt mark iniquities, O Lord, who shall stand?" Let us therefore prove ourselves worthy of that name which we have received. For whosoever is called by any other name besides this, he is not of God; for he has not received the prophecy which speaks thus concerning us: "The people shall be called by a new name, which the Lord shall name them, and shall be a holy people." This was first fulfilled in Syria; for "the disciples were called Christians at Antioch," when Paul and Peter were laying the foundations of the Church. Lay aside, therefore, the evil, the old, the corrupt leaven, and be ye changed into the new leaven of grace. Abide in Christ, that the stranger may not have dominion over you. It is absurd to speak of Jesus Christ with the tongue, and to cherish in the mind a Judaism which has now come to an end. For where there is Christianity there cannot be Judaism. For Christ is one, in whom every nation that believes, and every tongue that confesses, is gathered unto God. And those that were of a stony heart have become the children of Abraham, the friend of God; and in his seed all those have been blessed who were ordained to eternal life in Christ.

CHAPTER 11
I Write These Things To Warn You

These things[I address to you], my beloved, not that I know any of you to be in such a state; but, as less than any of you, I desire to guard you beforehand, that ye fall not upon the hooks of vain doctrine, but that you may rather attain to a full assurance in Christ, who was begotten by the Father before all ages, but was afterwards ye attain to full assurance in regard to the birth, and passion, and resurrection which took place in the time of the government of Pontius Pilate, being truly and certainly accomplished by Jesus Christ, who is our hope, from which may no one of you ever be turned aside. Born of the Virgin Mary without any intercourse with man. He also lived a holy life, and healed every kind of sickness and disease among the people, and wrought signs and wonders for the benefit of men; and to those who had fallen into the error of polytheism He made known the one and only true God, His Father, and underwent the passion, and endured the cross at the hands of the Christ-killing Jews, under Pontius Pilate the governor and Herod the king. He also died, and rose again, and ascended into the heavens to Him that sent Him, and is sat down at His right hand, and shall come at the end of the world, with His Father's glory, to judge the living and the dead, and to render to every one according to his works. He who knows these things with a full assurance, and believes them, is happy; even as ye are now the lovers of God and of Christ, in the full assurance of our hope, from

which may no one of us ever be turned aside!

CHAPTER 12
Ye Are Superior To Me

May I enjoy you in all respects, if indeed I be worthy! For though I am bound, I am not worthy to be compared to one of you that are at liberty. I know that ye are not puffed up, for ye have Jesus in yourselves. And all the more when I commend you, I know that ye cherish modesty of spirit; as it is written, "The righteous man is his own accuser;" and again, "Declare thou first thine iniquities, that thou mayest be justified;" and again, "When ye shall have done all things that are commanded you, say, We are unprofitable servants;" "for that which is highly esteemed among men is abomination in the sight of God." For says[the Scripture], "God be merciful to me a sinner." Therefore those great ones, Abraham and Job, styled themselves "dust and ashes before God. And David says, "Who am I before Thee, 0 Lord, that Thou hast glorified me hitherto?" And Moses, who was "the meekest of all men," saith to God, "I am of a feeble voice, and of a slow tongue." Be ye therefore also of a humble spirit, that ye may be exalted; for "he that abaseth himself shall be exalted, and he that exalteth himself shall be abased."]

CHAPTER 13
Be Established In Faith And Unity

Study, therefore, to be established in the doctrines of the Lord and the apostles, that so all things, whatsoever ye do, may prosper, both in the flesh and spirit, in faith and love, with your most admirable bishop, and the well-compacted spiritual crown of your presbytery, and the deacons who are according to God. Be ye subject to the bishop, and to one another, as Christ to the Father. that there may be a unity according to God among you.

... according to the flesh, and the apostles to Christ, and to the Father, and to the Spirit; that so there may be a union beth fleshly and spiritual.

CHAPTER 14
Your Prayers Requested

Knowing as I do that ye are full of all good, I have but briefly exhorted you in the love of Jesus Christ. Be mindful of me in your prayers, that I may attain to God; and of the Church which is in Syria, of whom I am not worthy to be called bishop. For I stand in need of your united prayer in God, and of your love, that the Church which is in Syria may be deemed worthy, by your good order, of being edified in Christ.

CHAPTER 15
Salutations

The Ephesians from Smyrna(whence I also write to you), who are here for the glory of God, as ye also are, who have in all things refreshed me, salute you, as does also Polycarp. The rest of the Churches, in honour of Jesus Christ, also salute you. Fare ye well in harmony, ye who have obtained the inseparable Spirit, in Christ Jesus, by the will of God.

Epistle of Ignatius to the Philadelphians

CHAPTER 1
Praise Of The Bishop

Having beheld your bishop, I know that he was not selected to undertake the ministry which pertains to the common [weal], either by himself or by men, or out of vainglory, but by the love of Jesus Christ, and of God the Father, who raised Him from the dead; at whose meekness I am struck with admiration, and who by His silence is able to accomplish more than they who talk a great deal. For he is in harmony with the commandments and ordinances of the Lord, even as the strings are with the harp, and is no less blameless than was Zacharias the priest. Wherefore my soul declares his mind towards God a happy one, knowing it to be virtuous and perfect, and that his stability as well as freedom from all anger is after the example of the infinite meekness of the living God.

CHAPTER 2
Maintain Union With The Bishop

Wherefore, as children of light and truth, flee from division and wicked doctrines; but where the shepherd is, there do ye as sheep follow. For there are many wolves that appear worthy of credit, who, by means of a pernicious pleasure, carry captives those that are running towards God; but in your unity they shall have no place. heretics, from whom "a defiling influence has gone forth into all the earth." But where the shepherd is, there do ye as sheep follow. For there are many wolves in sheep's clothing, who, by means of a pernicious pleasure, carry captive those that are running towards God; but in your unity they shall have no place.

CHAPTER 3
Avoid Schismatics

Keep yourselves, then, from those evil planes which Jesus Christ does not tend, bat that wild beast, the destroyer of men, because they are not the planting of the Father, but the seed of the wicked one. Not that I have found any division among you do I write these things; but I arm you beforehand, as the children of God. For as many as are of Christ are also with the bishop; but as many as fall away from him, and embrace communion with the accursed, these shall be cut off along with them. For they are not Christ's husbandry, but the seed of the enemy, from whom may you ever be delivered by the prayers of the shepherd, that most faithful and gentle shepherd who presides over you. I therefore exhort you in the Lord to receive with all tenderness those that repent and return to the unity of the Church, that through your kindness and forbearance they may recover themselves out of the snare of the devil, and becoming worthy of Jesus Christ, may obtain eternal salvation in the kingdom of Christ. Brethren, be not deceived. If any man follows him that separates from the truth, he shall not inherit the kingdom of God; and if any man does not stand aloof from the preacher of falsehood, he shall be condemned to hell. For it is obligatory neither to separate from the godly, nor to associate with the ungodly. If any one walks according to a strange opinion, he is not of Christ, nor a partaker of His passion; but is a fox, a destroyer of the vineyard of Christ. Have no fellowship with such a man, lest ye perish along with him, even should he be thy father, thy son, thy brother, or a member of thy family. For says [the Scripture], "Thine eye shall not spare him." You ought therefore to "hate those that hate God, and to waste away [with grief] on account of His enemies." I do not mean that you should beat them or persecute them, as do the Gentiles "that know not the Lord and God;" but that you should regard them as your enemies, and separate yourselves from them, while yet you admonish them, and exhort them to repentance, if it may be they will hear, if it may be they will submit themselves. For our God is a lover of mankind, and "will have all men to be saved, and to come to the knowledge of the truth." Wherefore "He makes His sun to rise upon the evil and on the good, and sendeth rain on the just and on the unjust;" of whose kindness the Lord, wishing us also to be imitators, says, "Be ye perfect, even as also your Father that is in heaven is perfect."

CHAPTER 4
Have But One Eucharist, Etc.

Take ye heed, then, to have but one Eucharist. For there is one flesh of our Lord Jesus Christ, and one cup to [show forth] the unity of His blood; one altar; as there is one bishop, along with the presbytery and deacons, my fellow-servants: that so, whatsoever ye do, ye may do it according to [the will of] God.

I have confidence of you m the Lord, that ye will be of no other mind. Wherefore I write boldly to your love, which is worthy of God, and exhort you to have but one faith, and one [kind of] preaching, and one Eucharist. For there is one flesh of the Lord Jesus Christ; and His blood which was shed for us is one; one loaf also is broken to all [the communicants], and one cup is distributed among them all: there is but one altar for the whole Church, and one bishop, with the presbytery and deacons, my fellow-servants. Since, also, there is but one unbegotten Being, God, even the Father; and one only-begotten Son, God, the Word and man; and one Comforter, the Spirit of truth; and also one preaching, and one faith, and one baptism; and one Church which the holy apostles established from one end of the earth to the other by the blood of Christ, and by their own sweat and toil; it behoves you also, therefore, as "a peculiar people, and a holy nation," to perform all things with harmony in Christ. Wives, be ye subject to your husbands in the fear of God; and ye virgins, to Christ in purity, not counting marriage an abomination, but desiring that which is better, not for the reproach of wedlock, but for the sake of meditating on the law. Children, obey your parents, and have an affection for them, as workers together with God for your birth [into the world]. Servants, be subject to your masters in God, that ye may be the freed-men of Christ. Husbands, love your wives, as fellow-servants of God, as your own body, as the partners of your life, and your co-adjutors in the procreation of children. Virgins, have Christ alone before your eyes, and His Father in your prayers, being enlightened by the Spirit. May I have pleasure in your purity, as that of Elijah, or as of Joshua the son of Nun, as of Melchizedek, or as of Elisha, as of Jeremiah, or as of John the Baptist, as of the beloved disciple, as of Timothy, as of Titus, as of Evodius, as of Clement, who departed this life in [perfect] chastity, Not, however, that I blame the other blessed [saints] because they entered into the married state, of which I have just spoken. For I pray that, being found worthy of God, I may be found at their feet in the kingdom, as at the feet of Abraham, and Isaac, and Jacob; as of Joseph, and Isaiah, and the rest of the prophets; as of Peter, and Paul, and the rest of the apostles, that were married men. For they entered into these marriages not for the sake of appetite, but out of regard for the propagation of mankind. Fathers, "bring up your children in the nurture and admonition of the Lord;" and teach them the holy Scriptures, and also trades, that they may not indulge in idleness. Now [the Scripture] says, "A righteous father educates [his children] well; his heart shall rejoice in a wise son."

Masters, be gentle towards your servants, as holy Job has taught you; for there is one nature, and one family of mankind. For "in Christ there is neither bond nor free." Let governors be obedient to Caesar; soldiers to those that command them; deacons to the presbyters, as to high-priests; the presbyters, and deacons, and the rest of the clergy, together with all the people, and the soldiers, and the governors, and Caesar [himself], to the bishop; the bishop to Christ, even as Christ to the Father. And thus unity is preserved throughout. Let not the widows be wanderers about, nor fond of dainties, nor gadders from house to house; but let them be like Judith, noted for her seriousness; and like Anna, eminent for her sobriety. I do not ordain these things as an apostle: for "who am I, or what is my father's house," that I should pretend to be equal in honour to them? But as your "fellow-soldier," I hold the position of one who [simply] admonishes you.

CHAPTER 5
Pray For Me

My brethren, I am greatly enlarged in loving you; and rejoicing exceedingly [over you], I seek to secure your safety. Yet it is not I, but the Lord Jesus through me; for whose sake being bound, I fear the more, for I am not yet perfect. But your prayer to God shall make me perfect, that I may attain that to which I have been called, while I flee to the Gospel as to the flesh of Jesus Christ, and to the apostles as the presbytery of the Church. I do also love the prophets as those who announced Christ, and as being partakers of the same Spirit with the apostles. For as the false prophets and the false apostles drew [to themselves] one and the same wicked, deceitful, and seducing spirit; so also did the prophets and the apostles receive from God, through Jesus Christ, one and the same Holy Spirit, who is good, and sovereign, and true, and the Author of [saving] knowledge. For there is one God of the Old and New Testament, "one Mediator between God and men," for the creation of both intelligent and sensitive beings, and in order to exercise a beneficial and suitable providence [over them]. There is also one Comforter, who displayed His power in Moses, and the prophets, and apostles. All the saints, therefore, were saved by Christ, hoping in Him, and waiting for Him; and they obtained through Him salvation, being holy ones, worthy of love and admiration, having testimony borne to them by Jesus Christ, in the Gospel of our common hope.

CHAPTER 6
Do Not Accept Judaism

But if any one preach the Jewish law unto you, listen not to him. For it is better to hearken to Christian doctrine from a man who has been circumcised, than to Judaism from one uncircumcised. But if either of such persons do not speak concerning Jesus Christ, they are in my judgment but as monuments and sepulchres of the dead, upon which are written only the names of men. Flee therefore the wicked devices and snares of the prince prophets, but denies Christ to be the Son of God, he is a liar, even as also is his father the devil, and is a Jew falsely so called, being possessed of mere carnal circumcision. If any one confesses Christ Jesus the Lord, but denies the God of the law and of the prophets, saying that the Father of Christ is not the Maker of heaven and earth, he has not continued in the truth any more than his father the devil, and is a disciple of Simon Magus, not of the Holy Spirit. If any one says there is one God, and also confesses Christ Jesus, but thinks the Lord to be a mere man, and not the only-begotten God, and Wisdom of this world, lest at any time being conquered by his artifices, ye grow weak in your love. But be ye all joined together with an undivided heart. And I thank my God that I have a good conscience in respect to you, and that no one has it in his power to boast, either privately or publicly, that I have burdened any one either in much or in little. And I wish for all among whom I have spoken, that they may not possess that for a testimony against them. Dom, and the Word of God, and deems Him to consist merely of a soul and body, such an one is a serpent, that preaches deceit and error for the destruction of men, And such a man is poor in understanding, even as by name he is an Ebionite. If any one confesses the truths mentioned, but calls lawful wedlock, and the procreation of children, destruction and pollution, or deems certain kinds of food abominable, such an one has the apostate dragon dwelling within him. If any one confesses the Father, and the Son, and the Holy Ghost, and praises the creation, but calls the incarnation merely an appearance, and is ashamed of the passion, such an one has denied the faith, not less than the Jews who killed Christ. If any one confesses these things, and that God the Word did dwell in a human body, being within it as the Word, even as the soul also is in the body, because it was God that inhabited it, and not a human soul, but affirms that unlawful unions are a good thing, and places the highest happiness in pleasure, as does the man who is falsely called a Nicolaitan, this person can neither be a lover of God, nor a lover of Christ, but is a corrupter of his own flesh, and therefore void of the Holy Spirit, and a stranger to Christ. All such persons are but monuments and sepulchres of the dead, upon which are written only the names of dead men. Flee, therefore, the wicked devices and snares of the spirit which now worketh in the children of this world,s lest at any time being overcome, ye grow weak in your love. But be ye all joined together with an undivided heart and a willing mind, "being of one accord and of one judgment," being always of the same opinion about the same things, both when you are at ease and in danger, both in sorrow and in joy. I thank God, through Jesus Christ, that I have a good conscience in respect to you, and that no one has it in his power to boast, either privately or publicly, that I have burdened any one either in much or in little. And I wish for all among whom I have spoken, that they may not possess that for a testimony against them.

CHAPTER 7
I Have Exhorted You To Unity

For though some would nave deceived me according to the flesh, yet my spirit is not deceived; for I have received it from God. For it knows both whence it comes and whither it goes, and detects the secrets [of the heart]. For when I was among you, I cried, I spoke with a loud voice--the word is not mine, but God's--Give heed to the bishop, and to the presbytery and deacons. But if ye suspect that I spake thus, as having learned beforehand the division caused by some among you, He is my witness, for whose sake I am in bonds, that I learned nothing of it from the mouth of any man. But the Spirit made an announcement to me, saying as follows: Do nothing without the bishop; keep your bodies as the temples of God; love unity; avoid divisions; be ye followers of Paul, and of the rest of the apostles, even as they also were of Christ.

CHAPTER 8
The Same Continued

I therefore did what belonged to me, as a man devoted to unity; adding this also, that where there is diversity of judgment, and wrath, and hatred, God does not dwell. To all them that repent, God grants forgiveness, if they with one consent return to the unity of Christ, and communion with the bishop. I trust to the grace of Jesus Christ, that He will free you from every bond of wickedness. I therefore exhort you that ye do nothing out of strife, but according to the doctrine of Christ. For I have heard some saying, If I do not find the Gospel in the archives, I will not believe it. To such persons I say that my archives are Jesus Christ, to disobey whom is manifest destruction. My authentic archives are His cross, and death, and resurrection, and the faith which bears on these things, by which I desire, through your prayers, to be justified. He who disbelieves the Gospel disbelieves everything along with it. For the archives ought not to be preferred to the Spirit. "It is hard to kick against the pricks;" it is hard to disbelieve Christ; it is hard to reject the preaching of the apostles.

CHAPTER 9
The Old Testament Is Good: The New Testament Is Better

The priests indeed, and the ministers of the word, are good; but the High Priest is better, to whom the holy of holies has been committed, and who alone has been entrusted with the secrets of God. The ministering powers of God are good. The Comforter is holy, and the Word is holy, the Son of the Father, by whom He made all things, and exercises a providence over them all. This is the Way which leads to the Father, the Rock, the Defence, the Key, the Shepherd, the Sacrifice, the Door of knowledge, through which have entered Abraham, and Isaac, and Jacob, Moses and all the company of the prophets, and these pillars of the world, the apostles, and the spouse of Christ, on whose account He poured out His own blood, as her marriage portion, that He might redeem her. All these things tend towards the unity of the one and only true God. But the Gospel possesses something transcendent [above the former dispensation], viz. the appearing of our Saviour Jesus Christ, His passion, and the resurrection itself. For those things which the prophets announced, saying, "Until He come for whom it is reserved, and He shall be the expectation of the Gentiles," have been fulfilled in the Gospel, [our Lord saying,] "Go ye and teach all nations, baptizing them in the name of the Father, and of the Son, and of the Holy Ghost." All then are good together, the law, the prophets, the apostles, the whole company[of others] that have believed through them: only if we love one another.

CHAPTER 10
Congratulate The Inhabintants Of Antioch
On The Close Of The Persecution

Since, according to your prayers, and the compassion which ye feel in Christ Jesus, it is reported to me that the Church which is at Antioch in Syria possesses peace, it will become you, as a Church of God, to elect a bishop to act as the ambassador of God[for you] to[the brethren] there, that it may be granted them to meet together, and to glorify the name of God. Blessed is he in Christ Jesus, who shall be deemed worthy of such a ministry; and if ye be zealous[in this matter], ye shall receive glory in Christ. And if ye are willing, it is not altogether beyond your power to do this, for the sake of God; as also the nearest Churches have sent, in some cases bishops, and in others presbyters and deacons.

CHAPTER 11
Thanks And Salutation

Now, as to Philo the deacon, a man of Cilicia, of high reputation, who still ministers to me in the word of God, along with Gaius and Agathopus, an elect man, who has followed me from Syria, not regarding his life, --these also bear testimony in your behalf. And I myself give thanks to God for you, because ye have received them: and the Lord will also receive you. But may those that dishonoured them be forgiven through the grace of Jesus Christ, "who wisheth not the death of the sinner, but his repentance." The love of the brethren at Troas salutes you; whence also I write to you by Burrhus, who was sent along with me by the Ephesians and Smyrnaeans, to show their respect: whom the Lord Jesus Christ will requite, in whom they hope, in flesh, and soul, and spirit, and faith, and love, and concord. Fare ye well in the Lord Jesus Christ, our common hope, in the Holy Ghost.

Epistle of Ignatius to the Philippians

CHAPTER 1
Reason For Writing The Epistle

Being mindful of your love and of your zeal in Christ, which ye have manifested towards us we thought it fitting to write to you, who display such a godly and spiritual love to the brethren, to put you in remembrance of your Christian course, "that ye all speak the same thing, being of one mind, thinking the same thing, and walking by the same rule of faith," as Paul admonished you. For if there is one God of the universe, the Father of Christ, "of whom are all things;" and one Lord Jesus Christ, our [Lord], "by whom are all things;" and also one Holy Spirit, who wrought in Moses, and in the prophets and apostles; and also one baptism, which is administered that we should have fellowship with the death of the Lord; and also one elect Church; there ought likewise to be but one faith in respect to Christ. For "there is one Lord, one faith, one baptism; one God and Father of all, who is through all, and in all."

CHAPTER 2
Unity Of The Three Divine Persons

There is then one God and Father, and not two or three; One who is; and there is no other besides Him, the only true [God]. For "the Lord thy God," saith [the Scripture], "is one Lord." And again, "Hath not one God created us? Have we not all one Father? And there is also one Son, God the Word. For "the only-begotten Son," saith [the Scripture], "who is in the bosom of the Father." And again, "One Lord Jesus Christ." And in another place, "What is His name, or what His Son's name, that we may know?" And there is also one

Paraclete. For "there is also," saith [the Scripture], "one Spirit," since "we have been called in one hope of our calling." And again, "We have drunk of one Spirit," with what follows. And it is manifest that all these gifts [possessed by believers] "worketh one and the self-same Spirit." There are not then either three Fathers, or three Sons, or three Paracletes, but one Father, and one Son, and one Paraclete. Wherefore also the Lord, when He sent forth the apostles to make disciples of all nations, commanded them to "baptize in the name of the Father, and of the Son, and of the Holy Ghost," not unto one [person] having three names, nor into three [persons] who became incarnate, but into three possessed of equal honour.

CHAPTER 3
Christ Was Truly Born, And Died

For there is but One that became incarnate, and that neither the Father nor the Paraclete, but the Son only, [who became so] not in appearance or imagination, but in reality. For "the Word became flesh." For "Wisdom builded for herself a house." And God the Word was born as man, with a body, of the Virgin, without any intercourse of man. For [it is written], "A virgin shall conceive in her womb, and bring forth a son." He was then truly born, truly grew up, truly ate and drank, was truly crucified, and died, and rose again. He who believes these things, as they really were, and as they really took place, is blessed. He who believeth them not is no less accursed than those who crucified the Lord. For the prince of this world rejoiceth when any one denies the cross, since he knows that the confession of the cross is his own destruction. For that is the trophy which has been raised up against his power, which when he sees, he shudders, and when he hears of, is afraid.

CHAPTER 4
The Malignity And Folly Of Satan

And indeed, before the cross was erected, he (Satan) was eager that it should be so; and he "wrought" [for this end] "in the children of disobedience." He wrought in Judas, in the Pharisees, in the Sadducees, in the old, in the young, and in the priests. But when it was just about to be erected, he was troubled, and infused repentance into the traitor, and pointed him to a rope to hang himself with, and taught him [to die by] strangulation. He terrified also the silly woman, disturbing her by dreams; and he, who had tried every means to have the cross prepared, now endeavoured to put a stop to its erection; not that he was influenced by repentance on account of the greatness of his crime (for in that case he would not be utterly depraved), but because he perceived his own destruction [to be at hand]. For the cross of Christ was the beginning of his condemnation the beginning of his death, the beginning of his destruction. Wherefore, also, he works in some that they should deny the cross, be ashamed of the passion, call the death an appearance, mutilate and explain away the birth of the Virgin, and calumniate the [human] nature s itself as being abominable. He fights along with the Jews to a denial of the cross, and with the Gentiles to the calumniating of Mary, who are heretical in holding that Christ possessed a mere phantasmal body. For the leader of all wickedness assumes manifold forms, beguiler of men as he is, inconsistent, and even contradicting himself, projecting one course and then following another. For he is wise to do evil, but as to what good may be he is totally ignorant. And indeed he is full of ignorance, on account of his voluntary want of reason: for how can he be deemed anything else who does not perceive reason when it lies at his very feet?

CHAPTER 5
Apostrophe To Satan

For if the Lord were a mere man, possessed of a soul and body only, why dost thou mutilate and explain away His being born with the common nature of humanity? Why dost thou call the passion a mere appearance, as if it were any strange thing happening to a [mere] man? And why dost thou reckon the death of a mortal to be simply an imaginary death? But if, [on the other hand,] He is both God and man, then why dost thou call it unlawful to style Him "the Lord of glory," who is by nature unchangeable? Why dost thou say that it is unlawful to declare of the Lawgiver who possesses a human soul, "The Word was made flesh," and was a perfect man, and not merely one dwelling in a man? But how came this magician into existence, who of old formed all nature that can be apprehended either by the senses or intellect, according to the will of the Father; and, when He became incarnate, healed every kind of disease and infirmity?

CHAPTER 6
Continuation

And how can He be but God, who raises up the dead, sends away the lame sound of limb, cleanses the lepers, restores sight to the blind, and either increases or transmutes existing substances, as the five loaves and the two fishes, and the water which became wine, and who puts to flight thy whole host by a mere word? And why dost thou abuse the nature of the Virgin, and style her members disgraceful, since thou didst of old display such in public processions, and didst order them to be exhibited naked, males in the sight of females, and females to stir up the unbridled lust of males? But now these are reckoned by thee disgraceful, and thou pretendest to be full of modesty, thou spirit of fornication, not knowing that then only anything becomes disgraceful when it is polluted by wickedness. But when sin is not present, none of the things that have been created are shameful, none of them evil, but all very good. But inasmuch as thou art blind, thou revilest these things.

CHAPTER 7
Continuation: Inconsistency Of Satan

And how, again, does Christ not at all appear to thee to be of the Virgin, but to be God over all, and the Almighty? Say, then, who sent Him? Who was Lord over Him ? And whose will did He obey? And what laws did He fulfil, since He was subject neither to the will nor power of any one? And while you deny that Christ was born, you affirm that the unbegotten was begotten, and that He who had no beginning was nailed to the cross, by whose permission I am unable to say. But thy changeable tactics do not escape me, nor am I ignorant that thou art wont to walk with slanting and uncertain steps. And thou art ignorant who really was born, thou who pretendest to know everything.

CHAPTER 8
Continuation: Ignorance Of Satan

For many things are unknown to thee; [such as the following]: the virginity of Mary; the wonderful birth; Who it was that became incarnate; the star which guided those who were in the east; the Magi who presented gifts; the salutation of the archangel to the Virgin; the marvellous conception of her that was betrothed; the announcement of the boy-forerunner respecting the son of the Virgin, and his leaping in the womb on account of what was foreseen; the songs of the angels over Him that was born; the glad tidings announced to the shepherds; the fear of Herod lest his kingdom should be taken from him; the command to slay the infants; the removal into Egypt, and the return from that country to the same region; the infant swaddling-bands; the human registration; the nourishing by means of milk; the name of father given to Him who did not beget; the manger because there was not room [elsewhere]; no human preparation [for the Child]; the gradual growth, human speech, hunger, thirst, journeyings, weariness; the offering of sacrifices and then also circumcision, baptism; the voice of God over Him that was baptized, as to who He was and whence [He had come]; the testimony of the Spirit and the Father from above; the voice of John the prophet when it signified the passion by the appellation of "the Lamb;" the performance of divers miracles, manifold healings; the rebuke of the Lord ruling both the sea and the winds; evil spirits expelled; thou thyself subjected to torture, and, when afflicted by the power of Him who had been manifested, not having it in thy power to do anything.

CHAPTER 9
Continuation: Ignorance Of Satan

Seeing these things, thou wast in utter perplexity. And thou wast ignorant that it was a virgin that should bring forth; but the angels song of praise struck thee with astonishment, as well as the adoration of the Magi, and the appearance of the star. Thou didst revert to thy state of [wilful] ignorance, because all the circumstances seemed to thee trifling; for thou didst deem the swaddling-bands, the circumcision, and the nourishment by means of milk contemptible: these things appeared to thee unworthy of God. Again, thou didst behold a man who remained forty days and nights without tasting human food, along with ministering gels at whose presence thou didst shudder, when first of all thou hadst seen Him baptized as a common man, and knewest not the reason thereof. But after His [lengthened] fast thou didst again assume thy wonted audacity, and didst tempt Him when hungry, as if He had been an ordinary man, not knowing who He was. For thou saidst, "If thou be the Son of God, command that these stones be made bread." Now, this expression, "If thou be the Son," is an indication of ignorance. For if thou hadst possessed real knowledge, thou wouldst have understood that the Creator can with equal ease both create what does not exist, and change that which already has a being. And thou temptedst by means of hunger Him who nourisheth all that require food. And thou temptedst the very "Lord of glory," forgetting in thy malevolence that "man shall not live by bread alone, but by every word that proceedeth out of the mouth of God." For if thou hadst known that He was the Son of God, thou wouldst also have understood that He who had kept his body from feeling any want for forty days and as many nights, could have also done the same for ever. Why, then, does He suffer hunger? In order to prove that He had assumed a body subject to the same feelings as those of ordinary men. By the first fact He showed that He was God, and by the second that He was also man.

CHAPTER 10
Continuation: Audacity Of Satan

Darest thou, then, who didst fall "as lightning from the very highest glory, to say to the Lord, "Cast thyself down from hence [to Him] to whom the things that are not are reckoned as if they were,(and to provoke to a display of vainglory Him that was free from all ostentation? And didst thou pretend to read in Scripture concerning Him: "For He hath given His angels charge concerning Thee, and in their hands they shall bear Thee up, lest thou shouldest dash Thy foot against a stone?" At the same time thou didst pretend to be ignorant of the rest, furtively concealing what [the Scripture] predicted concerning thee and thy servants: "Thou shalt tread upon the adder and the basilisk; the lion and the dragon shall thou trample under foot."

CHAPTER 11
Continuation: Audacity Of Satan

If, therefore, thou art trodden down under the feet of the Lord, how dost thou tempt Him that cannot be tempted, forgetting that precept of the law-giver, "Thou shall not tempt the Lord thy God?" Yea, thou even darest, most accursed one, to appropriate the works of God to thyself, and to declare that the dominion over these was delivered to thee. And thou dost set forth thine own fall as an example to the Lord, and dost promise to give Him what is really His own, if He would fall down and worship thee. And how didst thou not shudder, O thou spirit more wicked through thy malevolence than all other wicked spirits, to utter such words against the Lord? Through thine appetite was thou overcome, and through thy vainglory wast thou brought to dishonour: through avarice and ambition dost thou [now] draw on [others] to ungodliness. Thou, O Belial, dragon, apostate, crooked serpent, rebel against God, outcast from Christ, alien from the Holy Spirit, exile from the ranks of the angels, reviler of the laws of God, enemy of all that is lawful, who didst rise up against the first-formed of men, and didst drive forth [from obedience to] the commandment [of God] those who had in no respect injured thee; thou who didst raise up against Abel the murderous Cain; thou who didst take arms against Job: dost thou say to the Lord, "If Thou wilt fall down and worship me?" Oh what audacity! Oh what madness! Thou runaway slave, thou incorrigible slave, dost thou rebel against the good Lord? Dost thou say to so great a Lord, the God of all that either the mind or the senses can perceive, "If Thou wilt fall down and worship me?"

CHAPTER 12
The Meek Reply Of Christ

But the Lord is long-suffering, and does not reduce to nothing him who in his ignorance dares [to utter] such words, but meekly replies, "Get thee hence, Satan." He does not say, "Get thee behind Me," for it is not possible that he should be converted; but, "Begone, Satan," to the course which thou hast chosen. "Begone" to those things to which, through thy malevolence, thou hast been called. For I know Who I am, and by Whom I have been sent, and Whom it behoves Me to worship. For "thou shall worship the Lord thy God, and Him only shalt thou serve." I know the one [God]; I am acquainted with the only [Lord] from whom thou hast become an apostate. I am not an enemy of God; I acknowledge His pre-eminence; I know the Father, who is the author of my generation.

CHAPTER 13
Various Exhortations And Directions

These things, brethren, out of the affection which I entertain for you, I have felt compelled to write, exhorting you with a view to the glory of God, not as if I were a person of any consequence, but simply as a brother. Be ye subject to the bishop, to the presbyters, and to the deacons. Love one another in the Lord, as being the images of God. Take heed, ye husbands, that ye love your wives as your own members. Ye wives also, love your husbands, as being one with them in virtue of your union. If any one lives in chastity or continence, let him not be lifted up, lest he lose his reward. Do not lightly esteem the festivals. Despise not the period of forty days, for it comprises an imitation of the conduct of the Lord. After the week of the passion, do not neglect to fast on the fourth and sixth days, distributing at the same time of thine abundance to the poor. If any one fasts on the Lord's Day or on the Sabbath, except on the paschal Sabbath only, he is a murderer of Christ.

CHAPTER 14
Farewells And Cautions

Let your prayers be extended to the Church of Antioch, whence also I as a prisoner am being led to Rome. I salute the holy bishop Polycarp; I salute the holy bishop Vitalius, and the sacred presbytery, and my fellow-servants the deacons; in whose stead may my soul be found. Once more I bid farewell to the bishop, and to the presbyters in the Lord. If any one celebrates the passover along with the Jews, or receives the emblems of their feast, he is a partaker with those that killed the Lord and His apostles.

CHAPTER 15
Salutations And Conclusion

Philo and Agathopus the deacons salute you. I salute the company of virgins, and the order of widows; of whom may I have joy! I salute the people of the Lord, from the least unto the greatest. I have sent you this letter through Euphanius the reader, a man honoured of God, and very faithful, happening to meet with him at Rhegium, just as he was going on board ship. Remember my bonds that I may be made perfect in Christ. Fare ye well in the flesh, the soul, and the spirit, while ye think of things perfect, and turn yourselves away from the workers of iniquity, who corrupt the word of truth, and are strengthened inwardly by the grace of our Lord Jesus Christ.

Epistle of Ignatius to the Romans

CHAPTER 1
As A Prisoner, I Hope To See You

Through prayer to God I have obtained the privilege of seeing your most worthy faces, even as I earnestly begged might be granted me; for as a prisoner in Christ Jesus I hope to salute you, if indeed it be the will [of God] that I be thought worthy of attaining unto the end. For the beginning has been well ordered, if I may obtain grace to cling to my lot without hindrance unto the end. For I am afraid of your love, lest it should do me an injury. For it is easy for you to accomplish what you please;

CHAPTER 2
Do Not Save Me From Martyrdom

For it is not my desire that ye should please men, Out God, even as also ye do please Him. For neither shall I ever hereafter have such an opportunity of attaining to God; nor will ye, if ye shall now be silent, ever be entitled to s the honour of a better work. For if ye are silent concerning me, I shall become God's; but if ye show your love to my flesh, I shall again have to run my race. Pray, then, do not seek to confer any greater favour upon me than that I be sacrificed to God, while the altar is still prepared; that, being gathered together in love, ye may sing praise to the Father, through Christ Jesus, that God has deemed me, the bishop of Syria, worthy to be sent for from the east unto the west, and to become a martyr in behalf of His own precious sufferings, so as to pass from the world to God, that I may rise again unto Him.

CHAPTER 3
Pray Rather That I May Attain To Martydom

Ye have never envied any one; ye have taught others. Now I desire that those things may be confirmed [by your conduct], which in your instructions ye enjoin [on others]. Only request in my behalf both inward and outward strength, that I may not only speak, but [truly] will, so that I may not merely be called a Christian,   but really found to be one. For if I be truly found [a Christian], I may also be called one, and be then deemed faithful, when I shall no longer appear to the world. Nothing visible is eternal. "For the things which are seen are temporal, but the things which are not seen are eternal. The Christian is not the result of persuasion, but of power. When he is hated by the world, he is beloved of God. For says [the Scripture], "If ye were of this world, the world would love its own; but now ye are not of the world, but I have chosen you out of it: continue in fellowship with me."

CHAPTER 4
Allow Me To Fall A Prey To The Wild Beasts

I write to all the Churches, and impress on them all, that I shall willingly die for God, unless ye hinder me. I beseech of you not to show an unseasonable goodwill towards me. Suffer me to become food for the wild beasts, through whose instrumentality it will be granted me to attain to God. I am the wheat of God, and am ground by the teeth of the wild beasts, that I may be found the pure bread of God. Rather entice the wild beasts, that they may become my tomb, and may leave nothing of my body; so that when I have fallen asleep [in death], I may not be found troublesome to any one. Then shall I be a true disciple of Jesus Christ, when the world shall not see so much as my body. Entreat the Lord for me, that by these instruments I may be found a sacrifice to God. I do not, as Peter and Paul, issue commandments unto you. They were apostles of Jesus Christ, but I am the very least [of believers]: they were free, as the servants of God; while I am, even until now, a servant. But when I suffer, I shall be the freedman of Jesus Christ, and shall rise again emancipated in Him. And now, being in bonds for Him, I learn not to desire anything worldly or vain.

CHAPTER 5
I Desire To Die

From Syria even unto Rome I fight with beasts, both by land and sea, both by night and day, being bound to ten leopards, I mean a band of soldiers, who, even when they receive benefits, show themselves all the worse. But I am the more instructed by their injuries [to act as a disciple of Christ]; "yet am I not thereby justified." May I enjoy the wild beasts that are prepared for me; and I pray that they may be found eager to rush upon me, which also I will entice to devour me speedily, and not deal with me as with some, whom, out of fear, they have not touched. But if they be unwilling to assail me, I will compel them to do so. Pardon me [in this] I know what is for my benefit. Now I begin to be a disciple, and have no desire after anything visible or invisible, that I may attain to Jesus Christ.

CHAPTER 6
By Death I Shall Attain True Life

All the ends of the world, and all the kingdoms of this earth, shall profit me nothing. It is better for me to die for the sake of Jesus Christ, than to reign over all the ends of the earth. "For what is a man profited, if he gain the whole world, but lose his own soul?" I long after the Lord, the Son of the true God and Father, even Jesus Christ. Him I seek, who died for us and rose again. Pardon me, brethren: do not hinder me in attaining to life; for Jesus is the life of believers. Do not wish to keep me in a state of death, for life without Christ is death. While I desire to belong to God, do not ye give me over to the world. Suffer me to obtain pure light: when I have gone thither, I shall indeed be a man of God. Permit me to be an imitator of the passion of Christ, my God. If any one has Him within himself, let him consider what I desire, and let him have sympathy with me, as knowing how I am straitened.

CHAPTER 7
Reason Of Desiring To Die

The prince of this world would fain carry me away, and corrupt my disposition towards God. Let none of you, therefore, who are [in Rome] help him; rather be ye on my side, that is, on the side of God. Do not speak of Jesus Christ, and yet prefer this world to Him. Let not envy find a dwelling-place among you; nor even should I, when present with you, exhort you to it, be ye persuaded, but rather give credit to those things which I now write to you. For though I am alive while I write to you, yet I am eager to die for the sake of Christ. My love s has been crucified, and there is no fire in me that loves anything; but there is living water springing up in me, and which says to me inwardly, Come to the Father. I have no delight in corruptible food, nor in the pleasures of this life. I desire the bread of God, the heavenly bread, the bread of life, which is the flesh of Jesus Christ,

CHAPTER 8
Be Ye Favourable To Me

I no longer wish to live after the manner of men, and my desire shall be fulfilled if ye consent. "I am crucified with Christ: nevertheless I live; yet no longer I, since Christ liveth in me." I entreat you in this brief letter: do not refuse me; believe me that I love Jesus, who was delivered [to death] for my sake. "What shall I render to the Lord for all His benefits towards me ?" Now God, even the Father, and the Lord Jesus Christ, shall reveal these things to you, [so that ye shall know] that I speak truly. And do ye pray along with me, that I may attain my aim in the Holy Spirit. I have not written to you according to the flesh, but according to the will of God. If I shall suffer, ye have loved me; but if I am rejected, ye have hated me.

CHAPTER 9
Pray For The Church In Syria

Remember in your prayers the Church which is in Syria, which, instead of me, has now for its shepherd the Lord, who says, "I am the good Shepherd." And He alone will oversee it, as well as your love towards Him. But as for me, I am ashamed to be counted one of them; for I am not worthy, as being the very last of them, and one born out of due time. But I have obtained mercy to be somebody, if I shall attain to God. My spirit salutes you, and the love of the Churches which have received me in the name of Jesus Christ, and not as a mere passerby. For even those Churches which were not near to me in the way, have brought me forward, city by city.

CHAPTER 10
Conclusion

Now I write these things to you from Smyrna by the Ephesians, who are deservedly most happy. There is also with me, along with many others, Crocus, one dearly beloved by me. As to those who have gone before me from Syria to Rome for the glory of God, I believe that you are acquainted with them; to whom, [then,] do ye make known that I am at hand. For they are all worthy, both of God and of you; and it is becoming that you should refresh them in all things. I have written these things unto you on the day before the ninth of the Kalends of September. Fare ye well to the end, in the patience of Jesus Christ. Amen.

Epistle of Ignatius to the Smyrnaeans

CHAPTER 1
Thanks To God For Your Faith

I glorify the God and Father of our Lord Jesus Christ, who by Him has given you such wisdom. For I have observed that ye are perfected in an immoveable faith, as if ye were nailed to the cross of our Lord Jesus Christ, both in the flesh and in the spirit, and are established in love through the blood of Christ, being fully persuaded, in very truth, with respect to our Lord Jesus Christ, that He was the Son of God, "the first-born of every creature," God the Word, the only-begotten Son, and was of the seed of David according to the flesh, by the Virgin Mary; was baptized by John, that all righteousness might be fulfilled by Him; that He lived a life of holiness without sin, and was truly, under Pontius Pilate and Herod the tetrarch, nailed [to the cross] for us in His flesh. From whom we also derive our being, from His divinely-blessed passion, that He might set up a standard for the ages, through His resurrection, to all His holy and faithful [followers], whether among Jews or Gentiles, in the one body of His Church.

CHAPTER 2
Christ's True Passion

Now, He suffered all these things for us; and He suffered them really, and not in appearance only, even as also He truly rose again. But not, as some of the unbelievers, who are ashamed of the formation of man, and the cross, and death itself, affirm, that in appearance only, and not in truth, He took a body of the Virgin, and suffered only in appearance, forgetting, as they do, Him who said, "The Word was made flesh;" and again, "Destroy this temple, and in three days I will raise it up;" and once more, "If I be lifted up from the earth, I will draw all men unto Me." The Word therefore did dwell in flesh, for "Wisdom built herself an house." The Word raised up again His own temple on the third day, when it had been destroyed by the Jews fighting against Christ. The Word, when His flesh was lifted up, after the manner of the brazen serpent in the wilderness, drew all men to Himself for their eternal salvation.

CHAPTER 3
Christ Was Possessed Of A Body After His Resurrection

And I know that He was possessed of a body not only in His being born and crucified, but I also know that He was so after His resurrection, and believe that He is so now. When, for instance, He came to those who were with Peter, He said to them, "Lay hold, handle Me, and see that I am not an incorporeal spirit." "For a spirit hath not flesh and bones, as ye see Me have." And He says to Thomas, "Reach hither thy finger into the print of the nails, and reach hither thy hand, and thrust it into My side;" and immediately they believed that He was Christ. Wherefore Thomas also says to Him, "My Lord, and my God." And on this account also did they despise death, for it were too little to say, indignities and stripes. Nor was this all; but also after He had shown Himself to them, that He had risen indeed, and not in appearance only, He both ate and drank with them during forty entire days. And thus was He, with the flesh, received up in their sight unto Him that sent Him, being with that same flesh to come again, accompanied by glory and power. For, say the[holy] oracles, "This same Jesus, who is taken up from you into heaven, shall so come, in like manner as ye have seen Him go unto heaven." But if they say that He will come at the end of the world without a body, how shall those "see Him that pierced Him," and when they recognise Him, "mourn for themselves?" For incorporeal beings have neither form nor figure, nor the aspect of an animal possessed of shape, because their nature is in itself simple.

CHAPTER 4
Beware Of These Heretics

[A] ... guard you beforehand from those beasts in the shape of men, whom you must not only not receive, but, if it be possible, not even meet with; only you must pray to God for them, if by any means they may be brought to repentance, which, however, will be very difficult. Yet Jesus Christ, who is our true life, has the power of[effecting] this. But if these things were done by our Lord only in appearance, then am I also only in appearance bound. And why have I also surrendered myself to death, to fire, to the sword, to the wild beasts? But,[in fact,] he who is near to the sword is near to God; he that is among the wild beasts is in company with God; provided only he be so m the name of Jesus Christ. I undergo all these things that I may suffer together with Him, He who became a perfect man inwardly strengthening me.

[B] ... whom you must not only turn away, but even flee from them. Only you must pray for them, if by any means they may be brought to repentance. For if the Lord were in the body in appearance only, and were crucified in appearance only, then am I also bound in appearance only. And why have I also surrendered myself to death, to fire, to the sword, to the wild beasts? But, [in fact,] I endure all things for Christ, not in appearance only, but in reality, that I may suffer together with Him, while He Himself inwardly strengthens me; for of myself I have no such ability.

CHAPTER 5
Their Dangerous Errors

Some have ignorantly denied Him, and advocate falsehood rather than the truth. These persons neither have the prophecies persuaded, nor the law of Moses, nor the Gospel even to this day, nor the sufferings we have individually endured. For they think also the same thing regarding us. For what does it profit, if any one commends me, but blasphemes my Lord, not owning Him to be God incarnate? He that does not confess this, has in fact altogether denied Him, being enveloped in death. I have not, however, thought good to write the names of such persons, inasmuch as they are unbelievers; and far be it from me to make any mention of them, until they repent.

CHAPTER 6
Unbelievers In The Blood Of Christ Shall Be Condemned

Let no man deceive himself. Unless he believes that Christ Jesus has lived in the flesh, and shall confess His cross and passion, and the blood which He shed for the salvation of the world, he shall not obtain eternal life, whether he be a king, or a priest, or a ruler, or a private ... consequence, incur condemnation. "He that is able to receive it, let him receive it." Let not[high] place puff any one up: for that which is worth all is a faith and love, to which nothing is to be preferred. But consider those who are of a different opinion with respect to the grace of Christ which has come unto us, how opposed they are to the will of God. They have no regard for love; no care for the widow, or the orphan, or the oppressed; of the bond, or of the free; of the hungry, or of the thirsty. person, a master or a servant, a man or a woman. "He that is able to receive it, let him receive it." Let no man's place, or dignity, or riches, puff him up; and let no man's low condition or poverty abase him. For the chief points are faith towards God, hope towards Christ, the enjoyment of those good things for which we look, and love towards God and our neighbour. For, "Thou shall love the Lord thy God with all thy heart, and thy neighbour as thyself." And the Lord says, "This is life eternal, to know the only true God, and Jesus Christ whom He has sent." And again, "A new commandment give I unto you, that ye love one another. On these two commandments hang all the law and the prophets." Do ye, therefore, notice those who preach other doctrines, how they affirm that the Father of Christ cannot be known, and how they exhibit enmity and deceit in their dealings with one another. They have no regard for love; they despise the good things we expect hereafter; they regard present things as if they were durable; they ridicule him that is in affliction; they laugh at him that is in bonds.

CHAPTER 7
Let Us Stand Aloof From Such Heretics

They abstain from the Eucharist and from prayer, because they confess not the Eucharist to be the flesh of our Saviour Jesus Christ, which suffered for our sins, and which the Father, of His goodness, raised up again. Those, therefore, who speak against this gift of God, incur death in the midst of their disputes. But it were better for them to treat it with respect, that they also might rise again. It is fitting, therefore, that ye should keep aloof from such persons, and not to speak of them either in private or in public, but to give heed to the prophets, and above all, to the Gospel, in which the passion[of Christ] has been revealed to us, and the resurrection has been fully proved. But avoid all divisions, as the beginning of evils. They are ashamed of the cross; they mock at the passion; they make a jest of the resurrection. They are the offspring of that spirit who is the author of all evil, who led Adam, by means of his wife, to transgress the commandment, who slew Abel by the hands of Cain, who fought against Job, who was the accuser of Joshua the son of Josedech, who sought to "sift the faith" of the apostles, who stirred up the multitude of the Jews against the Lord, who also now "worketh in the children of disobedience; from whom the Lord Jesus Christ will deliver us, who prayed that the faith of the apostles might not fail, not because He was not able of Himself to preserve it, but because He rejoiced in the pre-eminence of the Father. It is fitting, therefore, that ye should keep aloof from such persons, and neither in private nor in public to talk with them; but to give heed to the law, and the prophets, and to those who have preached to you the word of salvation. But flee from all abominable heresies, and those that cause schisms, as the beginning of evils.

CHAPTER 8
Let Nothing Be Done Without The Bishop

See that ye all follow the bishop, even as Jesus Christ does the Father, and the presbytery as ye would the apostles; and reverence the deacons, as being the institution of God. Let no man do anything connected with the Church without the bishop. Let that be deemed a proper Eucharist, which is[administered] either by the bishop, or by one to whom he has entrusted it. Wherever the bishop shall appear, there let the multitude[of the people] also be; even as, wherever Jesus Christ is, there is the Catholic Church. It is not lawful without the bishop either to baptize or to celebrate a love-feast; but whatsoever he shall approve of, that is also pleasing to God, so that everything that is done may be secure and valid. even as where Christ is, there does all the heavenly host stand by, waiting upon Him as the Chief Captain of the Lord's might, and the Governor of every intelligent nature. It is not lawful without the bishop either to baptize, or to offer, or to present sacrifice, or to celebrate a love-feast. But that which seems good to him, is also well-pleasing to God, that everything ye do may be secure and valid.

CHAPTER 9
Honour The Bishop

Moreover, it is in accordance with reason that we should return to soberness[of conduct], and, while yet we have opportunity, exercise repentance towards God. For "in Hades there is no one who can confess his sins." For "behold the man, and his work is before him." And[the Scripture saith], "My son, honour thou God and the king." And say I, Honour thou God indeed, as the Author and Lord of all things, but the bishop as the high-priest, who bears the image of God--of God. inasmuch as he is a ruler, and of Christ, in his capacity of a priest. After Him, we must also honour the king. For there is no one superior to God, or even like to Him, among all the beings that exist. Nor is there any one in the Church greater than the bishop, who ministers as a priest to God for the salvation of the whole world. Nor, again, is there any one among rulers to be compared with the king, who secures peace and good order to those over whom he rules. He who honours the bishop shall be honoured by God, even as he that dishonours him shall be punished by God. For if he that rises up against kings is justly held worthy of punishment, inasmuch as he dissolves public order, of how much sorer punishment, suppose ye, shall he be thought worthy, who presumes to do anything without the bishop, thus both destroying the[Church's] unity, and throwing its order into confusion? For the priesthood is the very highest point of all good things among men, against which whosoever is mad enough to strive, dishonours not man, but God, and Christ Jesus, the First-born, and the only High Priest, by nature, of the Father. Let all things therefore be done by you with good order in Christ. Let the laity be subject to the deacons; the deacons to the presbyters; the presbyters to the bishop; the bishop to Christ, even as He is to the Father. As ye, brethren, have refreshed me, so will Jesus Christ refresh you. Ye have loved me when absent, as well as when present. God will recompense you, for whose sake ye have shown such kindness towards His prisoner. For even if I am not worthy of it, yet your zeal[to help me] is an admirable thing. For "he who honours a prophet in the name of a prophet, shall receive a prophet's reward." It is manifest also, that he who honours a prisoner of Jesus Christ shall receive the reward of the martyrs.

CHAPTER 10
Acknowledgment Of Their Kindness

Ye have done well in receiving Philo, and Gaius, and Agathopus, who, being the servants of Christ, have followed me for the sake of God, and who greatly bless the Lord in your behalf, because ye have in every way refreshed them. None of those things which ye have done to them shall be passed by without being reckoned unto you. "The Lord grant" to you "that ye may find mercy of the Lord in that day!" May my spirit be for you, and my bonds, which ye have not despised or been ashamed of. Wherefore, neither shall Jesus Christ, our perfect hope, be ashamed of you.

CHAPTER 11
Request To Them To Send A Messenger To Antioch

Your prayers have reached to the Church of Antioch, and it is at peace. Coming from that place bound, I salute all; I who am not worthy to be styled from thence, inasmuch as I am the least of them. Nevertheless, according to the will of God, I have been thought worthy[of this honour], not that I have any senses[of having deserved it], but by the grace of God, which I wish may be perfectly given to me, that through your prayers I may attain to God. In order, therefore, that your work may be complete both on earth and in heaven, it is fitting that, for the honour of God, your Church should elect some worthy delegate; so that he, journeying into Syria, may congratulate them that they are[now] at peace, and are restored to their proper greatness, and that their proper constitution has been re-established among them. What appears to me proper to be done is this, that you should send some one of your number with an epistle, so that, in company with them, he may rejoice over the tranquillity which, according to the will of God, they have obtained, and because that, through your prayers, I have secured Christ as a safe harbour. As persons who are perfect, ye should also aim at those things which are perfect. For when ye are desirous to do well, God is also ready to assist you.

CHAPTER 12
Salutations

The love of the brethren at Troas salutes you; whence also I write to The love of your brethren at Troas salutes you; whence also I write to you by Burgus, whom ye sent with you by Burrhus, whom ye sent with me, together with the Ephesians, your brethren, and who has in all things refreshed me. And I would that all may imitate him, as being a pattern of a minister of God. Grace will reward him in all things. I salute your most worthy bishop, and your very venerable presbytery, and your deacons, my fellow-servants, and all of you individually, as well as generally, in the name of Jesus Christ, and in His flesh and blood, in His passion and resurrection, both corporeal and spiritual, in union with God and you. Grace, mercy, peace, and patience, be with you for evermore! me, together with the Ephesians, your brethren, and who has in all things refreshed me. And I would that all may imitate him, as being a pattern of a minister of God. The grace of the Lord will reward him in all things. I salute your most worthy bishop Polycarp, and your venerable presbytery, and your Christ-bearing deacons, my fellow-servants, and all of you individually, as well as generally, in the name of Christ Jesus, and in His flesh and blood, in His passion and resurrection, both corporeal and spiritual, in union with God and you. Grace, mercy, peace, and patience, be with you in Christ for evermore! salute the families of my bretheren, with their wives and children, and the virgins who are called widows. Be ye strong, I pray, in the power of the Holy Ghost. Philo, who is with me, greets you. I salute the house of Tavias, and pray that it may be confirmed in faith and love, both corporeal and spiritual. I salute Alce, my well-beloved, and the incomparable Daphnus, and Eutecnus, and all by name. Fare ye well in the grace of God.

CHAPTER 13
Conclusion

I salute the families of my brethren, with their wives and children, and those that are ever virgins, and the widows. Be ye strong, I pray, in the power of the Holy Ghost. Philo, my fellow-servant, who is with me, greets you. I salute the house of Tavias, and pray that it may be confirmed in faith and love, both corporeal and spiritual. I salute Alce; my well-beloved, and the incomparable Daphnus, and Eutecnus, and all by name. Fare ye well in the grace of God, and of our Lord Jesus Christ, being filled with the Holy Spirit, and divine and sacred wisdom.

Epistle of Ignatius to the Trallians

CHAPTER 1
Acknowledgment Of Their Excellence

I know that ye possess an unblameable and sincere mind in patience, and that not only for present use, but as a permanent possession, as Polybius your bishop has shown me, who has come to Smyrna by the will of God the Father, and the Lord Jesus Christ, His Son, with the cooperation of the Spirit, and so sympathized in the joy which I, who am bound in Christ Jesus, possess, that I beheld your whole multitude in Him. Having therefore received through him the testimony of your goodwill according to God, I gloried to find that you were the followers of Jesus Christ the Saviour.

CHAPTER 2
Be Subject To The Bishop, Etc

Be ye subject to the bishop as to the Lord, for "he watches for your souls, as one that shall give account to God." Wherefore also, ye appear to me to live not after the manner of men, but according to Jesus Christ, who died for us, in order that, by believing in His death, ye may by baptism be made partakers of His resurrection. It is therefore necessary, whatsoever things ye do, to do nothing without the bishop. And be ye subject also to the presbytery, as to the apostles of Jesus Christ, who is be subject to the presbytery, as to the apostle of Jesus Christ, who is our hope, in whom, if we live, we shall [at last] be found. It is fitting also that the deacons, as being [the ministers] of the mysteries of Jesus Christ, should in every respect be pleasing to all. For they are not ministers of meat and drink, but servants of the Church of God. They are bound, therefore, to avoid all grounds of accusation [against them], as they would do fire. Our hope, in whom, if we live, we shall be found in Him. It behoves you also, in every way, to please the deacons, who are [ministers] of the mysteries of Christ Jesus; for they are not ministers of meat and drink, but servants of the Church of God. They are bound, therefore, to avoid all grounds of accusation [against them], as they would a burning fire. Let them, then, prove themselves to be such.

CHAPTER 3
Honour The Deacons, Etc.

And do ye reverence them as Christ Jesus, of whose place they are the keepers, even as the bishop is the representative of the Father of all things, and the presbyters are the sanhedrim of God, and assembly of the apostles of Christ. Apart from these there is no elect Church, no congregation of holy ones, no assembly of saints. I am persuaded that ye also are of this opinion. For I have received the manifestation s of your love, and still have it with me, in your bishop, whose very appearance is highly instructive, and his meekness of itself a power; whom I imagine even the ungodly must reverence. Loving you as I do, I avoid writing in any severer strain to you, that I may not seem harsh to any, or wanting [in tenderness]. I am indeed bound for the sake of Christ, but I am not yet worthy of Christ. But when I am perfected, perhaps I shall then become so. I do not issue orders like an apostle.

CHAPTER 4
I Have Need Of Humility

But I measure myself, that I may not perish through boasting: but it is good to glory in the Lord. And even though I were established in things pertaining to God, yet then would it befit me to be the more fearful, and not give heed to those that vainly puff me up. For those that commend me scourge me. [I do indeed desire to suffer], but I know not if I be worthy to do so. For the envy of the wicked one is not visible to many, but it wars against me. I therefore have need of meekness, by which the devil, the prince of this world, is brought to nought.

CHAPTER 5
I Will Not Teach You Profound Doctrines

For might not I write to you things more full of mystery? But I fear to do so, lest I should inflict injury on you who are but babes [in Christ]. Pardon me in this respect, lest, as not being able to receive their weighty import, ye should be strangled by them. For even I, though I am bound [for Christ], and am able to understand heavenly things, the angelic orders, and the different sorts of angels and hosts, the distinctions between powers and dominions, and the diversities between thrones and authorities, the mightiness of the Aeons, and the pre-eminence of the cherubim and seraphim, the sublimity of the spirit, the kingdom of the Lord, and above all, the incomparable majesty of Almighty God--though I am acquainted with these things, yet am I not therefore by any means perfect; nor am I such a disciple as Paul or Peter. For many things are yet wanting to me, that I may not fall short of God.

CHAPTER 6
Abstain From The Poison Of Heretics

I therefore, yet not l, out the love of Jesus Christ, "entreat you that ye all speak the same thing, and that there be no divisions among you; but that ye be perfectly joined together in the same mind, and in the same judgment." For there are some vain talkers and deceivers, not Christians, but Christ-betrayers, bearing about the name of Christ in deceit, and "corrupting the word" of the Gospel; while they intermix the poison of their deceit with their persuasive talk, as if they mingled aconite with sweet wine, that so he who drinks, being deceived in his taste by the very great sweetness of the draught, may incautiously meet with his death. One of the ancients gives us this advice, "Let no man be called good who mixes good with evil." For they speak of Christ, not that they may preach Christ, but that they may reject Christ; and they speak of the law, not that they may establish the law, but that they may proclaim things contrary to it. For they alienate Christ from the Father, and the law from Christ. They also calumniate His being born of the Virgin; they are ashamed of His cross; they deny His passion; and they do not believe His resurrection. They introduce God as a Being unknown; they suppose Christ to be unbegotten; and as to the Spirit, they do not admit that He exists. Some of them say that the Son is a mere man, and that the Father, Son, and Holy Spirit are but the same person, and that the creation is the work of God, not by Christ, but by some other strange power.

CHAPTER 7
The Same Continued

Be on your guard, therefore, against such persons. And this will be the case with you if you are not puffed up, and continue in intimate union with Jesus Christ our God, and the bishop, and the enactments of the apostles. He that is within the altar is pure, but he that is without is not pure; that is, he who does anything apart from the bishop, and presbytery, and deacons, such a man is not pure in his conscience. Self in his own works, is the brother of him that destroys himself." If, therefore, ye also put away conceit, arrogance, disdain, and haughtiness, it will be your privilege to be inseparably united to God, for "He is nigh unto those that fear Him." And says He, "Upon whom will I look, but upon him that is humble and quiet, and that trembles at my words?" And do ye also reverence your bishop as Christ Himself, according as the blessed apostles have enjoined you. He that is within the altar is pure, wherefore also he is obedient to the bishop and presbyters: but he that is without is one that does anything apart from the bishop, the presbyters, and the deacons. Such a person is defiled in his conscience, and is worse than an infidel. For what is the bishop but one who beyond all others possesses all power and authority, so far as it is possible   for a man to possess it, who according to his ability has been made an imitator of the Christ Of God? And what is the presbytery but a sacred assembly, the counsellors and assessors of the bishop? And what are the deacons but imitators of the angelic powers, fulfilling a pure and blameless ministry unto him, as the holy Stephen did to the blessed James, Timothy and Linus to Paul, Anencletus and Clement to Peter? He, therefore, that will not yield obedience to such, must needs be one utterly without God, an impious man who despises Christ, and depreciates His appointments.

Now I write these things unto you, not that I know there are any such persons among you; nay, indeed I hope that God will never permit any such report to reach my ears, He "who spared not His Son for the sake of His holy Church." But foreseeing the snares of the wicked one, I arm you beforehand by my admonitions, as my beloved and faithful children in Christ, furnishing you with the means of protection against the deadly disease of unruly men, by which do ye flee from the disease [referred to] by the good-will of Christ our Lord. Do ye therefore, clothing yourselves with meekness, become the imitators of His sufferings, and of His love, wherewith He loved us when He gave Himself a ransom for us, that He might cleanse us by His blood from our old ungodliness, and bestow life on us when we were almost on the point of perishing through the depravity that was in us. Let no one of you, therefore, cherish any grudge against his neighbour. For says our Lord, "Forgive, and it shall be forgiven unto you." Give no occasion to the Gentiles, lest "by means of a few foolish men the word and doctrine [of Christ.] be blasphemed." For says the prophet, as in the person of God, "Woe to him by whom my name is blasphemed among the Gentiles."

CHAPTER 9
Reference To The History Of Christ

Stop your ears, therefore, when any one speaks to you at variance with Jesus Christ, who was descended from David, and was also of Mary; who was truly born, and did eat and drink. He was truly persecuted under Pontius Pilate; He was truly crucified, and [truly] died, in the sight of beings in heaven, and on earth, and under the earth. He was also truly raised from the dead, His Father quickening Him, even as after the same manner His Father will so raise up us who believe in Him by Christ Jesus, apart from whom we do not possess the true life. Descended from David, and was also of Mary; who was truly begotten of God and of the Virgin, but not after the same manner. For indeed God and man are not the same. He truly assumed a body; for "the Word was made flesh," and lived upon earth without sin. For says He, "Which of you convicteth me of sin?" He did in reality both eat and drink. He was crucified and died under Pontius Pilate. He really, and not merely in appearance, was crucified, and died, in the sight of beings in heaven, and on earth, and under the earth. By those in heaven I mean such as are possessed of incorporeal natures; by those on earth, the Jews and Romans, and such persons as were present at that time when the Lord was crucified; and by those under the earth, the multitude that arose along with the Lord. For says the Scripture, "Many bodies of the saints that slept arose," their graves being opened. He descended, indeed, into Hades alone, but He arose accompanied by a multitude; and rent asunder that means of separation which had existed from the beginning of the world, and cast down its partition-wall. He also rose again in three days, the Father raising Him up; and after spending forty days with the apostles, He was received up to the Father, and "sat down at His right hand, expecting till His enemies are placed under His feet." On the day of the preparation, then, at the third hour, He received the sentence from Pilate, the Father permitting that to happen; at the sixth hour He was crucified; at the ninth hour He gave up the ghost; and before sunset He was buried. During the Sabbath He continued under the earth in the tomb in which Joseph of Arimathaea had laid Him. At the dawning of the Lord's day He arose from the dead, according to what was spoken by Himself, "As Jonah was three days and three nights in the whale's belly, so shall the Son of man also be three days and three nights in the heart of the earth." The day of the preparation, then, comprises the passion; the Sabbath embraces the burial; the Lord's Day contains the resurrection.

CHAPTER 10
The Reality Of Christ's Passion

But if, as some that are without God, that is, the unbelieving, say, He became man in appearance [only], that He did not in reality take unto Him a body, that He died in appearance [merely], and did not in very deed suffer, then for what reason am I now in bonds, and long to be exposed to the wild beasts? In such a case, I die in vain, and am guilty of falsehood against the cross of the Lord. Then also does the prophet in vain declare, "They shall look on Him whom they have pierced, and mourn over themselves as over one beloved." These men, therefore, are not less unbelievers than were those that crucified Him. But as for me, I do not place my hopes in one who died for me in appearance, but in reality. For that which is false is quite abhorrent to the truth. Mary then did truly conceive a body which had God inhabiting it. And God the Word was truly born of the Virgin, having clothed Himself with a body of like passions with our own. He who forms all men in the womb, was Himself really in the womb, and made for Himself a body of the seed of the Virgin, but without any intercourse of man. He was carried in the womb, even as we are, for the usual period of time; and was really born, as we also are; and was in reality nourished with milk, and partook of common meat and drink, even as we do. And when He had lived among men for thirty years, He was baptized by John, really and not in appearance; and when He had preached the Gospel three years, and done signs and wonders, He who was Himself the Judge was judged by the Jews, falsely so called, and by Pilate the governor; was scourged, was smitten on the cheek, was spit upon; He wore a crown of thorns and a purple robe; He was condemned: He was crucified in reality, and not in appearance, not in imagination, not in deceit.

He really died, and was buried, and rose from the dead, even as He prayed in a certain place, saying, "But do Thou, O Lord, raise me up again, and I shall recompense them." And the Father, who always hears Him, answered and said, "Arise, O God, and judge the earth; for Thou shall receive all the heathen for Thine inheritance." The Father, therefore, who raised Him up, will also raise us up through Him, apart from whom no one will attain to true life. For says He, "I am the life; he that believeth in me, even though he die, shall live: and every one that liveth and believeth in me, even though he die, shall live for ever." Do ye therefore flee from these ungodly heresies; for they are the inventions of the devil, that serpent who was the author of evil, and who by means of the woman deceived Adam, the father of our race.

CHAPTER 11
Avoid The Deadly Errors Of The Docetists

Flee, therefore, those evil offshoots [of Satan], which produce death-bearing fruit, whereof if any one tastes, he instantly dies. For these men are not the planting of the Father. For if they were, they would appear as branches of the cross, and their fruit would be incorruptible. By it He calls you through His passion, as being His members. The head, therefore, cannot be born by itself, without its members; God, who is [the Saviour] Himself, having promised their union.

Do ye also avoid those wicked offshoots of his, Simon his firstborn son, and Menander, and Basilides, and all his wicked mob of followers, the worshippers of a man, whom also the prophet Jeremiah pronounces accursed. Flee also the impure Nicolaitanes, falsely so called, who are lovers of pleasure, and given to calumnious speeches. Avoid also the children of the evil one, Theodotus and Cleobulus, who produce death-bearing fruit, whereof if any one tastes, he instantly dies, and that not a mere temporary death, but one that shall endure for ever. These men are not the planting of the Father, but are an accursed brood. And says the Lord, "Let every plant which my heavenly Father has not planted be rooted up." For if they had been branches of the Father, they would not have been "enemies of the cross of Christ," but rather of those who "killed the Lord of glory." But now, by denying the cross, and being ashamed of the passion, they cover the transgression of the Jews, those fighters against God, those murderers of the Lord; for it were too little to style them merely murderers of the prophets. But Christ invites you to [share in] His immortality, by His passion and resurrection, inasmuch as ye are His members.

CHAPTER 12
Continue In Unity And Love

I salute you from Smyrna, together with the Churches of God which are with me, whose rulers have refreshed me in every respect, both in the flesh and in the spirit. My bonds, which I carry about with me for the sake of Jesus Christ (praying that I may attain to God), exhort you. Continue in harmony among yourselves, and in supplication; for it becomes every one of you, and especially the presbyters, to refresh the bishop, to the honour of the Father, and to the honour of Jesus Christ and of the apostles. I entreat you in love to hear me, that I may not, by having thus written, be a testimony against you. And do ye also pray for me, who have need of your love, along with the mercy of God, that I may be thought worthy to attain the lot for which I am now designed, and that I may not be found reprobate.

CHAPTER 13
Conclusion

The love of the Smyrnaeans and Ephesians salutes you. Remember our Church which is in Syria, from which I am not worthy to receive my appellation, being the last of those of that place. Fare ye well in the Lord Jesus Christ, while ye continue subject to the bishop, and in like manner to the presbyters and to the deacons. And do ye, every man, love one another with an undivided heart. My spirit salutes you, not only now, but also when I shall have attained to God; for I am as yet exposed to danger. But the Father of Jesus Christ is faithful to fulfil both mine and your petitions: in whom may we be found without spot. May I have joy of you in the Lord.

The Epistle of Polycarp to the Philippians

CHAPTER 1
Praise Of The Philippians

I have greatly rejoiced with you in our Lord Jesus Christ, because ye have followed the example of true love [as displayed by God], and have accompanied, as became you, those who were bound in chains, the fitting ornaments of saints, and which are indeed the diadems of the true elect of God and our Lord; and because the strong root of your faith, spoken of in days long gone by, endureth even until now, and bringeth forth fruit to our Lord Jesus Christ, who for our sins suffered even unto death, [but] "whom God raised froth the dead, having loosed the bands of the grave." "In whom, though now ye see Him not, ye believe, and believing, rejoice with joy unspeakable and full of glory; " into which joy many desire to enter, knowing that "by grace ye are saved, not of works," but by the will of God through Jesus Christ.

CHAPTER 2
An Exhortation To Virtue

"Wherefore, girding up your loins," "serve the Lord in fear" and truth, as those who have forsaken the vain, empty talk and error of the multitude, and "believed in Him who raised up our Lord Jesus Christ from the dead, and gave IIim glory," and a throne at His right hand. To Him all things" in heaven and on earth are subject. Him every spirit serves. He comes as the Judge of the living and the dead. His blood will God require of those who do not believe in Him. But He who raised Him up from the dead will raise up us also, if we do His will, and walk in His commandments, and love what He loved, keeping ourselves from all unrighteousness, covetousness, love of money, evil speaking, falsewitness; "not rendering evil for evil, or railing for railing," or blow for blow, or cursing for cursing, but being mindful of what the Lord said in His teaching: "Judge not, that ye be not judged; forgive, and it shall be forgiven unto you; be merciful, that ye may obtain mercy; with what measure ye mete, it shall be measured to you again; and once more, "Blessed are the poor, and those that are persecuted for righteousness' sake, for theirs is the kingdom of God."

CHAPTER 3
Expressions Or Personal Unworthiness

These things, brethren, I write to you concerning righteousness, not because I take anything upon myself, but because ye have invited me to do so. For neither I, nor any other such one, can come up to the wisdom" of the blessed and glorified Paul. He, when among you, accurately and stedfastly taught the word of truth in the presence of those who were then alive. And when absent from you, he wrote you a letter, which, if you carefully study, you will find to be the means of building you up in that faith which has been given you, and which, being followed by hope, and preceded by love towards God, and Christ, and our neighbour, "is the mother of us all." For if any one be inwardly possessed of these graces, he hath fulfilled the command of righteousness, since he that hath love is far from all sin.

CHAPTER 4
Various Exhortations

"But the love of money is the root of all evils." Knowing, therefore, that "as we brought nothing into the world, so we can carry nothing out," let us arm ourselves with the armour of righteousness; and let us teach, first of all, ourselves to walk in the commandments of the Lord. Next, [teach] your wives [to walk] in the faith given to them, and in love and purity tenderly loving their own husbands in all truth, and loving all [others] equally in all chastity; and to train up their children in the knowledge and fear of God. Teach the widows to be discreet as respects the faith of the Lord, praying continually for all, being far from all slandering, evil-speaking, false-witnessing, love of money, and every kind of evil; knowing that they are the altar s of God, that He clearly perceives all things, and that nothing is hid from Him, neither reasonings, nor reflections, nor any one of the secret things of the heart.

CHAPTER 5
The Duties Of Deacons, Youths, And Virgins

Knowing, then, that "God is not mocked," we ought to walk worthy of His commandment and glory. In like manner should the deacons be blameless before the face of His righteousness, as being the servants of God and Christ, and not of men. They must not be slanderers, double-tongued, or lovers of money, but temperate in all things, compassionate, industrious, walking according to the truth of the Lord, who was the servant of all. If we please Him in this present world, we shall receive also the future world, according as He has promised to us that He will raise us again from the dead, and that if we live worthily of Him, "we shall also reign together with Him," provided only we believe. In like manner, let the young men also be blameless in all things, being especially careful to preserve purity, and keeping themselves in, as with a bridle, from every kind of evil. For it is well that they should be cut off from the lusts that are in the world, since "every lust warreth against the spirit;" and "neither fornicators, nor effeminate, nor abusers of themselves with mankind, shall inherit the kingdom of God," nor those who do things inconsistent and unbecoming. Wherefore, it is needful to abstain from all these things, being subject to the presbyters and deacons, as unto God and Christ. The virgins also must walk in a blameless and pure conscience.

CHAPTER 6
The Duties Of Presbyters And Others

And let the presbyters be compassionate and merciful to all, bringing back those that wander, visiting all the sick, and not neglecting the widow, the orphan, or the poor, but always "providing for that which is becoming in the sight of God and man ; " abstaining from all wrath, respect of persons, and unjust judgment; keeping far off from . all covetousness, not quickly crediting [an evil re port] against any one, not severe in judgment, as knowing that we are all under a debt of sin. If then we entreat the Lord to forgive us, we ought also ourselves to forgive; for we are before the eyes of our Lord and God, and "we must all appear at the judgment-seat of Christ, and must every one give an account of himself." Let us then serve Him in fear, and with all reverence, even as He Himself has commanded us, and as the apostles who preached the Gospel unto us, and the prophets who proclaimed beforehand the coming of the Lord [have alike taught us]. Let us be zealous in the pursuit of that which is good, keeping ourselves from causes of offence, from false brethren, and from those who in hypocrisy bear the name of the Lord, and draw away vain men into error.

CHAPTER 7
Avoid The Docetae, And Persevere In Fasting And Prayer

"For whosoever does not confess that Jesus Christ has come in the flesh, is antichrist;" and whosoever does not confess the testimony of the cross, is of the devil; and whosoever perverts the oracles of the Lord to his own lusts, and says that there is neither a resurrection nor a judgment, he is the first-born of Satan. Wherefore, forsaking the vanity of many, and their false doctrines, let us return to the word which has been handed down to us from the beginning; "watching unto prayer," and persevering in fasting; beseeching in our supplications the all-seeing God "not to lead us into temptation," as the Lord has said: "The spirit truly is willing, but the flesh is weak."

CHAPTER 8
Persevere In Hope And Patience

Let us then continually persevere in our hope, and the earnest of our righteousness, which is Jesus Christ, "who bore our sins in His own body on the tree," "who did no sin, neither was guile found in His mouth," but endured all things for us, that we might live in Him. Let us then be imitators of His patience; and if we suffer for His name's sake, let us glorify Him. For He has set us this example s in Himself, and we have believed that such is the case.

CHAPTER 9
Patience Inculcated

I exhort you all, therefore, to yield obedience to the word of righteousness, and to exercise all patience, such as ye have seen [set] before your eyes, not only in the case of the blessed Ignatius, and Zosimus, and Rufus, but also in others among yourselves, and in Paul himself, and the rest of the apostles. [This do] in the assurance that all these have not run in vain, but in faith and righteousness, and that they are [now] in their due place in the presence of the Lord, with whom also they suffered. For they loved not this present world, but Him who died for us, and for our sakes was raised again by God from the dead.

CHAPTER 10
Exhortation To The Practice Of Virtue

Stand fast, therefore, in these things, and follow the example of the Lord, being firm and unchangeable in the faith, loving the brotherhood, and being attached to one another, joined together in the truth, exhibiting the meekness of the Lord in your intercourse with one another, and despising no one. When you can do good, defer it not, because "alms delivers from death." "Be all of you subject one to another? having your conduct blameless among the Gentiles,"(that ye may both receive praise for your good works, and the Lord may not be blasphemed through you. But woe to him by whom the name of the Lord is blasphemed! Teach, therefore, sobriety to all, and manifest it also in your own conduct.

CHAPTER 11
Expression Of Grief On Account Of Valens

I am greatly grieved for Valens, who was once a presbyter among you, because he so little understands the place that was given him [in the Church]. I exhort you, therefore, that ye abstain from covetousness, and that ye be chaste and truthful. "Abstain from every form of evil." For if a man cannot govern himself in such matters, how shall he enjoin them on others? If a man does not keep himself from covetousness, he shall be defiled by idolatry, and shall be judged as one of the heathen. But who of us are ignorant of the judgment of the Lord? "Do we not know that the saints shall judge the world?" as Paul teaches. But I have neither seen nor heard of any such thing among you, in the midst of whom the blessed Paul laboured, and who are commended in the beginning of his Epistle. For he boasts of you in all those Churches which alone then knew the Lord; but we [of Smyrna] had not yet known Him. I am deeply grieved, therefore, brethren, for him (Valens) and his wife; to whom may the Lord grant true repentance! And be ye then moderate in regard to this matter, and "do not count such as enemies," but call them back as suffering and straying members, that ye may save your whole body. For by so acting ye shall edify yourselves.

CHAPTER 12
Exhortation To Various Graces

For I trust that ye are well versed in the Sacred Scriptures, and that nothing is hid from you; but to me this privilege is not yet granted. It is declared then in these Scriptures, "Be ye angry, and sin not," and, "Let not the sun go down upon your wrath." Happy is he who remembers this, which I believe to be the case with you. But may the God and Father of our Lord Jesus Christ, and Jesus Christ Himself, who is the Son of God, and our everlasting High Priest, build you up in faith and truth, and in all meekness, gentleness, patience, long-suffering, forbearance, and purity; and may He bestow on you a lot and portion among His saints, and on us with you, and on all that are under heaven, who shall believe in our Lord Jesus Christ, and in His Father, who "raised Him from the dead. Pray for all the saints. Pray also for kings, and potentates, and princes, and for those that persecute and hate you, and for the enemies of the cross, that your fruit may be manifest to all, and that ye may be perfect in Him.

CHAPTER 13
Concerning The Transmission Of Epistles

Both you and Ignatius wrote to me, that if any one went [from this] into Syria, he should carry your letter with him; which request I will attend to if I find a fitting opportunity, either personally, or through some other acting for me, that your desire may be fulfilled. The Epistles of Ignatius written by him to us, and all the rest [of his Epistles] which we have by us, we have sent to you, as you requested. They are subjoined to this Epistle, and by them ye may be greatly profited; for they treat of faith and patience, and all things that tend to edification in our Lord. Any more certain information you may have obtained respecting both Ignatius himself, and those that were with him, have the goodness to make known to us.

CHAPTER 14
Conclusion

These things I have written to you by Crescens, whom up to the present time I have recommended unto you, and do now recommend. For he has acted blamelessly among us, and I believe also among you. Moreover, ye will hold his sister in esteem when she comes to you. Be ye safe in the Lord Jesus Christ. Grace be with you all. Amen.

Epistle of the Apostles

The book which Jesus Christ revealed unto his disciples: and how that Jesus Christ revealed the book for the company (college) of the apostles, the disciples of Jesus Christ, even the book which is for all men. Simon and Cerinthus, the false apostles, concerning whom it is written that no man shall cleave unto them for there is in them deceit wherewith they bring men to destruction. (The book hath been written) that ye may be steadfast and not flinch nor be troubled, and depart not from the word of the Gospel which ye have heard. Like as we heard it, we keep it in remembrance and have written it for the whole world. We commend you our sons and our daughters in joy in the name of God the Father the Lord of the world, and of Jesus Christ. Let grace be multiplied upon you.

2. We, John, Thomas, Peter, Andrew, James, Philip, Bartholomew, Matthew, Nathanael, Judas Zelotes, and Cephas, write unto the churches of the east and the west, of the north and the south declaring and imparting unto you that which concerneth our Lord Jesus Christ: we do write according as we have seen and heard and touched him, after that he was risen from the dead: and how that he revealed unto us things mighty and wonderful and true.

3 This know we: that our Lord and Redeemer Jesus Christ is God the Son of God, who was sent of God the Lord of the whole world, the maker and creator of it, who is named by all names and high above all powers, Lord of lords, King of kings, Ruler of rulers, the heavenly one, that sitteth above the cherubim and seraphim at the right hand of the throne of the Father: who by his word made the heavens, and formed the earth and that which is in it, and set bounds to the sea that it should not pass: the deeps also and fountains,that they should spring forth and flow over the earth: the day and the night, the sun and the moon, did he establish, and the stars in the heaven: that did separate the light from the darkness: that called forth hell, and in

the twinkling of an eye ordained the rain of the winter, the snow (cloud), the hail, and the ice, and the days in their several seasons: that maketh the earth to quake and again establisheth it: that created man in his own image, after his likeness, and by the fathers of old and the prophets is it declared (or, and spake in parables with the fathers of old and the prophets in verity), of whom the apostles preached, and whom the disciples did touch. In God, the Lord, the Son of God, do we believe, that he is the word become flesh: that of Mary the holy virgin he took a body, begotten of the Holy Ghost, not of the will (lust) of the flesh, but by the will of God: that he was wrapped in swaddling clothes in Bethlehem and made manifest, and grew up and came to ripe age, when also we beheld it.

4. This did our Lord Jesus Christ, who was sent by Joseph and Mary his mother to be taught. [And] when he that taught him said unto him: Say Alpha: then answered he and said: Tell thou me first what is Beta (probably: Tell thou me first what is Beta. Cf. the Marcosian story quoted by Irenaeus (see above, Gospel of Thomas)- The story is in our texts of the Gospel of Thomas, and runs through all the Infancy Gospels). This thing which then came to pass Is true and of verity.

5. Thereafter was there a marriage in Cana of Galilee; and they bade him with his mother and his brethren, and he changed water into wine. He raised the dead, he caused the lame to walk: him whose hand was withered he caused to stretch it out, and the woman which had suffered an issue of blood twelve years touched the hem of his garment and was healed in the same hour. And when we marvelled at the miracle which was done, he said: Who touched me? Then said we: Lord, the press of men hath touched thee. But he answered and said unto us: I perceive that a virtue is gone out of me. Straightway that woman came before him, and answered and said unto him: Lord, I touched thee. And he answered and said unto her: Go, thy faith hath made thee whole. Thereafter he made the deaf to hear and the blind to see; out of them that were possessed he cast out the unclean spirits, and cleansed the lepers. The spirit which dwelt in a man, whereof the name was Legion, cried out against Jesus, saying: Before the time of our destruction is come, thou art come to drive us out. But the Lord Jesus rebuked him, saying: Go out of this man and do him no hurt. And he entered into the swine and drowned them in the water and they were choked.

Thereafter he did walk upon the sea, and the winds blew, and he cried out against them (rebuked them), and the waves of the sea were made calm. And when we his disciples had no money, we asked him: What shall we do because of the tax-gatherer? And he answered and told us: Let one of you cast an hook into the deep, and take out a fish, and he shall find therein a penny: that give unto the tax-gatherer for me and you. And thereafter when we had no bread, but only five loaves and two fishes, he commanded the people to sit them down, and the number of them was five thousand, besides children and women. We did set pieces of bread before them, and they ate and were filled, and there remained over, and we filled twelve baskets full of the fragments, asking one another and saying: What mean these five loaves? They are the symbol of our faith in the Lord of the Christians (in the great christendom), even in the Father, the Lord Almighty, and in Jesus Christ our redeemer, in the Holy Ghost the comforter, in the holy church, and in the remission of sins.

6. These things did our Lord and Saviour reveal unto us and teach us. And we do even as he, that ye may become partakers in the grace of our Lord and in our ministry and our giving of thanks (glory), and think upon life eternal. Be ye steadfast and waver not in the knowledge and confidence of our Lord Jesus Christ, and he will have mercy on you and save you everlastingly, world without end.

Here begins the Coptic text. (Translated from a different text)

7. Cerinthus and Simon are come to go to and fro in the world, but they are enemies of our Lord Jesus Christ, for they do pervert the word and the true thing, even (faith in) Jesus Christ. Keep yourselves therefore far from them, for death is in them, and great pollution and corruption, even in these on whom shall come judgement and the end and everlasting destruction.

8. Therefore have we not shrunk from writing unto you concerning the testimony of Christ our Saviour, of what he did, when we followed with him, how he enlightened our understanding . . . .

9. Concerning whom we testify that the Lord is he who was crucified by Pontius Pilate and Archelaus between the two thieves (and with them he was taken down from the tree of the cross, Eth.), and was buried in a place which is called the place of a skull (Kranion). And thither went three women, Mary, she that was kin to Martha, and Mary Magdalene (Sarrha, Martha, and Mary, Eth.), and took ointments to pour upon the body, weeping and mourning over that which was come to pass. And when they drew near to the sepulchre, they looked in and found not the body (Eth. they found the stone rolled

away and opened the entrance).

10. And as they mourned and wept, the Lord showed himself unto them and said to them: For whom weep ye? weep no more I am he whom ye seek. But let one of you go to your brethren and say: Come ye, the Master is risen from the dead. Martha (Mary, Eth.) came and told us. We said unto her: What have we to do with thee, woman? He that is dead and buried, is it possible that he should live? And we believed her not that the Saviour was risen from the dead. Then she returned unto the Lord and said unto him: None of them hath believed me, that thou livest. He said: Let another of you go unto them and tell them again. Mary (Sarrha, Eth.) came and told us again, and we believed her not; and she returned unto the Lord and she also told him.

11. Then said the Lord unto Mary and her sisters: Let us go unto them. And he came and found us within (sitting veiled or fishing, Eth.), and called us out, but we thought that it was a phantom and believed not that it was the Lord. Then said he unto us: Come, fear ye not. I am your master, even he, O Peter, whom thou didst deny thrice; and dost thou now deny again? And we came unto him, doubting in our hearts whether it were he. Then said he unto us: Wherefore doubt ye still, and are unbelieving? I am he that spake unto you of my flesh and my death and my resurrection. But that ye may know that I am he, do thou, Peter, put thy finger into the print of the nails in mine hands, and thou also, Thomas, put thy finger into the wound of the spear in my side; but thou, Andrew, look on my feet and see whether they press the earth; for it is written in the prophet: A phantom of a devil maketh no footprint on the earth.

12. And we touched him, that we might learn of a truth whether he were risen in the flesh; and we fell on our faces (and worshipped him) confessing our sin, that we had been unbelieving. Then said our Lord and Saviour unto us: Rise up, and I will reveal unto you that which is above the heaven and in the heaven, and your rest which is in the kingdom of heaven. For my Father hath given me power (sent me, Eth.) to take you up thither, and them also that believe on me.

13. Now that which he revealed unto us is this, which he spake: It came to pass when I was about (minded) to come hither from the Father of all things, and passed through the heavens, then did I put on the wisdom of the Father, and I put on the power of his might. I was in heaven, and I passed by the archangels and the angels in their likeness, like as if I were one of

them, among the princedoms and powers. I passed through them because I possessed the wisdom of him that had sent me. Now the chief captain of the angels, [is] Michael, and Gabriel and Uriel and Raphael followed me unto the fifth firmament (heaven), for they thought in their heart that I was one of them; such power was given me of my Father. And on that day did I adorn the archangels with a wonderful voice (so Copt.: Eth., Lat., I made them quake -amazed them), so that they should go unto the altar of the Father and serve and fulfil the ministry until I should return unto him. And so wrought I the likeness by my wisdom; for I became all things in all, that I might praise the dispensation of the Father and fulfil the glory of him that sent me (the verbs might well be transposed) and return unto him. (Here the Latin omits a considerable portion of text without notice, to near the beginning of c. 17.)

14. For ye know that the angel Gabriel brought the message unto Mary. And we answered: Yea, Lord. He answered and said unto us: Remember ye not, then, that I said unto you a little while ago: I became an angel among the angels, and I became all things in all? We said unto him: Yea, Lord. Then answered he and said unto us: On that day whereon I took the form of the angel Gabriel, I appeared unto Mary and spake with her. Her heart accepted me, and she believed (She believed and laughed, Eth.), and I formed myself and entered into her body. I became flesh, for I alone was a minister unto myself in that which concerned Mary (I was mine own messenger, Eth.) in the appearance of the shape of an angel. For so must I needs (or, was I wont to) do. Thereafter did I return to my Father (Copt. After my return to the Father, and run on).

15. But do ye commemorate my death. Now when the Passover (Easter, pascha) cometh, one of you shall be cast into prison for my names sake; and he will be in grief and sorrow, because ye keep the Easter while he is in pris-on and separated from you, for he will be sorrowful because he keepeth not Easter with you. And I will send my power in the form of mine angel Gabriel, and the doors of the prison shall open. And he shall come forth and come unto you and keep the night-watch with you until the cock crow. And when ye have accomplished the memorial which is made of me, and the Agape (love-feast), he shall again be cast into prison for a testimony, until he shall come out thence and preach that which I have delivered unto you.

And we said unto him: Lord, is it then needful that we should again take the cup and drink? (Lord, didst not thou thyself fulfil the drinking of the Passover? is it then needful that we should accomplish it again? Eth.) He said unto us: Yea, it is needful, until the day when I come again, with them that have been put to death for my sake (come with my wounds, Eth.).

16. Then said we to him: Lord, that which thou hast revealed unto us (revealest, Eth.) is great. Wilt thou come in the power of any creature or in an appearance of any kind? (In what power or form wilt thou come? Eth.) He answered and said unto us: Verily I say unto you, I shall come like the sun when it is risen, and my brightness will be seven times the brightness thereof! The wings of the clouds shall bear me in brightness, and the sign of the cross shall go before me, and I shall come upon earth to judge the quick and the dead.

17. We said unto him: Lord, after how many years shall this come to pass? He said unto us: When the hundredth part and the twentieth part is fulfilled, between the Pentecost and the feast of unleavened bread, then shall the coming of my Father be (so Copt.: When an hundred and fifty years are past, in the days of the feast of Passover and Pentecost, &c., Eth.: . . . (imperfect word) year is fulfilled, between the unleavened bread and Pentecost shall be the coming of my Father, lat.).3
We said unto him: Now sayest thou unto us: I will come; and how sayest thou: He that sent me is he that shall come? Then said he to us: I am wholly in the Father and my Father is in me. Then said we to him: Wilt thou indeed forsake us until thy coming? Where can we find a master? But he answered and said unto us: Know ye not, then, that like as until now I have been here, so also was I there, with him that sent me? And we said to him: Lord, is it then possible that thou shouldest be both here and there? But he answered us: I am wholly in the Father and the Father in me, because of (in regard of) the likeness of the form and the power and the fullness and the light and the full measure and the voice. I am the word, I am become unto him a thing, that is to say (word gone) of the thought, fulfilled in the type (likeness); I have come into the Ogdoad (eighth number), which is the Lord's day. [The Lord's day considered as the eighth day of the week.] (In place of these sentences Eth. has: I am of his resemblance and form, of his power and completeness, and of his light. I am his complete (fulfilled, entire) word.

18. But it came to pass after he was crucified, and dead and arisen again, when the work was fulfilled which was accomplished in the flesh, and he was crucified and the ascension come to pass at the end of the days, then said he thus, &c. It is an interpolation, in place of words which the translator did not understand, or found heretical.) But the whole fulfilment of the fulfilment shall ye see after the redemption which hath come to pass by me, and ye shall

see me, how I go up unto my Father which is in heaven. But behold, now, I give unto you a new commandment: Love one another and [a leaf lost in Copt.] obey one another, that peace may rule always among you. Love your enemies, and what ye would not that man do unto you, that do unto no man.

19. And this preach ye also and teach them that believe on me and preach the kingdom of heaven of my Father, and how my Father hath given me the power, that ye may bring near the children of my heavenly Father. Preach ye, and they shall obtain faith, that ye may be they for whom it is ordained that they shall bring his children unto heaven.

And we said unto him: Lord, unto thee it is possible to accomplish that whereof thou tellest us, but how shall we be able to do it? He said to us: Verily I say unto you, preach and proclaim as I command you, for I will be with you, for it is my good pleasure to be with you, that ye may be heirs with me in the kingdom of heaven, even the kingdom of him that sent me. Verily I say unto you, ye shall be my brethren and my friends for my Father hath found pleasure in you: and so also shall they be that believe on me by your means. Verily I say unto you such and so great joy hath my Father prepared for you that the angels and the powers desired and do desire to see it and look upon it; but it is not given unto them to behold the glory of my Father. We said unto him: Lord, what is this whereof thou speakest to us?

Copt. begins again: words are missing.

He answered us: Ye shall behold a light, more excellent than that which shineth . . . (shineth more brightly than the light, and is more perfect than perfection. And the Son shall become perfect through the Father who is Light, for the Father is perfect which bringeth to pass death and resurrection, and ye shall see a perfection more perfect than the perfect. And I am wholly at the right hand of the Father, even in him that maketh perfect. So Eth.: Copt. has gaps).

And we said unto him: Lord, in all things art thou become salvation and life unto us, for that thou makest known such a hope unto us. And he said to us: Be of good courage and rest in me. Verily I say unto you, your rest shall be above (?), in the place where is neither eating nor drinking, nor care (Copt. joy) nor sorrow, nor passing away of them that are therein: for ye shall have no part in (the things of earth, Eth.) but ye shall be received in the everlastingness of my Father. Like as I am in him, so shall ye also be in me.

Again we said unto him: In what form? in the fashion of angels, or in flesh? And he answered and said unto us: Lo, I have put on your flesh, wherein I was born and crucified, and am risen again through my Father which is in heaven, that the prophecy of David the prophet might be fulfilled, in regard of that which was declared concerning me and my death and resurrection, saying:

Lord, they are increased that fight with me, and many are they that are risen up against me. Many there be that say to my soul: There is no help for him in his God.But thou, O Lord, art my defender: thou art my worship, and the lifter up of my head.I did call upon the Lord with my voice and he heard me (out of the high place of his temple, Eth.). I laid me down and slept,and rose up again: for thou,O Lord, art my defender. I will not be afraid for ten thousands of the people, that have set themselves against me round about. Up, Lord, and help me, O my God: for thou hast smitten down all them that without cause are mine enemies: thou hast broken the teeth of the ungodly. Salvation belongeth unto the Lord, and his good pleasure is upon his people (Ps. iii. 1-8).

If, therefore, all the words which were spoken by the prophets have been fulfilled in me (for I myself was in them), how much more shall that which I say unto you come to pass indeed, that he which sent me may be glorified by you and by them that believe on me?

20. And when he had said this unto us, we said to him: In all things hast thou had mercy on us and saved us, and hast revealed all things unto us; but yet would we ask of thee somewhat if thou give us leave. And he said unto us: I know that ye pay heed, and that your heart is well-pleased when ye hear me: now concerning that which ye desire, I will speak good words unto you.

21. For verily I say unto you: Like as my Father hath raised me from the dead, so shall ye also rise (in the flesh, Eth.) and be taken up into the highest heaven, unto the place whereof I have told you from the beginning, unto the place which he who sent me hath prepared for you. And so will I accomplish all dispensations (all grace, Eth.), even I who am unbegotten and yet begotten of mankind, who am without flesh and yet have borne flesh : for to that end am I come, that (gap in Copt.: Eth. continues) ye might rise from the dead in your flesh, in the second birth, even a vesture that shall not decay, together with all them that hope and believe in him that sent me: for so is the will of my Father that I would give unto you, and unto them whom it pleaseth me, the hope of the kingdom.

Then said we unto him: Great is that which thou sufferest us to hope, and tellest us. And he answered and said: Believe ye that every thing that I tell you shall come to pass? We answered and said: Yea, Lord. (Copt. resumes for a few lines: then another gap. Follow Eth.) He said unto us: Verily I say unto you, that I have obtained the whole power of my Father, that I may bring back into light them that dwell in darkness, them that are in corruption into incorruption, them that are in death into life and that I may loose them that are in fetters. For that which is impossible with men, is possible with the Father. I am the hope of them that despair, the helper of them that have no saviour, the wealth of the poor, the health of the sick, and the resurrection of the dead.

22. When he had thus said, we said unto him: Lord, is it true that the flesh shall be judged together with the soul and the spirit and that the one part shall rest in heaven and the other part be punished everlastingly yet living? And he said unto us: (Copt. resumes) How long will ye inquire and doubt?

23. Again we said unto him: Lord, there is necessity upon us to inquire of thee -because thou hast commanded us to preach- that we ourselves may learn assuredly of thee and be profitable preachers, and that they which are instructed by us may believe in thee. Therefore must we needs inquire of thee.

24. He answered us and said: Verily I say unto you, the resurrection of the flesh shall come to pass with the soul therein and the spirit. And we said unto him: Lord, is it then possible that that which is dissolved and brought to nought should become whole? and we ask thee not as unbelieving, neither as if it were impossible unto thee; but verily we believe that that which thou sayest shall come to pass. And he was wroth with us and said: O ye of little faith, how long will ye ask questions? But what ye will, tell it me, and I myself will tell you without grudging: only keep ye my commandments and do that which I bid you, and turn not away your face from any man, that I turn not my face away from you, but without shrinking and fear and without respect of persons, minister ye in the way that is direct and narrow and strait. So shall my Father himself rejoice over you.

25. Again we said unto him: Lord, already are we ashamed that we question thee oft-times and burden thee. And he answered and said unto us: I know that in faith and with your whole heart ye do question me, therefore do I rejoice over you for verily I say unto you: I rejoice, and my Father that is in me, because ye question me; and your importunity (shamelessness) is unto me rejoicing and unto you it giveth life. And when he had so said unto us, we were glad that we had questioned him and we said to him: Lord, in all things

thou makest us alive and hast mercy on us. Wilt thou now declare unto us that which we shall ask thee? Then said he unto us: Is it the flesh that passeth away, or is it the spirit? We said unto him: The flesh is it that passeth away. Then said he unto us: That which hath fallen shall rise again, and that which was lost shall be found, and that which was weak shall recover, that in these things that are so created the glory of my Father may be revealed. As he hath done unto me, so will I do unto all that believe in me.

26. Verily I say unto you: the flesh shall arise, and the soul, alive, that their defence may come to pass on that day in regard of that that they have done, whether it be good or evil: that there may be a choosing-out of the faithful who have kept the commandments of my Father that sent me; and so shall the judgement be accomplished with strictness. For my Father said unto me: My Son, in the day of judgement thou shalt have no respect for the rich, neither pity for the poor, but according to the sins of every man shalt thou deliver him unto everlasting torment. But unto my beloved that have done the commandments of my Father that sent me will I give the rest of life in the kingdom of my Father which is in heaven, and they shall behold that which he hath given me. And he hath given me authority to do that which I will, and to give that which I have promised and determined to give and grant unto them.

27. For to that end went I down unto the place of Lazarus, and preached unto the righteous and the prophets, that they might come out of the rest which is below and come up into that which is above; and I poured out upon them with my right hand the water (?) (baptism, Eth.) of life and forgiveness and salvation from all evil, as I have done unto you and unto them that believe on me. But if any man believe on me and do not my commandments, although he have confessed my name, he hath no profit therefrom but runneth a vain race: for such will find themselves in perdition and destruction, because they have despised my commandments.

28. But so much the more have I redeemed you, the children of light, from all evil and from the authority of the rulers (archons), and every one that believeth on me by your means. For that which I have promised unto you will I give unto them also, that they may come out of the prison-house and the fetters of the rulers. We answered and said: Lord thou hast given unto us the rest of life and hast given us <Joy? by wonders, unto the confirmation of faith: wilt thou now preach the same unto us, seeing that thou hast preached it unto the and the prophets? Then said he unto us: Verily I say unto you, all

that have believed on me and that believe in him that sent me will I take up into the heaven, unto the place which my Father hath prepared for the elect, and I will give you the kingdom, the chosen kingdom, in rest, and everlasting life.

29. But all they that have offended against my commandments and have taught other doctrine, (perverting) the Scripture and adding thereto, striving after their own glory, and that teach with other words them that believe on me in uprightness, ie they make them fall thereby, shall receive everlasting punishment. We said unto him: Lord, shall there then be teaching by others, diverse from that which thou hast spoken unto us? He said unto us: It must needs be, that the evil and the good may be made manifest; and the judgement shall be manifest upon them that do these things, and according to their works shall they be judged and shall be delivered unto death.

Again we said unto him: Lord, blessed are we in that we see thee and hear thee declaring such things, for our eyes have beheld these great wonders that thou hast done. He answered and said unto us: Yea, rather blessed are they that have not seen and yet have believed for they shall be called children of the kingdom, and they shall be perfect among the perfect, and I will be unto them life in the kingdom of my Father.

Again we said unto him: Lord, how shall men be able to believe that thou wilt depart and leave us; for thou sayest unto us: There shall come a day and an hour when I shall ascend unto my Father?

30. But he said unto us: Go ye and preach unto the twelve tribes, and preach also unto the heathen, and to all the land of Israel from the east to the west and from the south unto the north, and many shall believe on the Son of God. But we said unto him: Lord, who will believe us, or hearken unto us, or (how shall we be able, Eth.) to teach the powers and signs and wonders which thou hast done? Then answered he and said to us: Go ye and preach the mercifulness of my Father, and that which he hath done through me will I myself do through you, for I am in you, and I will give you my peace, and I will give you a power of my spirit, that ye may prophesy to them unto life eternal. And unto the others also will I give my power, that they may teach the residue of the peoples.

31. And behold a man shall meet you, whose name is Saul which being interpreted is Paul: he is a Jew, circumcised according to the law, and he shall receive my voice from heaven with fear and terror and trembling. And his eyes shall be blinded and by your hands by the sign of the cross shall they be

protected (healed: other Eth. MSS. with spittle by your hands shall his eyes &c.). Do ye unto him all that I have done unto you. Deliver it (? the word of God) unto the other. And at the same time that man shall open his eyes and praise the Lord, even my Father which is in heaven. He shall obtain power among the people and shall preach and instruct; and many that hear him shall obtain glory and be redeemed. But thereafter shall men be wroth with him and deliver him into the hands of his enemies, and he shall bear witness before kings that are mortal, and his end shall be that he shall turn unto me, whereas he persecuted me at the first. He shall preach and teach and abide with the elect, as a chosen vessel and a wall that shall not be overthrown, yea, the last of the last shall become a preacher unto the Gentiles, made perfect by the will of my Father. Like as ye have learned from the Scripture that your fathers the prophets spake of me, and in me it is indeed fulfilled.

And he said unto us: Be ye also therefore guides unto them; and all things that I said unto you, and that ye write concerning me (tell ye them), that I am the word of the Father and that the Father is in me. Such also shall ye be unto that man, as becometh you. Instruct him and bring to his mind that which is spoken of me in the Scripture and is fulfilled, and thereafter shall he become the salvation of the Gentiles.

32. And we asked him: Lord, is there for us and for them the self-same expectation of the inheritance? He answered and said unto us: Are then the fingers of the hand like unto each other, or the ears of corn in the field, or do all fruit-trees bear the same fruit? Doth not every one bear fruit according to its nature? And we said unto him: Lord, wilt thou again speak unto us in parables? Then said he unto us: Lament not. Verily I say unto you, ye are my brethren, and my companions in the kingdom of heaven unto my Father, for so is his good pleasure. Verily I say unto you, unto them also whom ye teach and who believe on me will I give that expectation.

33. And we asked him again: When shall we meet with that man, and when wilt thou depart unto thy Father and our God and Lord? He answered and said unto us: That man will come out of the land of Cilicia unto Damascus of Syria, to root up the church which ye must found there. It is I that speak through you; and he shall come quickly: and he shall become strong in the faith, that the word of the prophet may be fulfilled, which saith: Behold, out of Syria will I begin to call together a new Jerusalem, and Sion will I subdue unto me, and it shall be taken, and the place which is childless shall be called the son and daughter of my Father, and my bride. For so hath it pleased him that sent me. But that man will I turn back, that he accomplish

not his evil desire, and the praise of my Father shall be perfected in him, and after that I am gone home and abide with my Father, I will speak unto him from heaven, and all things shall be accomplished which I have told you before concerning him.

34. And we said unto him again: Lord, so many great things hast thou told us and revealed unto us as never yet were spoken, and in all hast thou given us rest and been gracious unto us. After thy resurrection thou didst reveal unto us all things that we might be saved indeed; but thou saidst unto us only: There shall be wonders and strange appearances in heaven and on earth before the end of the world come. Tell us now, how shall we perceive it? And he answered us: I will teach it you; and not that which shall befall you only, but them also whom ye shall teach and who shall believe, as well as them who shall hear that man and believe on me. In those years and days shall it come to pass.

And we said again unto him: Lord, what shall come to pass? And he said unto us: Then shall they that believe and they that believe not hear (see Eth.) a trumpet in the heaven, a vision of great stars which shall be seen in the day, wonderful sights in heaven reaching down to the earth; stars which fall upon the earth like fire, and a great and mighty hail of fire (a star shining from the east unto this place, like unto fire, Eth. 2). The sun and the moon fighting one with the other, a continual rolling and noise of thunders and lightnings, thunder and earthquake; cities falling and men perishing in their overthrow, a continual dearth for lack of rain, a terrible pestilence and great mortality, mighty and untimely, so that they that die lack burial: and the bearing forth of brethren and sisters and kinsfolk shall be upon one bier. The kinsman shall show no favour to his kinsman,nor any man to his neighbour. And they that were overthrown shall rise up and behold them that overthrew them, that they lack burial, for the pestilence shall be full of hatred and pain and envy: and men shall take from one and give to another. And thereafter shall it wax yet worse than before. (Bewail ye them that have not hearkened unto my commandments, Eth. 2.)

35. Then shall my Father be wroth at the wickedness of men, for many are their transgressions, and the abomination of their uncleanness weigheth heavy upon them in the corruption of their life.

And we asked him: What of them that trust in thee? He answered and said unto us: Ye are yet slow of heart; and how long? Verily I say unto you, as the prophet David spake of me and of my people, so shall it be (?) for them also that believe on me. But they that are deceivers in the world and enemies of righteousness, upon them shall come the fulfilment of the prophecy of David, who said: Their feet are swift to shed blood, their tongue uttereth slander, adders' poison is under their lips. I behold thee companying with thieves, and partaking with adulterers, thou continuest speaking against thy brother and puttest stumbling blocks before thine own mother's son. What thinkest thou that I shall be like unto thee? Behold now how the prophet of God hath spoken of all, that all things may be fulfilled which he said aforetime.

36. And again we said unto him: Lord, will not then the nations say: Where is their God? And he answered and said unto us: Thereby shall the elect be known, that they being plagued with such afflictions, come forth. We said: Will then their departure out of the world be by a pestilence which giveth them pain? He answered us: Nay, but if they suffer such affliction, it will be a proving of them, whether they have faith and remember these my sayings, and fulfil my commandments. These shall arise, and short will be their expectation, that he may be glorified that sent me, and I with him. For he hath sent me unto you to tell you these things; and that ye may impart them unto Israel and the Gentiles and they may hear, and they also be redeemed and believe on me and escape the woe of the destruction. But whoso escapeth from the destruction of death, him will they take and hold him fast in the prison-house in torments like the torments of a thief.

And we said unto him: Lord, will they that believe be treated like the unbelievers, and wilt thou punish them that have escaped from the pestilence? And he said unto us: If they that believe in my name deal like the sinners, then have they done as though they had not believed. And we said again to him: Lord, have they on whom this lot hath fallen no life? He answered and said unto us: Whoso hath accomplished the praise of my Father, he shall abide in the resting-place of my Father.

37. Then said we unto him: Lord, teach us what shall come to pass thereafter? And he answered us: In those years and days shall war be kindled upon war; the four ends of the earth shall be in commotion and fight against each other. Thereafter shall be quakings of clouds (or, clouds of locusts), darkness, and dearth, and persecutions of them that believe on me and against the elect. Thereupon shall come doubt and strife and transgressions against one another. And there shall be many that believe on my name and yet follow after evil and spread vain doctrine. And men shall follow after them and their riches, and be subject unto their pride, and lust for drink, and bribery, and there shall be respect of persons among them.

38. But they that desire to behold the face of God and respect not the persons of the rich sinners, and are not ashamed before the people that lead them astray, but rebuke (?) them, they shall be crowned by the Father. And they also shall be saved that rebuke their neighbours, for they are sons of wisdom. and of faith. But if they become not children of wisdom, whoso hateth his brother and persecuteth him and showeth him no favour, him will God despise and reject.

But they that walk in truth and in the knowledge of the faith, and have love towards me -for they have endured insult- they shall be praised for that they walk in poverty and endure them that hate them and put them to shame. Men have stripped them naked, for they despised them because they continued in hunger and thirst, but after they have endured patiently, they shall have the blessedness of heaven, and they shall be with me for ever. But woe unto them that walk in pride and boasting, for their end is perdition.

39. And we said unto him: Lord, is this thy purpose, that thou leavest us, to come upon them? (Will all this come to pass, Eth.) He answered and said unto us: After what manner shall he judgement be? whether righteous or unrighteous? (In Copt. and Eth. the general sense is the same: but the answer of Jesus in the form of a question is odd, and there is probably a corruption.)

We said unto him: Lord, in that day they will say unto thee: Thou hast not distinguished between (probably: will they not say unto thee: Thou hast distinguished between) righteousness and unrighteousness, between the light and the darkness, and evil and good? Then said he: I will answer them and say: Unto Adam was power given to choose one of the two: he chose the light and laid his hand thereon, but the darkness he left behind him and cast away from him. Therefore have all men power to believe in the light which is life, and which is the Father that hath sent me. And every one that believeth and doeth the works of the light shall live in them, but if there be any that confesseth that he belongeth unto the light, and doeth the works of darkness, such an one hath no defence to utter, neither can he lift up his face to look upon the Son of God, which Son am I. For I will say unto him: As thou soughtest, so hast thou found, and as thou askedst, so hast thou received. Wherefore condemnest thou me, O man? Wherefore hast thou departed from me and denied me? And wherefore hast thou confessed me and yet denied me? hath not every man power to live and to die?

Whoso then hath kept my commandments shall be a son of the light, that is, of the Father that is in me. But because of them that corrupt my words am I come down from heaven. I am the word: I became flesh, and I wearied myself (or, suffered) and taught, saying: The heavy laden shall be saved, and they that are gone astray shall go astray for ever. They shall be chastised and tormented in their flesh and in their soul.

40. And we said unto him: O Lord, verily we are sorrowful for their sake. And he said unto us: Ye do rightly, for the righteous are sorry for the sinners, and pray for them, making prayer unto my Father. Again we said unto him: Lord, is there none that maketh intercession unto thee (so Eth.)? And he said unto us: Yea, and I will hearken unto the prayer of the righteous which they make for them.

When he had so said unto us, we said to him: Lord, in all things hast thou taught us and had mercy on us and saved us that we might preach unto them that are worthy to be saved, and that we might obtain a recompense with thee. (Shall we be partakers of a recompense from thee? Eth.)

41. He answered and said unto us: Go and preach, and ye shall be labourers, and fathers, and ministers. We said unto him: Thou art he (or, Art thou he) that shalt preach by us. (Lord, thou art our father. Eth.) Then answered he us, saying: Be not (or, Are not ye) all fathers or all masters. (Are then all fathers, or all servants, or all masters? Eth.) We said unto him: Lord, thou art he that saidst unto us: Call no man your father upon earth, for one is your Father, which is in heaven, and your master. Therefore sayest thou now unto us: Ye shall be fathers of many children, and servants and masters? He answered and said unto us: According as ye have said (Ye have rightly said, Eth.).

For verily I say unto you: whosoever shall hear you and believe on me, shall receive of you the light of the seal through me, and baptism through me: ye shall be fathers and servants and masters.

42. But we said unto him: Lord, how may it be that every one of us should be these three? He said unto us: Verily I say unto you: Ye shall be called fathers, because with praiseworthy heart and in love ye have revealed unto them the things of the kingdom of heaven. And ye shall be called servants, because they shall receive the baptism of life and the remission of their sins at my hand through you. And ye shall be called masters because ye have given them the word without grudging, and have admonished them, and when ye admonished them, they turned themselves (were converted). Ye were not afraid of their riches, nor ashamed before their face, but ye kept the commandments of my Father and fulfilled them. And ye shall have a great reward with my Father which is in heaven, and they shall have forgiveness of sins and everlasting life, and be partakers in the kingdom of heaven.

And we said unto him: Lord, even if every one of us had ten thousand tongues to speak withal, we could not thank thee, for that thou promisest such things unto us. Then answered he us, saying: Only do ye that which I say unto you, even as I myself also have done it.

43. And ye shall be like the wise virgins which watched and slept not, but went forth unto the lord into the bride chamber: but the foolish virgins were not able to watch, but slumbered. And we said unto him: Lord, who are the wise and who are the foolish? He said unto us: Five wise and five foolish; for these are they of whom the prophet hath spoken: Sons of ; God are they. Hear now their names.

But we wept and were troubled for them that slumbered. He said unto us: The five wise are Faith and Love and Grace and Peace and Hope. Now they of the faithful which possess this (these) shall be guides unto them that have believed on me and on him that sent me. For I am the Lord and I am the bridegroom whom they have received, and they have entered in to the house of the bridegroom and are laid down with me in the bridal chamber rejoicing. But the five foolish, when they had slept and had awaked, came unto the door of the bridal chamber and knocked, for the doors were shut. Then did they weep and lament that no man opened unto them.

We said unto him: Lord, and their wise sisters that were within in the bridegroom's house, did they continue without opening unto them, and did they not sorrow for their sakes nor entreat the bridegroom to open unto them? He answered us saying: They were not yet able to obtain favour for them. We said unto him: Lord, on what day shall they enter in for their sisters' sake? Then said he unto us: He that is shut out, is shut out. And we said unto him: Lord, is this word (determined?). Who then are the foolish? He said unto us: Hear their names. They are Knowledge, Understanding (Perception) Obedience, Patience, and Compassion. These are they that slumbered in them that have believed and confessed me but have not fulfilled my commandments.

44. On account of them that have slumbered, they shall remain outside the kingdom and the fold of the shepherd and his sheep. But whoso shall abide outside the sheepfold, him will the wolves devour, and he shall be (condemned?) and die in much affliction: in him shall be no rest nor endurance, and (Eth.) although he be hardly punished, and rent in pieces and devoured in long and evil torment, yet shall he not be able to obtain death quickly.

45. And we said unto him: Lord, well hast thou revealed all this unto us. Then answered he us, saying: Understand ye not (or. Ye understand not)

these words? We said unto him: Yea Lord. By five shall men enter into thy kingdom : notwithstanding, they that watched were with thee the Lord and bridegroom, even though they rejoiced not because of them that slumbered (yet will they have no pleasures because of, Eth.). He said unto us: They will indeed rejoice that they have entered in with the bridegroom the Lord; and they are sorrowful because of them that slumbered, for they are their sisters. For all ten are daughters of God, even the Father. Then said we unto him: Lord is it then for thee to show them favour on account of their sisters? (It becometh thy majesty to show them favour, Eth.) He said unto us: but his that sent me, and I am consenting with him (It is not yours, &c., Eth.).

46. But be ye upright and preach rightly and teach, and be not abashed by any man and fear not any man, and especially the rich, for they do not my commandments, but boast themselves (swell) in their riches. And we said unto him: Lord, tell us if it be the rich only. He answered, saying unto us: If any man who is not rich and possesseth a small livelihood giveth unto the poor and needy, men will call him a benefactor.

47. But if any man fall under the load of sin that he hath committed, then shall his neighbour correct him because of the good that he hath done unto his neighbour. And if his neighbour correct him and he return, he shall be saved, and he that corrected him shall receive a reward and live for ever. For a needy man, if he see him that hath done him good sin and correct him not, shall be judged with severe judgement. Now if a blind man lead a blind, they both fall into a ditch: and whoso respecteth persons for their sake, shall be as the two , as the prophet hath said: Woe unto them that respect persons and justify the ungodly for reward, even they whose God is their belly. Behold that judgement shall be their portion. For verily I say unto you: On that day will I neither have respect unto the rich nor pity for the poor.

48. If thou behold a sinner, admonish him betwixt him and thee: (if he hear thee, thou hast gained thy brother, Eth.) and if he hear thee not, then take to thee another, as many as three, and instruct thy brother: again, if he hear thee not, let him be unto thee

49. If thou hear aught against thy brother, give it no credence; slander not, and delight not in hearing slander. For thus it is written: Suffer not thine ear to receive aught against thy brother: but if thou seest aught correct him, rebuke him and convert him.

And we said unto him: Lord, thou hast in ail things taught us and warned us. But, Lord, concerning the believers, even them to whom it belongeth to believe in the preaching of thy name: is it determined that among them also there shall be doubt and division, jealousy confusion, hatred, and envy? For thou sayest: They shall find fault with one another and respect the person of them that sin, and hate them that rebuke them. And he answered and said unto us: How then shall the judgement come about, that the corn should be gathered into the garner and the chaff thereof cast into the fire?

50. They that hate such things, and love me and rebuke them that fulfil not my commandments, shall be hated and persecuted and despised and mocked. Men will of purpose speak of them that which is not true, and will band themselves together against them that love me. But these will rebuke them, that they may be saved. But them that will rebuke and chasten and warn them, them will they (the others) hate, and thrust them aside, and despise them, and hold themselves far from them that wish them good. But they that endure such things shall be like unto the martyrs with the Father, because they have striven for righteousness, and have not striven for corruption.

And we asked him: Lord, shall such things be among us? And he answered us: Fear not; it shall not be in many, but in a few. We said unto him: Yet tell us, in what manner it shall come to pass. And he said unto us: There shall come forth another doctrine, and a confusion, and because they shall strive after their own advancement, they shall bring forth an unprofitable doctrine. And therein shall be a deadly corruption (of uncleanness), and they shall teach it, and shall turn away them that believe on me from my commandments and cut them off from eternal life. But woe unto them that falsify this my word and commandment, and draw away them that hearken to them from the life of the doctrine and separate themselves from the commandment of life: for together with them they shall come into everlasting judgement.

51. And when he had said this, and had finished his discourse with us, he said unto us again: Behold, on the third day and at the third hour shall he come which hath sent me, that I may depart with him. And as he so spake, there was thunder and lightning and an earthquake, and the heavens parted asunder and there appeared a light (bright) cloud which bore him up. And there came voices of many angels, rejoicing and singing praises and saying: Gather us, O Priest, unto the light of the majesty. And when they drew nigh unto the firmament, we heard his voice saying unto us: Depart hence in peace.

Epistle to the Laodiceans

aul, an apostle not of men nor by man, but by Jesus Christ, unto the brethren that are at Laodicea.

2. Grace be unto you and peace from God the Father and the Lord Jesus Christ.

3. I give thanks unto Christ in all my prayers, that ye continue in him and persevere in his works, looking for the promise at the day of judgement.

4. Neither do the vain talkings of some overset you, which creep in, that they may turn you away from the truth of the Gospel which is preached by me.

5. And now shall God cause that they that are of me shall continue ministering unto the increase of the truth of the Gospel and accomplishing goodness, and the work of salvation, even eternal life.

6. And now are my bonds seen of all men, which I suffer in Christ, wherein I rejoice and am glad.

7. And unto me this is for everlasting salvation, which also is brought about by your prayers, and the ministry of the Holy Ghost, whether by life or by death.

8. For verily to me life is in Christ, and to die is joy.

9. And unto him (or And also) shall he work his mercy in you that ye may have the same love, and be of one mind.

10. Therefore, dearly beloved, as ye have heard in my presence so hold fast and work in the fear of God, and it shall be unto you for life eternal.

11. For it is God that worketh in you.

12. And do ye without afterthought whatsoever ye do.

13. And for the rest, dearly beloved, rejoice in Christ, and beware of them that are filthy in lucre.

14. Let all your petitions be made openly before God, and be ye steadfast in the mind of Christ.

15. And what things are sound and true and sober and just and to be

loved, do ye.

16. And what ye have heard and received, keep fast in your heart.

17. And peace shall be unto you.

18 . The saints salute you.

19. The grace of the Lord Jesus be with your spirit.

20. And cause this epistle to be read unto them of Colossae, and the epistle of the Colossians to be read unto you.

Excerpts from the Gospel of Mary

The Savior said, "All natures, all formed things, all creatures exist in and with one another and will again be resolved into their own roots, because the nature of matter is dissolved into the roots of its nature alone. He who has ears to hear, let him hear." [cf. Matt. 11:15, etc.].

Peter said to him, "Since you have now explained all things to us, tell us this: what is the sin of the world?" [cf. John 1:29]. The Savior said, "Sin as such does not exist, but you make sin when you do what is of the nature of fornication, which is called 'sin.' For this reason the Good came into your midst, to the essence of each nature, to restore it to its root." He went on to say, "For this reason you come into existence and die [...] whoever knows may know [...] a suffering which has nothing like itself, which has arisen out of what is contrary to nature. Then there arises a disturbance in the whole body. For this reason I said to you, Be of good courage [cf. Matt. 28:9], and if you are discouraged, still take courage over against the various forms of nature. He who has ears to hear, let him hear." When the Blessed One said this, he greeted all of them, saying "Peace be with you [cf. John 14:27]. Receive my peace for yourselves. Take heed lest anyone lead you astray with the words, 'Lo, here!' or 'Lo, there!' [cf. Matt. 24:5, 23; Luke 17:21] for the Son of Man is within you [cf. Luke 17:21]. Follow him; those who seek him will find him [cf. Matt. 7:7]. Go, therefore, and preach the Gospel of the Kingdom [cf. Matt. 4:23; 9:15; Mark 16:15]. I have left no commandment but what I have commanded you, and I have given you no law, as the lawgiver did, lest you be bound by it."

They grieved and mourned greatly, saying, "How shall we go to the Gentiles and preach the Gospel of the Kingdom of the Son of Man? If even he was not spared, how shall we be spared?"

Then Mary stood up and greeted all of them and said to her brethren, "Do not mourn or grieve or be irresolute, for his grace will be with you all and will defend you. Let us rather praise his greatness, for he prepared us and made us into men." When Mary said this, their hearts changed for the better, and they began to discuss the words of the [Savior].

Peter said to Mary, "Sister, we know that the Savior loved you more than other women [cf. John 11:5, Luke 10:38-42]. Tell us the words of the Savior which you have in mind since you know them; and we do not, nor have we heard of them."

Mary answered and said, "What is hidden from you I will impart to you." And she began to say the following words to them. "I," she said, "I saw the Lord in a vision and I said to him, 'Lord, I saw you today in a vision.' He answered and said to me, 'Blessed are you, since you did not waver at the sight of me. For where the mind is, there is your countenance' [cf. Matt. 6:21]. I said to him, 'Lord, the mind which sees the vision, does it see it through the soul or through the spirit?' The Savior answered and said, 'It sees neither through the soul nor through the spirit, but the mind, which is between the two, which sees the vision, and it is...'"

"...and Desire said, 'I did not see you descend; but now I see you rising. Why do you speak falsely, when you belong to me?' The soul answered and said, 'I saw you, but you did not see me or recognize me; I served you as a garment and you did not recognize me.' After it had said this, it went joyfully and gladly away. Again it came to the third power, Ignorance. This power questioned the soul: 'Whither are you going? You were bound in wickedness, you were bound indeed. Judge not' [cf. Matt. 7:1]. And the soul said, 'Why do you judge me, when I judged not? I was bound, though I did not bind. I was not recognized, but I recognized that all will go free, things both earthly and heavenly.' After the soul had left the third power behind, it rose upward, and saw the fourth power, which had seven forms. The first form is darkness, the second desire, the third ignorance, the fourth the arousing of death, the fifth is the kingdom of the flesh, the sixth is the wisdom of the folly of the flesh, the seventh is wrathful wisdom. These are the seven participants in wrath. They ask the soul, 'Whence do you come, killer of men, or where are you going, conqueror of space?' The soul answered and said, 'What seizes me is killed; what turns me about is overcome; my desire has come to an end and ignorance is dead. In a world I was saved from a world, and in a "type," from a higher "type" and from the fetter of the impotence of knowledge, the existence of which is temporal. From this time I will reach rest in the time of the moment of the Aeon in silence.'"

When Mary had said this, she was silent, since the Savior had spoken thus far with her. But Andrew answered and said to the brethren, 'Say what you think concerning what she said. For I do not believe that the Savior said this. For certainly these teachings are of other ideas."

Peter also opposed her in regard to these matters and asked them about the Savior. "Did he then speak secretly with a woman [cf. John 4:27], in preference to us, and not openly? Are we to turn back and all listen to her? Did he prefer her to us?" Then Mary grieved and said to Peter, "My brother Peter, what do you think? Do you think that I thought this up myself in my heart or that I am lying concerning the Savior?"

Levi answered and said to Peter, "Peter, you are always irate. Now I see that you are contending against the woman like the adversaries. But if the Savior made her worthy, who are you to reject her? Surely the Savior knew her very well [cf. Luke 10:38–42]. For this reason he loved her more than us [cf. John 11:5]. And we should rather be ashamed and put on the Perfect Man, to form us [?] as he commanded us, and proclaim the gospel, without publishing a further commandment or a further law than the one which the Savior spoke." When Levi had said this, they began to go out in order to proclaim him and preach him.

The First Epistle Of Clement To The Corinthians

CHAPTER 1
The Salutation & Praise Of The Corinthians Before The Breaking Forth Of Schism Among them

The Church of God which sojourns at Rome, to the Church of God sojourning at Corinth, to them that are called and sanctified by the will of God, through our Lord Jesus Christ: Grace unto you, and peace, from Almighty God through Jesus Christ, be multiplied.

Owing, dear brethren, to the sudden and successive calamitous events which have happened to ourselves, we feel that we have been somewhat tardy in turning our attention to the points respecting which you consulted us; and especially to that shameful and detestable sedition, utterly abhorrent to the elect of God, which a few rash and self-confident persons have kindled to such a pitch of frenzy, that your venerable and illustrious name, worthy to be universally loved, has suffered grievous injury. For who ever dwelt even for a short time among you, and did not find your faith to be as fruitful of virtue as it was firmly established? Who did not admire the sobriety and moderation of your godliness in Christ? Who did not proclaim the magnificence of your habitual hospitality? And who did not rejoice over your perfect and well-grounded knowledge? For ye did all things without respect of persons, and walked in the command-merits of God, being obedient to those who had the rule over you, and giving all fitting honour to the presbyters among you. Ye enjoined young men to be of a sober and serious mind; ye instructed your wives to do all things with a blameless, becoming, and pure conscience, loving their husbands as in duty bound; and ye taught them that, living in the rule of obedience, they should manage their household affairs becomingly, and be in every respect marked by discretion.

CHAPTER 2
Praise Of The Corinthians Continued

Moreover, ye were all distinguished by humility, and were in no respect puffed up with pride, but yielded obedience rather than extorted it, and were more willing to give than to receive? Content with the provision which God had made for you, and carefully attending to His words, ye were inwardly filled with His doctrine, and His sufferings were before your eyes. Thus a profound and abundant peace was given to you all, and ye had an insatiable desire for doing good, while a full outpouring of the Holy Spirit was upon you all. Full of holy designs, ye did, with true earnestness of mind and a godly confidence, stretch forth your hands to God

Almighty, beseeching Him to be merciful unto you, if ye had been guilty of any involuntary transgression. Day and night ye were anxious for the whole brotherhood, that the number of God's elect might be saved with mercy and a good conscience. Ye were sincere and uncorrupted, and forgetful of injuries between one another. Every kind of faction and schism was abominable in your sight. Ye mourned over the transgressions of your neighhours: their deficiencies you deemed your own. Ye never grudged any act of kindness, being "ready to every good work." Adorned by a thoroughly virtuous and religious life, ye did all things in the fear of God. The commandments and ordinances of the Lord were written upon the tablets of your hearts.

CHAPTER 3
The Sad State Of The Corinthian Church After Sedition Arose In It From Envy And Emulation

Every kind of honour and happiness was bestowed upon you, and then was fulfilled that which is written, "My beloved did eat and drink, and was enlarged and became fat, and kicked." Hence flowed emulation and envy, strife and sedition, persecution and disorder, war and captivity. So the worthless rose up against the honoured, those of no reputation against such as were renowned, the foolish against the wise, the young against those advanced in years. For this reason righteousness and peace are now far departed from you, inasmuch as every one abandons the fear of God, and is become blind in His faith, neither walks in the ordinances of His appointment, nor acts a part becoming a Christian but walks after his own wicked lusts, resuming the practice of an unrighteous and ungodly envy, by which death itself entered into the world.

CHAPTER 4
Many Evils Have Already Flowed From This Source In Ancient Times

For thus it is written: "And it came to pass after certain days, that Cain brought of the fruits of the earth a sacrifice unto God; and Abel also brought of the firstlings of his sheep, and of the fat thereof. And God had respect to Abel and to his offerings, but Cain and his sacrifices He did not regard. And Cain was deeply grieved, and his countenance fell. And God said to Cain, Why art thou grieved, and why is try countenance fallen? If thou offerest rightly, but dost not divide rightly, hast thou not sinned? Be at peace: thine offering returns to thyself, and thou shalt again possess it. And Cain said to Abel his brother, Let us go into the field. And it came to pass, while they were in the field, that Cain rose up against Abel his brother, and slew him." Ye see, brethren, how envy and jealousy led to the murder of a brother. Through envy, also, our father Jacob fled from the face of Esau his brother. Envy made Joseph be persecuted unto death, and to come into bondage. Envy compelled Moses to flee from the face of Pharaoh king of Egypt, when he heard these words from his fellow-countryman, "Who made thee a judge or a ruler over us? wilt thou kill me, as thou didst kill the Egyptian yesterday?" On account of envy, Aaron and Miriam had to make their abode without the camp. Envy brought down Dathan and Abiram alive to Hades, through the sedition which they excited against God's servant Moses. Through envy, David underwent the hatred not only of foreigners, but was also persecuted by Saul king of Israel.

CHAPTER 5
No Less Evils Have Arisen From The Same Source In The Most Recent Times, The Martyrdom Of Peter And Paul

But not to dwell upon ancient examples, let us come to the most recent spiritual heroes. Let us take the noble examples furnished in our own generation. Through envy and jealousy, the greatest and most righteous pillars[of the Church] have been persecuted and put to death. Let us set before our eyes the illustrious apostles. Peter, through unrighteous envy, endured not one or two, but numerous labours and when he had at length suffered martyrdom, departed to the place of glory due to him. Owing to envy, Paul also obtained the reward of patient endurance, after being seven times thrown into captivity, compelled to flee, and stoned. After preaching both in the east and west, he gained the illustrious reputation due to his faith, having taught righteousness to the whole world, and come to the extreme limit of the west, and suffered martyrdom under the prefects. Thus was he removed from the world, and went into the holy place, having proved himself a striking example of patience.

CHAPTER 6
Continuation: Several Other Martyrs

To these men who spent their lives in the practice of holiness, there is to be added a great multitude of the elect, who, having through envy endured many indignities and tortures, furnished. us with a most excellent example. Through envy, those women, the Danaids and Dircae, being persecuted, after they had suffered terrible and unspeakable torments, finished the course of their faith with stedfastness, and though weak in body, received a noble reward. Envy has alienated wives from their husbands, and changed that saying of our father Adam, "This is now bone of my bones, and flesh of my flesh." Envy and strife have overthrown great cities and rooted up mighty nations.

CHAPTER 7
An Exhortation To Repentance

These things, beloved, we write unto you, not merely to admonish you of your duty, but also to remind ourselves. For we are struggling on the same arena, and the same conflict is assigned to both of us. Wherefore let us give up vain and fruitless cares, and approach to the glorious and venerable rule of our holy calling. Let us attend to what is good, pleasing, and acceptable in the sight of Him who formed us. Let us look stedfastly to the blood of Christ, and see how precious that blood is to God, which, having been shed for our salvation, has set the grace of repentance before the whole world. Let us turn to every age that has passed, and learn that, from generation to generation, the Lord has granted a place of repentance to all such as would be converted unto Him. Noah preached repentance, and as many as listened to him were saved. Jonah proclaimed destruction to the Ninevites; but they, repenting of their sins, propitiated God by prayer, and obtained salvation, although they were aliens [to the covenant] of God.

CHAPTER 8
Continuation Respecting Repentance

The ministers of the grace of God have, by the Holy Spirit, spoken of repentance; and the Lord of all things has himself declared with an oath regarding it, "As I live, saith the Lord, I desire not the death of the sinner, but rather his repentance ; " adding, moreover, this gracious declaration Repent O house of Israel, of your iniquity. Say to the children of My people, Though your sins reach from earth to heaven, I and though they be redder than scarlet, and blacker than sackcloth, yet if ye turn to Me with your whole heart, and say, Father ! I will listen to you, as to a holy people." And in another place He speaks thus: "Wash you, and become clean; put away the wickedness of your souls from before mine eyes; cease from your evil ways, and learn to do well; seek out judgment, deliver the oppressed, judge the fatherless, and see that justice is done to the widow; and come, and let us reason together. He declares, Though your sins be like crimson, I will make them white as snow; though they be like scarlet, I will whiten them like wool. And if ye be willing and obey Me, ye shall eat the good of the land; but if ye refuse, and will not hearken unto Me, the sword shall devour you, for the mouth of the Lord hath spoken these things." Desiring, therefore, that all His beloved should be partakers of repentance, He has, by His almighty will, established [these declarations].

CHAPTER 9
Examples Of The Saints

Wherefore, let us yield obedience to His excellent and glorious will; and imploring His mercy and loving-kindness, while we forsake all fruitless labours, and strife, and envy, which leads to death, let us turn and have recourse to His compassions. Let us stedfastly contemplate those who have perfectly ministered to His excellent glory. Let us take (for instance) Enoch, who, being found righteous in obedience, was translated, and death was never known to happen to him? Noah, being found faithful, preached regeneration to the world through his ministry; and the Lord saved by him the animals which, with one accord, entered into the ark.

CHAPTER 10
Continuation Of The Above

Abraham, styled "the friend," was found faithful, inasmuch as he rendered obedience to the words of God. He, in the exercise of obedience, went out from his own country, and from his kindred, and from his father's house, in order that, by forsaking a small territory, and a weak family, and an insignificant house, he might inherit the promises of God. For God said to him, "Get thee out from thy country,, and from thy kindred, and from thy father's house, into the land which I shall show thee. And I will make thee a great nation, and will bless thee, and make thy name great, and thou shall be blessed. And I will bless them that bless thee, and curse them that curse thee; and in thee shall all the families of the earth be blessed." And again, on his departing from Lot, God said to him. "Lift up thine eyes, and look from the place where thou now art, northward, and southward, and eastward, and westward; for all the land which thou seest, to thee will I give it, and to thy seed for ever. And I will make thy seed as the dust of the earth, [so that] if a man can number the dust of the earth, then shall thy seed also be numbered." And again [the Scripture] saith, "God brought forth Abram, and spake unto him, Look up now to heaven, and count the stars if thou be able to number them; so shall thy seed be. And Abram believed God, and it was counted to him for righteousness." On account of his faith and hospitality, a son was given him in his old age; and in the exercise of obedience, he offered him as a sacrifice to God on one of the mountains which He showed him.

CHAPTER 11
Continuation: Lot

On account of his hospitality and godliness, Lot was saved out of Sodore when all the country round was punished by means of fire and brimstone, the Lord thus making it manifest that He does not forsake those that hope in Him, but gives up such as depart from Him to punishment and torture. For Lot's wife, who went forth with him, being of a different mind from himself and not continuing in agreement with him [as to the command which had been given them], was made an example of, so as to be a pillar of salt unto this day. This was   done that all might know that those who are of a double mind, and who distrust the power of God, bring down judgment on themselves? and become a sign to all succeeding generations.

CHAPTER 12
The Rewards Of Faith And Hospitality: Rahab

On account of her faith and hospitality, Rahab the harlot was saved. For when spies were sent by Joshua, the son of Nun, to Jericho, the king of the country ascertained that they were come to spy out their land, and sent men to seize them, in order that, when taken, they might be put to death. But the hospitable Rahab receiving them, concealed them on the roof of her house under some stalks of flax. And when the men sent by the king arrived and said "There came men unto thee who are to spy out our land; bring them forth, for so the king commands," she answered them, "The two men whom ye seek came unto me, but quickly departed again and are gone," thus not discovering the spies to them. Then she said to the men, "I know assuredly that the Lord your God hath given you this city, for the fear and dread of you have fallen on its inhabitants. When therefore ye shall have taken it, keep ye me and the house of my father in safety." And they said to her, "It shall be as thou hast spoken to us. As soon, therefore, as thou knowest that we are at hand, thou shall gather all thy family under thy roof, and they shall be preserved, but all that. are found outside of thy dwelling shall perish." Moreover, they gave her a sign to this effect, that she should hang forth from her house a scarlet thread. And thus they made it manifest that redemption should flow through the blood of the Lord to all them that believe and hope in God. Ye see, beloved, that there was not only faith, but prophecy, in this woman.

CHAPTER 13
An Exhortation To Humility

Let us therefore, brethren, be of humble mind, laying aside all haughtiness, and pride, and foolishness, and angry feelings; and let us act according to that which is written (for the Holy Spirit saith, "Let not the wise man glory in his wisdom, neither let the mighty man glory in his might, neither let the rich man Story in his riches; but let him that glorieth glory in the Lord, in diligently seeking Him, and doing judgment and righteousness"), being especially mindful of the words of the Lord Jesus which He spake, teaching us meekness and long-suffering. For thus He spoke: "Be ye merciful, that ye may obtain mercy; forgive, that it may be forgiven to you ; as ye do, so shall it be done unto you; as ye judge, so shall ye be judged; as ye are kind, so shall kindness be shown to you; with what measure ye mete, with the same it shall be measured to you." By this precept and by these rules let us stablish ourselves, that we walk with all humility in obedience to His holy words. For the holy word saith, "On whom shall I look, but on him that is meek and peaceable, and that trembleth at My words?"

CHAPTER 14
We Should Obey God Rather Than The Authors Of Sedition

It is right and holy therefore, men and brethren, rather to obey God than to follow those who, through pride and sedition, have become the leaders of a detestable emulation. For we shall incur no slight injury, but rather great danger, if we rashly yield ourselves to the inclinations of men who aim at exciting strife and tumults, so as to draw us away from what is good. Let us be kind one to another after the pattern of the tender mercy and benignity of our Creator. For it is written, "The kind-hearted shall inhabit the land, and the guiltless shall be left upon it, but transgressors shall be destroyed from off the face of it." And again [the Scripture] saith, "I saw the ungodly highly exalted, and lifted up like the cedars of Lebanon: I passed by, and, behold, he was not; and I diligently sought his place, and could not find it. Preserve innocence, and look on equity: for there shall be a remnant to the peaceful man."

CHAPTER 15
We Must Adhere To Those Who Cultivate Peace, Not To Those Who
Merely Pretend To Do So

Let us cleave, therefore, to those who cultivate peace with godliness, and not to those who hypocritically profess to desire it. For [the Scripture] saith in a certain place, "This people honoureth Me with their lips, but their heart is far from Me." And again: "They bless with their mouth, but curse with their heart." And again it saith, "They loved Him with their mouth, and lied to Him with their tongue; but their heart was not right with Him, neither were they faithful in His covenant." "Let the deceitful lips become silent," [and "let the Lord destroy all the lying lips,] and the boastful tongue of those who have said, Let us magnify our tongue; our lips are our own; who is lord over us? For the oppression of the poor, and for the sighing of the needy, will I now arise, saith the Lord: I will place him in safety; I will deal confidently with him."

CHAPTER 16
Christ As An Example Of Humility

For Christ is of those who are humble-minded, and not of those who exalt themselves over His flock. Our Lord Jesus Christ, the Sceptre of the majesty of God, did not come in the pomp of pride or arrogance, although

He might have done so, but in a lowly condition, as the Holy Spirit had declared regarding Him. For He says, "Lord, who hath believed our report, and to whom is the arm of the Lord revealed ? We have declared [our message] in His presence: He is, as it were, a child, and like a root in thirsty ground; He has no form nor glory, yea, we saw Him, and He had no form nor comeliness; but His form was without eminence, yea, deficient in comparison with the [ordinary] form of men. He is a man exposed to stripes and suffering,

anti acquainted with the endurance of grief: for His countenance was turned away; He was despised, and not esteemed. He bears our iniquities, and is in sorrow for our sakes; yet we supposed that [on His own account] He was exposed to labour, and stripes, and affliction. But He was wounded for our transgressions, and bruised for our iniquities. The chastisement of our peace was upon Him, and by His stripes we were healed. All we, like sheep, have gone astray; [every] man has wandered in his own way; and the Lord has delivered Him up for our sins, while He in the midst of His sufferings openeth not His mouth. He was brought as a sheep to the slaughter, and as a lamb before her shearer is dumb, so He openeth not His mouth. In His humiliation His judgment was taken away; who shall declare His generation? for His life is taken from the earth. For the transgressions of my people was He brought down to death. And I will give the wicked for His sepulchre, and the rich for His death? because He did no iniquity, neither was guile found in His mouth. And the Lord is pleased to purify Him by stripes. If ye make an offering for sin, your soul shall see a long-lived seed. And the Lord is pleased to relieve Him of the affliction of His soul, to show Him light, and to form Him with understanding, to justify the Just One who ministereth well to many; and the Himself shall carry their sins. On this account He shall inherit many, and shall divide the spoil of the strong; because His soul was delivered to death, and He was reckoned among the transgressors, and He bare the sins of many, and for their sins was He delivered." And again He saith, "I am a worm, and no man; a reproach of men, and despised of the people. All that see Me have derided Me; they have spoken with their lips; they have wagged their head, [saying] He hoped in God, let Him deliver Him, let Him save Him, since He delighteth in Him." Ye see, beloved, what is the example which has been given us; for if the Lord thus humbled Himself, what shall we do who have through Him come under the yoke of His grace ?

CHAPTER 17
The Saints As Examples Of Humility

Let us be imitators also of those who in goat-skins and sheep-skins went

215

about proclaiming the coming of Christ; I mean Elijah, Elisha, and Ezekiel among the prophets, with those others to whom a like testimony is borne [in Scripture]. Abraham was specially honoured, and was called the friend of God; yet he, earnestly regarding the glory of God, humbly declared, "I am but dust and ashes." Moreover, it is thus written of Job, "Job was a righteous man, and blameless, truthful, God-fearing, and one that kept himself from all evil." But bringing an accusation against himself, he said, " No man is free from defilement, even if his life be but of one day." Moses was called faithful in all God's house; and through his instrumentality, God punished Egypt with plagues and tortures. Yet he, though thus greatly honoured, did not adopt lofty language, but said, when the divine oracle came to him out of the bush, "Who am I, that Thou sendest me ? I am a man of a feeble voice and a slow tongue." And again he said, "I am but as the smoke of a pot."

CHAPTER 18
David As An Example Of Humility

But what shall we say concerning David, to whom such testimony was borne, and of whom God said, "I have found a man after Mine own heart, David the son of Jesse; and in everlasting mercy have I anointed him?" Yet this very man saith to God, "Have mercy on me, O Lord, according to Thy great mercy; and according to the multitude of Thy compassions, blot out my transgression. Wash me still more from mine iniquity, and cleanse me from my sin. For I acknowledge my iniquity, and my sin is ever before me. Against Thee only have I sinned, and done that which was evil in Thy sight; that Thou mayest be justified in Thy sayings, and mayest overcome when Thou art judged. For, behold, I was conceived in transgressions, and in my sins did my mother conceive me. For, behold, Thou hast loved truth; the secret and hidden things of wisdom hast Thou shown me. Thou shalt sprinkle me with hyssop, and I shall be cleansed; Thou shalt wash me, and I shall be whiter than snow. Thou shalt make me to hear joy and gladness; my bones, which have been humbled, shall exult. Turn away Thy face from my sins, and blot out all mine iniquities. Create in me a clean heart, O God, and renew a right spirit within me. Cast me not away from Thy presence, and take not Thy Holy Spirit from me. Restore to me the joy of Thy salvation, and establish me by Thy governing Spirit. I will teach transgressors Thy ways, and the ungodly shall be converted unto Thee. Deliver me from blood-guiltiness, O God, the God of my salvation: my tongue shall exult in Thy righteousness. O Lord, Thou shalt open my mouth, and my lips shall show forth Thy praise. For if Thou hadst desired sacrifice, I would have given it; Thou wilt not delight in burnt-offerings. The sacrifice [acceptable] to God is a bruised spirit; a broken and a contrite heart God will not despise."

CHAPTER 19
Imitating These Examples, Let Us Seek After Peace

Thus the humility and godly submission of so great and illustrious men have rendered not only us, but also all the generations before us, better; even as many as have received His oracles in fear and truth. Wherefore, having so many great and glorious examples set before us, let us turn again to the practice of that peace which from the beginning was the mark set before us; and let us look stedfastly to the Father and Creator of the universe, and cleave to His mighty and surpassingly great gifts and benefactions, of peace. Let us contemplate Him with our understanding, and look with the eyes of our soul to His long-suffering will. Let us reflect how free from wrath He is towards all His creation.

CHAPTER 20
The Peace And Harmony Of The Universe

The heavens, revolving under His government, are subject to Him in peace. Day and night run the course appointed by Him, in no wise hindering each other. The sun and moon, with the companies of the stars, roll on in harmony according to His command, within their prescribed limits, and without any deviation. The fruitful earth, according to His will, brings forth food in abundance, at the proper seasons, for man and beast and all the living beings upon it, never hesitating, nor changing any of the ordinances which He has fixed. The unsearchable places of abysses, and the indescribable arrangements of the lower world, are restrained by the same laws. The vast unmeasurable sea, gathered together by His working into various basins, never passes beyond the bounds placed around it, but does as He has commanded. For He said, "Thus far shalt thou come, and thy waves shall be broken within thee." The ocean, impassible to man, and the worlds beyond it, are regulated by the same enactments of the Lord. The seasons of spring, summer, autumn, and winter, peacefully give place to one another. The winds in their several quarters fulfil, at the proper time, their service without hindrance. The ever-flowing fountains, formed both for enjoyment and health, furnish without fail their breasts for the life of men. The very smallest of living beings meet together in peace and concord. All these the great Creator and Lord of all has appointed to exist in peace and harmony; while He does good to all, but most abundantly to us who have fled for refuge to His compassions through Jesus Christ our Lord, to whom be glory and majesty for ever and ever. Amen.

CHAPTER 21
Let Us Obey God, And Not The Authors Of Sedition

Take heed, beloved, lest His many kindnesses lead to the condemnation of us all. [For thus it must be] unless we walk worthy of Him, and with one mind do those things which are good and well-pleasing in His sight.   For [the Scripture] saith in a certain place, "The Spirit of the Lord is a candle searching the secret parts of the belly." Let us reflect how near He is, and that none of the thoughts or reasonings in which we engage are hid from Him. It is right, therefore, that we should not leave the post which His will has assigned us. Let us rather offend those men who are foolish, and inconsiderate, and lifted up, and who glory in the pride of their speech, than [offend] God. Let us reverence the Lord Jesus Christ, whose blood was given for us; let us esteem those who have the rule over us; let us honour the aged among us; let us train up the young men in the fear of God; let us direct our wives to that which is good. Let them exhibit the lovely habit of purity [in all their conduct];   let them show forth the sincere disposition of meekness; let them make manifest the command which they have of their tongue, by their manner of speaking; let them display their love, not by preferring one to another, but by showing equal affection to all that piously fear God. Let your children be partakers of true Christian training; let them learn of how great avail humility is with God--how much the spirit of pure affection can prevail with Him--how excellent and great His fear is, and how it saves all those who walk in it with a pure mind. For He is a Searcher of the thoughts and desires [of the heart]: His breath is in us; and when He pleases, He will take it away.

CHAPTER 22
These Exhortations Are Confirmed By The Chrisitan Faith, Which Proclaims The Misery Of Sinful Conduct

Now the faith which is in Christ confirms all these [admonitions]. For He Himself by the Holy Ghost thus addresses us: "Come, ye children, hearken unto Me; I will teach you the fear of the Lord. What man is he that desireth life, and loveth to see good days? Keep thy tongue from evil, and thy lips from speaking guile. Depart from evil, and do good; seek peace, and pursue it. The eyes of the Lord are upon the righteous, and His ears are [open] unto their prayers. The face of the Lord is against them that do evil, to cut off the remembrance of them from the earth. The righteous cried, and the Lord heard him, and delivered him out of all his troubles." "Many are the stripes [appointed for] the wicked; but mercy shall compass those about who hope in the Lord."

CHAPTER 23
Be Humble, And Believe That Christ Will Come Again

The all-merciful and beneficent Father has bowels [of compassion] towards those that fear Him, and kindly and lovingly bestows His favours upon those who come to Him with a simple mind. Wherefore let us not be double-minded; neither let our soul be lifted up on account of His exceedingly great and glorious gifts. Far from us be that which is written, "Wretched are they who are of a double mind, and of a doubting heart; who say, These things we have heard even in the times of our fathers; but, behold, we have grown old, and none of them has happened unto us." Ye foolish ones! compare yourselves to a tree: take [for instance] the vine. First of all, it sheds its leaves, then it buds, next it puts forth leaves, and then it flowers; after that comes the sour grape, and then follows the ripened fruit. Ye perceive how in a little time the fruit of a tree comes to maturity. Of a truth, soon and suddenly shall His will be accomplished, as the Scripture also bears witness, saying, "Speedily will He come, and will not tarry;" and, "The Lord shall suddenly come to His temple, even the Holy One, for whom ye look."

CHAPTER 24
God Continually Shows Us In Nature That There Will Be A Resurrection

Let us consider, beloved, how the Lord continually proves to us that there shall be a future resurrection, of which He has rendered the Lord Jesus Christ the first-fruits by raising Him from the dead. Let us contemplate, beloved, the resurrection which is at all times taking place. Day and night declare to us a resurrection. The night sinks to sleep, and the day arises; the day [again] departs, and the night comes on. Let us behold the fruits [of the earth], how the sowing of grain takes place. The sower goes forth, and casts it into the ground; and the seed being thus scattered, though dry and naked when it fell upon the earth, is gradually dissolved. Then out of its dissolution the mighty power of the providence of the Lord raises it up again, and from one seed many arise and bring forth fruit.

CHAPTER 25
The Phoenix, An Emblem Of Our Resurrection

Let us consider that wonderful sign [of the resurrection] which takes place in Eastern lands, that is, in Arabia and the countries round about. There is a certain bird which is called a phoenix. This is the only one of its kind, and lives five hundred years. And when the time of its dissolution draws near that it must die, it builds itself a nest of frankincense, and myrrh, and other spices, into which, when the time is fulfilled, it enters and dies. But as the flesh decays a certain kind of worm is produced, which, being nourished by the juices of the dead bird, brings forth feathers. Then, when it has acquired strength, it takes up that nest in which are the bones of its parent, and bearing these it passes from the land of Arabia into Egypt, to the city called Heliopolis. And, in open day, flying in the sight of all men, it places them on the altar of the sun, and having done this, hastens back to its former abode. The priests then inspect the registers of the dates, and find that it has returned exactly as the five hundredth year was completed.

CHAPTER 26
We Shall Rise Again, Then, As The Scriptures Also Testifies

Do we then deem it any great and wonderful thing for the Maker of all things to raise up again those that have piously served Him in the assurance of a good faith, when even by a bird He shows us the mightiness of His power to fulfil His promise ? For [the Scripture] saith in a certain place, "Thou shalt raise me up, and I shall confess unto Thee; "and again, "I laid me down, and slept; I awaked, because Thou art with me; "and again, Job says, "Thou shalt raise up this flesh of mine, which has suffered all these things."

CHAPTER 27
In The Hope Of The Resurrection, Let Us Cleave To The Omnipotent
And Omniscient God

Having then this hope, let our souls be bound to Him who is faithful in His promises, and just in His judgments. He who has commanded us not to lie, shall much more Himself not lie; for nothing is impossible with God, except to lie. Let His faith therefore be stirred up again within us, and let us consider that all things are nigh unto Him. By the word of His might He established all things, and by His word He can overthrow them. "Who shall say unto Him, What hast thou done ? or, Who shall resist the power of His strength?" When and as He pleases He will do all things, and none of the things determined by Him shall pass away? All things are open before Him, and nothing can be hidden from His counsel. "The heavens declare the glory of God, and the firmament showeth His handy-work. Day unto day uttereth speech, and night unto night showeth knowledge. And there are no words or speeches of which the voices are not heard."

CHAPTER 28
God Sees All Things: Therefore Let Us Avoid Transgression

Since then all things are seen and heard [by God], let us fear Him, and forsake those wicked works which proceed from evil desires; so that, through His mercy, we may be protected from the judgments to come. For whither can any of us flee from His mighty hand? Or what world will receive any of those who run away from Him ? For the Scripture saith in a certain place, "Whither shall I go, and where shall I be hid from Thy presence? If I ascend into heaven, Thou art there; if I go away even to the uttermost parts of the earth, there is Thy right hand; if I make my bed in the abyss, there is Thy Spirit." Whither, then, shall any one go, or   where shall he escape from Him who comprehends all things?

CHAPTER 29
Let Us Also Draw Near To God In Purity Of Heart

Let us then draw near to Him with holiness of spirit, lifting up pure and undefiled hands unto Him, loving our gracious and merciful Father, who has made us partakers in the blessings of His elect. For thus it is written, "When the Most High divided the nations, when He scattered the sons of Adam, He fixed the bounds of the nations according to the number of the angels of God. His people Jacob became the portion of the Lord, and Israel the lot of His inheritance." And in another place [the Scripture] saith, "Behold, the Lord taketh unto Himself a nation out of the midst of the nations, as a man takes the first-fruits of his threshing-floor; and from that nation shall come forth the Most Holy.

CHAPTER 30
Let Us Do Those Things That Please God, And Flee From Those He Hates, That We May Be Blessed

Seeing, therefore, that we are the portion of the Holy One, let us do all those things which pertain to holiness, avoiding all evil-speaking, all abominable and impure embraces, together with all drunkenness, seeking after change, all abominable lusts, detestable adultery, and execrable pride. "For God," saith [the Scripture], "resisteth the proud, but giveth grace to the humble." Let us cleave, then, to those to whom grace has been given by God. Let us clothe ourselves with concord and humility, ever exercising self-control, standing far off from all whispering and evil-speaking, being justified by our works, and not our words. For [the Scripture] saith, "He that speaketh much, shall also hear much in answer. And does he that is ready in speech deem himself righteous? Blessed is he that is born of woman, who liveth but a short time: be not given to much speaking." Let our praise be in God, and not of ourselves; for God hateth those that commend themselves. Let testimony to our good deeds be borne by others, as it was in the case of our righteous forefathers. Boldness, and arrogance, and audacity belong to those that are accursed of God; but moderation, humility, and meekness to such as are blessed by Him.

CHAPTER 31
Let Us See By What Means We May Obtain The Divine Blessing

Let us cleave then to His blessing, and consider what are the means of possessing it. Let us think over the things which have taken place from the beginning. For what reason was our father Abraham blessed? was it not because he wrought righteousness and truth through faith? Isaac, with perfect confidence, as if knowing what was to happen, cheerfully yielded himself as a sacrifice. Jacob, through reason of his brother, went forth with humility from his own land, and came to Laban and served him; and there was given to him the sceptre of the twelve tribes of Israel.

CHAPTER 32
We Are Justified Not By Our Own Works, But By Faith

Whosoever will candidly consider each particular, will recognise the greatness of the gifts which were given by him. For from him have sprung the priests and all the Levites who minister at the altar of God. From him also [was descended] our Lord Jesus Christ according to the flesh. From him [arose] kings, princes, and rulers of the race of Judah. Nor are his other tribes in small glory, inasmuch as God had promised, "Thy seed shall be as the stars of heaven." All these, therefore, were highly honoured, and made great, not for their own sake, or for their own works, or for the righteousness which they wrought, but through the operation of His will. And we, too, being called by His will in Christ Jesus, are not justified by ourselves, nor by our own wisdom, or understanding, or godliness, or works which we have wrought in holiness of heart; but by that faith through which, from the beginning, Almighty God has justified all men; to whom be glory for ever and ever. Amen.

CHAPTER 33
But Let Us Not Owe Up The Practice Of Good Works And Love. God Himself Is An Example To Us Of Good Works

What shall we do, then, brethren? Shall we become slothful in well-doing, and cease from the practice of love? God forbid that any such course should be followed by us! But rather let us hasten with all energy and readiness of mind to perform every good work. For the Creator and Lord of all Himself rejoices in His works. For by His infinitely great power He established the heavens, and by His incomprehensible wisdom He adorned them. He also divided the earth from the water which surrounds it, and fixed it upon the immoveable foundation of His own will. The animals also which are upon it He commanded by His own word into existence. So likewise, when He had formed the sea, and the living creatures which are in it, He enclosed them [within their proper bounds] by His own power. Above all, with His holy and undefiled hands He formed man, the most excellent [of His creatures], and truly great through the understanding given him--the express likeness of His own image. For thus says God: "Let us make man in Our image, and after Our likeness. So God made man; male and female He created them." Having thus finished all these things, He approved them, and blessed them, and said, "Increase and multiply." We see, then, how all righteous men have been adorned with good works, and how the Lord Himself, adorning Himself with His works, rejoiced. Having therefore such an example, let us without delay accede to His will, and let us work the work of righteousness with our whole strength.

CHAPTER 34
Great Is The Reward Of Good Works With God. Joined Together In Harmony, Let Us Implore That Reward From Him

The good servant receives the bread of his labour with confidence; the lazy and slothful cannot look his employer in the face. It is requisite, therefore, that we be prompt in the practice of well-doing; for of Him are all things.

And thus He forewarns us: "Behold, the Lord [cometh], and His reward is before His face, to render to every man according to his work." He exhorts us, therefore, with our whole heart to attend to this, that we be not lazy or slothful in any good work. Let our boasting and our confidence be in Him. Let us submit ourselves to His will. Let us consider the whole multitude of His angels, how they stand ever ready to minister to His will. For the Scripture saith, "Ten thousand times ten thousand stood around Him, and thousands of thousands ministered unto Him, and cried, Holy, holy, holy, [is] the Lord of Sabaoth; the whole creation is full of His glory." And let us therefore, conscientiously gathering together in harmony, cry to Him earnestly, as with one mouth, that we may be made partakers of His great and glorious promises. For [the Scripture] saith, "Eye hath not seen, nor ear heard, neither have entered into the heart of man, the things which He hath prepared for them that wait for Him."

CHAPTER 35
Immense Is This Reward. How Shall We Obtain It?

How blessed and wonderful, beloved, are the gifts of God! Life in immortality, splendour in righteousness, truth in perfect confidence, faith in assurance, self-control in holiness! And all these fall under the cognizance of our understandings [now]; what then shall those things be which are prepared for such as wait for Him? The Creator and Father of all worlds, the Most Holy, alone knows their amount and their beauty. Let us therefore earnestly strive to be found in the number of those that wait for Him, in order that we may share in His promised gifts. But how, beloved, shall this be done? If our understanding be fixed by faith rewards God; if we earnestly seek the things which are pleasing and acceptable to Him; if we do the things which are in harmony with His blameless will; and if we follow the way of truth, casting away from us all unrighteousness and iniquity, along with all covetousness, strife, evil practices, deceit, whispering, and evil-speaking, all hatred of God, pride and haughtiness, vainglory and ambition. For they that do such things are hateful to God; and not only they that do them, but also those that take pleasure in them that do them. For the Scripture saith, "But to the sinner God said, Wherefore dost thou declare my statutes, and take my covenant into thy mouth, seeing thou hatest instruction, and castest my words behind thee? When thou sawest a thief, thou consentedst with him, and didst make thy portion with adulterers. Thy mouth has abounded with wickedness, and thy tongue contrived deceit. Thou sittest, and speakest against thy brother; thou slanderest thine own mother's son. These things thou hast done, and I kept silence; thou thoughtest, wicked one, that I should be like to thyself. But I will reprove thee, and set thyself before thee. Consider now these things, ye that forget God, lest He tear you in pieces, like a lion, and there be none to deliver. The sacrifice of praise will glorify Me, and a way is there by which I will show him the salvation of God."

CHAPTER 36
All Blessings Are Given To Us Through Christ

This is the way, beloved, in which we find our Saviour, even Jesus Christ, the High Priest of all our offerings, the defender and helper of our infirmity. By Him we look up to the heights of heaven. By Him we behold, as in a glass, His immaculate and most excellent visage. By Him are the eyes of our hearts opened. By Him our foolish and darkened understanding blossoms up anew towards His marvellous light. By Him the Lord has willed that we should taste of immortal knowledge, "who, being the brightness of His majesty, is by so much greater than the angels, as He hath by inheritance obtained a more excellent name than they." For it is thus written, "Who maketh His angels spirits, and His ministers a flame of fire." But concerning His Son the Lord spoke thus: "Thou art my Son, to-day have I begotten Thee. Ask of Me, and I will give Thee the heathen for Thine inheritance, and the uttermost parts of the earth for Thy possession." And again He saith to Him, "Sit Thou at My right hand, until I make Thine enemies Thy footstool." But who are His enemies? All the wicked, and those who set themselves to oppose the will of God.

CHAPTER 37
Christ Is Our Leader, And We His Soldiers

Let us then, men and brethren, with all energy act the part of soldiers, in accordance with His holy commandments. Let us consider those who serve under our generals, with what order, obedience, and submissiveness they perform the things which are commanded them. All are not prefects, nor commanders of a thousand, nor of a hundred, nor of fifty, nor the like, but each one in his own rank performs the things commanded by the king and the generals. The great cannot subsist without the small, nor the small without the great. There is a kind of mixture in all things, and thence arises mutual advantage. Let us take our body for an example. The head is nothing without the feet, and the feet are nothing without the head; yea, the very smallest members of our body are necessary and useful to the whole body.

But all work harmoniously together, and are under one common rule for the preservation of the whole body.

CHAPTER 38
Let The Members Of The Church Submit Themselves, And No One Exalt Himself Above Another

Let our whole body, then, be preserved in, Christ Jesus; and let every one be subject to his neighbour, according to the special gift bestowed upon him. Let the strong not despise the weak, and let the weak show respect unto the strong. Let the rich man provide for the wants of the poor; and let the poor man bless God, because He hath given him one by whom his need may be supplied. Let the wise man display his wisdom, not by [mere] words, but through good deeds. Let the humble not bear testimony to himself, but leave witness to be borne to him by another. Let him that is pure in the flesh not grow proud of it, and boast, knowing that it was another who bestowed on him the gift of continence. Let us consider, then, brethren, of what matter we were made,--who and what manner of beings we came into the world, as it were out of a sepulchre, and from utter darkness. He who made us and fashioned us, having prepared His bountiful gifts for us before we were born, introduced us into His world. Since, therefore, we receive all these things from Him, we ought for everything to give Him thanks; to whom be glory for ever and ever. Amen.

CHAPTER 39
There Is No Reason For Self-Conceit

Foolish and inconsiderate men, who have neither wisdom nor instruction, mock and deride us, being eager to exalt themselves in their own conceits. For what can a mortal man do? or what strength is there in one made out of the dust? For it is written, "There was no shape before mine eyes, only I heard a sound, and a voice [saying], What then? Shall a man be pure before the Lord? or shall such an one be [counted] blameless in his deeds, seeing He does not confide in His servants, and has charged even His angels with perversity? The heaven is not clean in His sight: how much less they that dwell in houses of clay, of which also we ourselves were made! He smote them as a moth; and from morning even until evening they endure not. Because they could furnish no assistance to themselves, they perished. He breathed upon them, and they died, because they had no wisdom. But call now, if any one will answer thee, or if thou wilt look to any of the holy angels; for wrath destroys the foolish man, and envy killeth him that is in error. I have seen the foolish taking root, but their habitation was presently consumed. Let their sons be far from safety; let them be despised before the gates of those less than themselves, and there shall be none to deliver. For what was prepared for them, the righteous shall eat; and they shall not be delivered from evil."

CHAPTER 40
Let Us Preserve In The Church The Order Appointed By God

These things therefore being manifest to us, and since we look into the depths of the divine knowledge, it behoves us to do all things in [their proper] order, which the Lord has commanded us to perform at stated times. He has enjoined offerings [to be presented] and service to be performed [to Him], and that not thoughtlessly or irregularly, but at the appointed times and hours. Where and by whom He desires these things to be done, He Himself has fixed by His own supreme will, in order that all things being piously done according to His good pleasure, may be acceptable unto Him. Those, therefore, who present their offerings at the appointed times, are accepted and blessed; for inasmuch as they follow the laws of the Lord, they sin not. For his own peculiar services are assigned to the high priest, and their own proper place is prescribed to the priests, and their own special ministrations devolve on the Levites. The layman is bound by the laws that pertain to laymen.

CHAPTER 41
Continuation Of The Same Subject

Let every one of you, brethren, give thanks to God in his own order, living in all good conscience, with becoming gravity, and not going beyond the rule of the ministry prescribed to him. Not in every place, brethren, are the daily sacrifices offered, or the peace-offerings, or the sin-offerings and the trespass-offerings, but in Jerusalem only. And even there they are not offered in any place, but only at the altar before the temple, that which is offered being first carefully examined by the high priest and the ministers already mentioned. Those, therefore, who do anything beyond that which is agreeable to His will, are punished with death. Ye see, brethren, that the greater the knowledge that has been vouchsafed to us, the greater also is the danger to which we are exposed.

CHAPTER 42
The Order Of Ministers In The Church

The apostles have preached the Gospel to us from the Lord Jesus Christ; Jesus Christ [has done so from God. Christ therefore was sent forth by God, and the apostles by Christ. Both these appointments, then, were made in an orderly way, according to the will of God. Having therefore received their orders, and being fully assured by the resurrection of our Lord Jesus Christ, and established in the word of God, with full assurance of the Holy Ghost, they went forth proclaiming that the kingdom of God was at hand. And thus preaching through countries and cities, they appointed the first-fruits [of their labours], having first proved them by the Spirit, to be bishops and deacons of those who should afterwards believe. Nor was this any new thing, since indeed many ages before it was written concerning bishops and deacons. For thus saith the Scripture a certain place, "I will appoint their bishops in righteousness, and their deacons in faith."

CHAPTER 43
Moses Of Old Stilled The Contention Which Arose Concerning The Priestly Dignity

And what wonder is it if those in Christ who were entrusted with such a duty by God, appointed those [ministers] before mentioned, when the blessed Moses also, "a faithful servant in all his house," noted down in the sacred books all the injunctions which were given him, and when the other prophets also followed him, bearing witness with one consent to the ordinances which he had appointed? For, when rivalry arose concerning the priesthood, and the tribes were contending among themselves as to which of them should be adorned with that glorious title, he commanded the twelve princes of the tribes to bring him their rods, each one being inscribed with the name of the tribe. And he took them and bound them [together], and sealed them with the rings of the princes of the tribes, and laid them up in the tabernacle of witness on the table of God. And having shut the doors of the tabernacle, he sealed the keys, as he had done the rods, and said to them, Men and brethren, the tribe whose rod shall blossom has God chosen to fulfil the office of the priesthood, and to minister unto Him. And when the morning was come, he assembled all Israel, six hundred thousand men, and showed the seals to the princes of the tribes, and opened the tabernacle of witness, and brought forth the rods. And the rod of Aaron was found not only to have blossomed, but to bear fruit upon it. What think ye, beloved? Did not Moses know beforehand that this would happen? Undoubtedly he knew; but he acted thus, that there might be no sedition in Israel, and that the name of the true and only God might be glorified; to whom be glory for ever and ever. Amen.

CHAPTER 44
The Ordinances Of The Apostles, That There Might Be No Contention Respecting The Priestly Office

Our apostles also knew, through our Lord Jesus Christ, and there would be strife on account of the office of the episcopate. For this reason, therefore, inasmuch as they had obtained a perfect fore-knowledge of this, they appointed those [ministers] already mentioned, and afterwards gave instructions, that when these should fall asleep, other approved men should succeed them in their ministry. We are of opinion, therefore, that those appointed by them, or afterwards by other eminent men, with the consent of the whole Church, and who have blame-lessly served the flock of Christ in a humble, peaceable, and disinterested spirit, and have for a long time possessed the good opinion of all, cannot be justly dismissed from the ministry. For our sin will not be small, if we eject from the episcopate those who have blamelessly and holily fulfilled its duties. Blessed are those presbyters who, having finished their course before now, have obtained a fruitful and perfect departure [from this world]; for they have no fear lest any one deprive them of the place now appointed them. But we see that ye have removed some men of excellent behaviour from the ministry, which they fulfilled blamelessly and with honour.

CHAPTER 45
It Is The Part Of The Wicked To Vex The Righteous

Ye are fond of contention, brethren, and full of zeal about things which do not pertain to salvation. Look carefully into the Scriptures, which are the true utterances of the Holy Spirit. Observe that nothing of an unjust or counterfeit character is written in them. There you will not find that the righteous were cast off by men who themselves were holy. The righteous were indeed persecuted, but only by the wicked. They were cast into prison, but only by the unholy; they were stoned, but only by transgressors; they were slain, but only by the accursed, and such as had conceived an unrighteous envy against them. Exposed to such sufferings, they endured them gloriously. For what shall we say, brethren? Was Daniel s cast into the den of lions by such as feared God? Were Ananias, and Azarias, and Mishael shut up in a furnace of fire by those who observed the great and glorious worship of the Most High? Far from us be such a thought! Who, then, were they that did such things? The hateful, and those full of all wickedness, were roused to such a pitch of fury, that they inflicted torture on those who served God with a holy and blameless purpose [of heart], not knowing that the Most High is the Defender and Protector of all such as with a pure conscience venerate" His all-excellent name; to whom be glory for ever and ever. Amen. But they who with confidence endured [these things] are now heirs of glory and honour, and have been exalted and made illustrious by God in their memorial for ever and ever. Amen.

CHAPTER 46
Let Us Cleave To The Righteous: Your Strife Is Pernicious

Such examples, therefore, brethren, it is right that we should follow; since it is written, "Cleave to the holy, for those that cleave to them shall [themselves] be made holy." And again, in another place, [the Scripture] saith, "With a harmless man thou shalt prove thyself harmless, and with an elect man thou shalt be elect, and with a perverse man thou shalt show thyself perverse." Let us cleave, therefore, to the innocent and righteous, since these are the elect of God. Why are there strifes, and tumults, and divisions, and schisms, and wars among you? Have we not [all] one God and one Christ? Is there not one Spirit of grace poured out upon us? And have we not one calling in Christ? Why do we divide and tear to pieces the members of Christ, and raise up strife against our own body, and have reached such a height of madness as to forget that "we are members one of another?" Remember the words of our Lord Jesus Christ, how He said, "Woe to that man [by whom offences come]! It were better for him that he had never been born, than that he should cast a stumbling-block before one of my elect. Yea, it were better for him that a millstone should be hung about [his neck], and he should be sunk in the depths of the sea, than that he should cast a stumbling-block before one of my little ones. Your schism has subverted [the faith of] many, has discouraged many, has given rise to doubt in many, and has caused grief to us all. And still your sedition continueth.

CHAPTER 47
Your Recent Discord Is Worse Than The Former Which Took Place In The Times Of Paul

Take up the epistle of the blessed Apostle Paul. What did he write to you at the time when the Gospel first began to be preached? Truly, under the inspiration of the Spirit, he wrote to you concerning himself, and Cephas, and Apollos, because even then parties had been formed among you. But that inclination for one above another entailed less guilt upon you, inasmuch as your partialities were then shown towards apostles, already of high reputation, and towards a man whom they had approved. But now reflect who those are that have perverted you, and lessened the renown of your far-famed brotherly love. It is disgraceful, beloved, yea, highly disgraceful, and unworthy of your Christian profession, that such a thing should be heard of as that the most stedfast and ancient Church of the Corinthians should, on account of one or two persons, engage in sedition against its presbyters. And this rumour has reached not only us, but those also who are unconnected with us; so that, through your infatuation, the name of the Lord is blasphemed, while danger is also brought upon yourselves.

CHAPTER 48
Let us Return To The Practice Of Brotherly Love

Let us therefore, with all haste, put an end s to this [state of things]; and let us fall down before the Lord, and beseech Him with tears, that He would mercifully be reconciled to us, and restore us to our former seemly and holy practice of brotherly love. For [such conduct] is the gate of righteousness, which is set open for the attainment of life, as it is written, "Open to me the gates of righteousness; I will go in by them, and will praise the Lord: this is the gate of the Lord: the righteous shall enter in by it." Although, therefore, many gates have been set open, yet this gate of righteousness is that gate in Christ by which blessed are all they that have entered in and have directed their way in holiness and righteousness, doing all things without disorder. Let a man be faithful: let him be powerful in the utterance of knowledge; let him be wise in judging of words; let him be pure in all his deeds; yet the more he seems to be superior to others [in these respects], the more humble-minded ought he to be, and to seek the common good of all, and not merely his own advantage.

CHAPTER 49
The Praise Of Love

Let him who has love in Christ keep the commandments of Christ. Who can describe the [blessed] bond of the love of God? What man is able to tell the excellence of its beauty, as it ought to be told? The height to which love exalts is unspeakable. Love unites us to God. Love covers a multitude of sins.

Love beareth all things, is long-suffering in all things. There is nothing base, nothing arrogant in love. Love admits of no schisms: love gives rise to no seditions: love does all things in harmony. By love have all the elect of God been made perfect; without love nothing is well-pleasing to God. In love has the Lord taken us to Himself. On account of the Love he bore us, Jesus Christ our Lord gave His blood for us by the will of God; His flesh for our flesh, and His soul for our souls.

CHAPTER 50
Let us Pray To Be Thought Worthy Of Love

Ye see, beloved, how great and wonderful a thing is love, and that there is no declaring its perfection. Who is fit to be found in it, except such as God has vouchsafed to render so? Let us pray, therefore, and implore of His mercy, that we may live blameless in love, free from all human partialities for one above another. All the generations from Adam even unto this day have passed away; but those who, through the grace of God, have been made perfect in love, now possess a place among the godly, and shall be made manifest at the revelation of the kingdom of Christ. For it is written, "Enter into thy secret chambers for a little time, until my wrath and fury pass away; and I will remember a propitious day, and will raise you up out of your graves." Blessed are we, beloved, if we keep the commandments of God in the harmony of love; that so through love our sins may be forgiven us. For it is written, "Blessed are they whose transgressions are forgiven, and whose sins are covered. Blessed is the man whose sin the Lord will not impute to him, and in whose mouth there is no guile." This blessedness cometh upon those who have been chosen by God through Jesus Christ our Lord; to whom be glory for ever and ever. Amen.

CHAPTER 51
Let The Partakers In Strife Acknowledge Their Sins

Let us therefore implore forgiveness for all those transgressions which through any [suggestion] of the adversary we have committed. And those who have been the leaders of sedition and disagreement ought to have respect to the common hope. For such as live in fear and love would rather that they themselves than their neighbours should be involved in suffering. And they prefer to bear blame themselves, rather than that the concord which has been well and piously handed down to us should suffer. For it is better that a man should acknowledge his transgressions than that he should harden his heart, as the hearts of those were hardened who stirred up sedition against Moses the servant of God, and whose condemnation was made manifest [unto all]. For they went down alive into Hades, and death swallowed them up. Pharaoh with his army and all the princes of Egypt, and the chariots with their riders, were sunk in the depths of the Red Sea, and perished, for no other reason than that their foolish hearts were hardened, after so many signs and wonders had been wrought in the land of Egypt by Moses the servant of God.

CHAPTER 52
Such A Confession Is Pleasing To God

The Lord, brethren, stands in need of nothing; and He desires nothing of any one, except that confession be made to Him. For, says the elect David, "I will confess unto the Lord ; and that will please Him more than a young bullock that hath horns and hoofs. Let the poor see it, and be glad." And again he saith, "Offer unto God the sacrifice of praise, and pay thy vows unto the Most High. And call upon Me in the day of thy trouble: I will deliver thee, and thou shalt glorify Me." For "the sacrifice of God is a broken spirit."

CHAPTER 53
The Love Of Moses Towards His People

Ye understand, beloved, ye understand well the Sacred Scriptures, and ye have looked very earnestly into the oracles of God. Call then these things to your remembrance. When Moses went up into the mount, and abode there, with fasting and humiliation, forty days and forty nights, the Lord said unto him, "Moses, Moses, get thee down quickly from hence; for thy people whom thou didst bring out of the land of Egypt have committed iniquity. They have speedily departed from the way in which I commanded them to walk, and have made to themselves molten images." And the Lord said unto him, "I have spoken to thee once and again, saying, I have seen this people, and, behold, it is a stiff-necked people: let Me destroy them, and blot out their name from under heaven; and I will make thee a great and wonderful nation, and one much more numerous than this." But Moses said, "Far be it from Thee, Lord: pardon the sin of this people; else blot me also out of the book of the living." O marvellous love! O insuperable perfection! The servant speaks freely to his Lord, and asks forgiveness for the people, or begs that he himself might perish along with them.

CHAPTER 54
He Who Is Full Of Love Will Incur Every Loss, That Peace May Be Restored To The Church

Who then among you is noble-minded? who compassionate? who full of love? Let him declare, "If on my account sedition and disagreement and schisms have arisen, I will depart, I will go away whithersoever ye desire, and I will do whatever the majorit) commands; only let the flock of Christ live on terms of peace with the presbyters set over it." He that acts thus shall procure to himself great glory in the Lord; and every place will welcome him. For "the earth is the Lord's, and the fulness thereof." These things they who live a godly life, that is never to be repented of, both have done and always will do.

CHAPTER 55
Examples Of Such Love

To bring forward some examples from among the heathen: Many kings and princes, in times of pestilence, when they had been instructed by an oracle, have given themselves up to death, in order that by their own blood they might deliver their fellow-citizens [from destruction]. Many have gone forth from their own cities, that so sedition might be brought to an end within them. We know many among ourselves who have given themselves up to bonds, in order that they might ransom others. Many, too, have surrendered themselves to slavery, that with the price which they received for themselves, they might provide food for others. Many women also, being strengthened by the grace of God, have performed numerous manly exploits. The blessed Judith, when her city was besieged, asked of the elders permission to go forth into the camp of the strangers; and, exposing herself to danger, she went out for the love which she bare to her country and people then besieged; and the Lord delivered Holofernes into the hands of a woman. Esther also, being perfect in faith, exposed herself to no less danger, in order to deliver the twelve tribes of Israel from impending destruction. For with fasting and humiliation she entreated the everlasting God, who seeth all things; and He, perceiving the humility of her spirit, delivered the people for whose sake she had encountered peril.

CHAPTER 56
Let Us Admonish And Correct One Another

Let us then also pray for those who have fallen into any sin, that meekness and humility may be given to them, so that they may submit, not unto us, but to the will of God. For in this way they shall secure a fruitful and perfect remembrance from us, with sympathy for them, both in our prayers to God, and our mention of them to the saints. Let us receive correction, beloved, on account of which no one should feel displeased. Those exhortations by which we admonish one another are both good [in themselves] and highly profitable, for they tend to unite us to the will of God. For thus saith the holy Word: "The Lord hath severely chastened me, yet hath not given me over to death." "For whom the Lord loveth He chasteneth, and scourgeth every son whom He receiveth." "The righteous," saith it, "shall chasten me in mercy, and reprove me; but let not the oil of sinners make fat my head." And again he saith, "Blessed is the man whom the Lord reproveth, and reject not thou the warning of the Almighty. For He causes sorrow, and again restores [to gladness]; He woundeth, and His hands make whole. He shall deliver thee in six troubles, yea, in the seventh no evil shall touch thee. In famine He shall rescue thee from death, and in war He shall free thee from the power of the sword. From the scourge of the tongue will He hide thee, and thou shalt not fear when evil cometh. Thou shalt hugh at the unrighteous and the wicked, and shalt not be afraid of the beasts of the field. For the wild beasts shall be at peace with thee: then shalt thou know that thy house shall be in peace, and the habitation of thy tabernacle shall not fail? Thou shall know also that thy seed shall be great, and thy children like the grass of the field. And thou shall come to the grave like ripened corn which is reaped in its season, or like a heap of the threshing-floor which is gathered together at the proper time." Ye see, beloved, that protection is afforded to those that are chastened of the Lord; for since God is good, He corrects us, that we may be admonished by His holy chastisement.

CHAPTER 57
Let The Authors Of Sedition Submit Themselves

Ye therefore, who laid the foundation of this sedition, submit yourselves to the presbyters, and receive correction so as to repent, bending the knees of your hearts. Learn to be subject, laying aside the proud and arrogant self-confidence of your tongue. For it is better for you that ye should occupy a humble but honourable place in the flock of Christ, than that, being highly exalted, ye should be cast out from the hope of His people. For thus speaketh all-virtuous Wisdom: "Behold, I will bring forth to you the words of My Spirit, and I will teach you My speech. Since I called, and ye did not hear; I held forth My words, and ye regarded not, but set at naught My counsels, and yielded not at My reproofs; therefore I too will laugh at your destruction; yea, I will rejoice when ruin cometh upon you, and when sudden confusion overtakes you, when overturning presents itself like a tempest, or when tribulation and oppression fall upon you. For it shall come to pass, that when ye call upon Me, I will not hear you; the wicked shall seek Me, and they shall not find Me. For they hated wisdom, and did not choose the fear of the Lord; nor would they listen to My counsels, but despised My reproofs. Wherefore they shall eat the fruits of their own way, and they shall be filled with their own ungodliness."

CHAPTER 58
Blessings Sought For All That Call Upon God

May God, who seeth all things, and who is the Ruler of all spirits and the Lord of all flesh--who chose our Lord Jesus Christ and us through Him to be a peculiar people--grant to every soul that calleth upon His glorious and holy Name, faith, fear, peace, patience, long-suffering, self-control, purity, and sobriety, to the well-pleasing of His Name, through our High Priest and Protector, Jesus Christ, by whom be to Him glory, and majesty, and power, and honour, both now and for evermore. Amen.

CHAPTER 59
Exhortation To Speedily Send Back Word That Peace Has Been Restored. The Benediction

Send back speedily to us in peace and with joy these our messengers to you: Claudius Ephebus and Valerius Bito, with Fortunatus: that they may the sooner announce to us the peace and harmony we so earnestly desire and long for [among you], and that we may the more quickly rejoice over the good order re-established among you. The grace of our Lord Jesus Christ be with you, and with all everywhere that are the called of God through Him, by whom be to Him glory, honour, power, majesty, and eternal dominion, from everlasting to everlasting. Amen.

The first Gospel of the Infancy of Jesus Christ

CHAPTER I

he following accounts we found in the book of Joseph the high-priest, called by some Caiaphas:

2. He relates, that Jesus spake even when he was in the cradle, and said to his mother:

3. Mary, I am Jesus the Son of God, that word which thou didst bring forth according to the declaration of the angel Gabriel to thee, and my father hath sent me for the salvation of the world.

4. In the three hundred and ninth year of the era of Alexander, Augustus published a decree that all persons should go to be taxed in their own country.

5. Joseph therefore arose, and with Mary his spouse he went to Jerusalem, and then came to Bethlehem, that he and his family might be taxed in the city of his fathers.

6. And when they came by the cave, Mary confessed to Joseph that her time of bringing forth was come, and she could not go on to the city, and said, Let us go into this cave.

7. At that time the sun was very near going down.

8. But Joseph hastened away, that he might fetch her a mid-wife; and when he saw an old Hebrew woman who was of Jerusalem, he said to her, Pray come hither, good woman, and go into that cave, and you will there see a woman just ready to bring forth.

9. It was after sunset, when the old woman and Joseph with her reached the cave, and they both went into it.

10. And behold, it was all filled with lights, greater than the light of lamps

and candles, an, greater than the light of the sun itself.

11. The infant was then wrapped up in swaddling clothes, an sucking the breasts of his mother St. Mary.

12. When they both saw this light, they were surprised; the old woman asked St. Mary, Art thou the mother of this child ?

13. St. Mary replied, She was.

14. On which the old woman said, Thou art very different from all other women.

15. St. Mary answered, As there is not any child like to my son, so neither is there any woman like to his mother.

16. The old woman answered and said, O my Lady, I am come hither that I may obtain an everlasting reward.

17. Then our Lady, St. Mary said to her, Lay thine hand upon the infant; which, when she had done, she became whole

18. And as she was going forth, she said, From henceforth, all the days of my life, I will attend upon and be a servant of this infant.

19. After this, when the shepherds came, and had made a fire and they were exceedingly rejoicing, the heavenly host appeared to them, praising and adoring the supreme God.

20. And as the shepherds we engaged in the same employment, the cave at that time seemed like a glorious temple, because both the tongues of angels and men united to adore and magnify God, on account of the birth of the Lord Christ.

21. But when the old Hebrew woman saw all these evident miracles, she gave praises to God, and said, I thank thee, O God, thou God of Israel, for that mine eyes have seen the birth of the Saviour of the world.

II

1. And when the time of his circumcision was come, namely, the eighth day, on which the law commanded the child to be circumcised, they circumcised him in the cave.

2. And the old Hebrew woman took the foreskin (others say she took the navel-string), and preserved it in an alabaster-box of old oil of spikenard.

3. And she had a son who was a druggist, to whom she said, Take heed thou sell not this alabaster box of spikenard-ointment, although thou shouldst be, offered three hundred pence for it.

4. Now this is that alabaster box which Mary the sinner procured, and poured forth the ointment out of it upon the head and the feet of our Lord Jesus Christ, and wiped it off with the hairs of her head.

5. Then after ten days they brought him to Jerusalem, and on the fortieth day from his birth they presented him in the temple before the Lord, making the proper offerings for him, according to the requirement of the law of Moses: namely, that every male which opens the womb shall be called holy unto God.

6. At that time old Simeon saw him shining as a pillar of light, when St. Mary the Virgin, his mother, carried him in her arms, and was filled with the greatest pleasure at the sight.

7. And the angels stood around him, adoring him, as a king's guards stand around him.

8. Then Simeon going near to St. Mary, and stretching forth his hands towards her, said to the Lord Christ, Now, O my a Lord, thy servant shall depart in peace, according to thy word;

9. For mine eyes have seen thy mercy, which thou hast prepared for the salvation of all nations; a light to all people, and the glory of thy people Israel.

10. Hannah the prophetess was also present, and drawing near, she gave praises to God, and celebrated the happiness of Mary.

III

1. And it came to pass, when the Lord Jesus was born at Bethlehem, a city of Judea in the time of Herod the King; the wise men came from the East to Jerusalem, according to the prophecy of Zoradascht(Zoroaster), and brought with them offerings: namely, gold, frankincense, and myrrh, and worshipped him, and offered to him their gifts.

2. Then the Lady Mary took one of his swaddling clothes in which the infant was wrapped and gave it to them instead of a blessing, which they received from her as a most noble present.

3. And at the same time there appeared to them an angel in the form of that star which had before been their guide in their journey; the light of which they followed till they returned into their own country.

4. On their return their kings and princes came to them inquiring, What they had seen and done? What sort of journey and return they had? What company they had on the road?

5. But they produced the swaddling cloth which St. Mary had given to them, on account whereof they kept a feast.

6. And having, according to the custom of their country, made a fire, they worshipped it.

7. And casting the swaddling cloth into it, the fire took it, and kept it.

8. And when the fire was put out, they took forth the swaddling cloth

unhurt, as much as if the fire had not touched it.

9. Then they began to kiss it, and put it upon their heads and their eyes, saying, This is certainly an undoubted truth, and it is really surprising that the fire could not burn it, and consume it.

10. Then they took it, and with the greatest respect laid it up among their treasures.

IV

1. Now Herod, perceiving that the wise men did delay, and not return to him, called together the priests and wise men and said, Tell me in what place the Christ should be born?

2. And when they replied, in Bethlehem, a city of Judea, he began to contrive in his own mind the death of the Lord Jesus Christ.

3. But an angel of the Lord appeared to Joseph in his sleep and said, Arise, take the child and his mother, and go into Egypt as soon as the cock crows. So he arose, and went.

4. And as he was considering with himself about his journey, the morning came upon him.

5. In the length of the journey the girts of the saddle broke.

6. And now he drew near a great city, in which there was an idol, to which the other idol and gods of Egypt brought their offerings and vows.

7. And there was by this idol a priest ministering to it, who as often as Satan spoke out of that idol, related the things he said to the inhabitants of Egypt and those countries.

8. This priest had a son three years old, who was possessed with a great multitude of devil who uttered many strange things and when the devils seized him walked about naked with his clothes torn, throwing stones at those whom he saw.

9. Near to that idol was the inn of the city, into which when Joseph and St. Mary were come, and had turned into that inn, all the inhabitants of the city were astonished.

10. And all the magistrates and priests of the idols assembled before that idol, and made inquiry there, saying, What means all this consternation, and dread, which has fallen upon our country?

11. The idol answered them, The unknown God is come hither, who is truly God; nor is there any one besides him, who is worthy of divine worship; for he is truly the Son of God.

12. At the fame of him this country trembled, and at his coming it is under the present commotion and consternation; and we ourselves are affrighted

by the greatness of his power.

13. And at the same instant this idol fell down, and at his fall all the inhabitants of Egypt, besides others, ran together.

14. But the son of the priest, when his usual disorder came upon him, going into the inn, found there Joseph and St. Mary, whom all the rest had left behind and forsook.

15. And when the Lady St. Mary had washed the swaddling clothes of the Lord Christ, and hanged them out to dry upon a post, the boy possessed with the devil took down one of them, and put it upon his head.

16. And presently the devils began to come out of his mouth, and fly away in the shape of crows and serpents.

17. From that time the boy was healed by the power of the Lord Christ, and he began to sing praises, and give thanks to the Lord who had healed him.

18. When his father saw him restored to his former state of health, he said, My son, what has happened to thee, and by what means wert thou cured ?

19. The son answered, When the devils seized me, I went into the inn, and there found a very handsome woman with a boy, whose swaddling clothes she had just before washed, and hanged out upon a post.

20. One of these I took, and put it upon my head, and immediately the devils left me, and fled away.

21. At this the father exceedingly rejoiced, and said, My son, perhaps this boy is the son of the living God, who made the heavens and the earth.

22. For as soon as he came amongst us, the idol was broken and all the gods fell down, and were destroyed by a greater power.

23. Then was fulfilled the prophecy which saith, Out of Egypt I have called my son.

V

1. Now Joseph and Mary, when they heard that the idol was fallen down and destroyed were seized with fear and trembling, and said, When we were in the land of Israel, Herod, intending to kill Jesus, slew for that purpose all the infants at Bethlehem, and that neighbourhood.

2. And there is no doubt but the Egyptians if they come to hear that this idol is broken and fallen down, will burn us with fire.

3. They went therefore hence to the secret places of robbers, who robbed travellers as they pass by, of their carriages and their clothes, and carried them away bound.

4. These thieves upon their coming heard a great noise, such as the noise

of a king with a great army and many horses, and the trumpets sounding at his departure from his own city at which they were so affrighted as to leave all their booty behind them, and fly away in haste.

5. Upon this the prisoners arose, and loosed each other's bonds, and taking each man his bags, they went away, and saw Joseph and Mary coming towards them, and inquired, Where is that king, the noise of whose approach the robbers heard, and left us, so that we are now come off safe ?

6. Joseph answered, He will come after us.

VI

1. Then they went into another city where there was a woman possessed with a devil, and in whom Satan, that cursed rebel, had taken up his abode.

2. One night, when she went to fetch water, she could neither endure her clothes on, nor to be in any house; but as often as they tied her with chains or cords, she brake them, and went out into desert places, and sometimes standing where roads crossed, and in churchyards, would throw stones at men.

3. When St. Mary saw this woman, she pitied her; whereupon Satan presently left her, and fled away in the form of a young man, saying, Wo to me, because of thee, Mary, and thy son.

4. So the woman was delivered from her torment; but considering herself naked, she blushed, and avoided seeing any man, and having put on her clothes, went home, and gave an account of her case to her father and relations, who, as they were the best of the city, entertained St. Mary and Joseph with the greatest respect.

5. The next morning having received a sufficient supply of provisions for the road, they went from them, and about the evening of the day arrived at another town, where a marriage was then about to be solemnized; but by the arts of Satan and the practices of some sorcerers, the bride was become so dumb, that she could not so much as open her mouth.

6. But when this dumb bride saw the Lady St. Mary entering into the town, and carrying the Lord Christ in her arms, she stretched out her hands to the Lord Christ, and took him in her arms, and closely hugging him, very often kissed him, continually moving him and pressing him to her body.

7. Straightway the string of her tongue was loosed, and her ears were opened, and she began to sing praises unto God, who had restored her.

8. So there was great joy among the inhabitants of the town that night, who thought that God and his angels were come down among them.

9. In this place they abode three days, meeting with the greatest respect and most splendid entertainment.

10. And being then furnished by the people with provisions for the road, they departed and went to another city, in which they were inclined to lodge, because it was a famous place.

11. There was in this city a gentlewoman, who, as she went down one day to the river to bathe, behold cursed Satan leaped upon her in the form of a serpent.

12. And folded himself about her belly, and every night lay upon her.

13. This woman seeing the Lady St. Mary, and the Lord Christ the infant in her bosom, asked the Lady St. Mary, that she would give her the child to kiss, and carry in her arms.

14. When she had consented, and as soon as the woman had moved the child, Satan left her, and fled away, nor did the woman ever afterwards see him.

15. Hereupon all the neighbours praised the Supreme God, and the woman rewarded them with ample beneficence.

16. On the morrow the same woman brought perfumed water to wash the Lord Jesus; and when she had washed him, she preserved the water.

17. And there was a girl there, whose body was white with a leprosy, who being sprinkled with this water, and washed, was instantly cleansed from her leprosy.

18. The people therefore said Without doubt Joseph and Mary, and that boy are Gods, for they do not look like mortals.

19. And when they were making ready to go away, the girl, who had been troubled with the leprosy, came and desired they would permit her to go along with them; so they consented, and the girl went with them till they came to a city, in which was the palace of a great king, and whose house was not far from the inn.

20. Here they staid, and when the girl went one day to the prince's wife, and found her in a sorrowful and mournful condition, she asked her the reason of her tears.

21. She replied, Wonder not at my groans, for I am under a great misfortune, of which I dare not tell any one.

22. But, says the girl, if you will entrust me with your private grievance, perhaps I may find you a remedy for it.

23. Thou, therefore, says the prince's wife, shalt keep the secret, and not discover it to any one alive!

24. I have been married to this prince, who rules as king over large dominions, and lived long with him, before he had any child by me. At length I conceived by him, but alas! I brought forth a leprous son; which, when he saw, he would not own to be his, but said to me,

25. Either do thou kill him, or send him to some nurse in such a place, that he may be never heard of; and now take care of yourself; I will never see you more.

26. So here I pine, lamenting my wretched and miserable circumstances. Alas, my son! alas, my husband! Have I disclosed it to you?

27. The girl replied, I have found a remedy for your disease, which I promise you, for I also was leprous, but God hath cleansed me, even he who is called Jesus, the son of the Lady Mary.

28. The woman inquiring where that God was, whom she spake of, the girl answered He lodges with you here in the same house.

29. But how can this be? says she; where is he? Behold, replied the girl, Joseph and Mary; and the infant who is with them is called Jesus: and it is he who delivered me from my disease and torment.

30. But by what means, says she, were you cleansed from your leprosy? Will you not tell me that?

31. Why not? says the girl; I took the water with which his body had been washed, and poured it upon me, and my leprosy vanished.

32. The prince's wife then arose and entertained them, providing a great feast for Joseph among a large company of men.

33. And the next day took perfumed water to wash the Lord Jesus, and afterwards poured the same water upon her son, whom she had brought with her, and her son was instantly cleansed from his leprosy.

34. Then she sang thanks and praises unto God, and said, Blessed is the mother that bare thee, O Jesus!

35. Dost thou thus cure men of the same nature with thyself; with the water with which thy body is washed?

36. She then offered very large gifts to the Lady Mary, and sent her away with all imaginable respect.

VII

1. They came afterwards to another city, and had a mind to lodge there.

2. Accordingly they went to a man's house, who was newly married, but by the influence of sorcerers could not enjoy his wife:

3. But they lodging at his house that night, the man was freed of his disorder:

4. And when they were preparing early in the morning to go forward on their journey, the new married person hindered them, and provided a noble entertainment for them.

5. But going forward on the morrow, they came to another city, and saw

three women going from a certain grave with great weeping.

6. When St. Mary saw them she spake to the girl who was their companion, saying, Go and inquire of them, what is the matter with them, and what misfortune has befallen them?

7. When the girl asked them they made her no answer, but asked her again, Who are ye and where are ye going? For the day is far spent, and the night is at hand.

8. We are travellers, saith the girl, and are seeking for an inn to lodge at.

9. They replied, Go along with us, and lodge with us.

10. They then followed them and were introduced into a new house, well furnished with all sorts of furniture.

11. It was now winter-time and the girl went into the parlour where these women were and found them weeping and lamenting, as before.

12. By them stood a mule covered over with silk, and an ebony collar hanging down from his neck, whom they kissed, and were feeding.

13. But when the girl said, How handsome, ladies, that mule is! they replied with tears, and said, This mule, which you see, was our brother, born of this same mother as we:

14. For when our father died, and left us a very large estate, and we had only this brother, and we endeavoured to procure him a suitable match, and thought he should be married as other men, some giddy and jealous woman bewitched him without our knowledge.

15. And we, one night, a little before day, while the doors of the house were all fast shut, saw this our brother was changed into a mule, such as you now see him to be:

16. And we, in the melancholy condition in which you see us, having no father to comfort us, have applied to all the wise men, magicians, and diviners in the world, but they have been of no service to us.

17. As often therefore as we find ourselves oppressed with grief, we rise and go with this our mother to our father's tomb, where, when we have cried sufficiently we return home.

18. When the girl had heard this, she said, Take courage, and cease your fears, for you have a remedy for your afflictions near at hand, even among you and in the midst of your house,

19. For I was also leprous but when I saw this woman, and this little infant with her, whose name is Jesus, I sprinkled my body with the water with which his mother had washed him, and I was presently made well.

20. And I am certain that he is also capable of relieving you under your distress. Wherefore, arise, go to my mistress, Mary, and when you have brought her into your own parlour, disclose to her the secret, at the same

time, earnestly beseeching her to compassionate your case.

21. As soon as the women had heard the girl's discourse, they hastened away to the Lady St. Mary, introduced themselves to her, and sitting down before her, they wept.

22. And said, O our Lady St. Mary, pity your handmaids, for we have no head of our family no one older than us; no father, or brother to go in and out before us.

23. But this mule, which you see, was our brother, which some woman by witchcraft have brought into this condition which you see: we therefore entreat you to compassionate us.

24. Hereupon St. Mary was grieved at their case, and taking the Lord Jesus, put him upon the back of the mule.

25. And said to her son, O Jesus Christ, restore (or heal) according to thy extraordinary power this mule, and grant him to have again the shape of a man and a rational creature, as he had formerly.

26. This was scarce said by the Lady St. Mary, but the mule immediately passed into a human form, and became a young man without any deformity.

27. Then he and his mother and the sisters worshipped the Lady St. Mary, and lifting the child upon their heads, they kissed him, and said, Blessed is thy mother, O Jesus, O Saviour of the world! Blessed are the eyes which are so happy as to see thee.

28. Then both the sisters told their mother, saying, Of a truth our brother is restored to his former shape by the help of the Lord Jesus Christ, and the kindness of that girl, who told us of Mary and her son.

29. And inasmuch as our brother is unmarried, it is fit that we marry him to this girl their servant.

30. When they had consulted Mary in this matter, and she had given her consent, they made a splendid wedding for this girl.

31. And so their sorrow being turned into gladness, and their mourning into mirth, they began to rejoice. and to make merry, and sing, being dressed in their richest attire, with bracelets.

32. Afterwards they glorified and praised God, saying, O Jesus son of David who changest sorrow into gladness, and mourning into mirth!

33. After this Joseph and Mary tarried there ten days, then went away, having received great respect from those people

34. Who, when they took their leave of them, and returned home, cried,

35. But especially the girl.

VIII

1. In their journey from hence they came into a desert country, and were told it was infested with robbers; so Joseph and St. Mary prepared to pass through it in the night.

2. And as they were going along, behold they saw two robbers asleep in the road, and with them a great number of robbers, who were their confederates, also asleep.

3. The names of these two were Titus and Dumachus; and Titus said to Dumachus, I beseech thee let those persons go along quietly, that our company may not perceive anything of them:

4. But Dumachus refusing, Titus again said, I will give thee forty groats, and as a pledge take my girdle, which he gave him before he had done speaking, that he might not open his mouth, or make a noise.

5. When the Lady St. Mary saw the kindness which this robber did shew them, she said to him, The Lord God will receive thee to his right hand, and grant thee pardon of thy sins.

6. Then the Lord Jesus answered, and said to his mother, When thirty years are expired, O mother, the Jews will crucify me at Jerusalem;

7. And these two thieves shall be with me at the same time upon the cross, Titus on my right hand, and Dumachus on my left, and from that time Titus shall go before me into paradise:

8. And when she had said, God forbid this should be thy lot, O my son, they went on to a city in which were several idols which, as soon as they came near to it, was turned into hills of sand.

9. Hence they went to that sycamore tree, which is now called Matarea;

10. And in Matarea the Lord Jesus caused a well to spring forth, in which St. Mary washed his coat;

11. And a balsam is produced, or grows, in that country from the sweat which ran down there from the Lord Jesus.

12. Thence they proceeded to Memphis, and saw Pharaoh, and abode three years in Egypt.

13. And the Lord Jesus did very many miracles in Egypt, which are neither to be found in the Gospel of the Infancy nor in the Gospel of Perfection.

14. At the end of three years he returned out of Egypt, and when he came near to Judea, Joseph was afraid to enter;

15. For hearing that Herod was dead, and that Archelaus his son reigned in his stead, he was afraid;

16. And when he went to Judea, an angel of God appeared to him, and said, O Joseph, go into the city Nazareth, and abide there.

17. It is strange indeed that he who is the Lord of all countries, should be thus carried backward and forward through so many countries.

IX

1. When they came afterwards into the city Bethlehem, they found there several very desperate distempers, which became so troublesome to children by seeing them, that most of them died.

2. There was there a woman who had a sick son, whom she brought, when he was at the point of death, to the Lady St. Mary, who saw her when she was washing Jesus Christ.

3. Then said the woman, O my Lady Mary, look down upon this my son, who is afflicted with most dreadful pains.

4. St. Mary hearing her, said, Take a little of that water with which I have washed my son, and sprinkle it upon him.

5. Then she took a little of that water, as   St. Mary had commanded, and sprinkled it upon her son, who being wearied with his violent pains, had fallen asleep; and after he had slept a little, awaked perfectly well and recovered.

6. The mother being abundantly glad of this success, went again to St. Mary, and St. Mary said to her, Give praise to God, who hath cured this thy son.

7. There was in the same place another woman, a neighbour of her, whose son was now cured.

8. This woman's son was afflicted with the same disease, and his eyes were now almost quite shut, and she was lamenting for him day and night.

9. The mother of the child which was cured, said to her, Why do you not bring your son to St. Mary, as I brought my son to her, when he was in the agonies of death; and he was cured by that water, with which the body of her son Jesus was washed?

10. When the woman heard her say this, she also went, and having procured the same water, washed her son with it, whereupon his body and his eyes were instantly restored to their former state.

11. And when she brought her son to St. Mary, and opened his case to her, she commanded her to give thanks to God for the recovery of her son's health, and tell no one what had happened.

X

1. There were in the same city two wives of one man, who had each a son sick. One of them was called Mary and her son's name was Caleb.

2. She arose, and taking her son, went to the Lady St. Mary, the mother

of Jesus, and offered her a very handsome carpet, saying, O my Lady Mary accept this carpet of me, and instead of it give me a small swaddling cloth.

3. To this Mary agreed, and when the mother of Caleb was gone, she made a coat for her son of the swaddling cloth, put it on him, and his disease was cured; but the son of the other wife died.

4. Hereupon there arose between them, a difference in doing the business of the family by turns, each her week.

5. And when the turn of Mary the mother of Caleb came, and she was heating the oven to bake bread, and went away to fetch the meal, she left her son Caleb by the oven;

6. Whom, the other wife, her rival, seeing to be by himself took and cast him into the oven, which was very hot, and then went away.

7. Mary on her return saw her son Caleb lying in the middle of the oven laughing, and the oven quite as cold as though it had not been before heated, and knew that her rival the other wife had thrown him into the fire.

8. When she took him out she brought him to the Lady St Mary, and told her the story to whom she replied, Be quiet, I am concerned lest thou shouldest make this matter known.

9. After this her rival, the other wife, as she was drawing water at the well, and saw Caleb playing by the well, and that no one was near, took him, and threw him into the well.

10. And when some men came to fetch water from the well they saw the boy sitting on the superficies of the water, an drew him out with ropes, and were exceedingly surprised a the child, and praised God.

11. Then came the mother and took him and carried him to the Lady St. Mary, lamenting and saying, O my Lady, see what my rival hath done to my son, and how she hath cast him into the well, and I do not question but one time or other she will be the occasion of his death.

12. St. Mary replied to her God will vindicate your injured cause.

13. Accordingly a few days after, when the other wife came to the well to draw water, her foot was entangled in the rope, so that she fell headlong into the well, and they who ran to her assistance, found her skull broken, and bones bruised.

14. So she came to a bad end, and in her was fulfilled that saying of the author, They digged a well, and made it deep, but fell themselves into the pit which they prepared.

XI

1. Another woman in that city had likewise two sons sick.

2. And when one was dead, the other, who lay at the point of death, she took in her arms to the Lady St. Mary, and in a flood of tears addressed herself to her, saying,

3. O my Lady, help and relieve me; for I had two sons the one I have just now buried, the other I see is just at the point of death, behold how I (earnestly) seek favour from God, and pray to him.

4. Then she said, O Lord, thou art gracious, and merciful, and kind; thou hast given me two sons; one of them thou hast taken to thyself, O spare me this other.

5. St. Mary then perceiving the greatness of her sorrow, pitied her and said, Do thou place thy son in my son's bed, and cover him with his clothes.

6. And when she had placed him in the bed wherein Christ lay, at the moment when his eyes were just closed by death; as soon as ever the smell of the garments of the Lord Jesus Christ reached the boy, his eyes were opened, and calling with a loud voice to his mother, he asked for bread, and when he had received it, he sucked it.

7. Then his mother said, O Lady Mary, now I am assured that the powers of God do dwell in you, so that thy son can cure children who are of the same sort as himself, as soon as they touch his garments.

8. This boy who was thus cured, is the same who in the Gospel is called Bartholomew.

XII

1. Again there was a leprous woman who went to the Lady St. Mary, the mother of Jesus, and said, O my Lady, help me.

2. St. Mary replied, what help dost thou desire? Is it gold or silver, or that thy body be cured of its leprosy?

3. Who, says the woman, can grant me this?

4. St. Mary replied to her, Wait a little till I have washed my son Jesus, and put him to bed.

5. The woman waited, as she was commanded; and Mary when she had put Jesus in bed, giving her the water with which she had washed his body, said Take some of the water, and pour it upon thy body;

6. Which when she had done, she instantly became clean, and praised God, and gave thanks to him.

7. Then she went away, after she had abode with her three days:

8. And going into the city, she saw a certain prince, who had married another prince's daughter;

9. But when he came to see her, he perceived between her eyes the signs of

leprosy like a star, and thereupon declared the marriage dissolved and void.

10. When the woman saw these persons in this condition, exceedingly sorrowful, and shedding abundance of tears, she inquired of them the reason of their crying.

11. They replied, Inquire not unto our circumstances; for we are not able to declare our misfortunes into any person whatsoever.

12. But still she pressed and desired them to communicate their case to her, intimating, that perhaps she might be able to direct them to a remedy.

13. So when they shewed the young woman to her, and the signs of the leprosy, which appeared between her eyes,

14. She said, I also, whom ye see in this place, was afflicted with the same distemper, and going on some business to Bethlehem, I went into a certain cave, and saw a woman named Mary, who had a son called Jesus.

15. She seeing me to be leprous, was concerned for me, and gave me some water with which she had washed her son's body; with that I sprinkled my body, and became clean.

16. Then said these women, Will you, Mistress, go along with us, and shew the Lady St. Mary to us?

17. To which she consenting, they arose and went to the Lady St. Mary, taking with them very noble presents.

18. And when they came in and offered their presents to her they showed the leprous young woman what they brought with them to her.

19. Then said St. Mary, The mercy of the Lord Jesus Christ rest upon you;

20. And giving them a little of that water with which she had washed the body of Jesus Christ, she bade them wash the diseased person with it; which when they had done, she was presently cured;

21. So they, and all who were present, praised God; and being filled with joy, they went back to their own city, and gave praise to God on that account.

22. Then the prince hearing that his wife was cured, took her home and made a second marriage, giving thanks unto God for the recovery of his wife's health.

XIII

1. Again there was also a girl, who was afflicted by Satan;

2. For that cursed spirit did frequently appear to her in the shape of a dragon, and was inclined to swallow her up, and had so sucked out all her blood, that she looked like a dead carcase.

3. As often as she came to herself, with her hands wringed about her head she would cry out, and say, Wo, Wo is me, that there is no one to be found

who can deliver me from that impious dragon!

4. Her father and mother, and all who were about her and saw her, mourned and wept over her;

5. And all who were present would especially be under sorrow and in tears, when they heard her bewailing, and saying, My brethren and friends, is there no one who can deliver me from this murderer?

6. Then the prince's daughter, who had been cured of her leprosy, hearing the complaint of that girl, went upon the top of her castle, and saw her with her hand twisted about her head, pouring out a flood of tears, and all the people that were about her in sorrow.

7. Then she asked the husband of the possessed person, Whether his wife's mother was alive? He told her, That her father and mother were both alive.

8. Then she ordered her mother to be sent to her: to whom, when she saw her coming, she said, Is this possessed girl thy daughter? She moaning and bewailing said, Yes, madam, I bore her.

9. The prince's daughter answered, Disclose the secret of her case to me, for I confess to you that I was leprous, but the Lady Mary, the mother of Jesus Christ, healed me.

10. And if you desire your daughter to be restored to her former state, take her to Bethlehem, and inquire for Mary the mother of Jesus, and doubt not but your daughter will be cured; for I do not question but you will come home with great joy at your daughter's recovery.

11. As soon as ever she had done speaking, she arose and went with her daughter to the place appointed, and to Mary, and told her the case of her daughter.

12. When St. Mary had heard her story, she gave her a little of the water with which she had washed the body of her son Jesus, and bade her pour it upon the body of her daughter.

13. Likewise she gave her one of the swaddling cloths of the Lord Jesus, and said, Take this swaddling cloth and shew it to thine enemy as often as thou seest him; and she sent them away in peace.

14. After they had left that city and returned home, and the time was come in which Satan was wont to seize her, in the same moment this cursed spirit appeared to her in the shape of a huge dragon, and the girl seeing him was afraid.

15. The mother said to her, Be not afraid daughter; let him alone till he come nearer to thee! then shew him the swaddling cloth, which the Lady Mary gave us, and we shall see the event.

16. Satan then coming like a dreadful dragon, the body of the girl trembled for fear.

17. But as soon as she had put the swaddling cloth upon her head, and about her eyes, and shewed it to him, presently there issued forth from the swaddling cloth flames and burning coals, and fell upon the dragon.

18. Oh! how great a miracle was this, which was done: as soon as the dragon saw the swaddling cloth of the Lord Jesus, fire went forth and was scattered upon his head and eyes; so that he cried out with a loud voice, What have I to do with thee, Jesus, thou son of Mary, Whither shall I flee from thee?

19. So he drew back much affrighted, and left the girl.

20. And she was delivered from this trouble, and sang praises and thanks to God, and with her all who were present at the working of the miracle.

XIV

1. Another woman likewise lived there, whose son was possessed by Satan.

2. This boy, named Judas, as often as Satan seized him, was inclined to bite all that were present; and if he found no one else near him, he would bite his own hands and other parts.

3. But the mother of this miserable boy, hearing of St. Mary and her son Jesus, arose presently, and taking her son in her arms, brought him to the Lady Mary.

4. In the meantime, James and Joses had taken away the infant, the Lord Jesus, to play at a proper season with other children; and when they went forth, they sat down and the Lord Jesus with them.

5. Then Judas, who was possessed, came and sat down at the right hand of Jesus.

6. When Satan was acting upon him as usual, he went about to bite the Lord Jesus.

7. And because he could not do it, he struck Jesus on the right side, so that he cried out.

8. And in the same moment Satan went out of the boy, and ran away like a mad dog.

9. This same boy who struck Jesus, and out of whom Satan went in the form of a dog, was Judas Iscariot, who betrayed him to the Jews.

10. And that same side, on which Judas struck him, the Jews pierced with a spear.

XV

1. And when the Lord Jesus was seven years of age, he was on a certain day

with other boys his companions about the same age.

2. Who when they were at play, made clay into several shapes namely, asses, oxen, birds, and other figures,

3. Each boasting of his work and endeavouring to exceed the rest.

4. Then the Lord Jesus said to the boys, I will command these figures which I have made to walk.

5. And immediately they moved and when he commanded then to return, they returned.

6. He had also made the figure of birds and sparrows, which when he commanded to fly, did fly, and when he commanded to stand still, did stand still; and if he gave them meat and drink they did eat and drink.

7. When at length the boys went away, and related these things to their parents, their fathers said to them, Take heed children, for the future, of his company, for he is a sorcerer; shun and avoid him, and from henceforth never play with him.

8. On a certain day also when the Lord Jesus was playing with the boys, and running about he passed by a dyer's shop, who name was Salem.

9. And there were in his shop many pieces of cloth belonging to the people of that city, which they designed to dye of several colours.

10. Then the Lord Jesus going into the dyer's shop, took all the cloths, and threw them into the furnace.

11. When Salem came home and saw the cloths spoiled, he began to make a great noise, and to chide the Lord Jesus, saying

12. What hast thou done me, O thou Son of Mary? Thou hast injured both me and my neighbours; they all desired their cloths of a proper colour; but thou hast come, and spoiled them all.

13. The Lord Jesus replied, l will change the colour of every cloth to what colour thou desirest;

14. And then he presently began to take the cloths out of the furnace, and they were all dyed of those same colours which the dyer desired.

15. And when the Jews saw this surprising miracle, they praised God.

XVI

1. And Joseph, wheresoever he went in the city, took the Lord Jesus with him, where he was sent for to work to make gates, or milk-pails, or sieves, or boxes; the Lord Jesus was with him wheresoever he went.

2. And as often as Joseph had anything in his work, to make longer or shorter, or wider, or narrower, the Lord Jesus would stretch his hand towards it.

3. And presently it became as Joseph would have it.

4. So that he had no need to finish anything with his own hands, for he was not very skillful at his carpenter's trade

5. On a certain time the King of Jerusalem sent for him and said, I would have thee make me a throne of the same dimensions with that place in which I commonly sit.

6. Joseph obeyed, and forthwith began the work, and continued two years in the king's palace before he finished it.

7. And when he came to fix it in its place, he found it wanted two spans on each side of the appointed measure.

8. Which, when the king saw, he was very angry with Joseph;

9. And Joseph afraid of the king's anger, went to bed without his supper, taking not any thing to eat.

10. Then the Lord Jesus asked him, What he was afraid of?

11. Joseph replied, Because I have lost my labour in the work which I have been about these two years.

12. Jesus said to him, Fear not, neither be cast down;

13. Do thou lay hold on one side of the throne and I will the other, and we will bring it to its just dimensions.

14. And when Joseph had done as the Lord Jesus said, and each of them had with strength drawn his side, the throne obeyed, and was brought to the proper dimensions of the place:

15. Which miracle when they who stood by saw, they were astonished, and praised God.

16. The throne was made of the same wood, which was in being in Solomon's time, namely, wood adorned with various shapes and figures.

XVII

1. On another day the Lord Jesus going out into the street, and seeing some boys who were met to play, joined himself to their company:

2. But when they saw him, they hid themselves, and left him to seek for them:

3. The Lord Jesus came to the gate of a certain house, and asked some women who were standing there, Where the boys were gone?

4. And when they answered, That there was no one there; the Lord Jesus said, Who are those whom ye see in the furnace?

5. They answered, They were kids of three years old.

6. Then Jesus cried out aloud, and said, Come out hither, O ye kids, to your shepherd;

7. And presently the boys came forth like kids, and leaped about him; which when the women saw, they were exceedingly amazed, and trembled.

8. Then they immediately worshipped the Lord Jesus, and beseeched him, saying, O our Lord Jesus, son of Mary, thou art truly that good shepherd of Israel! have mercy on thy handmaids, who stand before thee, who do not doubt, but that thou, O Lord, art come to save, and not to destroy.

9. After that, when the Lord Jesus said, the children of Israel are like Ethiopians among the people; the women said, Thou Lord, knowest all things, nor is anything concealed from thee; but now we entreat thee, and beseech of thy mercy that thou wouldst restore those boys to their former state.

10. Then Jesus said, Come hither O boys, that we may go and play; and immediately, in the presence of these women, the kids were changed and returned into the shape of boys.

XVIII

1. In the month Adar Jesus gathered together the boys, and ranked them as though he had been a king.

2. For they spread their garments on the ground for him to sit on; and having made a crown of flowers, put it upon his head, and stood on his right and left as the guards of a king.

3. And if any one happened to pass by, they took him by force, and said, Come hither, and worship the king, that you may have a prosperous journey.

4. In the mean time, while these things were doing, there came certain men, carrying a boy upon a couch;

5. For this boy having gone with his companions to the mountain to gather wood, and having found there a partridge's nest, and put his hand in to take out the eggs, was stung by a poisonous serpent, which leaped out of the nest; so that he was forced to cry out for the help of his companions: who, when they came, found him lying upon the earth like a dead person.

6. After which his neighbours came and carried him back into the city.

7. But when they came to the place where the Lord Jesus was sitting like a king, and the other boys stood around him like his ministers, the boys made hast to meet him, who was bitten by the serpent, and said to his neighbours, Come and pay your respects to the king;

8. But when, by reason of their sorrow, they refused to come, the boys drew them, and forced them against their wills to come.

9. And when they came to the Lord Jesus, he inquired, On what account they carried that boy?

10. And when they answered, that a serpent had bitten him, the Lord Je-

sus said to the boys, Let us go and kill that serpent.

11. But when the parents of the boy desired to be excused, because their son lay at the point of death; the boys made answer, and said, Did not ye hear what the king said? Let us go and kill the serpent; and will not ye obey him?

12. So they brought the couch back again, whether they would or not.

13. And when they were come to the nest, the Lord Jesus said to the boys, Is this the serpent's lurking place? They said, It was.

14. Then the Lord Jesus calling the serpent, it presently came forth and submitted to him; to whom he said, Go and suck out all the poison which thou hast infused into that boy;

15. So the serpent crept to the boy, and took away all its poison again.

16. Then the Lord Jesus cursed the serpent so that it immediately burst asunder, and died.

17. And he touched the boy with his hand to restore him to his former health;

18. And when he began to cry, I the Lord Jesus said, Cease crying, for hereafter thou shalt be my disciple;

19. And this is that Simon the Canaanite, who is mentioned in the Gospel.

XIX

1. On another day Joseph sent his son James to gather wood and the Lord Jesus went with him;

2. And when they came to the place where the wood was, and James began to gather it, be- hold, a venomous viper bit him, so that he began to cry, and make a noise.

3. The Lord Jesus seeing him in this condition, came to him; and blowed upon the place where the viper had bit him, and it was instantly well.

4. On a certain day the Lord Jesus was with some boys, who were playing on the housetop, and one of the boys fell down, and presently died.

5. Upon which the other boys all running away, the Lord Jesus was left alone on the house-top.

6. And the boy's relations came to him and said to the Lord Jesus, Thou didst throw our son down from the housetop.

7. But he denying it, they cried out, Our son is dead, and this is he who killed him.

8. The Lord Jesus replied to them, Do not charge me with a crime, of which you are not able to convict me, but let us go ask the boy himself, who will bring the truth to light.

9. Then the Lord Jesus going down stood over the head of the dead boy,

and said with a loud voice, Zeinunus, Zeinunus, who threw thee down from the house top?

10. Then the dead boy answered, thou didst not throw me down, but such a one did.

11. And when the Lord Jesus bade those who stood by to take notice of his words, all who were present praised God on account of that miracle.

12. On a certain time the Lady St. Mary had commanded the Lord Jesus to fetch her some water out of the well;

13. And when he had gone to fetch the water, the pitcher, when it was brought up full, brake.

14. But Jesus spreading his mantle gathered up the water again, and brought it in that to his mother.

15. Who, being astonished at this wonderful thing, laid up this, and all the other things which she had seen, in her memory.

16. Again on another day the Lord Jesus was with some boys by a river and they drew water out of the river by little channels, and made little fish pools.

17. But the Lord Jesus had made twelve sparrows, and placed them about his pool on each side, three on a side.

18. But it was the Sabbath day, and the son of Hanani a Jew came by, and saw them making these things, and said, Do ye thus make figures of clay on the Sabbath? And he ran to them, and broke down their fish pools.

19. But when the Lord Jesus clapped his hands over the sparrows which he had made, they fled away chirping.

20. At length the son of Hanani coming to the fish-pool of Jesus to destroy it, the water vanished away, and the Lord Jesus said to him,

21. In like manner as this water has vanished, so shall thy life vanish; and presently the boy died.

22. Another time, when the Lord Jesus was coming home in the evening with Joseph, he met a boy, who ran so hard against him, that he threw him down;

23. To whom the Lord Jesus said, As thou hast thrown me down, so shalt thou fall, nor ever rise.

24. And that moment the boy fell down and died.

XX

1. There was also at Jerusalem one named Zaccheus, who was a school-master.

2. And he said to Joseph, Joseph, why dost thou not send Jesus to me, that

he may learn his letters?

3. Joseph agreed, and told St. Mary;

4. So they brought him to that master; who, as soon as he saw him, wrote out an alphabet for him.

5. And he bade him say Aleph; and when he had said Aleph, the master bade him pronounce Beth.

6. Then the Lord Jesus said to him, Tell me first the meaning of the letter Aleph, and then I will pronounce Beth.

7. And when the master threatened to whip him, the Lord Jesus explained to him the meaning of the letters Aleph and Beth;

8. Also which were the straight figures of the letters, which the oblique, and what letters had double figures; which had points, and which had none; why one letter went before another; and many other things he began to tell him, and explain, of which the master himself had never heard, nor read any book.

9. The Lord Jesus farther said the master, Take notice how I say to thee; then he began clearly and distinctly to say Aleph, Beth, Gimel, Daleth, and so on to the end of the alphabet.

10. At this the master was so surprised, that he said, I believe his boy was born before Noah;

11. And turning to Joseph, he said, Thou hast brought a boy to be to be taught, who is more learned than any master.

12. He said also unto St. Mary, This your son has no need of any learning.

13. They brought him then to a more learned master, who, when he saw him, said, say Aleph.

14. And when he had said Aleph, he master bade him pronounce Beth; to which the Lord Jesus replied, Tell me first the meaning of the letter Aleph, and then I will pronounce Beth.

15. But this master, when he lift up his hand to whip him, had his hand presently withered, and he died.

16. Then said Joseph to St. Mary, henceforth we will not allow him to go out of the house; for every one who displeases him is killed.

XXI

1. And when he was twelve years old, they brought him to Jerusalem to the feast; and when the feast was over, they returned.

2. But the Lord Jesus continued behind in the temple among the doctors and elders, and   learned men of Israel; to whom he proposed several questions of learning, and also gave them answers:

3. For he said to them, Whose son is the Messiah? They answered, the son of David:

4. Why then, said he, does he in the spirit call him Lord? when he saith, The Lord said to my Lord, sit thou at my right hand, till I have made thine enemies thy footstool.

5. Then a certain principal Rabbi asked him, Hast thou read books?

6. Jesus answered, he had read both books, and the things which a were contained in books.

7. And he explained to them the books of the law, and precepts, and statutes: and the mysteries which are contained in the books of the prophets; things which the mind of no creature a could reach.

8. Then said that Rabbi, I never yet have seen or heard of such knowledge! What do you think that boy will be!

9. When a certain astronomer, who was present, asked the Lord Jesus, Whether he had studied astronomy?

10. The Lord Jesus replied, and told him the number of the spheres and heavenly bodies, as also their triangular, square, and to sextile aspect; their progressive and retrograde motion; their size and several prognostication; and other things which the reason of man had never discovered.

11. There was also among them a philosopher well skilled in physic and natural philosophy, who asked the Lord Jesus Whether he had studied physic?

12. He replied, and explained to him physics and metaphysics.

13. Also those things which were above and below the power of nature;

14. The powers also of the body, its humours, and their effects.

15. Also the number of its members, and bones, veins, arteries, and nerves;

16. The several constitutions of body, hot and dry, cold and moist, and the tendencies of them;

17. How the soul operated upon the body;

18. What its various sensations and faculties were;

19. The faculty of speaking, anger, desire;

20. And lastly the manner of its composition and dissolution; and other things, which the understanding of no creature had ever reached.

21. Then that philosopher arose, and worshipped the Lord Jesus, and said, O Lord Jesus, from henceforth I will be thy disciple and servant.

22. While they were discoursing on these and such like things, the Lady St. Mary came in, having been three days walking about with Joseph, seeking for him.

23. And when she saw him sitting among the doctors, and in his turn proposing questions to them, and giving answers, she said to him, My son,

why hast thou done thus by us? Behold I and thy father have been at much pains in seeking thee.

24. He replied, Why did ye seek me? Did ye not know that I ought to be employed in my father's house?

25. But they understood not the words which he said to them

26. Then the doctors asked Mary, Whether this was her son? And when she said, He was, they said, O happy Mary, who hast borne such a son.

27. Then he returned with them to Nazareth, and obeyed them in all things.

28. And his mother kept all these things in her mind;

29. And the Lord Jesus grew in stature and wisdom, and favour with God and man.

XXII

1. Now from this time Jesus began to conceal his miracles and secret works,

2. And he gave himself to the study of the law, till he arrived to the end of his thirtieth year;

3. At which time the Father publicly owned him at Jordan, sending down this voice from heaven, This is my beloved son, in whom I am well pleased;

4. The Holy Ghost being also present in the form of a dove.

5. This is he whom we worship with all reverence, because he gave us our life and being, and brought us from our mother's womb.

6. Who, for our sakes, tooka human body, and hath redeemed us, so that he might so embrace us with everlasting mercy, and shew his free, large, bountiful grace and goodness to us.

7. To him be glory and praise, and power, and dominion, from henceforth and for evermore, Amen.

The end of the whole Gospel of the Infancy, by the assistance of the Supreme God, according to what we found in the original.

The Gospel of Bartholomew

It exists in three languages, and not, apparently, in a very original form in any of them: Greek is the original language, of which we have two manuscripts, at Vienna and Jerusalem; Latin 1, consisting of two leaves of extracts, of the ninth century; Latin 2, complete: see below; Slavonic (i-iv. 15). The Greek text may be as old as the fifth century; the Latin 2 of the sixth or seventh.

In the Revue Biblique for 1913 the Latin fragments and a fresh Greek text were published by MM. Wilmart and Tisserant, with the variants of the other authorities and in 1921-2 yet another text, a complete Latin one, appeared in the same periodical, edited by Professor Moricca from a manuscript in the Casanatensian library at Rome in which the text is, in parts, tremendously expanded. This copy is of the eleventh century and came from the monastery of Monte Amiata. The Latin is exceedingly incorrect, and there are many corruptions, and interpolations which extend to whole pages of closely printed text. Cite it as Lat. 2.

We take the Greek and Slavonic, where they exist, as the basis of this version, and add some passages from the Latin. The main topics, common to two or more of the texts, are:

i. The descent into Hell: the number of souls saved and lost.

ii. The Virgin's account of the Annunciation.

iii. The apostles see the bottomless pit.

iv. The devil is summoned and gives an account of his doings.

v. Questions about the deadly sins. Commission of the apostles to preach. Departure of Christ. (This reads like a late addition.)

GOSPEL (QUESTIONS) OF ST. BARTHOLOMEW

(the opening 3 verses are given from each of the three texts)

Greek.

1. After the resurrection from the dead of our Lord Jesus Christ, Bartholomew came unto the Lord and questioned him, saying: Lord, reveal unto me the mysteries of the heavens.

2. Jesus answered and said unto him: If I put off the body of the flesh, I shall not be able to tell them unto thee.

3. Om.

Slavonic.

1. Before the resurrection of our Lord Jesus Christ from the dead, the apostles said: Let us question the Lord: Lord, reveal unto us the wonders.

2. And Jesus said unto them: If I put off the body of the flesh, I cannot tell them unto you.

3. But when he was buried and risen again, they all durst not question him, because it was not to look upon him, but the fullness of his Godhead was seen.

4. But Bartholomew, &c.

Latin 2.

1. At that time, before the Lord Jesus Christ suffered, all the disciples were gathered together, questioning him and saying: Lord, show us the mystery in the heavens.

2. But Jesus answered and said unto them: If I put not off the body of flesh I cannot tell you.

3. But after that he had suffered and risen again, all the apostles, looking upon him, durst not question him, because his countenance was not as it had been aforetime, but showed forth the fullness of power.

Greek.

4. Bartholomew therefore drew near unto the Lord and said: I have a word to speak unto thee, Lord.

5. And Jesus said to him: I know what thou art about to say; say then what thou wilt, and I will answer thee.

6. And Bartholomew said: Lord, when thou wentest to be hanged upon the cross, I followed thee afar off and saw thee hung upon the cross, and the angels coming down from heaven and worshipping thee. And when there

came darkness,

7. I beheld, and I saw thee that thou wast vanished away from the cross and I heard only a voice in the parts under the earth, and great wailing and gnashing of teeth on a sudden. Tell me, Lord, whither wentest thou from the cross?

8. And Jesus answered and said: Blessed art thou, Bartholomew, my beloved, because thou sawest this mystery, and now will I tell thee all things whatsoever thou askest me.

9. For when I vanished away from the cross, then went I down into Hades that I might bring up Adam and all them that were with him, according to the supplication of Michael the archangel.

10. Then said Bartholomew: Lord, what was the voice which was heard?

11. Jesus saith unto him: Hades said unto Beliar: As I perceive, a God cometh hither. [Slavonic and latin 2 continue: And the angels cried unto the powers, saying: Remove your gates, ye princes, remove the everlasting doors, for behold the King of glory cometh down.

12. Hades said: Who is the King of glory, that cometh down from heaven unto us?

13. And when I had descended five hundred steps, Hades was troubled, saying: I hear the breathing of the Most High, and I cannot endure it. (latin 2. He cometh with great fragrance and I cannot bear it.)

14. But the devil answered and said: Submit not thyself, O Hades, but be strong: for God himself hath not descended upon the earth.

15. But when I had descended yet five hundred steps, the angels and the powers cried out: Take hold, remove the doors, for behold the King of glory cometh down. And Hades said: O, woe unto me, for I hear the breath of God.]

16-17 And Beliar said unto Hades: Look carefully who it is that , for it is Elias, or Enoch, or one of the prophets that this man seemeth to me to be. But Hades answered Death and said: Not yet are six thousand years accomplished. And whence are these, O Beliar; for the sum of the number is in mine hands.

[Slavonic. 16 And the devil said unto Hades: Why affrightest thou me, Hades? it is a prophet, and he hath made himself like unto God: this prophet will we take and bring him hither unto those that think to ascend into heaven. 17 And Hades said: Which of the prophets is it? Show me: Is it Enoch the scribe of righteousness? But God hath not suffered him to come down upon the earth before the end of the six thousand years. Sayest thou that it is Elias, the avenger? But before he cometh not down. What shall I do, whereas the destruction is of God: for surely our end is at hand? For I have the number (of the years) in mine hands.]

Greek.

18. Be not troubled, make safe thy gates and strengthen thy bars: consider, God cometh not down upon the earth.

19. Hades saith unto him: These be no good words that I hear from thee: my belly is rent, and mine inward parts are pained: it cannot be but that God cometh hither. Alas, whither shall I flee before the face of the power of the great king? Suffer me to enter into myself (thyself, Latin): for before (of, latin) thee was I formed.

20. Then did I enter in and scourged him and bound him with chains that cannot be loosed, and brought forth thence all the patriarchs and came again unto the cross.

21. Bartholomew saith unto him: [latin 2, I saw thee again, hanging upon the cross, and all the dead arising and worshipping thee, and going up again into their sepulchres.] Tell me, Lord, who was he whom the angels bare up in their hands, even that man that was very great of stature? [Slav., Latin. 2, And what spakest thou unto him that he sighed so sore?]

22. Jesus answered and said unto him: It was Adam the first-formed, for whose sake I came down from heaven upon earth. And I said unto him: I was hung upon the cross for thee and for thy children's sake. And he, when he heard it, groaned and said: So was thy good pleasure, O Lord.

23. Again Bartholomew said: Lord, I saw the angels ascending before Adam and singing praises.

24. But one of the angels which was very great, above the rest, would not ascend up with them: and there was in his hand a sword of fire, and he was looking steadfastly upon thee only.

Slavonic.

25. And all the angels besought him that he would go up with them, but he would not. But when thou didst command him to go up, I beheld a flame of fire issuing out of his hands and going even unto the city of Jerusalem.

26. And Jesus said unto him: Blessed art thou, Bartholomew my beloved because thou sawest these mysteries. This was one of the angels of vengeance which stand before my Father's throne: and this angel sent he unto me.

27. And for this cause he would not ascend up, because he desired to destroy all the powers of the world. But when I commanded him to ascend up, there went a flame out of his hand and rent asunder the veil of the temple,

and parted it in two pieces for a witness unto the children of Israel for my passion because they crucified me. (Lat. 1. But the flame which thou sawest issuing out of his hands smote the house of the synagogue of the Jews, for a testimony of me wherein they crucified me.)].

Greek.

28. And when he had thus spoken, he said unto the apostles: Tarry for me in this place, for today a sacrifice is offered in paradise.

29. And Bartholomew answered and said unto Jesus: Lord, what is the sacrifice which is offered in paradise? And Jesus said: There be souls of the righteous which to-day have departed out of the body and go unto paradise, and unless I be present they cannot enter into paradise.

30. And Bartholomew said: Lord, how many souls depart out of the world daily? Jesus saith unto him: Thirty thousand.

31. Bartholomew saith unto him: Lord, when thou wast with us teaching the word, didst thou receive the sacrifices in paradise? Jesus answered and said unto him: Verily I say unto thee, my beloved, that I both taught the word with you and continually sat with my Father, and received the sacrifices in paradise everyday.

32. Bartholomew answered and said unto him: Lord, if thirty thousand souls depart out of the world every day, how many souls out of them are found righteous? Jesus saith unto him: Hardly fifty [three] my beloved.

33. Again Bartholomew saith: And how do three only enter into paradise? Jesus saith unto him: The [fifty] three enter into paradise or are laid up in Abraham's bosom: but the others go into the place of the resurrection, for the three are not like unto the fifty.

34. Bartholomew saith unto him: Lord, how many souls above the number are born into the world daily? Jesus saith unto him: One soul only is born above the number of them that depart.[30, &c., Latin 1. Bartholomew said: How many are the souls which depart out of the body every day? Jesus said: Verily I say unto thee, twelve (thousand) eight hundred, four score and three souls depart out of the body every day.]

35. And when he had said this he gave them the peace, and vanished away from them.

II

1. The apostles were in the place [Cherubim, Cheltoura, Chritir] with Mary.

2. And Bartholomew came and said unto Peter and Andrew and John: Let

us ask her that is highly favoured how she conceived the incomprehensible, or how she bare him that cannot be carried, or how she brought forth so much greatness. But they doubted to ask her.

3. Bartholomew therefore said unto Peter: Thou that art the chief, and my teacher, draw near and ask her. But Peter said to John: Thou art a virgin and undefiled (and beloved) and thou must ask her.

4. And as they all doubted and disputed, Bartholomew came near unto her with a cheerful countenance and said to her: Thou that art highly favoured, the tabernacle of the Most High, unblemished we, even all the apostles, ask thee (or All the apostles have sent me to ask thee) to tell us how thou didst conceive the incomprehensible, or how thou didst bear him that cannot be carried, or how thou didst bring forth so much greatness.

5. But Mary said unto them: Ask me not (or Do ye indeed ask me) concerning this mystery. If I should begin to tell you, fire will issue forth out of my mouth and consume all the world.

6. But they continued yet the more to ask her. And she, for she could not refuse to hear the apostles, said: Let us stand up in prayer.

7. And the apostles stood behind Mary: but she said unto Peter: Peter, thou chief, thou great pillar, standest thou behind us? Said not our Lord: the head of the man is Christ ? now therefore stand ye before me and pray.

8. But they said unto her: In thee did the Lord set his tabernacle, and it was his good pleasure that thou shouldest contain him, and thou oughtest to be the leader in the prayer (al. to go with us to).

9. But she said unto them: Ye are shining stars, and as the prophet said, 'I did lift up mine eyes unto the hills, from whence shall come mine help'; ye, therefore, are the hills, and it behoveth you to pray.

10. The apostles say unto her: Thou oughtest to pray, thou art the mother of the heavenly king.

11. Mary saith unto them: In your likeness did God form the sparrows, and sent them forth into the four corners of the world.

12. But they say unto her: He that is scarce contained by the seven heavens was pleased to be contained in thee.

13. Then Mary stood up before them and spread out her hands toward the heaven and began to speak thus: Elphue Zarethra Charboum Nemioth Melitho Thraboutha Mephnounos Chemiath Aroura Maridon Elison Marmiadon Seption Hesaboutha Ennouna Saktinos Athoor Belelam Opheoth Abo Chrasar (this is the reading of one Greek copy: the others and the Slavonic have many differences as in all such cases: but as the original words-assuming them to have once had a meaning-are hopelessly corrupted, the matter is not of importance), which is in the Greek tongue(Hebrew, Slav.): O God the

exceeding great and all-wise and king of the worlds (ages), that art not to be described, the ineffable, that didst establish the greatness of the heavens and all things by a word, that out of darkness (or the unknown) didst constitute and fasten together the poles of heaven in harmony, didst bring into shape the matter that was in confusion, didst bring into order the things that were without order, didst part the misty darkness from the light, didst establish in one place the foundations of the waters, thou that makest the beings of the air to tremble, and art the fear of them that are on (or under) the earth, that didst settle the earth and not suffer it to perish, and filledst it, which is the nourisher of all things, with showers of blessing: (Son of) the Father, thou whom the seven heavens hardly contained, but who wast well-pleased to be contained without pain in me, thou that art thyself the full word of the Father in whom all things came to be: give glory to thine exceeding great name, and bid me to speak before thy holy apostles .

14. And when she had ended the prayer she began to say unto them: Let us sit down upon the ground; and come thou, Peter the chief, and sit on my right hand and put thy left hand beneath mine armpit; and thou, Andrew, do so on my left hand; and thou, John, the virgin, hold together my bosom; and thou, Bartholomew, set thy knees against my back and hold my shoulders, lest when I begin to speak my bones be loosed one from another.

15. And when they had so done she began to say: When I abode in the temple of God and received my food from an angel, on a certain day there appeared unto me one in the likeness of an angel, but his face was incomprehensible, and he had not in his hand bread or a cup, as did the angel which came to me aforetime.

16. And straightway the robe (veil) of the temple was rent and there was a very great earthquake, and I fell upon the earth, for I was not able to endure the sight of him.

17. But he put his hand beneath me and raised me up, and I looked up into heaven and there came a cloud of dew and sprinkled me from the head to the feet, and he wiped me with his robe.

18. And said unto me: Hail, thou that art highly favoured, the chosen vessel, grace inexhaustible. And he smote his garment upon the right hand and there came a very great loaf, and he set it upon the altar of the temple and did eat of it first himself, and gave unto me also.

19. And again he smote his garment upon the left hand and there came a very great cup full of wine: and he set it upon the altar of the temple and did drink of it first himself, and gave also unto me. And I beheld and saw the bread and the cup whole as they were.

20. And he said unto me: Yet three years, and I will send my word unto

thee and then shalt conceive my (or a) son, and through him shall the whole creation be saved. Peace be unto thee, my beloved, and my peace shall be with thee continually.

21. And when he had so said he vanished away from mine eyes, and the temple was restored as it had been before.

22. And as she was saying this, fire issued out of her mouth; and the world was at the point to come to an end: but Jesus appeared quickly (lat. 2, and laid his hand upon her mouth) and said unto Mary: Utter not this mystery, or this day my whole creation will come to an end (Lat. 2, and the flame from her mouth ceased). And the apostles were taken with fear lest haply the Lord should be wroth with them.

III

1. And he departed with them unto the mount Mauria (Lat. 2, Mambre), and sat in the midst of them.

2. But they doubted to question him, being afraid.

3. And Jesus answered and said unto them: Ask me what ye will that I should teach you, and I will show it you. For yet seven days, and I ascend unto my Father, and I shall no more be seen of you in this likeness.

4. But they, yet doubting, said unto him: Lord, show us the deep (abyss) according unto thy promise.

5. And Jesus said unto them: It is not good (Lat. 2, is good) for you to see the deep: notwithstanding, if ye desire it, according to my promise, come, follow me and behold.

6. And he led them away into a place that is called Cherubim (Cherukt Slav., Chairoudee Gr., Lat. 2 omits), that is the place of truth.

7. And he beckoned unto the angels of the West and the earth was rolled up like a volume of a book and the deep was revealed unto them.

8. And when the apostles saw it they fell on their faces upon the earth.

9. But Jesus raised them up, saying: Said I not unto you, 'It is not good for you to see the deep'. And again he beckoned unto the angels, and the deep was covered up.

IV

1. And he took them and brought them again unto the Mount of olives.

2. And Peter said unto Mary: Thou that art highly favoured, entreat the Lord that he would reveal unto us the things that are in the heavens.

3. And Mary said unto Peter: O stone hewn out of the rock, did not the

Lord build his church upon thee? Go thou therefore first and ask him.

4. Peter saith again: O tabernacle that art spread abroad .

5. Mary saith: Thou art the image of Adam: was not he first formed and then Eve? Look upon the sun, that according to the likeness of Adam it is bright. and upon the moon, that because of the transgression of Eve it is full of clay. For God did place Adam in the east and Eve in the west, and appointed the lights that the sun should shine on the earth unto Adam in the east in his fiery chariots, and the moon in the west should give light unto Eve with a countenance like milk. And she defiled the commandment of the Lord. Therefore was the moon stained with clay (Lat. 2, is cloudy) and her light is not bright. Thou therefore, since thou art the likeness of Adam, oughtest to ask him: but in me was he contained that I might recover the strength of the female.

6. Now when they came up to the top of the mount, and the Master was withdrawn from them a little space, Peter saith unto Mary: Thou art she that hast brought to nought the transgression of Eve, changing it from shame into joy; it is lawful, therefore, for thee to ask.

7. When Jesus appeared again, Bartholomew saith unto him: Lord, show us the adversary of men that we may behold him, of what fashion he is, and what is his work, and whence he cometh forth, and what power he hath that he spared not even thee, but caused thee to be hanged upon the tree.

8. But Jesus looked upon him and said: Thou bold heart! thou askest for that which thou art not able to look upon.

9. But Bartholomew was troubled and fell at Jesus' feet and began to speak thus: O lamp that cannot be quenched, Lord Jesu Christ, maker of the eternal light that hast given unto them that love thee the grace that beautifieth all, and hast given us the eternal light by thy coming into the world, that hast accomplished the work of the Father, hast turned the shame-facedness of Adam into mirth, hast done away the sorrow of Eve with a cheerful countenance by thy birth from a virgin: remember not evil against me but grant me the word of mine asking. (Lat. 2, who didst come down into the world, who hast confirmed the eternal word of the Father, who hast called the sadness of joy, who hast made the shame of Eve glad, and restored her by vouchsafing to be contained in the womb.)

10. And as he thus spake, Jesus raised him up and said unto him: Bartholomew, wilt thou see the adversary of men? I tell thee that when thou beholdest him, not thou only but the rest of the apostles and Mary will fall on your faces and become as dead corpses.

11. But they all said unto him: Lord, let us behold him.

12. And he led them down from the Mount of Olives and looked wrath-

fully upon the angels that keep hell (Tartarus), and beckoned unto Michael to sound the trumpet in the height of the heavens. And Michael sounded, and the earth shook, and Beliar came up, being held by 660 (560 Gr., 6,064 Lat. 1, 6,060 Lat. 2) angels and bound with fiery chains.

13. And the length of him was 1,600 cubits and his breadth 40 (Lat. 1, 300, Slav. 17) cubits (Lat. 2, his length 1,900 cubits, his breadth 700, one wing of him 80), and his face was like a lightning of fire and his eyes full of darkness (like sparks, Slav.). And out of his nostrils came a stinking smoke; and his mouth was as the gulf of a precipice, and the one of his wings was four-score cubits.

14. And straightway when the apostles saw him, they fell to the earth on their faces and became as dead.

15. But Jesus came near and raised the apostles and gave them a spirit of power, and he saith unto Bartholomew: Come near, Bartholomew, and trample with thy feet on his neck, and he will tell thee his work, what it is, and how he deceiveth men.

16. And Jesus stood afar off with the rest of the apostles.

17. And Barthololmew feared, and raised his voice and said: Blessed be the name of thine immortal kingdom from henceforth even for ever. And when he had spoken, Jesus permitted him, saying: Go and tread upon the neck of Beliar: and Bartholomew ran quickly upon him and trode upon his neck: and Beliar trembled. (For this verse the Vienna MS. has: And Bartholomew raised his voice and said thus: O womb more spacious than a city, wider than the spreading of the heavens, that contained him whom the seven heavens contain not, but thou without pain didst contain sanctified in thy bosom, &c.: evidently out of place. Latin 1 has only: Then did Antichrist tremble and was filled with fury.)

18. And Bartholomew was afraid, and fled, and said unto Jesus: Lord, give me an hem of thy garments (Lat. 2, the kerchief (?) from thy shoulders) that I may have courage to draw near unto him.

19. But Jesus said unto him: Thou canst not take an hem of my garments, for these are not my garments which I wore before I was crucified.

20. And Bartholomew said: Lord, I fear lest, like as he spared not thine angels, he swallow me up also.

21. Jesus saith unto him: Were not all things made by my word, and by the will of my Father the spirits were made subject unto Solomon? thou, therefore, being commanded by my word, go in my name and ask him what thou wilt. (lat. 2 omits 20.)

22. [And Bartholomew made the sign of the cross and prayed unto Jesus and went behind him. And Jesus said to him: Draw near. And as Bar-

tholomew drew near, fire was kindled on every side, so that his garments appeared fiery. Jesus saith to Bartholomew: As I said unto thee, tread upon his neck and ask him what is his power.] And Bartholomew went and trode upon his neck, and pressed down his face into the earth as far as his ears.

23. And Bartholomew saith unto him: Tell me who thou art and what is thy name. And he said to him: Lighten me a little, and I will tell thee who I am and how I came hither, and what my work is and what my power is.

24. And he lightened him and saith to him: Say all that thou hast done and all that thou doest.

25. And Beliar answered and said: If thou wilt know my name, at the first I was called Satanael, which is interpreted a messenger of God, but when I rejected the image of God my name was called Satanas, that is, an angel that keepeth hell (Tartarus).

26. And again Bartholomew saith unto him: Reveal unto me all things and hide nothing from me.

27. And he said unto him: I swear unto thee by the power of the glory of God that even if I would hide aught I cannot, for he is near that would convict me. For if I were able I would have destroyed you like one of them that were before you.

28. For, indeed, I was formed (al. called) the first angel: for when God made the heavens, he took a handful of fire and formed me first, Michael second [Vienna MS. here has these sentences: for he had his Son before the heavens and the earth and we were formed (for when he took thought to create all things, his Son spake a word), so that we also were created by the will of the Son and the consent of the Father. He formed, I say, first me, next Michael the chief captain of the hosts that are above], Gabriel third, Uriel fourth, Raphael fifth, Nathanael sixth, and other angels of whom I cannot tell the names. [Jerusalem MS., Michael, Gabriel, Raphael, Uriel, Xathanael, and other 6,000 angels. Lat. I, Michael the honour of power, third Raphael, fourth Gabriel, and other seven. Lat. 2, Raphael third, Gabriel fourth, Uriel fifth, Zathael sixth, and other six.] For they are the rod-bearers (lictors) of God, and they smite me with their rods and pursue me seven times in the night and seven times in the day, and leave me not at all and break in pieces all my power. These are the (twelve, lat. 2) angels of vengeance which stand before the throne of God: these are the angels that were first formed.

30. And after them were formed all the angels. In the first heaven are an hundred myriads, and in the second an hundred myriads, and in the third an hundred myriads, and in the fourth an hundred myriads, and in the fifth an hundred myriads, and in the sixth an hundred myriads, and in the seventh (an hundred myriads, and outside the seven heavens, Jerusalem MS.) is the

first firmament (flat surface) wherein are the powers which work upon men.

31. For there are four other angels set over the winds. The first angel is over the north, and he is called Chairoum (. . . broil, Jerusalem MS.; lat. 2, angel of the north, Mauch), and hath in his hand a rod of fire, and restraineth the super-fluity of moisture that the earth be not overmuch wet.

32. And the angel that is over the north is called Oertha (Lat. 2, Alfatha): he hath a torch of fire and putteth it to his sides, and they warm the great coldness of him that he freeze not the world.

33. And the angel that is over the south is called Kerkoutha (Lat. 2, Cedar) and they break his fierceness that he shake not the earth.

34. And the angel that is over the south-west is called Naoutha, and he hath a rod of snow in his hand and putteth it into his mouth, and quencheth the fire that cometh out of his mouth. And if the angel quenched it not at his mouth it would set all the world on fire.

35. And there is another angel over the sea which maketh it rough with the waves thereof.

36. But the rest I will not tell thee, for he that standeth by suffereth me not.

37. Bartholomew saith unto him: Flow chastisest thou the souls of men?

38. Beliar saith unto him: Wilt thou that I declare unto thee the punishment of the hypocrites, of the back-biters, of the jesters, of the idolaters,

and the covetous, and the adulterers, and the wizards, and the diviners, and of them that believe in us, and of all whom I look upon (deceive?)?

(38 Lat. 2: When I will show any illusion by them. But they that do these things, and they that consent unto them or follow them, do perish with me. 39 Bartholomew said unto him: Declare quickly how thou persuadest men not to follow God and thine evil arts, that are slippery and dark, that they should leave the straight and shining paths of the Lord.)

39. Bartholomew saith unto him: I will that thou declare it in few words.

40. And he smote his teeth together, gnashing them, and there came up out of the bottomless pit a wheel having a sword flashing with fire, and in the sword were pipes.

41. And I (he) asked him, saying: What is this sword?

42. And he said: This sword is the sword of the gluttonous: for into this pipe are sent they that through their gluttony devise all manner of sin; into the second pipe are sent the backbiters which backbite their neighbour secretly; into the third pipe are sent the hypocrites and the rest whom I overthrow by my contrivance.

(Lat. 2:40 And Antichrist said: I will tell thee. And a wheel came up out of the abyss, having seven fiery knives. The first knife hath twelve pipes (canales).. . .

42b. Antichrist answered: The pipe of fire in the first knife, in it are put the casters of lots and diviners and enchanters, and they that believe in them or have sought them, because in the iniquity of their heart they have invented false divinations. In the second pipe of fire are first the blasphemers ... suicides ... idolaters.... In the rest are first perjurers . . . (long enumeration).)

43. And Bartholomew said: Dost thou then do these things by thyself alone?

44. And Satan said: If I were able to go forth by myself, I would have destroyed the whole world in three days: but neither I nor any of the six hundred go forth. For we have other swift ministers whom we command, and we furnish them with an hook of many points and send them forth to hunt, and they catch for us souls of men, enticing them with sweetness of divers baits, that is by drunkenness and laughter, by backbiting, hypocrisy, pleasures, fornication, and the rest of the trifles that come out of their treasures. (Lat. 2 amplifies enormously.)

45. And I will tell thee also the rest of the names of the angels. The angel of the hail is called Mermeoth, and he holdeth the hail upon his head, and my ministers do adjure him and send him whither they will. And other angels are there over the snow, and other over the thunder, and other over the lightning, and when any spirit of us would go forth either by land or by sea, these angels send forth fiery stones and set our limbs on fire. (Lat. 2 enumerates all the transgressions of Israel and all possible sins in two whole pages.)

46. Bartholomew saith: Be still (be muzzled) thou dragon of the pit.

47. And Beliar said: Many things will I tell thee of the angels. They that run together throughout the heavenly places and the earthly are these: Mermeoth, Onomatath, Douth, Melioth, Charouth, Graphathas, Oethra, Nephonos, Chalkatoura. With them do fly (are administered?) the things that are in heaven and on earth and under the earth.

48. Bartholomew saith unto him: Be still (be muzzled) and be faint, that I may entreat my Lord.

49. And Bartholomew fell upon his face and cast earth upon his head and began to say: O Lord Jesu Christ, the great and glorious name. All the choirs of the angels praise thee, O Master, and I that am unworthy with my lips... do praise thee, O Master. Hearken unto me thy servant, and as thou didst choose me from the receipt of custom and didst not suffer me to have my conversation unto the end in my former deeds, O Lord Jesu Christ, hearken unto me and have mercy upon the sinners.

50. And when he had so said, the Lord saith unto him: Rise up, suffer him that groaneth to arise: I will declare the rest unto thee.

51. And Bartholomew raised up Satan and said unto him: Go unto thy

place, with thine angels, but the Lord hath mercy upon all his world.

(50, 51, again enormously amplified in lat. 2. Satan complains that he has been tricked into telling his secrets before the time. The interpolation is to some extent dated by this sentence: ' Simon Magus and Zaroes and Arfaxir and Jannes and Mambres are my brothers.' Zaroes and Arfaxatare wizards who figure in the Latin Acts of Matthew and of Simon and Jude (see below). 49 follows 51 in this text.)

52. But the devil said: Suffer me, and I will tell thee how I was cast down into this place and how the Lord did make man.

53. I was going to and fro in the world, and God said unto Michael: Bring me a clod from the four corners of the earth, and water out of the four rivers of paradise. And when Michael brought them God formed Adam in the regions of the east, and shaped the clod which was shapeless, and stretched sinews and veins upon it and established it with Joints; and he worshipped him, himself for his own sake first, because he was the image of God, therefore he worshipped him.

54. And when I came from the ends of the earth Michael said: Worship thou the image of God, which he hath made according to his likeness. But I said: I am fire of fire, I was the first angel formed, and shall worship clay and matter?

55. And Michael saith to me: Worship, lest God be wroth with thee. But I said to him: God will not be wroth with me; but I will set my throne over against his throne, and I will be as he is. Then was God wroth with me and cast me down, having commanded the windows of heaven to be opened.

56. And when I was cast down, he asked also the six hundred that were under me, if they would worship: but they said: Like as we have seen the first angel do, neither will we worship him that is less than ourselves. Then were the six hundred also cast down by him with me.

57. And when we were cast down upon the earth we were senseless for forty years, and when the sun shone forth seven times brighter than fire, suddenly I awaked; and I looked about and saw the six hundred that were under me senseless.

58. And I awaked my son Salpsan and took him to counsel how I might deceive the man on whose account I was cast out of the heavens.

59. And thus did I contrive it. I took a vial in mine hand and scraped the sweat from off my breast and the hair of mine armpits, and washed myself (Lat. 2, I took fig leaves in my hands and wiped the sweat from my bosom and below mine arms and cast it down beside the streams of waters. 59 is greatly prolonged in this text) in the springs of the waters whence the four rivers flow out, and Eve drank of it and desire came upon her: for if she had

not drunk of that water I should not have been able to deceive her.

60. Then Bartholomew commanded him to go into hell.

61. And Bartholomew came and fell at Jesus' feet and began with tears to say thus: Abba, Father, that art past finding out by us, Word of the Father, whom the seven heavens hardly contained, but who wast pleased to be contained easily and without pain within the body of the Virgin: whom the Virgin knew not that she bare: thou by thy thought hast ordained all things to be: thou givest us that which we need before thou art entreated.

62. Thou that didst wear a crown of thorns that thou mightest prepare for us that repent the

precious crown from heaven; that didst hang upon the tree, that (a clause gone): (lat. 2, that thou mightest turn from us the tree of lust and concupiscence (etc., etc.). The verse is prolonged for over 40 lines) (that didst drink wine mingled with gall) that thou mightest give us to drink of the wine of compunction, and wast pierced n the side with a spear that thou mightest fill us with thy body and thy blood:

63. Thou that gavest names unto the four rivers: to the first Phison, because of the faith (pistis) which thou didst appear in the world to preach; to the second Geon, for that man was made of earth (ge); to the third Tigris, because by thee was revealed unto us the consubstantial Trinity in the heavens (to make anything of this we must read Trigis); to the fourth Euphrates, because by thy presence in the world thou madest every soul to rejoice (euphranai) through the word of immortality.

64. My God, and Father, the greatest, my King: save, Lord, the sinners.

65. When he had thus prayed Jesus said unto him: Bartholomew, my Father did name me Christ, that I might come down upon earth and anoint every man that cometh unto me with the oil of life: and he did call me Jesus that I might heal every sin of them that know not . . . and give unto men (several corrupt words: the Latin has) the truth of God.

66. And again Bartholomew saith unto him: Lord, is it lawful for me to reveal these mysteries unto every man? Jesus saith unto him: Bartholomew, my beloved, as many as are faithful and are able to keep them unto themselves, to them mayest thou entrust these things. For some there are that be worthy of them, but there are also other some unto whom it is not fit to entrust them: for they are vain (swaggerers), drunkards, proud, unmerciful, partakers in idolatry, authors of fornication, slanderers, teachers of foolishness, and doing all works that are of the devil, and therefore are they not worthy that these should be entrusted to them.

68. And also they are secret, because of those that cannot contain them; for as many as can contain them shall have a part in them. Herein (Hither-

to?) therefore, my beloved, have I spoken unto thee, for blessed art thou and all thy kindred which of their choice have this word entrusted unto them; for all they that can contain it shall receive whatsoever they will in the of my judgement.

69. Then I, Bartholomew, which wrote these things in mine heart, took hold on the hand of the lord the lover of men and began to rejoice and to speak thus:

Glory be to thee, O Lord Jesus Christ, that givest unto all thy grace which all we have perceived. Alleluia. Glory be to thee, O Lord, the life of sinners.

Glory be to thee, O Lord, death is put to shame.

Glory be to thee, O Lord, the treasure of righteousness. For unto God do we sing.

70. And as Bartholomew thus spake again, Jesus put off his mantle and took a kerchief from the neck of Bartholomew and began to rejoice and say (70 lat. 2, Then Jesus took a kerchief (?) I and said: I am good: mild and gracious and merciful, strong and righteous, wonderful and holy): I am good. Alleluia. I am meek and gentle. Alleluia. Glory be to thee, O Lord: for I give gifts unto all them that desire me. Alleluia.

Glory be to thee, O Lord, world without end. Amen. Alleluia.

71. And when he had ceased, the apostles kissed him, and he gave them the peace of love.

VI

1. Bartholomew saith unto him: Declare unto us, Lord what sin is heavier than all sins?

2. Jesus saith unto him: Verily I say unto thee that hypocrisy and backbiting is heavier than all sins: for because of them, the prophet said in the psalm, that 'the ungodly shall not rise in the judgement, neither sinners in the council of the righteous', neither the ungodly in the judgement of my Father. Verily, verily, I say unto you, that every sin shall be forgiven unto every man, but the sin against the Holy Ghost shall not be forgiven.

3. And Bartholomew saith unto him: What is the sin against the Holy Ghost?

4. Jesus saith unto him: Whosoever shall decree against any man that hath served my holy Father hath blasphemed against the Holy Ghost: For every man that serveth God worshipfully is worthy of the Holy Ghost, and he that speaketh anything evil against him shall not be forgiven.

5. Woe unto him that sweareth by the head of God, yea woe (?) to him that sweareth falsely by him truly. For there are twelve heads of God the most

high: for he is the truth, and in him is no lie, neither forswearing.

6. Ye, therefore, go ye and preach unto all the world the word of truth, and thou, Bartholomew, preach this word unto every one that desireth it; and as many as believe thereon shall have eternal life.

7. Bartholomew saith: O Lord, and if any sin with sin of the body, what is their reward?

8. And Jesus said: It is good if he that is baptized present his baptism blameless: but the pleasure of the flesh will become a lover. For a single marriage belongeth to sobriety: for verily I say unto thee, he that sinneth after the third marriage (wife) is unworthy of God. (8 Lat. 2 is to this effect: . . . But if the lust of the flesh come upon him, he ought to be the husband of one wife. The married, if they are good and pay tithes, will receive a hundredfold. A second marriage is lawful, on condition of the diligent performance of good works, and due payment of tithes: but a third marriage is reprobated: and virginity is best.)

9. But ye, preach ye unto every man that they keep themselves from such things: for I depart not from you and I do supply you with the Holy Ghost. (lat. 2, At the end of 9, Jesus ascends in the clouds, and two angels appear and say: 'Ye men of Galilee', and the rest)

10. And Bartholomew worshipped him with the apostles, and glorified God earnestly, saying: Glory be to thee, Holy Father, Sun unquenchable, incomprehensible, full of light. Unto thee be glory, unto thee honour and adoration, world without end. Amen. (Lat. 2, End of the questioning of the most blessed Bartholomew and (or) the other apostles with the Lord Jesus Christ.)

THE BOOK OF THE RESURRECTION OF CHRIS
BY BARTHOLOMEW THE APOSTLE

This exists in Coptic only. There are several recensions of it: the most complete is in a manuscript recently acquired by the British Museum (Or. 6804), and translated first by W. E. Crum (Rustafjaell's light of Egypt, 1910) and then edited and translated by Sir E. A. Wallis Budge (Coptic Apocrypha in the dialect of Upper Egypt, 1913).

Christ is on the cross, but his side has been pierced, and he is dead.

A man in the crowd named Ananias, of Bethlehem, rushes to the cross and embraces and salutes the body breast to breast, hand to hand, and denounces the Jews. A voice comes from the body of Jesus and blesses Ananias, promising him incorruption and the name of ' the firstfruits of the immortal fruit '. The priests decide to stone Ananias: he utters words of exultation. The stoning produces no effect. They cast him into a furnace where he remains till Jesus has risen. At last they pierce him with a spear.

The Saviour takes his soul to heaven, and blesses him.

There can be but little matter lost between this and the opening of the British Museum MS., in the first lines of which the taking of Ananias' soul to heaven is mentioned.

We now take up the British Museum MS. as our basis. Certain passages of it are preserved in Paris fragments which partly overlap each other, and so three different texts exist for some parts: but it will not be important for our purpose to note many of the variations.

Joseph of Arimathaea buried the body of Jesus. Death came into Amente (the underworld), asking who the new arrival was, for he detected a disturbance.

He came to the tomb of Jesus with his six sons in the form of serpents. Jesus lay there (it was the second day, i. e. the Saturday) with his face and head covered with napkins.

Death addressed his son the Pestilence, and described the commotion which had taken place in his domain. Then he spoke to the body of Jesus and asked, 'Who art thou?' Jesus removed the napkin that was on his face and looked in the face of Death and laughed at him. Death and his sons fled. Then they approached again, and the same thing happened. He addressed Jesus again at some length, suspecting, but not certain, who he was.

Then Jesus rose and mounted into the chariot of the Cherubim. He wrought havoc in Hell, breaking the doors, binding the demons Beliar and Melkir (cf. Melkira in the Ascension of Isaiah), and delivered Adam and the holy souls.

Then he turned to Judas Iscariot and uttered a long rebuke, and described the sufferings which he must endure. Thirty names of sins are given, which are the snakes which were sent to devour him.

Jesus rose from the dead, and Abbaton (Death) and Pestilence came back to Amente to protect it, but they found it wholly desolate, only three souls were left in it (those of Herod, Cain, and Judas, says the Paris MS.).

Meanwhile the angels were singing the hymn which the Seraphim sing at dawn on the Lord's day over his body and his blood.

Early in the morning of the Lord's day the women went to the tomb. They were Mary Magdalene, Mary the mother of James whom Jesus delivered out of the hand of Satan, Salome who tempted him, Mary who ministered to him and Martha her sister, Joanna (al. Susanna) the wife of Chuza who had renounced the marriage bed, Berenice who was healed of an issue of blood in Capernaum, Lia (Leah) the widow whose son he raised at Nain, and the woman to whom he said, 'Thy sins which are many are forgiven thee'.

These were all in the garden of Philogenes, whose son Simeon Jesus healed when he came down from the Mount of Olives with the apostles (probably the lunatic boy at the Mount of Transfiguration).

Mary said to Philogenes: If thou art indeed he, I know thee. Philogenes said: Thou art Mary the mother of Thalkamarimath, which means joy, blessing, and gladness. Mary said: If thou have borne him away, tell me where thou hast laid him and I will take him away: fear not. Philogenes told how the Jews sought a safe tomb for Jesus that the body might not be stolen, and he offered to place it in a tomb in his own garden and watch over it: and they sealed it and departed. At midnight he rose and went out and found all the orders of angels: Cherubim Seraphim, Powers, and Virgins. Heaven opened, and the Father raised Jesus. Peter, too, was there and supported Philogenes, or he would have died.

The Saviour then appeared to them on the chariot of the Father and said to Mary: Mari Khar Mariath (Mary the mother of the Son of God). Mary answered: Rabbouni Kathiathari Mioth (The Son of God the Almighty, my Lord, and my Son.). A long address to Mary from Jesus follows, in the course of which he bids her tell his brethren, 'I ascend unto my Father and your Father', &c. Mary says: If indeed I am not permitted to touch thee, at least bless my body in which thou didst deign to dwell.

Believe me, my brethren the holy apostles, I, Bartholomew beheld the Son of God on the chariot of the Cherubim. All the heavenly hosts were about him. He blessed the body of Mary.

She went and gave the message to the apostles, and Peter blessed her, and they rejoiced.

Jesus and the redeemed souls ascended into Heaven, and the Father crowned him. The glory of this scene Bartholomew could not describe. It is here that he enjoins his son Thaddaeus not to let this book fall into the hands of the impure (quoted above).

Then follows a series of hymns sung in heaven, eight in all, which accompany the reception of Adam and the other holy souls into glory. Adam was eighty cubits high and Eve fifty. They were brought to the Father by Michael. Bartholomew had never seen anything to compare with the beauty and Glory of Adam, save that of Jesus. Adam was forgiven, and all the angels and saints rejoiced and saluted him, and departed each to their place.

Adam was set at the gate of life to greet all the righteous as they enter, and Eve was set over all the women who had done the will of God, to greet them as they come into the city of Christ.

As for me, Bartholomew, I remained many days without food or drink, nourished by the glory of the vision. The apostles thanked and blessed Bartholomew for what he had told them: he should be called the apostle of

the mysteries of God. But he protested: I am the least of you all, a humble workman. Will not the people of

the city say when they see me, 'Is not this Bartholomew the man of Italy, the gardener the dealer in vegetables? Is not this the man that dwelleth in the garden of Hierocrates the governor of our city? How has he attained this greatness?

The next words introduce a new section.

At the time when Jesus took us up into the Mount of Olives he spoke to us in an unknown tongue, which he revealed to us, saying: Anetharath (or Atharath Thaurath). The heavens were opened and we all went up into the seventh heaven (so the London MS.: in the Paris copy only Jesus went up, and the apostles gazed after him). He prayed the Father to bless us.

The Father, with the Son and the Holy Ghost, laid His hand on the head of Peter (and made him archbishop of the wholeworld: Paris B). All that is bound or loosed by him on earth shall be so in heaven; none who is not ordained by him shall be accepted. Each of the apostles was separately blessed (there are omissions of single names in one or other of the three texts). Andrew, James, John, Philip (the cross will precede him wherever he goes), Thomas, Bartholomew (he will be the depositary of the mysteries of the Son), Matthew (his shadow will heal the sick) James son of Alphaeus, Simon Zelotes, Judas of James, Thaddeus, Matthias who was rich and left all to follow Jesus).

And now, my brethren the apostles, forgive me: I, Bartholomew, am not a man to be honoured. The apostles kissed and blessed him. And then, with Mary, they offered the Eucharist.

The Father sent the Son down into Galilee to console the apostles and Mary: and he came and blessed them and showed them his wounds, and committed them to the care of Peter, and gave them their commission to preach. They kissed his side and sealed themselves with the blood that flowed thence. He went up to heaven.

Thomas was not with them, for he had departed to his city, hearing that his son Siophanes (Theophanes?) was dead: it was the seventh day since the death when he arrived. He went to the tomb and raised him in the name of Jesus.

Siophanes told him of the taking of his soul by Michael: how it sprang from his body and lighted on the hand of Michael, who wrapped it in a fine linen cloth: how he crossed the river of fire and it seemed to him as water, and was washed thrice in the Acherusian lake: how in heaven he saw the twelve splendid thrones of the apostles, and was not permitted to sit on his father's throne.

Thomas and he went into the city to the consternation of all who saw them. He, Siophanes, addressed the people and told his story: and Thomas baptized 12,000 of them, founded a church, and made Siophanes its bishop.

Then Thomas mounted on a cloud and it took him to the Molmtof Olives and to the apostles, who told him of the visit of Jesus: and he would not believe. Bartholomew admonished him. Then Jesus appeared, and made Thomas touch his wounds: and departed into heaven.

This is the second time that he showed himself to his disciples after that he had risen from the dead. This is the Book of the Resurrection of Jesus the Christ, our Lord, in joy and gladness. In peace. Amen.

Peter said to the apostles: Let us offer the offering before we separate. They prepared the bread, the cup, and incense.

Peter stood by the sacrifice and the others round the Table. They waited (break in the text: Budge and others suppose an appearance of Christ, but I do not think this is correct: 4 1/2 lines are gone then there are broken words): table . . . their hearts rejoiced . . . worshipped the Son of God. He took his seat . . . his Father (probably, who sitteth at the right hand of the Father). His Body was on the Table about which they were assembled; and they divided it. They saw the blood of Jesus pouring out as living blood down into the cup. Peter said: God hath loved us more than all, in letting us see these great honours: and our Lord Jesus Christ hath allowed us to behold and hath revealed to us the glory of his body and his divine blood. They partook of the body and blood-and then they separated and preached the word. (What is clearly indicated is a change in the elements: there is not room for a description of an appearance of Jesus: he says no word, and his departure is not mentioned.)

The Gospel of Nicodemus, or The Acts of Pilate

Memorials of our Lord Jesus Christ done in the time of Pontius Pilate

Prologue

I Ananias (Aeneas Copt., Emaus Lat.), the Protector, of praetorian rank, learned in the law, did from the divine scriptures recognize our Lord Jesus Christ and came near to him by faith and was accounted worthy of holy baptism: and I sought out the memorials that were made at that season in the time of our master Jesus Christ, which the Jews deposited with Pontius Pilate, and found the memorials in Hebrew (letters), and by the good pleasure of God I translated them into Greek (letters) for the informing of all them that call upon the name of our Lord Jesus Christ: in the reign of our Lord Flavius Theodosius, in the seventeenth year, and of Flavius Valentinianus the sixth, in the ninth indiction [corrupt: Lat. has the eighteenth year of Theodosius, when Valentinian was proclaimed Augustus, i. e. A. D. 425].

All ye therefore that read this and translate (or copy) it into other books, remember me and pray for me that God will be gracious unto me and be merciful unto my sins which I have sinned against him.

Peace be to them that read and that hear these things and to their servants. Amen.

In the fifteenth (al. nineteenth) year of the governance of Tiberius Caesar, emperor of the Romans, and of Herod, king of Galilee, in the nineteenth year of his rule, on the eighth of the Calends of April, which is the 25th of March, in the consulate of Rufus and Rubellio, in the fourth year of the two hundred and second Olympiad, Joseph who is Caiaphas being high priest of the Jews:

These be the things which after the cross and passion of the Lord Nicodemus recorded and delivered unto the high priest and the rest of the Jews: and the same Nicodemus set them forth in Hebrew (letters).

I

1. For the chief priests and scribes assembled in council, even Annas and Caiaphas and Somne (Senes,Summas) and Dothaim (Dothael, Dathaes, Datam) and Gamaliel, Judas, Levi and Nepthalim, Alexander and Jairus and the rest of the Jews, and came unto Pilate accusing Jesus for many deeds, saying: We know this man, that he is the son of Joseph the carpenter, begotten of Mary, and he saith that he is the Son of God and a king; more-over he doth pollute the sabbaths and he would destroy the law of our fathers.

Pilate saith: And what things are they that he doeth, and would destroy the law?

The Jews say: We have a law that we should not heal any man on the sabbath: but this man of his evil deeds hath healed the lame and the bent, the withered and the blind and the paralytic, the dumb and them that were possessed, on the sabbath day!

Pilate saith unto them: By what evil deeds?

They say unto him: He is a sorcerer, and by Beelzebub the prince of the devils he casteth out devils, and they are all subject unto him.

Pilate saith unto them: This is not to cast out devils by an unclean spirit, but by the god Asclepius.

2. The Jews say unto Pilate: We beseech thy majesty that he appear before thy judgement-seat and be heard. And Pilate called them unto him and said: Tell me, how can I that am a governor examine a king? They say unto him: We say not that he is a king, but he saith it of himself.

And Pilate called the messenger (cursor) and said unto him: Let Jesus be brought hither, but with gentleness. And the messenger went forth, and when he perceived Jesus he worshipped him and took the kerchief that was on his hand and spread it upon the earth and saith unto him: Lord, walk hereon and enter in, for the governor calleth thee. And when the Jews saw what the messenger had done, they cried out against Pilate saying: Wherefore didst thou not summon him by an herald to enter in, but by a messenger? for the messenger when he saw him worshipped him and spread out his kerchief upon the ground and hath made him walk upon it like a king!

3. Then Pilate called for the messenger and said unto him: Wherefore hast thou done this, and hast spread thy kerchief upon the ground and made Jesus to walk upon it? The messenger saith unto him: Lord governor, when thou sentest me to Jerusalem unto Alexander, I saw Jesus sitting upon an ass, and the children of the Hebrews held branches in their hands and cried out, and others spread their garments beneath him, saying: Save now, thou that art in the highest: blessed is he that cometh in the name of the Lord.

4. The Jews cried out and said unto the messenger: The children of the Hebrews cried out in Hebrew: how then hast thou it in the Greek? The messenger saith to them: I did ask one of the Jews and said: What is it that they cry out in Hebrew? and he interpreted it unto me.

Pilate saith unto them: And how cried they in Hebrew? The Jews say unto him: Hosanna membrome barouchamma adonai. Pilate saith unto them: And the Hosanna and the rest, how is it interpreted? The Jews say unto him: Save now, thou that art in the highest: blessed is he that cometh in the name of the Lord. Pilate saith unto them: If you yourselves bear witness of the words which were said of the children, wherein hath the messenger sinned? and they held their peace.

The governor saith unto the messenger: Go forth and bring him in after what manner thou wilt. And the messenger went forth and did after the former manner and said unto Jesus: Lord, enter in: the governor calleth thee.

5. Now when Jesus entered in, and the ensigns were holding the standards, the images (busts) of the standards bowed and did reverence to Jesus. And when the Jews saw the carriage of the standards, how they bowed themselves and did reverence unto Jesus, they cried out above measure against the ensigns. But Pilate said unto the Jews: Marvel ye not that the images bowed themselves and did reverence unto Jesus. The Jews say unto Pilate: We saw how the ensigns made them to bow and did reverence to him. And the governor called for the ensigns and saith unto them: Wherefore did ye so? They say unto Pilate: We are Greeks and servers of temples, and how could we do him reverence? for indeed, whilst we held the images they bowed of themselves and did reverence unto him.

6. Then saith Pilate unto the rulers of the synagogue and the elders of the people: Choose you out able and strong men and let them hold the standards, and let us see if they bow of themselves. And the elders of the Jews took twelve men strong and able and made them to hold the standards by

sixes, and they were set before the judgement-seat of the governor; and Pilate said to the messenger: Take him out of the judgement hall (praetorium) and bring him in again after what manner thou wilt. And Jesus went out of the judgement hall, he and the messenger. And Pilate called unto him them that before held the image and said unto them: I have sworn by the safety of Caesar that if the standards bow not when Jesus entereth in, I will cut off your heads.

And the governor commanded Jesus to enter in the second time. And the messenger did after the former manner and besought Jesus much that he would walk upon his kerchief; and he walked upon it and entered in. And when he had entered, the standards bowed themselves again and did reverence unto Jesus.

II

1. Now when Pilate saw it he was afraid, and sought to rise up from the judgement-seat. And while he yet thought to rise up, his wife sent unto him, saying: Have thou nothing to do with this just man, for I have suffered many things because of him by night. And Pilate called unto him all the Jews, and said unto them: Ye know that my wife feareth God and favoureth rather the customs of the Jews, with you? They say unto him: Yea, we know it. Pilate saith unto them: Lo, my wife hath sent unto me, saying: Have thou nothing to do with this just man: for I have suffered many things because of him by night. But the Jews answered and said unto Pilate: Said we not unto thee that he is a sorcerer? behold, he hath sent a vision of a dream unto thy wife.

2. And Pilate called Jesus unto him and said to him: What is it that these witness against thee? speakest thou nothing? But Jesus said: If they had not had power they would have spoken nothing; for every man hath power over his own mouth, to speak good or evil: they shall see to it.

3. The elders of the Jews answered and said unto Jesus: What shall we see? Firstly, that thou wast born of fornication; secondly, that thy birth in Bethlehem was the cause of the slaying of children; thirdly, that thy father Joseph and thy mother Mary fled into Egypt because they had no confidence before the people.

4. Then said certain of them that stood by, devout men of the Jews: We say not that he came of fornication; but we know that Joseph was betrothed unto Mary, and he was not born of fornication. Pilate saith unto those Jews which said that he came of fornication: This your saying is not true for there were espousals, as these also say which are of your nation. Annas and Caiaphas say unto Pilate: The whole multitude of us cry out that he was born of forni-

cation, and we are not believed: but these are proselytes and disciples of his. And Pilate called Annas and Caiaphas unto him and said to them: What be proselytes? They say unto him: They were born children of Greeks, and now are they become Jews. Then said they which said l that he was not born of fornication, even Lazarus, Asterius, Antonius, Jacob, Amnes, Zenas, Samuel, Isaac, Phinees, Crispus, Agrippa and Judas: We were not born proselytes (are not Greeks, Copt.), but we are children of Jews and we speak the truth; for verily we were present at the espousals of Joseph and Mary.

5. And Pilate called unto him those twelve men which said that he was not born of fornication, and saith unto them: I adjure you by the safety of Caesar, are these things true which ye have said, that he was not born of fornication? They say unto Pilate: We have a law that we swear not, because it is sin: But let them swear by the safety of Caesar that it is not as we have said, and we will be guilty of death. Pilate saith to Annas and Caiaphas: Answer ye nothing to these things? Annas and Caiaphas say unto Pilate: These twelve men are believed which say that he was not born of fornication, but the whole multitude of us cry out that he was born of fornication, and is a sorcerer, and saith that he is the Son of God and a king, and we are not believed.

6. And Pilate commanded the whole multitude to go out, saving the twelve men which said that he was not born of fornication and he commanded Jesus to be set apart: and Pilate saith unto them: For what cause do they desire to put him to death? They say unto Pilate: They have jealousy, because he healeth on the sabbath day. Pilate saith: For a good work do they desire to put him to death? They say unto him: Yea.

III

1. And Pilate was filled with indignation and went forth without the judgement hall and saith unto them: I call the Sun to witness that I find no fault in this man. The Jews answered and said to the governor: If this man were not a malefactor we would not have delivered him unto thee. And Pilate said: Take ye him and judge him according to your law. The Jews said unto Pilate: It is not lawful for us to put any man to death. Pilate said: Hath God forbidden you to slay, and allowed me?

2. And Pilate went in again into the judgement hall and called Jesus apart and said unto him: Art thou the King of the Jews? Jesus answered and said to Pilate: Sayest thou this thing of thyself, or did others tell it thee of me? Pilate answered Jesus: Am I also a Jew? thine own nation and the chief priests have delivered thee unto me: what hast thou done? Jesus answered: My kingdom is not of this world; for if my kingdom were of this world, my servants

would have striven that I should not be delivered to the Jews: but now is my kingdom not from hence. Pilate said unto him: Art thou a king, then? Jesus answered him: Thou sayest that I am a king; for this cause was I born and am come, that every one that is of the truth should hear my voice. Pilate saith unto him: What is truth? Jesus saith unto him: Truth is of heaven. Pilate saith: Is there not truth upon earth? Jesus saith unto Pilate: Thou seest how that they which speak the truth are judged of them that have authority upon earth.

IV

1. And Pilate left Jesus in the judgement hall and went forth to the Jews and said unto them: I find no fault in him. The Jews say unto him: This man said: I am able to destroy this temple and in three days to build it up.

Pilate saith: What temple? The Jews say: That which Solomon built in forty and six years but which this man saith he will destroy and build it in three days. Pilate saith unto them: I am guiltless of the blood of this just man: see ye to it. The Jews say: His blood be upon us and on our children.

2. And Pilate called the elders and the priests and Levites unto him and said to them secretly: Do not so: for there is nothing worthy of death whereof ye have accused him, for your accusation is concerning healing and profaning of the sabbath. The elders and the priests and Levites say: If a man blaspheme against Caesar, is he worthy of death or no? Pilate saith: He is worthy of death. The Jews say unto Pilate: If a man be worthy of death if he blaspheme against Caesar, this man hath blasphemed against God.

3. Then the governor commanded all the Jews to go out from the judgement hall, and he called Jesus to him and saith unto him: What shall I do with thee? Jesus saith unto Pilate: Do as it hath been given thee. Pilate saith: How hath it been given? Jesus saith: Moses and the prophets did foretell concerning my death and rising again. Now the Jews inquired by stealth and heard, and they say unto Pilate: What needest thou to hear further of this blasphemy? Pilate saith unto the Jews: If this word be of blasphemy, take ye him for his blasphemy, and bring him into your synagogue and judge him according to your law. The Jews say unto Pilate: It is contained in our law, that if a man sin against a man, he is worthy to receive forty stripes save one: but he that blasphemeth against God, that he should be stoned with stoning.

4. Pilate saith unto them: Take ye him and avenge yourselves of him in what manner ye will. The Jews say unto Pilate: We will that he be crucified. Pilate saith: He deserveth not to be crucified.

5. Now as the governor looked round about upon the multitude of the Jews which stood by, he beheld many of the Jews weeping, and said: Not all the multitude desire that he should be put to death. The elder of the Jews said: To this end have the whole multitude of us come Hither, that he should be put to death. Pilate saith to the Jews: Wherefore should he die? The Jews said: Because he called himself the Son of God, and a king.

V

1. But a certain man, Nicodemus, a Jew, came and stood before the governor and said: I beseech thee, good (pious) lord, bid me speak a few words. Pilate saith: Say on. Nicodemus saith: I said unto the elders and the priests and Levites and unto all the multitude of the Jews in the synagogue: Wherefore contend ye with this man? This man doeth many and wonderful signs, which no man hath done, neither will do: let him alone and contrive not any evil against him: if the signs which he doeth are of God, they will stand, but if they be of men, they will come to nought. For verily Moses, when he was sent of God into Egypt did many signs, which God commanded him to do before Pharaoh, king of Egypt; and there were there certain men servants of Pharaoh, Jannes and Jambres, and they also did signs not a few, of them which Moses did, and the Egyptians held them as gods, even Jannes and Jambres: and whereas the signs which they did were not of God, they perished and those also that believed on them. And now let this man go, for he is not worthy of death.

2. The Jews say unto Nicodemus: Thou didst become his disciple and thou speakest on his behalf. Nicodemus saith unto them: Is the governor also become his disciple, that he speaketh on his behalf? did not Caesar appoint him unto this dignity? And the Jews were raging and gnashing their teeth against Nicodemus.

Pilate saith unto them: Wherefore gnash ye your teeth against him, wherens ye have heard the truth? The Jews say unto Nicodemus: Mayest thou receive his truth and his portion. Nicodemus saith: Amen, Amen: may I receive it as ye have said.

VI

1. Now one of the Jews came forward and besought the governor that he might speak a word. The governor saith: If thou wilt say aught, speak on. And the Jew said: Thirty and eight years lay I on a bed in suffering of pains, and at the coming of Jesus many that were possessed and laid with divers diseases

291

were healed by him, and certain (faithful) young men took pity on me and carried me with my bed and brought me unto him; and when Jesus saw me he had compassion, and spake a word unto me: Take up thy bed and walk. And I took up my bed and walked. The Jews say unto Pilate: Ask of him what day it was whereon he was healed? He that was healed saith: On the sabbath. The Jews say: Did we not inform thee so, that upon the sabbath he healeth and casteth out devils?

2. And another Jew came forward and said: I was born blind: I heard words but I saw no man's face: and as Jesus passed by I cried with a loud voice: Have mercy on me, O son of David. And he took pity on me and put his hands upon mine eyes and I received sight immediately. And another Jew came forward and said: I was bowed and he made me straight with a word. And another said: I was a leper, and he healed me with a word.

VII

And a certain woman named Bernice (Beronice Copt., Veronica Lat.) crying out from afar off said: I had an issue of blood and touched the hem of his garment, and the flowing of my blood was stayed which I had twelve years. The Jews say: We have a law that a woman shall not come to give testimony.

VIII

And certain others, even a multitude both of men and women cried out, saying: This man is a prophet and the devils are subject unto him. Pilate saith to them which said: The devils are subject unto him: Wherefore were not your teachers also subject unto him? They say unto Pilate: We know not. Others also said: He raised up Lazarus which was dead out of his tomb after four days. And the governor was afraid and said unto all the multitude of the Jews: Wherefore will ye shed innocent blood?

IX

1. And he called unto him Nicodemus and those twelve men which said that he was not born of fornication, and said unto them: What shall I do, for there riseth sedition among the people? They say unto him: We know not, let them see to it. Again Pilate called for all the multitude of the Jews and saith: Ye know that ye have a custom that at the feast of unleavened bread I should release unto you a prisoner. Now I have a prisoner under condemnation in the prison, a murderer, Barabbas by name, and this Jesus also which standeth

before you, in whom I find no fault: Whom will ye that I release unto you? But they cried out: Barabbas. Pilate saith: What shall I do then with Jesus who is called Christ? The Jews say: Let him be crucified. But certain of the Jews answered: Thou art not a friend of Caesar's if thou let this man go; for he called himself the Son of God and a king: thou wilt therefore have him for king, and not Caesar.

2. And Pilate was wroth and said unto the Jews: Your nation is always seditious and ye rebel against your benefactors. The Jews say: Against what benefactors? Pilate saith: According as I have heard, your God brought you out of Egypt out of hard bondage, and led you safe through the sea as by dry land, and in the wilderness he nourished you with manna and gave you quails, and gave you water to drink out of a rock, and gave unto you a law. And in all these things ye provoked your God to anger, and sought out a molten calf, and angered your God and he sought to slay you: and Moses made supplication for you and ye were not put to death. And now ye do accuse me that I hate the king (emperor).

3. And he rose up from the judgement-seat and sought to go forth. And the Jews cried out, saying: We know our king, even Caesar and not Jesus. For indeed the wise men brought gifts from the east unto him as unto a king, and when Herod heard from the wise men that a king was born, he sought to slay him, and when his father Joseph knew that, he took him and his mother and they fled into Egypt. And when Herod heard it he destroyed the children of the Hebrews that were born in Bethlehem.

4. And when Pilate heard these words he was afraid. And Pilate silenced the multitude, because they cried still, and said unto them: So, then, this is he whom Herod sought? The Jews say: Yea, this is he. And Pilate took water and washed his hands before the sun, saying: I am innocent of the blood of this just man: see ye to it. Again the Jews cried out: His blood be upon us and upon our children.

5. Then Pilate commanded the veil to be drawn before the judgement-seat whereon he sat, and saith unto Jesus: Thy nation hath convicted thee (accused thee) as being a king: therefore have I decreed that thou shouldest first be scourged according to the law of the pious emperors, and thereafter hanged upon the cross in the garden wherein thou wast taken: and let Dysmas and Gestas the two malefactors be crucified with thee.

X

1. And Jesus went forth of the judgement hall and the two malefactors with him. And when they were come to the place they stripped him of his

garments and girt him with a linen cloth and put a crown of thorns about his head: likewise also they hanged up the two malefactors. But Jesus said: Father forgive them, for they know not what they do. And the soldiers divided his garments among them.

And the people stood looking upon him, and the chief priests and the rulers with them derided him, saying: He saved others let him save himself: if he be the son of God [let him come down from the cross]. And the soldiers also mocked him, coming and offering him vinegar with gall; and they said: If thou be the King of the Jews, save thyself.

And Pilate after the sentence commanded his accusation to be written for a title in letters of Greek and Latin and Hebrew according to the saying of the Jews: that he was the King of the Jews.

2. And one of the malefactors that were hanged [by name Gestas] spake unto him, saying: If thou be the Christ, save thyself, and us. But Dysmas answering rebuked him, saying: Dost thou not at all fear God, seeing thou art in the same condemnation? and we indeed justly, for we receive the due reward of our deeds; but this man hath done nothing amiss. And he said unto Jesus: Remember me, Lord, in thy kingdom. And Jesus said unto him: Verily, verily, I say unto thee, that today thou shalt be (art) with me in paradise.

XI

1. And it was about the sixth hour, and there was darkness over the land until the ninth hour, for the sun was darkened: and the veil of the temple was rent asunder in the midst. And Jesus called with a loud voice and said: Father, baddach ephkid rouel, which is interpreted: Into thy hands I commend my spirit. And having thus said he gave up the ghost. And when the centurion saw what was done, he glorified God, saying: This man was righteous. And all the multitudes that had come to the sight, when they beheld what was done smote their breasts and returned.

2. But the centurion reported unto the governor the things that had come to pass: and when the governor and his wife heard, they were sore vexed, and neither ate nor drank that day. And Pilate sent for the Jews and said unto them: Did ye see that which came to pass? But they said: There was an eclipse of the sun after the accustomed sort.

3. And his acquaintance had stood afar off, and the women which came with him from Galilee, beholding these things. But a certain man named Joseph, being a counsellor, of the city of Arimathaea, who also himself looked for the kingdom of God this man went to Pilate and begged the body of Jesus.

And he took it down and wrapped it in a clean linen cloth and laid it in a hewn sepulchre wherein was never man yet laid.

XII

1. Now when the Jews heard that Joseph had begged the body of Jesus, they sought for him and for the twelve men which said that Jesus was not born of fornication, and for Nicodemus and many others which had come forth before Pilate and declared his good works. But all they hid themselves, and Nicodemus only was seen of them, for he was a ruler of the Jews. And Nicodemus said unto them: How came ye into the synagogue? The Jews say unto him: How didst thou come into the synagogue? for thou art confederate with him, and his portion shall be with thee in the life to come. Nicodemus saith: Amen, Amen. Likewise Joseph also came forth and said unto them: Why is it that ye are vexed against me, for that I begged the body of Jesus? behold I have laid it in my new tomb, having wrapped it in clean linen, and I rolled a stone over the door of the cave. And ye have not dealt well with the just one, for ye repented not when ye had crucified him, but ye also pierced him with a spear.

But the Jews took hold on Joseph and commanded him to be put in safe-guard until the first day of the week: and they said unto him: Know thou that the time alloweth us not to do anything against thee, because the sabbath dawneth: but knew that thou shalt not obtain burial, but we will give thy flesh unto the fowls of the heaven. Joseph saith unto them: This is the word of Goliath the boastful which reproached the living God and the holy David. For God said by the prophet: Vengeance is mine, and I will recompense, saith the Lord. And now, lo, one that was uncircumcised, but circumcised in heart, took water and washed his hands before the sun, saying: I am Innocent of the blood of this just person: see ye to it. And ye answered Pilate and said: His blood be upon us and upon our children. And now I fear lest the wrath of the Lord come upon you and upon your children, as ye have said. But when the Jews heard these words they waxed bitter in soul, and caught hold on Joseph and took him and shut him up in an house wherein was no window, and guards were set at the door: and they sealed the door of the place where Joseph was shut up.

2. And upon the sabbath day the rulers of the synagogue and the priests and the Levites made an ordinance that all men should appear in the synagogue on the first day of the week. And all the multitude rose up early and took council in the synagogue by what death they should kill him. And when

the council was set they commanded him to be brought with great dishonour. And when they had opened the door they found him not. And all the people were beside themselves and amazed, because they found the seals closed, and Caiaphas had the key. And they durst not any more lay hands upon them that had spoken in the behalf of Jesus before Pilate.

XIII

1. And while they yet sat in the synagogue and marvelled because of Joseph, there came certain of the guard which the Jews had asked of Pilate to keep the sepulchre of Jesus lest peradventure his disciples should come and steal him away. And they spake and declared unto the rulers of the synagogue and the priests and the Levites that which had come to pass: how that there was a great earthquake, and we saw an angel descend from heaven, and he rolled away the stone from the mouth of the cave, and sat upon it. And he did shine like snow and like lightning, and we were sore afraid and lay as dead men. And we heard the voice of the angel speaking with the women which waited at the sepulchre, saying: Fear ye not: for I know that ye seek Jesus which was crucified. He is not here: he is risen, as he said. Come, see the place where the Lord lay, and go quickly and say unto his disciples that he is risen from the dead, and is in Galilee.

2. The Jews say: With what women spake he? They of the guard say: We know not who they were. The Jews say: At what hour was it? They of the guard say: At midnight. The Jews say: And wherefore did ye not take the women? They of the guard say: We were become as dead me through fear, and we looked not to see the light of the day; how then could we take them? The Jews say: As the Lord liveth, we believe you not. They of the guard say unto the Jews: So many signs saw ye in that man, and ye believed not, how then should ye believe us? verily ye sware rightly 'as the Lord liveth', for he liveth indeed. Again they of the guard say: We have heard that ye shut up him that begged the body of Jesus, and that ye sealed the door; and when ye had opened it ye found him not. Give ye therefore Joseph and we will give you Jesus. The Jews say: Joseph is departed unto his own city. They of the guard say unto the Jews: Jesus also is risen, as we have heard of the angel, and he is in Galilee.

3. And when the Jews heard these words they were sore afraid, saying: Take heed lest this report be heard and all men incline unto Jesus. And the Jews took counsel and laid down much money and gave it to the soldiers, saying: Say ye: While we slept his disciples came by night and stole him away. And if this come to the governor's hearing we will persuade him and secure

you. And they took the money and did as they were instructed. [And this their saying was published abroad among all men. lat.]

XIV

1. Now a certain priest named Phinees and Addas a teacher and Aggaeus (Ogias Copt., Egias lat.) a Levite came down from Galilee unto Jerusalem and told the rulers of the synagogue and the priests and the Levites, saying: We saw Jesus and his disciples sitting upon the mountain which is called Mamilch (Mambre or Malech lat., Mabrech Copt.), and he said unto his disciples: Go into all the world and preach unto every creature (the whole creation): he that believeth and is baptized shall be saved, but he that disbelieveth shall be condemned. [And these signs shall follow upon them that believe: in my name they shall cast out devils, they shall speak with new tongues, they shall take up serpents, and if they drink any deadly thing it shall not hurt them: they shall lay hands upon the sick and they shall recover.] And while Jesus yet spake unto his disciples we saw him taken up into heaven.

2. The elders and the priests and Levites say: Give glory to the God of Israel and make confession unto him: did ye indeed (or that ye did) hear and see those things which ye have told us? They that told them say: As the Lord God of our fathers Abraham, Isaac, and Jacob liveth, we did hear these things and we saw him taken up into heaven. The elders and the priests and the Levites say unto them: Came ye for this end, that ye might tell us, or came ye to pay your vows unto God? And they say: To pay our vows unto God. The elders and the chief priests and the Levites say unto them: If ye came to pay your vows unto God, to what purpose is this idle tale which ye have babbled before all the people? Phinees the priest and Addas the teacher and Aggaeus the Levite say unto the rulers of the synagogue and priests and Levites: If these words which ye have spoken and seen be sin, lo, we are before you: do unto us as seemeth good in your eyes. And they took the book of the law and adjured them that they should no more tell any man these words: and they gave them to eat and to drink, and put them out of the city: moreover they gave them money, and three men to go with them, and they set them on their way as far as Galilee, and they departed in peace.

3. Now when these men were departed into Galilee, the chief priests and the rulers of the synagogue and the elders gathered together in the synagogue, and shut the gate, and lamented with a great lamentation, saying: What is this sign which is come to pass in Israel? But Amlas and Caiaphas said: Wherefore are ye troubled? why weep ye? Know ye not that his disciples gave much

gold unto them that kept the sepulchre and taught them to say that an angel came down and rolled away the stone from the door of the sepulchre? But the priests and the elders said: Be it so, that his disciples did steal away his body; but how is his soul entered into his body, and how abideth he in Galilee? But they could not answer these things, and hardly in the end said: It is not lawful for us to believe the uncircumcised. [Lat. (and Copt., and Arm.): Ought we to believe the soldiers, that an angel came down from heaven and rolled away the stone from the door of the sepulchre? but in truth his disciples gave . . . sepulchre. Know ye not that it is not lawful for Jews to believe any word of the uncircumcised, knowing that they who received much good from us have spoken according as we taught them.]

XV

1. And Nicodemus rose up and stood before the council, saying: Ye say well. Know ye not, O people of the Lord, the men that came down out of Galilee, that they fear God and are men of substance, hating covetousness (a lie, Lat.), men of peace? And they have told you with an oath, saying: We saw Jesus upon the mount Mamilch with his disciples and that he taught them all things that ye heard of them, and, say they, we saw him taken up into heaven. And no man asked them in what manner he was taken up. For like as the book of the holy scriptures hath taught us that Elias also was taken up into heaven, and Eliseus cried out with a loud voice, and Elias cast his hairy cloak upon Eliseus, and Eliseus cast the cloak upon Jordan and passed over and went unto Jericho. And the sons of the prophets met him and said: Eliseus, where is thy lord Elias? and he said that he was taken up into heaven. And they said unto Eliseus: Hath not a spirit caught him up and cast him upon one of the mountains? but let us take our servants with us and seek after him. And they persuaded Eliseus and he went with them, and they sought him three days and found him not: and they knew that he had been taken up. And now hearken unto me, and let us send into all the coasts (al. mountains) of Israel and see whether the Christ were not taken up by a spirit and cast upon one of the mountains. And this saying pleased them all: and they sent into all the coasts (mountains, Lat.) and sought Jesus and found him not. But they found Joseph in Arimathaea, and no man durst lay hands upon him.

2. And they told the elders and the priests and the Levites, saying: We went about throughout all the coasts of Israel, and we found not Jesus; but Joseph we found in Arimathaea. And when they heard of Joseph they rejoiced and gave glory to the God of Israel. And the rulers of the synagogue and the priests and the Levites took counsel how they should meet with Joseph, and

they took a volume of paper and wrote unto Joseph these words:

Peace be unto thee. We know that we have sinned against God and against thee, and we have prayed unto the God of Israel that thou shouldest vouchsafe to come unto thy fathers and unto thy children (Lat. But thou didst pray unto the God of Israel, and he delivered thee out of our hands. Now therefore vouchsafe, &c.) for we are all troubled, because when we opened the door we found thee not: and we know that we devised an evil counsel against thee, but the Lord helped thee. And the Lord himself made of none effect (scattered) our counsel against thee, O father Joseph, thou that art honourable among all the people.

3. And they chose out of all Israel seven men that were friends of Joseph, whom Joseph also himself accounted his friends, and the rulers of the synagogue and the priests and the Levites said unto them: See: if he receive our epistle and read it, know that he will come with you unto us: but if he read it not, know that he is vexed with us, and salute ye him in peace and return unto us. And they blessed the men and let them go.

And the men came unto Joseph and did him reverence, and said unto him: Peace be unto thee. And he said: Peace be unto you and unto all the people of Israel. And they gave him the book of the epistle, and Joseph received it and read it and embraced (or kissed) the epistle and blessed God and said: Blessed be the Lord God, which hath redeemed Israel from shedding innocent blood; and blessed be the Lord, which sent his angel and sheltered me under his wings. (And he kissed them) and set a table before them, and they did eat and drink and lay there.

4. And they rose up early and prayed: and Joseph saddled his she-ass and went with the men, and they came unto the holy city, even Jerusalem. And all the people came to meet Joseph and cried: Peace be to thine entering-in. And he said unto all the people: Peace be unto you, and all the people kissed him. And the people prayed with Joseph, and they were astonished at the sight of him.

And Nicodemus received him into his house and made a great feast, and called Annas and Caiaphas and the elders and the priests and the Levites unto his house. And they made merry eating and drinking with Joseph. And when they had sung an hymn (or blessed God) every man went unto his house. But Joseph abode in the house of Nicodemus.

5. And on the morrow, which was the preparation, the rulers of the synagogue and the priests and the Levites rose up early and came to the house of

Nicodemus, and Nicodemus met them and said: Peace be unto you. And they said: Peace be unto thee and to Joseph and unto all thy house and to all the house of Joseph. And he brought them into his house. And the whole council was set, and Joseph sat between Annas and Caiaphas and no man durst speak unto him a word. And Joseph said: Why is it that ye have called me? And they beckoned unto Nicodemus that he should speak unto Joseph. And Nicodemus opened his mouth and said unto Joseph: Father, thou knowest that the reverend doctors and the priests and the Levites seek to learn a matter of thee. And Joseph said: Inquire ye. And Annas and Caiaphas took the book of the law and adjured Joseph saying: Give glory to the God of Israel and make confession unto him: [for Achar, when he was adjured of the prophet Jesus(-Joshua), foresware not himself but declared unto him all things and hid not a word from him: thou therefore also hide not from us so much as a word. And Joseph: I will not hide one word from you.] And they said unto him: We were greatly vexed because thou didst beg the body of Jesus and wrappedst it in a clean linen cloth and didst lay him in a tomb. And for this cause we put thee in safeguard in an house wherein was no window, and we put keys and seals upon the doors, and guards did keep the place wherein thou wast shut up. And on the first day of the week we opened it and found thee not, and we were sore troubled, and amazement fell upon all the people of the Lord until yesterday. Now, therefore, declare unto us what befell thee.

6. And Joseph said: On the preparation day about the tenth hour ye did shut me up, and I continued there the whole sabbath. And at midnight as I stood and prayed the house wherein ye shut me up was taken up by the four corners, and I saw as it were a flashing of light in mine eyes, and being filled with fear I fell to the earth. And one took me by the hand and removed me from the place whereon I had fallen; and moisture of water was shed on me from my head unto my feet, and an odour of ointment came about my nostrils. And he wiped my face and kissed me and said unto me: Fear not, Joseph: open thine eyes and see who it is that speaketh with thee. And I looked up and saw Jesus and I trembled, and supposed that it was a spirit: and I said the commandments: and he said them with me. And [as] ye are not ignorant that a spirit, if it meet any man and hear the commandments, straightway fleeth. And when I perceived that he said them with me, I said unto him:

Rabbi Elias? And he said unto me: I am not Elias. And I said unto him: Who art thou, Lord? And he said unto me: I am Jesus, whose body thou didst beg of Pilate, and didst clothe me in clean linen and cover my face with a napkin, and lay me in thy new cave and roll a great stone upon the door of the cave. And I said to him that spake with me: Show me the place where I laid thee. And he brought me and showed me the place where I laid him, and the linen cloth lay therein, and the napkin that was upon his face. And I knew that it was Jesus. And he took me by the hand and set me in the midst of mine house, the doors being shut, and laid me upon my bed and said unto me: Peace be unto thee. And he kissed me and said unto me: Until forty days be ended go not out of thine house: for behold I go unto my brethren into Galilee.

XVI

1. And when the rulers of the synagogue and the priests and the Levites heard these words of Joseph the became as dead men and fell to the ground, and they fasted until the ninth hour. And Nicodemus with Joseph comforted Annas and Caiaphas and the priests and the Levites, saying: Rise up and stand on your feet and taste bread and strengthen your souls, for tomorrow is the sabbath of the Lord. And they rose up and prayed unto God and did eat and drink, and departed every man to his house.

2. And on the sabbath the (al. our) teachers and the priests and Levites sat and questioned one another and said: What is this wrath that is come upon us? for we know his father and his mother. Levi the teacher saith: I know that his parents feared God and kept not back their vows and paid tithes three times a year. And when Jesus was born, his parents brought him up unto this place and gave sacrifices and burnt-offerings to God. And [when] the great teacher Symeon took him into his arms and said: Now lettest thou thy servant, Lord, depart in peace for mine eyes have seen thy salvation which thou hast prepared before the face of all peoples, a light to lighten the Gentiles and the glory of thy people Israel. And Symeon blessed them and said unto Mary his mother: I give thee good tidings concerning this child. And Mary said: Good, my lord? And Symeon said to her : Good. Behold, he is set for the fall and rising again of many in Israel, and for a sign spoken against: and a sword shall pierce through thine own heart also, that the thoughts of many hearts may be revealed.

3. They say unto Levi the teacher: How knowest thou these things? Levi saith unto them: Know ye not that from him I did learn the law? The council say unto him: We would see thy father. And they sent after his father, and asked of him, and he said to them: Why believed ye not my son? the blessed and righteous Symeon, he did teach him the law. The council saith: Rabbi Levi, is the word true which thou hast spoken? And he said: It is true.

Then the rulers of the synagogue and the priests and the Levites said among themselves: Come, let us send into Galilee unto the three men which came and told us of his teaching and his taking-up, and let them tell us how they saw him taken up. And this word pleased them all, and they sent the three men which before had gone with them into Galilee and said to them: Say unto Rabbi Addas and Rabbi Phinees and Rabbi Aggaeus: peace be to you and to all that are with you. Inasmuch as great questioning hath arisen in the council, we have sent unto you to call you unto this holy place of Jerusalem.

4. And the men went into Galilee and found them sitting and meditating upon the law, and saluted them in peace. And the men that were in Galilee said unto them that were come to them: Peace be upon all Israel. And they said: Peace be unto you. Again they said unto them: Wherefore are ye come? And they that were sent said: The council calleth you unto the holy city Jerusalem. And when the men heard that they were bidden by the council, they prayed to God and sat down to meat with the men and did eat and drink, and rose up and came in peace unto Jerusalem.

5. And on the morrow the council was set in the synagogue, and they examined them, saying: Did ye in very deed see Jesus sitting upon the mount Mamilch, as he taught his eleven disciples, and saw ye him taken up? And the men answered them and said: Even as we saw him taken up, even so did we tell it unto you.

6. Annas saith: Set them apart from one another, and let us see if their word agreeth. And they set them apart one from another, and they call Addas first and say unto him: How sawest thou Jesus taken up? Addas saith: While he yet sat upon the Mount Mamilch and taught his disciples, we saw a cloud that overshadowed him and his disciples: and the cloud carried him up into heaven, and his disciples lay (al. prayed, lying) on their faces upon the earth. And they called Phinees the priest, and questioned him also, saying: How sawest thou Jesus taken up? And he spake in like manner. And again they asked Aggaeus, and he also spake in like manner. And the council said: It is contained in the law of Moses: At the mouth of two or three shall every word be established.

Abuthem (Bouthem Gr., Abudem lat., Abuden, Abuthen Arm.,om. Copt.) the teacher saith: It is written in the law: Enoch walked with God and is not, because God took him. Jaeirus the teacher said: Also we have heard of the death of the holy Moses and have not seen him; for it is written in the law of the Lord: And Moses died at the mouth of the Lord, and no man knew of his sepulchre unto this day. And Rabbi Levi said: Wherefore was it that Rabbi Symeon said when he saw Jesus: Behold, this child is set for the fall and rising again of many in Israel and for a sign spoken against? And Rabbi Isaac said: It is written in the law: Behold I send my messenger before thy face, which shall go before thee to keep thee in every good way, for my name is named thereon.

7. Then said Annas and Caiaphas: Ye have well said those things which are written in the law of Moses, that no man saw the death of Enoch, and no man hath named the death of Moses. But Jesus spake before Pilate, and we know that we saw him receive buffets and spittings upon his face, and that the soldiers put on him a crown of thorns and that he was scourged and received condemnation from Pilate, and that he was crucified at the place of a skull and two thieves with him, and that they gave him vinegar to drink with gall, and that Longinus the soldier pierced his side with a spear, and that Joseph our honourable father begged his body, and that, as he saith, he rose again, and that (lit. as) the three teachers say: We saw him taken up into heaven, and that Rabbi Levi spake and testified to the things which were spoken by Rabbi Symeon, and that he said: Behold this child is set for the fall and rising again of many in Israel and for a sign spoken against.

And all the teachers said unto all the people of the Lord: If this hath come to pass from the Lord, and it is marvelous in our eyes, ye shall surely know, O house of Jacob, that it is written: Cursed is every one that hangeth upon a tree. And another scripture teacheth: The gods which made not the heaven and the earth shall perish.

And the priests and the Levites said one to another: If his memorial endure until the Sommos (Copt. Soum) which is called Jobel (i. e. the Jubilee), know ye that he will prevail for ever and raise up for himself a new people.

Then the rulers of the synagogue and the priests and the Levites admonished all Israel, saying: Cursed is that man who shall worship that which man's hand hath made, and cursed is the man who shall worship creatures beside the Creator. And all the people said: Amen, Amen.

And all the people sang an hymn unto the Lord and said: Blessed be the Lord who hath given rest unto the people of Israel according to all that he spake. There hath not one word fallen to the ground of all his good saying which he spake unto his servant Moses. The Lord our God be with us as he was with our fathers: let him not forsake us. And let him not destroy us from turning our heart unto him, from walking in all his ways and keeping his statutes and his judgements which he commanded our fathers. And the Lord shall be King over all the earth in that day. And there shall be one Lord and his name one, even the Lord our King: he shall save us.

There is none like unto thee, O Lord. Great art thou, O Lord, and great is thy name.

Heal us, O Lord, by thy power, and we shall be healed: save us, Lord, and we shall be saved: for we are thy portion and thine inheritance.

And the Lord will not forsake his people for his great name's sake, for the

Lord hath begun to make us to be his people.

And when they had all sung this hymn they departed every man to his house, glorifying God. [For his is the glory, world without end. Amen.]

ACTS OF PILATE

PART II. THE DESCENT INTO HELL

I

1. And Joseph arose and said unto Annas and Caiaphas: Truly and of right do ye marvel because ye have heard that Jesus hath been seen alive after death, and that he hath ascended into heaven. Nevertheless it is more marvelous that he rose not alone from the dead, but did raise up alive many other dead out of their sepulchres, and they have been seen of many in Jerusalem. And now hearken unto me; for we all know the blessed Simeon, the high priest which received the child Jesus in his hands in the temple. And this Simeon had two sons, brothers in blood and we all were at their falling asleep and at their burial. Go therefore and look upon their sepulchres: for they are open, because they have risen, and behold they are in the city of Arimathaea dwelling together in prayer. And indeed men hear them crying out, yet they speak with no man, but are silent as dead men. But come, let us go unto them and with all honour and gentleness bring them unto us, and if we adjure them, perchance they will tell us concerning the mystery of their rising again.

2. When they heard these things, they all rejoiced. And Annas and Caiaphas, Nicodemus and Joseph and Gamaliel went and found them not in their sepulchre, but they went unto the city of Arimathaea, and found them there, kneeling on their knees and giving themselves unto prayer. And they kissed them, and with all reverence and in the fear of God they brought them to Jerusalem into the synagogue. And they shut the doors and took the law of the Lord and put it into their hands, and adjured them by the God Adonai and the God of Israel which spake unto our fathers by the prophets, saying: Believe ye that it is Jesus which raised you from the dead? Tell us how ye have arisen from the dead.

3 .And when Karinus and Leucius heard this adjuration, they trembled in their body and groaned, being troubled in heart. And looking up together unto heaven they made the seal of the cross with their fingers upon their tongues, and forthwith they spake both of them, saying: Give us each a volume of paper, and let us write that which we have seen and heard. And they

gave them unto them, and each of them sat down and wrote, saying:

II

1. O Lord Jesu Christ, the life and resurrection of the dead (al. resurrection of the dead and the life of the living), suffer us to speak of the mysteries of thy majesty which thou didst perform after thy death upon the cross, inasmuch as we have been adjured by thy Name. For thou didst command us thy servants to tell no man the secrets of thy divine majesty which thou wroughtest in hell.

Now when we were set together with all our fathers in the deep, in obscurity of darkness, on a sudden there came a golden heat of the sun and a purple and royal light shining upon us. And immediately the father of the whole race of men, together with all the patriarchs and prophets, rejoiced, saying: This light is the beginning (author) of everlasting light which did promise to send unto us his co-eternal light. And Esaias cried out and said: This is the light of the Father, even the Son of God, according as I prophesied when I lived upon the earth: The land of Zabulon and the land of Nephthalim beyond Jordan, of Galilee of the Gentiles, the people that walked in darkness have seen a great light, and they that dwell in the land of the shadow of death, upon them did the light shine. And now hath it come and shone upon us that sit in death.

2. And as we all rejoiced in the light which shined upon us, there came unto us our father Simeon, and he rejoicing said unto us: Glorify ye the Lord Jesus Christ, the Son of God; for I received him in my hands in the temple when he was born a child, and being moved of the Holy Ghost I made confession and said unto him: Now have mine eyes seen thy salvation which thou hast prepared before the face of all people, a light to lighten the Gentiles, and to be the glory of thy people Israel. And when they heard these things, the whole multitude of the saints rejoiced yet more.

3. And after that there came one as it were a dweller in the wilderness, and he was inquired of by all: Who art thou? And he answered them and said: I am John, the voice and the prophet of the most High, which came before the face of his advent to prepare his ways, to give knowledge of salvation unto his people, for the remission of their sins. And when I saw him coming unto me, being moved of the Holy Ghost, I said: Behold the Lamb of God, behold him that taketh away the sins of the world. And I baptized him in the river of Jordan, and saw the Holy Ghost descending upon him in the likeness of a dove, and heard a voice out of heaven saying: This is my beloved Son, in

whom I am well pleased. And now have I come before his face, and come down to declare unto you that he is at hand to visit us, even the day spring, the Son of God, coming from on high unto us that sit in darkness and in the shadow of death.

III

1. And when father Adam that was first created heard this, even that Jesus was baptized in Jordan, he cried out to Seth his son, saying: Declare unto thy sons the patriarchs and the prophets all that thou didst hear from Michael the archangel, when I sent thee unto the gates of paradise that thou mightest entreat God to send thee his angel to give thee the oil of the tree of mercy to anoint my body when I was sick. Then Seth drew near unto the holy patriarchs and prophets, and said: When I, Seth, was praying at the gates of paradise, behold Michael the angel of the Lord appeared unto me, saying: I am sent unto thee from the Lord: it is I that am set over the body of man. And I say unto thee, Seth, vex not thyself with tears, praying and entreating for the oil of the tree of mercy, that thou mayest anoint thy father Adam for the pain of his body: for thou wilt not be able to receive it save in the last days and times, save when five thousand and five hundred (al. 5,952) years are accomplished: then shall the most beloved Son of God come upon the earth to raise up the body of Adam and the bodies of the dead, and he shall come and be baptized in Jordan. And when he is come forth of the water of Jordan, then shall he anoint with the oil of mercy all that believe on him, and that oil of mercy shall be unto all generations of them that shall be born of water and of the Holy Ghost, unto life eternal. Then shall the most beloved Son of God, even Christ Jesus, come down upon the earth and shall bring in our father Adam into paradise unto the tree of mercy.

And when they heard all these things of Seth, all the patriarchs and prophets rejoiced with a great rejoicing.

IV

1. And while all the saints were rejoicing, behold Satan the prince and chief of death said unto Hell: Make thyself ready to receive Jesus who boasteth himself that he is the Son of God, whereas he is a man that feareth death, and sayeth: My soul is sorrowful even unto death. And he hath been much mine enemy, doing me great hurt, and many that I had made blind, lame, dumb, leprous, and possessed he hath healed with a word: and some whom I have brought unto thee dead, them hath he taken away from thee.

2. Hell answered and said unto Satan the prince: Who is he that is so mighty, if he be a man that feareth death? for all the mighty ones of the earth are held in subjection by my power, even they whom thou hast brought me subdued by thy power. If, then, thou art mighty, what manner of man is this Jesus who, though he fear death, resisteth thy power? If he be so mighty in his manhood, verily I say unto thee he is almighty in his god-head, and no man can withstand his power. And when he saith that he feareth death, he would ensnare thee, and woe shall be unto thee for everlasting ages. But Satan the prince of Tartarus said: Why doubtest thou and fearest to receive this Jesus which is thine adversary and mine? For I tempted him, and have stirred up mine ancient people of the Jews with envy and wrath against him. I have sharpened a spear to thrust him through, gall and vinegar have I mingled to give him to drink, and I have prepared a cross to crucify him and nails to pierce him: and his death is nigh at hand, that I may bring him unto thee to be subject unto thee and me.

3. Hell answered and said: Thou hast told me that it is he that hath taken away dead men from me. For there be many which while they lived on the earth have taken dead men from me, yet not by their own power but by prayer to God, and their almighty God hath taken them from me. Who is this Jesus which by his own word without prayer hath drawn dead men from me? Perchance it is he which by the word of his command did restore to life Lazarus which was four days dead and stank and was corrupt, whom I held here dead. Satan the prince of death answered and said: It is that same Jesus. When Hell heard that he said unto him: I adjure thee by thy strength and mine own that thou bring him not unto me. For at that time I, when I heard the command of his word, did quake and was overwhelmed with fear, and all my ministries with me were troubled. Neither could we keep Lazarus, but he like an eagle shaking himself leaped forth with all agility and swiftness, and departed from us, and the earth also which held the dead body of Lazarus straightway gave him up alive. Wherefore now I know that that man which was able to do these things is a God strong in command and mighty in manhood, and that he is the saviour of mankind. And if thou bring him unto me he will set free all that are here shut up in the hard prison and bound in the chains of their sins that cannot be broken, and will bring them unto the life of his god head for ever.

V

1. And as Satan the prince, and Hell, spoke this together, suddenly there came a voice as of thunder and a spiritual cry: Remove, O princes, your gates,

and be ye lift up, ye everlasting doors, and the King of glory shall come in. When Hell heard that he said unto Satan the prince: Depart from me and go out of mine abode: if thou be a mighty man of war, fight thou against the King of glory. But what hast thou to do with him? And

Hell cast Satan forth out of his dwelling. Then said Hell unto his wicked ministers: Shut ye the hard gates of brass and put on them the bars of iron and withstand stoutly, lest we that hold captivity be taken captive.

2. But when all the multitude of the saints heard it, they spake with a voice of rebuking unto Hell: Open thy gates, that the King of glory may come in. And David cried out, saying: Did I not when I was alive upon earth, foretell unto you: Let them give thanks unto the Lord, even his mercies and his wonders unto the children of men; who hath broken the gates of brass and smitten the bars of iron in sunder? he hath taken them out of the way of their iniquity. And thereafter in like manner Esaias said: Did not I when I was alive upon earth foretell unto you: The dead shall arise, and they that are in the tombs shall rise again, and they that are in the earth shall rejoice, for the dew which cometh of the Lord is their healing? And again I said: O death, where is thy sting? O Hell, where is thy victory?

3. When they heard that of Esaias, all the saints said unto Hell: Open thy gates: now shalt thou be overcome and weak and without strength. And there came a great voice as of thunder, saying: Remove, O princes, your gates, and be ye lift up ye doors of hell, and the King of glory shall come in. And when Hell saw that they so cried out twice, he said, as if he knew it not: Who is the King of glory? And David answered Hell and said: The words of this cry do I know, for by his spirit I prophesied the same; and now I say unto thee that which I said before: The Lord strong and mighty, the Lord mighty in battle, he is the King of glory. And: The Lord looked down from heaven that he might hear the groanings of them that are in fetters and deliver the children of them that have been slain. And now, O thou most foul and stinking Hell, open thy gates, that the King of glory may come in. And as David spake thus unto Hell, the Lord of majesty appeared in the form of a man and lightened the eternal darkness and brake the bonds that could not be loosed: and the succour of his everlasting might visited us that sat in the deep darkness of our transgressions and in the shadow of death of our sins.

VI

1. When Hell and death and their wicked ministers saw that, they were stricken with fear, they and their cruel officers, at the sight of the brightness

308

of so great light in their own realm, seeing Christ of a sudden in their abode, and they cried out, saying: We are overcome by thee. Who art thou that art sent by the Lord for our confusion? Who art thou that without all damage of corruption, and with the signs (?) of thy majesty unblemished, dost in wrath condemn our power? Who art thou that art so great and so small, both humble and exalted, both soldier and commander, a marvelous warrior in the shape of a bondsman, and a King of glory dead and living, whom the cross bare slain upon it? Thou that didst lie dead in the sepulchre hast come down unto us living and at thy death all creation quaked and all the stars were shaken and thou hast become free among the dead and dost rout our legions. Who art thou that settest free the prisoners that are held bound by original sin and restorest them into their former liberty? Who art thou that sheddest thy divine and bright light upon them that were blinded with the darkness of their sins? After the same manner all the legions of devils were stricken with like fear and cried out all together in the terror of their confusion, saying: Whence art thou, Jesus, a man so mighty and bright in majesty, so excellent without spot and clean from sin? For that world of earth which hath been always subject unto us until now, and did pay tribute to our profit, hath never sent unto us a dead man like thee, nor ever dispatched such a gift unto Hell. Who then art thou that so fearlessly enterest our borders, and not only fearest not our torments, but besides essayest to bear away all men out of our bonds? Peradventure thou art that Jesus, of whom Satan our prince said that by thy death of the cross thou shouldest receive the dominion of the whole world.

2. Then did the King of glory in his majesty trample upon death, and laid hold on Satan the prince and delivered him unto the power of Hell, and drew Adam to him unto his own brightness.

VII

1. Then Hell, receiving Satan the prince, with sore reproach said unto him. O prince of perdition and chief of destruction, Beelzebub, the scorn of the angels and spitting of the righteous why wouldest thou do this? Thou wouldest crucify the King of glory and at his decease didst promise us great spoils of his death: like a fool thou knewest not what thou didst. For behold now, this Jesus putteth to flight by the brightness of his majesty all the darkness of death, and hath broken the strong depths of the prisons, and let out the prisoners and loosed them that were bound. And all that were sighing in our torments do rejoice against us, and at their prayers our dominions are vanquished and our realms conquered, and now no nation of men feareth

us any more. And beside this, the dead which were never wont to be proud triumph over us, and the captives which never could be joyful do threaten us. O prince Satan, father of all the wicked and ungodly and renegades wherefore wouldest thou do this? They that from the beginning until now have despaired of life and salvation-now is none of their wonted roarings heard, neither doth any groan from them sound in our ears, nor is there any sign of tears upon the face of any of them. O prince Satan, holder of the keys of hell, those thy riches which thou hadst gained by the tree of transgression and the losing of paradise, thou hast lost by the tree of the cross, and all thy gladness hath perished. When thou didst hang up Christ Jesus the King of glory thou wroughtest against thyself and against me. Henceforth thou shalt know what eternal torments and infinite pains thou art to suffer in my keeping for ever. O prince Satan, author of death and head of all pride, thou oughtest first to have sought out matter of evil in this Jesus: Wherefore didst thou adventure without cause to crucify him unjustly against whom thou foundest no blame, and to bring into our realm the innocent and righteous one, and to lose the guilty and the ungodly and unrighteous of the whole world? And when Hell had spoken thus unto Satan the prince, then said the King of glory unto Hell: Satan the prince shall be in thy power unto all ages in the stead of Adam and his children, even those that are my righteous ones.

VIII

1. And the Lord stretching forth his hand, said: Come unto me, all ye my saints which bear mine image and my likeness. Ye that by the tree and the devil and death were condemned, behold now the devil and death condemned by the tree. And forthwith all the saints were gathered in one under the hand of the Lord. And the Lord holding the right hand of Adam, said unto him: Peace be unto thee with all thy children that are my righteous ones. But Adam, casting himself at the knees of the Lord entreated him with tears and beseechings, and said with a loud voice: I will magnify thee, O Lord, for thou hast set me up and not made my foes to triumph over me: O Lord my God I cried unto thee and thou hast healed me; Lord, thou hast brought my soul out of hell, thou hast delivered me from them that go down to the pit. Sing praises unto the Lord all ye saints of his, and give thanks unto him for the remembrance of his holiness. For there is wrath in his indignation and life is in his good pleasure. In like manner all the saints of God kneeled and cast themselves at the feet of the Lord, saying with one accord: Thou art come, O redeemer of the world: that which thou didst foretell by the law and by thy prophets, that hast thou accomplished in deed. Thou hast redeemed

the living by thy cross, and by the death of the cross thou hast come down unto us, that thou mightest save us out of hell and death through thy majesty. O Lord, like as thou hast set the name of thy glory in the heavens and set up thy cross for a token of redemption upon the earth, so, Lord, set thou up the sign of the victory of thy cross in hell, that death may have no more dominion.

2. And the Lord stretched forth his hand and made the sign of the cross over Adam and over all his saints, and he took the right hand of Adam and went up out of hell, and all the saints followed him. Then did holy David cry aloud and say: Sing unto the Lord a new song, for he hath done marvelous things. His right hand hath wrought salvation for him and his holy arm. The Lord hath made known his saving health, before the face of all nations hath he revealed his righteousness. And the whole multitude of the saints answered, saying: Such honour have all his saints. Amen, Alleluia.

3. And thereafter Habacuc the prophet cried out and said: Thou wentest forth for the salvation of thy people to set free thy chosen. And all the saints answered, saying: Blessed is he that cometh in the name of the Lord. God is the Lord and hath showed us light. Amen, Alleluia. Likewise after that the prophet Micheas also cried, saying: What God is like thee, O Lord, taking away iniquity and removing sins? and now thou withholdest thy wrath for a testimony that thou art merciful of free will, and thou dost turn away and have mercy on us, thou forgivest all our iniquities and hast sunk all our sins in the depths of the sea, as thou swarest unto our fathers in the days of old. And all the saints answered, saying: This is our God for ever and ever, he shall be our guide, world without end. Amen, Alleluia. And so spake all the prophets, making mention of holy words out of their praises, and all the saints followed the Lord, crying Amen, Alleluia.

IX

1. But the Lord holding the hand of Adam delivered him unto Michael the archangel, and all the saints followed Michael the archangel, and he brought them all into the glory and beauty (grace) of paradise. And there met with them two men, ancients of days, and when they were asked of the saints: Who are ye that have not yet been dead in hell with us and are set in paradise in the body? then one of them answering, said: I am Enoch which was translated hither by the word of the Lord, and this that is with me is Elias the Thesbite which was taken up in a chariot of fire: and up to this day we have not tasted death, but we are received unto the coming of Antichrist to fight against him with signs and wonders of God, and to be slain of him in Jerusa-

lem, and after three days and a half to be taken up again alive on the clouds.

X

1. And as Enoch and Elias spake thus with the saints, behold there came another man of vile habit, bearing upon his shoulders the sign of the cross; whom when they beheld, all the saints said unto him: Who art thou? for thine appearance is as of a robber; and wherefore is it that thou bearest a sign upon thy shoulders? And he answered them and said: Ye have rightly said: for I was a robber, doing all manner of evil upon the earth. And the Jews crucified me with Jesus, and I beheld the wonders in the creation which came to pass through the cross of Jesus when he was crucified, and I believed that he was the maker of all creatures and the almighty king, and I besought him, saying: Remember me, Lord, when thou comest into thy kingdom. And forthwith he received my prayer, and said unto me: Verily I say unto thee, this day shalt thou be with me in paradise: and he gave me the sign of the cross, saying: Bear this and go unto paradise, and if the angel that keepeth paradise suffer thee not to enter in, show him the sign of the cross; and thou shalt say unto him: Jesus Christ the Son of God who now is crucified hath sent me. And when I had so done, I spake all these things unto the angel that keepeth paradise; and when he heard this of me, forthwith he opened the door and brought me in and set me at the right hand of paradise, saying: Lo now, tarry a little, and Adam the father of all mankind will enter in with all his children that are holy and righteous, after the triumph and glory of the ascending up of Christ the Lord that is crucified. When they heard all these words of the robber, all the holy patriarchs and prophets said with one voice: Blessed be the Lord Almighty, the Father of eternal good things, the Father of mercies, thou that hast given such grace unto thy sinners and hast brought them again into the beauty of paradise and into thy good pastures: for this is the most holy life of the spirit. Amen, Amen.

XI

1. These are the divine and holy mysteries which we saw and heard, even I, Karinus, and Leucius: but we were not suffered to relate further the rest of the mysteries of God, according as Michael the archangel strictly charged us, saying: Ye shall go with your brethren unto Jerusalem and remain in prayer, crying out and glorifying the resurrection of the Lord Jesus Christ, who hath raised you from the dead together with him: and ye shall not be speaking with any man, but sit as dumb men, until the hour come when the Lord

himself suffereth you to declare the mysteries of his god head. But unto us Michael the archangel gave commandment that we should go over Jordan unto a place rich and fertile, where are many which rose again together with us for a testimony of the resurrection of Christ the Lord. For three days only were allowed unto us who rose from the dead, to keep the passover of the Lord in Jerusalem with our kindred (parents) that are living for a testimony of the resurrection of Christ the Lord: and we were baptized in the holy river of Jordan and received white robes, every one of us. And after the three days, when we had kept the passover of the Lord, all they were caught up in the clouds which had risen again with us, and were taken over Jordan and were no more seen of any man. But unto us it was said that we should remain in the city of Arimathaea and continue in prayer.

These be all things which the Lord bade us declare unto you: give praise and thanksgiving (confession) unto him, and repent that he may have mercy upon you. Peace be unto you from the same Lord Jesus Christ which is the Saviour of us all. Amen.

And when they had finished writing all things in the several volumes of paper they arose; and Karinus gave

that which he had written into the hands of Annas and Caiaphas and Gamaliel; likewise Leucius gave that which he had written into the hands of Nicodemus and Joseph. And suddenly they were transfigured and became white exceedingly and were no more seen. But their writings were found to be the same (lit. equal), neither more nor less by one letter.

And when all the synagogue of the Jews heard all these marvelous sayings of Karinus and Leucius, they said one to another: Of a truth all these things were wrought by the Lord, and blessed be the Lord, world without end, Amen. And they went out all of them in great trouble of mind, smiting their breasts with fear and trembling, and departed every man unto his own home.

And all these things which were spoken by the Jews in their synagogue, did Joseph and Nicodemus forthwith declare unto the governor. And Pilate himself wrote all the things that were done and said concerning Jesus by the Jews, and laid up all the words in the public books of his judgement hall (praetorium).

XII

1. After these things Pilate entered into the temple of the Jews and gathered together all the chief of the priests, and the teachers (grammaticos) and scribes and doctors of the law, and went in with them into the holy place of the temple and commanded all the doors to be shut, and said unto them: We

have heard that ye have in this temple a certain great Bible; wherefore I ask you that it be presented before us. And when that great Bible adorned with gold and precious jewels was brought by four ministers, Pilate said to them all: I adjure you by the God of your fathers which commanded you to build this temple in the place of his sanctuary, that ye hide not the truth from me. Ye know all the things that are written in this Bible; but tell me now if ye have found in the scriptures that this Jesus whom ye have crucified is the Son of God which should come for the salvation of mankind, and in what year of the times he must come. Declare unto me whether ye crucified him in ignorance or knowingly.

And Annas and Caiaphas when they were thus adjured commanded all the rest that were will them to go out of the temple; and they themselves shut all the doors of the temple and of the sanctuary, and said unto Pilate: Thou hast adjured us, O excellent judge, by the building of this temple to make manifest unto thee the truth and reason (or a true account). After that we had crucified Jesus, knowing not that he was the Son of God, but supposing that by some chance he did his wondrous works, we made a great assembly (synagogue) in this temple; and as we conferred one with another concerning the signs of the mighty works which Jesus had done, we found many witnesses of our own nation who said that they had seen Jesus alive after his passion, and that he was passed into the height of the heaven. Moreover, we saw two witnesses whom Jesus raised from the dead, who declared unto us many marvelous things which Jesus did among the dead, which things we have in writing in our hands. Now our custom is that every year before our assembly we open this holy Bible and inquire the testimony of God. And we have found in the first book of the Seventy how that Michael the angel spake unto the third son of Adam the first man concerning the five thousand and five hundred years, wherein should come the most beloved Son of God, even Christ: and furthermore we have thought that peradventure this same was the God of Israel which said unto Moses: Make thee an ark of the covenant in length two cubits and a half, and in breadth one cubit and a half, and in height one cubit and a half. For by those five cubits and a half we have understood and known the fashion of the ark of the old covenant, for that in five thousand and a half thousand years Jesus Christ should come in the ark of his body: and we have found that he is the God of Israel, even the Son of God. For after his passion, we the chief of the priests, because we marvelled at the signs which came to pass on his account did open the Bible, and searched out all the generations unto the generation of Joseph, and Mary the mother of Christ, taking her to be the seed of David: and we found that from the day when God made the heaven and the earth and the first man, from that time unto the Flood are 2,212 years: and from the Flood unto the building of the tower 531 years: and from the building of the tower unto Abraham 606 years: and from Abraham unto the coming of the children of Israel out of Egypt 470 years: and from the going of the children of Israel out of Egypt unto the building of the temple 511 years: and from the building of the temple unto the destruction of the same temple 464 years: so far found we in the Bible of Esdras: and inquiring from the burning of the temple unto the coming of Christ and his birth we found it to be 636 years, which together were five thousand and five hundred years like as we found it written in the Bible that Michael the archangel declared before unto Seth the third son of Adam, that after five thousand and a half thousand years Christ the Son of God hath (? should) come. Hitherto have we told no man, lest there should be a schism in our synagogues; and now, O excellent judge, thou hast adjured us by this holy Bible of the testimonies of God, and we do declare it unto thee: and we also have adjured thee by thy life and health that thou declare not these words unto any man in Jerusalem.

XIII

1. And Pilate, when he heard these words of Annas and Caiaphas, laid them all up amongst the acts of the Lord and Saviour in the public books of his judgement hall, and wrote a letter unto Claudius the king of the city of Rome, saying:

[The following Epistle or Report of Pilate is inserted in Greek into the late Acts of Peter and Paul (_ 40) and the Pseudo-Marcellus Passion of Peter and Paul (_ 19). We thus have it in Greek and Latin, and the Greek is used here as the basis of the version.]

Pontius Pilate unto Claudius, greeting.

There befell of late a matter which I myself brought to light (or made trial of): for the Jews through envy have punished themselves and their posterity with fearful judgements of their own fault; for whereas their fathers had promises (al. had announced unto them) that their God would send them out of heaven his holy one who should of right be called their king, and did promise that he would send him upon earth by a virgin; he, then (or this God of the Hebrews, then), came when I was governor of Judaea, and they beheld him enlightening the blind, cleansing lepers, healing the palsied, driving devils out of men, raising the dead, rebuking the winds, walking upon the waves of the sea dry-shod, and doing many other wonders, and all the people of the Jews calling him the Son of God: the chief priests therefore, moved with envy against him, took him and delivered him unto me and brought against him one false accusation after another, saying that he was a sorcerer and did things contrary to their law.

But I, believing that these things were so, having scourged him, delivered him unto their will: and they crucified him, and when he was buried they set guards upon him. But while my soldiers watched him he rose again on the third day: yet so much was the malice of the Jews kindled that they gave money to the soldiers, saying: Say ye that his disciples stole away his body. But they, though they took the money, were not able to keep silence concerning that which had come to pass, for they also have testified that they saw him arisen and that they received money from the Jews. And these things have I reported for this cause, lest some other should lie unto thee (lat. lest any lie otherwise) and thou shouldest deem right to believe the false tales of the Jews.

The Gospel of Peter - Last

Introduction

The early testimonies about this book have been set forth already. The present fragment was discovered in 1884 in a tomb at Akhmimin Egypt. The manuscript is a little book containing a portion of the Book of Enoch in Greek.

FRAGMENT I

But of the Jews no man washed his hands, neither did Herod nor any one of his judges: and whereas they would not wash, Pilate rose up. And then Herod the king commanded that the Lord should be taken into their hands, saying unto them: All that I commanded you to do unto him, do ye

2. Now there stood there Joseph the friend of Pilate and of the Lord, and he, knowing that they were about to crucify him, came unto Pilate and begged the body of Jesus for burial. And Pilate sending unto Herod, begged his body. And Herod said: Brother Pilate, even if none had begged for him, we should have buried him, since also the Sabbath dawneth, for it is written in the law that the sun should not set upon one that hath been slain (murdered).

3. And he delivered him unto the people before the first day of (or on the day before the) unleavened bread, even their feast. And they having taken the Lord pushed him as they ran, and said: Let us hale the Son of God, now that we have gotten authority over him. And they put on him a purple robe, and made him sit upon the seat of judgement, saying: Give righteous judgement, thou King of Israel. And one of them brought a crown of thorns and set it upon the Lord's head; and others stood and did spit in his eyes, and

others buffeted his cheeks; and others did prick him with a reed, and some of them scourged him, saying With this honour let us honour (or at this price let us value) the son of God.

4. And they brought two malefactors, and crucified the Lord between them. But he kept silence, as one feeling no pain. And when they set the cross upright, they wrote thereon: This is the King of Israel. And they laid his garments before him, and divided them among themselves and cast the lot upon them. But one of those malefactors reproached them, saying: We have thus suffered for the evils which we have done; but this man which hath become the saviour of men, wherein hath he injured you? And they were wroth with him, and commanded that his legs should not be broken, that so he might die in torment.

5. Now it was noonday, and darkness prevailed over all Judaea: and they were troubled and in an agony lest the sun should have set, for that he yet lived: for it is written for them that the sun should not set upon him that hath been slain (murdered). And one of them said: Give ye him to drink gall with vinegar: and they mingled it and gave him to drink: and they fulfilled all things and accomplished their sins upon their own heads. And many went about with lamps, supposing that it was night: and some fell. And the Lord cried out aloud saying: My power, my power, thou hast forsaken me. And when he had so said, he was taken up. And in the same hour was the veil of the temple of Jerusalem rent in two.

6. And then they plucked the nails from the hands of the Lord and laid him upon the earth: and the whole earth was shaken, and there came a great fear on all. Then the sun shone forth, and it was found to be the ninth hour. And the Jews rejoiced, and gave his body unto Joseph to bury it, because he had beheld all the good things which he did. And he took the Lord and washed him and wrapped him in linen and brought him unto his own sepulchre, which is called the Garden of Joseph.

7. Then the Jews and the elders and the priests, when they perceived how great evil they had done themselves, began to lament and to say: Woe unto our sins: the judgement and the end of Jerusalem is drawn nigh. But I with my fellows was in grief, and we were wounded in our minds and would have hid ourselves; for we were sought after by them as malefactors, and as thinking to set the temple on fire. And beside all these things we were fasting, and we sat mourning and weeping night and day until the Sabbath.

8. But the scribes and Pharisees and elders gathered one with another, for they had heard that all the people were murmuring and beating their breasts, saying: If these very great signs have come to pass at his death, behold how righteous he was. And the elders were afraid and came unto Pilate, entreating

him and saying: Give us soldiers that we (or they) may watch his sepulchre for three days, lest his disciples come and steal him away and the people suppose that he is risen from the dead, and do us hurt. And Pilate gave them Petronius the centurion with soldiers to watch the sepulchre; and the elders and scribes came with them unto the tomb, and when they had rolled a great stone to keep out (al. together with) the centurion and the soldiers, then all that were there together set it upon the door of the tomb; and plastered thereon seven seals; and they pitched a tent there and kept watch.

9. And early in the morning as the Sabbath dawned, there came a multitude from Jerusalem and the region roundabout to see the sepulchre that had been sealed. Now in the night whereon the Lord's day dawned, as the soldiers were keeping guard two by two in every watch, there came a great sound in the heaven, and they saw the heavens opened and two men descend thence, shining with (lit. having) a great light, and drawing near unto the sepulchre. And that stone which had been set on the door rolled away of itself and went back to the side, and the sepulchre was

10. opened and both of the young men entered in. When therefore those soldiers saw that, they waked up the centurion and the elders (for they also were there keeping watch); and while they were yet telling them the things which they had seen, they saw again three men come out of the sepulchre, and two of them sustaining the other (lit. the one), and a cross following, after them. And of the two they saw that their heads reached unto heaven, but of him that was led by them that it overpassed the heavens. And they heard a voice out of the heavens saying: Hast thou (or Thou hast) preached unto them that sleep? And an answer was heard from the cross, saying: Yea.

11. Those men therefore took counsel one with another to go and report these things unto Pilate. And while they yet thought thereabout, again the heavens were opened and a man descended and entered into the tomb. And they that were with the centurion (or the centurion and they that were with him) when they saw that, hasted to go by night unto Pilate and left the sepulchre whereon they were keeping watch, and told all that they had seen, and were in great agony, saying: Of a truth he was the son of God. Pilate answered and said: I am clear from the blood of the son of God, but thus it seemed good unto you. Then all they came and besought him and exhorted him to charge the centurion and the soldiers to tell nothing of that they had seen: For, said they, it is expedient for us to incur the greatest sin before God, rather than to (and not to) fall into the hands of the people of the Jews and to be stoned. Pilate therefore charged the centurion and the soldiers that they should say nothing.

12. Now early on the Lord's day Mary Magdalene, a disciple (fem.) of the Lord-which, being afraid because of the Jews, for they were inflamed with anger, had not performed at the sepulchre of the Lord those things which women are accustomed to do unto them that die and are beloved of them-took with her the women her friends and came unto the tomb where he was laid. And they feared lest the Jews should see them, and said: Even if we were not able to weep and lament him on that day whereon he was crucified, yet let us now do so at his tomb. But who will roll away for us the stone also that is set upon the door of the tomb, that we may enter in and sit beside him and perform that which is due? for the stone was great, and we fear lest any man see us. And if we cannot do so, yet let us cast down at the door these things which we bring for a memorial of him, and we will weep and lament until we come unto our house.

13. And they went and found the sepulchre open : and they drew near and looked in there, and saw there a young man sitting in the midst of the sepulchre, of a fair countenance and clad in very bright raiment, which said unto them: Wherefore are ye come? whom seek ye? not him that was crucified? He is risen and is departed; but if ye believe it not, look in and see the place where he lay, that he is not here: for he is risen and is departed thither whence he was sent. Then the women were affrighted and fled.

14. Now it was the last day of unleavened bread, and many were coming forth of the city and returning unto their own homes because the feast was at an end. But we, the twelve disciples of the Lord, were weeping and were in sorrow, and each one being grieved for that which had befallen departed unto his own house. But I, Simon Peter, and Andrew my brother, took our nets and went unto the sea: and there was with us Levi the son of Alphaeus, whom the Lord (For Fragment II see Apocalypse of Peter.)

The Gospel of Phillip

Hebrew makes another Hebrew, and such a person is called proselyte. But a proselyte does not make another proselyte. Some both exist just as they are and make others like themselves, while others simply exist. The slave seeks only to be free, but he does not hope to acquire the estate of his master. But the son is not only a son but lays claim to the inheritance of the father. Those who are heirs to the dead are themselves dead, and they inherit the dead. Those who are heirs to what is living are alive, and they are heirs to both what is living and the dead. The dead are heirs to nothing. For how can he who is dead inherit? If he who is dead inherits what is living he will not die, but he who is dead will live even more.

A Gentile does not die, for he has never lived in order that he may die. He who has believed in the truth has found life, and this one is in danger of dying, for he is alive. Ever since Chirst came the world is created, the cities adorned, the dead carried out. When we were Hebrews we were orphans and had only our mother, but when we became Christians we had both father and mother.

Those who sow in winter reap in summer. The winter is the world, the summer the other Aeon. Let us sow in the world that we may reap in the summer. Because it is not fitting for us not to pray in the winter. Summer follows winter. But if any man reap in the winter hw will not actually reap but pluck out, since this sort of thing will not provide him a harvest. It is not only noc that the fruit will not come forth, but also on the Sabbath his field will be barren.

Christ came to ransom some, to save others, to redeem others. He ransomed those who were strangers and made them his own. And he set his own apart, those whom he gave as a pledge in his will. It was not only when he appeared that he voluntarily laid down his life, but he voluntarily laid down his life from the very day the world came into being. Then he came forth in order to take it, since it has been given as a pledge. It fell into the hands of robbers and was taken captive , but he saved it. He redeemed the good people in the world as well as the evil.

Light and Darkness, life and death, right and left, are brothers of one another. They are inseparable.Because of this neither are the good good, nor evil evil, nor is life life, nor death death. For this reason each one will dissolve into its original nature. But those who are exalted above the world are indissoluble, eternal.

Names given to worldly things are very deceptive for they divert our thoughts from what is correct to what is incorrect. Thus one who hears the word God does not perceive what is correct, but perceives what is incorrect. So also with the Father and the Son and Holy Spirit and life and light and ressurrection and the Church(Ekklesia) and all the rest - people do not perceive what is correct. The names which are heard in the world to deceive. If they were in the Aeon, they would at no time be used as names in the world.Nor were they set among worldly things. They have an end in the Aeon.

One single name is not uttered in the world, the name which the Father gave to the Son, the name above all things; the name of the Father. For the Son would not become Father unless he wears the name of the Father. Thos who have this name know it, buut they do not speak it. But those who do not have it do not know it.

But truth brought names into existennce in the world because it is not possible to teach without names. Truth is one single thing and it is also many things for our sakes who learn this one thing in love through many things. The powers wanted to deceive man, since they saw that he had kinship with those that are truly good. They took the name of those that are good and gave it to those who are not good, so that through the names they might deceive him and bind them to those that are not good. And afterward, if they do them a favor, they will be made to remove them from those that are not good and place them among those that are good. These things they knew, for they wanted to take the free man and make him a slave to them forever.

These are the powers which contend against man, not wishing him to be saved. For if man is saved, there will not be any sacrifices and animals will not be offered to the powers. They were indeed offering them up alive, but then they offered them up they died. As for (the Son of?) man, they offered him up to God dead, and he lived.

Before Christ came there was no bread in the world, just as Paradise, the place were Adam was, had many trees to nourish the animals but no wheat to sustain man. Man used to feed like the animals, but when Christ came, the perfect man, he brought bread from heaven in order that man might be nourished with the food of man. The powers thought that it was by their own power and will they were doing what they did ,but the Holy Spirit in secret accomplished everything through them as it wished. Truth, which existed since the beginning, is sown everywhere. And many see it as it is sown, but few are they who see it as it is reaped.

Some said,Mary conceived by the Holy Spirit, they are in error. They do not know what they are saying.When did a woman ever conceive by a woman? Mary is the virgin whom no power defiled. She is a great anathema to the Hebrews, who are the apostles and apostolic men. This virgin whom no power defiled; the powers defiled themselves. And the Lord would not have said My Father who is in Heaven[Matt16:17] unless he had had another father, but he would have said simply My father.

The Lord said to the disciples Bring out from every other hourse Bring into the house of the Father. But do not take anything in the house of the Father nor carry it off.

Jesus is a hidden name; Christ is a revealed name for this reason:Jesus does not exist in any other language, but his name is always Jesus as he is called. Christ is also his name; in Syriac it is Messiah, in Greek it is Christ. Certainly all the others have it according to their own language.The Nazarene is he who reveals what is hidden. Christ has everything in himself - man, angel, mystery, and the Father.

Those who say that the Lord died first and then rose up are in error, for he rose up first and then died. If one does not first attain the ressurection will he not die? As God lives, he would already be dead.

No one will hide a large valuable objectin something large, but many a time one has tossed countless thousands into a thing worth a penny. Compare the Soul. It is a precious thing and it came to be in a contemptible body.

Some are afraid lest they rise naked. Because of this they wish to rise in the flesh, and they do not know that it is those who wear the flesh who are naked. It is those who [...] to unclothe themselves who are not naked.Flesh and Blood shall not be able to inherit the kingdom of God[1Cor15:50] What is this which will not inherit? This which is on us. But what is this very thing which will inherit? It is that which belongs to Jesus and his blood. Because of this he said He who shall not eat my flesh and drink my blood has not life in him[John6:53] What is it? His flesh is the word, and his blood is the Holy Spirit. He who have received these has food and he has drink and clothing. I find fault with the others who say that it will not rise. Then both of them are at fault. You say that the flesh will not rise. But tell me what will rise, that we may honour you. You say the Spirit in the flesh, and it is also this light in the flesh. But this too is a matter which is in the flesh, for whatever you shall say, you say nothing outside the flesh.It is necessary to rise in this flesh, since everything exists in it.In this world those who put on garments are better than the garments. In the Kingdom of Heaven the garments are better than those that put them on.

It is through water and fire that the whole place is purified - the visible by the visible, the hidden by the hidden. There are some things hidden through those visible. There is water in the water, there is fire in the chrism. Jesus took them all by stealth, for he did not reveal himself in the manner in which he was, but it was in the manner in which they would be able to see him that he revealed himself. He revealed himself to them all. He revealed himself as great to the great. He revealed himself as small to the small. He revealed himself to the angels as an angel. Because of this his word hid itself from everyone. Some indeed saw him, thinking that they were seeing themselves, but when he appeared to his disciples in glory on the mount he was not small. He became great, but he made the disciples great,that they might be able to see his greatness. He said on that day in the Thanksgiving You who have joined the perfect, the light, with the Holy Spirit, unite the angels with us also, the images. Do not despise the lamb, for without it, it is not possible to see the king.No one will be able to go in to the king if he is naked.

The heavenly man has many more sons than the earthly man.If the sons if Adam are many, although they die, how much more the sons of the perfect manm they who do not die but are always begotten. The father makes a son, and the son has not the power to make a son. For he who has been begotten has not the power to beget, but the sons gets brothers for himself, not sons. All who are begotten in the world in a natural way, and the others in a spiritual way. Those who are begotten by him cry out from that place to the perfect man, because they are nourished on the promise concerning the heavenly place. If the word has gone out from that place it would become perfect. For it is by a kiss that the perfect conceive and give birth. For this reason we also kiss one another. We receive conception from the grace which is in each other.

There were three who always walked with the Lord; Mary, his mother, and his sister and Magdalene, the one who was his companion. His sister and his mother and his companion were each a Mary.

The Father and the Son is both single names, the Holy Spirit is a double name. For they are everywhere: they apore in the concealed, they are in the revealed. The Holy Spirit is the revealed: it is below. It is in the concealed: it is above.

The saints are served by evil powers, for they are blinded by the Holy Spirit into thinking that they are serving an ordinary man whenever they do something for the saints. Because of this a disciple asked the Lord one day for something of this world. He said to him: Ask your mother, and she will give you of the things which are another`s.

The apostles said to the disciples:May our offering obtain salt They called Sophia salt. Without it no offering is acceptable. But Sophia is without child. For this reason she is called a trace of salt . But where they will be in their own way, the Holy Spirit will also be, and her children are many.

What the father possesses belongs to the son, and the son himself, so long as he is small, is not entrusted with what is his. But when he becomes a man his father give him all that he possesses. Those who have gone astray, whom the spirit itself begets, usaully go astray because of the Spirit. Thus, by this one and the same breath, the fire blazes and is put out.

Echamoth is one thing and Echmoth, another. Echamoth is Wisdom simply, but Echmoth is the Wisdom of death which is the one who knows death [called The little wisdom]. There are domestic animals like the bull and the ass and others of this kind. Others are wild and live apart in the deserts. Man ploughs the field by means of the domestic animals, and from this he feeds both himself and the animals, wether tame or wild. Compare the perfect man. It is through powers which are submissive that he ploughs, prepairing for everything to come into being. For it is because of this that the whole place stands, wether good or evil, the right and the left. The Holy Spirit shepherds everyone and rules all the powers, the tame ones and the wild ones, as well as those which are unique. For indeed she gathers them and shuts them inn, in order that these, even if they wish, will not be able to escape. He who has been created us beautiful, and you would find his sons noble creations. If he was not created, but begotten, you would find that his seed was noble. But now he was created and he begot. What nobility is this? First, adultery came into being, afterward murder. And he was begotten in adultery, for he was the child of the Serpent. So he became a murderer, just like his father, and he killed his brother. Indeed, every act of sexual intercourse which has accured between those who are unlike one another is adultery.

God is a dyer. As the good dyes which are called true, dissolve with the things dyed in them, so it is with those whom God has dyed.Since the dyes is immortal, they are immortal by means of his co,ors. Now God dips what he dips in water. It is not possible for anyone to see anything of the things that actually exist unless he becomes like them. This is not the way with man in the world: he sees the sun without being a sun; and he sees the heaven and the earth and all other things, but he is not these things. You saw the Spirit, and you became spirit. You saw Christ and you became Christ [a christian]. You saw the Father and you shall become Father. So in this place you see everything and do not see yourself; but in that place you do see yourself - and what you see you shall become.

Faith receives, Love gives. No one will be able to receive without faith.No one will be able to give without love. Because of this, in order that we may indeed receive, we believe; but it is so that we may love and give, since if one does not give in love, he has no profit from what he has given. He who has not received the Lord is still a Hebrew.

The apostles who were before us had these names for him: Jesus,the Nazorean, Messiah, that is , Jesus, the Nazorean, Christ The last name is Christ, the first is Jesus, that in the middle is the Nazarne Messiah has two meanings, both the Christ and the measured. Jesus in Hebrew is the redemption Nazara is the Truth. The Nazarene then, is the Truth.Christ has been measured. The Nazarene and Jesus are they who have been measured.

When the pearl is cast down into the mud it does not become greatly despised, nor if it is anointed with balsam oil will it become more precious. But it always has value in the eyes of the owner. Compare the Sons of God, whatever they may be. They still have value in the eyes of their Father.

God is a man-eater. For this reason men are sacrificed to him. Before men were sacrificed animals were being sacrificed, since those to whom they were sacrificed were not gods. Glass decanters and earthenware jugs are both made by means of fire. But if glass decanters break they are done over, for they came into being through a breath. If earthenware jugs break, however, they are destroyed, for they came into being without breath.

An ass which turns a millstone did a hundred miles of walking. When it was loosened, it found that it was still at the same place. There are men who make many journeys, but make no progress towards a destination. When evening came upon them, they saw neither city nor village, neither creation nor nature, power nor angel. In vain have the wretches labored.

The eucharist is Jesus. For he is called in Syriac Pharisatha which is the one who is spread out for Jesus came crufifying the world. The Lord went into the dye works of Levi. He took seventy-two different colors and threw them into the vat. He took them out all white. And he said, Even so the Son of Man come as a dyer

As for the Wisdom who is called the barren she is the mother of the angels.And the companion of the Saviour is Mary Magdalene. But Christ loved her more than all the disciples and used to kiss her often on the mouth. The rest of the disciples were offended by it and expressed disapproval. They said to him Why do you love her more than all of us? The Saviour answered and said to them,Why do I not love you like her?.When a blind man and one who sees are together in the darkness, they are no different from one another. When the light comes, then he who sees will see the light, and he who is blind will remain in the darkness. The Lord said Blessed is he who is before he came into being. For he who is, has been and shall be The superiority of man is not obvious to the eye but lies in what is hidden from view. Consequently, he has mastery over the animals which are stronger than he is and great in terms of the obvious and the hidden. This enables them to survive. But if man is separated from them, they slay one another and bite one another. They ate one another because they did not find any food. But now they have found food because man tilled the soil.

If one goes down into the water and comes up again without having received anything, and says I am a Chrjstian he has borrowed the name at interest. But if he receives the Holy Spirit, he has the name as a gift. He who has received a gift does not have to give it back, but of him who has borrowed it at interest, payment is demanded. This is the way it happens to one when one experiences a mystery. Great is the mystery of marriage! For without it the world would not have existed. Now the existence of the world depends on man, and the existence of man on marriage. Think of the undefiled relationship, for it possesses a great power. Its image consists of a defilement of the form.

As for the unclean spirits, there are males among them and there are females. The males are they which unite with the souls which inhabit a female form, but the females are they which are mingled with those in a male form, through one who was disobedient. And none shall be able to escape them, since they detain him if he does not receive a male power or a female power - the bridegroom and the bride.One receives them from the mirrored bridal chamber. When the wanton women see a male sitting alone, they leap down on him and play with him and defile him. So also the lecherous men, when they see a beautiful woman sitting alone, they persuade her and comple her, wishing to defile her. But if they see the man and his wife sitting beside one another, the female cannot come into the man, nor can the male come into a woman. So if the image and the angel are united with one another, neither can any venture to go into the man or the woman.

He who comes out of the world can no longer be detained, because he was in the world. It is evident that he is above desire and fear. He is master over nature. He is superior to envy. If anyone else comes, they seize him and throttle him. And how will this one be able to escape the great grasping powers? How will he be able to hide from them? Often some come and say We are faithful in order that they may be able to escape the unclean spirits and the demons. For if they had the Holy Spirit no unclean spirit would cleave to them. Fear not the flesh nor love it. If you fear it, it will gain mastery over you. If you love it, it will swallow and paralyzr you. Either will he be in this world or in the ressurrection ot in the places of the middle.God forbid that I be found in them! In this world there is good and evil.Its good is not good, and its evil not evil. But there is evil after this world which is truly evil - what is called the Middle,It is death. While we are in this world it is fitting for us to acquire the ressurrection for ourselves, so that when we strip off the flesh we may be found in rest and not walk in the Middle.For many go astray on the way. For it is good to come forth from the world before one has sinned.

Some neither desire to sin nor are able to sin. Others, even if they desire to sin, are not better off for not having done it, for this desire makes them sinners. But even if some do not desire to sin, rightousness will be concealed for them both - those who desire not and do not. An apostolic man in a vision saw some people shut up in a house afire and bound with fiery chains, lying in flaming ointment. And he said to them Why are they not able to be saved? They answered They did not desire it. They received this place as punishment,what is called the outer darkness, because he is thrown out into it. It is from water and fire that the soul and the spirit came into being. It is from water and fire and light that the son of the bridal chamber came into being. The fire is the chrism, the light is the fire. I am not referring to that fire which has no form, but the other fire whose for are white, which is bright and beautiful, and which gives beauty.

Truth did not come into the world naked, but it came in types and images. One will receive the truth in any other way. There is a rebirth and an image of rebirth.It is certainly necessary that they should be born again through the image. The bridegroom and the image must enter through the image into the truth: this is the restoration. It is appropiate that those who do not have it only acquire the name of the Father and the Son, and the Holy Spirit, but that the have acquired it on their own. If one does not acquire the name for himself, the name Christian will also be taken from him. But one receives them in the aromatic unction of the power of the cross.This power the apostles called the right and the left For this person is no longer a Christian but a Christ.

The Lord did everything in a mystery, a baptism and a chrism and a eucharist and a redemption and a bridal chamber. The Lord said,I came to make the things below like the things above, and the things outside like the inside. I came to unite them bil that place He revealed himself in this place through types and images. Those who say, There is a heavenly man and there is one above him are wrong.For he who is revealed in Heaven is that heavenly man, the one who is called the one who is below, and he to whom the hidden belongs is that one who is above him. For it is good that they should say, The inner and outer, with what is outside the outer. Because of this the

Lord called destruction the the outer darkness; there is not another outside of it. He said,My Father who is secret. He said , Go into your chamber and shut the door behind you, and pray to your Father who is secret[Matt6:6], the one who is within them all. But that which is within them all is the fullness. Beyond it there is nothing else within it. This is that of which they say, That which is above them.

Before Christ some came from a place they were no longer able to enter, and they went where they were no longer able to come out. The Christ came. Those who went in he brought out, and those who went out, he brought in. When Eve was still with Adam, death did not exist. When she was separated from him, death came into being. If he again becomes complete and attains his former self, death will be no more.

My God, my God, why, O Lord, have you forsaken me? [Mark15:23].It was on the cross that he said these words, for it was there he was divided.

Everyone who has been begotten through him who destroys did not emanate from God.

The Lord rose from the dead. He became as he used to be, but now his body was perfect. He did indeed possess flesh, but this flesh is true flesh. Our flesh is not true, but we only possess an image of that which is true. A bridal chamber is not for the animals, nor is it for the slaves, nor for the defiled women, but it is for free men and virgins. Through the Holy Spirit we are indeed begotten again, but we are begotten through Christ in the two. We are anointed through the Spirit. When we were begotten by we were united. None shall be able to see himself either in the water or in a mirror without the light. Nor again will you be able to see in light without mirror or water. For this reason it is fitting to baptize in the two, in the light and in the water. Now the light is the chrism.

There were three buildings specifically for sacrifice in Jerusalem. The one facing the west was called The Holy. Another facing the South was called The Holy of the Holy. The third facing the East was called The Holy of the Holies, the place where only the high priest enters. Baptism is the Holy building. Redemption is the Holy of the Holy building. The Holy of the Holies is the bridal chamber. Baptism includes ressurrection and the redemption; the redemption takes place in the bridal chamber. But the bridal chamber is in that which is superior to it and the others, because you will not find anything like it. Those who are familiar with it are those who prays in the Holy in Jerusalem. There are some in Jerusalem, awaiting the Kingdom of Heaven. These are called the Holy of the Holies because before the veil was rent we had no other bridal chamber except for the image of the bridal chamber which is above. Because of this, its veil was rent from top to bottom. For it was fitting for some from below to go upward.

The powers do not see those who are clothed in the perfect light, and consequently are not able to detain them. One will clothe himself in this light sacramentally in the union.

If the woman had not separated from the man, she would not die with the man. His separation became the beginning of death. Because of this Christ came to repair the separation which was from the beginning and to again unite the two, to give life to those who died as a result of the separation and unite them. But the woman is united to her husband in the bridal chamber. Indeed, those who have united in the bridal chamber will no longer be separated. Thus Eve separated from Adam because she was never united with him in the bridal chamber.

The soul of Adam came into being by means of a breath(pneuma), which is a synonym for spirit(Pneuma). The Spirit given him is his mother. His soul was replaced by a spirit. When he was united to the spirit, he spoke words incomprehensible to the powers. They envied him because they were separated from the spiritual union. This separation afforded them the opportunity to fashion for themselves the symbolic bridal chamber so that men would be defiled.

Jesus revealed himself at the Jordan: it was the fullness of the Kingdom of Heaven.He who was begotten before everything was begotten anew. He who was once anointed was anointed anew. He who was redeemed in turn redeemed others.

Is it permitted to utter a mystery? The Father of everything united with the virgin who came down, and a fire shone for him on that day. He appeared in the great bridal chamber. Therefore his body came into being on that very day.It left the bridal chamber as one who came into being from the bridegroom and the bride. So Jesus established everything in it through these. It is fitting for each of the disciples to enter into his rest.

Adam came into being from two virgins, from the Spirit and from the virgin of earth.Christ therefore, was born from a virgin to rectify the Fall which occured in the beginning.

There are two trees growing in Paradise. One bears animals, the other bears men. Adam ate from the tree which bore animals. He became an animal and he brought forth animals. For this reason the children of Adam worship animals. The tree whose gifte Adam ate is the Tree of Knowledge. That is why sins increased. If he ate the fruit of the other tree, that is to say, the Tree of Life, the one which bears men, then the gods would worship man. For in the beginning God created man. But now men create God. That is the way it is in the world - men make gods and worship their creation. It would be fitting for the gods to worship men!

Surely what a man accomplishes depends on his abilities. We even refer to one's accomplishments as abilities. Among his accomplishments are his children. They originate in a moment of ease. Thus his abilities determine what he may accomplish,, but this ease is clearly evident in the children.You will find that this applies directly to the image. Here is the man made after the image, accomplishing things with his physical strenght but produving his children with ease. In this world slaves serve the free. In the Kingdom of Heaven the free will minister to the slaves: the children of the bridal chamber will minister to the children of the marriage. The children of the bridal chamber have just one name. Together they shall share rest. They need take no other form because they have contemplation, comprehending by insight. They are numorous because they do not put their treasure in the things below, which are despised, but in the glories which are above, though they did not yet know them.

Those who will be baptized go down into the water. But Christ, by coming out of the water, will consecrate it, so that they who have received the baptism in his name may be perfect. For he said,Thus we should fulfill all righteousness[Matt3:15]

Those who say they will die first and then rise are in error. If they do not first receive the ressurrection while they live, when they die they will receive nothing. So also when speaking about baptism they say Baptism is a great thing because if people receive it it they will live. Phillip the apostle said, Joseph the carpenter planted a garden because he needed wood for his trade. it was he who made the cross from the trees which he planted. His own offspring hung on that which he planted. His offspring was Jesus and the planting was the cross. But the Tree of Life is in the middle of the Garden. However,it is from the olive tree that we got the chrism, and from the chrism, the ressurrection.

This world is a corpse-eater. All the things eaten in it themselves die also. Truth is a life-eater. Therefore no one nourished by truth will die. It was from that place that Jesus came and brought food.To those who so desired he gave life, that they might not die.

God planted a Garden. Man was put into the Garden. There were many trees there for him, and man lived in this place with the blessing of the image of God.The things which are in it I will eat as I wish. This garden is the place where they will say to me, O man , eat this or do not eat that, just as you wish This is the place where I will eat all things, since the Tree of Knowledge is there. That one killed Adam, but here the Tree of Knowledge made men alive. The law was the tree. It has power to give the knowledge of good and evil. It neither removed him from evil, nor did it set him in the good, but it created death for those who ate it, For when he said, Eat this, do not eat that, it became the beginning of death.

The chrism is superior to the baptism, for it is from the word Chrism that we have been called Christians certainly not because of the word baptism. And it is because of the chrism that the Christ has his name. For the Father anointed the Son, and the Son anointed the apostles, and the apostles anointed us. He who has been anointed possesses everything, he possesses the ressurrection, the light, the cross, the Holy Spirit. The Father gave him this in the bridal chamber; he merely accepted the gift. The Father was in the Son and the Son in the Father. This is the Kingdom of Heaven.

The Lord have said it well, Some have entered the Kingdom of Heaven laughing and they have come out.. They do not remain there - the one because he is not a Christian, the other because he regrets his action afterward. And as soon as Christ went down into the water, he came out laughing at everything of this world, not because he considers it a trifle, but because he is full of contempt for it. He who wants to enter the Kingdom of Heaven will attain it. If he despises everything of this world and scorrns it as a trifle, he will come out laughing. So it is also with the bread and the cup and the oil, even though there is another one superior to these.

The world came about through a mistake. For he who created it wanted to create it imperishable and immortal. He fell short of attaining his desire. For the world never was imperishable, but sons are. Nothing will be able to receive imperishability if it does not first become a son.But he who has not the ability to receive, how much more will he be unable to give?

The Cup of prayer contains wine and water, since it is appointed as the type of the blood for which thanks is given. And it is full of the Holy Spirit, and it belongs to the wholly perfect man. When we drink this, we shall receive for ourselves the perfect man. The living water is a body. It is neccessary that we put on the living man. Therefore, when he is about to go down into the water, he unclothes himself, in order that he may put on the living man.

A horse sires a horse, a man begets man, a god brings forth a god. Compare the bridegroom and the bride. Their children were conceived in the bridal chamber.No Jew was ever born to Greek parents as long as the world has existed. And, as a Christian people. we ourselves do not descend from the Jews.There was another people and these blessed ones are referred to as The chosen people of the Living God and The true man and Son of Man and the seed of the Son of Man. In the world it is called this true people. Where they are, there are the sons of the bridal chamber.

Whereas in this world the union is one of husband with wife - a case of strenght complemented with weakness - in the Aeon the form of the union is different, although we refer to them by the same names. There are other names,however, they are superior to every other name that is named and are stronger than the strong. For where there is a show of strenght, there those who excel in strenght appear. These are not separate things, but both of them are this one single thing. This is the one which will not be able to rise above the heart of flesh.

Is it not necessary for all those who possess everything to know themselves? Some indeed, if they do not know themselves, will not enjoy their possessions. Not only will they be unable to detain the perfect man, but they will not be able to see him, for if they see him they will detain him. There is no other way for a person to acquire this quality except by putting on the perfect light and become perfect oneself. Everyone who has put this on will enter the kingdom. This is the perfect light, and it is necessary that we, by all means, become perfect men before we leave the world. He who has received everything and has not rid himself of these places will not be able ti share in that place, but will go to the Middle as imperfect. Only Jesus knows the end of this person.

The priest is completely holy, down to his very body. For if he has taken the bread, will he consecrate it? Or the cup or anything else that he gets, does he consecrate them? Then how will he not consecrate the body also? By perfecting the water of baptism, Jesus emptied it of death. Thus we do go down into the water, but we do not go down into death in order that we may not be poured out into the spirit of the world. When this spirit blows, it brings the winter. When the Holy Spirit breathes, the summer comes.

He who has knowledge of the truth is a free man, but the free man does not sin, for He who sins is the slave of sin[John8:34] Truth is the mother, knowledge the father. Those who think that sinning does not apply for them are called free by the world. Knowledge of the truth merely makes such people arrogant, which is what the words, it makes them free mean. It even gives them a sense of superiority over the whole world. But Love builds up [1Cor8:1].In fact, he who is really free through knowledge is a slave because of love for those who have not yet been able to attain the freedom which comes from knowledge. Knowledge makes them capable of becoming free. Love never calls somethings its own, and yet it may actually possess that very thing.It never says,This is mine but All these are yours. Spiritual love is wine and fragrance. All those who anoints themselves with it take pleasure in it. While those who are anointed are present, those nearby profit from the fragrance. If those anointed with ointment withdraw from them and leave, then those anointed, who merely stand nearby, still remain in their bad odor.The samaritan gave nothing but wine and oil to the wounded man. It is nothing other than the ointment. It healed the wounds, for love covers a multitude of sins[1Pet4:8]

The children a woman bears resemble the man who loves her. If her husband loves her, then they resemble her husband. If it is an adulterer, then they resemble the adulterer. Frequently, if a woman sleep with her husband out of necessity, while her heart is with the adulterer with whim she usually has intercourse , the child she will bear is born resembling the adulterer. Now you who live together with the Son of God, love not the world, but love the Lord.

The human being has intercourse with the human being. The horse has intercourse with the horse, the ass with the ass. Members of a race usually have associated with those of like race. So spirit mingles with spirit, and thought consorts with thought, and light shares with light. If you are born a human being, it is the human being which will love you.If you become a spirit, it is the spirit which will be joined to you. If you become thought, it is thought which will mingle with you. If you become light, it is light which will share with you. If you become one of those who belong above,it is those who belong above who will rest in you. If you become horse or ass or bull or dog or sheep or another of the animals which are outside and below, then neither human bein nor spirit nor thought nor light will be able to love you. Neither those who belong above nor those who belong within will be able to rest in you, and you have no part in them. He who is a slave against his will, will be able to become free.

Farming in the world requires the cooperation of four essential elements.A harvest is gathered into the barn only as a result of the natural action of water, earth, wind and light. God`s farming likewise has four element - faith, hope, love, and knowledge. Faith is our earth, that in which we take root.And hope is the water through which we are nourished.Love is the wind through which we grow.Knowledge is the light through which we ripen. Grace exists in four ways; it is earthborn, it is heavenly; it comes from the highest heaven; and it resides in truth.

Blessed is the one who on no occasion caused a soul distress. That person is Jesus Christ.He came to the whole place and did not burden anyone.Therefore the blessed is the one who is like this, because he is a perfect man.This indeed is the Word.Tell us about it, since it is difficult to define.How shall we be able to accomplish such a great thing? How whill he give everyone comfort? Above all, it is not proper to cause anyone distress - whether the person is great or small, unbeliever or believer - and then give comfort only to those who take satisfaction in good deeds.Some find it advantageous to give comfort to the one who has fared well.He who does good deeds cannot give comfort to such people, for it goes against his will. He is unable to cause distress, however, since he does not afflict them.To be sure, the one who fares well sometimes causes people distress . not that he intends to do so; rather, it is their own wickedness which is responsible for their distress.He who possesses the qualities of the perfect man rejoice in the good.Some, however, are terribly distressed by all this.

There was a householder who had every conceiveable thing, be it son or slave or cattle or dog or pig or corn or barley or chaff or gress or castor oil or meat and acorn.Now he was a sensible fellow and he knew what the food of each one was.He himself served the children bread and meat.He served the slaves castor oil and meal. Anf he threw barley and chaff and grass to the cattle. He threw bones to the dogs, and to the pigs he threw acorns and scraps of bread. Compare the disciple of God: if he is a sensible fellow he understands what discipleship is all about.The bodily forms will not deceive him, but he will look at the condition of the soul of each one and speak with him.There are many animals in the world which arc in a human form.When he identifies them, to the swine he will throw acorns, to the cattle he will throw barley and chaff and grass, to the dogs he will throw bones.To the slaves he will give only the elementary lessons, but to the children he will give the complete instruction.

There is the Son of man and there is the son of the Son of man. The Lord is the Son of man, and the son of the Son of man is he who created through the Son of man.The Son of man received from God the capacity to create. He also has the ability to beget.He who has received the ability to create is a creature.He who has received the ability to beget is an offspring.He who creates cannot beget. He who begets also has the ability to create.Now they say, He who creates begets.But his so-called offspring is merely a creature. Therefore his children are not offspring but creatures.He who create works openly; he himself is visible. He who begets, begets in private; he is himself hidden, since he is superior to every image.He who creates, creates openly. But one who begets, begets children in private.No one will be able to know when the husband and the wife have intercourse with one another, except the two in them.Indeed, marriage in the world is a mystery for those who have taken a wife.If there is a hidden quality to the marriage of defilement, how much more is the undefiled marriage a true mystery!It is not fleshly but pure.It belongs not to desire but to the will.It belongs not to the darkness or the night but to the day and the light.If a marriage is open to the public, it has become prostitution, and the bride plays the harlot not only when she is impregnated by another man but even if she slips out of her bedroom and is seen.Let her show herself only to the father and her mother and the friend of the bridegroom and the sons of the bridegroom. There are permitted to enter every day into the bridal chamber. But let the others yearn to listen to her voice and to enjoy her ointment, and let them feed from the crumbs that fall from the table, like dogs.Bridegrooms and brides belong to the bridal chamber. No one shall be able to see the bridegroom with the bride unless one becomes one.

When Abraham rejoiced that he was to see what he was to see, he circumcised the flesh of the foreskin, teaching us that it is proper to destroy the flesh.

Most things in the world, as long as their inner parts are hidden, stand upright and live. If they are revealed they die, as is illustrated by the visible man: as long as the intestines of the man are hidden, the man is alive; when his intestines are exposed and come out of him, the man will die. So also with the tree: while its root is hidden it sprouts and grows. If its root is exposed, the tree dries up.So it is with every birth that is in the world, not only with the revealed but with the hidden.For so long as the root of wickedness is hidden, it is strong.But when it is recognized, it is dissolved.When it is revealed, it perishes.That is why the word say, Already the axe is laid at the root of the tree[Matt3:10] It will not merely cut - what is cut sprouts again - but the ax penetrates deeply until it brings up the root.Jesus pulled out the root of the whole place, while others only did it partially. As for ourselves, let each one of us dig down after the root of evil which is within one, and let one pluck it out of one`s heart from the root.It will be plucked out if we recognize it. But if we are ignorant of it, it takes root in us and produces its fruit in our heart. It masters us.We are its slaves.It takes us captive, to make us do what we do not want; and what we do want we do not do. It is powerful because we have not recognized it. While it exists it is active.Ignorance is the mother of all evil.Ignorance will eventuate in death, because thos who come from ignorance neither were nor are nor shall be.But those who are in the truth will be perfect when all the truth is revealed.For truth is like ignorance: while it is hidden it rests in itself, but when it is revealed and is recognized, it is praised inasmuch as it is stronger than ignorance and the error. It gives freedom.The word said, If you know the truth, the truth will make you free[John8:32] Ignorance is a slave.Knowledge is freedom.If we know the truth, we shall find the fruits of the truth within us.If we are joined to it, it will bring fulfillment.

At the present time we have the manifest things of creation. We say, The strong are they who are held in high regard.And the obscure are the weak who are despised. Contrast the manifest things of truth: they are weak and despised, while the hidden things are strong and held in high regard. The mysteries of truth are revealed, though in type and image. The bridal chamber, however, remains hidden.It is the Holy in the Holy.The veil at first concealed how God controlled the creation, but when the veil is rent and the things inside are revealed, this house will be left desolate, or rather - it will be destroyed. But the whole inferior godhead will flee from these places into the holy of holies, for it wil not be able to mix with the unmixed light and the flawless fullness, but will be under the wings of the cross and its arms. This asrk will be its salvation when the flood of water(?) surges over them.If some belong to the order of the priesthood, they will be able to go within the veil with the high priest. For this reason the veil was not rent at the top only since it would have been revealed only to those below. But it was rent from the top to bottom.Those above opened to us who are below, in order that we may go into the secret of truth. This truly is what is held in high regard, since it is strong! But we shall go into there by means of lowly types and forms of weakness.They are lowly indeed when compared with the perfect glory. There is glory which surpasses glory.There is power which surpasses power. Therefore, the perfect things have opened to us, together with the hidden things of truth.The holies of the holies were revealed, and the bridal chamber invited us in.

As long as it is hidden, wickedness is indeed ineffectual, but it has not been removed from the midst of the seed of the Holy Spirit. They are slaves of evil.But when it is revealed, then the perfect light will flow out on everyone.And all those who are in it will receive the chrism. Then the slaves will be free and the captives ransomed.Every plant which my father in heaven has not planted will be plucked out[Matt15:13]. Those who are seperated will be united and will be filled.Every one who will enter the bridal chamber will kindle the light, for it burns just as in the marriages which are observed, though they happen at night.That fire burns only at night and is put out.But the mysteries of this marriage are perfected rather in the day and the light. Neither that day nor its light ever sets.If anyone becomes a son of the bridal chamber, he will receive the light.If anyone does not receive it while he is in these places, he will not be able to receive it in the other place.He who will receive the light will not be seen, nor can he be detained. And none shall be able to torment a person like this even while he dwells in the world.And again, when he leaves the world he has allready received the truth in the images.The world has become the Aeon, for the Aeon if fullness for him.This is the way it is: it is revealed to him alone, not hidden in the darkness and the night, but hidden in a perfect day and a holy light.

The Gospel of Pseudo-Matthew

(Gospel of the Birth of Mary)

ere beginneth the book of the Birth of the Blessed Mary and the Infancy of the Saviour. Written in Hebrew by the Blessed Evangelist Matthew, and translated into Latin by the Blessed Presbyter Jerome.

To their well-beloved brother Jerome the Presbyter, Bishops Cromatius and Heliodorus in the Lord, greeting. The birth of the Virgin Mary, and the nativity and infancy of our Lord Jesus Christ, we find in apocryphal books. But considering that in them many things contrary to our faith are written, we have believed that they ought all to be rejected, lest perchance we should transfer the joy of Christ to Antichrist. While, therefore, we were considering these things, there came holy men, Parmenius and Varinus, who said that your Holiness had found a Hebrew volume, written by the hand of the most blessed Evangelist Matthew, in which also the birth of the virgin mother herself, and the infancy of our Saviour, were written. And accordingly we entreat your affection by our Lord Jesus Christ Himself, to render it from the Hebrew into Latin, not so much for the attainment of those things which are the insignia of Christ, as for the exclusion of the craft of heretics, who, in order to teach bad doctrine, have mingled their own lies with the excellent nativity of Christ, that by the sweetness of life they might hide the bitterness of death. It will therefore become your purest piety, either to listen to us as your brethren entreating, or to let us have as bishops exacting, the debt of affection which you may deem due.

REPLY TO THEIR LETTER BY JEROME

To my lords the holy and most blessed Bishops Cromatius and Heliodorus, Jerome, a humble servant of Christ, in the Lord greeting.

He who digs in ground where he knows that there is gold, does not instantly snatch at whatever the uptorn trench may pour forth; but, before the stroke of the quivering spade raises aloft the glittering mass, he meanwhile lingers over the sods to turn them over and lift them up, and especially he who has not added to his gains. An arduous task is enjoined upon me, since what your Blessedness has commanded me, the holy Apostle and Evangelist Matthew himself did not write for the purpose of publishing. For if he had not done it somewhat secretly, he would have added it also to his Gospel which he published. But he composed this book in Hebrew; and so little did he publish it, that at this day the book written in Hebrew by his own hand is in the possession of very religious men, to whom in successive periods of time it has been handed down by those that were before them. And this book they never at any time gave to any one to translate. And so it came to pass, that when it was published by a disciple of Manichaeus named Leucius, who also wrote the falsely styled Acts of the Apostles, this book afforded matter, not of edification, but of perdition; and the opinion of the Synod in regard to it was according to its deserts, that the ears of the Church should not be open to it. Let the snapping of those that bark against us now cease; for we do not add this little book to the canonical writings, but we translate what was written by an Apostle and Evangelist, that we may disclose the falsehood of heresy. In this work, then, we obey the commands of pious bishops as well as oppose impious heretics. It is the love of Christ, therefore, which we fulfil, believing that they will assist us by their prayers, who through our obedience attain to a knowledge of the holy infancy of our Saviour.

There is extant another letter to the same bishops, attributed to Jerome:

You ask me to let you know what I think of a book held by some to be about the nativity of St. Mary. And so I wish you to know that there is much in it that is false. For one Seleucus, who wrote the Sufferings of the Apostles, composed this book. But, just as he wrote what was true about their powers, and the miracles they worked, but said a great deal that was false about their doctrine; so here too he has invented many untruths out of his own head. I shall take care to render it word for word, exactly as it is in the Hebrew, since it is asserted that it was composed by the holy Evangelist Matthew, and written in Hebrew, and set at the head of his Gospel. Whether this be true or not, I leave to the author of the preface and the trustworthiness of the writer: as for myself, I pronounce them doubtful; I do not affirm that they are clearly false. But this I say freely-- and I think none of the faithful will deny it -- that, whether these stories be true or inventions, the sacred nativity of St. Mary was preceded by great miracles, and succeeded by the greatest; and so by those who believe that God can do these things, they can be believed and read without damaging their faith or imperilling their souls. In short, so far as I can, following the sense rather than the words of the writer, and sometimes walking in the same path, though not in the same footsteps, sometimes digressing a little, but still keeping the same road, I shall in this way keep by the style of the narrative, and shall say nothing that is not either written there, or might, following the same train of thought, have been written.

CHAPTER 1

In those days there was a man in Jerusalem, Joachim by name, of the tribe of Judah. He was the shepherd of his own sheep, fearing the Lord in integrity and singleness of heart. He had no other care than that of his herds, from the produce of which he supplied with food all that feared God, offering double gifts in the fear of God to all who laboured in doctrine, and who ministered unto Him. Therefore his lambs, and his sheep, and his wool, and all things whatsoever he possessed, he used to divide into three portions: one he gave to the orphans, the widows, the strangers, and the poor; the second to those that worshipped God; and the third he kept for himself and all his house. And as he did so, the Lord multiplied to him his herds, so that there was no man like him in the people of Israel. This now he began to do when he was fifteen years old. And at the age of twenty he took to wife Anna, the daughter of Achar, of his own tribe, that is, of the tribe of Judah, of the family of David. And though they had lived together for twenty years, he had by her neither sons nor daughters.

CHAPTER 2

And it happened that, in the time of the feast, among those who were offering incense to the Lord, Joachim stood getting ready his gifts in the sight of the Lord. And the priest, Ruben by name, coming to him, said: It is not lawful for thee to stand among those who are doing sacrifice to God, because God has not blessed thee so as to give thee seed in Israel. Being therefore put to shame in the sight of the people, he retired from the temple of the

Lord weeping, and did not return to his house, but went to his flocks, taking with him his shepherds into the mountains to a far country, so that for five months his wife Anna could hear no tidings of him. And she prayed with tears, saying: O Lord, most mighty God of Israel, why hast Thou, seeing that already Thou hast not given me children, taken from me my husband also? Behold, now five months that I have not seen my husband; and I know not where he is tarrying; nor, if I knew him to be dead, could I bury him. And while she wept excessively, she entered into the court of His house; and she fell on her face in prayer, and poured out her supplications before the Lord. After this, rising from her prayer, and lifting her eyes to God, she saw a sparrow's nest in a laurel tree, and uttered her voice to the Lord with groaning, and said: Lord God Almighty, who hast given offspring to every creature, to beasts wild and tame, to serpents, and birds, and fishes, and they all rejoice over their young ones, Thou hast shut out me alone from the gift of Thy benignity. For Thou, O God, knowest my heart, that from the beginning of my married life I have vowed that, if Thou, O God, shouldst give me son or daughter, I would offer them to Thee in Thy holy temple. And while she was thus speaking, suddenly an angel of the Lord appeared before her, saying: Be not afraid, Anna, for there is seed for thee in the decree of God; and all generations even to the end shall wonder at that which shall be born of thee. And when he had thus spoken, he vanished out of her sight. But she, in fear and dread because she had seen such a sight, and heard such words, at length went into her bed-chamber, and threw herself on the bed as if dead. And for a whole day and night she remained in great trembling and in prayer. And after these things she called to her her servant, and said to her: Dost thou see me deceived in my widowhood and in great perplexity, and hast thou been unwilling to come in to me? Then she, with a slight murmur, thus answered and said: If God hath shut up thy womb, and hath taken away thy husband from thee, what can I do for thee? And when Anna heard this, she lifted up her voice, and wept aloud.

CHAPTER 3

At the same time there appeared a young man on the mountains to Joachim while he was feeding his flocks, and said to him: Why dost thou not return to thy wife? And Joachim said: I have had her for twenty years, and it has not been the will of God to give me children by her. I have been driven with shame and reproach from the temple of the Lord: why should I go back to her, when I have been once cast off and utterly despised? Here then will I remain with my sheep; and so long as in this life God is willing to grant me light, I shall willingly, by the hands of my servants, bestow their portions upon the poor, and the orphans, and those that fear God. And when he had thus spoken, the young man said to him: I am an angel of the Lord, and I have to-day appeared to thy wife when she was weeping and praying, and have consoled her; and know that she has conceived a daughter from thy seed, and thou in thy ignorance of this hast left her. She will be in the temple of God, and the Holy Spirit shall abide in her; and her blessedness shall be greater than that of all the holy women, so that no one can say that any before her has been like her, or that any after her in this world will be so. Therefore go down from the mountains, and return to thy wife, whom thou wilt find with child. For God hath raised up seed in her, and for this thou wilt give God thanks; and her seed shall be blessed, and she herself shall be blessed, and shall be made the mother of eternal blessing. Then Joachim adored the angel, and said to him: If I have found favour in thy sight, sit for a little in my tent, and bless thy servant. And the angel said to him: Do not say servant, but fellow-servant; for we are the servants of one Master. But my food is invisible, and my drink cannot be seen by a mortal. Therefore thou oughtest not to ask me to enter thy tent; but if thou wast about to give me anything, offer it as a burnt-offering to the Lord. Then Joachim took a lamb without spot, and said to the angel: I should not have dared to offer a burnt-offering to the Lord, unless thy command had given me the priest's right of offering. And the angel said to him: I should not have invited thee to offer unless I had known the will of the Lord. And when Joachim was offering the sacrifice to God, the angel and the odour of the sacrifice went together straight up to heaven with the smoke.

Then Joachim, throwing himself on his face, lay in prayer from the sixth hour of the day even until evening. And his lads and hired servants who were with him saw him, and not knowing why he was lying down, thought that he was dead; and they came to him, and with difficulty raised him from the ground. And when he recounted to them the vision of the angel, they were struck with great fear and wonder, and advised him to accomplish the vision of the angel without delay, and to go back with all haste to his wife. And when Joachim was turning over in his mind whether he should go back or not, it happened that he was overpowered by a deep sleep; and, behold, the angel who had already appeared to him when awake, appeared to him in his sleep, saying: I am the angel appointed by God as thy guardian: go down with confidence, and return to Anna, because the deeds of mercy which thou and thy wife Anna have done have been told in the presence of the Most High; and to you will God give such fruit as no prophet or saint has ever had from the beginning, or ever will have. And when Joachim awoke out of his sleep, he called all his herdsmen to him, and told them his dream. And they worshipped the Lord, and said to him: See that thou no further despise the words of the angel. But rise and let us go hence, and return at a quiet pace, feeding our flocks.

And when, after thirty days occupied in going back, they were now near at hand, behold, the angel of the Lord appeared to Anna, who was standing and praying, and said: Go to the gate which is called Golden, and meet thy husband in the way, for to-day he will come to thee. She therefore went towards him in haste With her maidens, and, praying to the Lord, she stood a long time in the gate waiting for him. And when she was wearied with long waiting, she lifted up her eyes and saw Joachim afar off coming with his flocks; and she ran to him and hung on his neck, giving thanks to God, and saying: I was a widow, and behold now I am not so: I was barren, and behold I have now conceived. And so they worshipped the Lord, and went into their own house. And when this was heard of, there was great joy among all their neighbours and acquaintances, so that the whole land of lsrael congratulated them.

CHAPTER 4

After these things, her nine months being fulfilled, Anna brought forth a daughter, and called her Mary. And having weaned her in her third year, Joachim, and Anna his wife, went together to the temple of the Lord to offer sacrifices to God, and placed the infant, Mary by name, in the community of virgins, in which the virgins remained day and night praising God. And when she was put down before the doors of the temple, she went up the fifteen steps so swiftly, that she did not look back at all; nor did she, as children are wont to do, seek for her parents. Whereupon her parents, each of them anxiously seeking for the child, were both alike astonished, until they found her in the temple, and the priests of the temple themselves wondered.

CHAPTER 5

Then Anna, filled with the Holy Spirit, said before them all: The Lord Almighty, the God of Hosts, being mindful of His word, hath visited His people with a good and holy visitation, to bring down the hearts of the Gentiles who were rising against us, and turn them to Himself. He hath opened His ears to our prayers: He hath kept away from us the exulting of all our enemies. The barren hath become a mother, and hath brought forth exultation and gladness to lsrael. Behold the gifts which I have brought to offer to my Lord, and mine enemies have not been able to hinder me. For God hath turned their hearts to me, and Himself hath given me everlasting joy.

CHAPTER 6

And Mary was held in admiration by all the people of Israel; and when she was three years old, she walked with a step so mature, she spoke so perfectly, and spent her time so assiduously in the praises of God, that all were astonished at her, and wondered; and she was not reckoned a young infant, but as it were a grown-up person of thirty years old. She was so constant in prayer, and her appearance was so beautiful and glorious, that scarcely any one could look into her face. And she occupied herself constantly with her wool-work, so that she in her tender years could do all that old women were not able to do. And this was the order that she had set for herself: From the morning to the third hour she remained in prayer; from the third to the ninth she was occupied with her weaving; and from the ninth she again applied herself to prayer. She did not retire from praying until there appeared to her the angel of the Lord, from whose hand she used to receive food; and thus she became more and more perfect in the work of God. Then, when the older virgins rested from the praises of God, she did not rest at all; so that in the praises and vigils of God none were found before her, no one more learned in the wisdom of the law of God, more lowly in humility, more elegant in singing, more perfect in all virtue. She was indeed stedfast, immoveable, unchangeable, and daily advancing to perfection. No one saw her angry, nor heard her speaking evil. All her speech was so full of grace, that her God was acknowledged to be in her tongue. She was always engaged in prayer and in searching the law, and she was anxious lest by any word of hers she should sin with regard to her companions. Then she was afraid lest in her laughter, or the sound of her beautiful voice, she should commit any fault, or lest, being elated, she should display any wrong- doing or haughtiness to one of her equals. She blessed God without intermission; and lest perchance, even in her salutation, she might cease from praising God; if any one saluted her, she used to answer by way of salutation: Thanks be to God. And from her the custom first began of men saying, Thanks be to God, when they saluted each other. She refreshed herself only with the food which she daily received from the hand of the angel; but the food which she obtained from the priests she divided among the poor. The angels of God were often seen speaking with her, and they most diligently obeyed her. If any one who was unwell touched her, the same hour he went home cured.

CHAPTER 7

Then Abiathar the priest offered gifts without end to the high priests, in order that he might obtain her as wife to his son. But Mary forbade them, saying: It cannot be that I should know a man, or that a man should know me. For all the priests and all her relations kept saying to her: God is worshipped in children and adored in posterity, as has always happened among the sons of Israel. But Mary answered and said unto them: God is worshipped in chastity, as is proved first of all. For before Abel there was none righteous among men, and he by his offerings pleased God, and was without mercy slain by him who displeased Him. Two crowns, therefore, he received -- of oblation and of virginity, because in his flesh there was no pollution. Elias also, when he was in the flesh, was taken up in the flesh, because he kept his flesh unspotted. Now I, from my infancy in the temple of God, have learned that virginity can be sufficiently dear to God. And so, because I can offer what is dear to God, I have resolved in my heart that I should not know a man at all.

CHAPTER 8

Now it came to pass, when she was fourteen s years old, and on this account there was occasion for the Pharisees' saying that it was now a custom that no woman of that age should abide in the temple of God, they fell upon the plan of sending a herald through all the tribes of Israel, that on the third day all should come together into the temple of the Lord. And when all the people had come together, Abiathar the high priest rose, and mounted on a higher step, that he might be seen and heard by all the people; and when great silence had been obtained, he said: Hear me, O sons of Israel, and receive my words into your ears. Ever since this temple was built by Solomon, there have been in it virgins, the daughters of kings and the daughters of prophets, and of high priests and priests; and they were great, and worthy of admiration. But when they came to the proper age they were given in marriage, and followed the course of their mothers before them, and were pleasing to God. But a new order of life has been found out by Mary alone, who promises that she will remain a virgin to God. Wherefore it seems to me, that through our inquiry and the answer of God we should try to ascertain to whose keeping she ought to be entrusted. Then these words found favour with all the synagogue. And the lot was east by the priests upon the twelve tribes, and the lot fell upon the tribe of Judah. And the priest said: To-morrow let every one who has no wife come, and bring his rod in his hand. Whence it happened that Joseph brought his rod along with the young men. And the rods having been handed over to the high priest, he offered a sacrifice to the Lord God, and inquired of the Lord. And the Lord said to him: Put all their rods into the holy of holies of God, and let them remain there, and order them to come to thee on the morrow to get back their rods; and the man from the point of whose rod a dove shall come forth, and fly towards heaven, and in whose hand the rod, when given back, shall exhibit this sign, to him let Mary be delivered to be kept.

On the following day, then, all having assembled early, and an incense-offering having been made, the high priest went into the holy of ho-lies, and brought forth the rods. And when he had distributed the rods, and the dove came forth out of none of them, the high priest put on the twelve bells and the sacerdotal robe; and entering into the holy of holies, he there made a burnt-offering, and poured forth a prayer. And the angel of the Lord appeared to him, saying: There is here the shortest rod, of which thou hast made no account: thou didst bring it in with the rest, but didst not take it out with them. When thou hast taken it out, and hast given it him whose it is, in it will appear the sign of which I spoke to thee. Now that was Joseph's rod; and because he was an old man, he had been cast off, as it were, that he might not receive her, but neither did he himself wish to ask back his rod. And when he was humbly standing last of all, the high priest cried out to him with a loud voice, saying: Come, Joseph, and receive thy rod; for we are waiting for thee. And Joseph came up trembling, because the high priest had called him with a very loud voice. But as soon as he stretched forth his hand, and laid hold of his rod, immediately from the top of it came forth a dove whiter than snow, beautiful exceedingly, which, after long flying about the roofs of the temple, at length flew towards the heavens. Then all the people congratulated the old man, saying: Thou hast been made blessed in thine old age, O father Joseph, seeing that God hath shown thee to be fit to receive Mary. And the priests having said to him, Take her, because of all the tribe of Judah thou alone hast been chosen by God; Joseph began bashfully to address them, saying: I am an old man, and have children; why do you hand over to me this infant, who is younger than my grandsons? Then Abiathar the high priest said to him: Remember, Joseph, how Dathan and Abiron and Core perished, because they despised the will of God. So will it happen to thee, if thou despise this which is commanded thee by God. Joseph answered him: I indeed do not despise the will of God; but I shall be her guardian until I can ascertain concerning the will of God, as to which of my sons can have her as his wife. Let some virgins of her companions, with whom she may meanwhile spend her time, be given for a consolation to her. Abiathar the high priest answered and said: Five virgins indeed shall be given her for consolation, until the appointed day come in which thou mayst receive her; for to no other can she be joined in marriage.

Then Joseph received Mary, with the other five virgins who were to be with her in Joseph's house. These virgins were Rebecca, Sephora, Susanna, Abigea, and Cael; to whom the high priest gave the silk, and the blue, and the fine linen, and the scarlet, and the purple, and the fine flax. For they cast lots among themselves what each virgin should do, and the purple for the veil of the temple of the Lord fell to the lot of Mary. And when she had got it, those virgins said to her: Since thou art the last, and humble, and younger than all, thou hast deserved to receive and obtain the purple. And thus saying, as it were in words of annoyance, they began to call her queen of virgins. While, however, they were so doing, the angel of the Lord appeared in the midst of them, saying: These words shall not have been uttered by way of annoyance, but prophesied as a prophecy most true. They trembled, therefore, at the sight of the angel, and at his words, and asked her to pardon them, and pray for them.

CHAPTER 9

And on the second day, while Mary was at the fountain to fill her pitcher, the angel of the Lord appeared to her, saying: Blessed art thou, Mary; for in thy womb thou hast prepared an habitation for the Lord. For, lo, the light from heaven shall come and dwell in thee, and by means of thee will shine over the whole world.

Again, on the third day, while she was working at the purple with her fingers, there entered a young man of ineffable beauty. And when Mary saw him, she exceedingly feared and trembled. And he said to her: Hail, Mary, full of grace; the Lord is with thee: blessed art thou among women, and blessed is the fruit of thy womb. And when she heard these words, she trembled, and was exceedingly afraid. Then the angel of the Lord added: Fear not, Mary; for thou hast found favour with God: Behold, thou shalt conceive in thy womb, and shalt bring forth a King, who fills not only the earth, but the heaven, and who reigns from generation to generation.

CHAPTER 10

While these things were doing, Joseph was occupied with his work, house-building, in the districts by the sea-shore; for he was a carpenter. And after nine months he came back to his house, and found Mary pregnant. Wherefore, being in the utmost distress, he trembled and cried out, saying: O

Lord God, receive my spirit; for it is better for me to die than to live any longer. And the virgins who were with Mary said to him: Joseph, what art thou saying? We know that no man has touched her; we can testify that she is still a virgin, and untouched. We have watched over her; always has she continued with us in prayer; daily do the angels of God speak with her; daily does she receive food from the hand of the Lord. We know not how it is possible that there can be any sin in her. But if thou wishest us to tell thee what we suspect, nobody but the angel of the Lord has made her pregnant. Then said Joseph: Why do you mislead me, to believe that an angel of the Lord has made her pregnant? But it is possible that some one has pretended to be an angel of the Lord, and has beguiled her. And thus speaking, he wept, and said:

With what face shall I look at the temple of the Lord, or with what face shall I see the priests of God? What am I to do? And thus saying, he thought that he would flee, and send her away.

CHAPTER 11

And when he was thinking of rising up and hiding himself, and dwelling in secret, behold, on that very night, the angel of the Lord appeared to him in sleep, saying: Joseph, thou son of David, fear not; receive Mary as thy wife: for that which is in her womb is of the Holy Spirit. And she shall bring forth a son, and His name shall be called Jesus, for He will save His people from their sins. And Joseph, rising from his sleep, gave thanks to God, and spoke to Mary and the virgins who were with her, and told them his vision. And he was comforted about Mary, saying: I have sinned, in that I suspected thee at all.

CHAPTER 12

After these things there arose a great report that Mary was with child. And Joseph was seized by the officers of the temple, and brought along with Mary to the high priest. And he with the priests began to reproach him, and to say: Why hast thou beguiled so great and so glorious a virgin, who was fed like a dove in the temple by the angels of God, who never wished either to see or to have a man, who had the most excellent knowledge of the law of God? If thou hadst not done violence to her, she would still have remained in her virginity. And Joseph vowed, and swore that he had never touched her at all. And Abiathar the high priest answered him: As the Lord liveth, I will give thee to drink of the water of drinking of the Lord, and immediately thy sin will appear.

Then was assembled a multitude of people which could not be numbered, and Mary was brought to the temple. And the priests, and her relatives, and her parents wept, and said to Mary: Confess to the priests thy sin, thou that wast like a dove in the temple of God, and didst receive food from the hands of an angel. And again Joseph was summoned to the altar, and the water of drinking of the Lord was given him to drink. And when any one that had lied drank this water, and walked seven times round the altar, God used to show some sign in his face. When, therefore, Joseph had drunk in safety, and had walked round the altar seven times, no sign of sin appeared in him. Then all the priests, and the officers, and the people justified him, saying: Blessed art thou, seeing that no charge has been found good against thee. And they summoned Mary, and said: And what excuse canst thou have? or what greater sign can appear in thee than the conception of thy womb, which betrays thee? This only we require of thee, that since Joseph is pure regarding thee, thou confess who it is that has beguiled thee. For it is better that thy confession should betray thee, than that the wrath of God should set a mark on thy face, and expose thee in the midst of the people. Then Mary said, stedfastly and without trembling: O Lord God, King over all, who knowest all secrets, if there be any pollution in me, or any sin, or any evil desires, or unchastity, expose me in the sight of all the people, and make me an example of punishment to all. Thus saying, she went up to the altar of the Lord boldly, and drank the water of drinking, and walked round the altar seven times, and no spot was found in her.

And when all the people were in the utmost astonishment, seeing that she was with child, and that no sign had appeared in her face, they began to be disturbed among themselves by conflicting statements: some said that she was holy and unspotted, others that she was wicked and defiled. Then Mary, seeing that she was still suspected by the people, and that on that account she did not seem to them to be wholly cleared, said in the hearing of all, with a loud voice, As the Lord Adonai liveth, the Lord of Hosts before whom I stand, I have not known man; but I am known by Him to whom from my earliest years I have devoted myself. And this vow I made to my God from my infancy, that I should remain unspotted in Him who created me, and I trust that I shall so live to Him alone, and serve Him alone; and in Him, as long as I shall live, will I remain unpolluted. Then they all began to kiss her feet and to embrace her knees, asking her to pardon them for their wicked suspicions. And she was led down to her house with exultation and joy by the people, and the priests, and all the virgins. And they cried out, and said: Blessed be the name of the Lord for ever, because He hath manifested thy holiness to all His people Israel.

CHAPTER 13

And it came to pass some little time after, that an enrolment was made according to the edict of Caesar Augustus, that all the world was to be enrolled, each man in his native place. This enrolment was made by Cyrinus, the governor of Syria, It was necessary, therefore, that Joseph should enrol with the blessed Mary in Bethlehem, because to it they belonged, being of the tribe of Judah, and of the house and family of David. When, therefore, Joseph and the blessed Mary were going along the road which leads to Bethlehem, Mary said to Joseph: I see two peoples before me, the one weeping, and the other rejoicing. And Joseph answered: Sit still on thy beast, and do not speak superfluous words. Then there appeared before them a beautiful boy, clothed in white raiment, who-said to Joseph: Why didst thou say that the words which Mary spoke about the two peoples were superfluous? For she saw the people of the Jews weeping, because they have departed from their God; and the people of the Gentiles rejoicing, because they have now been added and made near to the Lord, according to that which He promised to our fathers Abraham, Isaac, and Jacob: for the time is at hand when in the seed of Abraham all nations shall be blessed.

And when he had thus said, the angel ordered the beast to stand, for the time when she should bring forth was at hand; and he commanded the blessed Mary to come down off the animal, and go into a recess under a cavern, in which there never was light, but always darkness, because the light of day could not reach it. And when the blessed Mary had gone into it, it began to shine with as much brightness as if it were the sixth hour of the day. The light from God so shone in the cave, that neither by day nor night was light wanting as long as the blessed Mary was there. And there she brought forth a son, and the angels surrounded Him when He was being born. And as soon as He was born, He stood upon His feet, and the angels adored Him, saying: Glory to God in the highest, and on earth peace to men of good pleasure. Now, when the birth of the Lord was at hand, Joseph had gone away to seek midwives. And when he had found them, he returned to the cave, and found with Mary the infant which she had brought forth. And Joseph said to the blessed Mary: I have brought thee two midwives--Zelomi and Salome; and they are standing outside before the entrance to the cave, not daring to come in hither, because of the exceeding brightness. And when the blessed Mary heard this, she smiled; and Joseph said to her: Do not smile; but prudently allow them to visit thee, in case thou shouldst require them for thy cure. Then she ordered them to enter. And when Zelomi had come in, Salome having stayed without, Zelomi said to Mary: Allow me to touch thee. And when she had permitted her to make an examination, the midwife cried out with a loud voice, and said: Lord, Lord Almighty, mercy on us! It has never been heard or thought of, that any one should have her breasts full of milk, and that the birth of a son should show his mother to be a virgin. But there has been no spilling of blood in his birth, no pain in bringing him forth. A virgin has conceived, a virgin has brought forth, and a virgin she remains. And hearing these words, Salome said: Allow me to handle thee, and prove whether Zelomi have spoken the truth. And the blessed Mary allowed her to handle her. And when she had withdrawn her hand from handling her, it dried up, and through excess of pain she began to weep bitterly, and to be in great distress, crying out, and saying: O Lord God, Thou knowest that I have always feared Thee, and that without recompense I have cared for all the poor; I have taken nothing from the widow and the orphan, and the needy have I not sent empty away. And, behold, I am made wretched because of mine unbelief, since without a cause I wished to try Thy virgin.

And while she was thus speaking, there stood by her a young man in shining garments, saying: Go to the child, and adore Him, and touch Him with thy hand, and He will heal thee, because He is the Saviour of the world, and of all that hope in Him. And she went to the child with haste, and adored Him, and touched the fringe of the cloths in which He was wrapped, and instantly her hand was cured. And going forth, she began to cry aloud, and to tell the wonderful things which she had seen, and which she had suffered, and how she had been cured; so that many through her statements believed.

And some shepherds also affirmed that they had seen angels singing a hymn at midnight, praising and blessing the God of heaven, and saying: There has been born the Saviour of all, who is Christ the Lord, in whom salvation shall be brought back to Israel.

Moreover, a great star, larger than any that had been seen since the beginning of the world, shone over the cave from the evening till the morning. And the prophets who were in Jerusalem said that this star pointed out the birth of Christ, who should restore the promise not only to Israel, but to all nations.

CHAPTER 14

And on the third day after the birth of our Lord Jesus Christ, the most blessed Mary went forth out of the cave, and entering a stable, placed the child in the stall, and the ox and the ass adored Him. Then was fulfilled that which was said by Isaiah the prophet, saying: The ox knoweth his owner, and the ass his master's crib. The very animals, therefore, the ox and the ass, having Him in their midst, incessantly adored Him. Then was fulfilled that which was said by Abacuc the prophet, saying: Between two animals thou art made manifest. In the same place Joseph remained with Mary three days.

CHAPTER 15

And on the sixth day they entered Bethlehem, where they spent the seventh day. And on the eighth day they circumcised the child, and called His name Jesus; for so He was called by the angel before He was conceived in the womb. Now, after the days of the purifation of Mary were fulfilled according to the law of Moses, then Joseph took the infant to the temple of the Lord. And when the infant had received parhithomus, --parhithomus, that is, circumcision--they offered for Him a pair of turtle-doves, or two young pigeons.

Now there was in the temple a man of God, perfect and just, whose name was Symeon, a hundred and twelve years old. He had received the answer from the Lord, that he should not taste of death till he had seen Christ, the Son of God, living in the flesh. And having seen the child, he cried out with a loud voice, saying: God hath visited His people, and the Lord hath fulfilled His promise. And he made haste, and adored Him. And after this he took Him up into his cloak and kissed His feet, and said: Lord, now lettest Thou Thy servant depart in peace, according to Thy word: for mine eyes have seen Thy salvation, which Thou hast prepared before the face of all peoples, to be a light to lighten the Gentiles, and the glory of Thy people Israel.

There was also in the temple of the Lord, Anna, a prophetess, the daughter of Phanuel, of the tribe of Asher, who had lived with her husband seven years from her virginity; and she had now been a widow eighty-four years. And she never left the temple of the Lord, but spent her time in fasting and prayer. She also likewise adored the child, saying: In Him is the redemption of the world.

CHAPTER 16

And when the second year was past, Magi came from the east to Jerusalem, bringing great gifts. And they made strict inquiry of the Jews, saying: Where is the king who has been born to you? for we have seen his star in the east, and have come to worship him. And word of this came to King Herod, and so alarmed him that he called together the scribes and the Pharisees, and the teachers of the people, asking of them where the prophets had foretold that Christ should be born. And they said: In Bethlehem of Judah. For it is written: And thou Bethelehem, in the land of Judah, art by no means the least among the princes of Judah; for out of thee shall come forth a Leader who shall rule my people Israel. Then King Herod summoned the magi to him, and strictly inquired of them when the star appeared to them. Then, sending them to Bethlehem, he said: Go and make strict inquiry about the child; and when ye have found him, bring me word again, that I may come and worship him also. And while the magi were going on their way, there appeared to them the star, which was, as it were, a guide to them, going before them until they came to where the child was. And when the magi saw the star, they rejoiced with great joy; and going into the house, they saw the child Jesus sitting in His mother's lap. Then they opened their treasures, and presented great gifts to the blessed Mary and Joseph. And to the child Himself they offered each of them a piece of gold. And likewise one gave gold, another frankincense, and the third myrrh. And when they were going to return to King Herod, they were warned by an angel in their sleep not to go back to Herod; and they returned to their own country by another road.

CHAPTER 17

And when Herod saw that he had been made sport of by the magi, his heart swelled with rage, and he sent through all the roads, wishing to seize them and put them to death. But when he could not find them at all; he sent anew to Bethlehem and all its borders, and slew all the male children whom he found of two years old and under, according to the time that he had ascertained from the magi.

Now the day before this was done Joseph was warned in his sleep by the angel of the Lord, who said to him: Take Mary and the child, and go into Egypt by the way of the desert. And joseph went according to the saying of the angel.

CHAPTER 18

And having come to a certain cave, and wishing to rest in it, the blessed Mary dismounted from her beast, and sat down with the child Jesus in her bosom. And there were with Joseph three boys, and with Mary a girl, going on the journey along with them. And, lo, suddenly there came forth from the cave many dragons; and when the children saw them, they cried out in great terror. Then Jesus went down from the bosom of His mother, and stood on His feet before the dragons; and they adored Jesus, and thereafter retired. Then was fulfilled that which was said by David the prophet, saying: Praise the Lord from the earth, ye dragons; ye dragons, and all ye deeps And the young child Jesus, walking before them, commanded them to hurt no man. But Mary and Joseph were very much afraid lest the child should be hurt by the dragons. And Jesus said to them: Do not be afraid, and do not consider me to be a little child; for I am and always have been perfect; and all the beasts of the forest must needs be tame before me.

CHAPTER 19

Lions and panthers adored Him likewise, and accompanied them in the desert. Wherever Joseph and the blessed Mary went, they went before them showing them the way, and bowing their heads; and showing their submission by wagging their tails, they adored Him with great reverence. Now at first, when Mary saw the lions and the panthers, and various kinds of wild beasts, coming about them, she was very much afraid. But the infant Jesus looked into her face with a joyful countenance, and said: Be not afraid, mother; for they come not to do thee harm, but they make haste to serve both thee and me. With these words He drove all fear from her heart. And the lions kept walking with them, and with the oxen, and the asses, and the beasts of burden which carried their baggage, and did not hurt a single one of them, though they kept beside them; but they were tame among the sheep and the rams which they had brought with them from Judaea, and which they had with them. They walked among wolves, and feared nothing; and no one of them was hurt by another. Then was fulfilled that which was spoken by the prophet: Wolves shall feed with lambs; the lion and the ox shall eat straw together. There were together two oxen drawing a waggon with provision for the journey, and the lions directed them in their path.

CHAPTER 20

And it came to pass on the third day of their journey, while they were walking, that the blessed Mary was fatigued by the excessive heat of the sun in the desert; and seeing a palm tree, she said to Joseph: Let me rest a little under the shade of this tree. Joseph therefore made haste, and led her to the palm, and made her come down from her beast. And as the blessed Mary was sitting there, she looked up to the foliage of the palm, and saw it full of fruit, and said to Joseph: I wish it were possible to get some of the fruit of this palm. And Joseph said to her: I wonder that thou sayest this, when thou seest how high the palm tree is; and that thou thinkest of eating of its fruit. I am thinking more of the want of water, because the skins are now empty, and we have none wherewith to refresh ourselves and our cattle. Then the child

Jesus, with a joyful countenance, reposing in the bosom of His mother, said to the palm: O tree, bend thy branches, and refresh my mother with thy fruit. And immediately at these words the palm bent its top down to the very feet of the blessed Mary; and they gathered from it fruit, with which they were all refreshed. And after they had gathered all its fruit, it remained bent down, waiting the order to rise from Him who bad commanded it to stoop. Then Jesus said to it: Raise thyself, O palm tree, and be strong, and be the companion of my trees, which are in the paradise of my Father; and open from thy roots a vein of water which has been hid in the earth, and let the waters flow, so that we may be satisfied from thee. And it rose up immediately, and at its root there began to come forth a spring of water exceedingly clear and cool and sparkling. And when they saw the spring of water, they rejoiced with great joy, and were satisfied, themselves and all their cattle and their beasts. Wherefore they gave thanks to God.

CHAPTER 21

And on the day after, when they were setting out thence, and in the hour in which they began their journey, Jesus turned to the palm, and said: This privilege I give thee, O palm tree, that one of thy branches be carried away by my angels, and planted in the paradise of my Father. And this blessing I will confer upon thee, that it shall be said of all who conquer in any contest, You have attained the palm of victory. And while He was thus speaking, behold, an angel of the Lord appeared, and stood upon the palm tree; and taking off one of its branches, flew to heaven with the branch in his hand. And when they saw this, they fell on their faces, and became as it were dead. And Jesus said to them: Why are your hearts possessed with fear? Do you not know that this palm, which I have caused to be transferred to paradise, shall be prepared for all the saints in the place of delights, as it has been prepared for us in this place of the wilderness? And they were filled with joy; and being strengthened, they all rose up.

CHAPTER 22

After this, while they were going on their journey, Joseph said to Jesus: Lord, it is a boiling heat; if it please Thee, let us go by the sea-shore, that we may be able to rest in the cities on the coast. Jesus said to him: Fear not, Joseph; I will shorten the way for you, so that what you would have taken thirty days to go over, you shall accomplish in this one day. And while they were thus speaking, behold, they looked forward, and began to see the mountains and cities of Egypt.

And rejoicing and exulting, they came into the regions of Hermopolis, and entered into a certain city of Egypt which is called Sotinen; and because they knew no one there from whom they could ask hospitality, they went into a temple which was called the Capitol of Egypt. And in this temple there had been set up three hundred and fifty-five idols, to each of which on its own day divine honours and sacred rites were paid. For the Egyptians belonging to the same city entered the Capitol, in which the priests told them how many sacrifices were offered each day, according to the honour in which the god was held.

CHAPTER 23

And it came to pass, when the most blessed Mary went into the temple with the little child, that all the idols prostrated themselves on the ground, so that all of them were lying on their faces shattered and broken to pieces; and thus they plainly showed that they were nothing. Then was fulfilled that which was said by the prophet Isaiah: Behold, the Lord will come upon a swift cloud, and will enter Egypt, and all the handiwork of the Egyptians shall be moved at His presence.

CHAPTER 24

Then Affrodosius, that governor of the city, when news of this was brought to him, went to the temple with all his army. And the priests of the temple, when they saw Affrodosius with all his army coming into the temple, thought that he was making haste only to see vengeance taken on those on whose account the gods had fallen down. But when he came into the temple, and saw all the gods lying prostrate on their faces, he went up to the blessed Mary, who was carrying the Lord in her bosom, and adored Him, and said to all his army and all his friends: Unless this were the God of our gods, our gods would not have fallen on their faces before Him; nor would they be lying prostrate in His presence: wherefore they silently confess that He is their Lord. Unless we, therefore, take care to do what we have seen our gods doing, we may run the risk of His anger, and all come to destruction, even as it happened to Pharaoh king of the Egyptians, who, not believing in powers so mighty, was drowned in the sea, with all his army. Then all the people of that same city believed in the Lord God through Jesus Christ.

CHAPTER 25

After no long time the angel said to Joseph: Return to the land of Judah, for they are dead who sought the child's life.

CHAPTER 26

And it came to pass, after Jesus had returned out of Egypt, when He was in Galilee, and entering on the fourth year of His age, that on a Sabbath-day He was playing with some children at the bed of the Jordan. And as He sat there, Jesus made to Himself seven pools of clay, and to each of them He made passages, through which at His command He brought water from the torrent into the pool, and took it back again. Then one of those children, a son of the devil, moved with envy, shut the passages which supplied the pools with water, and overthrew what Jesus had built up. Then said Jesus to him: Woe unto thee, thou son of death, thou son of Satan! Dost thou destroy the works which I have wrought? And immediately he who had done this died. Then with great uproar the parents of the dead boy cried out against Mary and Joseph, saying to them: Your son has cursed our son, and he is dead. And when Joseph and Mary heard this, they came forthwith to Jesus, on account of the outcry of the parents of the boy, and the gathering together of the Jews. But Joseph said privately to Mary: I dare not speak to Him; but do thou admonish Him, and say: Why hast Thou raised against us the hatred of the people; and why must the troublesome hatred of men be borne by us? And His mother having come to Him, asked Him, saying: My Lord, what was it that he did to bring about his death? And He said: He deserved death, because he scattered the works that I had made. Then His mother asked Him, saying: Do not so, my Lord, because all men rise up against us. But He, not wishing to grieve His mother, with His right foot kicked the hinder parts of the dead boy, and said to him: Rise, thou son of iniquity for thou art not worthy to enter into the rest of my Father, because thou didst destroy the works which I had made. Then he who had been dead rose up, and went away. And Jesus, by the word of His power, brought water into the pools by the aqueduct.

CHAPTER 27

And it came to pass, after these things, that in the sight of all Jesus took clay froth the pools which He had made, and of it made twelve sparrows. And it was the Sabbath when Jesus did this, and there were very many children with Him. When, therefore, one of the Jews had seen Him doing this, he said to Joseph: Joseph, dost thou not see the child

Jesus working on the Sabbath at what it is not lawful for him to do? for he has made twelve sparrows of clay. And when Joseph heard this, he reproved him, saying: Wherefore doest thou on the Sabbath such things as are not lawful for us to do? And when Jesus heard Joseph, He struck His hands together, and said to His sparrows: Fly! And at the voice of His command they began to fly. And in the sight and hearing of all that stood by, He said to the birds: Go and fly through the earth, and through all the world, and live. And when those that were there saw such miracles, they were filled with great astonishment. And some praised and admired Him, but others reviled Him. And certain of them went away to the chief priests and the heads of the Pharisees, and reported to them that Jesus the son of Joseph had done great signs and miracles in the sight of all the people of Israel. And this was reported in the twelve tribes of Israel.

CHAPTER 28

And again the son of Annas, a priest of the temple, who had come with Joseph, holding his rod in his hand in the sight of all, with great fury broke down the dams which Jesus had made with His own hands, and let out the water which He had collected in them from the torrent. Moreover, he shut the aqueduct by which the water came in, and then broke it down. And when Jesus saw this, He said to that boy who had destroyed His dams: O most wicked seed of iniquity! O son of death! O workshop of Satan! verily the fruit of thy seed shall be without strength, and thy roots without moisture, and thy branches withered, bearing no fruit. And immediately, in the sight of all, the boy withered away, and died.

CHAPTER 29

Then Joseph trembled, and took hold of Jesus, and went with Him to his own house, and His mother with Him. And, behold, suddenly from the opposite direction a boy, also a worker of iniquity, ran up and came against the shoulder of Jesus, wishing to make sport of Him, or to hurt Him, if he could. And Jesus said to him: Thou shall not go back safe and sound from the way that thou goest. And immediately he fell down, and died. And the parents of the dead boy, who had seen what happened, cried out, saying: Where does this child come from? It is manifest that every word that he says is true; and it is often accomplished before he speaks. And the parents of the dead boy came to Joseph, and said to him: Take away that Jesus from this place, for he cannot live with us in this town; or at least teach him to bless, and not to curse. And Joseph came up to Jesus, and admonished Him, saying: Why doest thou such things? For already many are in grief and against thee, and hate us on thy account, and we endure the reproaches of men because of thee. And Jesus answered and said unto Joseph: No one is a wise son but he whom his father hath taught, according to the knowledge of this time; and a father's curse can hurt none but evil-doers. Then they came together against Jesus, and accused him to Joseph. When Joseph saw this, he was in great terror, fearing the violence and uproar of the people of Israel. And the same hour Jesus seized the dead boy by the ear, and lifted him up from the earth in the sight of all: and they saw Jesus speaking to him like a father to his son. And his spirit came back to him, and he revived. And all of them wondered.

CHAPTER 30

Now a certain Jewish schoolmaster named Zachyasheard Jesus thus speaking; and seeing that He could not be overcome, from knowing the power that was in Him,he became angry, and began rudely and foolishly, and without fear, to speak against Joseph. And he said: Dost thou not wish to entrust me with thy son, that he may be instructed in human learning and in reverence? But I see that Mary and thyself have more regard for your son than for what the elders of the people of Israel say against him. You should have given more honour to us, the elders of the whole church of Israel, both that he might be on terms of mutual affection with the children, and that among us he might be instructed in Jewish learning. Joseph, on the other hand, said to him: And is there any one who can keep this child, and teach him? But if thou canst keep him and teach him, we by no means hinder him from being taught by thee those things which are learned by all. And Jesus, having heard what Zachyas had said, answered and said unto him: The precepts of the law which thou hast just spoken of, and all the things that thou hast named, must be kept by those who are instructed in human learning; but I am a stranger to your law-courts, because I have no father after the flesh. Thou who readest the law, and art learned in it, abidest in the law; but I was before the law, But since thou thinkest that no one is equal to thee in learning, thou shalt be taught by me, that no other can teach anything but those things which thou hast named. But he alone can who is worthy.For when I shall be exalted on earth, I will cause to cease all mention of your genealogy. For thou knowest not when thou wast born: I alone know when you were born, and how long your life on earth will be. Then all who heard these words were struck with astonishment, and cried out: Oh! oh! oh! this marvellously great and wonderful mystery. Never have we heard the like! Never has it been heard from any one else, nor has it been said or at any time heard by the prophets, or the Pharisees, or the scribes. We know whence he is sprung, and he is scarcely five years old; and whence does he speak these words? The Pharisees answered: We have never heard such words spoken by any other child so young. And Jesus answered and said unto them: At this do ye wonder, that such things are said by a child? Why, then, do ye not believe me in those things which I have said to you? And you all wonder because I said to you that I know when you were born. I will tell you greater things, that you may wonder more. I have seen Abraham, whom you call your father, and have spoken with him; and he has seen me.And when they heard this they held their tongues, nor did any of them dare to speak. And Jesus said to them: I have been among you with children, and you have not known me; I have spoken to you as to wise men, and you have not understood my words; because you are younger than I am, and of little faith.

CHAPTER 31

A second time the master Zachyas, doctor of the law, said to Joseph and Mary: Give me the boy, and I shall hand him over to master Levi, who shall teach him his letters and instruct him. Then Joseph and Mary, soothing Jesus, took Him to the schools, that He might be taught His letters by old Levi. And as soon as He went in He held His tongue. And the master Levi said one letter to Jesus, and, beginning from the first letter Aleph, said to Him: Answer. But Jesus was silent, and answered nothing. Wherefore the preceptor Levi was angry, and seized his storax-tree rod, and struck Him on the head. And Jesus said to the teacher Levi: Why dost thou strike me? Thou shall know in truth, that He who is struck can teach him who strikes Him more than He can be taught by him. For I can teach you those very things that yon are saying. But all these are blind who speak and hear, like sounding brass or tinkling cymbal, in which there is no perception of those things which are meant by their sound.And Jesus in addition said to Zachyas: Every letter from Aleph even to Thetis known by its arrangement. Say thou first, therefore, what Thet is, and I will tell thee what Aleph is. And again Jesus said to them: Those who do not know Aleph, how can they say Thet, the hypocrites? Tell me what the first one, Aleph, is; and I shall then believe you when you have said Beth. And Jesus began to ask the names of the letters one by one, and said: Let the master of the law tell us what the first letter is, or why it has many triangles, gradate, subacute, mediate, obduced, produced, erect, prostrate, curvistrate. And when Levi heard this, he was thunderstruck at such an arrangement of the names of the letters. Then he began in the heating of all to cry out, and say: Ought such a one to live on the earth? Yea, he ought to be hung on the great cross. For he can put out fire, and make sport of other modes of punishment. I think that he lived before the flood, and was born before the deluge. For what womb bore him? or what mother brought him forth? or what breasts gave him suck? I flee before him; I am not able to withstand the words from his mouth, but my heart is astounded to hear such words. I do not think that any man can understand what he says, except God were with him. Now I, unfortunate wretch, have given myself up to be a laughing- stock to him. For when I thought I had a scholar, I, not knowing him, have found my master. What shall I say? I cannot withstand the words of this child: I shall now flee from this town, because I cannot understand them. An old man like me has been beaten by a boy, because I can find neither beginning nor end of what he says. For it is no easy matter to find a beginning of himself.I tell you of a certainty, I am not lying, that to my eyes the proceedings of this boy, the commencement of his conversation, and the upshot of his intention, seem to have nothing in common with mortal man. Here then I do not know whether he be a wizard or a god; or at least an angel of God speaks in him. Whence he is, or where he comes from, or who he will turn out to be, I know not. Then Jesus, smiling at him with a joyful countenance, said in a commanding voice to all the sons of Israel standing by and hearing: Let the unfruitful bring forth fruit, and the blind see, and the lame walk right, and the poor enjoy the good things of this life, and the dead live, that each may return to his original state, and abide in Him who is the root of life and of perpetual sweetness. And when the child Jesus had said this, forthwith all who had fallen under malignant diseases were restored. And they did not dare to say anything more to Him, or to hear anything from Him.

CHAPTER 32

After these things, Joseph and Mary departed thence with Jesus into the city of Nazareth; and He remained there with His parents. And on the first of the week, when Jesus was playing with the children on the roof of a certain house, it happened that one of the children pushed another down from the roof to the ground, and he was killed. Anod the parents of the dead boy, who had not seen this, cried out against Joseph and Mary, saying: Your son has thrown our son down to the ground, and he is dead. But Jesus was silent, and answered them nothing. And Joseph and Mary came in haste to Jesus.; and His mother asked Him, saying: My lord, tell me if thou didst throw him down. And immediately Jesus went down from the roof to the ground, and called the boy by his name, Zeno. And he answered Him: My lord. And Jesus said to him: Was it I that threw thee down from the roof to the ground? And he said: No, my lord. And the parents of the boy who had been dead wondered, and honoured Jesus for the miracle that had been wrought. And Joseph and Mary departed thence with Jesus to Jericho.

CHAPTER 33

Now Jesus was six years old, and His mother sent Him with a pitcher to the fountain to draw water with the children. And it came to pass, after He had drawn the water, that one of the children came against Him, and struck the pitcher, and broke it. But Jesus stretched out the cloak which He had on, and took up in His cloak as much water as there had been in the pitcher, and carried it to His mother. And when she saw it she wondered, and reflected within herself, and laid up all these things in her heart.

CHAPTER 34

Again, on a certain day, He went forth into the field, and took a little wheat from His mother's barn, and sowed it Himself. And it sprang up, and grew, and multiplied exceedingly. And at last it came to pass that He Himself reaped it, and gathered as the produce of it three kors,and gave it to His numerous acquaintances.

CHAPTER 35

There is a road going out of Jericho and leading to the river Jordan, to the place where the children of Israel crossed: and there the ark of the covenant is said to have rested. And Jesus was eight years old, and He went out of Jericho, and went towards the Jordan. And there was beside the road, near the bank of the Jordan, a cave where a lioness was nursing her cubs; and no one was safe to walk that way. Jesus then, coming from Jericho, and knowing that in that cave the lioness had brought forth her young, went into it in the sight of all. And when the lions saw Jesus, they ran to meet Him, and adored Him. And Jesus was sitting in the cavern, and the lion's cubs ran hither and thither round His feet, fawning upon Him, and sporting. And the older lions, with their heads bowed down, stood at a distance, and adored Him, and fawned upon Him with their tails. Then the people who were standing afar off, not seeing Jesus, said: Unless he or his parents had committed grievous sins, he would not of his own accord have offered himself up to the lions. And when the people were thus reflecting within themselves, and were lying under great sorrow, behold, on a sudden, in the sight of the people, Jesus came out of the cave, and the lions went before Him, and the lion's cubs played with each other before His feet. And the parents of Jesus stood afar off, with their heads bowed down, and watched; likewise also the people stood at a distance, on account of the lions; for they did not dare to come close to them. Then Jesus began to say to the people: How much better are the beasts than you, seeing that they recognise their Lord, and glorify Him; while you men, who have been made after the image and likeness of God, do not know Him! Beasts know me, and are tame; men see me, and do not acknowledge me.

CHAPTER 36

After these things Jesus crossed the Jordan, in the sight of them all, with the lions; and the water of the Jordan was divided on the right hand and on the left. Then He said to the lions, in the hearing of all: Go in peace, and hurt no one; but neither let man injure you, until you return to the place whence you have come forth. And they, bidding Him farewell, not only with their gestures but with their voices, went to their own place. But Jesus returned to His mother.

CHAPTER 37

Now Joseph was a carpenter, and used to make nothing else of wood but ox-yokes, and ploughs, and implements of husbandry, and wooden beds. And it came to pass that a certain young man ordered him to make for him a couch six cubits long. And Joseph commanded his servant to cut the wood with an iron saw, according to the measure which he had sent. But he did not keep to the prescribed measure, but made one piece of wood shorter than the other. And Joseph was in perplexity, and began to consider what he was to do about this. And when Jesus saw him in this state of cogitation, seeing that it was a matter of impossibility to him, He addresses him with words of comfort, saying: Come, let us take hold of the ends of the pieces of wood, and let us put them together, end to end, and let us fit them exactly to each other, and draw to us, for we shall be able to make them equal. Then Joseph did what he was bid, for he knew that He could do whatever He wished. And Joseph took hold of the ends of the pieces of wood, and brought them together against the wall next himself, and Jesus took hold of the other ends of the pieces of wood, and drew the shorter piece to Him, and made it of the same length as the longer one. And He said to Joseph: Go and work, and do what thou hast promised to do. And Joseph did what he had promised.

CHAPTER 38

And it came to pass a second time, that Joseph and Mary were asked by the people that Jesus should be taught His letters in school. They did not refuse to do so; and according to the commandment of the elders, they took Him to a master to be instructed in human learning. Then the master began to teach Him in an imperious tone, saying: Say Alpha. And Jesus said to him: Do thou tell me first what Betha is, and I will tell thee what Alpha is. And upon this the master got angry and struck Jesus; and no sooner had he struck Him, than he fell down dead.

And Jesus went home again to His mother. And Joseph, being afraid, called Mary to him, and said to her: Know of a surety that my soul is sorrowful even unto death on account of this child. For it is very likely that at some time or other some one will strike him in malice, and he will die. But Mary answered and said: O man of God! do not believe that this is possible. You may believe to a certainty that He who has sent him to be born among men will Himself guard him from all mischief, and will in His own name preserve him from evil.

CHAPTER 39

Again the Jews asked Mary and Joseph a third time to coax Him to go to another master to learn. And Joseph and Mary, fearing the people, and the overbearing of the princes, and the threats of the priests, led Him again to school, knowing that He could learn nothing from man, because He had perfect knowledge from God only. And when Jesus had entered the school, led by the Holy Spirit, He took the book out of the hand of the master who was teaching the law, and in the sight and hearing of all the people began to read, not indeed what was written in their book; but He spoke in the Spirit of the living God, as if a stream of water were gushing forth from a living fountain, and the fountain remained always full. And with such power He taught the people the great things of the living God, that the master himself fell to the ground and adored Him. And the heart of the people who sat and heard Him saying such things was turned into astonishment. And when Joseph heard of this, he came running to Jesus, fearing that the master himself was dead. And when the master saw him, he said to him: Thou hast given me not a scholar, but a master; and who can withstand his words? Then was fulfilled that which was spoken by the Psalmist: The river of God is full of water: Thou hast prepared them corn, for so is the provision for it.

CHAPTER 40

After these things Joseph departed thence with Mary and Jesus to go into Capernaum by the sea-shore, on account of the malice of his adversaries. And when Jesus was living in Capernaum, there was in the city a man named Joseph, exceedingly rich. But he had wasted away under his infirmity, and died, and was lying dead in his couch. And when Jesus heard them in the city mourning, and weeping, and lamenting over the dead man, He said to Joseph: Why dost thou not afford the benefit of thy favour to this man, seeing that he is called by thy name? And Joseph answered him: How have I any power or ability to afford him a benefit? And Jesus said to him: Take the handkerchief which is upon thy head, and go and put it on the face of the dead man, and say to him: Christ heal thee; and immediately the dead man will be healed, and will rise from his couch. And when Joseph heard this, he went away at the command of Jesus, and ran, and entered the house of the dead man, and put the handkerchief which he was wearing on his head upon the face of him who was lying in the couch, and said: Jesus heal thee. And forthwith the dead man rose from his bed, and asked who Jesus was.

CHAPTER 41

And they went away from Capernaum into the city which is called Bethlehem; and Joseph lived with Mary in his own house, and Jesus with them. And on a certain day Joseph called to him his first-born son James,and sent him into the vegetable garden to gather vegetables for the purpose of making broth. And Jesus followed His brother James into the garden; but Joseph and Mary did not know this. And while James was collecting the vegetables, a viper suddenly came out of a hole and struck his hand, and he began to cry out from excessive pain. And, becoming exhausted, he said, with a bitter cry: Alas! alas! an accursed viper has struck my hand. And Jesus, who was standing opposite to him, at the bitter cry ran up to James, and took hold of his hand; and all that He did was to blow on the hand of James, and cool it: and immediately James was healed, and the serpent died. And Joseph and Mary did not know what had been done; but at the cry of James, and the command of Jesus, they ran to the garden, and found the serpent already dead, and James quite cured.

CHAPTER 42

And Joseph having come to a feast with his sons, James, Joseph, and Judah, and Simeon and his two daughters, Jesus met them, with Mary His mother, along with her sister Mary of Cleophas, whom the Lord God had given to her father Cleophas and her mother Anna, because they had offered Mary the mother of Jesus to the Lord. And she was called by the same name, Mary, for the consolation of her parents. And when they had come together, Jesus sanctified and blessed them, and He was the first to begin to eat and drink; for none of them dared to eat or drink, or to sit at table, or to break bread, until He had sanctified them, and first done so. And if He happened to be absent, they used to wait until He should do this. And when He did not wish to come for refreshment, neither Joseph nor Mary, nor the sons of Joseph, His brothers, came. And, indeed, these brothers, keeping His life as a lamp before their eyes, observed Him, and feared Him. And when Jesus slept, whether by day or by night, the brightness of God shone upon Him. To whom be all praise and glory for ever and ever. Amen, amen.

The Gospel of the Lord

The written account of the life of Jesus Christ, preserved in its original greek by Marcion, son of Philologus, bishop of Sinope. 130 anno domine, Rome - version 1.00 - contains five chapters of twenty-one .

CHAPTER 1

n the fifteenth year of the reign of Tiberius Caesar,

2. [Pontius Pilatus being the Governor of Judaea,] Jesus came down to Capernaum, a city in Galilee, and was

3. teaching on the sabbath days : and they were astonished at his doctrine : for his word was in authority.

4. And in the synagogue there was a man which had a spirit of an unclean demon, and he cried out with a loud

5. voice, Saying, "let us alone ; what have we to do with thee, Jesus? art thou come to destroy us? I know thee

6. who thou art : the Holy One of God." And Jesus rebuked him, saying ; "Hold thy peace, and come out of him." And when the demon had thrown him into the midst,

7. he came out of him, having done no hurt. And amazement came upon all, and they spake together saying to one another, what is this word? For in authority and power he commandeth the unclean spirits,

8. and they come out. And a rumour of him went out into every place of the country round about,

9. And he arose out of the synagogue, and entered into the house of Simon.

And Simon's mother in law was taken with a great fever : and they besought him for her.

10. And he stood over her, and rebuked the fever : and it left her : and immidately she arose and ministered unto them.

11. And he came to Nazareth, and went into the

12. synagogue [on the Sabbath day] and sat down. And the eyes of all in the synagogue fastened on him,

13-14. And he began to speak to them; and all wondered

15. at the words which proceedeth from his mouth. And he said unto them, " Ye will surely say unto me this parable, Physician, heal thyself; whatsoever we have

16. heard done at Capernaum, do also here. But I tell you of a truth, many widows were in Israel in the days of Elijah, when the heaven was shut up three years and six months,

17. when great famine occured throughout all the land: and unto none of them was Elijah sent, but only to Sarepta ,

18. a city of Sidon, unto a woman that was a widow. And many lepers were in Israel in the time of Elisha the prophet : and none of them was cleansed, but only

19. Naaman the syrian". And they were all filled with wrath

20. in the synagogue, when they heard these things, and rose up, and thrust him out of the city, and led him unto the brow of the hill whereon their city was built, to cast

21. him down headlong. But he passing through the midst of them went his way.

22. And when the sun was setting, all as many as had any sick with divers diseases brought them unto him; and he laid his hands on every one of them, and healed them.

23. And demons also came out of many, crying out, saying, "Thou art Son of God" and he rebuked them

suffered them not to speak; for they knew that he was the Christ.

24. And when it was day, he departed and went into a desert place: and the multitudes sought him, and came unto

him, and stayed him, that he should not depart from

25. them. And he said unto them, "I must announce as good tidings the kingdom of God to the other cities also:

for therefore am i sent.

26. And he was preaching in the synagogues of Galilee.

CHAPTER 2

1. Now it came to pass, that, as the multitude pressed upn him to hear the word of God, he was standing by

2. the lake of Gennesaret, and saw two boats standing by the lake: but the

fdishermen were gone out of them,

3. and were washing their nets. And he entered into one of the boats, which was Simon`s , and asked him to thrust out a litle from land. And he sat down, and

4. taught the multitudes out of the boat. Now when he had left speaking, he said unto Simon, "Put put into the

5. deep, and let down your nets a draught". And Simon answering said unto him, "Master, we have toiled all the night, and taken nothing ; but at thy word I will let down

6. the net." When they had this done, they inclosed a

7. great multitude of fishes: and their nets were breaking. And they beckoned unto their partners, in the other boat, that they should come and help them out. And they came, and

8. filled both the boats, so that they began to sink. When Simon Peter saw it, he fell down at Jesus` knees, saying,

9. "Depart from me; for I am a sinful man , O Lord." For amazement overcame him, and all that were with him, at

10. the draught of the fishes which they had taken: which were partners with Simon. And Jesus said unto Simon, "fear not ; from henceforth thou shalt be taking men

11. alive." And when they had brought their boats to land, they left all, and followed him.

12. And it came to pass, when he was in one of the cities, behold a man full of leprosy: who seeing Jesus fell on his face, and besought him, saying ; "Lord, if thou wilt, thou

13. canst make me clean." And he put forth his hand, and touched him, saying, " I will : be thou cleansed" And

14. immediately the leprosy departed from the man. And he charged him to tell no man; but go, and shew thyself to the priest, and offer for thy cleansing, according as Moses

15. commanded, that this may be a testimony to you. But so much the more went there a fame abroad of him: and many multitidues came together to hear, and to be healed

16. by him for their infirmities. And he himself was withdrawing in the wilderness, praying.

17. And it came to pass on one of the days that he was teaching, and there were Pharisees and doctors of the law sitting vtm which were come out of every village of Galilee, Judaea, and Jerusalem: and the power of the

18. Lord was with Him tohcal them. And behold, men brought in a bed a man that was palsied; and they sought

19. to bring him in, and to lay him before him. And not finding by what way they might bring him in because of the multitude, they went up to the housetop, and let him down through the tiles with his couch into the midst before

20. Jesus. And seeing their faith, he said unto him , "Man, thy

21. sins are forgiven thee." And the scribes and the Pharisees began to reason, saying, "Who is this which speaketh blasphemies? Who can forgive sin, but God alone?

22. But Jesus perceiving their reasoning answered and said unto them, "What reasen ye in your hearts?

23. Whether is easier, to say, Thy sins are forgiven thee ; or

24. to say ; Rise up and walk? But that ye may know that the Son of man hath authority upon earth to forgive sins (he said unto the palsied man) I say unto thee, Arise

25. and take up they couch, and go to thine house. And immediately he rose up before them, and took up that whereon he lay, and departed to his house, glorifying

26. God. And amazement took hold on all, and they glorified God, and were filled with fear, saying, "We have seen strange things today".

27. And after these things he went forth, and saw a publican, named Levi, sitting at the place of toll : and he

28. said unto him, "Follow me." And he left all, rose up, and

29. followed him. And Levi made him a great feast in his hourse : and there was a great company of publicans and

30. of others that were reclining with them. And their scribes and the Pharisees murmured against his disciples, saying, "Why do ye year and drink with publicans and

31. sinners?" And Jesus answering said unto them, "They that are whole have no need of a physiciian ; but they

32. that are sick. I am not come to call the righteous, but

33. sinners to repentance. And they said unto him, "Why do the disciples of John fast often, and make prayers, and likewise the disciples of the Pharisees; but thine eat and

34. drink? And he said unto them, "Can ye make the sons of the bridal chamber fast, while the bridegroom is with

35. them? But the days will come; and when the bridegroom shall be taken away from them, then will they fast in

36. those days." And he spake also a parable unto them; "No man putteth a piece of new garment upon an old garment; else both the new maketh a rent, and the piece that was taken out of the new agreeth not with the

37. old. And no man puttteth new wine into old wine-skins, else the new wine will burst the skins; and itself will be

38. spilled, and the skins will perish. But new wine must be put into new wine-skins, and both are preserved.

39. No man also having drunk old wine straigtway desireth new ; for he saith, the old is better.

CHAPTER 3

1. And it came to pass on the second sabbath after the first, that he was going through the corn fields : and his disciples plucked the ears of cornm and did eat, rubbing them in

2. their hands. And certain of the Pharisees said unto them, "Why do ye that which is not lawful to do

3. on the sabbath day?" And Jesus answering them, said, "Have ye not read even this what David did, when himself was

4. an hungered, and they which were with him ; how they went into the house of God, and did take and eat the shewbread, and gave also to them that were with him ; which it is not lawful to eat but for the priests alone?"

5. And he said unto them, "That the Son of man is Lord even of the sabbath"

6. And it came to pass also on another Sabbath, that he entered into the synagogue and taught; and there were a

7. a man there and his right hand was withered. And the scribes and Pharisees watched him, whether he would heal on the sabbath day; that they might find an

8. accusation against him. But he knew their reasonings, and said to the man which had the withered man, "Rise up, and stand forth in the midst. And he rose and stood

9. forth. Then said Jesus unto them, "I will ask you something; Is it lawful on the sabbath to do good

10. or to do evil? To save life, or to destroy it?" And looking round about upon them all, he said unto the man, "stretch forth thy hand." and he did so : and his hand was

11. restored as the other. And they were filled with madness; and commanded one with another what they might do to Jesus.

12. And it came to pass in those days, that he went out into the mountains to pray, and was passing the whole night

13. in prayer to God. And when it was day, he called unto him his disciples: and he chose from them twelve.

14. whom he also named ; apostles ; Simon (whom was also named Peter), and Andrew his brother, James and John, Phillip

15. and Bartholomew, Matthew and Thomas, James the son

16. of Alphaeas, and Simon whom they called Zelotes, and Judas the brother of James, and Judas Iscarioth , which also became a

17. traitor. And he came down among them, and stood on a level place, and the multitude of his disciples, and a great number of people out of all Judaea and Jerusalem, and from the sea coast of Tyre and Sidon, which came to hear

18. him, and to be healed of their diseases; and they that were troubled by unclean spirits: and they were healed.

19. And the whole multitude sought to touch him : for power went out of him, and healed them all.

20. And he lifted up his eyes on his disciples, and said: "Blessed are ye poor: for your`s is the kingdom of God.

21. Blessed are ye that hunger now : for ye shall be filled. Blessed are ye that weep now : for ye shall laught.

22. Blessed are ye, when men shall hate you, and when they shall separate you from their company, and shall reproach you, and cast out your name as evil, for the Son of man`s

23. sake. Rejoice ye in that day, and leap for you : for , behold, your reward is great in heaven: for according to

24. these things did their fathers unto the prophets. But woe unto you that are rich! for ye have consolation

25. in full. Woe unto you that are full! for ye shall hunger. Woe unto you that laugh now! for ye

26. shall mourn and weep. Woe unto you, when all men shall speak well of you! for according to these things did their fathers to the false prophets.

27. But I say unto you that hear, Love your enemies, do

28. good to them which hate you, bless them that curse you,

29. and pray for them which despitefully use you.Unto him that smiteth thee on the one cheek, offer also the other ; and from him that taketh away thy cloke, withhold

30. not thy coat also. Give every man that asketh of thee: and of him that taketh away thy goods ask them.

31. not again. and as ye would that men should do to you,

32. do ye also to them likewise. And if ye love them which love you, what thank have ye? for sinners also love those

33. that love them. And if ye do good to them which do good to you, what thank have ye? for sinners also do

34. the same. And if ye lend to them of whom ye hope to receive, what thank have ye? for sinners also lend to

35. sinners, to receive equal things.But love ye your enemies, and do good, and lend, hoping for nothing again : and your reward shall be great , and ye shall be sons of the Highest : for he is kind unto the unthankful and to

36. the evil. Be ye therefore merciful, as your Father also is

37. merciful. And Judge not, and ye shall not be judged : condemn not, and ye shall not be condemned : release

38. and ye shall be released : Give, and it shall be given unto you ; good measure, pressed down, and shaken together, and running over, shall they give into your bosom. For with the same measure that ye mete withal it shall be measured to you again."

39. And he spake a parable unto them, "Can the blind lead

40. the blind? shall they not both fall into the ditch? The disciple is not above his teacher : but every one that is

41 perfect shall be as his teacher. And why beholdest thou the mote that is in thy brothers eye, but perceivest

42. not the beam that is in thine won eye? Either how canst thou say to thy brother, Brother, let me pull the mote that is in thine eye, when thou thyself beholdest not the beam in thine own eye? Thou hypocrite, cast out first the beam out of thine own eye, and then shall you see clearly to pull out the mote that is in thy brother`s eye!.

43. For there is no good tree that maketh corrupt fruit ; nor

44. corrupt tree that maketh good fruit. For each tree is known by its fruit. For of thorns do they not gather figs, nor of a bramble bush gather they grapes.

45. The good man out of the good treasure of his heart bringeth forth that which is truely good : and the evil man out of the evil treasure of his heart bringeth forth that which is evil : for out of the abundance of the heart his

46. mouth speaketh. And why call ye me, Lord, Lord , and

47. do not do the things which I say? Everyone that cometh to me, and heareth my sayings, and doeth them, I will

48. shew you to whom he is like : He is like a man building a house, who digged and went deep, and laid a foundation on the rock : and when the flood arose, the stream beat vehemtly upon the house, and had not strenght to shake it: for it was founded upon the

49. rock. But he that heareth, and doeth not, is like a man that without a foundation built a house upon the earth; against which the stream did beat vehemently, and immediately it fell, and the ruin of that house was great.

CHAPTER 4

1. Now when he had completed all his sayings in the ears of the people, he entered into Capernaum.

2. And a certain centurion's servant was sick, and going to

3. die ; and he was precious unto him. And when he heard of Jesus, he sent unto him elders of the Jews

4. asking him that he would come and save his servant. And when they came to Jesus, they besought him earnestly , saying, That he was worthy for whom he should do this:

5. "For he loveth our nation, and he hath built us the

6. synagogue". Then Jesus went with them. And when he was now not far from the house, the centurion sent friends to him,saying unto him : "Lord, trouble not thyself; for I am not worthy that thou shouldest enter under my roof.

7. Wherefore neither thoughtr I myself worthy to come unto thee: but say in a word, and my boy shall be healed.

8. For I aslo am a man set under authority, having under me soliders, and I say unto this one , Go, and he goeth ; and to another, Come, and he cometh ; and to my servant , Do

9. this, and he doeth it". And when Jesus heard these things, he marveled at him, and turned, and said unto the multitude that followed him, "I say unto you, not even in

10. Israel have I found so great faith." And they that were sent, returned to the house, and found the sick servant whole.

11. And it came to pass the day after, that he was going into a city called Nain,; and many of his disciples were

12. going with him, and a great multitude. Now when he came night to the gate of the city, behold, a dead man was being carried out, the only son of his mother, and she was a widow : and a considerable multitude of the

13. city was with her. And when the Lord saw her, he had

14. compassion on her, and said unto her, "Weep not." And he came and touched the bier : and they that bare him stood still. And he said, "Young man, I say unto thee, Arise!"

15. And the dead man sat up, and began to speak. And

16. he delivered him to his mother. And fear took hold on all: and they glorified God, saying, That a great prophet is risen up among us ; and, That God hath

17. visited his people. And this rumour of him went forth in the whole of Judaea, and in all region round about.

18. And the disciples of John told him of all these

19. things. And John calling unto him a certain two of his disciples sent them to Jesus, saying, "Art thou he that

20. cometh? or are we to look for another?" And when the men were come unto him, they said, "John the Baptist hath sent us unto thee, saying ; Art thou he that cometh?

21. or are we to look for another?" And in that same hour he cured many infirmities and plagues and of evil spirits;

22. and unto many blind he gave sight. And Jesus answering said unto them, "Go your way, and tell John what things ye have seen and heard : that the blind receive their sight, the lame walk, the lepers are cleansed, the deaf hear, the dead are raised, the poor have good tidings

23. announced to them. And blessed is he, whosoever shall not be offended in me."

24. And when the messengers of John were departed, he began to say unto the multitudes concerning John What are ye come into the wilderness to gaze at? A reed

25. shaken with the wind? But what are ye come out to see? A man clothed in soft rainment? Behold, they which are in gorgeous apparel, and delicacy, are kings'

26. courts. But what are ye come out to see? A Prophet? Yea , I say unto you, and much more than a prophet.

27. This is he, of whom it is written, "Behold, I send my messenger before thy face, which shall prepare thy way

28. before thee." For I say unto you, Among those that are born from women, a greater prophet than John the Baptist, there is none : but he that is less in the Kingdom of God

29. is greater than he". And all the people when they heard it, and the publicans, justified God, being baptised with

30. the baptism of John. But the Pharisees and lawyer rejected the counsel of God unto themselves, being not

31. baptised of him. And the Lord said, "Whereunto then shall I liken the men of this generation? and to what are

32. they like? They are like unto children sitting in the marketplace, and calling to one another, and saying :, We piped unto you, and ye did not dance, we mourned

33. you, and ye did not weep. For John the Baptist is come neither eating bread nor drinking wine, and ye say, He

34. hath a demon. The Son of man is coming eating and drinking, and ye say, Behold a gluttonous man, and a

35. winebibber, a friend of publicans and sinners! And wisdom was justified of all her children".

36. And one of the Pharisees desired him that he would eat with him. And he went into the Pharisee`s house, and

37. reclined to meat. And behold, a woman of the city, which was a sinner, when she knew that he was reclining in the Pharisee`s house, brought an alabaster box of ointment

38. and stood at his feet behind him weeping, and began to wet his feet with the tears,, and did wipe them with the hairs of her head, and kissed his feet, and anointed

39. them with the ointment. Now when the Pharisee which had bidden him saw it, he spake to himself, saying, "This man, if he were a prophet, would have known who and what manner manner of woman this is that touched him :

40. for she is a sinner. And Jesus answering said unto him, "Simon, I have somewhat to say unto thee." And he saith,

41. "Teacher, say on." "A certain money-lender had two debtors : the one owed five hundred denarii, and

42. the other fifty. And when they had not whewewith to pay, he forgave them both. Tell me therefore, which

43. of them will love him more?" Simon answered and said, "I suppose that he, to whom he forgave the more." And he said unto

44. him, "Thou hast rightly judged"And he turned to the woman, and said unto Simon, "Seest thou this woman? I entered into thine house : water for my feet thou gavest me not : but she hath wetted my feet with tears, and wiped

45. them with the hairs of her head. A kiss thou gavest me not : but she since the time I came hath not ceased

46. kissing my feet. My head with oil thou didst not anoint: but this woman hath anointed my feet with ointment.

47. For the sake of which I say unto thee ; Her sins which are many are forgiven; for she loved much : but to

48. whom little is forgiven, the same loveth little". And he

49. said unto her, " Thy sins are forgiven." And they that were reclining with him began to say among themselves,

50. "Who is this that even forgiveth sins?" And he said to the woman "Thy faith has saved thee, go in peace."

CHAPTER 5

1. And it came to pass afterward, that he made his way through city and village, preaching and announcing as good

tidings the kingdom of God : and the twelve were

2. with him. And certain women, which had been healed of evil spirits and infirmities, Mary called Magdalene, from

3. whom seven demons had gone out , and Joannah the wife of Chuza, Herod`s steward, and Susanna, and many others, which ministered unto him of their possessions.

4. And when a great multitude were coming together, and they of every city were come to him, he spake by a

5. parable : "The sower went out to sow his seed : and as he sowed, some fell by the way side : and it was trodden

6. down, and the fowls of the heaven devoured it. And other fell upon the rock, and when sprung up, it withered away,

7. because it lacked moisture. And other fell in the midst of the thorns ; and the thorns sprang up with it, and

8. choked it. And other fell on the good ground, and when sprung up, it made fruit and hundredfold". And when he said these things, he cried," He that hath ears to hear, let him hear!"

9. And his disciples asked him, saying, "What might this

10. parable be?" And he said, "Unto you it is given to know the mysteries of the Kingdom of God: but to the rest in parables; that seeing they may not see, and hearing

11. that they may not understand. Now the parable is this :

12. The seed is the word of God. Those by the way side are they that hear ; then cometh the devil, and taketh away the word from their hearts, lest they should believe and

13. be saved. Those on the rock are they, which , when they hear, receive the word with joy ; and these have no root, which for a while believe, and in time of temptation fall

14. away. And that which fell among thorns, these are they, which, when they have heard , go, and are choked with cares and riches and pleasures of this life , and bring

15. no fruit of perfection. But that on the good ground, these are, whoever in an honest and good heart, having heard the word, keep hold of it, and bring forth fruit in patience.

16. No man, when he hath lighted a lamp, covereth it with a vessel, or putteth it under a bed; but setteth it on a lamp-stand, that they which enter

in may see the light.

17. For there is no secret thing, that shall not be made manifest ; nor hidden, that shall not be known and come

18. into view. Take heed therefore how ye hear : for whosoever hath, to him shall be given: and whosoever hath not, even what he seemed to have shall be taken from him."

19. And it was told him by certain which said, "Thy mother and thy brethren stand without, desiring to see thee"

20. And he answered and said unto them , " Who is my mother and who is my brethren? My mother and my brethren are these, which hear the word of God, and do it!"

21. Now it came to pass on one of the days, that he went into a boat and his disciples : and he said unto them, "Let us go over unto the other side of the lake". And they

22. launched forth. But as they sailed he fell asleep : and there came down a storm of wind on the lake; and they were filling with water, and were in jeopardy,

23.
And they came to him, and awoke him, saying, "Master, master, we perish" And he arose, and rebuked the wind and the raging of the water : and they ceased, and there

24. was a calm. And he said unto them, " Where is your faith?" And they were frightened and wondered, saying one to another, "Who then is this? for he commandeth even the winds and water, and they obey him?"

25. And they sailed down to the country of the Gandarenes,

26. which is over against Galilee. And when he went forth to land, there met him out of the city a certain man, which had demons long time, and wore no cloke, neither abode

27. in a house, but among the tombs. When he saw Jesus, he cried out, and fell down before him, and with a loud voice said, "What have I to do with thee, Jesus, thou Son of

28. God most high? I beseech thee, torment me not." (For he had commanded the unclean spirit to come out of the man. For oftentimes it had caught him : and he was guarded and bound with chains and in fetters: and he brake the bands asunder, and was driven of the demon

29. into the deserts) And Jesus asked him , saying, "What is

30. thy name?" And he said, "Legion" because many demons were entered into him. And they besought him that he

31. would not command them to go out into the abyss. And there was an herd of many swine feeding of the mountain: and they besought him that he

would suffer them to enter into them. And he suffered them.

32. Then went the demons out of the man, and entered into the swine : and the herd ran violently down the

33. steep place into the lake, and were drowned. When they that fed them saw what was done, they fled, and went and told it

34. in the city and in the country. Then they went out to see what was done; and came to Jesus, and found the man, from whom the demons were departed, sitting at the feet of Jesus, clothed, and in his right mind : and they

35. were afraid. They also which saw it told them by what means he that was possessed of the demons was saved.

36. Then the whole multitude of the country of the Gandarenes round about him asked him to depart from them; for they were holden with great fear: and he entered into the

37. boat, and returned back again. Now the man, from whom the demons had departed, besought him that he might be with him : but Jesus sent him away, saying

38. "Return to thine house, and recount how great things God hath done unto thee." And he went his way, publishing throughout the whole city how great things Jesus had done unto him.

39. And it came to pass, that, when Jesus returned, the multitude welcomed him : for they were all waiting for

40. him. And, behold, there came a man whose name was Jairus, and he was a ruler of the synagogue : and he fell down at Jesus` feet , and besought him that he would

41. come into his house : For he had an only daughter, about twelve years of age, and she was dying. But as he went the multitudes thronged him.

42. And a woman having an issue of blood twelve years, which had spent all her living upon physicians, neither

43. could be healed if any, came behind him, and touched the border of his garment ; and immediately her issue of

44. blood stanched. And Jesus said, "Who touched me?" When all denied, Peter and they that were with him said, "Master , the multitude throng thee, and press thee, and

45. sayest thou, "Who touched me?" And Jesus said, "Somebody touched me : for I perceived that power had gone

46. out of me." And when the woman saw that shw was not hid, she came trembling , and falling down before him, she declared unto him before all the people for what reason she touched him, and how she was healed immediately.

47. And he said unto her, "Daughter , be of good comfort : thy faith hath

saved thee ; go into peace"

48. While he yet spake , theere cometh one from the ruler of the synagogue`s house, saying to him, "The daughter is

49. dead ; trouble not the Teacher." But when Jesus heard it, he answered him, saying, "Fear not, believe only,

50. and she shall be saved." And when he came into the house, he suffered no man to go in, save Peter, and James, and John, and the father and the mother of the maiden.

51. And all were weeping, and bewailing her, but he said :

52. "Weep not : she is not dead, but sleepeth." And they

53. laughed to scorn him, knowing that she was dead. And he put them all out, and took her by the hand, and called

54. saying, "Maid, arise". And her spirit came again, and she arose staightway ; and he commanded that something be

55. given her to eat. And her parents were astonished : but he charged them to tell no man what was done.

The Gospel of the Nativity of Mary

CHAPTER 1

The blessed and glorious ever-virgin Mary, sprung from the royal stock and family of David, born in the city of Nazareth, was brought up at Jerusalem in the temple of the Lord. Her father was named Joachim, and her mother Anna. Her father's house was from Galilee and the city of Nazareth, but her mother's family from Bethlehem. Their life was guileless and right before the Lord, and irreproachable and pious before men. For they divided all their substance into three parts. One part they spent upon the temple and the temple servants; another they distributed to strangers and the poor; the third they reserved, for themselves and the necessities of their family. Thus, dear to God, kind to men, for about twenty years they lived in their own house, a chaste married life, without having any children. Nevertheless they vowed that, should the Lord happen to give them offspring, they would deliver it to the service of the Lord; on which account also they used to visit the temple of the Lord at each of the feasts during the year.

CHAPTER 2

And it came to pass that the festival of the dedication was at hand; wherefore also Joachim went up to Jerusalem with some men of his own tribe. Now at that time Issachar was high priest there. And when he saw Joachim with his offering among his other fellow- citizens, he despised him, and spurned his gifts, asking why he, who had no offspring, presumed to stand among those who had; saying that his gifts could not by any means be acceptable to God, since He had deemed him unworthy of off-spring: for the Scripture said, Cursed is every one who has not begot a male or a female in Israel. He said, therefore, that he ought first to be freed from this curse by the begetting of children; and then, and then only, that be should come into the presence of the Lord with his offerings. And Joachim, covered with shame from this reproach that was thrown in his teeth, retired to the shepherds, who were in their pastures with their flocks; nor would he return home, test perchance he might be branded with the same reproach by those of his own tribe, who were there at the time, and had heard this from the priest.

CHAPTER 3

Now, when he had been there for some time, on a certain day when he was alone, an angel of the Lord stood by him in a great light. And when he was disturbed at his appearance, the angel who had appeared to him restrained his fear, saying: Fear not, Joachim, nor be disturbed by my appearance; for I am the angel of the Lord, sent by Him to thee to tell thee that thy prayers have been heard, and that thy charitable deeds have gone up into His presence. For He hath seen thy shame, and hath heard the reproach of unfruitfulness which has been unjustly brought against thee. For God is the avenger of sin, not of nature: and, therefore, when He shuts up the womb of any one, He does so that He may miraculously open it again; so that that which is born may be acknowledged to be not of lust, but of the gift of God. For was it not the case that the first mother of your nation--Sarah--was barren up to her eightieth year? And, nevertheless, in extreme old age she brought forth Isaac, to whom the promise was renewed of the blessing of all nations. Rachel also, so favoured of the Lord, and so beloved by holy Jacob, was long barren; and yet she brought forth Joseph, who was not only the lord of Egypt, but the deliverer of many nations who were ready to perish of hunger. Who among the judges was either stronger than Samson, or more holy than Samuel? And yet the mothers of both were barren. If, therefore, the reasonableness of my words does not persuade thee, believe in fact that conceptions very late in life, and births in the case of women that have been barren, are usually attended with something wonderful. Accordingly thy wife Anna will bring forth a daughter to thee, and thou shall call her name Mary: she shall be, as you have vowed, consecrated to the Lord from her infancy, and she shall be filled with the Holy Spirit, even from her mother's womb. She shall neither eat nor drink any unclean thing, nor shall she spend her life among the crowds of the people without, but in the temple of the Lord, that it may not be possible either to say, or so much as to suspect, any evil concerning her. Therefore, when she has grown up, just as she herself shall be miraculously born of a barren woman, so in an incomparable manner she, a virgin, shall bring forth the Son of the Most High, who shall be called Jesus, and who, according to the etymology of His name, shall be the Saviour of all nations. And this shall be the sign to thee of those things which I announce: When thou shalt come to the Golden gate in Jerusalem, thou shalt there meet Anna thy wife, who, lately anxious from the delay of thy return, will then rejoice at the sight of thee. Having thus spoken, the angel departed from him.

CHAPTER 4

Thereafter he appeared to Anna his wife, saying: Fear not, Anna, nor think that it is a phantom which thou seest. For I am that angel who has presented your prayers and alms before God; and now have I been sent to you to announce to you that thou shalt bring forth a daughter, who shall be called Mary, and who shall be blessed above all women. She, full of the favour of the Lord even from her birth, shall remain three years in her father's house until she be weaned. Thereafter, being delivered to the service of the Lord, she shall not depart from the temple until she reach the years of discretion. There, in fine, serving God day and night in fastings and prayers, she shall abstain from every unclean thing; she shall never know man, but alone, without example, immaculate, uncorrupted, without intercourse with man, she, a virgin, shall bring forth a son; she, His hand-maiden, shall bring forth the Lord--both in grace, and in name, and in work, the Saviour of the world. Wherefore arise, and go up to Jerusalem; and when thou shalt come to the gate which, because it is plated with gold, is called Golden, there, for a sign, thou shalt meet thy husband, for whose safety thou hast been anxious. And when these things shall have so happened, know that what I announce shall without doubt be fulfilled.

CHAPTER 5

Therefore, as the angel had commanded, both of them setting out from the place where they were, went up to Jerusalem; and when they had come to the place pointed out by the angel's prophecy, there they met each other. Then, rejoicing at seeing each other, and secure in the certainty of the promised offspring, they gave the thanks due to the Lord, who exalteth the humble. And so, having worshipped the Lord, they returned home, and awaited in certainty and in gladness the divine promise. Anna therefore conceived, and brought forth a daughter; and according to the command of the angel, her parents called her name Mary.

CHAPTER 6

And when the circle of three years had rolled round, and the time of her weaning was fulfilled, they brought the virgin to the temple of the Lord with offerings. Now there were round the temple, according to the fifteen Psalms of Degrees, fifteen steps going up; for, on account of the temple having been built on a mountain, the altar of burnt-offering, which stood outside, could not be reached except by steps. On one of these, then, her parents placed the little girl, the blessed virgin Mary. And when they were putting off the clothes which they had worn on the journey, and were putting on, as was usual, others that were neater and cleaner, the virgin of the Lord went up all the steps, one after the other, without the help of any one leading her or lifting her, in such a manner that, in this respect at least, you would think that she had already attained full age. For already the Lord in the infancy of His virgin wrought a great thing, and by the indication of this miracle foreshowed how great she was to be. Therefore, a sacrifice having been offered according to the custom of the law, and their vow being perfected, they left the virgin within the enclosures of the temple, there to be educated with the other virgins, and themselves returned home.

CHAPTER 7

But the virgin of the Lord advanced in age and in virtues; and though, in the words of the Psalmist, her father and mother had forsaken her, the Lord took her up. For daily was she visited by angels, daily did she enjoy a divine vision, which preserved her from all evil, and made her to abound in all good. And so she reached her fourteenth year; and not only were the wicked unable to charge her with anything worthy of reproach, but all the good, who knew her life and conversation, judged her to be worthy of admiration. Then the high priest publicly announced that the virgins who were publicly settled in the temple, and had reached this time of life, should return home and get married, according to the custom of the nation and the ripeness of their years. The others readily obeyed this command; but Mary alone, the virgin of the Lord, answered that she could not do this, saying both that her parents had devoted her to the service of the Lord, and that, moreover, she herself had made to the Lord a vow of virginity, which she would never violate by any intercourse with man. And the high priest, being placed in great perplexity of mind, seeing that neither did he think that the vow should be broken contrary to the Scripture, which says, Vow and pay, nor did he dare to introduce a custom unknown to the nation, gave order that at the festival, which was at hand, all the chief persons from Jerusalem and the neighbour-hood should be present, in order that from their advice he might know what was to be done in so doubtful a case. And when this took place, they resolved unanimously that the Lord should be consulted upon this matter. And when they all bowed themselves in prayer, the high priest went to consult God in the usual way. Nor had they long to wait: in the hearing of all a voice issued from the oracle and from the mercy-seat, that, according to the prophecy of Isaiah, a man should be sought out to whom the virgin ought to be entrusted and espoused. For it is clear that Isaiah says: A rod shall come forth from the root of Jesse, and a flower shall ascend from his root; and the Spirit of the Lord shall rest upon him, the spirit of wisdom and understanding, the spirit of counsel and strength, the spirit of wisdom and piety; and he shall be filled with the spirit of the fear of the Lord. According to this prophecy, therefore, he predicted that all of the house and family of David that were unmarried and fit for marriage should bring there rods to the altar; and that he whose rod after it was brought should produce a flower, and upon the end of whose rod the Spirit of the Lord should settle in the form of a dove, was the man to whom the virgin ought to be entrusted and espoused.

CHAPTER 8

Now there was among the rest Joseph, of the house and family of David, a man of great age: and when all brought there rods, according to the order, he alone withheld his. Wherefore, when nothing in conformity with the divine voice appeared, the high priest thought it necessary to consult God a second time; and He answered, that of those who had been designated, he alone to whom the virgin ought to be espoused had not brought his rod. Joseph, therefore, was found out. For when he had brought his rod, and the dove came from heaven; and settled upon the top of it, it clearly appeared to all that he was the man to whom the virgin should be espoused. Therefore, the usual ceremonies of betrothal having been gone through, he went back to the city of Bethlehem to put his house in order, and to procure things necessary for the marriage. But Mary, the virgin of the Lord, with seven other virgins of her own age, and who had been weaned at the same time, whom she had received from the priest, returned to the house of her parents in Galilee.

CHAPTER 9

And in those days, that is, at the time of her first coming into Galilee, the angel Gabriel was sent to her by God, to announce to her the conception of the Lord, and to explain to her the manner and order of the conception. Accordingly, going in, he filled the chamber where she was with a great light; and most courteously saluting her, he said: Hail, Mary! O virgin highly favoured by the Lord, virgin full of grace, the Lord is with thee; blessed art thou above all women, blessed above all men that have been hitherto born. And the virgin, who was already well acquainted with angelic faces, and was not unused to the light from heaven, was neither terrified by the vision of the angel, nor astonished at the greatness of the light, but only perplexed by his words; and she began to consider of what nature a salutation so unusual could be, or what it could portend, or what end it could have. And the angel, divinely inspired, taking up this thought, says: Fear not, Mary, as if anything contrary to thy chastity were hid under this salutation. For in choosing chastity, thou hast found favour with the Lord; and therefore thou, a virgin, shalt conceive without sin, and shalt bring forth a son. He shall be great, because He shall rule from sea to sea, and from the river even to the ends of the earth; and He shall be called the Son of the Most High, because He who is born on earth in humiliation, reigns in heaven in exaltation; and the Lord God will give Him the throne of His father David, and He shall reign in the house of Jacob for ever, and of His kingdom there shall be no end; forasmuch as He is King of kings and Lord of lords, and His throne is from everlasting to everlasting. The virgin did not doubt these words of the angel; but wishing to know the manner of it, she answered: How can that come to pass? For while, according to my vow, I never know man, how can I bring forth without the addition of man's seed? To this the angel says: Think not, Mary, that thou shalt conceive in the manner of mankind: for without any intercourse with man, thou, a virgin, wilt conceive; thou, a virgin, wilt bring forth; thou, a virgin, wilt nurse: for the Holy Spirit shall come upon thee, and the power of the Most High shall overshadow thee, without any of the heats of lust; and therefore that which shall be born of thee shall alone be holy, because it alone, being conceived and born without sin, shall be called the Son of God. Then Mary stretched forth her hands, and raised her eyes to heaven, and said: Behold the hand-maiden of the Lord, for I am not worthy of the name of lady; let it be to me according to thy word.

CHAPTER 10

Joseph therefore came from Judaea into Galilee, intending to marry the virgin who had been betrothed to him; for already three months had elapsed, and it was the beginning of the fourth since she had been betrothed to him. In the meantime, it was evident from her shape that she was pregnant, nor could she conceal this from Joseph. For in consequence of his being betrothed to her, coming to her more freely and speaking to her more familiarly, he found out that she was with child. He began then to be in great doubt and perplexity, because he did not know what was best for him to do. For, being a just man, he was not willing to expose her; nor, being a pious man, to injure her fair fame by a suspicion of fornication. He came to the conclusion, therefore, privately to dissolve their contract, and to send her away secretly. And while he thought on these things, behold, an angel of the Lord appeared to him in his sleep, saying: Joseph, thou son of David, fear not; that is, do not have any suspicion of fornication in the virgin, or think any evil of her; and fear not to take her as thy wife: for that which is begotten in her, and which now vexes thy soul, is the work not of man, but of the Holy Spirit. For she alone of all virgins shall bring forth the Son of God, and thou shalt call His name Jesus, that is, Saviour; for He shall save His people from their sins. Therefore Joseph, according to the command of the angel, took the virgin as his wife; nevertheless he knew her not, but took care of her, and kept her in chastity. And now the ninth month from her conception was at hand, when Joseph, taking with him his wife along with what things he needed, went to Bethlehem, the city from which he came. And it came to pass, while they were there, that her days were fulfilled that she should bring forth; and she brought forth her first-born son, as the holy evangelists have shown, our Lord Jesus Christ, who with the Father and the Son and the Holy Ghost lives and reigns God from everlasting to everlasting.

The Gospel of Thomas
"The Scholars' Translation"

hese are the secret sayings that the living Jesus spoke and Didymos Judas Thomas recorded. 1 And he said, "Whoever discovers the interpretation of these sayings will not taste death."

2. Jesus said, "Those who seek should not stop seeking until they find. When they find, they will be disturbed. When they are disturbed, they will marvel, and will reign over all. [And after they have reigned they will rest.]"

3. Jesus said, "If your leaders say to you, 'Look, the (Father's) kingdom is in the sky,' then the birds of the sky will precede you. If they say to you, 'It is in the sea,' then the fish will precede you. Rather, the kingdom is within you and it is outside you.

When you know yourselves, then you will be known, and you will understand that you are children of the living Father. But if you do not know yourselves, then you live in poverty, and you are the poverty."

4. Jesus said, "The person old in days won't hesitate to ask a little child seven days old about the place of life, and that person will live.

For many of the first will be last, and will become a single one."

5. Jesus said, "Know what is in front of your face, and what is hidden from you will be disclosed to you. For there is nothing hidden that will not be revealed. [And there is nothing buried that will not be raised."]

6. His disciples asked him and said to him, "Do you want us to fast? How should we pray? Should we give to charity? What diet should we observe?"

Jesus said, "Don't lie, and don't do what you hate, because all things are disclosed before heaven. After all, there is nothing hidden that will not be revealed, and there is nothing covered up that will remain undisclosed."

7. Jesus said, "Lucky is the lion that the human will eat, so that the lion becomes human. And foul is the human that the lion will eat, and the lion still will become human."

8. And he said, The person is like a wise fisherman who cast his net into the sea and drew it up from the sea full of little fish. Among them the wise fisherman discovered a fine large fish. He threw all the little fish back into the sea, and easily chose the large fish. Anyone here with two good ears had better listen!

9. Jesus said, Look, the sower went out, took a handful (of seeds), and scattered (them). Some fell on the road, and the birds came and gathered them. Others fell on rock, and they didn't take root in the soil and didn't produce heads of grain. Others fell on thorns, and they choked the seeds and worms ate them. And others fell on good soil, and it produced a good crop: it yielded sixty per measure and one hundred twenty per measure.

10. Jesus said, "I have cast fire upon the world, and look, I'm guarding it until it blazes."

11. Jesus said, "This heaven will pass away, and the one above it will pass away.

The dead are not alive, and the living will not die. During the days when you ate what is dead, you made it come alive. When you are in the light, what will you do? On the day when you were one, you became two. But when you become two, what will you do?"

12. The disciples said to Jesus, "We know that you are going to leave us. Who will be our leader?"

Jesus said to them, "No matter where you are you are to go to James the Just, for whose sake heaven and earth came into being."

13. Jesus said to his disciples, "Compare me to something and tell me what I am like." Simon Peter said to him, "You are like a just messenger."

Matthew said to him, "You are like a wise philosopher."

Thomas said to him, "Teacher, my mouth is utterly unable to say what you are like."

Jesus said, "I am not your teacher. Because you have drunk, you have become intoxicated from the bubbling spring that I have tended."

And he took him, and withdrew, and spoke three sayings to him. When Thomas came back to his friends they asked him, "What did Jesus say to you?"

Thomas said to them, "If I tell you one of the sayings he spoke to me, you will pick up rocks and stone me, and fire will come from the rocks and devour you."

14. Jesus said to them, "If you fast, you will bring sin upon yourselves, and if you pray, you will be condemned, and if you give to charity, you will harm your spirits.

When you go into any region and walk about in the countryside, when people take you in, eat what they serve you and heal the sick among them.

After all, what goes into your mouth will not defile you; rather, it's what comes out of your mouth that will defile you."

15. Jesus said, "When you see one who was not born of woman, fall on your faces and worship. That one is your Father."

16. Jesus said, "Perhaps people think that I have come to casy peace upon the world. They do not know that I have come to cast conflicts upon the earth: fire, sword, war.

For there will be five in a house: there'll be three against two and two against three, father against son and son against father, and they will stand alone.

17. Jesus said, "I will give you what no eye has seen, what no ear has heard, what no hand has touched, what has not arisen in the human heart."

18. The disciples said to Jesus, "Tell us, how will our end come?"

Jesus said, "Have you found the beginning, then, that you are looking for the end? You see, the end will be where the beginning is.

Congratulations to the one who stands at the beginning: that one will know the end and will not taste death."

19. Jesus said, "Congratulations to the one who came into being before coming into being.

If you become my disciples and pay attention to my sayings, these stones will serve you.

For there are five trees in Paradise for you; they do not change, summer or winter, and their leaves do not fall. Whoever knows them will not taste death."

20. The disciples said to Jesus, "Tell us what Heaven's kingdom is like."

He said to them, It's like a mustard seed, the smallest of all seeds, but when it falls on prepared soil, it produces a large plant and becomes a shelter for birds of the sky.

21. Mary said to Jesus, "What are your disciples like?"

He said, They are like little children living in a field that is not theirs. when the owners of the field come, they will say, "Give us back our field." They take off their clothes in front of them in order to give it back to them, and they return their field to them.

For this reason I say, if the owners of a house know that a thief is coming, they will be on guard before the thief arrives and will not let the thief break into their house (their domain) and steal their possessions.

As for you, then, be on guard against the world. Prepare yourselves with great strength, so the robbers can't find a way to get to you, for the trouble you expect will come.

Let there be among you a person who understands.

When the crop ripened, he came quickly carrying a sickle and harvested it. Anyone here with two good ears had better listen!

22. Jesus saw some babies nursing. He said to his disciples, "These nursing babies are like those who enter the kingdom."

They said to him, "Then shall we enter the kingdom as babies?"

Jesus said to them, "When you make the two into one, and when you make the inner like the outer and the outer like the inner, and the upper like the lower, and when you make male and female into a single one, so that the male will not be male nor the female be female, when you make eyes in place of an eye, a hand in place of a hand, a foot in place of a foot, an image in place of an image, then you will enter [the kingdom]."

23. Jesus said, "I shall choose you, one from a thousand and two from ten thousand, and they will stand as a single one."

24. His disciples said, "Show us the place where you are, for we must seek it."

He said to them, "Anyone here with two ears had better listen! There is light within a person of light, and it shines on the whole world. If it does not shine, it is dark."

25. Jesus said, "Love your friends like your own soul, protect them like the pupil of your eye."

26. Jesus said, "You see the sliver in your friend's eye, but you don't see the timber in your own eye. When you take the timber out of your own eye, then you will see well enough to remove the sliver from your friend's eye."

27. "If you do not fast from the world, you will not find the kingdom. If you do not observe the sabbath as a sabbath you will not see the Father."

28. Jesus said, "I took my stand in the midst of the world, and in flesh I appeared to them. I found them all drunk, and I did not find any of them thirsty. My soul ached for the children of humanity, because they are blind in their hearts and do not see, for they came into the world empty, and they also seek to depart from the world empty.

But meanwhile they are drunk. When they shake off their wine, then they will change their ways."

29. Jesus said, "If the flesh came into being because of spirit, that is a marvel, but if spirit came into being because of the body, that is a marvel of marvels.

Yet I marvel at how this great wealth has come to dwell in this poverty."

30. Jesus said, "Where there are three deities, they are divine. Where there are two or one, I am with that one."

31. Jesus said, "No prophet is welcome on his home turf; doctors don't

cure those who know them."

32. Jesus said, "A city built on a high hill and fortified cannot fall, nor can it be hidden."

33. Jesus said, "What you will hear in your ear, in the other ear proclaim from your rooftops.

After all, no one lights a lamp and puts it under a basket, nor does one put it in a hidden place. Rather, one puts it on a lampstand so that all who come and go will see its light."

34. Jesus said, "If a blind person leads a bind person, both of them will fall into a hole."

35. Jesus said, "One can't enter a strong person's house and take it by force without tying his hands. Then one can loot his house."

36. Jesus said, "Do not fret, from morning to evening and from evening to morning, [about your food--what you're going to eat, or about your clothing--] what you are going to wear. [You're much better than the lilies, which neither card nor spin.

As for you, when you have no garment, what will you put on? Who might add to your stature? That very one will give you your garment.]"

37. His disciples said, "When will you appear to us, and when will we see you?"

Jesus said, "When you strip without being ashamed, and you take your clothes and put them under your feet like little children and trample then, then [you] will see the son of the living one and you will not be afraid."

38. Jesus said, "Often you have desired to hear these sayings that I am speaking to you, and you have no one else from whom to hear them. There will be days when you will seek me and you will not find me."

39. Jesus said, "The Pharisees and the scholars have taken the keys of knowledge and have hidden them. They have not entered nor have they allowed those who want to enter to do so.

As for you, be as sly as snakes and as simple as doves."

40. Jesus said, "A grapevine has been planted apart from the Father. Since it is not strong, it will be pulled up by its root and will perish."

41. Jesus said, "Whoever has something in hand will be given more, and whoever has nothing will be deprived of even the little they have."

42. Jesus said, "Be passersby."

43. His disciples said to him, "Who are you to say these things to us?" "You don't understand who I am from what I say to you.

Rather, you have become like the Judeans, for they love the tree but hate its fruit, or they love the fruit but hate the tree."

44. Jesus said, "Whoever blasphemes against the Father will be forgiv-

en, and whoever blasphemes against the son will be forgiven, but whoever blasphemes against the holy spirit will not be forgiven, either on earth or in heaven."

45. Jesus said, "Grapes are not harvested from thorn trees, nor are figs gathered from thistles, for they yield no fruit.

Good persons produce good from what they've stored up; bad persons produce evil from the wickedness they've stored up in their hearts, and say evil things. For from the overflow of the heart they produce evil."

46. Jesus said, "From Adam to John the Baptist, among those born of women, no one is so much greater than John the Baptist that his eyes should not be averted.

But I have said that whoever among you becomes a child will recognize the kingdom and will become greater than John."

47. Jesus said, "A person cannot mount two horses or bend two bows.

And a slave cannot serve two masters, otherwise that slave will honor the one and offend the other. "Nobody drinks aged wine and immediately wants to drink young wine. Young wine is not poured into old wineskins, or they might break, and aged wine is not poured into a new wineskin, or it might spoil. An old patch is not sewn onto a new garment, since it would create a tear."

48. Jesus said, "If two make peace with each other in a single house, they will say to the mountain, 'Move from here!' and it will move."

49. Jesus said, "Congratulations to those who are alone and chosen, for you will find the kingdom. For you have come from it, and you will return there again."

50. Jesus said, "If they say to you, 'Where have you come from?' say to them, 'We have come from the light, from the place where the light came into being by itself, established [itself], and appeared in their image.'

If they say to you, 'Is it you?' say, 'We are its children, and we are the chosen of the living Father.' If they ask you, 'What is the evidence of your Father in you?' say to them, 'It is motion and rest.'"

51. His disciples said to him, "When will the rest for the dead take place, and when will the new world come?"

He said to them, "What you are looking forward to has come, but you don't know it."

52. His disciples said to him, "Twenty-four prophets have spoken in Israel, and they all spoke of you." He said to them, "You have disregarded the living one who is in your presence, and have spoken of the
dead."

53. His disciples said to him, "is circumcision useful or not?"

He said to them, "If it were useful, their father would produce children already circumcised from their mother. Rather, the true circumcision in spirit has become profitable in every respect."

54. Jesus said, "Congratulations to the poor, for to you belongs Heaven's kingdom."

55. Jesus said, "Whoever does not hate father and mother cannot be my disciple, and whoever does not hate brothers and sisters, and carry the cross as I do, will not be worthy of me."

56. Jesus said, "Whoever has come to know the world has discovered a carcass, and whoever has discovered a carcass, of that person the world is not worthy."

57. Jesus said, The Father's kingdom is like a person who has [good] seed. His enemy came during the night and sowed weeds among the good seed. The person did not let the workers pull up the weeds, but said to them, "No, otherwise you might go to pull up the weeds and pull up the wheat along with them." For on the day of the harvest the weeds will be conspicuous, and will be pulled up and burned.

58. Jesus said, "Congratulations to the person who has toiled and has found life."

59. Jesus said, "Look to the living one as long as you live, otherwise you might die and then try to see the living one, and you will be unable to see."

60. He saw a Samaritan carrying a lamb and going to Judea. He said to his disciples, "that person ... around the lamb." They said to him, "So that he may kill it and eat it." He said to them, "He will not eat it while it is alive, but only after he has killed it and it has become a carcass."

They said, "Otherwise he can't do it."

He said to them, "So also with you, seek for yourselves a place for rest, or you might become a carcass and be eaten."

61. Jesus said, "Two will recline on a couch; one will die, one will live."

Salome said, "Who are you mister? You have climbed onto my couch and eaten from my table as if you are from someone."

Jesus said to her, "I am the one who comes from what is whole. I was granted from the things of my Father." "I am your disciple."

"For this reason I say, if one is whole, one will be filled with light, but if one is divided, one will be filled with darkness."

62. Jesus said, "I disclose my mysteries to those [who are worthy] of [my] mysteries. Do not let your left hand know what your right hand is doing."

63. Jesus said, There was a rich person who had a great deal of money. He said, "I shall invest my money so that I may sow, reap, plant, and fill my storehouses with produce, that I may lack nothing." These were the things he

was thinking in his heart, but that very night he died. Anyone here with two ears had better listen!

64. Jesus said, A person was receiving guests. When he had prepared the dinner, he sent his slave to invite the guests. The slave went to the first and said to that one, "My master invites you." That one said, "Some merchants owe me money; they are coming to me tonight. I have to go and give them instructions. Please excuse me from dinner." The slave went to another and said to that one, "My master has invited you." That one said to the slave, "I have bought a house, and I have been called away for a day. I shall have no time." The slave went to another and said to that one, "My master invites you." That one said to the slave, "My friend is to be married, and I am to arrange the banquet. I shall not be able to come. Please excuse me from dinner." The slave went to another and said to that one, "My master invites you." That one said to the slave, "I have bought an estate, and I am going to collect the rent. I shall not be able to come. Please excuse me." The slave returned and said to his master, "Those whom you invited to dinner have asked to be excused." The master said to his slave, "Go out on the streets and bring back whomever you find to have dinner."

Buyers and merchants [will] not enter the places of my Father.

65. He said, A [...] person owned a vineyard and rented it to some farmers, so they could work it and he could collect its crop from them. He sent his slave so the farmers would give him the vineyard's crop. They grabbed him, beat him, and almost killed him, and the slave returned and told his master. His master said, "Perhaps he didn't know them." He sent another slave, and the farmers beat that one as well. Then the master sent his son and said, "Perhaps they'll show my son some respect." Because the farmers knew that he was the heir to the vineyard, they grabbed him and killed him. Anyone here with two ears had better listen!

66. Jesus said, "Show me the stone that the builders rejected: that is the keystone."

67. Jesus said, "Those who know all, but are lacking in themselves, are utterly lacking."

68. Jesus said, "Congratulations to you when you are hated and persecuted; and no place will be found, wherever you have been persecuted."

69. Jesus said, "Congratulations to those who have been persecuted in their hearts: they are the ones who have truly come to know the Father.

Congratulations to those who go hungry, so the stomach of the one in want may be filled."

70. Jesus said, "If you bring forth what is within you, what you have will save you. If you do not have that within you, what you do not have within

you [will] kill you."

71. Jesus said, "I will destroy [this] house, and no one will be able to build it [...]."

72. A [person said] to him, "Tell my brothers to divide my father's possessions with me." He said to the person, "Mister, who made me a divider?"

He turned to his disciples and said to them, "I'm not a divider, am I?"

73. Jesus said, "The crop is huge but the workers are few, so beg the harvest boss to dispatch workers to the fields."

74. He said, "Lord, there are many around the drinking trough, but there is nothing in the well."

75. Jesus said, "There are many standing at the door, but those who are alone will enter the bridal suite."

76. Jesus said, The Father's kingdom is like a merchant who had a supply of merchandise and found a peal.

That merchant was prudent; he sold the merchandise and bought the single pearl for himself.

So also with you, seek his treasure that is unfailing, that is enduring, where no moth comes to eat and no worm destroys."

77. Jesus said, "I am the light that is over all things. I am all: from me all came forth, and to me all attained. Split a piece of wood; I am there.

Lift up the stone, and you will find me there."

78. Jesus said, "Why have you come out to the countryside? To see a reed shaken by the wind? And to see a person dressed in soft clothes, [like your] rulers and your powerful ones? They are dressed in soft clothes, and they cannot understand truth."

79. A woman in the crowd said to him, "Lucky are the womb that bore you and the breasts that fed you." He said to [her], "Lucky are those who have heard the word of the Father and have truly kept it. For there will be days when you will say, 'Lucky are the womb that has not conceived and the breasts that have not given milk.'"

80. Jesus said, "Whoever has come to know the world has discovered the body, and whoever has discovered the body, of that one the world is not worthy."

81. Jesus said, "Let one who has become wealthy reign, and let one who has power renounce ."

82. Jesus said, "Whoever is near me is near the fire, and whoever is far from me is far from the kingdom."

83. Jesus said, "Images are visible to people, but the light within them is hidden in the image of the Father's light. He will be disclosed, but his image is hidden by his light."

84 .Jesus said, "When you see your likeness, you are happy. But when you see your images that came into being before you and that neither die nor become visible, how much you will have to bear!"

85. Jesus said, "Adam came from great power and great wealth, but he was not worthy of you. For had he been worthy, [he would] not [have tasted] death."

86. Jesus said, "[Foxes have] their dens and birds have their nests, but human beings have no place to lay down and rest."

87. Jesus said, "How miserable is the body that depends on a body, and how miserable is the soul that depends on these two."

88. Jesus said, "The messengers and the prophets will come to you and give you what belongs to you. You, in turn, give them what you have, and say to yourselves, 'When will they come and take what belongs to them?'"

89. Jesus said, "Why do you wash the outside of the cup? Don't you understand that the one who made the inside is also the one who made the outside?"

90. Jesus said, "Come to me, for my yoke is comfortable and my lordship is gentle, and you will find rest for yourselves."

91. They said to him, "Tell us who you are so that we may believe in you."

He said to them, "You examine the face of heaven and earth, but you have not come to know the one who is in your presence, and you do not know how to examine the present moment.

92. Jesus said, "Seek and you will find.

In the past, however, I did not tell you the things about which you asked me then. Now I am willing to tell them, but you are not seeking them."

93. "Don't give what is holy to dogs, for they might throw them upon the manure pile. Don't throw pearls [to] pigs, or they might ... it [...]."

94. Jesus [said], "One who seeks will find, and for [one who knocks] it will be opened."

95. [Jesus said], "If you have money, don't lend it at interest. Rather, give [it] to someone from whom you won't get it back."

96. Jesus [said], The Father's kingdom is like [a] woman. She took a little leaven, [hid] it in dough, and made it into large loaves of bread. Anyone here with two ears had better listen!

97. Jesus said, The [Father's] kingdom is like a woman who was carrying a [jar] full of meal. While she was walking along [a] distant road, the handle of the jar broke and the meal spilled behind her [along] the road. She didn't know it; she hadn't noticed a problem. When she reached her house, she put the jar down and discovered that it was empty.

98. Jesus said, The Father's kingdom is like a person who wanted to kill someone powerful. While still at home he drew his sword and thrust it into the wall to find out whether his hand would go in. Then he killed the powerful one.

99. The disciples said to him, "Your brothers and your mother are standing outside."

He said to them, "Those here who do what my Father wants are my brothers and my mother. They are the ones who will enter my Father's kingdom."

100. They showed Jesus a gold coin and said to him, "The Roman emperor's people demand taxes from us." He said to them, "Give the emperor what belongs to the emperor, give God what belongs to God, and give me what is mine."

101. "Whoever does not hate [father] and mother as I do cannot be my [disciple], and whoever does [not] love [father and] mother as I do cannot be my [disciple]. For my mother [...], but my true [mother] gave me life."

102. Jesus said, "Damn the Pharisees! They are like a dog sleeping in the cattle manger: the dog neither eats nor [lets] the cattle eat."

103. Jesus said, "Congratulations to those who know where the rebels are going to attack. [They] can get going, collect their imperial resources, and be prepared before the rebels arrive."

104. They said to Jesus, "Come, let us pray today, and let us fast."

Jesus said, "What sin have I committed, or how have I been undone? Rather, when the groom leaves the bridal suite, then let people fast and pray."

105. Jesus said, "Whoever knows the father and the mother will be called the child of a whore."

106. Jesus said, "When you make the two into one, you will become children of Adam, and when you say, 'Mountain, move from here!' it will move."

107. Jesus said, The kingdom is like a shepherd who had a hundred sheep. One of them, the largest, went astray. He left the ninety- nine and looked for the one until he found it. After he had toiled, he said to the sheep, 'I love you more than the ninety- nine.'

108. Jesus said, "Whoever drinks from my mouth will become like me; I myself shall become that person, and the hidden things will be revealed to him."

109. Jesus said, The (Father's) kingdom is like a person who had a treasure hidden in his field but did not know it. And [when] he died he left it to his [son]. The son [did] not know about it either. He took over the field and sold it. The buyer went plowing, [discovered] the treasure, and began to lend money at interest to whomever he wished.

110. Jesus said, "Let one who has found the world, and has become

wealthy, renounce the world."

111. Jesus said, "The heavens and the earth will roll up in your presence, and whoever is living from the living one will not see death."

Does not Jesus say, "Those who have found themselves, of them the world is not worthy"?

112. Jesus said, "Damn the flesh that depends on the soul. Damn the soul that depends on the flesh."

113. His disciples said to him, "When will the kingdom come?"

"It will not come by watching for it. It will not be said, 'Look, here!' or 'Look, there!' Rather, the Father's kingdom is spread out upon the earth, and people don't see it."

[Saying added to the original collection at a later date:]

114. Simon Peter said to them, "Make Mary leave us, for females don't deserve life." Jesus said, "Look, I will guide her to make her male, so that she too may become a living spirit resembling you males. For every female who makes herself male will enter the kingdom of Heaven."

Hermas

1:Heading Vision 1

he master, who reared me, had sold me to one Rhoda in Rome. After many years, I met her again, and began to love her as a sister.

1:2 After a certain time I saw her bathing in the river Tiber; and I gave her my hand, and led her out of the river. So, seeing her beauty, I reasoned in my heart, saying, "Happy were I, if I had such an one to wife both in beauty and in character." I merely reflected on this and nothing more.

1:3 After a certain time, as I was journeying to Cumae, and glorifying God's creatures for their greatness and splendor and power, as I walked I fell asleep. And a Spirit took me, and bore me away through a pathless tract, through which no man could pass: for the place was precipitous, and broken into clefts by reason of the waters. When then I had crossed the river, I came into the level country, and knelt down, and began to pray to the Lord and to confess my sins.

1:4 Now, while I prayed, the heaven was opened, and I see the lady, whom I had desired, greeting me from heaven, saying, "Good morrow, Hermas."

1:5 And, looking at her, I said to her, "Lady, what doest thou here?" Then she answered me, "I was taken up, that I might convict thee of thy sins before the Lord."

1:6 I said to her, "Dost thou now convict me?" "Nay, not so," said she, "but hear the words, that I shall say to thee. God, Who dwelleth in the heavens, and created out of nothing the things which are, and increased and multiplied them for His holy Church's sake, is wroth with thee, for that thou didst sin against me."

1:7 I answered her and said, "Sin against thee? In what way? Did I ever speak an unseemly word unto thee? Did I not always regard thee as a goddess? Did I not always respect thee as a sister? How couldst thou falsely charge me, lady, with such villainy and uncleanness?

1:8 "Laughing she saith unto me, "The desire after evil entered into thine heart. Nay, thinkest thou not that it is an evil deed for a righteous man, if the evil desire should enter into his heart? It is indeed a sin and a great one too," saith she; "for the righteous man entertaineth righteous purposes. While then his purposes are righteous, his repute stands steadfast in the heavens, and he finds the Lord easily propitiated in all that he does. But they that entertain evil purposes in their hearts, bring upon themselves death an captivity, especially they that claim for themselves this present work and boast in its riches, and cleave not to the good things that are to come.

1:9 Their souls shall rue it, seeing that they have no hope, but have abandoned themselves and their life. But do thou pray unto God and He shall heal thine own sins, and those of thy whole house, and of all the saints."

1:10 As soon as she had spoken these words the heavens were shut and I was given over to horror and grief Then I said within myself "If this sin is recorded against me, how can I be saved? Or how shall I propitiate God for my sins which are full-blown? Or with which words shall I entreat the Lord that He may be propitious unto me?

1:11 While I was advising and discussing these matters in my heart, I see, before me a great white chair of snow-white wool; and there came an aged lady in glistening raiment, having a book in her hands, and she sat down alone, and she saluted me, "Good morrow, Hermas." Then I grieved and weeping, said, "Good morrow, lady."

1:12 And she said to me "Why so gloomy, Hermas, thou that art patient and good-tempered and art always smiling? Why so downcast in thy looks, and far from cheerful?" And I said to her, "Because of an excellent lady's saying that I had sinned against her."

1:13 Then she said, "Far be this thing from the servant of God! Nevertheless the thought did enter into thy heart concerning her. Now to the servants of God such a purpose bringeth sin. For it is an evil and mad purpose to overtake a devout spirit that hath been already approved, that it should desire an evil deed, and especially if it be Hermas the temperate, who abstaineth from every evil desire, and is full of all simplicity and of great guilelessness.

1:14 "Yet it is not for this that God is wroth with thee, but that thou mayest convert thy family, that hath done wrong against the Lord and against you their parents. But out of fondness for thy children thou didst not admonish thy family, but didst suffer it to become fearfully corrupt. Therefore the Lord is wroth with thee. But He will heal all thy past sins, which have been committed in thy family; for by reason of their sins and iniquities thou hast been corrupted by the affairs of this world.

1:15 But the great mercy of the Lord had pity on thee and thy family, and will strengthen thee, and establish thee in His glory. Only be not thou careless, but take courage, and strengthen thy family. For as the smith hammering his work conquers the task which he wills, so also doth righteous discourse repeated daily conquer all evil. Cease not therefore to reprove thy children; for I know that if they shall repent with all their heart, they shall be written in the books of life with the saints."

1:16 After these words of hers had ceased, she saith unto me, "Wilt thou listen to me as I read?" Then say I, "Yes, lady." She saith to me, "Be attentive, and hear the glories of God" I listened with attention and with wonder to that which I had no power to remember; for all the words were terrible, such as man cannot bear. The last words however I remembered, for they were suitable for us and gentle.

1:17 "Behold, the God of Hosts, Who by His invisible and mighty power and by His great wisdom created the world, and by His glorious purpose clothed His creation with comeliness, and by His strong word fixed the heaven, and founded the earth upon the waters, and by His own wisdom and providence formed His holy Church, which also He blessed-behold, He removeth the heavens and the mountains and the hills and the seas, and all things are made level for His elect, that He may fulfill to them the promise which He promised with great glory and rejoicing, if so be that they shall keep the ordinances of God, which they received, with great faith."

1:18 When then she finished reading and arose from her chair, there came four young men, and they took away the chair, and departed towards the East.

1:19 Then she calleth me unto her, and she touched my breast, and saith to me, "Did my reading please thee?" And I say unto her, "Lady, these last words please me, but the former were difficult and hard." Then she spake to me, saying, "These last words are for the righteous, but the former are for the heathen and the rebellious."

1:20 While she yet spake with me, two men appeared, and took her by the arms, and they departed, whither the chair also had gone, towards the East. And she smiled as she departed and, as she was going, she saith to me, "Play the man, Hermas."

1 2:0 Heading Vision 2

(Again of his neglect in correcting his talkative wife; and of his lewd sons.)

1 2:1 I was on the way to Cumae, at the same season as last year, and called to mind my last year's vision as I walked; and again a Spirit taketh me, and carrieth me away to the same place as last year.

1 2:2 When then I arrived at the place, I fell upon my knees, and began to pray to the Lord, and to glorify His name, for that he counted me worthy, and made known unto me my former sins.

1 2:3 But after I had risen up from prayer, I behold before me the aged lady, whom also I had seen last year, walking and reading a little book.

1 2:4 And she saith to me, "Canst thou report these things to the elect of God?" I say unto her, "Lady, I cannot recollect so much; but give me the little book, that I may copy it."

1 2:5 "Take it," saith she, "and be sure and return it to me."

1 2:6 I took it, and retiring to a certain spot in the country I copied it letter for letter: for I could not make out the syllables.

1 2:7 When then I had finished the letters of the book, suddenly the book was snatched out of my hand; but by whom I did not see.

1 2:8 Now after fifteen days, when I had fasted and entreated the Lord earnestly, the knowledge of the writing was revealed to me. And this is what was written:--

1 2:9 "Thy seed, O Hermas, have sinned against God, and have blasphemed the Lord, and have betrayed their parents through great wickedness, yea, they have got the name of betrayers of parents, and yet they did not profit by their betrayal;

1 2:10 And they still further added to their sins wanton deeds and reckless wickedness; and so the measure of their transgressions was filled up. But make these words known to all thy children, and to thy wife who shall be as thy sister; for she too refraineth not from using her tongue, wherewith she doeth evil.

1 2:11 But, when she hears these apords, she will refrain, and will find mercy.

1 2:12 After that thou hast made known unto them all these words, which the Master commanded me that they should be revealed unto thee.

1 2:13 Then all their sins which they sinned aforetime are forgiven to them; yea, and to all the saints that have sinned unto this day, if they repent

with their whole heart, and remove double-mindedness from their heart.

1 2:14 For the Master sware by His own glory, as concerning His elect; that if, now that this day has been set as a limit, sin shall hereafter be committed, they shall not find salvation;

1 2:15 For repentance for the righteous hath an end; the days of repentance are accomplished for all the saints; whereas for the Gentiles (heathen), there is repentance until the last day.

1 2:16 Thou shalt therefore say unto the elders of the Church, that they direct their paths in righteousness, that they may receive in full the promises with abundant glory.

1 2:17 Ye therefore that work righteousness be steadfast, and be not double-minded, that ye may have admission with the holy angels.

1 2:18 Blessed are ye, as many as endure patiently the great tribulation that cometh, and as many as shall not deny their life.

1 2:19 For the Lord swear concerning His Son, that those who denied their Lord should be rejected from their life, even they that are now about to deny Him in the coming days;

1 2:20 But those who shall never deny him, he will of his exceeding great mercy be favourable unto them.

1 2:21 But to those who denied Him aforetime, to them mercy was given of His great loving kindness.

1 2:22 "But do thou, Hermas, no longer bear a grudge against thy children, neither suffer thy sister to have her way, so that they may be purified from their former sins.

1 2:23 For they shall be chastised with a righteous chastisement, unless thou bear a grudge against them thyself. The bearing of a grudge worketh death.

1 2:24 But thou, O Hermas, hast had great tribulations of thine own, by reason of the transgressions of thy family, because thou hadst no care for them. For thou wast neglectful of them, and wast mixed up with thine evil transactions.

1 2:25 But herein is thy salvation, in that thou didst not depart from the living God, and in thy simplicity and thy great continence. These have saved thee, if thou abidest therein;

1 2:26 Yea, they shall save all who do such things, and walk in guilelessness and simplicity.

1 2:27 These men prevail over all wickedness, and continue unto life eternal.

1 2:28 Blessed are all they that work righteousness. They shall never be destroyed.

1 2:29 But thou shalt say to Maximus, "Behold tribulation cometh (upon thee), if thou think fit to deny a second time.

1 2:30 The Lord is nigh unto them that turn unto him, as it is written in the book of Heldam (Eldad) and Modal (Modat), who prophesied to the people of Israel in the wilderness."

1 2:31 Now, brethren, a revelation was made unto me in my sleep by a youth of exceeding fair form, who said to me, "Whom thinkest thou the aged woman, from whom thou receivedst the book, to be?" I say, "The Sybil"

1 2:32 "Thou art wrong," saith he, "she is not." "Who then is she?" I say. "The Church of God," saith he.

1 2:33 I said unto him, "Wherefore then is she aged?" "Because," saith he, "she was created before all things; therefore is she aged; and for her sake the world was framed."

1 2:34 And afterwards I saw a vision in my house. The aged woman came, and asked me, if I had already given the book to the elders of the church? I said that I had not given it.

1 2:35 "Thou hast done well," she said, "for I have words to add. When then I shall have finished all the words, it shall be made known by thy means to all the elect.

1 2:36 Thou shalt therefore write two little books, and shalt send one to Clement, and one to Grapte. So Clement shall send to the foreign cities, for this is his duty; while Grapte shall instruct the widows and the orphans.

1 2:37 But thou shalt read (the book) to this city along with the elders that preside over the Church.

1 3:0 Vision 3

(Of the building of the church triumphant, and of the severalsorts of reprobates.)

1 3:1 The third vision, which I saw, brethren, was as follows.

1 3:2 After fasting often, and entreating the Lord to declare unto me the revelation which He promised to show me by the mouth of the aged woman, that very night the aged woman was seen of me, and she said to me,

1 3:3 "Seeing that thou art so importunate and eager to know all things, come into the country where thou abidest, and about the sixth hour, I will appear, and will show thee what thou oughtest to see."

1 3:4 I asked her, saying, "Lady, to what part of the country?" "Where thou wilt," saith she. I selected a beautiful and retired spot; but before I spoke to her and named the spot, she saith to me, "I will come, whither thou willest."

1 3:5 I went then, brethren, into the country, and I counted up the hours, and came to the place where I appointed her to come,

1 3:6 And I see an ivory couch placed there, and on the couch there lay a linen cushion, and on the cushion was spread a coverlet of fine linen of flax.

1 3:7 When I saw these things so ordered, and no one in the place, I was amazed, and a fit of trembling seized me, and my hair stood on end; and a fit of shuddering came upon me, because I was alone.

1 3:8 When then I recovered myself, and remembered the glory of God, and took courage, I knelt down and confessed my sins to the Lord once more, as I had done on the former occasion.

1 3:9 Then she came with six young men, the same whom I had seen before, and she stood by me, and listened attentively to me, as I prayed and confessed my sins to the Lord.

1 3:10 And she touched me, and said: "Hermas, make an end of constantly entreating for thy sins; entreat also for righteousness, that thou mayest take some part forthwith to thy family."

1 3:11 Then she raiseth me by the hand, and leadeth me to the couch, and saith to the young men, "Go ye, and build."

1 3:12 And after the young men had retired and we were left alone, she saith to me, "Sit down here." I say to her, "Lady, let the elders sit down first." "Do as I bid thee," saith she, "sit down."

1[9]y:9 When then I wanted to sit down on the right side, she would not allow me, but beckoned me with her hand that I should sit on the left side. As then I was musing thereon, and was sad because she would not permit me to sit on the right side, she saith to me, "Art thou sad, Hermas? The place on the right side is for others, even for those who have already been well-pleasing to God, and have suffered for the Name's sake. But thou lackest much that thou shouldest sit with them; but as thou abidest in thy simplicity, even so, and thou shalt sit with them, thou and as many as shall have done their deeds, and have suffered what they suffered."

1[10]:1 "What did they suffer?" say I. "Listen," saith she. "Stripes, imprisonments, great tribulations, crosses, wild beasts, for the Name's sake. Therefore to them belongs the right side of the Holiness--to them, and to all who shall suffer for the Name. But for the rest is the left side. Howbeit, to both, to them that sit on the right, and to them that sit on the left, are the same gifts, and the same promises, only they sit on the right and have a certain glory.

1[10]:2 Thou indeed art very desirous to sit on the right with them, but thy shortcomings are many; yet thou shalt be purified from thy shortcomings; yea, and all that are not double-minded shall be purified from all their sins unto this day."

1[10]:3 When she had said this, she wished to depart; but, falling at her feet, I entreated her by the Lord that she would show me the vision which she promised.

1[10]:4 Then she again took me by the hand, and raiseth me, and seateth me on the couch at the left hand, while she herself sat on the right. And lifting up a certain glistening rod, she saith to me, "Seest thou a great thing?" I say to her, "Lady, I see nothing." She saith to me, "Look thou; dost thou not see in front of thee a great tower being builded upon the waters, of glistening square stones?"

1[10]:5 Now the tower was being builded foursquare by the six young men that came with her. And countless other men were bringing stones, some of them from the deep, and others from the land, and were handing them to the six young men. And they took them and builded.

1[10]:6 The stones that were dragged from the deep they placed in every case, just as they were, into the building, for they had been shaped, and they fitted in their joining with the other stones; and they adhered so closely one with another that their joining could not possibly be detected; and the building of the tower appeared as if it were built of one stone. Hermas

2[10]:7 But of the other stones which were brought from the dry land, some they threw away, and some they put into the building; and others they broke in pieces, and threw to a distance from the tower.

1[10]:8 Now many other stones were lying round the tower, and they did not use them for the building; for some of them were mildewed, and others had cracks in them, and others were too short, and others were white and round, and did not fit into the building. Hermas

2[10]:9 And I saw other stones thrown to a distance from the tower, and coming to the way, and yet not staying in the way, but rolling to where there was no way; and others falling into the fire and burning there; and others falling near the waters, and yet not able to roll into the water, although they desired to roll and to come to the water.

3[11]:1 When she had shown me these things, she wished to hurry away. I say to her, "Lady, what advantage is it to me to have seen these things, and yet not to know what the things mean? "She answered and said unto me, "Thou art an over-curious fellow, in desiring to know all that concerns the tower." "Yea, lady," I said, "that I may announce it to my brethren, and that they [may be the more gladdened and] when they hear [these things] they may know the Lord in great glory." Then said she,

3[11]:2 "Many shall hear; but when they hear, some of them shall be glad, and others shall weep. Yet even these latter, if they hear and repent, shall likewise be glad. Hear thou therefore the parables of the tower; for I will reveal all things unto thee. And trouble me no more about revelation; for these revelations have an end, seeing that they have been completed. Nevertheless thou wilt not cease asking for revelations; for thou art shameless."

3[11]:3 The tower, which thou seest building, is myself, the Church, which was seen of thee both now and aforetime. Ask, therefore, what thou willest concerning the tower, and I will reveal it unto thee, that thou mayest rejoice with the saints."

3[11]:4 I say unto her, "Lady, since thou didst hold me worthy once for all, that thou shouldest reveal all things to me, reveal them." Then she saith to me, "Whatsoever is possible to be revealed to thee, shall be revealed. Only let thy heart be with God, and doubt not in thy mind about that which thou seest."

3[11]:5 I asked her, "Wherefore is the tower builded upon waters, lady?" "I told thee so before," said she, "and indeed thou dost enquire diligently. So by thy enquiry thou discoverest the truth. Hear then why the tower is builded upon waters; it is because your life is saved and shall be saved by water. But the tower has been founded by the word of the Almighty and Glorious Name, and is strengthened by the unseen power of the Master."

4[12]:1 I answered and said unto her, "Lady, this thing is great and marvelous. But the six young men that build, who are they, lady?" "These are the holy angels of God, that were created first of all, unto whom the Lord delivered all His creation to increase and to build it, and to be masters of all creation. By their hands therefore the building of the tower will be accomplished."

4[12]:2 "And who are the others who are bringing the stones in?" "They also are holy angels of God; but these six are superior to them. The building of the tower then shall be accomplished, and all alike shall rejoice in the (completed) circle of the tower, and shall glorify God that the building of the tower was accomplished."

4[12]:3 I enquired of her, saying, "Lady, I could wish to know concerning the end of the stones, and their power, of what kind it is." She answered and said unto me, "It is not that thou of all men art especially worthy that it should be revealed to thee; for there are others before thee, and better than thou art, unto whom these visions ought to have been revealed. But that the name of God may be glorified, it hath been revealed to thee, all shall be revealed, for the sake of the doubtful-minded, who question in their hearts whether these things are so or not. Tell them that all these things are true, and that there is nothing beside the truth, but that all are steadfast, and valid, and established on a firm foundation.

5[13]:1 "Hear now concerning the stones that go to the building The stones that are squared and white, and that fit together in their joints, these are the apostles and bishops and teachers and deacons, who walked after the holiness of God, and exercised their office of bishop and teacher and deacon in purity and sanctity for the elect of God, some of them already fallen on sleep, and others still living. And because they always agreed with one another, they both had peace among themselves and listened one to another. Therefore their joinings fit together in the building of the tower."

5[13]:2 "But they that are dragged from the deep, and placed in the building, and that fit together in their joinings with the other stones that are already builded in, who are they?" "These are they that suffered for the name of the Lord."

5[13]:3 "But the other stones that are brought from the dry land, I would fain know who these are, lady." She said, "Those that go to the building, and yet are not hewn, these the Lord hath approved because they walked in the uprightness of the Lord, and rightly performed His commandments."

5[13]:4 "But they that are brought and placed in the building, who are they?" "They are young in the faith, and faithful; but they are warned by the angels to do good, because wickedness was found in them."

5[13]:5 "But those whom they rejected and threw away, who are they?" "These have sinned, and desire to repent, therefore they were not cast to a great distance from the tower, because they will be useful for the building, if they repent. They then that shall repent, if they repent, will be strong in the faith, if they repent now while the tower is building. But if the building shall be finished, they have no more any place, but shall be castaways. This privilege only they have, that they lie near the tower.

5[13]:6 But wouldst thou know about them that are broken in pieces, and cast away far from the tower? These are the sons of lawlessness. They received the faith in hypocrisy, and no wickedness was absent from them. Therefore they have not salvation, for they are not useful for building by reason of their wickednesses. Therefore they were broken up and thrown far away by reason of the wrath of the Lord, for they excited Him to wrath.

5[13]:7 But the rest whom thou hast seen lying in great numbers, not going to the building, of these they that are mildewed are they that knew the truth, but did not abide in it, nor cleave to the saints. Therefore they are useless."

5[13]:8 "But they that have the cracks, who are they?" "These are they that have discord in their hearts against one another, and are not at peace among themselves; who have an appearance of peace, but when they depart from one another, their wickednesses abide in their hearts. These are the cracks which the stones have.

5[13]:9 But they that are broken off short, these have believed, and have their greater part in righteousness, but have some parts of lawlessness; therefore they are too short, and are not perfect."

5[13]:10 "But the white and round stones, which did not fit into the building, who are they, lady?" She answered and said to me, "How long art thou foolish and stupid, and enquirest everything, and understandest nothing? These are they that have faith, but have also riches of this world. When tribulation cometh, they deny their Lord by reason of their riches and their business affairs."

5[13]:11 And I answered and said unto her, "When then, lady, will they be useful for the building?" "When," she replied, "their wealth, which leadeth their souls astray, shall be cut away, then will they be useful for God. For just as the round stone, unless it be cut away, and lose some portion of itself, cannot become square, so also they that are rich in this world, unless their riches be cut away, cannot become useful to the Lord.

5[13]:12 Learn first from thyself When thou hadst riches, thou wast useless; but now thou art useful and profitable unto life. Be ye useful unto God, for thou thyself also art taken from the same stones.

...

7[15]:1 "But the other stones which thou sawest cast far away from the tower and falling into the way and rolling out of the way into the regions where there is no way, these are they that have believed, but by reason of their double heart they abandon their true way. Thus thinking that they can find a better way, they go astray and are sore distressed, as they walk about in the regions where there is no way.

7[15]:2 But they that fall into the fire and are burned, these are they that finally rebelled from the
living God, and it no more entered into their hearts to repent by reason of the lusts of their wantonness and of the wickednesses which they wrought.

7[15]:3 But the others, which are near the waters and yet cannot roll into the water, wouldest thou know who are they? These are they that heard the word, and would be baptized unto the name of the Lord. Then, when they call to their remembrance the purity of the truth, they change their minds, and go back again after their evil desires."

7[15]:4 So she finished the explanation of the tower.

7[15]:5 Still importunate, I asked her further, whether for all these stones that were rejected and would not fit into the building of the tower that was repentance, and they had a place in this tower. "They can repent," she said, "but they cannot be fitted into this tower.

7[15]:6 Yet they shall be fitted into another place much more humble, but not until they have undergone torments, and have fulfilled the days of their sins. And they shall be changed for this reason, because they participated in the Righteous Word; and then shall it befall them to be relieved from their torments, if the evil deeds, that they have done, come into their heart; but if these come not into their heart, they are not saved by reason of the hardness of their hearts."

8[16]:1 When then I ceased asking her concerning all these things, she saith to me; "Wouldest thou see something else?" Being very desirous of beholding, I was greatly rejoiced that I should see it.

8[16]:2 She looked upon me, and smiled, and she saith to me, "Seest thou seven women round the tower?" "I see them, lady," say I. "This tower is supported by them by commandment of the Lord.

8[16]:3 Hear now their employments. The first of them, the woman with the strong hands, is called Faith; through her are saved the elect of God.

8[16]:4 And the second, that is girded about and looketh like a man, is called Continence; she is the daughter of Faith. Whosoever then shall follow her, becometh happy in his life, for he shall refrain from all evil deeds, believing that, if he refrain from every evil desire, he shall inherit eternal life."

8[16]:5 "And the others, lady, who be they?" "They are daughters one of the other. The name of the one is Simplicity, of the next, Knowledge, of the next, Guilelessness, of the next, Reverence, of the next, Love. When then thou shalt do all the works of their mother, thou canst live."

8[16]:6 "I would fain know, lady," I say, "what power each of them possesseth." "Listen then," saith she, "to the powers which they have.

8[16]:7 Their powers are mastered each by the other, and they follow each other, in the order in which they were born. From Faith is born Continence, from Continence Simplicity, from Simplicity Guilelessness, from Guilelessness Reverence, from Reverence Knowledge, from Knowledge Love. Their works then are pure and reverent and divine.

8[16]:8 Whosoever therefore shall serve these women, and shall have strength to master their works, shall have his dwelling in the tower with the saints of God."

8[16]:9 Then I asked her concerning the seasons, whether the consummation is even now. But she cried aloud, saying, "Foolish man, seest thou not that the tower is still a-building? Whensoever therefore the tower shall be finished building, the end cometh; but it shall be built up quickly. Ask me no more questions: this reminder is sufficient for you and for the saints, and is the renewal of your spirits.

8[16]:10 But it was not revealed to thyself alone, but in order that thou mightest show these things unto all. After three days--

8[16]:11 for thou must understand first, and I charge thee, Hermas, first with these words, which I am about to speak to thee--(I charge thee to) tell all these things into the ears of the saints, that hearing them and doing them they may be purified from their wickednesses, and thyself also with them."

9[17]:1 "Hear me, my children. I brought you up in much simplicity and guilelessness and reverence, through the mercy of the Lord, Who instilled righteousness into you, that ye might be justified and sanctified from all wickedness and all crookedness. But ye will not to cease from your wickedness.

9[17]:2 Now then hear me and be at peace among yourselves, and have regard one to another, and assist one another, and do not partake of the creatures of God alone in abundance, but share them also with those that are in want.

9[17]:3 For some men through their much eating bring weakness on the flesh, and injure their flesh: whereas the flesh of those who have nought to eat is injured by their not having sufficient nourishment, and their body is ruined.

9[17]:4 This exclusiveness therefore is hurtful to you that have and do not share with them that are in want.

9[17]:5 Look ye to the judgment that cometh. Ye then that have more than enough, seek out them that are hungry, while the tower is still unfinished; for after the tower is finished, ye will desire to do good, and will find no place for it.

9[17]:6 Look ye therefore, ye that exult in your wealth, lest they that are in want shall moan, and their moaning shall go up unto the Lord, and ye with your [abundance of good things be shut outside the door of the tower.

9[17]:7 Now therefore I say unto you that are rulers of the Church, and that occupy the chief seats; be not ye like unto the sorcerers. The sorcerers indeed carry their drugs in boxes, but ye carry your drug and your poison in your heart.

9[17]:8 Ye are case-hardened, and ye will not cleanse your hearts and mix your wisdom together in a clean heart, that ye may obtain mercy from the Great King.

9[17]:9 Look ye therefore, children, lest these divisions of yours deprive you of your life.

9[17]:10 How is it that ye wish to instruct the elect of the Lord, while ye yourselves have no instruction? Instruct one another therefore, and have peace among yourselves, that I also may stand gladsome before the Father, and give an account concerning you all to your Lord."

10[18]:1 When then she ceased speaking with me, the six young men, who were building, came, and took her away to the tower, and other four lifted the couch, and took it also away to the tower. I saw not the face of these, for they were turned away.

10[18]:2 And, as she went, I asked her to reveal to me concerning the three forms, in which she had appeared to me. She answered and said to me; "As concerning these things thou must ask another, that they may be revealed to thee."

10[18]:3 Now she was seen of me, brethren, in my first vision of last year, as a very aged woman and seated on a chair.

10[18]:4 In the second vision her face was youthful, but her flesh and her hair were aged, and she spake to me standing; and she was more gladsome than before.

10[18]:5 But in the third vision she was altogether youthful and of exceeding great beauty, and her hair alone was aged; and she was gladsome exceedingly and seated on a couch. Touching these things I was very greatly anxious to learn this revelation.

10[18]:6 And I see the aged woman in a vision of the night, saying to me, "Every enquiry needs humility. Fast therefore, and thou shalt receive what thou askest from the Lord."

10[18]:7 So I fasted one day; and that very night there appeared unto me a young man, and he saith to me, "Seeing that thou askest me revelations offhand with entreaty, take heed lest by thy much asking thou injure thy flesh.

10[18]:8 Sufficient for thee are these revelations. Canst thou see mightier revelations than those thou hast seen?"

10[18]:9 I say unto him in reply, "Sir, this one thing alone I ask, concerning the three forms of the aged woman, that a complete revelation may be vouchsafed me." He saith to me in answer, How long are ye without understanding? It is your double-mindedness that maketh you of no understanding, and because your heart is not set towards the Lord."

10[18]:10 I answered and said unto him again, "From thee, Sir, we shall learn the matters more accurately."

11[19]:1 Listen," saith he, "concerning the three forms, of which thou enquirest.

11[19]:2 In the first vision wherefore did she appear to thee an aged woman and seated on a chair? Because your spirit was aged, and already decayed, and had no power by reason of your infirmities and acts of double-mindedness.

11[19]:3 For as aged people, having no longer hope of renewing their youth, expect nothing else but to fall asleep, so ye also, being weakened with the affairs of this world gave yourselves over to repining, and cast not your cares on the Lord; but your spirit was broken, and ye were aged by your sorrows."

11[19]:4 "Wherefore then she was seated on a chair, I would fain know, Sir." "Because every weak person sits on a chair by reason of his weakness, that the weakness of his body may be supported. So thou hast the symbolism of the first vision."

12[20]:1 "But in the second vision thou sawest her standing, and with her countenance more youthful and more gladsome than before; but her flesh and her hair aged. Listen to this parable also," saith he.

12[20]:2 "Imagine an old man, who has now lost all hope of himself by reason of his weakness and his poverty, and expecteth nothing else save the last day of his life. Suddenly an inheritance is left him. He heareth the news, riseth up and full of joy clothes himself with strength, and no longer lieth down, but standeth up, and his spirit, which was now broken by reason of his former circumstances, is renewed again, and he no longer sitteth, but taketh courage; so also was it with you, when you heard the revelation which the Lord revealed unto you.

12[20]:3 For He had compassion on you, and renewed your spirits, and ye laid aside your maladies, and strength came to you, and ye were made powerful in the faith, and the Lord rejoiced to see you put on your strength. And therefore He showed you the building of the tower; yea, and other things also shall He show you, if with your whole heart ye be at peace among yourselves.

13[21]:1 But in the third vision ye saw her younger and fair and gladsome, and her form fair.

13[21]:2 For just as when to some mourner cometh some piece of good tidings, immediately he forgetteth his former sorrows, and admitteth nothing but the tidings which he hath heard, and is strengthened thenceforth unto that which is good, and his spirit is renewed by reason of the joy which he hath received; so also ye have received a renewal of your spirits by seeing these good things.

13[21]:3 And whereas thou sawest her seated on a couch, the position is a firm on; for the couch has four feet and standeth firmly; for the world too Is upheld by means of four elements.

13[21]:4 They then that have fully repented shall be young again, and founded firmly, seeing that they have repented with their whole heart. There thou hast the revelation entire and complete. Thou shalt ask nothing more as touching revelation-- but if anything be lacking still, it shall be revealed unto thee."

1 22]:Heading Vision 4

1[22]:1 The fourth vision which I saw, brethren, twenty days after the former vision which came unto me, for a type of the impending tribulation.

1[22]:2 I was going into the country by the Companion Way. From the high road, it is about ten stades; and the place is easy for traveling.

1[22]:3 While then I am walking alone, I entreat the Lord that He will accomplish the revelations and the visions which He showed me through His holy Church, that He may strengthen me and may give repentance to His servants which have stumbled, that His great and glorious Name may be glorified, for that He held me worthy that He should show me His marvels.

1[22]:4 And as I gave glory and thanksgiving to Him, there answered me as it were the sound of a voice, "Be not of doubtful mind, Hermas." I began to question in myself and to say, "How can I be of doubtful mind, seeing that I am so firmly founded by the Lord, and have seen glorious things?"

1[22]:5 And I went on a little, brethren, and behold, I see a cloud of dust rising as it were to heaven, and I began to say within myself, "Can it be that cattle are coming, and raising a cloud of dust?" for it was just about a stade from me.

1[22]:6 As the cloud of dust waxed greater and greater, I suspected that it was something supernatural. Then the sun shone out a little, and behold, I see a huge beast like some sea-monster, and from its mouth fiery locusts issued forth. And the beast was about a hundred feet in length,

and its head was as it were of pottery.

1[22]:7 And I began to weep, and to entreat the Lord that He would rescue me from it. And I remembered the word which I had heard, "Be not of doubtful mind, Hermas."

1[22]:8 Having therefore, brethren, put on the faith of the Lord and called to mind the mighty works that He had taught me, I took courage and gave myself up to the beast. Now the beast was coming on with such a rush, that it might have ruined a city.

1[22]:9 I come near it, and, huge monster as it was, it stretcheth itself on the ground, and merely put forth its tongue, and stirred not at all until I had passed by it.

1[22]:10 And the beast had on its head four colors; black then fire and blood color, then gold, then white.

2[23]:1 Now after I had passed the beast, and had gone forward about thirty feet, behold, there meeteth me a virgin arrayed as if she were going forth from a bridal-chamber all in white and with white sandals, veiled up to her forehead, and her head-covering consisted of a turban, and her hair was white.

2[23]:2 I knew from the former Visions that it was the Church, and I became more cheerful. She saluteth me, saying, "Good morrow, my good man"; and I saluted her in turn, "Lady, good morrow."

2[23]:3 She answered and said unto me, "Did nothing meet thee? "I say unto her, Lady, such a huge beast, that could have destroyed whole peoples: but, by the power of the Lord and by His great mercy, I escaped it."

2[23]:4 "Thou didst escape it well," saith she, "because thou didst cast thy care upon God, and didst open thy heart to the Lord, believing that thou canst be saved by nothing else but by His great and glorious Name. Therefore the Lord sent His angel, which is over the beasts, whose name is Segri, and shut his mouth that it might not hurt thee. Thou hast escaped a great tribulation by reason of thy faith, and because, though thou sawest so huge a beast, thou didst not doubt in thy mind.

2[23]:5 Go therefore, and declare to the elect of the Lord His mighty works, and tell them that this beast is a type of the great tribulation which is to come. If therefore ye prepare yourselves beforehand, and repent (and turn) unto the Lord with your whole heart, ye shall be able to escape it, if your heart be made pure and without blemish, and if for the remaining days of your life ye serve the Lord blamelessly. Cast your cares upon the Lord and He will set them straight.

2[23]:6 Trust ye in the Lord, ye men of doubtful mind, for He can do all things, yea, He both turneth away His wrath from you, and again He sendeth forth His plagues upon you that are of doubtful mind. Woe to them that hear these words and are disobedient; it were better for them that they had not been born."

3[24]:1 I asked her concerning the four colors, which the beast had upon its head. Then she answered me and said, "Again thou art curious about such matters." "Yes, lady," said I, "make known unto me what these things are."

3[24]:2 "Listen," said she; "the black is this world in which ye dwell;

3[24]:3 and the fire and blood color showeth that this world must perish by blood and fire;

3[24]:4 and the golden part are ye that has escaped from this world. For as the gold is tested by the fire and is made useful, so ye also [that dwell in it] are being tested in yourselves. Ye then that abide and pass through the fire will be purified by it. For as the old loses its dross. so Ye also shall cast away all sorrow and tribulation, and shall be purified, and shall be useful for the building of the tower.

3[24]:5 But the white portion is the coming age, in which the elect of God shall dwell; because the elect of God shall be without spot and pure unto life eternal.

3[24]:6 Wherefore cease not thou to speak in the ears of the saints. Ye have now the symbolism also of the tribulation which is coming in power. But if ye be willing, it shall be nought. Remember ye the things that are written beforehand."

3[24]:7 With these words she departed, and I saw not in what direction she departed; for a noise was made: and I turned back in fear, thinking that the beast was coming.

5[25]:Heading Revelation 5

5[25]:1 As I prayed in the house, and sat on the couch, there entered a man glorious in his visage, in the garb of a shepherd, with a white skin wrapped about him, and with a wallet on his shoulders and a staff in his hand. And he saluted me, and I saluted him in return.

5[25]:2 And he immediately sat down by my side, and he saith unto me, "I was sent by the most holy angel, that I might dwell with thee the remaining days of thy life."

5[25]:3 I thought he came to tempt me, and I say unto him, "Why, who art thou? For I know," say I, "unto whom I was delivered." He saith to me, "Dost thou not recognize me?" "No," I say. "I," saith he, "am the shepherd, unto whom thou wast delivered."

5[25]:4 While he was still speaking, his form was changed, and I recognized him as being the same, to whom I was delivered; and straightway I was confounded, and fear seized me, and I was altogether overwhelmed with distress that I had answered him so wickedly and senselessly.

5[25]:5 But he answered and said unto me, "Be not confounded, but strengthen thyself in my commandments which I am about to command thee. For I was sent," saith he, "that I might show thee again all the things which thou didst see before, merely the heads which are convenient for you. First of all, write down my commandments and my parables; and the other matters thou shalt write down as I shall show them to thee. The reason why," saith he, "I command thee to write down first the commandments and parables is, that thou mayest read them off-hand, and mayest be able to keep them."

5[25]:6 So I wrote down the commandments and parables, as he commanded me.

5[25]:7 If then, when ye hear them, ye keep them and walk in them, and do them with a pure heart, ye shall receive from the Lord all things that He promised you; but if, when ye hear them, ye do not repent, but still add to your sins, ye shall receive from the Lord the opposite. All these the shepherd, the angel of repentance. commanded me to write.

1[26]:Heading Mandate 1

1[26]:1 "First of all, believe that God is One, even He who created all things and set them in order, and brought all things from non-existence into being, Who comprehendeth all things, being alone incomprehensible.

1[26]:2 Believe Him therefore, and fear Him, and in this fear be continent. Keep these things, and thou shalt cast off all wickedness from thyself, and shalt clothe thyself with every excellence of righteousness, and shalt live unto God, if thou keep this commandment."

1[27]:Heading Mandate 2

1[27]:1 He saith to me; "Keep simplicity and be guileless, and thou shalt be as little children, that know not the wickedness which destroyeth the life of men.

1[27]:2 First of all, speak evil of no man, neither take pleasure in listening to a slanderer. Otherwise thou that hearest too shalt be responsible for the sin of him that speaketh the evil, if thou believest the slander, which thou hearest; for in believing it thou thyself also wilt have a grudge against thy brother. So then shalt thou be responsible for the sin of him that speaketh the evil.

1[27]:3 Slander is evil; it is a restless demon, never at peace, but always having its home among factions. Refrain from it therefore, and thou shalt have success at all times with all men.

1[27]:4 But clothe thyself in reverence, wherein is no evil stumbling-block, but all things are smooth and gladsome. Work that which is good, and of thy labors, which God giveth thee, give to all that are in want freely, not questioning to whom thou shalt give, and to whom thou shalt not give. Give to all; for to all God desireth that there should be given of His own bounties.

1[27]:5 They then that receive shall render an account to God why they received it, and to what end; for they that receive in distress shall not be judged, but they that receive by false pretence shall pay the penalty.

1[27]:6 He then that giveth is guiltless; for as he received from the Lord the ministration to perform it, he hath performed it in sincerity, by making no distinction to whom to give or not to give. This ministration then, when sincerely performed, becomes glorious in the sight of God. He therefore that ministereth thus sincerely shall live unto God.

1[27]:7 Therefore keep this commandment, as I have told thee, that thine own repentance and that of thy household may be found to be sincere, and [thy] heart pure and undefiled."

1[28]:Heading Mandate 3

1[28]:1 Again he saith to me; "Love truth, and let nothing but truth proceed out of thy mouth, that the Spirit which God made to dwell in this flesh, may be found true in the sight of all men; and thus shall the Lord, Who dwelleth in thee, be glorified; for the Lord is true in every word, and with Him there is no falsehood

1[28]:2 They therefore that speak lies set the Lord at nought, and become robbers of the Lord, for they do not deliver up to Him the deposit which they received. For they received of Him a spirit free from lies. This if they shall return a lying spirit, they have defiled the commandment of the Lord and have become robbers."

1[28]:3 When then I heard these things, I wept bitterly. But seeing me weep he saith, "Why weepest thou?" "Because, Sir," say I "I know not if I can be saved." "Why so?" saith he. "Because, Sir," I say, "never in my life spake I a true word, but I always lied deceitfully with all men and dressed up my falsehood as truth before all men; and no man ever contradicted me, but confidence was placed in my word. How then, Sir," say I, "can I live, seeing that I have done these things?"

1[28]:4 "Your supposition," he saith, "is right and true, for it behoved thee as a servant of God to walk in truth, and no complicity with evil should abide with the Spirit of truth, nor bring grief to the Spirit which is holy and true." "Never, Sir," say I, "heard I clearly words such as these."

1[28]:5 "Now then," saith he, "thou hearest. Guard them, that the former falsehoods also which thou spakest in thy business affairs may themselves become credible, now that these are found true; for they too can become trustworthy. If thou keep these things, and from henceforward speak nothing but truth, thou shalt be able to secure life for thyself And whosoever shall hear this command, and abstain from falsehood, that most pernicious habit, shall live unto God."

1[29]:Heading Mandate 4

1[29]:1 "I charge thee, "saith he, "to keep purity, and let not a thought enter into thy heart concerning another's wife, or concerning fornication, or concerning any such like evil deeds; for in so doing thou commitest a great sin. But remember thine own wife always, and thou shalt never go wrong.

1[29]:2 For should this desire enter into thine heart, thou wilt go wrong, and should any other as evil as this, thou commitest sin. For this desire in a servant of God is a great sin; and if any man doeth this evil deed, he worketh out death for himself.

1[29]:3 Look to it therefore. Abstain from this desire; for, where holiness dwelleth, there lawlessness ought not to enter into the heart of a righteous man."

1[29]:4 I say to him, "Sir, permit me to ask thee a few more questions" "Say on," saith he. "Sir," say I, "if a man who has a wife that is faithful in the Lord detect her in adultery, doth the husband sin in living with her?"

1[29]:5 "So long as he is ignorant," saith he, "he sinneth not; but if the husband know of her sin, and the wife repent not, but continue in her fornication, and her husband live with her, he makes himself responsible for her sin and an accomplice in her adultery."

1[29]:6 "What then, Sir," say I, "shall the husband do, if the wife continue in this case?" "Let him divorce her," saith he, "and let the husband abide alone: but if after divorcing his wife he shall marry another, he likewise committeth adultery."

1[29]:7 "If then, Sir," say I, "after the wife is divorced, she repent and desire to return to her own husband, shall she not be received?"

1[29]:8 "Certainly," saith he, "if the husband receiveth her not, he sinneth and bringeth great sin upon himself; nay, one who hath sinned and repented must be received, yet not often; for there is but one repentance for the servants of God. For the sake of her repentance therefore the husband ought not to marry. This is the manner of acting enjoined on husband and wife.

1[29]:9 Not only," saith he, "is it adultery, if a man pollute his flesh, but whosoever doeth things like unto the heathen committeth adultery. If therefore in such deeds as these likewise a man continue and repent not, keep away from him, and live not with him. Otherwise, thou also art a partaker of his sin.

1[29]:10 For this cause ye were enjoined to remain single, whether husband or wife; for in such cases repentance is possible.

1[29]:11 I," said he, "am not giving an excuse that this matter should be concluded thus, but to the end that the sinner should sin no more. But as concerning his former sin, there is One Who is able to give healing; it is He Who hath authority over all things."

2[30]:1 I asked him again, saying, "Seeing that the Lord held me worthy that thou shouldest always dwell with me, suffer me still to say a few words, since I understand nothing, and my heart has been made dense by my former deeds. Make me to understand, for I am very foolish, and I apprehend absolutely nothing."

2[30]:2 He answered and said unto me, "I," saith he, "preside over repentance, and I give understanding to all who repent. Nay, thinkest thou not," saith he, "that this very act of repentance is understanding? To repent is great understanding," saith he. "For the man that hath sinned understandeth that he hath done evil before the Lord, and the deed which he hath done entereth into his heart, and he repenteth, and doeth no more evil, but doeth good lavishly, and humbleth his own soul and putteth it to torture because it sinned. Thou seest then that repentance is great understanding."

2[30]:3 "It is on this account therefore, Sir," say I, "that I enquire everything accurately of thee; first, because I am a sinner; secondly, because I know not what deeds I must do that I may live, for my sins are many and various."

2[30]:4 "Thou shalt live," saith he, "if thou keep my commandments and walk in them and whosoever shall hear these commandments and keep them, shall live unto God."

3[31]:1 "I will still proceed, Sir," say I, "to ask a further question." "Speak on," saith he. "I have heard, Sir," say I, "from certain teachers, that there is no other repentance, save that which took place when we rent down into the water and obtained remission of our former sins."

3[31]:2 He saith to me; "Thou hast well heard; for so it is. For he that hath received remission of sins ought no longer to sin, but to dwell in purity.

3[31]:3 But, since thou enquirest all things accurately, I will declare unto thee this also, so as to give no excuse to those who shall hereafter believe or those who have already believed, on the Lord. For they that have already believed, or shall hereafter believe, have not repentance for sins, but have only remission of their former sins.

3[31]:4 To those then that were called before these days the Lord has appointed repentance. For the Lord, being a discerner of hearts and foreknowing all things, perceived the weakness of men and the manifold wiles of the devil, how that he will be doing some mischief to the servants of God, and will deal wickedly with them.

3[31]:5 The Lord then, being very compassionate, had pity on His handiwork, and appointed this (opportunity of) repentance, and to me was given the authority over this repentance.

3[31]:6 But I say unto you," saith he, "if after this great and holy calling any one, being tempted of the devil, shall commit sin, he hath only one (opportunity of) repentance. But if he sin off-hand and repent, repentance is unprofitable for such a man; for he shall live with difficulty."

3[31]:7 I say unto him, "I was quickened unto life again, when I heard these things from thee so precisely. For I know that, if I shall add no more to my sins, I shall be saved." "Thou shalt be saved," he saith, "thou and all, as many as shall do these things."

4[32]:1 I asked him again, saying, "Sir, since once thou dost bear with me, declare unto me this further matter also." "Say on," saith he. "If a wife, Sir," say I, "or, it may be, a husband fall asleep, and one of them marry, doth the one that marrieth sin?"

4[32]:2 "He sinneth not," saith he, "but if he remain single, he investeth himself with more exceeding honor and with great glory before the Lord; yet even if he should marry, he sinneth not.

4[32]:3 Preserve purity and holiness therefore, and thou shalt live unto God. All these things, which I speak and shall hereafter speak unto thee, guard from this time forward, from the day when thou wast committed unto me, and I will dwell in thy house.

4[32]:4 But for thy former transgressions there shall be remission, if thou keepest my commandments. Yea, and all shall have remission, if they keep these my commandments, and walk in this purity."

Hermas 1[33]:Heading Mandate 5

1[33]:1 "Be thou long-suffering and understanding," he saith, "and thou shalt have the mastery over all evil deeds, and shalt work all righteousness.

1[33]:2 For if thou art long-suffering, the Holy Spirit that abideth in thee shall be pure, not being darkened by another evil spirit, but dwelling in a large room shall rejoice and be glad with the vessel in which he dwelleth, and shall serve God with much cheerfulness, having prosperity in himself.

1[33]:3 But if any angry temper approach, forthwith the Holy Spirit, being delicate, is straitened, not having [the] place clear, and seeketh to retire from the place; for he is being choked by the evil spirit, and has no room to minister unto the Lord, as he desireth, being polluted by angry temper. For the Lord dwelleth in long-suffering, but the devil in angry temper.

1[33]:4 Thus that both the spirits then should be dwelling together is inconvenient and evil for that man in whom they dwell.

1[33]:5 For if you take a little wormwood, and pour it into a jar of honey, is not the whole of the honey spoiled, and all that honey ruined by a very small quantity of wormwood? For it destroyeth the sweetness of the honey, and it no longer hath the same attraction for the owner, because it is rendered bitter and hath lost its use. But if the wormwood be not put into the honey, the honey is found sweet and becomes useful to its owner.

1[33]:6 Thou seest [then] that long-suffering is very sweet, beyond the sweetness of honey, and is useful to the Lord, and He dwelleth in it. But angry, temper is bitter and useless. If then angry temper be mixed with long-suffering, long-suffering is polluted and the man's intercession is no longer useful to God."

1[33]:7 "I would fain know, Sir," say I, "the working of angry temper, that I may guard myself from it." "Yea, verily," saith he, "if thou guard not thyself from it--thou and thy family--thou hast lost all thy hope. But guard thyself from it; for I am with thee. Yea, and all men shall hold aloof from it, as many as have repented with their whole heart. For I will be with them and will preserve them; for they all were justified by the most holy angel.

2[34]:1 "Hear now," saith he, "the working of angry temper, how evil it is, and how it subverteth the servants of God by its own working, and how it leadeth them astray from righteousness. But it doth not lead astray them that are full in the faith, nor can it work upon them, because the power of the Lord is with them; but them that are empty and double-minded it leadeth astray.

2[34]:2 For when it seeth such men in prosperity it insinuates itself into the heart of the man, and for no cause whatever the man or the woman is em-bittered on account of worldly matters, either about meats, or some triviality, or about some friend, or about giving or receiving, or about follies of this kind. For all these things are foolish and vain and senseless and inexpedient for the servants of God.

2[34]:3 But long-suffering is great and strong, and has a mighty and vigorous power, and is prosperous in great enlargement, gladsome, exultant, free from care, glorifying the Lord at every season, having no bitterness in itself, remaining always gentle and tranquil. This long-suffering therefore dwelleth with those whose faith is perfect.

2[34]:4 But angry temper is in the first place foolish, fickle and senseless; then from foolishness is engendered bitterness, and from bitterness wrath, and from wrath anger, and from anger spite; then spite being composed of all these evil elements becometh a great sin and incurable.

2[34]:5 For when all these spirits dwell in one vessel, where the Holy Spirit also dwelleth, that vessel cannot contain them, but overfloweth.

2[34]:6 The delicate spirit therefore, as not being accustomed to dwell with an evil spirit nor with harshness, departeth from a man of that kind, and seeketh to dwell with gentleness and tranquillity.

2[34]:7 Then, when it hath removed from that man, in whom it dwells, that man becometh emptied of the righteous spirit, and henceforward, being filled with the evil spirits, he is unstable in all his actions, being dragged about hither and thither by the evil spirits, and is altogether blinded and bereft of his good intent. Thus then it happeneth to all persons of angry temper.

2[34]:8 Refrain therefore from angry temper, the most evil of evil spirits. But clothe thyself in long-suffering, and resist angry temper and bitterness, and thou shalt be round in company with the holiness which is beloved of the Lord. See then that thou never neglect this commandment; for if thou master this commandment, thou shalt be able likewise to keep the remaining commandments, which I am about to give thee. Be strong in them and endowed with power; and let all be endowed with power, as many as desire to walk in them."

Hermas 1[35]:Heading Mandate 6

1[35]:1 I charged thee," saith he, "in my first commandment to guard faith and fear and temperance." "Yes, Sir," say I. "But now," saith he, "I wish to show thee their powers also, that thou mayest understand what is the power and effect of each one of them. For their effects are two fold. Now they are prescribed alike to the righteous and the unrighteous.

1[35]:2 Do thou therefore trust righteousness, but trust not unrighteousness; for the way of righteousness is straight, but the way of unrighteousness is crooked. But walk thou in the straight [and level] path, and leave the crooked one alone.

1[35]:3 For the crooked way has no tracks, but only pathlessness and many stumbling stones, and is rough and thorny. So it is therefore harmful to those who walk in it.

1[35]:4 But those who walk in the straight way walk on the level and without stumbling: for it is neither rough nor thorny. Thou seest then that it is more expedient to walk in this way."

1[35]:5 "I am pleased, Sir," say I, "to walk in this way." "Thou shalt walk," he saith, "yea, and whosoever shall turn unto the Lord with his whole heart shall walk in it.

2[36]:1 "Hear now," saith he, "concerning faith. There are two angels with a man, one of righteousness and one of wickedness."

2[36]:2 "How then, Sir," say I, "shall I know their workings, seeing that both angels dwell with me?"

2[36]:3 "Hear," saith he, "and understand their workings. The angel of righteousness is delicate and bashful and gentle and tranquil. When then this one enters into thy heart, forthwith he speaketh with thee of righteousness, of purity, of holiness, and of contentment, of every righteous deed and of every glorious virtue. When all these things enter into thy heart, know that the angel of righteousness is with thee. [These then are the works of the angel of righteousness.] Trust him therefore and his works.

2[36]:4 Now see the works of the angel of wickedness also. First of all, he is quick tempered and bitter and senseless, and his works are evil, overthrowing the servants of God. Whenever then he entereth into thy heart, know him by his works."

2[36]:5 "How I shall discern him, Sir," I reply, "I know not." Listen," saith he. "When a fit of angry temper or bitterness comes upon thee, know that he is in thee. Then the desire of much business and the costliness of many viands and drinking bouts and of many drunken fits and of various luxuries which are unseemly, and the desire of women, and avarice, and haughtiness and boastfulness, and whatsoever things are akin and like to these--when then these things enter into thy heart, know that the angel of wickedness is with thee.

2[36]:6 Do thou therefore, recognizing his works, stand aloof from him, and trust him in nothing, for his works are evil and inexpedient for the servants of God. Here then thou hast the workings of both the angels. Understand them, and trust the angel of righteousness.

2[36]:7 But from the angel of wickedness stand aloof, for his teaching is evil in every matter; for though one be a man of faith, and the desire of this angel enter into his heart, that man, or that woman, must commit some sin.

2[36]:8 And if again a man or a woman be exceedingly wicked, and the works of the angel of righteousness come into that man's heart, he must of necessity do something good.

2[36]:9 Thou seest then," saith he, "that it is good to follow the angel of righteousness, and to bid farewell to the angel of wickedness.

2[36]:10 This commandment declareth what concerneth faith, that thou mayest trust the works of the angel of righteousness, and doing them mayest live unto God. But believe that the works of the angel of wickedness are difficult; so by not doing them thou shalt live unto God."

Hermas 1[37]:Heading Mandate 7

1[37]:1 "Fear the Lord," saith he, "and keep His commandments. So keeping the commandments of God thou shalt be powerful in every deed, and thy doing shall be incomparable. For whilst thou fearest the Lord, thou shalt do all things well. But this is the fear wherewith thou oughtest to be afraid, and thou shalt be saved.

1[37]:2 But fear not the devil; for, if thou fear the Lord, thou shalt be master over the devil, for there is no power in him. [For] in whom is no power, neither is there fear of him; but in whom power is glorious, of him is fear likewise. For every one that hath power hath fear, whereas he that hath no power is despised of all.

1[37]:3 But fear thou the works of the devil, for they are evil. While then thou fearest the Lord, thou wilt fear the works of the devil, and wilt not do them, but abstain from them.

1[37]:4 Fear therefore is of two kinds. If thou desire to do evil, fear the Lord, and thou shalt not do it. If again thou desire to do good, fear the Lord and thou shalt do it. Therefore the fear of the Lord is powerful and great and glorious. Fear the Lord then, and thou shalt live unto Him; yea, and as many of them that keep His commandments as shall fear Him, shall live unto God."

1[37]:5 "Wherefore, Sir," say I, "didst thou say concerning those that keep His commandments, "They shall live unto God"?" "Because," saith he, "every creature feareth the Lord, but not every one keepeth His commandments. Those then that fear Him and keep His commandments, they have life unto God; but they that keep not His commandments have no life in them."

Hermas 1[38]:Heading Mandate 8

1[38]:1 "I told thee," saith he, "that the creatures of God are twofold; for temperance also is twofold. For in some things it is right to be temperate, but in other things it is not right."

1[38]:2 "Make known unto me, Sir," say I, "in what things it is right to be temperate, and in what things it is not right." "Listen," saith he. "Be temperate as to what is evil, and do it not; but be not temperate as to what is good, but do it. For if thou be temperate as to what is good, so as not to do it, thou committest a great sin; but if thou be temperate as to what is evil, so as not to do it, thou doest great righteousness. Be temperate therefore in abstaining from all wickedness, and do that which is good."

1[38]:3 "What kinds of wickedness, Sir," say I, "are they from which we must be temperate and abstain?" "Listen," saith he; "from adultery and fornication, from the lawlessness of drunkenness, from wicked luxury, from many viands and the costliness of riches, and vaunting and haughtiness and pride, and from falsehood and evil speaking and hypocrisy, malice and all blasphemy.

1[38]:4 These works are the most wicked of all in the life of men. From these works therefore the servant of God must be temperate and abstain; for he that is not temperate so as to abstain from these cannot live unto God. Listen then to what follows upon these."

1[38]:5 "Why, are there still other evil deeds, Sir?" say I. "Aye, saith he, "there are many, from which the servant of God must be temperate and abstain; theft, falsehood, deprivation, false witness, avarice, evil desire, deceit, vain-glory, boastfulness, and whatsoever things are like unto these.

1[38]:6 Thinkest thou not that these things are wrong, yea, very wrong," [saith he,] "for the servants of God? In all these things he that serveth God must exercise temperance. Be thou temperate, therefore, and refrain from all these things, that thou mayest live unto God, and be enrolled among those who exercise self-restraint in them. These then are the things from which thou shouldest restrain thyself

1[38]:7 Now hear," saith he, "the things, in which thou shouldest not exercise self restraint, but do them. Exercise no self-restraint in that which is good, but do it."

1[38]:8 "Sir," say I, "show me the power of the good also, that I may walk in them and serve them, that doing them it may be possible for me to be saved." "Hear," saith he, "the works of the good likewise, which thou must do, and towards which thou must exercise no self-restraint.

1[38]:9 First of all, there is faith, fear of the Lord, love, concord, words of righteousness, truth, patience; nothing is better than these in the life of men. If a man keep these, and exercise not self-restraint from them, he becomes blessed in his life.

1[38]:10 Hear now what follow upon these; to minister to widows, to visit the orphans and the needy, to ransom the servants of God from their afflictions, to be hospitable (for in hospitality benevolence from time to time has a place), to resist no man, to be tranquil, to show yourself more submissive than all men, to reverence the aged, to practice righteousness, to observe brotherly feeling, to endure injury, to be long-suffering, to bear no grudge, to exhort those who are sick at soul, not to cast away those that have stumbled from the faith, but to convert them and to put courage Into them, to reprove sinners, not to oppress debtors and indigent persons, and whatsoever actions are like these.

1[38]:11 Do these things," saith he, "seem to thee to be good?" "Why, what, Sir," say I, "can be better than these?" "Then walk in them," saith he, "and abstain not from them, and thou shalt live unto God.

1[38]:12 Keep this commandment therefore. If thou do good and abstain not from it, thou shalt live unto God; yea, and all shall live unto God who act so. And again if thou do not evil, and abstain from it, thou shalt live unto God; yea, and all shall live unto God, who shall keep these commandments, and walk in them."

Hermas 1[39]:Heading Mandate 9

1[39]:1 He saith to me; "Remove from thyself a doubtful mind and doubt not at all whether to ask of God, saying within thyself, "How can I ask thing of the Lord and receive it, seeing that I have committed so many sins against Him?"

1[39]:2 Reason not thus, but turn to the Lord with thy whole heart, and ask of Him nothing wavering, and thou shalt know His exceeding compassion, that He will surely not abandon thee, but will fulfill the petition of thy soul.

1[39]:3 For God is not as men who bear a grudge, but Himself is without malice and hath compassion on His creatures.

1[39]:4 Do thou therefore cleanse thy heart from all the vanities of this life, and from the things mentioned before; and ask of the Lord, and thou shalt receive all things, and shalt lack nothing of all thy petitions, if thou ask of the Lord nothing wavering.

1[39]:5 But if thou waver in thy heart, thou shalt surely receive none of thy petitions. For they that waver towards God, these are the doubtful-minded, and they never obtain any of their petitions.

1[39]:6 But they that are complete in the faith make all their petitions trusting in the Lord, and they receive, because they ask without wavering, nothing doubting; for every doubtful-minded man, if he repent not, shall hardly be saved.

1[39]:7 Cleanse therefore thy heart from doubtful-mindedness, and put on faith, for it is strong, and trust God that thou wilt receive all thy petitions which thou askest; and if after asking anything of the Lord, thou receive thy petition somewhat tardily, be not of doubtful mind because thou didst not receive the petition of thy soul at once. For assuredly it is by reason of some temptation or some transgression, of which thou art ignorant, that thou receivest thy petition so tardily.

1[39]:8 Do thou therefore cease not to make thy soul's petition, and thou shalt receive it. But if thou grow weary, and doubt as thou askest, blame thyself and not Him that giveth unto thee. See to this doubtful-mindedness; for it is evil and senseless, and uprooteth many from the faith, yea, even very faithful and strong men. For indeed this doubtful-mindedness is a daughter of the devil, and worketh great wickedness against the servants of God.

1[39]:9 Therefore despise doubtful-mindedness and gain the mastery over it in everything, clothing thyself with faith which is strong and powerful. For faith promiseth all things, accomplisheth all things; but doubtful-mindedness, as having no confidence in itself, fails in all the works which it doeth.

1[39]:10 Thou seest then," saith he, "that faith is from above from the Lord, and hath great power; but doubtful-mindedness is an earthly spirit from the devil, and hath no power.

1[39]:11 Do thou therefore serve that faith which hath power, and hold aloof from the doubtful-mindedness which hath no power; and thou shalt live unto God; yea, and all those shall live unto God who are so minded."

Hermas 1[40]:Heading Mandate 10

1[40]:1 "Put away sorrow from thyself," saith he, "for she is the sister of doubtful-mindedness and of angry temper."

1[40]:2 "How, Sir," say I, "is she the sister of these? For angry temper seems to me to be one thing, doubtful-mindedness another, sorrow another." "Thou art a foolish fellow," saith he, "[and] perceivest not that sorrow is more evil than all the spirits, and is most fatal to the servants of God, and beyond all the spirits destroys a man, and crushes out the Holy Spirit and yet again saves it."

1[40]:3 "I, Sir," say I, "am without understanding, and I understand not these parables. For how it can crush out and again save, I do not comprehend."

1[40]:4 "Listen," saith he. "Those who have never investigated concerning the truth, nor enquired concerning the deity, but have merely believed, and have been mixed up in business affairs and riches and heathen friendships, and many other affairs of this world--as many, I say, as devote themselves to these things, comprehend not the parables of the deity; for they are darkened by these actions, and are corrupted and become barren.

1[40]:5 As good vineyards, when they are treated with neglect, are made barren by the thorns and weeds of various kinds, so men who after they have believed fall into these many occupations which were mentioned before, lose their understanding and comprehend nothing at all concerning righteousness; for if they hear concerning the deity and truth, their mind is absorbed in their occupations, and they perceive nothing at all.

1[40]:6 But they that have the fear of God, and investigate concerning deity and truth, and direct their heart towards the Lord, perceive and understand everything that is said to them more quickly, because they have the fear of the Lord in themselves; for where the Lord dwelleth, there too is great understanding. Cleave therefore unto the Lord, and thou shalt understand and perceive all things.

2[41]:1 "Hear now, senseless man," saith he, "How sorrow crusheth out the Holy Spirit, and again saveth it.

2[41]:2 When the man of doubtful mind sets his hand to any action, and fails in it owing to his doubtful-mindedness, grief at this entereth into the man, and grieveth the Holy Spirit, and crusheth it out.

2[41]:3 Then again when angry temper cleaveth to a man concerning any matter, and he is much embittered, again sorrow entereth into the heart of the man that was ill-tempered, and he is grieved at the deed which he hath done, and repenteth that he did evil.

2[41]:4 This sadness therefore seemeth to bring salvation, because he repented at having done the evil. So both the operations sadden the Spirit; first, the doubtful mind saddens the Spirit, because it succeeded not in its business, and the angry temper again, because it did what was evil. Thus both are saddening to the Holy Spirit, the doubtful mind and the angry temper.

2[41]:5 Put away therefore from thyself sadness, and afflict not the Holy Spirit that dwelleth in thee, lest haply He intercede with God [against thee], and depart from thee.

2[41]:6 For the Spirit of God, that was given unto this flesh, endureth not sadness neither constraint.

3[42]:1 "Therefore clothe thyself in cheerfulness, which hath favor with Cod always, and is acceptable to Him, and rejoice in it. For every cheerful man worketh good, and thinketh good, and despiseth sadness;

3[42]:2 but the sad man is always committing sin. In the first place he committeth sin, because he grieveth the Holy Spirit, which was given to the man being a cheerful spirit; and in the second place, by grieving the Holy Spirit he doeth lawlessness, in that he doth not intercede with neither confess unto God. For the intercession of a sad man hath never at any time power to ascend to the altar of God."

3[42]:3 "Wherefore," say I, "doth not the intercession of him that is saddened ascend to the altar?" "Because," saith he, "sadness is seated at his heart. Thus sadness mingled with the intercession doth not suffer the intercession to ascend pure to the altar. For as vinegar when mingled with wine in the same (vessel) hath not the same pleasant taste, so likewise sadness mingled with the Holy Spirit hath not the same intercession.

3[42]:4 Therefore cleanse thyself from this wicked sadness, and thou shalt live unto God; yea, and all they shall live unto God, who shall cast away sadness from themselves and clothe themselves in all cheerfulness."

Hermas 1[43]:Heading Mandate 11

1[43]:1 He shewed me men seated on a couch, and another man seated on a chair. And he saith to me, "Seest thou those that are seated on the couch?" "I see them, Sir," say I. "These," saith he, "are faithful, but he that sitteth on the chair is a false prophet who destroyeth the mind of the servants of God--I mean, of the doubtful-minded, not of the faithful.

1[43]:2 These doubtful-minded ones then come to him as to a soothsayer and enquire of him what shall befall them. And he, the false prophet, having no power of a divine Spirit in himself, speaketh with them according to their enquiries [and according to the lusts of their wickedness], and filleth their souls as they themselves wish.

1[43]:3 For being empty himself he giveth empty answers to empty enquirers; for what-ever enquiry may be made of him, he answereth according to the emptiness of the man. But he speaketh also some true words; for the devil filleth him with his own spirit, if so be he shall be able to break down some of the righteous.

1[43]:4 So many therefore as are strong in the faith of the Lord, clothed with the truth, cleave not to such spirits, but hold aloof from them; but as many as are doubters and frequently change their minds, practice soothsaying like the Gentiles, and bring upon themselves greater sin by their idolatries. For he that consulteth a false prophet on any matter is an idolater and emptied of the truth, and senseless.

1[43]:5 For no Spirit given of God needeth to be consulted; but, having the power of deity, speaketh all things of itself, because it is from above, even from the power of the divine Spirit.

1[43]:6 But the spirit which is consulted, and speaketh according to the desires of men, is earthly and fickle, having no power; and it speaketh not at all, unless it be consulted."

1[43]:7 "How then, Sir," say I, "shall a man know who of them is a prophet, and who a false prophet?" "Hear," saith he, "concerning both the prophets; and, as I shall tell thee, so shalt thou test the prophet and the false prophet. By his life test the man that hath the divine Spirit.

1[43]:8 In the first place, he that hath the [divine] Spirit, which is from above, is gentle and tranquil and humble-minded, and abstaineth from all wickedness and vain desire of this present world, and holdeth himself inferior to all men, and giveth no answer to any man when enquired of, nor speaketh in solitude (for neither doth the Holy Spirit speak when a man wisheth Him to speak); but the man speaketh then when God wisheth him to speak.

1[43]:9 When then the man who hath the divine Spirit cometh into an assembly of righteous men, who have faith in a divine Spirit, and intercession is made to God by the gathering of those men, then the angel of the prophetic spirit, who is attached to him, filleth the man, and the man, being filled with the Holy Spirit, speaketh to the multitude, according as the Lord willeth.

1[43]:10 In this way then the Spirit of the deity shall be manifest. This then is the greatness of the power as touching the Spirit of the deity of the Lord.

1[43]:11 Hear now," saith he, "concerning the earthly and vain spirit, which hath no power but is foolish.

1[43]:12 In the first place, that man who seemeth to have a spirit exalteth himself, and desireth to have a chief place, and straight-way he is impudent and shameless and talkative and conversant in many luxuries and in many other deceits and receiveth money for his prophesying, and if he receiveth not, he prophesieth not. Now can a divine Spirit receive money and prophesy? It is not possible for a prophet of God to do this, but the spirit of such prophets is earthly.

1[43]:13 In the next place, it never approacheth an assembly of righteous men; but avoideth them, and cleaveth to the doubtful-minded and empty, and prophesieth to them in corners, and deceiveth them, speaking all things in emptiness to gratify their desires; for they too are empty whom it answereth. For the empty vessel placed together with the empty is not broken, but they agree one with the other.

1[43]:14 But when he comes into an assembly full of righteous men who have a Spirit of deity, and intercession is made from them, that man is emptied, and the earthly spirit fleeth from him in fear, and that man is struck dumb and is altogether broken in pieces, being unable to utter a word.

1[43]:15 For, if you pack wine or oil into a closet, and place an empty vessel among them, and again desire to unpack the closet, the vessel which you place there empty, empty in like manner you will find it. Thus also the empty prophets, whenever they come unto the spirits of righteous men, are found just such as they came.

1[43]:16 I have given thee the life of both kinds of prophets. Therefore test, by his life and his works, the man who says that he is moved by the Spirit.

1[43]:17 But do thou trust the Spirit that cometh from God, and hath power; but in the earthly and empty spirit put no trust at all; for in it there is no power, for it cometh from the devil.

1[43]:18 Listen [then] to the parable which I shall tell thee. Take a stone, and throw it up to heaven--see if thou canst reach it; or again, take a squirt of water, and squirt it up to heaven--see if thou canst bore through the heaven."

1[43]:19 "How, Sir," say I, "can these things be? For both these things which thou hast mentioned are beyond our power." "Well then," saith he, "just as these things are beyond our power, so likewise the earthly spirits have no power and are feeble.

1[43]:20 Now take the power which cometh from above. The hail is a very, small grain, and yet, when it falleth on a man's head, what pain it causeth! Or again, take a drop which falls on the ground from the tiles, and bores through the stone.

1[43]:21 Thou seest then that the smallest things from above falling on the earth have great power. So likewise the divine Spirit coming from above is powerful. This Spirit therefore trust, but from the other hold aloof."

Hermas 1[44]:Heading Mandate 12

1[44]:1 He saith to me; "Remove from thyself all evil desire, and clothe thyself in the desire which is good and holy; for clothed with this desire thou shalt hate the evil desire, and shalt bridle and direct it as thou wilt.

1[44]:2 For the evil desire is wild, and only tamed with difficulty; for it is terrible, and by its wildness is very costly to men; more especially if a servant of God get entangled in it, and have no understanding, he is put to fearful costs by it. But it is costly to such men as are not clothed in the good desire, but are mixed up with this life "These men then it hands over to death."

1[44]:3 "Of what sort, Sir," say I, "are the works of the evil desire, which hand over men to death? Make them known to me, that I may hold aloof from them." Listen," [saith he,] "through what works the evil desire bringeth death to the servants of God.

2[45]:1 "Before all is desire for the wife or husband of another, and for extravagance of wealth, and for many needless dainties, and for drinks and other luxuries, many and foolish. For even luxury is foolish and vain for the servants of God.

2[45]:2 These desires then are evil, and bring death to the servants of God. For this evil desire is a daughter of the devil. Ye must, therefore, abstain from the evil desires, that so abstaining ye may live unto God.

2[45]:3 But as many as are mastered by them, and resist them not, are done to death utterly; for these desires are deadly.

2[45]:4 But do thou clothe thyself in the desire of righteousness, and, having armed thyself with the fear of the Lord, resist them. For the fear of God dwelleth in the good desire. If the evil desire shall see thee armed with the fear of God and resisting itself, it shall flee far from thee, and shall no more be seen of thee, being in fear of thine arms.

2[45]:5 Do thou therefore, when thou art crowned for thy victory over it, come to the desire of righteousness, and deliver to her the victor's prize which thou hast received, and serve her, according as she herself desireth. If thou serve the good desire, and art subject to her, thou shalt have power to master the evil desire, and to subject her, according as thou wilt."

3[46]:1 "I would fain know, Sir," say I, "in what ways I ought to serve the good desire." "Listen," saith he; "practice righteousness and virtue, truth and the fear of the Lord, faith and gentleness, and as many good deeds as are like these. Practicing these thou shalt be well-pleasing as a servant of God, and shalt live unto Him; yea, and every one who shall serve the good desire shall live unto God."

3[46]:2 So he completed the twelve commandments, and he saith to me; Thou hast these commandments; walk in them, and exhort thy hearers that their repentance may become pure for the rest of the days of their life.

3[46]:3 This ministration, which I give thee, fulfill thou with all diligence to the end, and thou shalt effect much. For thou shalt find favor among those who are about to repent, and they shall obey thy words. For I will be with thee, and will compel them to obey thee."

3[46]:4 I say to him; "Sir, these commandments are great and beautiful and glorious, and are able to gladden the heart of the man who is able to observe them. But I know not whether these commandments can be kept by a man, for they are very hard." Hermas 3[46]:5 He answered and said unto me; "If thou set it before thyself that they can be kept, thou wilt easily keep them, and they will not be hard; but if it once enter into thy heart that they cannot be kept by a man, thou wilt not keep them.

3[46]:6 But now I say unto thee; if thou keep them not. but neglect them thou shalt not have salvation, neither thy children nor thy household, since thou hast already pronounced judgment against thyself that these commandments cannot be kept by a man."

4[47]:1 And these things he said to me very angrily, so that I was confounded, and feared him exceedingly; for his form was changed, so that a man could not endure his anger.

4[47]:2 And when he saw that I was altogether disturbed and confounded, he began to speak more kindly [and cheerfully] to me, and he saith; "Foolish fellow, void of understanding and of doubtful mind, perceivest thou not the glory of God, how great and mighty and marvelous it is, how that He created the world for man's sake, and subjected all His creation to man, and gave all authority to him, that he should be master over all things under the heaven?

4[47]:3 If then," [he saith,] "man is lord of all the creatures of God and mastereth all things, cannot he also master these commandments Aye," saith he, "the man that hath the Lord in his heart can master [all things and] all these commandments.

4[47]:4 But they that have the Lord on their lips, while their heart is hardened, and are far from the Lord, to them these commandments are hard and inaccessible.

4[47]:5 Therefore do ye, who are empty and fickle in the faith, set your Lord in your heart, and ye shall perceive that nothing is easier than these commandments, nor sweeter, nor more gentle.

4[47]:6 Be ye converted, ye that walk after the commandments of the devil, (the commandments which are so) difficult and bitter and wild and riotous; and fear not the devil, for there is no power in him against you.

4[47]:7 For I will be with you, I, the angel of repentance, who have the mastery over him. The devil hath fear alone, but his fear hath no force. Fear him not therefore; and he will flee from you."

5[48]:1 I say to him, "Sir, listen to a few words from me." "Say what thou wilt," saith he. "Man, Sir," I say, "is eager to keep the commandments of God, and there is no one that asketh not of the Lord that he may be strengthened in His commandments, and be subject to them; but the devil is hard and overmastereth them."

5[48]:2 "He cannot," saith he, "overmaster the servants of God, who set their hope on Him with their whole heart. The devil can wrestle with them, but he cannot overthrow them. If then ye resist him, he will be vanquished and will flee from you disgraced. But as many," saith he, "as are utterly empty, fear the devil as if he had power.

5[48]:3 When a man has filled amply sufficient jars with good wine, and among these jars a few are quite empty, he comes to the jars, and does not examine the full ones, for he knows that they are full; but he examineth the empty ones, fearing lest they have turned sour. For empty jars soon turn sour, and the taste of the wine is spoilt.

5[48]:4 So also the devil cometh to all the servants of God tempting them. As many then as are complete in the faith, oppose him mightily, and he departeth from them, not having a place where he can find an entrance. So he cometh next to the empty ones, and finding a place goeth into them, and further he doeth what he willeth in them, and they become submissive slaves to him.

6[49]:1 "But I, the angel of repentance, say unto you; Fear not the devil; for I was sent," saith he, "to be with you who repent with your whole heart, and to strengthen you in the faith.

6[49]:2 Believe, therefore, on God, ye who by reason of your sins have despaired of your life, and are adding to your sins, and weighing down your life; for if ye turn unto the Lord with your whole heart, and work righteousness the remaining days of your life, and serve Him rightly according to His will, He will give healing to your former sins, and ye shall have power to master the works of the devil. But of the threatening of the devil fear not at all; for he is unstrung, like the sinews of a dead man.

6[49]:3 Hear me therefore, and fear Him, Who is able to do all things, to save and to destroy, and observe these commandments, and ye shall live unto God."

6[49]:4 I say to him, "Sir, now am I strengthened in all the ordinances of the Lord, because thou art with me; and I know that thou wilt crush all the power of the devil, and we shall be masters over him, and shall prevail over all his works. And I hope, Sir, that I am now able to keep these commandments which thou hast commanded, the Lord enabling me."

6[49]:5 "Thou shalt keep them," saith he, "if thy heart be found pure with the Lord; yea, and all shall keep them, as many as shall purify their hearts from the vain desires of this world, and shall live unto God."

Hermas 1[50]:Heading Parables Which He Spake With Me

1[50]:1 He saith to me; "Ye know that ye, who are the servants of God, are dwelling in a foreign land; for your city is far from this city. If then ye know your city, in which ye shall dwell, why do ye here prepare fields and expensive displays and buildings and dwelling-chambers which are superfluous?

1[50]:2 He, therefore, that prepareth these things for this city does not purpose to return to his own city.

1[50]:3 O foolish and double-minded and miserable man, perceivest thou not that all these things are foreign, and are under the power of another For the lord of this city shall say, "I do not wish thee to dwell in my city; go forth from this city, for thou dost not conform to my laws."

1[50]:4 Thou, therefor who hast fields and dwellings and many other possessions, when thou art cast out by him, what wilt thou do with thy field and thy house am all the other things that thou preparedst for thyself? For the lord of this country saith to thee justly, "Either conform to my laws, or depart from my country."

1[50]:5 What then shalt thou do, who art under law in thine own city? For the sake of thy fields and the rest of thy possessions wilt thou altogether repudiate thy law, and walk according to the law of this city? Take heed, lest it be inexpedient to repudiate the law; for if thou shouldest desire to return again to thy city, thou shall surely not be received [because thou didst repudiate the law of the city], and shalt be shut out from it.

1[50]:6 Take heed therefore; as dwelling in a strange land prepare nothing more for thyself but a competency which is sufficient for thee, and make ready that, whensoever the master of this city may desire to cast thee out for thine opposition to his law, thou mayest go forth from his city and depart into thine own city and use thine own law joyfully, free from all insult.

1[50]:7 Take heed therefore, ye that serve God and have Him in your heart: work the "works of God being mindful of His commandments and of the promises which He made, and believe Him that He will perform them, if His commandments be kept.

1[50]:8 Therefore, instead of
fields buy ye souls that are in trouble, as each is able, and visit widows and orphans, and neglect them not; and spend your riches and all your displays, which ye received from God, on fields and houses of this kind.

1[50]:9 For to this end the Master enriched you, that ye might perform these ministrations for Him. It is much better to purchase fields [and possessions] and houses of this kind, which thou wilt find in thine own city, when thou visitest it.

1[50]:10 This lavish expenditure is beautiful and joyous, not bringing sadness or fear, but bringing joy. The expenditure of the heathen then practice not ye; for it is not convenient for you the servants of God.

1[50]:11 But practice your own expenditure, in which ye can rejoice; and do not corrupt, neither touch that which is another man's, nor lust after it for it is wicked to lust after other men's possessions. But perform thine own task, and thou shalt be saved."

Hermas 1[51]:Heading Another Parable

1[51]:1 As I walked in the field, and noticed an elm and a vine, and was distinguishing them and their fruits, the shepherd appeareth to me and saith; "What art thou meditating within thyself?" "I am thinking, [Sir,]" say I, "about the elm and the vine, that they are excellently suited the one to the other."

1[51]:2 "These two trees," saith he, "are appointed for a type to the servants of God." "I would fain know, [Sir,]" say I, "the type contained in these trees, of which thou speakest." "Seest thou," saith he, "the elm and the vine ?" "I see them, Sir," say I.

1[51]:3 "This vine," saith he, "beareth fruit, but the elm is an unfruitful stock. Yet this vine, except it climb up the elm, cannot bear much fruit when it is spread on the ground; and such fruit as it beareth is rotten, because it is not suspended upon the elm. When then the vine is attached to the elm, it beareth fruit both from itself and from the elm.

1[51]:4 Thou seest then that the elm also beareth [much] fruit, not less than the vine, but rather more." How more, Sir?" say I. "Because," saith he, "the vine, when hanging upon the elm, bears its fruit in abundance, and in good condition; but, when spread on the ground, it beareth little fruit, and that rotten. This parable therefore is applicable to the servants of God, to poor and to rich alike."

1[51]:5 "How, Sir?" say I; "instruct me." "Listen," saith he; the rich man hath much wealth, but in the things of the Lord he is poor, being distracted about his riches, and his confession and intercession with the Lord is very scanty; and even that which he giveth is mall and weak and hath not power above. When then the rich man goeth up to the poor, and assisteth him in his needs, believing that for what he doth to the poor man he shall be able to obtain a reward with God--because the poor man is rich in intercession [and confession], and his intercession hath great power with God--the rich man then supplieth all things to the poor man without wavering.

1[51]:6 But the poor man being supplied by the rich maketh intercession for him, thanking God for him that gave to him. And the other is still more zealous to assist the poor man, that he may be continuous in his life: for he knoweth that the intercession of the poor man is acceptable and rich before God.

1[51]:7 They both then accomplish their work; the poor man maketh intercession, wherein he is rich [which he received of the Lord]; this he rendereth again to the Lord Who supplieth him with it. The rich man too in like manner furnisheth to the poor man, nothing doubting, the riches which he received from the Lord. And this work great and acceptable with God, because (the rich man) hath understanding concerning his riches, and worketh for the poor man from the bounties of the Lord, and accomplisheth the ministration of the Lord rightly.

1[51]:8 In the sight of men then the elm seemeth not to bear fruit, and they know not, neither perceive, that if there cometh a drought the elm having water nurtureth the vine, and the vine having a constant supply of water beareth fruit two fold, both for itself and for the elm. So likewise the poor, by interceding with the Lord for the rich, establish their riches, and again the rich, supplying their needs to the poor, establish their souls.

1[51]:9 So then both are made partners in the righteous work. He then that doeth these things shall not be abandoned of God, but shall be written in the books of the living.

1[51]:10 Blessed are the rich, who understand also that they are enriched from the Lord. For they that have this mind shall be able to do some good work."

Hermas 1[52]:Heading Another Parable

1[52]:1 He showed me many trees which had no leaves, but they seemed to me to be, as it were, withered; for they were all alike. And he saith to me; "Seest thou these trees?" "I see them, Sir," I say, "they are all alike, and are withered." He answered and said to me; "These trees that thou seest are they that dwell in this world."

1[52]:2 "Wherefore then, Sir," say I, "are they as if they were withered, and alike?" "Because," saith he, "neither the righteous are distinguishable, nor the sinners in this world, but they are alike. For this world is winter to the righteous, and they are not distinguishable, as they dwell with the sinners.

1[52]:3 For as in the winter the trees, having shed their leaves, are alike, and are not distinguishable, which are withered, and which alive, so also in this world neither the just nor the sinners are distinguishable, but they are all alike."

Hermas 1[53]:Heading Another Parable

1[53]:1 He showed me many trees again, some of them sprouting, and others withered, and he saith to me; "Seest thou," saith he, "these trees?" "I see them, Sir," say I, "some of them sprouting, and others withered."

1[53]:2 "These trees," saith he, "that are sprouting are the righteous, who shall dwell in the world to come; for the world to come is summer to the righteous, but winter to the sinners. When then the mercy of the Lord shall shine forth, then they that serve God shall be made manifest; yea, and all men shall be made manifest.

1[53]:3 For as in summer the fruits of each several tree are made manifest, and are recognized of what sort they are, so also the fruits of the righteous shall be manifest, and all [even the very smallest] shall be known to be flourishing in that world.

1[53]:4 But the Gentiles and the sinners, just as thou sawest the trees which were withered, even such shall they be found, withered and unfruitful in that world, and shall be burnt up as fuel, and shall be manifest, because their practice in their life hath been evil. For the sinners shall be burned, because they sinned and repented not; and the Gentiles shall be burned, because they knew not Him that created them.

1[53]:5 Do thou therefore bear fruit, that in that summer thy fruit may be known. But abstain from overmuch business, and thou shalt never fill into any sin. For they that busy themselves overmuch, sin much also, being distracted about their business, and in no wise serving their own Lord.

1[53]:6 How then," saith he, "can such a man ask anything of the Lord and receive it, seeing that he serveth not the Lord? [For] they that serve Him, these shall receive their petitions, but they that serve not the Lord, these shall receive nothing.

1[53]:7 But if any one work one single action, he is able also to serve the Lord; for his mind shall not be corrupted from (following) the Lord, but he shall serve Him, because he keepeth his mind pure.

1[53]:8 If therefore thou doest these things, thou shalt be able to bear fruit unto the world to come; yea, and whosoever shall do these things, shall bear fruit."

Hermas 1[54]:1 Another Parable

1[54]:1 As I was fasting and seated on a certain mountain, and giving thanks to the Lord for all that He had done unto me, I see the shepherd seated by me and saying; "Why hast thou come hither in the early morn?" "Because, Sir," say I, "I am keeping a station."

1[54]:2 "What," saith he, "is a station?" "I am fasting, Sir," say I. "And what," saith he, "is this fast [that ye are fasting]?" "As I was accustomed, Sir," say I, "so I fast."

1[54]:3 "Ye know not," saith he, "how to fast unto the Lord, neither is this a fast, this unprofitable fast which ye make unto Him." "wherefore, Sir," say I, "sayest thou this?" "I tell thee," saith he, "that this is not a fast, wherein ye think to fast; but I will teach thee what is a complete fast and acceptable to the Lord. Listen," saith he;

1[54]:4 "God desireth not such a vain fast; for by so fasting unto God thou shalt do nothing for righteousness. But fast thou [unto God] such a fast as this;

1[54]:5 do no wickedness in thy life, and serve the Lord with a pure heart; observe His commandments and walk in His ordinances, and let no evil desire rise up in thy heart; but believe God. Then, if thou shalt do these things, and fear Him, and control thyself from every evil deed, thou shalt live unto God; and if thou do these things, thou shalt accomplish a great fast, and one acceptable to God.

Hermas 2[55]:1 "Hear the parable which I shall tell thee relating to fasting.

2[55]:2 A certain man had an estate, and many slaves, and a portion of his estate he planted as a vineyard; and choosing out a certain slave who was trusty and well-pleasing (and) held in honor, he called him to him and saith unto him; "Take this vineyard [which I have planted], and fence it [till I come], but do nothing else to the vineyard. Now keep this my commandment, and thou shalt be free in my house." Then the master of the servant went away to travel abroad.

2[55]:3 When then he had gone away, the servant took and fenced the vineyard; and having finished the fencing of the vineyard, he noticed that the vineyard was full of weeds.

2[55]:4 So he reasoned within himself, saying, "This command of my lord I have carried out I will next dig this vineyard, and it shall be neater when it is digged; and when it hath no weeds it will yield more fruit, because not choked by the weeds." He took and digged the vineyard, and all the weeds that were in the vineyard he plucked up. And that vineyard became very neat and flourishing, when it had no weeds to choke it.

2[55]:5 After a time the master of the servant [and of the estate] came, and he went into the vineyard. And seeing the vineyard fenced neatly, and digged as well, and [all] the weeds plucked up, and the vines flourishing, he rejoiced [exceedingly] at what his servant had done.

2[55]:6 So he called his beloved son, who was his heir, and the friends who were his advisers, and told them what he had commanded his servant, and how much he had found done. And they rejoiced with the servant at the testimony which his master had borne to him.

2[55]:7 And he saith to them; "I promised this servant his freedom, if he should keep the commandment which I commanded him; but he kept my commandment and did a good work besides to my vineyard, and pleased me greatly. For this work therefore which he has done, I desire to make him joint-heir with my son, because, when the good thought struck him, he did not neglect it, but fulfilled it."

2[55]:8 In this purpose the son of the master agreed with him, that the servant should be made joint-heir with the son.

2[55]:9 After some few days, his master made a feast, and sent to him many dainties from the feast. But when the servant received [the dainties sent to him by the master], he took what was sufficient for him, and distributed the rest to his fellow servants.

2[55]:10 And his fellow-servants, when they received the dainties, rejoiced, and began to pray for him, that he might find greater favor with the master, because he had treated them so handsomely.

2[55]:11 All these things which had taken place his master heard, and again rejoiced greatly at his deed. So the master called together again his friends and his son, and announced to them the deed that he had done with regard to his dainties which he had received; and they still more approved of his resolve, that his servant should be made joint-heir with his son."

3[56]:1 I say, "Sir, I understand not these parables, neither can I apprehend them, unless thou explain them for me."

3[56]:2 "I will explain everything to thee," saith he; "and will show thee whatsoever things I shall speak with thee. Keep the commandments of the Lord, and thou shalt be well-pleasing to God, and shalt be enrolled among the number of them that keep His commandments.

3[56]:3 But if thou do any good thing outside the commandment of God, thou shalt win for thyself more exceeding glory, and shalt be more glorious in the sight of God than thou wouldest otherwise have been. If then, while thou keepest the commandments of God, thou add these services likewise, thou shalt rejoice, if thou observe them according to my commandment."

3[56]:4 I say to him, "Sir, whatsoever thou commandest me, I will keep it; for I know that thou art with me." "I will be with thee," saith he, "because

thou hast so great zeal for doing good; yea, and I will be with all," saith he, "whosoever have such zeal as this.

3[56]:5 This fasting," saith he, "if the commandments of the Lord are kept, is very good. This then is the way, that thou shalt keep this fast which thou art about to observe].

3[56]:6 First of all, keep

thyself from every evil word and every evil desire, and purify thy heart from all the vanities of this world. If thou keep these things, this fast shall be perfect for thee.

3[56]:7 And thus shalt thou do. Having fulfilled what is written, on that day on which thou fastest thou shalt taste nothing but bread and water; and from thy meats, which thou wouldest have eaten, thou shalt reckon up the amount of that day's expenditure, which thou wouldest have incurred, and shalt give it to a widow, or an orphan, or to one in want, and so shalt thou humble thy soul, that he that hath received from thy humiliation may satisfy his own soul, and may pray for thee to the Lord.

3[56]:8 If then thou shalt so accomplish this fast, as I have commanded thee, thy sacrifice shall be acceptable in the sight of God, and this fasting shall be recorded; and the service so performed is beautiful and joyous and acceptable to the Lord.

3[56]:9 These things thou shalt so observe, thou and thy children and thy whole household; and, observing them, thou shalt be blessed; yea, and all those, who shall hear and observe them, shall be blessed, and whatsoever things they shall ask of the Lord, they shall receive."

4[57]:1 I entreated him earnestly, that he would show me the parable of the estate, and of the   master, and of the vineyard, and of the servant that fenced the vineyard, [and of the fence,] and of the weeds which were plucked up out of the vineyard, and of the son, and of the friends, the advisers. For I understood that all these things are a parable.

4[57]:2 But he answered and said unto me; "Thou art exceedingly impor-tunate in enquiries. Thou oughtest not," [saith he,] "to make any enquiry at all; for if it be right that a thing be explained unto thee, it shall be explained." I say to him; "Sir, whatsoever things thou showest unto me and dost not ex-plain, I shall have seen them in vain, and without understanding what they are. In like manner also, if thou speak parables to me and interpret them not, I shall have heard a thing in vain from thee."

4[57]:3 But he again answered, and said unto me; "Whosoever," saith he, "is a servant of God, and hath his own Lord in his heart, asketh understanding of Him, and receiveth it, and interpreteth every parable, and the words of the Lord which are spoken in parables are made known unto him. But as many as are sluggish and idle in intercession, these hesitate to ask of the Lord.

4[57]:4 But the Lord is abundant in compassion, and giveth to them that ask of Him without ceasing. But thou who hast been strengthened by the holy angel, and hast received from him such (powers of intercession and art not idle, wherefore dost thou not ask understanding of the Lord, and obtain it from Him)."

4[57]:5 I say to him, "Sir, I that have thee with me have (but) need to ask thee and enquire of thee; for thou showest me all things, and speakest with me; but if I had seen or heard them apart from thee I should have asked of the Lord, that they might be shown to me."

5[58]:1 "I told thee just now," saith he, "that thou art unscrupulous and importunate, in enquiring for the interpretations of the parables. But since thou art so obstinate, I will interpret to thee the parable of the estate and all the accompaniments thereof, that thou mayest make them known unto all. Hear now," saith he, "and understand them.

5[58]:2 The estate is this world, and the lord of the estate is He that created all things, and set them in order, and endowed them with power; and the servant is the Son of God, and the vines are this people whom He Himself planted;

5[58]:3 and the fences are the [holy] angels of the Lord who keep together His people; and the weeds, which are plucked up from the vineyard, are the transgressions of the servants of God; and the dainties which He sent to him from the feast are the commandments which He gave to His people through His Son; and the friends and advisers are the holy angels which were first created; and the absence of the master is the time which remaineth over until His coming."

5[58]:4 I say to him; "Sir, great and marvelous are all things and all things are glorious; was it likely then," say I, "that I could have apprehended them?" "Nay, nor can any other man, though he be full of understanding, apprehend them." "Yet again, Sir," say I, "explain to me what I am about to enquire of thee."

5[58]:5 "Say on," he saith, "if thou desirest anything." "Wherefore, Sir,]" say I, "is the Son of God represented in the parable in the guise of a servant?"

6[59]:1 "Listen," said he; "the Son of God is not represented in the guise of a servant, but is represented in great power and lordship." "How, Sir?" say I; "I comprehend not."

6[59]:2 "Because," saith he, "God planted the vineyard, that is, He created the people, and delivered them over to His Son. And the Son placed the angels in charge of them, to watch over them; and the Son Himself cleansed their sins, by laboring much and enduring many toils; for no one can dig without toil or labor.

6[59]:3 Having Himself then cleansed the sins of His people, He showed them the paths of life, giving them the law which He received from His Father. Thou seest," saith he, "that He is Himself Lord of the people, having received all power from His Father.

6[59]:4 But how that the lord took his son and the glorious angels as advisers concerning the inheritance of the servant, listen.

6[59]:5 The Holy Pre-existent Spirit. Which created the whole creation, God made to dwell in flesh that He desired. This flesh, therefore, in which the Holy Spirit dwelt, was subject unto the Spirit, walking honorably in holiness and purity, without in any way defiling the Spirit.

6[59]:6 When then it had lived honorably in chastity, and had labored with the Spirit, and had cooperated with it in everything, behaving itself boldly and bravely, He chose it as a partner with the Holy Spirit; for the career of this flesh pleased [the Lord], seeing that, as possessing the Holy Spirit, it was not defiled upon the earth.

6[59]:7 He therefore took the son as adviser and the glorious angels also, that this flesh too, having served the Spirit unblamably, might have some place of sojourn, and might not seem to hare lost the reward for its service; for all flesh, which is found undefiled and unspotted, wherein the Holy Spirit dwelt, shall receive a reward.

6[59]:8 Now thou hast the interpretation of this parable also."

7[60]:1 "I was right glad, Sir," say I, "to hear this interpretation." "Listen now," saith he, "Keep this thy flesh pure and undefiled, that the Spirit which dwelleth in it may bear witness to it, and thy flesh may be justified.

7[60]:2 See that it never enter into thine heart that this flesh of thine is perishable, and so thou abuse it in some defilement. [For] if thou defile thy flesh, thou shalt defile the Holy Spirit also; but if thou defile the flesh, thou shalt not live."

7[60]:3 "But if, Sir," say I, "there has been any ignorance in times past, before these words were heard, how shall a man who has defiled his flesh be saved?" "For the former deeds of ignorance," saith he, "God alone hath power to give healing; for all authority is His.

7[60]:4 [But now keep thyself, and the Lord Almighty, Who is full of compassion, will give healing for thy former deeds of ignorance,] if henceforth thou defile not thy flesh, neither the Spirit; for both share in common, and the one cannot be defiled without the other. Therefore keep both pure, and thou shalt live unto God."

Hermas 1[61]:Heading Parable 6

1[61]:1 As I sat in my house, and glorified the Lord for all things that I had seen, and was considering concerning the commandments, how that they were beautiful and powerful and gladsome and glorious and able to save a man's soul, I said within myself; "Blessed shall I be, if I walk in these commandments; yea, and whosoever shall walk in them shall be blessed."

1[61]:2 As I spake these things within myself, I see him suddenly seated by me, and saying as follows; "Why art thou of a doubtful mind concerning the commandments, which I commanded thee? They are beautiful. Doubt not at all; but clothe thyself in the faith of the Lord, and thou shalt walk in them. For I will strengthen thee in them.

1[61]:3 These commandments are suitable for those who meditate repentance; for if they walk not in them, their repentance is in vain.

1[61]:4 Ye then that repent, cast away the evil doings of this world which crush you; and, by putting on every excellence of righteousness, ye shall be able to observe these commandments, and to add no more to your sins. If then ye add no further sin at all, ye will depart from your former sins. Walk then in these my commandments, and ye shall live unto God. These things have [all] been told you from me."

1[61]:5 And after he had told these things to me, he saith to me, "Let us go into the country, and I will show thee the shepherds of the sheep." "Let us go, Sir," say I. And we came to a certain plain, and he showeth me a young man, a shepherd, clothed in a light cloak, of saffron color; Hermas

1[61]:6 and he was feeding a great number of sheep, and these sheep were, as it were, well fed and very frisky, and were gladsome as they skipped about hither and thither; and the shepherd himself was all gladsome over his flock; and the very visage of the shepherd was exceedingly gladsome; and he ran about among the sheep.

2[62]:1 And he saith to me; "Seest thou this shepherd?" "I see him Sir," I say. "This," saith he, "is the angel of self-indulgence and of deceit. He crusheth the souls of the servants of God, and perverteth them from the truth, leading them astray with evil desires, wherein they perish.

2[62]:2 For they forget the commandments of the living God, and walk in vain deceits and acts of self-indulgence, and are destroyed by this angel, some of them unto death, and others unto corruption."

2[62]:3 I say to him, "Sir, I comprehend not what means "unto death," and what "unto corruption". "Listen," saith he; "the sheep which thou sawest gladsome and skipping about, these are they who have been turned asunder from God utterly, and have delivered themselves over to the lusts of this world. In these, therefore, there is not repentance unto life. For the Name of God is being blasphemed through them. The life of such persons is death.

2[62]:4 But the sheep, which thou sawest not skipping about, but feeding in one place, these are they that have delivered themselves over to acts of self-indulgence and deceit, but have not uttered any blasphemy against the Lord. These then have been corrupted from the truth. In these there is hope of repentance, wherein they can live. Corruption then hath hope of a possible renewal, but death hath eternal destruction."

2[62]:5 Again we went forward a little way, and he showeth me a great shepherd like a wild man in appearance, with a white goatskin thrown about him; and he had a kind of wallet on his shoulders, and a staff very hard and with knots in it, and a great whip. And his look was very sour, so that I was afraid of him because of his look.

2[62]:6 This shepherd then kept receiving from the young man, the shepherd, those sheep that were frisky and well fed, but not skipping about, and putting them in a certain spot, which was precipitous and covered with thorns and briars, so that the sheep could not disentangle themselves from the thorns and briars, but [became entangled among the thorns and briars.

2[62]:7 And so they] pastured entangled in the thorns and briars, and were in great misery with being beaten by him; and he kept driving them about to and fro, and giving them no rest, and all together those sheep had not a happy time.

3[63]:1 When then I saw them so lashed with the whip and vexed, I was sorry for their sakes, because they were so tortured and had no rest at all.

3[63]:2 I say to the shepherd who was speaking with me; "Sir, who is this shepherd, who is [so] hard-hearted and severe, and has no compassion at all for these sheep?" "This," saith he, "is the angel of punishment, and he is one of the just angels, and presides over punishment.

3[63]:3 So he receiveth those who wander away from God, and walk after the lusts and deceits of this life, and punisheth them, as they deserve, with fearful and various punishments."

3[63]:4 "I would fain learn, Sir," said I, "of what sort are these various punishments." "Listen," saith he; "the various tortures and punishments are tortures belonging to the present life; for some are punished with losses, and others with want, and others with divers maladies, and others with [every kind] of unsettlement, and others with insults from unworthy persons and with suffering in many other respects.

3[63]:5 For many, being unsettled in their plans, set their hands to many things, and nothing ever goes forward with them. And then they say that they do not prosper in their doings, and it doth not enter into their hearts that they have done evil deeds, but they blame the Lord.

3[63]:6 When then they are afflicted with every kind of affliction, then they are delivered over to me for good instruction, and are strengthened in the faith of the Lord, and serve the Lord with a pure heart the remaining days of their life. But, if they repent, the evil works which they have done rise up in their hearts, and then they glorify God, saying that He is a just Judge, and that they suffered justly each according to his doings. And they serve the Lord thenceforward with a pure heart, and are prosperous in all their doings, receiving from the Lord whatsoever things they may ask; and then they glorify the Lord because they were delivered over unto me, and they no longer suffer any evil thing."

4[63]:1 I say unto him; "Sir, declare unto me this further matter." "What enquirest thou yet?" saith he. "Whether, Sir," say I, "they that live in self-indulgence and are deceived undergo torments during the same length of time as they live in self-indulgence and are deceived." He saith to me, "They undergo torments for the same length of time."

4[63]:2 "Then, Sir," say I, "they undergo very slight torments; for those who are living thus in self-indulgence and forget God ought to have been tormented seven-fold."

4[63]:3 He saith to me, "Thou art foolish, and comprehendest not the power of the torment" "True," say I, "for if I had comprehended it, I should not have asked thee to declare it to me." "Listen," saith he, "to the power of both, [of the self-indulgence and of the torment].

4[63]:4 The time of the self-indulgence and deceit is one hour. But an hour of the torment hath the power of thirty days. If then one live in self indulgence and be deceived for one day, and be tormented for one day, the day of the torment is equivalent to a whole year. For as many days then as a man lives in self-indulgence, for so many years is he tormented. Thou seest then," saith he, "that the time of the self-indulgence and deceit is very short, but the time of the punishment and torment is long."

5[65]:1 "Inasmuch, Sir," say I, "as I do not quite comprehend concerning the time of the deceit and self-indulgence and torment, show me more clearly."

5[65]:2 He answered and said unto me; "Thy stupidity cleaveth to thee;

and thou wilt not cleanse thy heart and serve God Take heed," [saith he,] "lest haply the time be fulfilled, and thou be found in thy foolishness. Listen then," [saith he,] "even as thou wishest, that thou mayest comprehend the matter.

5[65]:3 He that liveth in self-indulgence and is deceived for one day, and doeth what he wisheth, is clothed in much folly and comprehendeth not the thing which he doeth; for on the morrow he forgetteth what he did the day before. For self-indulgence and deceit have no memories, by reason of the folly, wherewith each is clothed; but when punishment and torment cling to a man for a single day, he is punished and tormented for a whole year long; for punishment and torment have long memories.

5[65]:4 So being tormented and punished for the whole year, the man remembers at length the self-indulgence and deceit, and perceiveth that it is on their account that he is suffering these ills. Every man, therefore, that liveth in self-indulgence and is deceived, is tormented in this way because, though possessing lire, they have delivered themselves over unto death."

5[65]:5 "What kinds of self-indulgence, Sir," say I, "are harmful?" "Every action," saith he, "is self-indulgence to a man, which he does with pleasure; for the irascible man, when he gives the reins to his passion, is self-indulgent; and the adulterer and the drunkard and the slanderer and the liar and the miser and the defrauder and he that doeth things akin to these, giveth the reins to his peculiar passion; therefore he is self-indulgent in his action.

5[65]:6 All these habits of self-indulgence are harmful to the servants of God; on account of these deceits therefore they so suffer who are punished and tormented.

5[65]:7 But there are habits of self-indulgence like-wise which save men; for many are self-indulgent in doing good, being carried away by the pleasure it gives to themselves. This self-indulgence then is expedient for the servants of God, and bringeth life to a man of this disposition; but the harmful self-indulgences afore-mentioned bring to men torments and punishments; and if they continue in them and repent not, they bring death upon themselves."

Hermas 1[66]:Heading Parable 7

1[66]:1 After a few days I saw him on the same plain, where also I had seen the shepherds, and he saith to me, "What seekest thou?" "I am here, Sir," say I, "that thou mayest bid the shepherd that punisheth go out of my house; for he afflicteth me much." "It is necessary for thee," saith he, "to be afflicted; for so," saith he, "the glorious angel ordered as concerning thee, for he wisheth thee to be proved." "Why, what so evil thing have I done, Sir," say I, "that I should be delivered over to this angel?"

1[66]:2 "Listen," saith he. "Thy sins are many, yet not so many that thou shouldest be delivered over to this angel; but thy house has committed great iniquities and sins, and the glorious angel was embittered at their deeds, and for this cause he bade thee be afflicted for a certain time, that they also might repent and cleanse themselves from every lust of this world. When therefore they shall repent and be cleansed, then shall the angel of punishment depart."

1[66]:3 I say to him; "Sir, if they perpetrated such deeds that the glorious angel is embittered, what have I done?" "They cannot be afflicted otherwise," saith he, "unless thou, the head of the [whole] house, be afflicted; for if thou be afflicted, they also of necessity will be afflicted; but if thou be prosperous, they can suffer no affliction."

1[66]:4 "But behold, Sir," say I, "they have repented with their whole heart." "I am quite aware myself," saith he, "that they have repented with their whole heart; well, thinkest thou that the sins of those who repent are forgiven forthwith? Certainly not; but the person who repents must torture his own soul, and must be thoroughly humble in his every action, and be afflicted with all the divers kinds of affliction; and if he endure the afflictions which come upon him, assuredly He Who created all things and endowed them with power will be moved with compassion and will bestow some remedy.

1[66]:5 And this (will God do), if in any way He perceive the heart of the penitent pure from every evil thing. But it is expedient for thee and for thy house that thou shouldest be afflicted now. But why speak I many words to thee? Thou must be afflicted as the angel of the Lord commanded, even he that delivered thee unto me; and for this give thanks to the Lord, in that He deemed thee worthy that I should reveal unto thee beforehand the affliction, that foreknowing it thou might endure it with fortitude."

1[66]:6 I say to him; "Sir, be thou with me, and I shall be able to endure all affliction [easily]." "I will be with thee," saith he; "and I will ask the angel that punisheth to afflict thee more lightly; but thou shalt be afflicted for a short time, and thou shalt be restored again to thy house. Only continue to be humble and to minister unto the Lord with a pure heart, thou and thy children and thy house, and walk in my commandments which I command thee, and thus it will be possible for thy repentance to be strong and pure.

1[66]:7 And if thou keep these commandments with thy household, all affliction shall hold aloof from thee; yea, and affliction," saith he, "shall hold aloof from all whosoever shall walk in these my commandments."

Hermas 1[67]:Heading Parable 8

1[67]:1 He showed me a [great] willow, overshadowing plains and mountains, and under the shadow of the willow all have come who are called by the name of the Lord.

1[67]:2 And by the willow there stood an angel of the Lord, glorious and very tall, having a great sickle, and he was lopping branches from the willow, and giving them to the people that sheltered beneath the willow; and he gave them little rods about a cubit long.

1[67]:3 And after all had taken the rods, the angel laid aside the sickle, and the tree was sound, just as I had seen it.

1[67]:4 Then I marvelled within myself, saying, "How is the tree sound after so many branches have been lopped off?" The shepherd saith to me, "Marvel not that the tree remained sound, after so many branches were lopped off but wait until thou seest all things, and it shall be shown to thee what it is."

1[67]:5 The angel who gave the rods to the people demanded them back from them again, and according as they had received them, so also they were summoned to him, and each of them returned the several rods. But the angel of the Lord took them, and examined them.

1[67]:6 From some he received the rods withered and eaten as it were by grubs: the angel ordered those who gave up rods like these to stand apart.

1[67]:7 And others gave them up withered, but not grub-eaten; and these again he ordered to stand apart.

1[67]:8 And others gave them up half-withered; these also stood apart.

1[67]:9 And others gave up their rods half-withered and with cracks; these also stood apart.

1[67]:10 And others gave up their rods green and with cracks; these also stood apart. And others gave up their rods one half withered and one half green; these also stood apart.

1[67]:11 And others brought their rods two parts of the rod green, and the third part withered; these also stood apart. And others gave them up two parts withered, and the third part green; these also stood apart.

1[67]:12 And others gave up their rods nearly all green, but a very small portion of their rods was withered, just the end; but they had cracks in them; these also stood apart.

1[67]:13 And in those of others there was a very small portion green, but the rest of the rods was withered; these also stood apart.

1[67]:14 And others came bringing their rods green, as they received them from the angel; and the most part of the multitude gave up their rods in this state; and the angel rejoiced exceedingly at these; these also stood apart.

1[67]:15 And others gave up their rods green and with shoots, these also stood apart; and at these again the angel rejoiced exceedingly.

1[67]:16 And others gave up their rods green and with shoots; and their shoots had, as it were, a kind of fruit. And those men were exceeding gladsome, whose rods were found in this state. And over them the angel exulted, and the shepherd was very gladsome over them.

2[68]:1 And the angel of the Lord commanded crowns to be brought. And crowns were brought, made as it were of palm branches; and he crowned the men that had given up the rods which had the shoots and some fruit, and sent them away into the tower.

2[68]:2 And the others also he sent into the tower, even those who had given up the rods green and with shoots, but the shoots were without fruit; and he set a seal upon them.

2[68]:3 And all they that went into the tower had the same raiment, white as snow.

2[68]:4 And those that had given up their rods green as they received them, he sent away, giving them a [white] robe, and seals.

2[68]:5 After the angel had finished these things, he saith to the shepherd; "I go away; but these thou shalt send away to (their places within) the walls, according as each deserveth to dwell; but examine their rods carefully), and so send them away. But be careful in examining them. Take heed lest any escape thee," saith he. "Still if any escape thee, I will test them at the altar." When he had thus spoken to the shepherd, he departed.

2[68]:6 And, after the angel had departed, the shepherd saith to me; "Let us take the rods of all and plant them, to see whether any of them shall be able to live." I say unto him, "Sir, these withered things, how can they live?"

2[68]:7 He answered and said unto me; "This tree is a willow, and this class of trees clingeth to life. If then the rods shall be planted and get a little moisture, many of them will live. And afterwards let us try to pour some water also over them. If any of them shall be able to live, I will rejoice with it; but if it live not, I at least shall not be found neglectful."

2[68]:8 So the shepherd bade me call them, just as each one of them was stationed. And they came row after row, and they delivered up the rods to the shepherd. And the shepherd took the rods, and planted them in rows, and after he had planted them, he poured much water over them, so that the rods could not be seen for the water.

2[68]:9 And after he had watered the rods, he saith to me; "Let us go now, and after days let us return and inspect all the rods; for He Who created this tree willeth that all those who have received rods from this tree should live. And I myself hope that these little rods, after they have got moisture and been watered, will live the greater part of them."

3[69]:1 I say to him; "Sir, inform me what this tree is. For I am perplexed herewith, because, though so many branches were cut off, the tree is sound, and nothing appears to have been cut from it; I am therefore perplexed thereat."

3[69]:2 "Listen," saith he; "this great tree which overshadows plains and mountains and all the earth is the law of God which was given to the whole world; and this law is the Son of Cod preached unto the ends of the earth. But the people that are under the shadow are they that have heard the preaching, and believed on Him;

3[69]:3 but the great and glorious angel is Michael, who hath the power over this people and is their captain. For this is he that putteth the law into the hearts of the believers; therefore he himself inspecteth them to whom he gave it, to see whether they have observed it.

3[69]:4 But thou seest the rods of every one; for the rods are the law. Thou seest these many rods rendered useless, and thou shalt notice all those that have not observed the law, and shalt see the abode of each severally."

3[69]:5 I say unto him; "Sir, wherefore did he send away some into the tower, and leave others for thee?" "As many," saith he, "as transgressed the law which they received from him, these he left under my authority for repentance; but as many as already satisfied the law and have observed it, these he has under his own authority."

3[69]:6 "Who then, Sir," say I, "are they that have been crowned and go into the tower?" ["As many," saith he, "as wrestled with the devil and overcame him in their wrestling, are crowned:] these are they that suffered for the law.

3[69]:7 But the others, who likewise gave up their rods green and with shoots, though not with fruit, are they that were persecuted for the law, but did not suffer nor yet deny their law.

3[69]:8 But they that gave them up green just as they received them, are sober and righteous men, who walked altogether in a pure heart and have kept the commandments of the Lord. But all else thou shalt know, when I have examined these rods that have been planted and watered."

4[70]:1 And after a few days we came to the place, and the shepherd sat down in the place of the angel, while I stood by him. And he saith to me; "Gird thyself with a garment of raw flax, and minister to me." So I girded myself with a clean garment of raw flax made of coarse material.

4[70]:2 And when he saw me girded and ready to minister to him "Call," saith he, "the men whose rods have been planted, according to the rank as each presented their rods." And I went away to the plain, and called them all;

and they stood all of them according to their ranks.

4[70]:3 He saith to them; "Let each man pluck out his own rod, and bring it to me." Those gave them up first, who had the withered and chipped rods, and they were found accordingly withered and chipped. He ordered them to stand apart.

4[70]:4 Then those gave them up, who had the withered but not chipped; and some of them gave up the rods green, and others withered and chipped as by grubs. Those then that gave them up green he ordered to stand apart; but those that gave them up withered and chipped he ordered to stand with the first.

4[70]:5 Then those gave them up who had the half-withered and with cracks; and many of them gave them up green and without cracks; and some gave them up green and with shoots, and fruits on the shoots, such as those had who went into the tower crowned; and some gave them up withered and eaten, and some withered and uneaten, and some such as they were, half-withered and with cracks. He ordered them to stand each one apart, some in their proper ranks, and others apart.

5[71]:1 Then those gave them up who had their rods green, but with cracks. These all gave them up green, and stood in their own company. And the shepherd rejoiced over these, because they all were changed and had put away their cracks.

5[71]:2 And those gave them up likewise who had the one half green and the other half withered. The rods of some were found entirely green, of some half-withered, of some withered and eaten, and of some green and with shoots. These were all sent away each to his company.

5[71]:3 Then those gave them up who had two parts green and the third withered; many of them gave them up green, and many half-withered, and others withered and eaten. These all stood in their own company.

5[71]:4 Then those gave them up who had two parts withered and the third part green. Many of them gave them up half-withered, but some withered and eaten, others half-withered and with cracks, and a few green. These all stood in their own company. Hermas 5[71]:5 Then those gave them up who had their rods green, but a very small part [withered] and with cracks. Of these some gave them up green, and others green and with shoots. These also went away to their own company.

5[71]:6 Then those gave them up who had a very small part green and the other parts withered. The rods of these were found for the most part green and with shoots and fruit on the shoots, and others altogether green. At these rods the shepherd rejoiced very [greatly], because they were found so. And these went away each to his own company.

6[72]:1 After [the shepherd] had examined the rods of all, he saith to me, "I told thee that this tree clingeth to life. Seest thou," saith he, "how many repented and were saved?" "I see, Sir," say I. "It is," saith he, that thou mayest see the abundant compassion of the Lord, how great and glorious it is, and He hath given (His) Spirit to those that are worthy of repentance."

6[72]:2 "Wherefore then, Sir," say I, "did they not all repent?" "To those, whose heart He saw about to become pure and to serve Him with all the heart, to them He gave repentance; but those whose craftiness and wickedness He saw, who intend to repent in hypocrisy, to them He gave not repentance, lest haply they should again profane His name."

6[72]:3 I say unto him, "Sir, now then show me concerning those that have given up their rods, what manner of man each of them is, and their abode, that when they hear this, they that believed and have received the seal and have broken it and did not keep it sound may fully understand what they are doing, and repent, receiving from thee a seal, and may glorify the Lord, that He had compassion upon them and sent thee to renew their spirits."

6[72]:4 "Listen," saith he; "those whose rods were found withered and grub-eaten, these are the renegades and traitors to the Church, that blasphemed the Lord in their sins, and still further were ashamed of the Name of the Lord, which was invoked upon them. These then perished altogether unto God. But thou seest how not one of them repented,

although they heard the words which thou spakest to them, which I commanded thee. From men of this kind life departed.

6[72]:5 But those that gave up the _withered_ and undecayed (rods), these also are near them; for they were hypocrites, and brought in strange doctrines, and perverted the servants of God, especially them that had sinned, not permitting them to repent, but persuading them with their foolish doctrines. These then have hope of repenting.

6[72]:6 But thou seest that many of them have indeed repented from the time when thou spakest to them my commandments; yea, and (others) still will repent. And as many as shall not repent, have lost their life; but as many of them as repented, became good; and their dwelling was placed within the first walls, and some of them even ascended into the tower. Thou seest then," [saith he,] "that repentance from sins bringeth life, but not to repent bringeth death.

7[73]:1 "But as many as gave up (the rods) half-withered, and with cracks in them, hear also concerning these. Those whose rods were half-withered throughout are the double-minded; for they neither live nor are dead.

7[73]:2 But those that have them half-withered and cracks in them, these are both double-minded and slanderers, and are never at peace among themselves but always causing dissensions. Yet even to these," [saith he,] "repentance is given. Thou seest," [saith he,] "that some of them have repented; and there is still," saith he, "hope of repentance among them.

7[73]:3 And as many of them," saith he, "as have repented, have their abode within the tower; but as many of them as have repented tardily shall abide within the walls; and as many as repent not, but continue in their doings, shall die the death.

7[73]:4 But   they that have given up their rods green and with cracks, these were found faithful and good at all times, [but] they have a certain emulation one with another about first places and about glory of some kind or other; but all these are foolish in having (emulation) one with another about first places.

7[73]:5 Yet these also, when they heard my commandments, being good, purified themselves and repented quickly. They have their habitation, therefore, within the tower. But if any one shall again turn to dissension, he shall be cast out from the tower and shall lose his life.

7[73]:6 Life is for all those that keep the commandments of the Lord.

But in the commandments there is nothing about first places, or about glory of any kind, but about long-suffering and humility in man. In such men, therefore, is the life of the Lord, but in factious and lawless men is death.

8[74]:1 "But they that gave up their rods half green and half withered, these are they that are mixed up in business and cleave not to the saints. Therefore the one half of them liveth, but the other half is dead.

8[74]:2 Many then when they heard my commandments repented. As many then as repented, have their abode within the tower. But some of them altogether stood aloof These then have no repentance; for by reason of their business affairs they blasphemed the Lord and denied Him. So they lost their life for the wickedness that they committed.

8[74]:3 But many of them were doubtful-minded. These still have place for repentance, if they repent quickly, and their dwelling shall be within the tower; and if they repent tardily, they shall dwell within the walls; but if they repent not, they too have lost their life.

8[74]:4 But they that have given up two parts green and the third part withered, these are they that have denied with manifold denials.

8[74]:5 Many of them therefore repented and departed to dwell inside the tower; but many utterly rebelled from God; these lost their life finally. And some of them were double-minded and caused dissensions. For these then there is repentance, if they repent speedily and continue not in their pleasures; but if they continue in their doings, they likewise procure for themselves death.

9[75]:1 "But they that have given up their rods two thirds withered and one third green, these are men who have been believers, but grew rich and became renowned among the Gentiles. They clothed themselves with great pride and became high-minded, and abandoned the truth and did not cleave to the righteous, but lived together after the manner of the Gentiles, and this path appeared the more pleasant unto them; yet they departed not from God, but continued in the faith, though they wrought not the works of the faith.

9[75]:2 Many of them therefore repented, and they had their habitation within the tower.

9[75]:3 But others at the last living with the Gentiles, and being corrupted by the vain opinions of the Gentiles, departed from God, and worked the works of the Gentiles. These therefore were numbered with the Gentiles.

9[75]:4 But others of them were doubtful-minded, not hoping to be saved by reason of the deeds that they had done; and others were double-minded and made divisions among themselves. For these then that were double-minded by reason of their doings there is still repentance; but their repentance ought to be speedy, that their dwelling may be within the tower; but for those who repent not, but continue in their pleasures, death is nigh.

10[76]:1 "But they that gave up their rods green, yet with the extreme ends withered and with cracks; these were found at all times good and faithful and glorious in the sight of God, but they sinned to a very slight degree by reason of little desires and because they had somewhat against one another. But, when they heard my words, the greater part quickly repented, and their dwelling was assigned within the tower.

10[76]:2 But some of them were double-minded, and some being double-minded made a greater dissension. In these then there is still a hope of repentance, because they were found always good; and hardly shall one of them die.

10[76]:3 But they that gave up their rods withered, yet with a very small part green, these are they that believed, but practiced the works of lawlessness. Still they never separated from God, but bore the Name gladly, and gladly received into their houses the servants of God. So hearing of this repentance they repented without wavering, and they practice all excellence and righteousness.

10[76]:4 And some of them even suffer persecution willingly, knowing the deeds that they did. All these then shall have their dwelling within the tower."

11[77]:1 And after he had completed the interpretations of all the rods, he saith unto me; "Go, and tell all men to repent, and they shall live unto God; for the Lord in His compassion sent me to give repentance to all, though some of them do not deserve it for their deeds; but being long-suffering the Lord willeth them that were called through His Son to be saved."

11[77]:2 I say to him; "Sir, I hope that all when they hear these words will repent; for I am persuaded that each one, when he fully knows his own deeds and fears God, will repent."

11[77]:3 He answered and said unto me; "As many," [saith he,] "as [shall repent] from their whole heart [and] shall cleanse themselves from all the evil deeds aforementioned, and shall add nothing further to their sins, shall receive healing from the Lord for their former sins, unless they be double-minded concerning these commandments, and they shall live unto God. [But as many," saith he, "as shall add to their sins and walk in the lusts of this world, shall condemn themselves to death.]

11[77]:4 But do thou walk in my commandments, and live [unto God; yea, and as many as shall walk in them and shall do rightly, shall live unto God."]

11[77]:5 Having shown me all these things [and told me them] he saith to me; "Now the rest will I declare (unto thee) after a few days."

Hermas 1[78]:Heading Parable 9

1[78]:1 After I had written down the commandments and parables of the shepherd, the angel of repentance, he came to me and saith to me; "I wish to show thee all things that the Holy Spirit, which spake with thee in the form of the Church, showed unto thee. For that Spirit is the Son of God.

1[78]:2 For when thou wast weaker in the flesh, it was not declared unto thee through an angel; but when thou wast enabled through the Spirit, and didst grow mighty in thy strength so that thou couldest even see an angel, then at length was manifested unto thee, through the Church, the building of the tower. In fair and seemly manner hast thou seen all things, (instructed) as it were by a virgin; but now thou seest (being instructed) by an angel, though by the same Spirit;

1[78]:3 yet must thou learn everything more accurately from me. For to this end also was I appointed by the glorious angel to dwell in thy house, that thou mightest see all things mightily, in nothing terrified, even as before."

1[78]:4 And he took me away into Arcadia, to a certain rounded mountain, and set me on the top of the mountain, and showed me a great plain, and round the plain twelve mountains, the mountains having each a different appearance.

1[78]:5 The first was black as soot; the second was bare, without vegetation; the third was thorny and full of briars;

1[78]:6 the fourth had the vegetation half-withered, the upper part of the grass green, but the part by the roots withered, and some of the grass became withered, whenever the sun had scorched it;

1[78]:7 the fifth mountain had green grass and was rugged; the sixth mountain was full with clefts throughout, some small and some great, and the clefts had vegetation, but the grass was not very luxuriant, but rather as if it had been withered;

1[78]:8 the seventh mountain had smiling vegetation, and the whole mountain was in a thriving condition, and cattle and birds of every kind did feed upon that mountain; and the more the cattle and the birds did feed, so much the more did the herbage of that mountain flourish. The eighth mountain was full of springs, and every kind of creature of the Lord did drink of the springs on that mountain.

1[78]:9 the ninth mountain had no water at all, and was entirely desert; and it had in it wild beasts and deadly reptiles, which destroy mankind. The tenth mountain had very large trees and was umbrageous throughout, and beneath the shade lay sheep resting and feeding.

1[78]:10 the eleventh mountain was thickly wooded all over, and the trees thereon were very productive, decked with divers kinds of fruits, so that one seeing them would desire to eat of their fruits. The twelfth mountain was altogether white and its aspect was cheerful; and the mountain was most beauteous in itself.

2[79]:1 And in the middle of the plain he showed me a great white rock, rising up from the plain. The rock was loftier than the mountains, being four-square, so that it could contain the whole world.

2[79]:2 Now this rock was ancient, and had a gate hewn out of it; but the gate seemed to me to have been hewed out quite recently. And the gate glistened beyond the brightness of the sun, so that I marvelled at the brightness of the gate.

2[79]:3 And around the gate stood twelve virgins. The four then that stood at the corners seemed to me to be more glorious (than the   rest); but the others likewise were glorious; and they stood at the four quarters of the gate, and virgins stood in pairs between them.

2[79]:4 And they were clothed in linen tunics and girt about in seemly fashion, having their right shoulders free, as if they intended to carry some burden. Thus were they prepared, for they were very cheerful and eager.

2[79]:5 After I had seen these things, I marvelled in myself at the greatness and the glory of what I was seeing And again I was perplexed concerning the virgins, that delicate as they were they stood up like men, as if they intended to carry the whole heaven.

2[79]:6 And the shepherd saith unto me; "Why questionest thou within thyself and art perplexed, and bringest sadness on thyself? For whatsoever things thou canst not comprehend, attempt them not, if thou art prudent; but entreat the Lord, that thou mayest receive understanding to comprehend them.

2[79]:7 What is behind thee thou canst not see, but what is before thee thou beholdest. The things therefore which thou canst not see, let alone, and trouble not thyself (about them; but the things which thou seest, these master, and be not over curious about the rest; but I will explain unto thee all things whatsoever I shall show thee. Have an eye therefore to what remaineth."

3[80]:1 I saw six men come, tall and glorious and alike in appearance and they summoned a multitude of men. And the others also which came were tall men and handsome and powerful. And the six men ordered them to build a tower above the gate. And there arose a great noise from those men who had come to build the tower, as they ran hither and thither round the gate.

3[80]:2 For the virgins standing round the gate told the men to hasten to build the tower. Now the virgins had spread out their hands, as if they would take something from the men.

3[80]:3 And the six men ordered stones to come up from a certain deep place, and to go to the building of the tower. And there went up ten stones square and polished, [not] hewn from a quarry.

3[80]:4 And the six men called to the virgins, and ordered them to carry all the stones which should go unto the building of the tower, and to pass through the gate and to hand them to the men that were about to build the tower.

3[80]:5 And the virgins laid the first ten stones that rose out of the deep on each other, and they carried them together, stone by stone.

4[81]:1 And just as they stood together around the gate, in that order they carried them that seemed to be strong enough and had stooped under the corners of the stone, while the others stooped at the sides of the stone. And so they carried all the stones. And they carried them right through the gate, as they were ordered, and handed them to the men for the tower; and these took the stones and builded.

4[81]:2 Now the building of the tower was upon the great rock and above the gate. Those ten stones then were

joined together, and they covered the whole rock. And these formed a foundation for the building of the tower. And [the rock and] the gate supported the whole tower.

4[81]:3 And, after the ten stones, other twenty-five stones came up from the deep, and these were fitted into the building of the tower, being carried by the virgins, like the former. And after these thirty-five stones came up. And these likewise were fitted into the tower. And after these came up other forty stones. and these all were put into the building of the tower. So four rows were made in the foundations of the tower.

4[81]:4 And (the stones) ceased coming up from the deep, and the builders likewise ceased for a little. And again the six men ordered the multitude of the people to bring in stones from the mountains for the building of the tower.

4[81]:5 They were brought in accordingly from all the mountains, of various colors, shaped by the men, and were handed to the virgins; and the virgins carried them right through the gate, and handed them in for the building of the tower. And when the various stones were placed in the building, they became all alike and white, and they lost their various colors.

4[81]:6 But some stones were handed in by the men for the building, and these did not become bright; but just as they were placed, such likewise were they found; for they were not handed in by the virgins, nor had they been carried in through the gate. These stones then were unsightly in the building of the tower.

4[81]:7 Then the six men, seeing the stones that were unsightly in the building, ordered them to be removed and carried [below] into their own place whence they were brought.

4[81]:8 And they say to the men who were bringing the stones in; "Abstain for your parts altogether from handing in stones for the building; but place them by the tower, that the virgins may carry them through the gate, and hand them in for the building. For if," [say they,] they be not carried in through the gate by the hands of these virgins, they cannot change their colors. Labor not therefore," [say they,] "in vain."

5[82]:1 And the building was finished on that day, yet was not the tower finally completed, for it was to be carried up [still] higher; and there was a cessation in the building. And the six men ordered the builders to retire for a short time [all of them], and to rest; but the virgins they ordered not to retire from the tower. And methought the virgins were left to guard the tower.

5[82]:2 And after all had retired Land rested], I say to the shepherd; "How is it, Sir," say I, "that the building of the tower was not completed?" "The tower," he saith, "cannot yet be finally completed, until its master come and test this building, that if any stones be found crumbling, he may change them; for the tower is being built according to His will."

5[82]:3 "I would fain know, Sir," say I, "what is this building of this tower, and concerning the rock and gate, and the mountains, and the virgins, and the stones that came up from the deep, and were not shaped, but went just as they were into the building;

5[82]:4 and wherefore ten stones were first placed in the foundations, then twenty-five, then thirty-five, then forty, and concerning the stones that had gone to the building and were removed again and put away in their own place--concerning all these things set my soul at rest, Sir, and explain them to me."

5[82]:5 "If," saith he, "thou be not found possessed of an idle curiosity, thou shalt know all things. For after a few days we shall come here, and thou shalt see the sequel that overtaketh this tower and shalt understand all the parables accurately."

5[82]:6 And after a few days we came to the place where we had sat, and he saith to me, "Let us go to the tower; for the owner of the tower cometh to inspect it." And we came to the tower, and there was no one at all by it, save the virgins alone.

5[82]:7 And the shepherd asked the virgins whether the master of the tower had arrived. And they said that he would be there directly to inspect the building.

6[83]:1 And, behold, after a little while I see an array of many men coming, and in the midst a man of such lofty stature that he overtopped the tower.

6[83]:2 And the six men who superintended the building walked with him on the right hand and on the left, and all they that worked at the building were with him, and many other glorious attendants around him. And the virgins that watched the tower ran up and kissed him, and they began to walk by his side round the tower.

6[83]:3 And that man inspected the building so carefully, that he felt each single stone; and he held a rod in his hand and struck each single stone that was built in.

6[83]:4 And when he smote,

some of the stones became black as soot, others mildewed, others cracked, others broke off short, others became neither white nor black, others rough and not fitting in with the other stones, and others with many spots; these were the varied aspects of the stones which were found unsound for the building.

6[83]:5 So he ordered all these to be removed from the tower, and to be placed by the side of the tower, and other stones to be brought and put into their place.

6[83]:6 And the builders asked him from what mountain he desired stones to be brought and put into their place. And he would not have them brought from the mountains, but ordered them to be brought from a certain plain that was nigh at hand.

6[83]:7 And the plain was dug, and stones were found there bright and square, but some of them too were round. And all the stones which there were anywhere in that plain were brought every one of them, and were carried through the gate by the virgins.

6[83]:8 And the square stones were hewed, and set in the place of those which had been removed; but the round ones were not placed in the building, because they were too hard to be shaped, and to work on them was slow. So they were placed by the side of the tower, as though they were intended to be shaped and placed in the building; for they were very bright.

7[84]:1 So then, having accomplished these things, the glorious man who was lord of the whole tower called the shepherd to him, and delivered unto him all the stones which lay by the side of the tower, which were cast out from the building, and saith unto him;

7[84]:2 "Clean these stones carefully, and set them in the building of the tower, these, I mean, which can fit with the rest; but those which will not fit, throw far away from the tower."

7[84]:3 Having given these orders to the shepherd, he departed from the tower with all those with whom he had come. And the virgins stood round the tower watching it.

7[84]:4 I say to the shepherd, "How can these stones go again to the building of the tower, seeing that they have been disapproved?" He saith unto me in answer; "Seest thou", saith he, "these stones?" I see them, Sir," say I. "I myself," saith he, "will shape the greater part of these stones and put them into the building, and they shall fit in with the remaining stones."

7[84]:5 "How, Sir," say I, "can they, when they are chiseled, fill the same space?" He saith unto me in answer, "As many as shall be found small, shall be put into the middle of the building; but as many as are larger, shall be placed nearer the outside, and they will bind them together."

7[84]:6 With these words he saith to me, "Let us go away, and after two days let us come and clean these stones, and put them into the building; for all things round the tower must be made clean, lest haply the master come suddenly and find the circuit of the tower dirty, and he be wroth, and so these stones shall not go to the building of the tower, and I shall appear to be careless in my master's sight."

7[84]:7 And after two days we came to the tower, and he saith unto me; "Let us inspect all the stones, and see those which can go to the building." I say to him, "Sir, let us inspect them."

8[85]:1 And so commencing first we began to inspect the black stones; and just as they were when set aside from the building, such also they were found. And the shepherd ordered them to be removed from the tower and to be put on one side.

8[85]:2 Then he inspected those that were mildewed, and he took and shaped many of them, and ordered the virgins to take them up and put them into the building. And the virgins took them up and placed them in the building of the tower in a middle position. But the rest he ordered to be placed with the black ones; for these also were found black.

8[85]:3 Then he began to inspect those that had the cracks; and of these he shaped many, and he ordered them to be carried away by the hands of the virgins for the building. And they were placed towards the outside, because they were found to be sounder. But the rest could not be shaped owing to the number of the cracks. For this reason therefore they were cast aside from the building of the tower.

8[85]:4 Then he proceeded to inspect the stunted (stones), and many among them were found black, and some had contracted great cracks; and he ordered these also to be placed with those that had been cast aside. But those of them which remained he cleaned and shaped, and ordered to be placed in the building So the virgins took them up, and fitted them into the middle of the building of the tower; for they were somewhat weak.

8[85]:5 Then he began to inspect those that were half white and half black, and many of them were (now) found black; and he ordered these also to be taken up with those that had been cast aside. But all the rest were [found white, and were] taken up by the virgins; for being white they were fitted by [the virgins] them[selves] into the building. But they were placed towards the outside, because they were found sound, so that they could hold together those that were placed in the middle; for not a single one of them was too short.

8[85]:6 Then he began to inspect the hard and rough; and a few of them were cast away, because they could not be shaped; for they were found very hard. But the rest of them were shaped [and taken up by the virgins] and fitted into the middle of the building of the tower; for they were somewhat weak.

8[85]:7 Then he proceeded to inspect those that had the spots, and of these some few had turned black and were cast away among the rest; but the remainder were found bright and sound, and these were fitted by the virgins into the building; but they were placed towards the outside, owing to their strength.

9[86]:1 Then he came to inspect the white and round stones, and he saith unto me; "What shall we do with these stones?" "How do I know, Sir?" say I [And he saith to me,] "Perceivest thou nothing concerning them?"

9[86]:2 "I, Sir," say I, "do not possess this art, neither am I a mason, nor can I understand." Seest thou not," saith he, "that they are very round; and if I wish to make them square, very much must needs be chiseled off from them? Yet some of them must of necessity be placed into the building."

9[86]:3 "If then, Sir," say I, "it must needs be so, why distress thyself, and why not choose out for the building those thou willest, and fit them into it?" He chose out from them the large and the bright ones, and shaped them; and the virgins took them up, and fitted them into the outer parts of the building.

9[86]:4 But the rest, which remained over, were taken up, and put aside into the plain whence they were brought; they were not however cast away, "Because," saith he, there remaineth still a little of the tower to be builded. And the master of the tower is exceedingly anxious that these stones be fitted into the building, for they are very bright."

9[86]:5 So twelve women were called, most beautiful in form, clad in black, [girded about and having the shoulders bare,] with their hair hanging loose. And these women, methought, had a savage look. And the shepherd ordered them to take up the stones which had been cast away from the building, and to carry them off to the same mountains from which also they had been brought;

9[86]:6 and they took them up joyfully, and carried away all the stones and put them in the place whence they had been taken. And after all the stones had been taken up, and not a single stone still lay round the tower, the shepherd saith unto me; "Let us go round the tower, and see that there is no defect in it." And I proceeded to go round it with him.

9[86]:7 And when the shepherd saw that the tower was very comely in the building, he was exceedingly glad; for the tower was so well builded, that when I saw it I coveted the building of it; for it was builded, as it were, of one stone, having one fitting in it. And the stone-work appeared as if hewn out of the rock; for it seemed to me to be all a single stone.

10[87]:1 And I, as I walked with him, was glad to see so brave a sight. And the shepherd saith to me; "Go and bring plaster and fine clay, that I may fill up the shapes of the stones that have been taken up and put into the building; for all the circuit of the tower must be made smooth."

10[87]:2 And I did as he bade, and brought them to him. "Assist me," saith he, "and the work will speedily be accomplished." So he filled in the shapes of the stones which had gone to the building, and ordered the circuit of the tower to be swept and made clean.

10[87]:3 And the virgins took brooms and swept, and they removed all the rubbish from the tower, and sprinkled water, and the site of the tower was made cheerful and very seemly.

10[87]:4 The shepherd saith unto me, "All," saith he, "hath now been cleaned. If the lord come to inspect the tower, he hath nothing for which to blame us." Saying this, he desired to go away.

10[87]:5 But I caught hold of his wallet, and began to adjure him by the Lord that he would explain to me [all] what he had showed me. He saith to me; "I am busy for a little while, and then I will explain everything to thee. Await me here till I come."

10[87]:6 I say to him; "Sir, when I am here alone what shall I do?" "Thou art not alone," saith he; "for these virgins are here with thee." "Commend me then to them," say I. The shepherd calleth them to him and saith to them; "I commend this man to you till I come," and he departed.

10[87]:7 So I was alone with the virgins; and they were most cheerful, and kindly disposed to Me especially the four of them that were the more glorious in appearance.

11[88]:1 The virgins say to me; "Today the shepherd cometh not here." "What then shall I do?" say I. "Stay for him," say they, "till eventide; and if he come, he will speak with thee; but if he come not, thou shalt stay here with us till he cometh."

11[88]:2 I say to them; "I will await him till evening, and if he come not, I will depart home and return early in the morning." But they answered and said unto me; "To us thou wast entrusted; thou canst not depart from us."

11[88]:3 "Where then," say I, "shall I remain?" "Thou shalt pass the night with us," say they as a brother, not as a husband; for thou art our brother, and henceforward we will dwell with thee; for we love thee dearly." But I was ashamed to abide with them.

11[88]:4 And she that seemed to be the chief of them began to kiss and to embrace me; and the others seeing her embrace me, they too began to kiss me, and to lead me round the tower, and to sport with me.

11[88]:5 And I had become as it were a younger man, and I commenced myself likewise to sport with them. For some of them began to dance, [others to skip,] others to sing. But I kept silence and walked with them round the tower, and was glad with them.

11[88]:6 But when evening came I wished to go away home; but they would not let me go, but detained me. And I stayed the night with them, and I slept by the side of the tower.

11[88]:7 For the virgins spread their linen tunics on the ground, and made me lie down in the midst of them, and they did nothing else but pray; and I prayed with them without ceasing, and not less than they. And the virgins rejoiced that I so prayed. And I stayed there with the virgins until the morning till the second hour.

11[88]:8 Then came the shepherd, and saith to the virgins; "Have ye done him any injury?" "Ask him," say they. I say to him, "Sir, I was rejoiced to stay with them." "On what didst thou sup?" saith he "I supped, Sir," say I, "on the words of the Lord the whole night through." "Did they treat thee well?" saith he. "Yes, Sir," say I.

11[88]:9 "Now," saith he, "what wouldest thou hear first?" "In the order as thou showedst to me, Sir, from the beginning," say I; "I request thee, Sir, to explain to me exactly in the order that I shall enquire of thee." According as thou desirest," saith he, "even so will I interpret to thee, and I will conceal nothing whatever from thee."

12[89]:1 "First of all, Sir," say I, "explain this to me. The rock and the gate, what is it?" "This rock," saith he, "and gate is the Son of God." "How, Sir," say I, "is the rock ancient, but the gate recent?" "Listen," saith he, "and understand, foolish man.

12[89]:2 The Son of God is older than all His creation, so that He became the Father's adviser in His creation. Therefore also He is ancient." "But the gate, why is it recent, Sir?" say I.

12[89]:3 "Because," saith he, "He was made manifest in the last days of the consummation; therefore the gate was made recent, that they which are to be saved may enter through it into the kingdom of God.

12[89]:4 Didst thou see," saith he, "that the stones which came through the gate have gone to the building of the tower, but those which came not through it were cast away again to their own place?” “I saw, Sir,” say I. “Thus,” saith he, “no one shall enter into the kingdom of God, except he receive the name of His Son.

12[89]:5 For if thou wishest to enter into any city, and that city is walled all round and has one gate only, canst thou enter into that city except through the gate which it hath?” “Why, how, Sir,” say I, “is it possible otherwise?” “If then thou canst not enter into the city except through the gate itself, even so,” saith he, “a man cannot enter into the kingdom of God except by the name of His Son that is beloved by Him.

12[89]:6 Didst thou see,” saith he, “the multitude that is building the tower?” “I saw it, Sir,” say I. “They,” saith he, are all glorious angels. With these then the Lord is walled around. But the gate is the Son of God; there is this one entrance only to the Lord. No one then shall enter in unto Him otherwise than through His Son.

12[89]:7 Didst thou see,” saith he, “the six men, and the glorious and mighty man in the midst of them, him that walked about the tower and rejected the stones from the building?” “I saw him, Sir,” say I.

12[89]:8 “The glorious man,” saith he, “is the Son of God, and those six are the glorious angels who guard Him on the right hand and on the left. Of these glorious angels not one,” saith he, “shall enter in unto God without Him; whosoever shall not receive His name, shall not enter into the kingdom of God.”

13[90]:1 “But the tower,” say I, “what is it?” “The tower,” saith he, “why, this is the Church.

13[90]:2 “And these virgins, who are they?” “They,” saith he, “are holy spirits; and no man can otherwise be found in the kingdom of God, unless these shall clothe him with their garment; for if thou receive only the name, but receive not the garment from them, thou profitest nothing. For these virgins are powers of the Son of God. If [therefore] thou bear the Name, and bear not His power, thou shalt bear His Name to none effect.

13[90]:3 And the stones,” saith he, “which thou didst see cast away, these bare the Name, but clothed not themselves with the raiment of the virgins.” “Of what sort, Sir,” say I, “is their raiment?” “The names themselves,” saith he, “are their raiment. Whosoever beareth the Name of the Son of God, ought to bear the names of these also; for even the Son Himself beareth the names of these virgins.

13[90]:4 As many stones,” saith he, “as thou sawest enter into the building of the tower, being given in by their hands and waiting for the building, they have been clothed in the power of these virgins.

13[90]:5 For this cause thou seest the tower made a single stone with the rock. So also they that have believed in the Lord through His Son and clothe themselves in these spirits, shall become one spirit and one body, and their garments all of one color. But such persons as bear the names of the virgins have their dwelling in the tower."

13[90]:6 "The stones then, Sir," say I, "which are cast aside, wherefore were they cast aside? For they passed through the gate and were placed in the building of the tower by the hands of the virgins." "Since all these things interest thee," saith he, "and thou enquirest diligently, listen as touching the stones that have been cast aside.

13[90]:7 These all," [saith he,] "received the name of the Son of God, and received likewise the power of these virgins. When then they received these spirits, they were strengthened, and were with the servants of God, and they had one spirit and one body [and one garment]; for they had the same mind, and they wrought righteousness.

13[90]:8 After a certain time then they were persuaded by the women whom thou sawest clad in black raiment, and having their shoulders bare and their hair loose, and beautiful in form. When they saw them they desired them, and they clothed themselves with their power, but they stripped off from themselves the power of the virgins.

13[90]:9 They then were cast away from the house of God, and delivered to these (women). But they that were not deceived by the beauty of these women remained in the house of God. So thou hast," saith he, "the interpretation of them that were cast aside."

14[90]:1 What then, Sir," say I, "if these men, being such as they are, should repent and put away their desire for these women, and return unto the virgins, and walk in their power and in their works? Shall they not enter into the house of God?"

14[90]:2 "They shall enter," saith he, "if they shall put away the works of these women, and take again the power of the virgins, and walk in their works. For this is the reason why there was also a cessation in the building, that, if these repent, they may go into the building of the tower; but if they repent not, then others will go, and these shall be cast away finally."

14[90]:3 For all these things I gave thanks unto the Lord, because He had compassion on all that called upon His name, and sent forth the angel of repentance to us that had sinned against Him, and refreshed our spirit, and, when we were already ruined and had no hope of life, restored our life.

14[90]:4 "Now, Sir," say I, "show me why the tower is not built upon the ground, but upon the rock and upon the gate." "Because thou art senseless," saith he, "and without understanding [thou askest the question]." "I am obliged, Sir," say I, "to ask all questions of thee, because I am absolutely unable to comprehend anything at all; for all are great and glorious and difficult for men to understand."

14[90]:5 "Listen," saith he. "The name of the Son of God is great and incomprehensible, and sustaineth the whole world. If then all creation is sustained by the   Son [of God], what thinkest thou of those that are called by Him, and bear the name of the Son of God, and walk according to His commandments?

14[90]:6 Seest thou then what manner of men He sustaineth? Even those that bear His name with their whole heart. He Himself then is become their foundation, and He sustaineth them gladly, because they are not ashamed to bear His name."

15[92]:1 "Declare to me, Sir," say I, "the names of the virgins, and of the women that are clothed in the black garments." "Hear," saith he, "the names of the more powerful virgins, those that are stationed at the corners.

15[92]:2 The first is Faith, and the second, Continence, and the third, Power, and the fourth, Long-suffering. But the others stationed between them have these names--Simplicity, Guilelessness, Purity, Cheerfulness, Truth, Understanding, Concord, Love. He that beareth these names and the name of the Son of God shall be able to enter into the kingdom of God.

15[92]:3 Hear," saith he, "likewise the names of the women that wear the black garments. Of these also four are more powerful than the rest; the first is Unbelief; the second, Intemperance; the third, Disobedience; the fourth, Deceit; and their followers are called, Sadness, Wickedness, Wantonness, Irascibility, Falsehood, Folly, Slander, Hatred. The servant of God that beareth these names shall see the kingdom of God, but shall not enter into it."

15[92]:4 "But the stones, Sir," say I, "that came from the deep, and were fitted into the building, who are they?" "The first," saith he, "even the ten, that were placed in the foundations, are the first generation; the twenty-five are the second generation of righteous men; the thirty-five are God's prophets and His ministers; the forty are apostles and teachers of the preaching of the Son of God."

15[92]:5 "Wherefore then, Sir," say I, "did the virgins give in these stones also for the building of the tower and carry them through the gate?"

15[92]:6 "Because these first," saith he, "bore these spirits, and they never separated the one from the other, neither the spirits from the men nor the men from the spirits, but the spirits abode with them till they fell asleep; and if they had not had these spirits with them, they would not have been found useful for the building of this tower."

16[92]:1 "Show me still further, Sir," say I. "What desirest thou to know besides?" saith he. "Wherefore, Sir," say I, "did the stones come up from the deep, and wherefore were they placed into the building, though they bore these spirits?"

16[92]:2 "It was necessary for them," saith he, "to rise up through water, that they might be made alive; for otherwise they could not enter into the kingdom of God, except they had put aside the deadness of their [former] life.

16[92]:3 So these likewise that had fallen asleep received the seal of the Son of God and entered into the kingdom of God. For before a man," saith he, "has borne the name of [the Son of] God, he is dead; but when he has received the seal, he layeth aside his deadness, and resumeth life.

16[92]:4 The seal then is the water: so they go down into the water dead, and they come up alive. "thus to them also this seal was preached, and they availed themselves of it that they might enter into the kingdom of God."

16[92]:5 "Wherefore, Sir," say I, "did the forty stones also come up with them from the deep, though they had already received the seal?" "Because," saith he, "these, the apostles and the teachers who preached the name of the Son of God, after they had fallen asleep in the power and faith of the Son of God, preached also to them that had fallen asleep before them, and themselves gave unto them the seal of the preaching.

16[92]:6 Therefore they went down with them into the water, and came up again. But these went down alive [and again came up alive]; whereas the others that had fallen asleep before them went down dead and came up alive.

156[92]:7 So by their means they were quickened into life, and came to the full knowledge of the name of the Son of God. For this cause also they came up with them, and were fitted with them into the building of the tower and were builded with them, without being shaped; for they fell asleep in righteousness and in great purity. Only they had not this seal. Thou hast then the interpretation of these things also." "I have, Sir," say I.

17[94]:1 "Now then, Sir, explain to me concerning the mountains. Wherefore are their forms diverse the one from the other, and various?" "Listen," saith he. "These twelve mountains are [twelve] tribes that inhabit the whole world. To these (tribes) then the Son of God was preached by the Apostles."

17[94]:2 But explain to me, Sir, why they are various--these mountains--and each has a different appearance." "Listen," saith he. "These twelve tribes which inhabit the whole world are twelve nations; and they are various in understanding and in mind. As various, then, as thou sawest these mountains to be, such also are the varieties in the mind of these nations, and such their understanding. And I will show unto thee the conduct of each."

17[94]:3 "First, Sir," say I, "show me this, why the mountains being so various, yet, when their stones were set into the building, became bright and of one color, just like the stones that had come up from the deep."

17[94]:4 "Because," saith he, "all the nations that dwell under heaven, when they heard and believed, were called by the one name of [the Son of] God. So having received the seal, they had one understanding and one mind, and one faith became theirs and [one] love, and they bore the spirits of the virgins along with the Name; therefore the building of the tower became of one color, even bright as the sun.

17[94]:5 But after they entered in together, and became one body, some of them defiled themselves, and were cast out from the society of the righteous, and became again such as they were before, or rather even worse." Hermas

18[95]:1 "How, Sir," say I, "did they become worse, after they had fully known God?" "He that knoweth not God," saith he, "and committeth wickedness, hath a certain punishment for his wickedness; but he that knoweth God fully ought not any longer to commit wickedness, but to do good.

18[95]:2 If then he that ought to do good committeth wickedness, does he not seem to do greater wickedness than the man that knoweth not God? Therefore they that have not known God, and commit wickedness, are condemned to death; but they that have known God and seen His mighty works, and yet commit wickedness, shall receive a double punishment, and shall die eternally. In this way therefore shall the Church of God be purified.

18[95]:3 And as thou sawest the stones removed from the tower and delivered over to the evil spirits, they too shall be cast out; and there shall be one body of them that are purified, just as the tower, after it had been purified, became made as it were of one stone. Thus shall it be with the Church of God also, after she hath been purified, and the wicked and hypocrites and blasphemers and double-minded and they that commit various kinds of wickedness have been cast out.

18[95]:4 When these have been cast out, the Church of God shall be one body, one understanding, one mind, one faith, one love. And then the Son of God shall rejoice and be glad in them, for that He hath received back His people pure." "Great and glorious, Sir," say I, "are all these things.

18[95]:5 Once more, Sir," [say I,] "show me the force and the doings of each one of the mountains, that every soul that trusteth in the Lord, when it heareth, may glorify His great and marvelous and glorious name." "Listen," saith he, "to the variety of the mountains and of the twelve nations.

19[96]:1 "From the first mountain, which was black, they that have believed are such as these; rebels and blasphemers against the Lord, and betrayers of the servants of God. For these there is no repentance, but there is death. For this cause also they are black; for their race is lawless.

19[96]:2 And from the second mountain, the bare one, they that believed are such as these; hypocrites and teachers of wickedness. And these then are like the former in not having the fruit of righteousness. For, even as their mountain is unfruitful, so likewise such men as these have a name indeed, but they are void of the faith, and there is no fruit of truth in them. For these then repentance is offered, if they repent quickly; but if they delay, they will have their death with the former."

19[96]:3 "Wherefore, Sir," say I, "is repentance possible for them, but not for the former ? For their doings are almost the same." "On this account," he saith, "is repentance offered for them, because they blasphemed not their Lord, nor became betrayers of the servants of God; yet from desire of gain they played the hypocrite, and taught each other [after] the desires of sinful men. But they shall pay a certain penalty; yet repentance is ordained for them, because they are not become blasphemers or betrayers.

20[97]:1 "And from the third mountain, which had thorns and briars, they that believed are such as these; some of them are wealthy and others are entangled in many business affairs. The briars are the wealthy, and the thorns are they that are mixed up in various business affairs.

20[97]:2 These [then, that are mixed up in many and various business affairs,] cleave [not] to the servants of God, but go astray, being choked by their affairs, but the wealthy unwillingly cleave to the servants of God, fearing lest they may be asked for something by them. Such men therefore shall hardly enter into the kingdom of God.

20[97]:3 For as it is difficult to walk on briars with bare feet, so also it is difficult for such men to enter the kingdom of God.

20[97]:4 But for all these repentance is possible, but it must be speedy, that in respect to what they omitted to do in the former times, they may now revert to (past) days, and do some good. If then they shall repent and do some good, they shall live unto God; but if they continue in their doings, they shall be delivered over to those women, the which shall put them to death.

21[97]:1 "And from the fourth mountain, which had much vegetation, the upper part of the grass green and the part towards the roots withered, and some of it dried up by the sun, they that believed are such as these; the double-minded, and they that have the Lord on their lips, but have Him not in their heart. Hermas

21[97]:2 Therefore their foundations are dry and without power, and their words only live, but their works are dead. Such men are neither alive nor dead. They are, therefore, like unto the double-minded; for the double-minded are neither green nor withered; for they are neither alive nor dead.

21[97]:3 For as their grass was withered up when it saw the sun, so also the double-minded, when they hear of tribulation, through their cowardice worship idols and are ashamed of the name of their Lord.

21[97]:4 Such are neither alive nor dead. Yet these also, if they repent quickly, shall be able to live; but if they repent not, they are delivered over already to the women who deprive them of their life.

22[99]:1 "And from the fifth mountain, which had green grass and was rugged, they that believed are such as these; they are faithful, but slow to learn and stubborn and self-pleasers, desiring to know all things, and yet they know nothing at all.

22[99]:2 By reason of this their stubbornness, understanding stood aloof from them, and a foolish senselessness entered into them; and they praise themselves as having understanding, and they desire to be self-appointed teachers, senseless though they are.

22[99]:3 Owing then to this pride of heart many, while they exalted themselves, have been made empty; for a mighty demon is stubbornness and vain confidence. Of these then many were cast away, but some repented and believed, and submitted themselves to those that had understanding, having learnt their own senselessness.

22[99]:4 Yea, and to the rest that belong to this class repentance is offered; for they did not become wicked, but rather foolish and without understanding. If these then shall repent, they shall live unto God; but if they repent not, they shall have their abode with the women who work evil against them.

23[100]:1 "But they that believed from the sixth mountain, which had clefts great and small, and in the clefts herbage withered, are such as these;

23[100]:2 they that have the small clefts, these are they that have aught against one another, and from their backbitings they are withered in the faith; but many of these repented Yea, and the rest shall repent, when they hear my commandments; for their backbitings are but small, and they shall quickly repent.

23[100]:3 But they that have great clefts, these are persistent in their back-bitings and bear grudges, nursing wrath against one another. These then were thrown right away from the tower and rejected from its building. Such persons therefore shall with difficulty live.

23[100]:4 If God and our Lord, Who ruleth over all things and hath the authority over all His creation, beareth no grudge against them that confess their sins, but is propitiated, doth man, who is mortal and full of sins, bear a grudge against man, as though he were able to destroy or save him?

23[100]:5 I say unto you--I, the angel of repentance--unto as many as hold this heresy, put it away from you and repent, and the Lord shall heal your former sins, if ye shall purify yourselves from this demon; but if not, ye shall be delivered unto him to be put to death.

24[101]:1 " And from the seventh mountain, on which was herbage green and smiling, and the whole mountain thriving, and cattle of every kind and the fowls of heaven were feeding on the herbage on that mountain, and the green herbage, on which they fed, only grew the more luxuriant, they that believed are such as these;

24[101]:2 they were ever simple and guileless and blessed, having nothing against one another, but rejoicing always in the servants of God, and clothed in the Holy Spirit of these virgins, and having compassion always on every man, and out of their labors they supplied every man's need without reproach and without misgiving.

24[101]:3 The Lord then seeing their simplicity and entire childliness made them to abound in the labors of their hands, and bestowed favor on them in all their doings.

24[101]:4 But I say unto you that are such--I, the angel of repentance--remain to the end such as ye are, and your seed shall never be blotted out. For the Lord hath put you to the proof, and enrolled you among our number, and your whole seed shall dwell with the Son of God; for of His Spirit did ye receive.

25[102]:1 "And from the eighth mountain, where were the many springs, and all the creatures of the Lord did drink of the springs, they that believed are such as these;

25[102]:2 apostles and teachers, who preached unto the whole world, and who taught the word of the Lord in soberness and purity, and kept back no part at all for evil desire, but walked always in righteousness and truth, even as also they received the Holy Spirit. Such therefore shall have their entrance with the angels.

26[103]:1 "And from the ninth mountain, which was desert, which had [the] reptiles and wild beasts in it which destroy mankind, they that believed are such as these;

26[103]:2 they that have the spots are deacons that exercised their office ill, and plundered the livelihood of widows and orphans, and made gain for themselves from the ministrations which they had received to perform. If then they abide in the same evil desire, they are dead and there is no hope of life for them; but if they turn again and fulfill their ministrations in purity, it shall be possible for them to live.

26[103]:3 But they that are mildewed, these are they that denied and turned not again unto their Lord, but having become barren and desert, because they cleave not unto the servants of God but remain alone, they destroy their own souls.

26[103]:4 For as a vine left alone in a hedge, if it meet with neglect, is destroyed and wasted by the weeds, and in time becometh wild and is no longer useful to its owner, so also men of this kind have given themselves up in despair and become useless to their Lord, by growing wild.

26[103]:5 To these then repentance cometh, unless they be found to have denied from the heart; but if a man be found to have denied from the heart, I know not whether it is possible for him to live.

26[103]:6 And this I say not in reference to these days, that a man after denying should receive repentance; for it is impossible for him to be saved who shall now deny his Lord; but for those who denied Him long ago repentance seemeth to be possible. If a man therefore will repent, let him do so speedily before the tower is completed; but if not, he shall be destroyed by the women and put to death.

26[103]:7 And the stunted, these are the treacherous and backbiters; and the wild beasts which thou sawest on the mountain are these. For as wild beasts with their venom poison and kill a man, so also do the words of such men poison and kill a man.

26[103]:8 These then are broken off short from their faith through the conduct which they have in themselves; but some of them repented and were saved; and the rest that are of this kind can be saved, if they repent; but if they repent not, they shall meet their death from those women of whose power they are possessed.

27[104]:1 "And from the tenth mountain, where were trees sheltering certain sheep, they that believed are such as these;

27[104]:2 bishops, hospitable persons, who gladly received into their houses at all times the servants of God without hypocrisy. [These bishops] at all times without ceasing sheltered the needy and the widows in their ministration and conducted themselves in purity at all times.

27[104]:3 These [all] then shall be sheltered by the Lord for ever. They therefore that have done these things are glorious in the sight of God, and their place is even now with the angels, if they shall continue unto the end serving the Lord.

28[104]:1 "And from the eleventh mountain, where were trees full of fruit, decked with divers kinds of fruits, they that believed are such as these;

28[104]:2 they that suffered for the Name [of the Son of God], who also suffered readily with their whole heart, and yielded up their lives."

28[104]:3 "Wherefore then, Sir," say I, "have all the trees fruits, but some of their fruits are more beautiful than others?" "Listen," saith he; "all as many as ever suffered for the Name's sake are glorious in the sight of God, and the sins of all these were taken away, because they suffered for the name of the Son of God. Now here why their fruits are various, and some surpassing others.

28[104]:4 "As many," saith he, "as were tortured and denied not, when brought before the magistery, but suffered readily, these are the more glorious in the sight of the Lord; their fruit is that which surpasseth. But as many as become cowards, and were lost in uncertainty, and considered in their hearts whether they should deny or confess, and yet suffered, their fruits are less, because this design entered into their heart; for this design is evil, that a servant should deny his own lord.

28[104]:5 See to it, therefore, ye who entertain this idea, lest this design remain in your hearts, and ye die unto God. But ye that suffer for the Name's sake ought to glorify God, because God deemed you worthy that ye should bear this name, and that all your sins should be healed.

28[104]:6 Reckon yourselves blessed therefore; yea, rather think that ye have done a great work, if any of you shall suffer for God's sake. The Lord bestoweth life upon you, and ye percieved it not; for your sins weighed you down, and if ye had not suffered for the Name [of the Lord], ye had died unto God by reason of your sins.

28[104]:7 These things I say unto you that waver as touching denial and confession. Confess that ye have the Lord, lest denying Him ye be delivered into prison.

28[104]:8 If the Gentiles punish their slaves, if any one deny his lord, what think ye the Lord will do unto you, He who has authority over all things? Away with these designs from your hearts, that ye may live forever unto God."

29[104]:1 "And from the twelfth mountain, which was white, they that believed are such as these; they that are as very babes, into whose heart no guile entereth, neither lernt they what wickedness is, but they remained as babes forever.

29[104]:2 Such as these then dwell without doubt in the kingdom of God, because they defiled the commandments of God in nothing, but continued as babes all the days of their life in the same mind.

29[104]:3 As many of you therefore as shall continue," saith he, "and shall be as infants not having guile, shall be glorious [even] than all them that have been mentioned before; for all infants are glorious in the sight of God, and stand first in His sight. Blessed then are ye, as many as have put away wickedness from you, and have clothed yourselves in guilelessness: ye shall live unto God cheifest of all."

29[104]:4 After he had finished the parables of the mountains, I say unto him, "Sir, now explain to me concerning the stones that were taken from the plain and placed in the building in the room of the stoes that were taken from the tower, and concerning the round (stones) which were placed in the building, and concerning those that were still round".

30[104]:1 "Hear," saith he, "likewise concerning all these things. The stones which were taken from the plain and placed in the building of the tower in the room of those that were rejected, are the roots of this white mountain.

30[104]:2 When then they that believed from this mountain were all found guiltless, the lord of the tower ordered these from the roots of the mountain to be put into the building of the tower. For He knew that if these stones should go into the building [of the tower], they would remain bright and not one of them would turn black.

30[104]:3 But if he added (stones) from other mountains, he would have been obliged to visit the tower again, and to purify it. Now all these have been found white, who have believed and who shall believe; for they are of the same kind. Blessed is this kind, for it is innocent!

30[104]:4 Hear now likewise concerning those round and bright stones. All these are from the white mountain. Now here wherefore they have been found round. Their riches have darkened and obscured them a little from the truth.

30[104]:5 When therefore the Lord percieved their mind, *that they could favor the truth,* and likewise remain good, He commanded their possessions to be cut off from them, yet not to be taken away altogether, so that they might be able to do some good with that which hath been left to them, and might live unto God for that they come of a good kind. So therefore they have been cut away a little, and placed in the building of this tower".

31[104]:1 "But the other (stones), which have remained round and have not been fitted into the building, because they have not yet received the seal, have been replaced in their own possession, for they were found very round.

31[104]:2 For this world and the vanities of their possessions must be cut off from them, and then they will fit into the kingdom of God. For it is necessary that they should enter into the kingdom of God; because the Lord hath blessed this innocent kind. Of this kind then not one shall perish. Yea, even though any one of them being tempted by the most wicked devil have committed any fault, he shall return speedily unto his Lord.

31[104]:3 Blessed I pronounced you all to be--I the angel of repentance--whoever of you are guileless as infants, because your part is good and honorable in the sight of God.

31[104]:4 Moreover I bid all of you, whoever have received this seal, keep guilelessness, and bear no grudge, and continue not in your wickedness nor in the memory of the offenses of bitterness; but become of one spirit,   and heal these evil clefts and take them away from among you, that the owner of the flocks may rejoice concerning them.

31[104]:5 For he will rejoice, if he find all things whole. But if he find any part of the flock scattered, woe unto the shepherds.

31[104]:6 For if the shepherds themselves shall have been found scattered, how will they answer for the flocks? Will they say that they were harassed by the flock? No credence will be given them. For it is an incredible thing that a shepherd should be injured by his flock; and he will be punished the more because of his falsehood. And I am the shepherd, and it behoveth me most strongly to render an account for you.

32[109]:1 "Amend yourselves therefore, while the tower is still in course of building.

32[109]:2 The Lord dwelleth in men that love peace; for to Him peace is dear; but from the contentious and them that are given up to wickedness He keepeth afar off. Restore therefore to Him your spirit whole as ye received it.

32[109]:3 For suppose thou hast given to a fuller a new garment whole, and desirest to receive it back again whole, but the fuller give it back to thee torn, wilt thou receive it thus? Wilt thou not at once blaze out and attack him with reproaches, saying; "The garment which I gave thee was whole; wherefore hast thou rent it and made it useless? See, by reason of the rent, which thou hast made in it, it cannot be of use." Wilt thou not then say all this to a fuller even about a rent which he has made in thy garment?

32[109]:4 If therefore thou art thus vexed in the matter of thy garment, and complainest because thou receivest it not back whole, what thinkest thou the Lord will do to thee, He, Who gave thee the spirit whole, and thou hast made it absolutely useless, so that it cannot be of any use at all to its Lord? For its use began to be useless, when it was corrupted by thee. Will not therefore the Lord of this spirit for this thy deed punish [thee with death]?"

32[109]:5 "Certainly," I said, "all those, whomsoever He shall find continuing to bear malice, He will punish." "Trample not," said he, "upon His mercy, but rather glorify Him, because He is so long-suffering with your sins, and is not like unto you. Practice then repentance which is expedient for you.

33[110]:1 "All these things which are written above I, the shepherd, the angel of repentance, have declared and spoken to the servants of God. If then ye shall believe and hear my words, and walk in them, and amend your ways, ye shall be able to live. But if ye continue in wickedness and in bearing malice, no one of this kind shall live unto God. All things which were to be spoken by me have (now) been spoken to you."

33[110]:2 The shepherd said to me, "Hast thou asked me all thy questions?" And I said, "Yes, Sir." "Why then hast thou not enquired of me concerning the shape of the stones placed in the building, in that we filled up their shapes?" And I said, "I forgot, Sir."

33[110]:3 "Listen now," said he, "concerning them. These are they that have heard my commandments now, and have practiced repentance with their whole heart. So when the Lord saw that their repentance was good and pure, and that they could continue therein, he ordered their former sins to be blotted out. These shapes then were their former sins, and they have been chiseled away that they might not appear."

Hermas 1[111]:Heading Parable 10

1[111]:1 After I had written out this book completely, the angel who had delivered me to the shepherd came to the house where I was, and sat upon a couch, and the shepherd stood at his right hand. Then he called me, and spake thus unto me;

1[111]:2 "I delivered thee," said he, "and thy house to this shepherd, that thou mightest be protected by him." "True, Sir," I said "If therefore," said he, "thou desirest to be protected from all annoyance and all cruelty, to have also success in every good work and word, and all the power of righteousness, walk in his commandments, which I have given thee, and thou shalt be able to get the mastery over all wickedness.

1[111]:3 For if thou keep his commandments, all evil desire and the sweetness of this world shall be subject unto thee; moreover success shall attend thee in every good undertaking. Embrace his gravity and self-restraint, and tell it out unto all men that he is held in great honor and dignity with the Lord, and is a ruler of great authority, and powerful in his office. To him alone in the whole world hath authority over repentance been assigned. Seemeth he to thee to be powerful? Yet ye despise the gravity and moderation which he useth towards you."

2[112]:1 I say unto him; "Ask him, Sir, himself, whether from the time that he hath been in my house, I have done ought out of order, whereby I have offended him."

2[112]:2 "I myself know," said he, "that thou hast done nothing out of order, nor art about to do so. And so I speak these things unto thee, that thou mayest persevere. For he hath given a good account of thee unto me. Thou therefore shalt speak these words to others, that they too who have practiced or shall practice repentance may be of the same mind as thou art; and he may give a good report of them to me, and I unto the Lord."

2[112]:3 "I too, Sir," I say, "declare to every man the mighty works of the Lord; for I hope that all who have sinned in the past, if they hear these things, will gladly repent and recover life."

2[112]:4 "Continue therefore," said he, "in this ministry, and complete it unto the end. For whosoever fulfill his commandments shall have life; yea such a man (shall have) great honor with the Lord. But whosoever keep not his commandments, fly from their life, and oppose him, and follow not his commandments, but deliver themselves over to death; and each one becometh guilty of his own blood. But I bid thee obey these commandments, and thou shalt have a remedy for thy sins.

3[113]:1 "Moreover, I have sent these virgins unto thee, that they may dwell with thee; for I have seen that they are friendly towards thee. Thou hast them therefore as helpers, that thou mayest be the better able to keep his commandments; for it is impossible that these commandments be kept without the help of these virgins. I see too that they are glad to be with thee. But I will charge them that they depart not at all from thy house.

3[113]:2 Only do thou purify thy house; for in a clean house they will gladly dwell. For they are clean and chaste and industrious, and have favor in the sight of the Lord. If, therefore, they shall find thy house pure, they will continue with thee; but if the slightest pollution arise, they will depart from thy house at once. For these virgins love not pollution in any form."

3[113]:3 I said unto him, "I hope, Sir, that I shall please them, so that they may gladly dwell in my house for ever; and just as he to whom thou didst deliver me maketh no complaint against me, so they likewise shall make no complaint."

3[113]:4 He saith unto the shepherd, "I perceive," saith he, "that he wishes to live as the servant of God, and that he will keep these commandments, and will place these virgins in a clean habitation."

3[113]:5 With these words he again delivered me over to the shepherd, and called the virgins, and said to them; "Inasmuch as I see that ye are glad to dwell in this man's house, I commend to you him and his house, that ye depart not at all from his house." But they heard these words gladly.

4[114]:1 He said then to me, "Quit you like a man in this ministry; declare to every man the mighty works of the Lord, and thou shalt have favor in this ministry. Whosoever therefore shall walk in these commandments, shall live and be happy in his life; but whosoever shall neglect them, shall not live, and shall be unhappy in his life.

4[114]:2 Charge all men who are able to do right, that they cease not to practice good works; for it is useful for them. I say moreover that every man ought to be rescued from misfortune; for he that hath need, and suffereth misfortune in his daily life, is in great torment and want.

4[114]:3 Whosoever therefore rescueth from penury a life of this kind, winneth great joy for himself. For he who is harassed by misfortune of this sort is afflicted and tortured with equal torment as one who is in chains. For many men on account of calamities of this kind, because they can bear them no longer, lay violent hands on themselves. He then who knows the calamity of a man of this kind and rescueth him not, committeth great sin, and becometh guilty of the man's blood.

4[114]:4 Do therefore good works, whoever of you have received (benefits) from the Lord, lest, while ye delay to do them, the building of the tower be completed. For it is on your account that the work of the building has been interrupted. Unless then ye hasten to do right, the tower will be completed, and ye shut out."

4[114]:5 When then he had finished speaking with me, he rose from the couch and departed, taking with him the shepherd and the virgins. He said however unto me, that he would send the shepherd and the virgins back again to my house.

The History of Joseph the Carpenter

In the name of God, of one essence and three persons

The History of the death of our father, the holy old man, Joseph the carpenter. May his blessings and prayers preserve us all, O brethren! Amen.

His whole life was one hundred and eleven years, and his departure from this world happened on the twenty-sixth of the month Abib, which answers to the month Ab. May his prayer preserve us! Amen. And, indeed, it was our Lord Jesus Christ Himself who related this history to His holy disciples on the Mount of Olives, and all Joseph's labour, and the end of his days. And the holy apostles have preserved this conversation, and have left it written down in the library at Jerusalem. May their prayers preserve us! Amen.

1. It happened one day, when the Saviour, our Master, God, and Saviour Jesus Christ, was sitting along with His disciples, and they were all assembled on the Mount of Olives, that He said to them: O my brethren and friends, sons of the Father who has chosen you from all men, you know that I have often told you that I must be crucified, and must die for the salvation of Adam and his posterity, and that I shall rise from the dead. Now I shall commit to you the doctrine of the holy gospel formerly announced to you, that you may declare it. throughout the whole world. And I shall endow you with power from on high, and fill you with the Holy Spirit. And you shall declare to all nations repentance and remission of sins. For a single cup of water, if a man shall find it in the world to come, is greater and better than all the wealth of this whole world. And as much ground as one foot can occupy in the house of my Father, is greater and more excellent than all the riches of the

earth. Yea, a single hour in the joyful dwelling of the pious is more blessed and more precious than a thousand years among sinners: inasmuch as their weeping and lamentation shall not come to an end, and their tears shall not cease, nor shall they find for themselves consolation and repose at any time for ever. And now, O my honoured members, go declare to all nations, tell them, and say to them: Verily the Saviour diligently inquires into the inheritance which is due, and is the administrator of justice. And the angels will cast down their enemies, and will fight for them in the day of conflict. And He will examine every single foolish and idle word which men speak, and they shall give an account of it. For as no one shall escape death, so also the works of every man shall be laid open on the day of judgment, whether they have been good or evil. Tell them also this word which I have said to you to-day: Let not the strong man glory in his strength, nor the rich man in his riches; but let him who wishes to glory, glory in the Lord.

2. There was a man whose name was Joseph, sprung from a family of Bethlehem, a town of Judah, and the city of King David. This same man, being well furnished with wisdom and learning, was made a priest in the temple of the Lord. He was, besides. skilful in his trade, which was that of a carpenter; and after the manner of all men, he married a wife. Moreover, he begot for himself sons and daughters, four sons, namely, and two daughters. Now these are their names--Judas, Justus, James, and Simon. The names of the two daughters were Assia and Lydia. At length the wife of righteous Joseph, a woman intent on the divine glory in all her works, departed this life. But Joseph, that righteous man, my father after the flesh, and the spouse of my mother Mary, went away with his sons to his trade, practising the art of a carpenter.

3. Now when righteous Joseph became a widower, my mother Mary, blessed, holy, and pure, was already twelve years old. For her parents offered her in the temple when she was three years of age, and she remained in the temple of the Lord nine years. Then when the priests saw that the virgin, holy and God-fearing, was growing up, they spoke to each other, saying: Let us search out a man, righteous and pious, to whom Mary may be entrusted until the time of her marriage; lest, if she remain in the temple, it happen to her as is wont to happen to women, and lest on that account we sin, and God be angry with us.

4. Therefore they immediately sent out, and assembled twelve old men of the tribe of Judah. And they wrote down the names of the twelve tribes of Israel. And the lot fell upon the pious old man, righteous Joseph. Then the priests answered, and said to my blessed mother: Go with Joseph, and be with him till the time of your marriage. Righteous Joseph therefore received

my mother, and led her away to his own house. And Mary found James the Less in his father's house, broken-hearted and sad on account of the loss of his mother, and she brought him up. Hence Mary was called the mother of James. Thereafter Joseph left her at home, and went away to the shop where he wrought at his trade of a carpenter. And after the holy virgin had spent two years in his house her age was exactly fourteen years, including the time at which he received her.

5. And I chose her of my own will, with the concurrence of my Father, and the counsel of the Holy Spirit. And I was made flesh of her, by a mystery which transcends the grasp of created reason. And three months after her conception the righteous man Joseph returned from the place where he worked at his trade; and when he found my virgin mother pregnant, he was greatly perplexed, and thought of sending her away secretly. But from fear, and sorrow, and the anguish of his heart, he could endure neither to eat nor drink that day.

6. But at mid-day there appeared to him in a dream the prince of the angels, the holy Gabriel, furnished with a command from my Father; and he said to him: Joseph, son of David, fear not to take Mary as thy wife: for she has conceived of the Holy Spirit; and she will bring forth a son, whose name shall be called Jesus. He it is who shall rule all nations with a rod of iron. Having thus spoken, the angel departed from him. And Joseph rose from his sleep, and did as the angel of the Lord had said to him; and Mary abode with him.

7. Some time after that, there came forth an order from Augustus Caesar the king, that all the habitable world should be enrolled, each man in his own city. The old man therefore, righteous Joseph, rose up and took the virgin Mary and came to Bethlehem, because the time of her bringing forth was at hand. Joseph then inscribed his name in the list; for Joseph the son of David, whose spouse Mary was, was of the tribe of Judah. And indeed Mary, my mother, brought me forth in Bethlehem, in a cave near the tomb of Rachel the wife of the patriarch Jacob, the mother of Joseph and Benjamin.

8. But Satan went and told this to Herod the Great, the father of Archelaus. And it was this same Herod who ordered my friend and relative John to be beheaded. Accordingly he searched for me diligently, thinking that my kingdom was to be of this world. But Joseph, that pious old man, was warned of this by a dream. Therefore he rose and took Mary my mother, and I lay in her bosom. Salome also was their fellow-traveller. Having therefore set out from home, he retired into Egypt, and remained there the space of one whole year, until the hatred of Herod passed away.

9. Now Herod died by the worst form of death, atoning for the shedding

of the blood of the children whom he wickedly cut off, though there was no sin in them. And that impious tyrant Herod being dead, they returned into the land of Israel, and lived in a city of Galilee which is called Nazareth. And Joseph, going back to his trade of a carpenter, earned his living by the work of his hands; for, as the law of Moses had commanded, he never sought to live for nothing by another's labour.

10. At length, by increasing years, the old man arrived at a very advanced age. He did not, however, labour under any bodily weakness, nor had his sight failed, nor had any tooth perished from his mouth. In mind also, for the whole time of his life, he never wandered; but like a boy he always in his business displayed youthful vigour, and his limbs remained unimpaired, and free from all pain. His life, then, in all, amounted to one hundred and eleven years, his old age being prolonged to the utmost limit.

11. Now Justus and Simeon, the eider sons of Joseph, were married, and had families of their own. Both the daughters were likewise married, and lived in their own houses. So there remained in Joseph's house, Judas and James the Less, and my virgin mother. I moreover dwelt along with them, not otherwise than if I had been one of his sons. But I passed all my life without fault. Mary I called my mother, and Joseph father, and I obeyed them in all that they said; nor did I ever contend against them, but complied with their commands, as other men whom earth produces are wont to do; nor did I at any time arouse their anger, or give any word or answer in opposition to them. On the contrary, I cherished them with great love, like the pupil of my eye.

12. It came to pass, after these things, that the death of that old man, the pious Joseph, and his departure from this world, were approaching, as happens to other men who owe their origin to this earth. And as his body was verging on dissolution, an angel of the Lord informed him that his death was now close at hand. Therefore fear and great perplexity came upon him. So he rose up and went to Jerusalem; and going into the temple of the Lord, he poured out his prayers there before the sanctuary, and said:

13. O God! author of all consolation, God of all compassion, and Lord of the whole human race; God of my soul, body, and spirit; with supplications I reverence thee, O Lord and my God. If now my days are ended, and the time draws near when I must leave this world, send me, I beseech Thee, the great Michael, the prince of Thy holy angels: let him remain with me, that my wretched soul may depart from this afflicted body without trouble, without terror and impatience. For great fear and intense sadness take hold of all bodies on the day of their death, whether it be man or woman, beast wild or tame, or whatever creeps on the ground or flies in the air. At the last all

creatures under heaven in whom is the breath of life are struck with horror, and their souls depart from their bodies with strong fear and great depression. Now therefore, O Lord and my God, let Thy holy angel be present with his help to my soul and body, until they shall be dissevered from each other. And let not the face of the angel, appointed my guardian from the day of my birth, be turned away from me; but may he be the companion of my journey even until he bring me to Thee: let his countenance be pleasant and gladsome to me, and let him accompany me in peace. And let not demons of frightful aspect come near me in the way in which I am to go, until I come to Thee in bliss. And let not the doorkeepers hinder my soul from entering paradise. And do not uncover my sins, and expose me to condemnation before Thy terrible tribunal. Let not the lions rush in upon me; nor let the waves of the sea of fire overwhelm my soul--for this must every soul pass through--before I have seen the glory of Thy Godhead. O God, most righteous Judge, who in justice and equity wilt judge mankind, and wilt render unto each one according to his works, O Lord and my God, I beseech Thee, be present to me in Thy compassion, and enlighten my path that I may come to Thee; for Thou art a fountain overflowing with all good things, and with glory for evermore Amen.

14. It came to pass thereafter, when he returned to his own house in the city of Nazareth, that he was seized by disease, and had to keep his bed. And it was at this time that he died, according to the destiny of all mankind. For this disease was very heavy upon him, and he had never been ill, as he now was, from the day of his birth. And thus assuredly it pleased Christ to order the destiny of righteous Joseph. He lived forty years unmarried; thereafter his wife remained under his care forty-nine years, and then died. And a year after her death, my mother, the blessed Mary, was entrusted to him by the priests, that he should keep her until the time of her marriage. She spent two years in his house; and in the third year of her stay with Joseph, in the fifteenth year of her age, she brought me forth on earth by a mystery which no creature can penetrate or understand, except myself, and my Father and the Holy Spirit, constituting one essence with myself.

15. The whole age of my father, therefore, that righteous old man, was one hundred and eleven years, my Father in heaven having so decreed. And the day on which his soul left his body was the twenty-sixth of the month Abib. For now the fine gold began to lose its splendour, and the silver to be worn down by use--I mean his understanding and his wisdom. He also loathed food and drink, and lost all his skill in his trade of carpentry, nor did he any more pay attention to it. It came to pass, then, in the early dawn of the twenty-sixth day of Abib, that Joseph, that righteous old man, lying in his bed, was

giving up his unquiet soul. Wherefore he opened his mouth with many sighs, and struck his hands one against the other, and with a loud voice cried out, and spoke after the following manner:--

16. Woe to the day on which I was born into the world! Woe to the womb which bare me! Woe to the bowels which admitted me! Woe to the breasts which suckled me! Woe to the feet upon which I sat and rested! Woe to the hands which carried me and reared me until I grew up! For I was conceived in iniquity, and in sins did my mother desire me. Woe to my tongue and my lips, which have brought forth and spoken vanity, detraction, falsehood, ignorance, derision, idle tales, craft, and hypocrisy! Woe to mine eyes, which have looked upon scandalous things! Woe to mine ears, which have delighted in the words of slanderers! Woe to my hands, which have seized what did not of right belong to them! Woe to my belly and my bowels, which have lusted after food unlawful to be eaten! Woe to my throat, which like a fire has consumed all that it found! Woe to my feet, which have too often walked in ways displeasing to God! Woe to my body; and woe to my miserable soul, which has already turned aside from God its Maker! What shall I do when I arrive at that place where I must stand before the most righteous Judge, and when He shall call me to account for the works which I have heaped up in my youth? Woe to every man dying in his sins! Assuredly that same dreadful hour, which came upon my father Jacob, when his soul was flying forth from his body, is now, behold, near at hand for me. Oh! how wretched I am this day, and worthy of lamentation! But God alone is the disposer of my soul and body; He also will deal with them after His own good pleasure.

17. These are the words spoken by Joseph, that righteous old man. And I, going in beside him, found his soul exceedingly troubled, for he was placed in great perplexity. And I said to him: Hail! my father Joseph, thou righteous man; how is it with thee? And he answered me: All hail! my well-beloved son. Indeed, the agony and fear of death have already environed me; but as soon as I heard Thy voice, my soul was at rest. O Jesus of Nazareth! Jesus, my Saviour! Jesus, the deliverer of my soul! Jesus, my protector! Jesus! O sweetest name in my mouth, and in the mouth of all those that love it! O eye which seest, and ear which hearest, hear me! I am Thy servant; this day I most humbly reverence Thee, and before Thy face I pour out my tears. Thou art altogether my God; Thou art my Lord, as the angel has told me times without number, and especially on that day when my soul was driven about with perverse thoughts about the pure and blessed Mary, who was carrying Thee in her womb, and whom I was thinking of secretly sending away. And while I was thus meditating, behold, there appeared to me in my rest angels of the Lord, saying to me in a wonderful mystery: O Joseph, thou son of Da-

vid, fear not to take Mary as thy wife; and do not grieve thy soul, nor speak unbecoming words of her conception, because she is with child of the Holy Spirit, and shall bring forth a son, whose name shall be called Jesus, for He shall save His people from their sins. Do not for this cause wish me evil, O Lord! for I was ignorant of the mystery of Thy birth. I call to mind also, my Lord, that day when the boy died of the bite of the serpent. And his relations wished to deliver Thee to Herod, saying that Thou hadst killed him; but Thou didst raise him from the dead, and restore him to them. Then I went up to Thee, and took hold of Thy hand, saying: My son, take care of thyself. But Thou didst say to me in reply: Art thou not my father after the flesh? I shall teach thee who I am. Now therefore, O Lord and my God, do not be angry with me, or condemn me on account of that hour. I am Thy servant, and the son of Thine handmaiden; but Thou art my Lord, my God and Saviour, most surely the Son of God.

18. When my father Joseph had thus spoken, he was unable to weep more. And I saw that death now had dominion over him. And my mother, virgin undefiled, rose and came to me, saying: O my beloved son, this pious old man Joseph is now dying. And I answered: Oh my dearest mother, assuredly upon all creatures produced in this world the same necessity of death lies; for death holds sway over the whole human race. Even thou, O my virgin mother, must look for the same end of life as other mortals. And yet thy death, as also the death of this pious man, is not death, but life enduring to eternity. Nay more, even I must die, as concerns the body which I have received from thee. But rise, O my venerable mother, and go in to Joseph, that blessed old man, in order that thou mayst see what will happen as his soul ascends from his body.

19. My undefiled mother Mary, therefore, went and entered the place where Joseph was. And I was sitting at his feet looking at him, for the signs of death already appeared in his countenance. And that blessed old man raised his head, and kept his eyes fixed on my face; but he had no power of speaking to me, on account of the agonies of death, which held him in their grasp. But he kept fetching many sighs. And I held his hands for a whole hour; and he turned his face to me, and made signs for me not to leave him. Thereafter I put my hand upon his breast, and perceived his soul now near his throat, preparing to depart from its receptacle.

20. And when my virgin mother saw me touching his body, she also touched his feet. And finding them already dead and destitute of heat, she said to me: O my beloved son, assuredly his feet are already beginning to stiffen, and they are as cold as snow. Accordingly she summoned his sons and daughters, and said to them: Come, as many as there are of you, and go to

your father; for assuredly he is now at the very point of death. And Assia, his daughter, answered and said: Woe's me, O my brothers, this is certainly the same disease that my beloved mother died of. And she lamented and shed tears; and all Joseph's other children mourned along with her. I also, and my mother Mary, wept along with them.

21. And turning my eyes towards the region of the south, I saw Death already approaching, and all Gehenna with him, closely attended by his army and his satellites; and their clothes, their faces, and their mouths poured forth flames. And when my father Joseph saw them coming straight to him, his eyes dissolved in tears, and at the same time he groaned after a strange manner. Accordingly, when I saw the vehemence of his sighs, I drove back Death and all the host of servants which accompanied him. And I called upon my good Father, saying:--

22. O Father of all mercy, eye which seest, and ear which hearest, hearken to my prayers and supplications in behalf of the old man Joseph; and send Michael, the prince of Thine angels, and Gabriel, the herald of light, and all the light of Thine angels, and let their whole array walk with the soul of my father Joseph, until they shall have conducted it to Thee. This is the hour in which my father has need of compassion. And I say unto you, that all the saints, yea, as many men as are born in the world, whether they be just or whether they be perverse, must of necessity taste of death.

23. Therefore Michael and Gabriel came to the soul of my father Joseph, and took it, and wrapped it in a shining wrapper. Thus he committed his spirit into the hands of my good Father, and He bestowed upon him peace. But as yet none of his children knew that he had fallen asleep. And the angels preserved his soul from the demons of darkness which were in the way, and praised God even until they conducted it into the dwelling-place of the pious.

24. Now his body was lying prostrate and bloodless; wherefore I reached forth my hand, and put right his eyes and shut his mouth, and said to the virgin Mary: O my mother, where is the skill which he showed in all the time that he lived in this world? Lo! it has perished, as if it had never existed. And when his children heard me speaking with my mother, the pure virgin, they knew that he had already breathed his last, and they shed tears, and lamented. But I said to them: Assuredly the death of your father is not death, but life everlasting: for he has been freed from the troubles of this life, and has passed to perpetual and everlasting rest. When they heard these words, they rent their clothes, and wept.

25. And, indeed, the inhabitants of Nazareth and of Galilee, having heard of their lamentation, flocked to them, and wept from the third hour even to the ninth. And at the ninth hour they all went together to Joseph's bed. And

they lifted his body, after they had anointed it with costly unguents. But I entreated my Father in the prayer of the celestials--that same prayer which with any own hand I made before I was carried in the womb of the virgin Mary, my mother. And as soon as I had finished it, and pronounced the amen, a great multitude of angels came up; and I ordered two of them to stretch out their shining garments, and to wrap in them the body of Joseph, the blessed old man.

26. And I spoke to Joseph, and said: The smell or corruption of death shall not have dominion over thee, nor shall a worm ever come forth from thy body. Not a single limb of it shall be broken, nor shall any hair on thy head be changed. Nothing of thy body shall perish, O my father Joseph, but it will remain entire and uncorrupted even until the banquet of the thousand years. And whosoever shall make an offering on the day of thy remembrance, him will I bless and recompense in the congregation of the virgins; and whosoever shall give food to the wretched, the poor, the widows, and orphans from the work of his hands, on the day on which thy memory shall be celebrated, and in thy name, shall not be in want of good things all the days of his life. And whosoever shall have given a cup of water, or of wine, to drink to the widow or orphan in thy name, I will give him to thee, that thou mayst go in with him to the banquet of the thousand years. And every man who shall present an offering on the day of thy commemoration will I bless and recompense in the church of the virgins: for one I will render unto him thirty, sixty, and a hundred. And whosover shall write the history of thy life, of thy labour, and thy departure from this world, and this narrative that has issued from my mouth, him shall I commit to thy keeping as long as he shall have to do with this life. And when his soul departs from the body, and when he must leave this world, I will bum the book of his sins, nor will I torment him with any punishment in the day of judgment; but he shall cross the sea of flames, and shall go through it without trouble or pain. And upon every poor man who can give none of those things which I have mentioned this is incumbent: viz., if a son is born to him, he shall call his name Joseph. So there shall not take place in that house either poverty or any sudden death for ever.

27. Thereafter the chief men of the city came together to the place where the body of the blessed old man Joseph had been laid, bringing with them burial-clothes; and they wished to wrap it up in them after the manner in which the Jews are wont to arrange their dead bodies. And they perceived that he kept his shroud fast; for it adhered to the body in such a way, that when they wished to take it off, it was found to be like iron--impossible to be moved or loosened. Nor could they find any ends in that piece of linen, which struck them with the greatest astonishment. At length they carried

him out to a place where there was a cave, and opened the gate, that they might bury his body beside the bodies of his fathers. Then there came into my mind the day on which he walked with me into Egypt, and that extreme trouble which he endured on my account. Accordingly, I bewailed his death for a long time; and lying upon his body, I said:--

28. O Death! who makest all knowledge to vanish away, and raisest so many tears and lamentations, surely it is God my Father Himself who hath granted thee this power. For men die for the transgression of Adam and his wife Eve, and Death spares not so much as one. Nevertheless, nothing happens to any one, or is brought upon him, without the command of my Father. There have certainly been men who have prolonged their life even to nine hundred years; but they died. Yea, though some of them have lived longer, they have, notwithstanding, succumbed to the same fate; nor has any one of them ever said: I have not tasted death. For the Lord never sends the same punishment more than once, since it hath pleased my Father to bring it upon men. And at the very moment when it, going forth, beholds the command descending to it from heaven, it says: I will go forth against that man, and will greatly move him. Then, without delay, it makes an onset on the soul, and obtains the mastery of it, doing with it whatever it will. For, because Adam did not the will of my Father, but transgressed His commandment, the wrath of my Father was kindled against him, and He doomed him to death; and thus it was that death came into the world. But if Adam had observed my Father's precepts, death would never have fallen to his lot. Think you that I can ask my good Father to send me a chariot of fire, which may take up the body of my father Joseph, and convey it to the place of rest, in order that it may dwell with the spirits? But on account of the transgression of Adam, that trouble and violence of death has descended upon all the human race. And it is for this cause that I must die according to the flesh, for my work which I have created, that they may obtain grace.

29. Having thus spoken, I embraced the body of my father Joseph, and wept over it; and they opened the door of the tomb, and placed his body in it, near the body of his father Jacob. And at the time when he fell asleep he had fulfilled a hundred and eleven years. Never did a tooth in his mouth hurt him, nor was his eyesight rendered less sharp, nor his body bent, nor his strength impaired; but he worked at his trade of a carpenter to the very last day of his life; and that was the six-and-twentieth of the month Abib.

30. And we apostles, when we heard these things from our Saviour, rose up joyfully, and prostrated ourselves in honour of Him, and said: O our Saviour, show us Thy grace. Now indeed we have heard the word of life: nevertheless we wonder, O our Saviour, at the fate of Enoch and Elias, inasmuch

as they had not to undergo death. For truly they dwell in the habitation of the righteous even to the present day, nor have their bodies seen corruption. Yet that old man Joseph the carpenter was, nevertheless, Thy father after the flesh. And Thou hast ordered us to go into all the world and preach the holy Gospel; and Thou hast said: Relate to them the death of my father Joseph, and celebrate to him with annual solemnity a festival and sacred day. And whosoever shall take anything away from this narrative, or add anything to it, commits sin. We wonder especially that Joseph, even from that day on which Thou wast born in Bethlehem, called Thee his son after the flesh. Wherefore, then, didst Thou not make him immortal as well as them, and Thou sayest that he was righteous and chosen?

31. And our Saviour answered and said: Indeed, the prophecy of my Father upon Adam, for his disobedience, has now been fulfilled. And all things are arranged according to the will and pleasure of my Father. For if a man rejects the commandment of God, and follows the works of the devil by committing sin, his life is prolonged; for be is preserved in order that he may perhaps repent, and reflect that he must be delivered into the hands of death. But if any one has been zealous of good works, his life also is prolonged, that, as the fame of his old age increases, upright men may imitate him. But when you see a man whose mind is prone to anger, assuredly his days are shortened; for it is these that are taken away in the flower of their age. Every prophecy, therefore, which my Father has pronounced concerning the sons of men, must be fulfilled in every particular. But with reference to Enoch and Elias, and how they remain alive to this day, keeping the same bodies with which they were born; and as to what concerns my father Joseph, who has not been allowed as well as they to remain in the body: indeed, though a man live in the world many myriads of years, nevertheless at some time or other he is compelled to exchange life for death. And I say to you, O my brethren, that they also, Enoch and Elias, must towards the end of time return into the world and die--in the day, namely, of commotion, of terror, of perplexity, and affliction. For Antichrist will slay four bodies, and will pour out their blood like water, because of the reproach to which they shall expose him, and the ignominy with which they, in their lifetime, shall brand him when they reveal his impiety.

32. And we said: O our Lord, our God and Saviour, who are those four whom Thou hast said Antichrist will cut off from the reproach they bring upon him? The Lord answered: They are Enoch, Elias, Schila, and Tabitha. When we heard this from our Saviour, we rejoiced and exulted; and we offered all glory and thanksgiving to the Lord God, and our Saviour Jesus Christ. He it is to whom is due glory, honour, dignity, dominion, power, and

praise, as well as to the good Father with Him, and to the Holy Spirit that giveth life, henceforth and in all time for evermore. Amen.

The Book of John the Evangelist

I, John, your brother and partaker in tribulation, and that shall be also a partaker in the kingdom of heaven, when I lay upon breast of our Lord Jesus Christ and said unto him: Lord, who is he that shall betray thee? [and] he answered and said: He that dippeth his hand with me in the dish: then Satan entered unto him and he sought how he might betray me.

And I said: Lord, before Satan fell, in what glory abode he with thy Father? And he said unto me: In such glory was he that he commanded the powers of the heavens: but I sat with my Father, and he did order all the followers of the Father, and went down from heaven unto the deep and ascended up out of the deep unto the throne of the invisible Father. And he saw the glory of him that moveth the heavens, and he thought to set his seat above the clouds of heaven and desired to be like unto the Most High.

And when he had descended into the air, he said unto the angel of the air: Open unto me the gates of the air. And he opened them unto him. And he sought to go further downward and found the angel which held the waters, and said unto him: Open unto me the gates of the waters. And he opened to him. And he passed through and found all the face of the earth covered with waters. And he passed through beneath the earth and found two fishes lying upon the waters, and they were as oxen yoked for ploughing, holding the whole earth by the commandment of the invisible Father, from the west even unto the sunrising. And when he had gone down he found clouds hanging which held the waters of the sea. And he went down yet further and found hell, that is the gehenna of fire and thereafter he could go down no further because of the flame of the burning fire. And Satan returned back and filled up (passed over again) the paths and entered in unto the angel of the air and to him that was over the waters, and said unto them: All these things are mine: if ye will hearken unto me, I will set my seat in the clouds and be like the Most High, and I will take the waters from this upper firmament and gather together the other parts (places) of the sea, and thereafter there shall be no water upon the face of all the earth, and I will reign with you world without end.

And when he had said thus unto the angels, he went up unto the other angels, even unto the fifth heaven, and thus spake he unto each of them: How much owest thou unto thy lord? He said: An hundred measures (cors) of wheat. And he said unto him: Take pen and ink and write sixty. And unto others he said: And thou, how much owest thou unto thy lord? and he answered: An hundred jars of oil. And he said: Sit down and write fifty. And as he went up through all the heavens he said thus, even unto the fifth heaven, seducing the angels of the invisible Father. And there came forth a voice out of the throne of the Father, saying: What doest thou, O denier of the Father, seducing the angels? doer of iniquity, that thou hast devised do quickly.

Then the Father commanded his angels, saying: Take away their garments. And the angels took away their garments and their thrones and their crowns from all the angels that hearkened unto him.

And I asked of the Lord: When Satan fell, in what place dwelt he? And he answered me: My Father changed his appearance because of his pride, and the light was taken from him, and his face became like unto heated iron, and his face became wholly like that of a man: and he drew with his tail the third part of the angels of God, and was cast out from the seat of God and from the stewardship of the heavens. And Satan came down into this firmament, and he could find (make) no rest for himself nor for them that were with him. And he asked the Father saying: Have patience with me and I will pay thee all. And the Father had mercy on him and gave him rest and them that were with him, as much as they would even unto seven days.

And so sat he in the firmament and commanded the angel that was over the air and him that was over the waters, and they raised the earth up and it appeared dry: and he took the crown of the angel that was over the waters, and of the half thereof he made the light of the moon and of the half the light of the stars: and of the precious stones he made all the hosts of the stars.

And thereafter he made the angels his ministers according to the order of the form of the Most High, bind by the commandment of the invisible Father he made thunder, rain, hail, and snow.

And he sent forth angels to be ministers over them. And he commanded the earth to bring forth every beast for food (fatling), and every creeping thing, and trees and herbs: and he commanded the sea to bring forth fishes, and the fowls of the heaven.

And he devised furthermore and made man in his likeness, and commanded the (or an) angel of the third heaven to enter into the body of clay. And he took thereof and made another body in the form of a woman, and commanded the (or an) angel of the second heaven to enter into the body of the woman. But the angel lamented when they beheld a mortal shape upon them and that they were unlike in shape. And he commanded them to do the deed of the flesh in the bodies of clay, and they knew not how to commit sin.

Then did the contriver of evil devise in his mind to make paradise, and he brought the man and woman into it. And he Commanded to bring a reed, and the devil planted it in the midst of paradise, and so did the wicked devil hide his device that they knew not his deceit. And he came in and spake unto them, saying: Of every fruit which is in paradise eat ye, but of the fruit of the knowledge of good and evil eat not. Notwithstanding, the devil entered into a wicked serpent and seduced the angel that was in the form of the woman, and he wrought his lust with Eve in the Song of the serpent. And therefore are they called sons of the devil and sons of the serpent that do the lust of the devil their father, even unto the end of this world. And again the devil poured out upon the angel that was in Adam the poison of his lust, and it begetteth the sons of the serpent and the sons of the devil even unto the end of this world.

And after that I, John, asked of the Lord, saying: How say men that Adam and Eve were created by God and set in paradise to keep the commandments of the Father, and were delivered unto death? And the Lord said to me: Hearken, John, beloved of my Father; foolish men say thus in their deceitfulness that my Father made bodies of clay: but by the Holy Ghost made he all the powers of the heavens, and holy ones were found having bodies of clay because of their transgression, and therefore were delivered unto death.

And again I, John, asked the Lord: How beginneth a man to be in the Spirit (to have a spirit) in a body of flesh? And the Lord said unto me: Certain of the angels which fell do enter unto the bodies of women, and receive flesh from the lust of the flesh, and so is a spirit born of spirit, and flesh of flesh, and so is the kingdom of Satan accomplished in this world and among all nations.

And he said to me: My Father hath suffered him to reign seven days, which are seven ages.

And I asked the Lord and said: What shall be in that time? And he said to me: From the time when the devil fell from the glory of the Father and (lost) his own glory, he sat upon the clouds, and sent his ministers, even angels flaming with fire, unto men from Adam even unto Henoch his servant. And he raised up Henoch upon the firmament and showed him his godhead and commanded pen and ink to be given him: and he sat down and wrote threescore and seven books. And he commanded that he should take them to the earth and deliver them unto his sons. And Henoch let his books down upon the earth and delivered them unto his sons, and began to teach them to perform the custom of sacrifice, and unrighteous mysteries, and so did he hide the kingdom of heaven from men. And he said unto them: Behold that I am your god and beside me is none other god. And therefore did my Father send me into the world that I might make it known unto men, that they might know the evil device of the devil.

And then when he perceived that I had come down out of heaven into the world, he sent an angel and took of three sorts of wood and gave them unto Moses that I might be crucified, and now are they reserved for me. But then (now) did the devil proclaim unto him (Moses) his godhead, and unto his people, and commanded a law to be given unto the children of Israel, and brought them out through the midst of the sea which was dried up.

When my Father thought to send me into the world, he sent his angel before me, by name Mary, to receive me. And I when I came down entered in by the ear and came forth by the ear.

And Satan the prince of this world perceived that I was come to seek and save them that were lost, and sent his angel, even Helias the prophet, baptizing with water: who is called John the Baptist. And Helias asked the prince of this world: How can I know him? Then his lord said: On whom soever thou shalt see the spirit descending like a dove and resting upon him, he it is that baptizeth with the Holy Ghost unto forgiveness of sins: thou wilt be able to destroy him and to save. And again I, John, asked the Lord: Can a man be saved by the baptism of John without thy baptism? And the Lord answered: Unless I have baptized him unto forgiveness of sins, by the baptism of water can no man see the kingdom of heaven: for I am the bread of life that came down from the seventh heaven and they that eat my flesh and drink my blood, they shall be called the sons of God.

And I asked the Lord and said: What meaneth it, to eat my flesh and drink my blood? (An answer and question seem to have fallen out.) And the Lord said unto me: Before the falling of the devil with all his host from the glory of the Father [in prayer], they did glorify the Father in their prayers thus, saying: Our Father, which art in heaven; and so did all their songs come up before the throne of the Father. But when they had fallen, after that they are not able to glorify God with that prayer.

And I asked the Lord: How do all men receive the baptism of John, but thine not at all? And the Lord answered: Because their deeds are evil and they come not unto the light.

The disciples of John marry and are given in marriage; but my disciples neither marry nor are given in marriage, but are as the angels of God in heaven. But I said: If, then, it be sin to have to do with a woman, it is not good to marry. And the Lord said unto me: Not every one can receive this saying (&c., Matt. xix.11, 12).

I asked the Lord concerning the day of judgement: What shall be the sign of thy coming? And he answered and said unto me: When the numbers of the righteous shall be accomplished that is, the number of the righteous that are crowned, that have fallen, then shall Satan be loosed out of his prison, having great wrath, and shall make war with the righteous, and they shall cry unto the Lord with a loud voice. And immediately the Lord shall command an angel to blow with the trumpet, and the voice of the archangel shall be heard in the trumpet from heaven even unto hell.

And then shall the sun be darkened and the moon shall not give her light, and the stars shall fall, and the four winds shall be loosed from their foundations, and shall cause the earth and the sea and the mountains to quake together. And the heaven shall immediately shake and the sun shall be darkened, and it shall shine even to the fourth hour. Then shall appear the sign of the Son of man, and all the holy angels with him, and he shall set his seat upon the clouds, and sit on the throne of his majesty with the twelve apostles on the twelve seats of their glory. And the books shall be opened and he shall judge the whole world and the faith which he proclaimed. And then shall the Son of man send his angels, and they shall gather his elect from the four winds from the heights of the heavens unto the boundaries of them, and shall bring them to seek.

Then shall the Son of God send the evil spirits, to bring all nations before him, and shall say unto them: Come, ye that did say: We have eaten and drunk and received the gain of this world. And after that they shall again be brought, and shall all stand before the judgement seat, even all nations, in fear. And the books of life shall be opened and all nations shall show forth their ungodliness. And he shall glorify the righteous for their patience: and glory and honour and incorruption shall be the reward of their good works: but as for them that kept the commandments of the angels and obeyed unrighteously, indignation and trouble and anguish shall take hold on then.

And the Son of God shall bring forth the elect out of the midst of the sinners and say unto them: Come, ye blessed of my Father, inherit the kingdom prepared for you from the foundation of the world. Then shall he say unto the sinners: Depart from me, ye cursed, into everlasting fire, which was prepared for the devil and   his angels. And the rest, beholding the last cutting off, shall cast the sinners into hell by the commandment of the invisible

Father. Then shall the spirits of them that believe not go forth out of the prisons, and then shall my voice be heard, and there shall be one fold and one shepherd: and the darkness and obscurity shall come forth out of the lower parts of the earth -that is to say, the darkness of the gehenna of fire- and shall burn all things from below even to the air of the firmament. And the Lord shall be in the firmament and even to the lower parts of the earth. (read And the distance from the firmament unto the lower parts of the earth shall be) as if a man of thirty years old should take up a stone and cast it down, hardly in three years would it reach the bottom: so great is the depth of the pit and of the fire wherein the sinners shall dwell. And then shall Satan and all his host be bound and cast into the lake of fire. And the Son of God shall walk with his elect above the firmament and shall shut up the devil, binding him with strong chains that cannot be loosed. At that time the sinners, weeping and mourning, shall say: O earth, swallow us up and cover us in death. And then shall the righteous shine as the sun in the kingdom of their Father. And he shall bring them before the throne of the invisible Father, saying: Behold, I and my children whom God hath given me. O righteous one, the world hath not known thee, but I have known thee in truth, because thou hast sent me. And then shall the Father answer his Son and say: My beloved Son, sit thou on my right hand until I make thine enemies the footstool of thy feet, which have denied me and said: We are gods, and beside us there is none other god: which have slain thy prophets and persecuted thy righteous ones, and thou hast persecuted them even unto the outer darkness: there shall be weeping and gnashing of teeth.

And then shall the Son of God sit on the right hand of his Father, and the Father shall command his angels, and they shall minister unto them (i.e. the righteous) and set them among the choirs of the angels, to clothe them with incorruptible garments, and shall give them crowns that fade not and seats that cannot be moved. And God shall be in the midst of them; and they shall not hunger nor thirst any more, neither shall the sun light on them nor any heat. And God shall wipe away every tear from their eyes. And he shall reign with his holy Father, and of his kingdom there shall be no end for ever and ever.

The Letter of Aristeas

Since I have collected Material for a memorable history of my visit to Eleazar the High priest of the Jews, and because you, Philocrates, as you lose no opportunity of reminding me, have set great store upon receiving an account of the motives and object of my mission, I have attempted to draw up a clear exposition of the matter for you, for I perceive that you possess a natural love of learning,   a quality which is the highest possession of man -to be constantly attempting ' to add to his stock of knowledge and acquirements ' whether through the study of history or by actually participating in the events themselves. It is by this means, by taking up into itself the noblest elements, that the soul is established in purity, and having fixed its aim on piety, the noblest goal of all, it uses this as its infallible guide and so acquires a definite purpose.

It was my devotion to the pursuit of religious knowledge that led me to undertake the embassy to the man I have mentioned, who was held in the highest esteem by his own citizens and by others both for his virtue and his majesty and who had in his possession documents of the highest value to the Jews in his own country and in foreign lands for the interpretation of the divine law, for their laws are written on leather parchments in Jewish characters. This embassy then I undertook with enthusiasm, having first of all found an opportunity of pleading with the king on behalf of the Jewish captives who had been transported from Judea to Egypt by the king's father, when he first obtained possession of this city and conquered the land of Egypt. It is worth while that I should tell you this story, too, since I am convinced that you, with your disposition towards holiness and your sympathy with men who are living in accordance with the holy law, will all the more readily listen to the account which I purpose to set forth, since you yourself have lately come to us from the island and are anxious to hear everything that tends to build up the soul. On a former occasion, too I sent you a record of the facts which I thought worth relating about the Jewish race, -the record which I had obtained from the most learned high priests of the most learned land of Egypt. As you are so eager to acquire the knowledge of those things which can benefit the mind, I feel it incumbent upon me to impart to you all the information in my power. I should feel the same duty towards all who possessed the same disposition but I feel it especially towards you since you have aspirations which are so noble, and since you are not only my brother in character no less than in blood but are one with me as well in the pursuit of goodness. For neither the pleasure derived from gold nor any other of the possessions which are prized by shallow minds confers the same benefit as the pursuit of culture and the study which we expend in securing it. But that I may not weary you by a too lengthy introduction, I will proceed at once to the substance of my narrative.

Demetrius of Phalerum, the president of the king's library, received vast sums of money, for the purpose of collecting together, as far as he possibly could, all the books in the world. By means of purchase and transcription, he carried out, to the best of his ability, the purpose of the king. On one occasion when I was present he was asked, How many thousand books are there in the library? And he replied, ' More than two hundred thousand, O king, and I shall make endeavour in the immediate future to gather together the remainder also, so that the total of five hundred thousand may be reached. I am told that the laws of the Jews are worth transcribing and deserve a place in your library.' ' What is to prevent you from doing this? ' replied the king. ' Everything that is necessary has been placed at your disposal.' 'They need to be translated,' answered Demetrius, ' for in the country of the Jews they use a peculiar alphabet (just as the Egyptians, too, have a special form of letters) and speak a peculiar dialect. They are supposed to use the Syriac tongue, but this is not the case; their language is quite different.' And the king when he understood all the facts of the case ordered a letter to be written to the Jewish High Priest that his purpose (which has already been described) might be accomplished.

Thinking that the time had come to press the demand, which I had often laid before Sosibius of Tarentum and Andreas, the chief of the bodyguard, for the emancipation of the Jews who had been transported from Judea by the king's father -for when by a combination of good fortune and courage he had brought his attack on the whole district of Coele -Syria and Phoenicia to a successful issue, in the process of terrorizing the country into subjection, he transported some of his foes and others he reduced to captivity. The number of those whom he transported from the country of the Jews to Egypt amounted to no less than a hundred thousand. Of these he armed thirty thousand picked men and settled them in garrisons in the country districts. (And even before this time large numbers of Jews had come into Egypt with the Persian, and in an earlier period still others had been sent to Egypt to help Psammetichus in his campaign against the king of the Ethiopians. But these were nothing like so numerous as the captives whom Ptolemy the son of Lagus transported.) As I have already said Ptolemy picked out the best of these, the men who were in the prime of life and distinguished for their courage, and armed them, but the great mass of the others, those who were too old or too young for this purpose, and the women too, he reduced to slavery, not that he wished to do this of his own free will, but he was compelled by his soldiers who claimed them as a reward for the services which they had rendered in war. Having, as has already been stated, obtained an opportunity for securing their emancipation, I addressed the king with the following arguments. ' Let us not be so unreasonable as to allow our deeds to give the lie to our words. Since the law which we wish not only to transcribe but also to translate belongs to the whole Jewish race, what justification shall we be able to find for our embassy while such vast numbers of them remain in a state of slavery in your kingdom ? In the perfection and wealth of your clemency release those who are held in such miserable bondage, since as I have been at pains to discover, the God who gave them their law is the God who maintains your kingdom. They worship the same God -the Lord and Creator of the Universe, as all other men, as we ourselves, O king, though we call him by different names, such as Zeus or Dis. This name was very appropriately bestowed upon him by our first ancestors, in order to signify that He through whom all things are endowed with life and come into being, is necessarily the ruler and lord of the Universe. Set all mankind an example of magnanimity by releasing those who are held in bondage.'

After a brief interval, while I was offering up an earnest prayer to God that He would so dispose the mind of the king that all the captives might be set at liberty-(for the human race, being the creation of God, is swayed and influenced by Him. Therefore with many divers prayers I called upon Him who ruleth the heart that the king might be constrained to grant my request. For I had great hopes with regard to the salvation of the men since I was assured that God would grant a fulfilment of my prayer. For when men from pure motives plan some action in the interest of righteousness and the performance of noble deeds, Almighty God brings their efforts and purposes to a successful issue) -the king raised his head and looking up at me with a cheerful countenance asked, ' How many thousands do you think they will number?' Andreas, who was standing near, replied, 'A little more than a hundred thousand.' ' It is a small boon indeed,' said the king, ' that Aristeas asks of us ! ' Then Sosibius and some others who were present said, ' Yes, but it will be a fit tribute to your magnanimity for you to offer the enfranchisement of these men as an act of devotion to the supreme God. You have been greatly honoured by Almighty God and exalted above all your forefathers in glory and it is only fitting that you should render to Him the greatest thank offering in your power.' Extremely pleased with these arguments he gave orders that an addition should be made to the wages of the soldiers by the amount of the redemption money that twenty drachmae should be paid to the owners for every slave, that a public order should be issued and that registers of the captives should be attached to it. He showed the greatest enthusiasm in the business, for it was God who had brought our purpose to fulfilment in its entirety and constrained him to redeem not only those who had come into Egypt with the army of his father but any who had come before that time or had been subsequently brought into the kingdom. It was pointed out to him that the ransom money would exceed four hundred talents.

I think it will be useful to insert a copy of the decree, for in this way the magnanimity of the king, who was empowered by God to save such vast multitudes, will be made clearer and more manifest. The decree of the king ran as follows: 'All who served in the army of our father in the campaign against Syria and Phoenicia and in the attack upon the country of the Jews and became possessed of Jewish captives and brought them back to the city of Alexandria and the land of Egypt or sold them to others -and in the same way any captives who were in our land before that time or were brought hither afterwards- all who possess such captives are required to set them at liberty at once, receiving twenty drachmae per head as ransom money. The soldiers will receive this money as a gift added to their wages, the others from the king's treasury. We think that it was against our father's will and against all propriety that they should have been made captives and that the devastation of their land and the transportation of the Jews to Egypt was an act of military wantonness. The spoil which fell to the soldiers on the field of battle was all the booty which they should have claimed. To reduce the people to slavery in addition was an act of absolute injustice. Wherefore since it is acknowledged that we are accustomed to render justice to all men and especially to those who are unfairly in a condition of servitude, and since we strive to deal fairly with all men according to the demands of justice and piety, we have decreed, in reference to the persons of the Jews who are in any condition of bondage in any part of our dominion, that those who possess them shall receive the stipulated sum of money and set them at liberty and that no man shall show any tardiness in discharging his obligations. Within three days after the publication of this decree, they must make lists of slaves for the officers appointed to carry out our will, and immediately produce the persons of the captives. For we consider that it will be advantageous to us and to our affairs that the matter should be brought to a conclusion. Any one who likes may give information about any who disobey the decree on condition that if the man is proved guilty he will become his slave; his property, however, will be handed over to the royal treasury.'

When the decree was brought to be read over to the king for his approval, it contained all the other provisions except the phrase ' any captives who were in the land before that time or were brought hither afterwards,' and in his magnanimity and the largeness of his heart the king inserted this clause and gave orders that the grant of money required for the redemption should be deposited in full with the paymasters of the forces and the royal bankers, and so the matter was decided and the decree ratified within seven days. The grant for the redemption amounted to more than six hundred and sixty talents; for many infants at the breast were emancipated together with their mothers. When the question was raised whether the sum of twenty talents was to be paid for these, the king ordered that it should be done, and thus he carried out his decision in the most comprehensive way. When this had been done, he ordered Demetrius to draw up a memorial with regard to the transcription of the Jewish books. For all affairs of state used to be carried out by means of decrees and with the most painstaking accuracy by these Egyptian kings, and nothing was done in a slipshod or haphazard fashion. And so I have inserted copies of the memorial and the letters, the number of the presents sent and the nature of each, since every one of them excelled in magnificence and technical skill. The following is a copy of the memorial. The Memorial of Demetrius to the great king. ' Since you have given me instructions, O king, that the books which are needed to complete your library should be collected together, and that those which are defective should be repaired, I have devoted myself with the utmost care to the fulfilment of your wishes, and I now have the following proposal to lay before you. The books of the law of the Jews (with some few others) are absent from the library. They are written in the Hebrew characters and language and have been carelessly interpreted, and do not represent the original text as I am informed by those who know; for they have never had a king's care to protect them. It is necessary that these should be made accurate for your library since the law which they contain, in as much as it is of divine origin, is full of wisdom and free from all blemish. For this reason literary men and poets and the mass of historical writers have held aloof from referring to these books and the men who have lived and are living in accordance with them, because their conception of life is so sacred and religious, as Hecataeus of Abdera says. If it please you, O king, a letter shall be written to the High Priest in Jerusalem, asking him to send six elders out of every tribe -men who have lived the noblest life and are most skilled in their law -that we may find out the points in which the majority of them are in agreement, and so having obtained an accurate translation may place it in a conspicuous place in a manner worthy of the work itself and your purpose. May continual prosperity be yours ! '

When this memorial had been presented, the king ordered a letter to be written to Eleazar on the matter, giving also an account of the emancipation of the Jewish captives. And he gave fifty talents weight of gold and seventy talents of silver and a large quantity of precious stones to make bowls and vials and a table and libation cups. He also gave orders to those who had the custody of his coffers to allow the artificers to make a selection of any materials they might require for the purpose, and that a hundred talents in money should be sent to provide sacrifices for the temple and for other needs. I shall give you a full account of the workmanship after I have set before you copies of the letters. The letter of the king ran as follows:

' King Ptolemy sends greeting and salutation to the High Priest Eleazar. Since there are many Jews settled in our realm who were carried off from Jerusalem by the Persians at the time of their power and many more who came with my father into Egypt as captives -large numbers of these he placed in the army and paid them higher wages than usual, and when he had proved the loyalty of their leaders he built fortresses and placed them in their charge that the native Egyptians might be intimidated by them. And I, when I ascended the throne, adopted a kindly attitude towards all my subjects, and more particularly to those who were citizens of yours- I have set at liberty more than a hundred thousand captives, paying their owners the appropriate market price for them, and if ever evil has been done to your people through the passions of the mob, I have made them reparation. The motive which prompted my action has been the desire to act piously and render unto the supreme God a thank offering for maintaining my kingdom in peace and great glory in all the world. Moreover those of your people who were in the prime of life I have drafted into my army, and those who were fit to be attached to my person and worthy of the confidence of the court, I have established in official positions. Now since I am anxious to show my gratitude to these men and to the Jews throughout the world and to the generations yet to come, I have determined that your law shall be translated from the Hebrew tongue which is in use amongst you into the Greek language, that these books may be added to the other royal books in my library. It will be a kindness on your part and a regard for my zeal if you will select six elders from each of your tribes, men of noble life and skilled in your law and able to interpret it, that in questions of dispute we may be able to discover the verdict in which the majority agree, for the investigation is of the highest possible importance. I hope to win great renown by the accomplishment of this work. I have sent Andreas, the chief of my bodyguard, and Aristeas -men whom I hold in high esteem- to lay the matter before you and present you with a hundred talents of silver, the firstfruits of my offering for the temple and the sacrifices and other religious rites. If you will write to me concerning your wishes in these matters, you will confer a great favour upon me and afford me a new pledge of friendship, for all your wishes shall be carried out as speedily as possible. Farewell.'

To this letter Eleazar replied appropriately as follows: ' Eleazar the High priest sends greetings to King Ptolemy his true friend. My highest wishes are for your welfare and the welfare of Queen Arsinoe your sister and your children. I also am well. I have received your letter and am greatly rejoiced by your purpose and your noble counsel. I summoned together the whole people and read it to them that they might know of your devotion to our God. I showed them too the cups which you sent, twenty of gold and thirty of silver, the five bowls and the table of dedication, and the hundred talents of silver for the offering of the sacrifices and providing the things of which the temple stands in need. These gifts were brought to me by Andreas, one of your most honoured servants, and by Aristeas, both good men and true, distinguished by their learning, and worthy in every way to be the representatives of your high principles and righteous purposes. These men imparted to me your message and received from me an answer in agreement with your letter. I will consent to everything which is advantageous to you even though your request is very unusual. For you have bestowed upon our citizens great and never to be forgotten benefits in many (ways). Immediately therefore I offered sacrifices on behalf of you, your sister, your children, and your friends, and all the people prayed that your plans might prosper continually, and that Almighty God might preserve your kingdom in peace with honour, and that the translation of the holy law might prove advantageous to you and be carried out successfully. In the presence of all the people I selected six elders from each tribe, good men and true, and I have sent them to you with a copy of our law. It will be a kindness, O righteous king, if you will give instruction that as soon as the translation of the law is completed, the men shall be restored again to us in safety. Farewell.'

The following are the names of the elders: Of the first tribe, Joseph, Ezekiah, Zachariah, John, Ezekiah, Elisha. Of the second tribe, Judas, Simon, Samuel, Adaeus, Mattathias, Eschlemias. Of the third tribe, Nehemiah, Joseph, Theodosius, Baseas, Ornias, Dakis. Of the fourth tribe, Jonathan, Abraeus, Elisha, Ananias, Chabrias.... Of the fifth tribe, Isaac, Jacob, Jesus, Sabbataeus, Simon, Levi. Of the sixth tribe, Judas, Joseph, Simon, Zacharias, Samuel, Selemias. Of the seventh tribe, Sabbataeus, Zedekiah, Jacob, Isaac,

Jesias, Natthaeus. Of the eighth tribe Theodosius, Jason, Jesus, Theodotus, John, Jonathan. Of the ninth tribe, Theophilus, Abraham Arsamos, Jason, Endemias, Daniel. Of the tenth tribe, Jeremiah, Eleazar, Zachariah, Baneas, Elisha, Dathaeus. Of the eleventh tribe, Samuel, Joseph, Judas, Jonathes, Chabu, Dositheus. Of the twelfth tribe, Isaelus, John, Theodosius, Arsamos, Abietes, Ezekiel. They were seventy-two in all. Such was the answer which Eleazar and his friends gave to the king's letter.

I will now proceed to redeem my promise and give a description of the works of art. They were wrought with exceptional skill, for the king spared no expense and personally superintended the workmen individually. They could not therefore scamp any part of the work or finish it off negligently.

First of all I will give you a description of the table. The king was anxious that this piece of work should be of exceptionally large dimensions, and he caused enquiries to be made of the Jews in the locality with regard to the size of the table already in the temple at Jerusalem. And when they described the measurements, he proceeded to ask whether he might make a larger structure. And some of the priests and the other Jews replied that there was nothing to prevent him. And he said that he was anxious to make it five times the size, but he hesitated lest it should prove useless for the temple services. He was desirous that his gift should not merely be stationed in the temple, for it would afford him much greater pleasure if the men whose duty it was to offer the fitting sacrifices were able to do so appropriately on the table which he had made. He did not suppose that it was owing to lack of gold that the former table had been made of small size, but there seems to have been, he said, some reason why it was made of this dimension. For had the order been given, there would have been no lack of means. Wherefore we must not transgress or go beyond the proper measure. At the same time he ordered them to press into service all the manifold forms of art, for he w as a man of the most lofty conceptions and nature had endowed him with a keen imagination which enabled him to picture the appearance which would be presented by the finished work. He gave orders too, that where there were no instructions laid down in the Jewish Scriptures, everything should be made as beautiful as possible. When such instructions were laid down, they were to be carried out to the letter.

They made the table two cubits long (one cubit broad) one and a half cubits high, fashioning it of pure solid gold. What I am describing was not thin gold laid over another foundation, but the whole structure was of massive gold welded together. And they made a border of a hand's breadth round about it. And there was a wreath of wave-work, engraved in relief in the form of ropes marvelously wrought on its three sides. For it was triangular in shape and the style of the work was exactly the same on each of the sides, so that whichever side they were turned, they presented the same appearance. Of the two sides under the border, the one which sloped down to the table was a very beautiful piece of work, but it was the outer side which attracted the gaze of the spectator. Now the upper edge of the two sides, being elevated, was sharp since, as we have said, the rim was three-sided, from whatever point of view one approached it. And there were layers of precious stones on it in the midst of the embossed cord-work, and they were interwoven with one another by an inimitable artistic device. For the sake of security they were all fixed by golden needles which were inserted in perforations in the stones. At the sides they were clamped together by fastenings to hold them firm. On the part of the border round the table which slanted upwards and met the eyes, there was wrought a pattern of eggs in precious stones, elaborately engraved by a continuous piece of fluted relief-work, closely connected together round the whole table. And under the stones which had been arranged to represent eggs the artists made a crown containing all kinds of fruits, having at its top clusters of grapes and ears of corn, dates also and apples, and pomegranates and the like, conspicuously arranged. These fruits were wrought out of precious stones, of the same colour as the fruits themselves and they fastened them edgeways round all the sides of the table with a band of gold. And after the crown of fruit had been put on, underneath there was inserted another pattern of eggs in precious stones, and other fluting and embossed work, that both sides of the table might be used, according to the wishes of the owners and for this reason the wave-work and the border were extended down to the feet of the table. They made and fastened under the whole width of the table a massive plate four fingers thick, that the feet might be inserted into it, and clamped fast with linch-pins which fitted into sockets under the border, so that which ever side of the table people preferred, might be used. Thus it became manifestly clear that the work was intended to be used either way. On the table itself they engraved a ' maeander ', having precious stones standing out in the middle of it, rubies and emeralds and an onyx too and many other kinds of stones which excel in beauty. And next to the ' maeander ' there was placed a wonderful piece of network, which made the centre of the table appear like a rhomboid in shape, and on it a crystal and amber, as it is called, had been wrought, which produced an incomparable impression on the beholders. They made the feet of the table with heads like lilies, so that they seemed to be like lilies bending down beneath the table, and the parts which were visible represented leaves which stood upright. The basis of the foot on the ground consisted of a ruby and measured a hand's breadth high all round. It had the appearance of a shoe and was eight fingers broad. Upon it the whole expanse of the foot rested.

And they made the foot appear like ivy growing out of the stone, interwoven with akanthus and surrounded with a vine which encircled it with clusters of grapes, which were worked in stones, up to the top of the foot. All the four feet were made in the same style, and everything was wrought and fitted so skillfully, and such remarkable skill and knowledge were expended upon making it true to nature, that when the air was stirred by a breath of wind, movement was imparted to the leaves, and everything was fashioned to correspond with the actual reality which it represented. And they made the top of the table in three parts like a triptychon, and they were so fitted and dovetailed together with spigots along the whole breadth of the work, that the meeting of the joints could not be seen or even discovered. The thickness of the table was not less than half a cubit, so that the whole work must have cost many talents. For since the king did not wish to add to its size he expended on the details the same sum of money which would have been required if the table could have been of larger dimensions. And everything was completed in accordance with his plan, in a most wonderful and remarkable way, with inimitable art and incomparable beauty.

Of the mixing bowls, two were wrought (in gold), and from the base to the middle were engraved with relief work in the pattern of scales, and between the scales precious stones were inserted with great artistic skill. Then there was a ' maeander ' a cubit in height, with its surface wrought out of precious stones of many colours, displaying great artistic effort and beauty. Upon this there was a mosaic, worked in the form of a rhombus, having a net-like appearance and reaching right up to the brim. In the middle, small shields which were made of different precious stones, placed alternately and varying in kind, not less than four fingers broad enhanced the beauty of their appearance. On the top of the brim there was an ornament of lilies in bloom, and intertwining clusters of grapes were engraven all round. Such then was the construction of the golden bowls, and they held more than two firkins each. The silver bowls had a smooth surface, and were wonderfully made as if they were intended for looking-glasses, so that everything which was brought near to them was reflected even more clearly than in mirrors. But it is impossible to describe the real impression which these works of art produced upon the mind when they were finished. For, when these vessels had been completed and placed side by side, first a silver bowl and then a golden, then another silver, and then another golden, the appearance they presented is altogether indescribable, and those who came to see them were not able to tear themselves from the brilliant sight and entrancing, spectacle. The impressions produced by the spectacle were various in kind. When men looked at the golden vessels, and their minds made a complete survey of each detail of workmanship, their souls were thrilled with wonder. Again when a man wished to direct his gaze to the silver vessels, as they stood before him, everything seemed to flash with light round about the place where he was standing, and afforded a still greater delight to the onlookers. So that it is really impossible to describe the artistic beauty of the works.

The golden vials they engraved in the centre with vine wreaths. And about the rims they wove a wreath of ivy and myrtle and olive in relief work and inserted precious stones in it. The other parts of the relief work they wrought in different patterns, since they made it a point of honour to complete everything in a way worthy of the majesty of the king. In a word it may be said that neither in the king's treasury nor in any other, were there any works which equaled these in costliness or in artistic skill. For the king spent no little thought upon them, for he loved to gain glory for the excellence of his designs. For oftentimes he would neglect his official business, and spend his time with the artists in his anxiety that they should complete everything in a manner worthy of the place to which the gifts were to be sent. So everything was carried out on a grand scale, in a manner worthy of the king who sent the gifts and of the high priest who was the ruler of the land. There was no stint of precious stones, for not less than five thousand were used and they were all of large size. The most exceptional artistic skill was employed, so that the cost of the stones and the workmanship was five times as much as that of the gold.

I have given you this description of the presents because I thought it was necessary. The next point in the narrative is an account of our journey to Eleazar, but I will first of all give you a description of the whole country. When we arrived in the land of the Jews we saw the city situated in the middle of the whole of Judea on the top of a mountain of considerable altitude. On the summit the temple had been built in all its splendour. It was surrounded by three walls more than seventy cubits high and in length and breadth corresponding to the structure of the edifice. All the buildings were characterized by a magnificence and costliness quite unprecedented. It was obvious that no expense had been spared on the door and the fastenings, which connected it with the door-posts, and the stability of the lintel. The style of the curtain too was thoroughly in proportion to that of the entrance. Its fabric owing to the draught of wind was in perpetual motion, and as this motion was communicated from the bottom and the curtain bulged out to its highest extent, it afforded a pleasant spectacle from which a man could scarcely tear himself away. The construction of the altar was in keeping with the place itself and with the burnt offerings which were consumed by fire upon it, and the approach to it was on a similar scale. There was a gradual slope up to it, conveniently arranged for the purpose of decency, and the ministering priests were robed in linen garments, down to their ankles. The Temple faces the east and its back is toward the west. The whole of the floor is paved with stones and slopes down to the appointed places, that water may be conveyed to wash away the blood from the sacrifices, for many thousand beasts are sacrificed there on the feast days. And there is an inexhaustible supply of water, because an abundant natural spring gushes up from within the temple area. There are moreover wonderful and indescribable cisterns underground, as they pointed out to me, at a distance of five furlongs all round the site of the temple, and each of them has countless pipes so that the different streams converge together. And all these were fastened with lead at the bottom and at the sidewalls, and over them a great quantity of plaster had been spread, and every part of the work had been most carefully carried out. There are many openings for water at the base of the altar which are invisible to all except to those who are engaged in the ministration, so that all the blood of the sacrifices which is collected in great quantities is washed away in the twinkling of an eye. Such is my opinion with regard to the character of the reservoirs and I will now show you how it was confirmed. They led me more than four furlongs outside the city and bade me peer down towards a certain spot and listen to the noise that was made by the meeting of the waters, so that the great size of the reservoirs became manifest to me, as has already been pointed out.

The ministration of the priests is in every way unsurpassed both for its physical endurance and for its orderly and silent service. For they all work spontaneously, though it entails much painful exertion, and each one has a special task allotted to him. The service is carried on without interruption -some provide the wood, others the oil, others the fine wheat flour, others the spices; others again bring the pieces of flesh for the burnt offering, exhibiting a wonderful degree of strength. For they take up with both hands the limbs of a calf, each of them weighing more than two talents, and throw them with each hand in a wonderful way on to the high place of the altar and never miss placing them on the proper spot. In the same way the pieces of the sheep and also of the goats are wonderful both for their weight and their fatness. For those, whose business it is, always select the beasts which are without blemish and specially fat, and thus the sacrifice which I have described, is carried out. There is a special place set apart for them to rest in, where those who are relieved from duty sit. When this takes place, those who have already rested and are ready to assume their duties rise up spontaneously since there is no one to give orders with regard to the arrangement of the sacrifices. The most complete silence reigns so that one might imagine that there was not a single person present, though there are actually seven hundred men engaged in the work, besides the vast number of those who are occupied in bringing up the sacrifices. Everything is carried out with reverence and in a way worthy of the great God.

We were greatly astonished, when we saw Eleazar engaged in the ministration, at the mode of his dress, and the majesty of his appearance, which was revealed in the robe which he wore and the precious stones upon his person. There were golden bells upon the garment which reached down to his feet, giving forth a peculiar kind of melody, and on both sides of them there were pomegranates with variegated flowers of a wonderful hue. He was girded with a girdle of conspicuous beauty, woven in the most beautiful colours. On his breast he wore the oracle of God, as it is called, on which twelve stones, of different kinds, were inset, fastened together with gold, containing the names of the leaders of the tribes, according to their original order, each one flashing forth in an indescribable way its own particular colour. On his head he wore a tiara, as it is called, and upon this in the middle of his forehead an inimitable turban, the royal diadem full of glory with the name of God inscribed in sacred letters on a plate of gold . . . having been judged worthy to wear these emblems in the ministrations. Their appearance created such awe and confusion of mind as to make one feel that one had come into the presence of a man who belonged to a different world. I am convinced that any one who takes part in the spectacle which I have described will be filled with astonishment and indescribable wonder and be profoundly affected in his mind at the thought of the sanctity which is attached to each detail of the service.

But in order that we might gain complete information, we ascended to the summit of the neighbouring citadel and looked around us. It is situated in a very lofty spot, and is fortified with many towers, which have been built up to the very top of immense stones, with the object, as we were informed, of guarding the temple precincts, so that if there were an attack, or an insurrection or an onslaught of the enemy, no one would be able to force an entrance within the walls that surround the temple. On the towers of the citadel engines of war were placed and different kinds of machines, and the position was much higher than the circle of walls which I have mentioned. The towers were guarded too by most trusty men who had given the utmost proof of their loyalty to their country. These men were never allowed to leave the citadel, except on feast days and then only in detachments. nor did they permit any stranger to enter it. They were also very careful when any command came from the chief officer to admit any visitors to inspect the place, as our own experience taught us. They were very reluctant to admit us, -though we were but two unarmed men- to view the offering of the sacrifices. And they asserted that they were bound by an oath when the trust was committed to them, for they had all sworn and were bound to carry out the oath sacredly to the letter, that though they were five hundred in number they would not permit more than five men to enter at one time. The citadel was the special protection of the temple and its founder had fortified it so strongly that it might efficiently protect it.

The size of the city is of moderate dimensions. It is about forty furlongs in circumference, as far as one could conjecture. It has its towers arranged in the shape of a theatre, with thoroughfares leading between them now the cross roads of the lower towers are visible but those of the upper towers are more frequented. For the ground ascends, since the city is built upon a mountain. There are steps too which lead up to the cross roads, and some people are always going up, and others down and they keep as far apart from each other as possible on the road because of those who are bound by the rules of purity, lest they should touch anything which is unlawful. It was not without reason that the original founders of the city built it in due proportions, for they possessed clear insight with regard to what was required. For the country is extensive and beautiful. Some parts of it are level, especially the districts which belong to Samaria, as it is called, and which border on the land of the Idumeans, other parts are mountainous, especially (those which are contiguous to the land of Judea). The people therefore are bound to devote themselves to agriculture and the cultivation of the soil that by this means they may have a plentiful supply of crops. In this way cultivation of every kind is carried on and an abundant harvest reaped in the whole of the aforesaid land. The cities which are large and enjoy a corresponding prosperity are well-populated, but they neglect the country districts, since all men are inclined to a life of enjoyment, for every one has a natural tendency towards the pursuit of pleasure. The same thing happened in Alexandria, which excels all cities in size and prosperity. Country people by migrating from the rural districts and settling in the city brought agriculture into disrepute: and so to prevent them from settling in the city, the king issued orders that they should not stay in it for more than twenty days. And in the same way he gave the judges written instructions, that if it was necessary to issue a summons against any one who lived in the country, the case must be settled within five days. And since he considered the matter one of great importance, he appointed also legal officers for every district with their assistants, that the farmers and their advocates might not in the interests of business empty the granaries of the city, I mean, of the produce of husbandry. I have permitted this digression because it was Eleazar who pointed out with great clearness the points which have been mentioned. For great is the energy which they expend on the tillage of the soil. For the land is thickly planted with multitudes of olive trees, with crops of corn and pulse, with vines too, and there is abundance of honey. Other kinds of fruit trees and dates do not count compared with these. There are cattle of all kinds in great quantities and a rich pasturage for them. Wherefore they rightly recognize that the country districts need a large population, and the relations between the city and the villages are properly regulated. A great quantity of spices and precious stones and gold is brought into the country by the Arabs. For the country is well adapted not only for agriculture but also for commerce, and the city is rich in the arts and lacks none of the merchandise which is brought across the sea. It possesses too suitable and commodious harbours at Askalon, Joppa, and Gaza, as well as at Ptolemais which was founded by the King and holds a central position compared with the other places named, being not far distant from any of them. The country produces everything in abundance, since it is well watered in all directions and well protected from storms. The river Jordan, as it is called, which never runs dry, flows through the land. Originally (the country) contained not less than million acres-though afterwards the neighbouring peoples made incursions against it -and, men were settled upon it in farms of a hundred acres each. The river like the Nile rises in harvest- time and irrigates a large portion of the land. Near the district belonging to the people of Ptolemais it issues into another river and this flows out into the sea. Other mountain torrents, as they are called, flow down into the plain and encompass the parts about Gaza and the district of Ashdod. The country is encircled by a natural fence and is very difficult to attack and cannot be assailed by large forces, owing to the narrow passes, with their overhanging precipices and deep ravines, and the rugged character of the mountainous regions which surround all the land. We were told that from the neighbouring mountains of Arabia copper and iron were formerly obtained. This was stopped, however, at the time of the Persian rule, since the authorities of the time spread abroad a false report that the working of the mines was useless and expensive, in order to prevent their country from being destroyed by the mining in these districts and possibly taken away from them owing to the Persian rule, since by the assistance of this false report they found an excuse for entering the district.

I have now, my dear brother Philocrates, given you all the essential information upon this subject in brief form. I shall describe the work of translation in the sequel. The High priest selected men of the finest character and the highest culture, such as one would expect from their noble parentage. They were men who had not only acquired proficiency in Jewish literature, but had studied most carefully that of the Greeks as well. They were specially qualified therefore for serving on embassies and they undertook this duty whenever it was necessary. They possessed a great facility for conferences and the discussion of problems connected with the law. They espoused the middle course -and this is always the best course to pursue. They abjured the rough and uncouth manner, but they were altogether above pride and never assumed an air of superiority over others, and in conversation they were ready to listen and give an appropriate answer to every question. And all of them carefully observed this rule and were anxious above everything else to excel each other in its observance and they were all of them worthy of their leader and of his virtue. And one could observe how they loved Eleazar by their unwillingness to be torn away from him and how he loved them. For besides the letter which he wrote to the king concerning their safe return, he also earnestly besought Andreas to work for the same end and urged me, too, to assist to the best of my, ability and although we promised to give our best attention to the matter, he said that he was still greatly distressed, for he knew that the king out of the goodness of his nature considered it his highest privilege, whenever he heard of a man who was superior to his fellows in culture and wisdom, to summon him to his court. For I have heard of a fine saying of his to the effect that by securing just and prudent men about his person he would secure the greatest protection for his kingdom, since such friends would unreservedly give him the most beneficial advice. And the men who were now being sent to him by Eleazar undoubtedly possessed these qualities. And he frequently asserted upon oath that he would never let the men go if it were merely some private interest of his own that constituted the impelling motive-but it was for the common advantage of all the citizens that he was sending them. For, he explained, the good life consists in the keeping of the enactments of the law, and this end is achieved much more by hearing than by reading. From this and other similar statements it was clear what his feelings towards them were.

It is worth while to mention briefly the information which he gave in reply to our questions. For I suppose that most people feel a curiosity with regard to some of the enactments in the law, especially those about meats and drinks and animals recognized as unclean. When we asked why, since there is but one form of creation, some animals are regarded as unclean for eating, and others unclean even to the touch (for though the law is scrupulous on most points, it is specially scrupulous on such matters as these) he began his reply as follows: ' You observe,' he said, ' what an effect our modes of life and our associations produce upon us; by associating with the bad, men catch their depravities and become miserable throughout their life; but if they live with the wise and prudent, they find the means of escaping from ignorance and amending their lives. Our Lawgiver first of all laid down the principles of piety and righteousness and inculcated them point by point, not merely by prohibitions but by the use of examples as well, demonstrating the injurious effects of sin and the punishments inflicted by God upon the guilty. For he proved first of all that there is only one God and that his power is manifested throughout the universe, since every place is filled with his sovereignty and none of the things which are wrought in secret by men upon the earth escapes His knowledge. For all that a man does and all that is to come to pass in the future are manifest to Him. Working out these truths carefully and having made them plain he showed that even if a man should think of doing evil -to say nothing of actually effecting it,- he would not escape detection, for he made it clear that the power of God pervaded the whole of the law. Beginning from this starting point he went on to show that all mankind except ourselves believe in the existence of many gods, though they themselves are much more powerful than the beings whom they vainly worship. For when they have made statues of stone and wood, they say that they are the images of those who have invented something useful for life and they worship them, though they have clear proof that they possess no feeling. For it would be utterly foolish to suppose that any one became a god in virtue of his inventions. For the inventors simply took certain objects already created and by combining them together, showed that they possessed a fresh utility: they did not themselves create the substance of the thing, and so it is a vain and foolish thing for people to make gods of men like themselves. For in our times there are many who are much more inventive and much more learned than the men of former days who have been deified, and yet they would never come to worship them. The makers and authors of these myths think that they are the wisest of the Greeks. Why need we speak of other infatuated people, Egyptians and the like, who place their reliance upon wild beasts and most kinds of creeping things and cattle, and worship them, and offer sacrifices to them both while living and when dead ?'

'Now our Lawgiver being a wise man and specially endowed by God to understand all things, took a comprehensive view of each particular detail, and fenced us round with impregnable ramparts and walls of iron, that we might not mingle at all with any of the other nations, but remain pure in body and soul, free from all vain imaginations, worshiping the one Almighty God above the whole creation. Hence the leading Egyptian priests having looked carefully into many matters, and being cognizant with (our) affairs, call us " men of God ". This is a title which does not belong to the rest of mankind but only to those who worship the true God. The rest are men not of

God but of meats and drinks and clothing. For their whole disposition leads them to find solace in these things.

Among our people such things are reckoned of no account. but throughout their whole life their main consideration is the sovereignty of God. Therefore lest we should be corrupted by any abomination, or our lives be perverted by evil communications, he hedged us round on all sides by rules of purity, affecting alike what we eat, or drink, or touch, or hear, or see. For though, speaking generally, all things are alike in their natural constitution, since they are all governed by one and the same power, yet there is a deep reason in each individual case why we abstain from the use of certain things and enjoy the common use of others. For the sake of illustration I will run over one or two points and explain them to you. For you must not fall into the degrading idea that it was out of regard to mice and weasels and other such things that Moses drew up his laws with such exceeding care. All these ordinances were made for the sake of righteousness to aid the quest for virtue and the perfecting of character. For all the birds that we use are tame and distinguished by their cleanliness, feeding on various kinds of grain and pulse, such as for instance pigeons, turtle-doves, locusts, partridges, geese also, and all other birds of this class. But the birds which are forbidden you will find to be wild and carnivorous, tyrannizing over the others by the strength which they possess, and cruelly obtaining food by preying on the tame birds enumerated above and not only so, but they seize lambs and kids, and injure human beings too, whether dead or alive, and so by naming them unclean, he gave a sign by means of them that those, for whom the legislation was ordained, must practice righteousness in their hearts and not tyrannize over any one in reliance upon their own strength nor rob them of anything, but steer their course of life in accordance with justice, just as the tame birds, already mentioned, consume the different kinds of pulse that grow upon the earth and do not tyrannize to the destruction of their own kindred. Our legislator taught us therefore that it is by such methods as these that indications are given to the wise, that they must be just and effect nothing by violence, and refrain from tyrannizing over others in reliance upon their own strength. For since it is considered unseemly even to touch such unclean animals, as have been mentioned, on account of their particular habits, ought we not to take every precaution lest our own characters should be destroyed to the same extent ? Wherefore all the rules which he has laid down with regard to what is permitted in the case of these birds and other animals, he has enacted with the object of teaching us a moral lesson. For the division of the hoof and the separation of the claws are intended to teach us that we must discriminate between our individual actions with a view to the practice of virtue. For the strength of our whole body and its activity depend upon our shoulders and limbs. Therefore he compels us to recognize that we must perform all our actions with discrimination according to the standard of righteousness -more especially because we have been distinctly separated from the rest of mankind. For most other men defile themselves by promiscuous intercourse, thereby working great iniquity, and whole countries and cities pride themselves upon such vices. For they not only have intercourse with men but they defile their own mothers and even their daughters. But we have been kept separate from such sins. And the people who have been separated in the aforementioned way are also characterized by the Lawgiver as possessing the gift of memory. For all animals " which are cloven-footed and chew the cud "represent to the initiated the symbol of memory. For the act of chewing the cud is nothing else than the reminiscence of life and existence. For life is wont to be sustained by means of food wherefore he exhorts us in the Scripture also in these words: ' Thou shalt surely remember the Lord that wrought in thee those great and wonderful things". For when they are properly conceived, they are manifestly great and glorious; first the construction of the body and the disposition of the food and the separation of each individual limb and, far more, the organization of the senses, the operation and invisible movement of the mind, the rapidity of its particular actions and its discovery of the arts, display an infinite resourcefulness. Wherefore he exhorts us to remember that the aforesaid parts are kept together by the divine power with consummate skill. For he has marked out every time and place that we may continually remember the God who rules and preserves (us). For in the matter of meats and drinks he bids us first of all offer part as a sacrifice and then forthwith enjoy our meal. Moreover, upon our garments he has given us a symbol of remembrance, and in like manner he has ordered us to put the divine oracles upon our gates and doors as a remembrance of God. And upon our hands, too, he expressly orders the symbol to be fastened, clearly showing that we ought to perform every act in righteousness, remembering (our own creation), and above all the fear of God. He bids men also, when lying down to sleep and rising up again, to meditate upon the works of God, not only in word, but by observing distinctly   the change and impression produced upon them, when they are going to sleep, and also their waking, how divine and incomprehensible the change from one of these states to the other is. The excellency of the analogy in regard to discrimination and memory has now been pointed out to you, according to our interpretation of " the cloven hoof and the chewing of the cud ". For our laws have not been drawn up at random or in accordance with the first casual thought that occurred to the mind, but with a view to truth and the indication of right reason. For by means of the directions which he gives with regard to meats and drinks and particular cases of touching, he bids us neither to do nor listen to anything, thoughtlessly nor to resort to injustice by the abuse of the power of reason. In the case of the wild animals, too, the same principle may be discovered. For the character of the weasel and of mice and such animals as these, which are expressly mentioned, is destructive. Mice defile and damage everything, not only for their own food but even to the extent of rendering absolutely useless to man whatever it falls in their way to damage. The weasel class, too, is peculiar: for besides what has been said, it has a characteristic which is defiling: It conceives through the ears and brings forth through the mouth. And it is for this reason that a like   practice is declared unclean in men. For by embodying in speech all that they receive through the ears, they involve others in evils and work no ordinary impurity, being themselves altogether defiled by the pollution of impiety. And your king, as we are informed, does quite right in destroying such men.'

Then I said ' I suppose you mean the informers, for he constantly exposes them to tortures and to painful forms of death.' 'Yes,' he replied, 'these are the men I mean, for to watch for men's destruction is an unholy thing. And our law forbids us to injure any one either by word or deed. My brief account of these matters ought to have convinced you, that all our regulations have been drawn up with a view to righteousness, and that nothing has been enacted in the Scripture thoughtlessly or without due reason, but its purpose is to enable us throughout our whole life and in all our actions to practice righteousness before all men, being mindful of Almighty God. And so concerning meats and things unclean, creeping things, and wild beasts, the whole system aims at righteousness and righteous relationships between man and man.'

He seemed to me to have made a good defense on all the points; for in reference also to the calves and rams and goats which are offered, he said that it was necessary to take them from the herds and flocks, and sacrifice tame animals and offer nothing wild, that the offerers of the sacrifices might understand the symbolic meaning of the lawgiver and not be under the influence of an arrogant self-consciousness. For he, who offers a sacrifice makes an offering also of his own soul in all its moods.

I think that these particulars with regard to our discussion are worth narrating and on account of the sanctity and natural meaning of the law, I have been induced to explain them to you clearly, Philocrates, because of your own devotion to learning.

And Eleazar, after offering the sacrifice, and selecting the envoys, and preparing many gifts for the king, despatched us on our journey in great security. And when we reached Alexandria, the king, was at once informed of our arrival. On our admission to the palace, Andreas and I warmly greeted the king and handed over to him the letter written by Eleazar. The king was very anxious to meet the envoys, and gave orders that all the other officials should be dismissed and the envoys summoned to his presence at once. Now this excited general surprise, for it is customary for those who come to seek an audience with the king on matters of importance to be admitted to his presence on the fifth day, while envoys from kings or very important cities with difficulty secure admission to the Court in thirty days -but these men he counted worthy of greater honour, since he held their master in such high esteem, and so he immediately dismissed those whose presence he regarded as superfluous and continued walking about until they came in and he was able to welcome them.

When they entered with the gifts which had been sent with them and the valuable parchments, on which the law was inscribed in gold in Jewish characters, for the parchment was wonderfully prepared and the connexion between the pages had been so effected as to be invisible, the king as soon as he saw them began to ask them about the books. And when they had taken the rolls out of their coverings and unfolded the pages, the king stood still for a long time and then making obeisance about seven times, he said: ' I thank you, my friends, and I thank him that sent you still more, and most of all God, whose oracles these are.' And when all, the envoys and the others who were present as well, shouted out at one time and with one voice: ' God save the King! ' he burst into tears of joy. For his exaltation of soul and the sense of the overwhelming honour which had been paid him compelled him to weep over his good fortune. He commanded them to put the rolls back in their places and then after saluting the men, said: ' It was right, men of God, that I should first of all pay my reverence to the books for the sake of which I summoned you here and then, when I had done that, to extend the right-hand of friendship to you. It was for this reason that I did this first. I have enacted that this day, on which you arrived, shall be kept as a great day and it will be celebrated annually throughout my life time. It happens also that it is the anniversary of my naval victory over Antigonus. Therefore I shall be glad to feast with you to-day.' 'Everything that you may have occasion to use ', he said, ' shall be prepared (for you) in a befitting manner and for me also with you.' After they had expressed their delight, he gave orders that the best quarters near the citadel should be assigned to them, and that preparations should be made for the banquet.

And Nicanor summoned the lord high steward, Dorotheus, who was the special officer appointed to look after the Jews, and commanded him to make the necessary preparation for each one. For this arrangement had been made by the king and it is an arrangement which you see maintained to-day. For as many cities (as) have (special) customs in the matter of drinking, eating, and reclining, have special officers appointed to look after their requirements. And whenever they come to visit the kings, preparations are made in accordance with their own customs, in order that there may be no discomfort to disturb the enjoyment of their visit. The same precaution was taken in the case of the Jewish envoys. Now Dorotheus who was the patron appointed to look after Jewish guests was a very conscientious man. All the stores which were under his control and set apart for the reception of such guests, he brought out for the feast. He arranged the seats in two rows in accordance with the king's instructions. For he had ordered him to make half the men sit at his right hand and the rest behind him, in order that he might not withhold from them the highest possible honour. When they had taken their seats he instructed Dorotheus to carry out everything in accordance with the customs which were in use amongst his Jewish guests. Therefore he dispensed with the services of the sacred heralds and the sacrificing priests and the others who were accustomed to offer the prayers, and called upon one of our number, Eleazar, the oldest of the Jewish priests, to offer prayer instead. And he rose up and made a remarkable prayer. ' May Almighty God enrich you, O king with all the good things which He has made and may He grant you and your wife and your children and your comrades the continual possession of them as long as you live ! ' At these words a loud and joyous applause broke out which lasted for a considerable time, and then they turned to the enjoyment of the banquet which had been prepared. All the arrangements for service at table were carried out in accordance with the injunction of Dorotheus. Among the attendants were the royal pages and others who held places of honour at the king's court.

Taking an opportunity afforded by a pause in the banquet the king asked the envoy who sat in the seat of honour (for they were arranged according to seniority), How he could keep his kingdom unimpaired to the end? After pondering for a moment he replied, 'You could best establish its security if you were to imitate the unceasing benignity of God. For if you exhibit clemency and inflict mild punishments upon those who deserve them in accordance with their deserts, you will turn them from evil and lead them to repentance.' The king praised the answer and then asked the next man, How he could do everything for the best in all his actions? And he replied, ' If a man maintains a just bearing towards all, he will always act rightly on every occasion, remembering that every thought is known to God. If you take the fear of God as your starting-point, you will never miss the goal.

The king complimented this man, too, upon his answer and asked another,

How he could have friends like-minded with himself? He replied, 'If they see you studying the interests of the multitudes over whom you rule; you will do well to observe how God bestows his benefits on the human race, providing for them health and food and all other things in due season.' After expressing his agreement with the reply, the king asked the next guest, How in giving audiences and passing judgments he could gain the praise even of those who failed to win their suit ? And he said, ' If you are fair in speech to all alike and never act insolently nor tyrannically in your treatment of   offenders. And you will do this if you watch the method by which God acts. The petitions of the worthy are always fulfilled, while those who fail to obtain an answer to their prayers are informed by means of dreams or events of what was harmful in their requests and that God does not smite them according to their sins or the greatness of His strength, but acts with forbearance towards them.'

The king praised the man warmly for his answer and asked the next in order, How he could be invincible in military affairs ? And he replied, ' If he did not trust entirely to his multitudes or his warlike forces, but called upon God continually to bring his enterprises to a successful issue, while he him self discharged all his duties in the spirit of justice.' Welcoming this answer, he asked another how he might become an object of dread to his enemies. And he replied, ' If while maintaining a vast supply of arms and forces he remembered that these things were powerless to achieve a permanent and conclusive result. For even God instils fear into the minds of men by granting reprieves and making merely a display of the greatness of his power.'

This man the king praised and then said to the next, What is the highest good in life? And he answered ' To know that God is Lord of the Universe, and that in our finest achievements it is not we who attain success but God who by his power brings all things to fulfilment and leads us to the goal.'

The king exclaimed that the man had answered well and then asked the next How he could keep all his possessions intact and finally hand them down to his successors in the same condition? And he answered ' By praying constantly to God that you may be inspired with high motives in all your undertakings and by warning your descendants not to be dazzled by fame or wealth, for it is God who bestows all these gifts and men never by themselves win the supremacy'.

The king expressed his agreement with the answer and enquired of the next guest, How he could bear with equanimity whatever befell him? And he said, ' If you have a firm grasp of the thought that all men are appointed by God to share the greatest evil as well as the greatest good, since it is impossible for one who is a man to be exempt from these. But God, to whom we ought always to pray, inspires us with courage to endure.'

Delighted with the man's reply, the king said that all their answers had been good. ' I will put a question to one other', he added, ' and then I will stop for the present: that we may turn our attention to the enjoyment of the feast and spend a pleasant time.' Thereupon he asked the man, What is the true aim of courage ? And he answered, ' If a right plan is carried out in the hour of danger in accordance with the original intention. For all things are accomplished by God to your advantage, O king, since your purpose is good.'

When all had signified by their applause their agreement with the answer, the king said to the philosophers (for not a few of them were present), ' It is my opinion that these men excel in virtue and possess extraordinary knowledge, since on the spur of the moment they have given fitting answers to these questions which I have put to them, and have all made God the starting-point of their words.'

And Menedemus, the philosopher of Eretria, said, 'True, O King -for since the universe is managed by providence and since we rightly perceive that man is the creation of God, it follows that all power and beauty of speech proceed from God.' When the king had nodded his assent to this sentiment, the speaking ceased and they proceeded to enjoy themselves. When evening came on, the banquet ended.

On the following day they sat down to table again and continued the banquet according to the same arrangements. When the king thought that a fitting opportunity had arrived to put inquiries to his guests, he proceeded to ask further questions of the men who sat next in order to those who had given answers on the previous day. He began to open the conversation with the eleventh man, for there were ten who had been asked questions on the former occasion. When silence was established, he asked How he could continue to be rich ? After a brief reflection, the man who had been asked the question replied If he did nothing unworthy of his position, never acted licentiously, never lavished expense on empty and vain pursuits, but by acts of benevolence made all his subjects well disposed towards himself. For it is God who is the author of all good things and Him man must needs obey.' The king bestowed praise upon him and then asked another How he could maintain the truth ? In reply to the question he said, ' By recognizing that a lie brings great disgrace upon all men, and more especially upon kings. For since they have the power to do whatever they wish, why should they resort to lies ? In addition to this you must always remember, O King, that God is a lover of the truth.'

The king received the answer with great delight and looking at another said, 'What is the teaching of wisdom? ' And the other replied, ' As you wish that no evil should befall you, but to be a partaker of all good things, so you should act on the same principle towards your subjects and offenders, and you should mildly admonish the noble and good. For God draws all men to himself by his benignity.'

The king praised him and asked the next in order How he could be the friend of men ? And he replied, ' By observing that the human race increases and is born with much trouble and great suffering: wherefore you must not lightly punish or inflict torments upon them, since you know that the life of men is made up of pains and penalties. For if you understood everything you would be filled with pity, for God also is pitiful.'

The king received the answer with approbation and inquired of the next 'What is the most essential qualification for ruling ? ' ' To keep oneself ', he answered, ' free from bribery and to practice sobriety during the greater part of one's life, to honour righteousness above all things, and to make friends of men of this type. For God, too, is a lover of justice.'

Having signified his approval, the king said to another 'What is the true mark of piety?' And he replied, 'To perceive that God constantly works in the Universe and knows all things, and no man who acts unjustly and works wickedness can escape His notice. AS God is the benefactor of the whole world, so you, too, must imitate Him and be void of offence.'

The king signified his agreement and said to another ' What is the essence of kingship ? ' And he replied, ' To rule oneself well and not to be led astray by wealth or fame to immoderate or unseemly desires, this is the true way of ruling if you reason the matter well out. For all that you really need is yours, and God is free from need and benignant withal. Let your thoughts be such as become a man, and desire not many things but only such as are necessary for ruling.'

The king praised him and asked another man How his deliberations might be for the best ? and he replied, 'If he constantly set justice before him in everything and thought that injustice was equivalent to deprivation of life. For God always promises the highest blessings to the just.'

Having praised him, the king asked the next How he could be free from disturbing thoughts ill his sleep ? And he replied, ' You have asked me a question which is very difficult to answer, for we cannot bring our true selves into play during the hours of sleep, but are held fast in these by imaginations that cannot be controlled by reason. For our souls possess the feeling that they actually see the things that enter into our consciousness during sleep. But we make a mistake if we suppose that we are actually sailing on the sea in boats or flying through the air or traveling to other regions or anything else of the kind. And yet we actually do imagine such things to be taking place. So far as it is possible for me to decide, I have reached the following conclusion. You must in every possible way, O King, govern your words and actions by the rule of piety that you may have the consciousness that you are maintaining virtue and that you never choose to gratify yourself at the expense of reason and never by abusing your power do despite to righteousness. For the mind mostly busies itself in sleep with the same things with which it occupies itself when awake. And he who has all his thoughts and actions set towards the noblest ends establishes himself in righteousness both when he is awake and when he is asleep. Wherefore you must be steadfast in the constant discipline of self.'

The king bestowed praise on the man and said to another-' since you are the tenth to answer, when you have spoken, we will devote ourselves to the banquet.' And then he put the question, How can I avoid doing anything unworthy of myself? And he replied, 'Look always to your own fame and your own supreme position, that you may speak and think only such things as are consistent therewith, knowing that all your subjects think and talk about you. For you must not appear to be worse than the actors, who study carefully the role, which it is necessary for them to play, and shape all their actions in accordance with it. You are not acting a part, but are really a king, since God has bestowed upon you a royal authority in keeping with your character.'

When the king had applauded loud and long in the most gracious way, the guests were urged to seek repose. So when the conversation ceased, they devoted themselves to the next course of the feast.

On the following day, the same arrangement was observed, and when the king found an opportunity of putting questions to the men, he questioned the first of those who had been left over for the next interrogation, What is the highest form of government? And he replied, 'To rule oneself and not to be carried away by impulses. For all men possess a certain natural bent of mind.

It is probable that most men have an inclination towards food and drink and pleasure, and kings a bent towards the acquisition of territory and great renown. But it is good that there should be moderation in all things. What God gives, that you must take and keep, but never yearn for things that are beyond your reach.'

Pleased with these words, the king asked the next How he could be free from envy ? And he after a brief pause replied, ' If you consider first of all that it is God who bestows on all kings glory and great wealth and no one is king by his own power. All men wish to share this glory but cannot, since it is the gift of God.'

The king praised the man in a long speech and then asked another How he could despise his enemies? And he replied, ' If you show kindness to all men and win their friendship, you need fear no one. To be popular with all men is the best of good gifts to receive from God.'

Having praised this answer the king ordered the next man to reply to the question, How he could maintain his great renown ? and he replied that ' If you are generous and large-hearted in bestowing kindness and acts of grace upon others, you will never lose your renown, but if you wish the aforesaid graces to continue yours, you must call upon God continually.'

The king expressed his approval and asked the next, To whom ought a man to show liberality? And he replied, ' All men acknowledge that we ought to show liberality to those who are well disposed towards us, but I think that we ought to show the same keen spirit of generosity to those who are opposed to us that by this means we may win them over to the right and to what is advantageous to ourselves. But we must pray to God that this may be accomplished, for he rules the minds of all men.'

Having expressed his agreement with the answer, the king asked the sixth to reply to the question, To whom ought we to exhibit gratitude ? And he replied, 'To our parents continually, for God has given us a most important commandment with regard to the honour due to parents. In the next place He reckons the attitude of friend towards friend for He speaks of " a friend which is as thine own soul". You do well in trying to bring all men into friendship with yourself.'

The king spoke kindly to him and then asked the next, What is it that resembles beauty in value? And he said, 'Piety, for it is the pre-eminent form of beauty, and its power lies in love, which is the gift of God. This you have already acquired and with it all the blessings of life.'

The king in the most gracious way applauded the answer and asked another How, if he were to fail, he could regain his reputation again in the same degree ? And he said, ' It is not possible for you to fail, for you have sown in all men the seeds of gratitude which produce a harvest of goodwill, and this is mightier than the strongest weapons and guarantees the greatest security. But if any man does fail, he must never again do those things which caused his failure, but he must form friendships and act justly. For it is the gift of God to be able to do good actions and not the contrary.'

Delighted with these words, the king asked another How he could be free from grief? And he replied, ' If he never injured any one, but did good to everybody and followed the pathway of righteousness, for its fruits bring freedom from grief. But we must pray to God that unexpected evils such as death or disease or pain or anything of this kind may not come upon us and injure us. But since you are devoted to piety, no such misfortune will ever come upon you.'

The king bestowed great praise upon him and asked the tenth, What is the highest form of glory ? And he said, ' To honour God, and this is done not with gifts and sacrifices but with purity of soul and holy conviction, since all things are fashioned and governed by God in accordance with His will. Of this purpose you are in constant possession as all men can see from your achievements in the past and in the present.'

With loud voice the king greeted them all and spoke kindly to them, and all those who were present expressed their approval, especially the philosophers. For they were far superior to them [i.e. the philosophers] both in conduct and in argument, since they always made God their starting point. After this the king to show his good feeling proceeded to drink the health of his guests.

On the following day the same arrangements were made for the banquet, and the king, as soon as an opportunity occurred, began to put questions to the men who sat next to those who had already responded, and he said to the first ' Is wisdom capable of being taught ? ' And he said, ' The soul is so constituted that it is able by the divine power to receive all the good and reject the contrary.'

The king expressed approval and asked the next man, What is it that is most beneficial to health ? And he said, 'Temperance, and it is not possible to acquire this unless God create a disposition towards it.'

The king spoke kindly to the man and said to another, ' How can a man worthily pay the debt of gratitude to his parents ? ' And he said, ' By never causing them pain, and this is not possible unless God dispose the mind to the pursuit of the noblest ends.'

The king expressed agreement and asked the next How he could become an eager listener? And he said, ' By remembering that all knowledge is useful, because it enables you by the help of God in a time of emergency to select some of the things which you have learned and apply them to the crisis which confronts you. And so the efforts of men are fulfilled by the assistance of God.'

The king praised him and asked the next How he could avoid doing anything contrary to law ? And he said, ' If you recognize that it is God who has put the thoughts into the hearts of the lawgivers that the lives of men might be preserved, you will follow them.'

The king acknowledged the man's answer and said to another, ' What is the advantage of kinship ? ' And he replied, ' If we consider that we ourselves are afflicted by the misfortunes which fall upon our relatives and if their sufferings become our own -then the strength of kinship is apparent at once, for it is only when such feeling is shown that we shall win honour and esteem in their eyes. For help, when it is linked with kindliness, is of itself a bond which is altogether indissoluble. And in the day of their prosperity we must not crave their possessions, but must pray God to bestow all manner of good upon them.'

And having accorded to him the same praise as to the rest, the king asked another How he could attain freedom from fear ? And he said, ' When the mind is conscious that it has wrought no evil, and when God directs it to all noble counsels.'

The king expressed his approval and asked another How he could always maintain a right judgement ? And he replied, ' If he constantly set before his eyes the misfortunes which befall men and recognized that it is God who takes away prosperity from some and brings others to great honour and glory.'

The king gave a kindly reception to the man and asked the next to answer the question How he could avoid a life of ease and pleasure ? And he replied, ' If he continually remembered that he was the ruler of a great empire and the lord of vast multitudes, and that his mind ought not to be occupied with other things, but he ought always to be considering how he could best promote their welfare. He must pray, too, to God that no duty might be neglected.'

Having bestowed praise upon him, the king asked the tenth How he could recognize those who were dealing treacherously with him ? And he replied to the question, ' If he observed whether the bearing of those about him was natural and whether they maintained the proper rule of precedence at receptions and councils, and in their general intercourse, never going beyond the bounds of propriety in congratulations or in other matters of deportment. But God will incline your mind, O King, to all that is noble.' When the king had expressed his loud approval and praised them all individually (amid the plaudits of all who were present), they turned to the enjoyment of the feast.

And on the next day, when the opportunity offered, the king asked the next man, What is the grossest form of neglect ? And he replied, ' If a man does not care for his children and devote every effort to their education. For w always pray to God not so much for ourselves as for our children that every blessing may be theirs. Our desire that our children may possess self-control is only realized by the power of God.'

The king said that he had spoken well and then asked another How he could be patriotic ? ' By keeping before your mind,' he replied, the thought that it is good to live and die in one's own country. Residence abroad brings contempt upon the poor and shame upon the rich as though they had been banished for a crime. If you bestow benefits upon all, as you continually do,

God will give you favour with all and you will be accounted patriotic.'

After listening to this man, the king asked the next in order How he could live amicably with his wife ? And he answered, ' By recognizing that woman-kind are by nature headstrong and energetic in the pursuit of their own desires, and subject to sudden changes of opinion through fallacious reasoning, and their nature is essentially weak. It is necessary to deal wisely with them and not to provoke strife. For the successful conduct of life the steersman must know the goal toward which he ought to direct his course. It is only by calling upon the help of God that men can steer a true course of life at all times.'

The king expressed his agreement and asked the next How he could be free from error ? And he replied, ' If you always act with deliberation and never give credence to slanders, but prove for yourself the things that are said to you and decide by your own judgement the requests which are made to you and carry out everything in the light of your judgement, you will be free from error, O King. But the knowledge and practice of these things is the work of the Divine power.'

Delighted with these words, the king asked another How he could be free from wrath ? And he said in reply to the question, ' If he recognized that he had power over all even to inflict death upon them, if he gave way to wrath, and that it would be useless and pitiful if he, just because he was lord, deprived many of life. What need was there for wrath, when all men were in subjection and no one was hostile to him ? It is necessary to recognize that God rules the whole world in the spirit of kindness and without wrath at all, and you,' said he, ' O king, must of necessity copy His example.

The king said that he had answered well and then inquired of the next man, What is good counsel ? ' To act well at all times and with due reflection,' he explained, ' comparing what is advantageous to our own policy with the injurious effects that would result from the adoption of the opposite view, in order that by weighing every point we may be well advised and our purpose may be accomplished. And most important of all, by the power of God every plan of yours will find fulfilment because you practice piety.'

The king said that this man had answered well, and asked another What is philosophy? And he explained, ' To deliberate well in reference to any question that emerges and never to be carried away by impulses, but to ponder over the injuries that result from the passions, and to act rightly as the circumstances demand, practicing moderation. But we must pray to God to instil into our mind a regard for these things.'

The king signified his consent and asked another How he could meet with recognition when traveling abroad ? ' By being fair to all men,' he replied, ' and by appearing to be inferior rather than superior to those amongst whom he was traveling. For it is a recognized principle that God by His very nature accepts the humble. And the human race loves those who are willing to be in subjection to them.'

Having expressed his approval at this reply, the king asked another How he could build in such a way that his structures would endure after him ? And he replied to the question, ' If his creations were on a great and noble scale, so that the beholders would spare them for their beauty, and if he never dismissed any of those who wrought such works and never compelled others to minister to his needs without wages. For observing how God provides for the human race, granting them health and mental capacity and all other gifts, he himself should follow His example by rendering to men a recompense for their arduous toil. For it is the deeds that are wrought in righteousness that abide continually.'

The king said that this man, too, had answered well and asked the tenth, What is the fruit of wisdom ? And he replied, ' That a man should be conscious in himself that he has wrought no evil and that he should live his life in the truth, since it is from these, O mighty King, that the greatest joy and steadfastness of soul and strong faith in God accrue to you if you rule your realm in piety.' And when they heard the answer they all shouted with loud acclaim, and afterwards the king in the fullness of his joy began to drink their healths.

And on the next day the banquet followed the same course as on previous occasions, and when the opportunity presented itself the king proceeded to put questions to the remaining guests, and he said to the first, ' How can a man keep himself from pride ? ' And he replied, ' If he maintains equality and remembers on all occasions that he is a man ruling over men. And God brings the proud to nought, and exalts the meek and humble.'

 The king spoke kindly to him and asked the next, Whom ought a man to select as his counselors ? and he replied, ' Those who have been tested in many affairs and maintain unmingled goodwill towards him and partake of his own disposition. And God manifests Himself to those who are worthy that these ends may be attained.'

The king praised him and asked another, What is the most necessary possession for a king ? ' The friendship and love of his subjects,' he replied, ' for it is through this that the bond of goodwill is rendered indissoluble. And it is God who ensures that this may come to pass in accordance with your wish.'

 The king praised him and inquired of another, What is goal of speech? And he replied, 'To convince your opponent by showing him his mistakes in a well-ordered array of arguments. For in this way you will win your hearer, not by opposing him, but by bestowing praise upon him with a view to persuading him. And it is by the power of God that persuasion is accomplished.'

The king said that he had given a good answer, and asked another How he could live amicably with the many different races who formed the population of his kingdom ? ' By acting the proper part towards each,' he replied, ' and taking righteousness as your guide, as you are now doing with the help of the insight which God bestows upon you.'

The king was delighted by this reply, and asked another ' Under what circumstances ought a man to suffer grief ? ' ' In the misfortunes that befall our friends,' he replied, when we see that they are protracted and irremediable. Reason does not allow us to grieve for those who are dead and set free from evil, but all men do grieve over them because they think only of themselves and their own advantage. It is by the power of God alone that we can escape all evil.'

The king said that he had given a fitting answer, and asked another, How is reputation lost? And he replied, When pride and unbounded self-confidence hold sway, dishonour and loss of reputation are engendered. For God is the Lord of all reputation and bestows it where He will.'

The king gave his confirmation to the answer, and asked the next man, To whom ought men to entrust themselves ? ' To those,' he replied, who serve you from goodwill and not from fear or self-interest, thinking only of their own gain. For the one is the sign of love, the other the mark of ill-will and time-serving. For the man who is always watching, for his own gain is a traitor at heart. But you possess the affection of all your subjects by the help of the good counsel which God bestows upon you.'

The king said that he had answered wisely, and asked another, What is it that keeps a kingdom safe? And he replied to the question, ' Care and forethought that no evil may be wrought by those who are placed in a position of authority over the people, and this you always do by the help of God who inspires you with grave judgement '.

The king spoke words of encouragement to him, and asked another, What is it that maintains gratitude and honour ? And he replied, ' virtue, for it is the creator of good deeds, and by it evil is destroyed, even as you exhibit nobility of character towards all by the gift which God bestows upon you.'

The king graciously acknowledged the answer and asked the eleventh (since there were two more than seventy), How he could in time of war maintain tranquillity of soul ? And he replied, ' By remembering that he had done no evil to any of his subjects, and that all would fight for him in return for the benefits which they had received, knowing that even if they lose their lives, you will care for those dependent on them. For you never fail to make reparation to any-such is the kind-heartedness with which God has inspired you.' The king loudly applauded them all and spoke very kindly to them and then drank a long draught to the health of each, giving himself up to enjoyment, and lavishing the most generous and joyous friendship upon his guests.

On the seventh day much more extensive preparations were made, and many others were present from the different cities (among them a large number of ambassadors). When an opportunity occurred, the king asked the first of those who had not yet been questioned How he could avoid being deceived by fallacious reasoning ? and he replied, ' By noticing carefully the speaker, the thing spoken, and the subject under discussion, and by putting the same questions again after an interval in different forms. But to possess an alert mind and to be able to form a sound judgement in every case is one of the good gifts of God, and you possess it, O King.'

The king loudly applauded the answer and asked another, Why is it that the majority of men never become virtuous ? ' Because,' he replied, ' all men are by nature intemperate and inclined to pleasure. Hence, injustice springs up and a flood of avarice. The habit of virtue is a hindrance to those who are devoted to a life of pleasure because it enjoins upon them the preference of temperance and righteousness. For it is God who is the master of these things.'

The king said that he had answered well, and asked, What ought kings to obey ? And he said, ' The laws, in order that by righteous enactments they may restore the lives of men. Even as you by such conduct in obedience to the Divine command have laid up in store for yourself a perpetual memorial.'

The king said that this man, too, had spoken well, and asked the next, Whom ought we to appoint as governors? And he replied, 'All who hate wickedness, and imitating your own conduct act righteously that they may maintain a good reputation constantly. For this is what you do, O mighty King,' he said, ' and it is God who has bestowed upon you the crown of righteousness.'

The king loudly acclaimed the answer and then looking at the next man said, Whom ought we to appoint as officers over the forces?' And he explained, ' Those who excel in courage and righteousness and those who are more anxious about the safety of their men than to gain a victory by risking their lives through rashness. For as God acts well towards all men, so too you in imitation of Him are the benefactor of all your subjects.'

The king said that he had given a good answer and asked another, What man is worthy of admiration ? And he replied, The man who is furnished with reputation and wealth and power and possesses a soul equal to it all. You yourself show by your actions that you are most worthy of admiration through the help of God who makes you care for these things.'

The king expressed his approval and said to another 'To what affairs ought kings to devote most time ? ' And he replied, ' To reading and the study of the records of official journeys, which are written in reference to the various kingdoms, with a view to the reformation and preservation of the subjects. And it is by such activity that you have attained to a glory which has never been approached by others, through the help of God who fulfils all your desires.'

The king spoke enthusiastically to the man and asked another How ought a man to occupy himself during his hours of relaxation and recreation? And he replied, 'To watch those plays which can be acted with propriety and to set before one's eyes scenes taken from life and enacted with dignity and decency is profitable and appropriate. For there is some edification to be found even in these amusements, for often some desirable lesson is taught by the most insignificant affairs of life. But by practicing the utmost propriety in all your actions, you have shown that you are a philosopher and you are honoured by God on account of your virtue.'

The king, pleased with the words which had just been spoken, said to the ninth man, How ought a man to conduct himself at banquets? And he replied, ' You should summon to your side men of learning and those who are able to give you useful hints with regard to the affairs of your kingdom and the lives of your subjects (for you could not find any theme more suitable or more educative than this) since such men are dear to God because they have trained their minds to contemplate the noblest themes-as you indeed are doing yourself, since all your actions are directed by God.'

Delighted with the reply, the king inquired of the next man, What is best for the people? That a private citizen should be made king over them or a member of the royal family ? And he replied, He who is best by nature. For kings who come of royal lineage are often harsh and severe towards their subjects. And still more is this the case with some of those who have risen from the ranks of private citizens, who after having experienced evil and borne their share of poverty, when they rule over multitudes turn out to be more cruel than the godless tyrants. But, as I have said, a good nature which has been properly trained is capable of ruling, and you are a great king, not so much because you excel in the glory of your rule and your wealth but rather because you have surpassed all men in clemency and philanthropy, thanks to God who has endowed you with these qualities.'

The king spent some time in praising this man and then asked the last of all, What is the greatest achievement in ruling an empire ? And he replied, ' That the subjects should continually dwell in a state of peace, and that justice should be speedily administered in cases of dispute.

These results are achieved through the influence of the ruler, when he is a man who hates evil and loves the good and devotes his energies to saving the lives of men, just as you consider injustice the worst form of evil and by your just administration have fashioned for yourself an undying reputation, since God bestows upon you a mind which is pure and untainted by any evil.'

And when he ceased, loud and joyful applause broke out for some considerable time. When it stopped the king took a cup and gave a toast in honour of all his guests and the words which they had uttered. Then in conclusion he said, ' I have derived the greatest benefit from your presence.

I have profited much by the wise teaching which you have given me in reference to the art of ruling.' Then he ordered that three talents of silver should be presented to each of them, and appointed one of his slaves to deliver over the money. All at once shouted their approval, and the banquet became a scene of joy, while the king gave himself up to a continuous round of festivity.

I have written at length and must crave your pardon, Philocrates. I was astonished beyond measure at the men and the way in which on the spur of the moment they gave answers which really needed a long time to devise. For though the questioner had given great thought to each particular question, those who replied one after the other had their answers to the questions ready at once and so they seemed to me and to all who were present and especially to the philosophers to be worthy of admiration. And I suppose that the thing will seem incredible to those who will read my narrative in the future. But it is unseemly to misrepresent facts which are recorded in the public archives. And it would not be right for me to transgress in such a matter as this. I tell the story just as it happened, conscientiously avoiding any error. I was so impressed by the force of their utterances, that I made an effort to consult those whose business it was to make a record of all that happened at the royal audiences and banquets. For it is the custom, as you know, from the moment the king begins to transact business until the time when he retires to rest, for a record to be taken of all his sayings and doings-a most excellent and useful arrangement.

For on the following day the minutes of the doings and sayings of the previous day are read over before business commences, and if there has been any irregularity, the matter is at once set right.

I obtained therefore, as has been said, accurate information from the public records, and I have set forth the facts in proper order since I know how eager you are to obtain useful information.

Three days later Demetrius took the men and passing along the sea-wall, seven stadia long, to the island, crossed the bridge and made for the northern districts of Pharos. There he assembled them in a house, which had been built upon the sea-shore, of great beauty and in a secluded situation, and invited them to carry out the work of translation, since everything that they needed for the purpose was placed at their disposal. So they set to work comparing their several results and making them agree, and whatever they agreed upon was suitably copied out under the direction of Demetrius.

And the session lasted until the ninth hour; after this they were set free to minister to their physical needs. Everything they wanted was furnished for them on a lavish scale. In addition to this Dorotheus made the same preparations for them daily as were made for the king himself-for thus he had been commanded by the king. In the early morning they appeared daily at the Court, and after saluting the king went back to their own place. And as is the custom of all the Jews, they washed their hands in the sea and prayed to God and then devoted themselves to reading and translating the particular passage upon which they were engaged, and I put the question to them, Why it was that they washed their hands before they prayed? And they explained that it was a token that they had done no evil (for every form of activity is wrought by means of the hands) since in their noble and holy way they regard everything as a symbol of righteousness and truth.

As I have already said, they met together daily in the place which was delightful for its quiet and its brightness and applied themselves to their task. And it so chanced that the work of translation was completed in seventy-two days, just as if this had been arranged of set purpose.

When the work was completed, Demetrius collected together the Jewish population in the place where the translation had been made, and read it over to all, in the presence of the translators, who met with a great reception also from the people, because of the great benefits which they had conferred upon them. They bestowed warm praise upon Demetrius, too, and urged him to have the whole law transcribed and present a copy to their leaders.

After the books had been read, the priests and the elders of the translators and the Jewish community and the leaders of the people stood up and said, that since so excellent and sacred and accurate a translation had been made, it was only right that it should remain as it was and no alteration should be made in it. And when the whole company expressed their approval, they bade them pronounce a curse in accordance with their custom upon any one who should make any alteration either by adding anything or changing in any way whatever any of the words which had been written or making any omission. This was a very wise precaution to ensure that the book might be preserved for all the future time unchanged.

When the matter was reported to the king, he rejoiced greatly, for he felt that the design which he had formed had been safely carried out. The whole book was read over to him and he was greatly astonished at the spirit of the lawgiver. And he said to Demetrius, ' How is it that none of the historians or the poets have ever thought it worth their while to allude to such a wonderful achievement ? ' And he replied, ' Because the law is sacred and of divine origin. And some of those who formed the intention of dealing with it have been smitten by God and therefore desisted from their purpose.' He said that he had heard from Theopompus that he had been driven out of his mind for more than thirty days because he intended to insert in his history some of the incidents from the earlier and somewhat unreliable translations of the law.

When he had recovered a little, he besought God to make it clear to him why the misfortune had befallen him. And it was revealed to him in a dream, that from idle curiosity he was wishing to communicate sacred truths to common men, and that if he desisted he would recover his health. I have heard, too, from the lips of Theodektes, one of the tragic poets, that when he was about to adapt some of the incidents recorded in the book for one of his plays, he was affected with cataract in both his eyes. And when he perceived the reason why the misfortune had befallen him, he prayed to God for many days and was afterwards restored.

And after the king, as I have already said, had received the explanation of Demetrius on this point, he did homage and ordered that great care should be taken of the books, and that they should be sacredly guarded. And he urged the translators to visit him frequently after their return to Judea, for it was only right, he said, that he should now send them home. But when they came back, he would treat them as friends, as was right, and they would receive rich presents from him. He ordered preparations to be made for them to return home, and treated them most munificently. He presented each one of them with three robes of the finest sort, two talents of gold, a sideboard weighing one talent, all the furniture for three couches.

And with the escort he sent Eleazar ten couches with silver legs and all the necessary equipment, a sideboard worth thirty talents, ten robes, purple, and a magnificent crown, and a hundred pieces of the finest woven linen, also bowls and dishes, and two golden beakers to be dedicated to God.

He urged him also in a letter that if any of the men preferred to come back to him, not to hinder them. For he counted it a great privilege to enjoy the society of such learned men, and he would rather lavish his wealth upon them than upon vanities.

And now Philocrates, you have the complete story in accordance with my promise. I think that you find greater pleasure in these matters than in the writings of the mythologists. For you are devoted to the study of those things which can benefit the soul, and spend much time upon it. I shall attempt to narrate whatever other events are worth recording, that by perusing them you may secure the highest reward for your zeal.

† Biblical Apocrypha †

narrate whatever other events are worth recording, that by perusing them you may secure the highest reward for your zeal.

The Letter of Peter to Phillip

eter, the apostle of Jesus Christ, to Philip, our beloved brother and our fellow apostle, and (to) the brethren who are with you: greetings!

Now I want you to know, our brother, that we received orders from our Lord and the Savior of the whole world that we should come together to give instruction and preach in the salvation which was promised us by our Lord Jesus Christ. But as for you, you were separate from us, and you did not desire us to come together and to know how we should organize ourselves in order that we might tell the good news. Therefore would it be agreeable to you, our brother, to come according to the orders of our God Jesus?"

When Philip had received these (words), and when he had read them, he went to Peter rejoicing with gladness. Then Peter gathered the others also. They went upon the mountain which is called "the (mount) olives," the place where they used to gather with the blessed Christ when he was in the body.

Then, when the apostles had come together, and had thrown themselves upon their knees, they prayed thus saying, "Father, Father, Father of the light, who possesses the incorruptions, hear us just as thou hast taken pleasure in thy holy child Jesus Christ. For he became for us an illuminator in the darkness. Yea hear us!"

And they prayed again another time, saying, "Son of life, Son of immortality, who is in the light, Son, Christ of immortality, our Redeemer, give us power, for they seek to kill us!"

Then a great light appeared so that the mountains shone from the sight of him who had appeared. And a voice called out to them saying, "Listen to my words that I may speak to you. Why are you asking me? I am Jesus Christ who am with you forever."

Then the apostles answered and said, "Lord, we would like to know the deficiency of the aeons and their pleroma." And: "How are we detained in this dwelling place?" Further: "How did we come to this place?" And: "In what manner shall we depart?" Again: "How do we have the authority of boldness?" And: "Why do the powers fight against us?"

Then a voice came to them out of the light saying, "It is you yourselves who are witnesses that I spoke all these things to you. But because of your unbelief I shall speak again. First of all concerning the deficiency of the aeons, this is the deficiency, when the disobedience and the foolishness of the mother appeared without the commandment of the majesty of the Father. She wanted to raise up aeons. And when she spoke, the Arrogant One followed. And when she left behind a part, the Arrogant One laid hold of it, and it became a deficiency. This is the deficiency of the aeons. Now when the Arrogant One had taken a part, he sowed it. And he placed powers over it and authorities. And he enclosed it in the aeons which are dead. And all the powers of the world rejoiced that they had been begotten. But they do not know the pre-existent Father, since they are strangers to him. But this is the one to whom they gave power and whom they served by praising him. But he, the Arrogant One, became proud on account of the praise of the powers. He became an envier and he wanted to make an image in the place of an image, and a form in the place of a form. And he commissioned the powers within his authority to mold mortal bodies. And they came to be from a misrepresentation, from the semblance which had merged."

"Next concerning the pleroma: I am the one who was sent down in the body because of the seed which had fallen away. And I came down into their mortal mold. But they did not recognize me; they were thinking of me that I was a mortal man. And I spoke with him who belongs to me, and he harkened to me just as you too who harkened today. And I gave him authority in order that he might enter into the inheritance of his fatherhood. And I took [...] they were filled [...] in his salvation. And since he was a deficiency, for this reason he became a pleroma."

"It is because of this that you are being detained, because you belong to me. When you strip off from yourselves what is corrupted, then you will become illuminators in the midst of mortal men."

"And this (is the reason) that you will fight against the powers, because they do not have rest like you, since they do not wish that you be saved."

Then the apostles worshiped again saying, "Lord, tell us: In what way shall we fight against the archons, since the archons are above us?"

Then a voice called out to them from the appearance saying, "Now you will fight against them in this way, for the archons are fighting against the inner man. And you are to fight against them in this way: Come together and teach in the world the salvation with a promise. And you, gird yourselves with the power of my Father, and let your prayer be known. And he, the Father, will help you as he has helped you by sending me. Be not afraid, I am with you forever, as I previously said to you when I was in the body." Then there came lightning and thunder from heaven, and what appeared to them in that place was taken up to heaven.

Then the apostles gave thanks to the Lord with every blessing. And they returned to Jerusalem. And while coming up they spoke with each other on the road concerning the light which had come. And a remark was made concerning the Lord. It was said, "If he, our Lord, suffered, then how much (must) we (suffer)?"

Peter answered saying, "He suffered on our behalf, and it is necessary for us too to suffer because of our smallness." Then a voice came to them saying, "I have told you many times: it is necessary for you to suffer. It is necessary that they bring you to synagogues and governors, so that you will suffer. But he who does not suffer and does not [...] the Father [...] in order that he may [...]."

And the apostles rejoiced greatly and came up to Jerusalem. And they came up to the temple and gave instruction in salvation in the name of the Lord Jesus Christ. And they healed a multitude.

And Peter opened his mouth, he said to his (fellow) disciples, "Did our Lord Jesus, when he was in the body, show us everything? For he came down. My brothers, listen to my voice." And he was filled with a holy spirit. He spoke thus: "Our illuminator, Jesus, came down and was crucified. And he bore a crown of thorns. And he put on a purple garment. And he was crucified on a tree and he was buried in a tomb. And he rose from the dead. My brothers, Jesus is a stranger to this suffering. But we are the ones who have suffered through the transgression of the mother. And because of this, he did everything like us. For the Lord Jesus, the Son of the immeasurable glory of the Father, he is the author of our life. My brothers, let us therefore not obey these lawless ones, and walk in [...]."

[...] Then Peter gathered together the others also, saying, "O, Lord Jesus Christ, author of our rest, give us a spirit of understanding in order that we also may perform wonders."

Then Peter and the other apostles saw him, and they were filled with a holy spirit, And each one performed healings. And they parted in order to preach the Lord Jesus. And they came together and greeted each other saying, "Amen."

Then Jesus appeared saying to them, "Peace to you all and everyone who believes in my name. And when you depart, joy be to you and grace and power. And be not afraid; behold, I am with you forever."

Then the apostles parted from each other into four words in order to preach. And they went by a power of Jesus, in peace.

The Letter of Pontius Pilate, Which He Wrote to the Roman Emperor, Concerning our Lord Jesus Christ.

Upon Jesus Christ, whose case I had dearly set forth to thee in my last, at length by the will of the people a bitter punishment has been inflicted, myself being in a sort unwilling and rather afraid. A man, by Hercules, so pious and strict, no age has ever had nor will have. But wonderful were the efforts of the people themselves, and the unanimity of all the scribes and chief men and elders, to crucify this ambassador of truth, notwithstanding that their own prophets, and after our manner the sibyls, warned them against it: and supernatural signs appeared while he was hanging, and, in the opinion of philosophers, threatened destruction to the whole world. His disciples are flourishing, in their work and the regulation of their lives not belying their master; yea, in his name most beneficent. Had I not been afraid of the rising of a sedition among the people, who were just on the point of breaking out, perhaps this man would still have been alive to us; although, urged more by fidelity to thy dignity than induced by my own wishes, I did not according to my strength resist that innocent blood free from the whole charge brought against it, but unjustly, through the malignity of men, should be sold and suffer, yet, as the Scriptures signify, to their own destruction.

Farewell,

28th March.

The Letters of Herod and Pilate

Connecting Roman History with the death of Christ at Jerusalem

LETTER OF HEROD TO PILATE THE GOVERNOR OF JERUSALEM

I am in great anxiety. I write these things unto thee, that when thou hast heard them thou mayest be grieved for me. For as my daughter Herodias, who is dear to me, was playing upon a pool of water which had ice upon it, it broke under her, and all her body went down, and her head was cut off and remained on the surface of the ice.

And behold, her mother is holding her head upon her knees in her lap, and my whole house is in great sorrow. For I, when I heard of the man Jesus, wished to come to thee, that I might see him alone, and hear his word, whether it was like that of the sons of men. And it is certain that because of the many evil things which were done by me to John the Baptist, and because I mocked the Christ, behold I receive the reward of righteousness, for I have shed much blood of others' children upon the earth. Therefore the judgments of God are righteous; for every man receives according to his thought.

But since thou wast worthy to see that God-man, therefore it becometh you to pray for me. My son Azbonius also is in the agony of the hour of death.

And I too am in affliction and great trial, because I have the dropsy; and am in great distress, because I persecuted the introducer of baptism by water, which was John. Therefore, my brother, the judgments of God are righteous.

And my wife, again, through all her grief for her daughter, is become blind in her left eye, because we desired to blind the Eye of righteousness. There is no peace to the doers of evil, saith the Lord. For already great affliction cometh upon the priests and upon the writers of the law; because they delivered unto thee the Just One. For this is the consummation of the world, that they consented that the Gentiles should become heirs. For the children of light shall be cast out, for they have not observed the things which were preached concerning the Lord, and concerning his Son.

Therefore gird up thy loins, and receive righteousness, thou with thy wife remembering Jesus night and day; and the kingdom shall belong to you Gentiles, for we the (chosen) people have mocked the Righteous One.

Now if there is place for our request, 0 Pilate, because we were at one time in power, bury my household carefully; for it is right that we should be buried by thee, rather than by the priests, whom, after a little time, as the Scriptures say, at the coming of Jesus Christ, vengeance shall overtake.

Fare thee well, with Procla thy wife.

I send thee the earrings of my daughter and my own ring, that they may be unto thee a memorial of my decease. For already do worms begin to issue from my body, and lo, I am receiving temporal judgment, and I am afraid of the judgment to come. For in both we stand before the works of the living God; but this judgment, which is temporal, is for a time, while that to come is judgment for ever.

End of the Letter to Pilate the Governor.

LETTER OF PILATE TO HEROD THE TETRARCH

Know and see, that in the day when thou didst deliver Jesus unto me, I took pity on myself, and testified by washing my hands (that I was innocent), concerning him who rose from the grave after three days, and had performed thy pleasure in him, for thou didst desire me to be associated with thee in his crucifixion. But I now learn from the executioners and from the soldiers who watched his sepulchre that he rose from the dead.

And I have especially confirmed what was told me, that he appeared bodily in Galilee, in the same form, and with the same voice, and with the same doctrine, and with the same disciples, not having changed in anything, but preaching with boldness his resurrection, and an everlasting kingdom.

And behold, heaven and earth rejoice; and behold, Procla my wife is believing in the visions which appeared unto her, when thou sentest that I should deliver Jesus to the people of Israel, because of the ill-will they had.

Now when Procla, my wife, heard that Jesus was risen, and had appeared in Galilee, she took with her Longinus the centurion and twelve soldiers, the same that had watched at the sepulchre, and went to greet the face of Christ, as if to a great spectacle, and saw him with his disciples.

Now while they were standing, and wondering, and gazing at him, he looked at them, and said to them, What is it? Do ye believe in me? Procla, know that in the covenant which God gave to the fathers, it is said that every body which had perished should live by means of my death, which ye have seen. And now, ye see that I live, whom ye crucified. And I suffered many things, till that I was laid in the sepulchre. But now, hear me, and believe in my Father - God who is in me. For I loosed the cords of death, and brake the gates of Sheol; and my coming shall be hereafter.

And when Procla my wife and the Romans heard these things, they came and told me, weeping; for they also were against him, when they devised the evils which they had done unto him. So that, I also was on the couch of my bed in affliction, and put on a garment of mourning, and took unto me fifty Romans with my wife and went into Galilee.

And when I was going in the way I testified these things; that Herod did these things by me, that he took counsel with me, and constrained me to arm my hands against him, and to judge him that judgeth all, and to scourge the Just One, Lord of the just. And when we drew nigh to him, O Herod, a great voice was heard from heaven, and dreadful thunder, and the earth trembled, and gave forth a sweet smell, like unto which was never perceived even in the temple of Jerusalem. Now while I stood in the way, our Lord saw me as he stood and talked with his disciples. But I prayed in my heart, for I knew that it was he whom ye delivered unto me, that he was Lord of created things and Creator of all. But we, when we saw him, all of us fell upon our faces before his feet. And I said with a loud voice, I have sinned, O Lord, in that I sat and judged thee, who avengest all in truth. And lo, I know that thou art God, the Son of God, and I beheld thy humanity and not thy divinity. But Herod, with the children of Israel, constrained me to do evil unto thee. Have pity, therefore, upon me, O God of Israel !

And my wife, in great anguish, said, God of heaven and of earth, God of Israel, reward me not according to the deeds of Pontius Pilate, nor according to the will of the children of Israel, nor according to the thought of the sons of the priests; but remember my husband in thy glory!

Now our Lord drew near and raised up me and my wife, and the Romans; and I looked at him and saw there were on him the scars of his cross. And be said, That which all the righteous fathers hoped to receive, and saw not - in thy time the Lord of Time, the Son of Man, the Son of the Most High, who is for ever, arose from the dead, and is glorified on high by all that he created, and established for ever and ever.

1. Justinus, one of the writers that were in the days of Augustus and Tiberius and Gaius, wrote in his third discourse: Now Mary the Galilaean, who bare the Christ that was crucified in Jerusalem, had not been with a husband. And Joseph did not abandon her; but Joseph continued in sanctity without a wife, he and his five sons by a former wife; and Mary continued without a husband.

2. Theodorus wrote to Pilate the Governor: Who was the man, against whom there was a complaint before thee, that he was crucified by the men of Palestine? If the many demanded this righteously, why didst thou not consent to their righteousness? And if they demanded this unrighteously, how didst thou transgress the law and command what was far from righteousness?

Pilate sent to him: - Because he wrought signs I did not wish to crucify him: and since his accusers said, He calleth himself a king, I crucified him.

3. Josephus saith: Agrippa, the king, was clothed in a robe woven with silver, and saw the spectacle in the theatre of Caesarea. When the people saw that his raiment flashed, they said to him,

Hitherto we feared thee as a man: henceforth thou art exalted above the nature of mortals. And he saw an angel standing over him, and he smote him as unto death.

End of the Letter of Pilate to Herod.

The Epistle of Pontius Pilate, which he wrote to the Roman Emperor concerning our Lord Jesus Christ

pon Jesus Christ, whom I fully made known to thee in my last, a bitter punishment hath at length been inflicted by the will of the people although I was unwilling and apprehensive. In good truth, no age ever had or will have a man so good and strict.

But the people made a wonderful effort, and all their scribes, chiefs and elders agreed to crucify this ambassador of truth, their own prophets, like the Sibyls with us, advising the contrary; and when he was hanged supernatural signs appeared, and in the judgment of philosophers menaced the whole world with ruin.

His disciples flourish, not belying their master by their behavior and continence of life; nay, in his name they are most beneficent. Had I not feared a sedition might arise among the people, who were almost furious, perhaps this man would have yet been living with us. Although, being rather compelled by fidelity to thy dignity, than led by my own inclination, I did not strive with all my might to prevent the sale and suffering of righteous blood, guiltless of every accusation, unjustly, indeed, through the maliciousness of men, and yet, as the Scriptures interpret, to their own destruction.

Farewell.

The 5th of the Calends of April.

The report of Pilate the Governor, concerning our Lord Jesus Christ, which was sent to Augustus Caesar in Rome

In those days, when our Lord Jesus Christ was crucified under Pontius Pilate, the governor of Palestine and Phoenicia, the things here recorded came to pass in Jerusalem, and were done by the Jews against the Lord. Pilate therefore sent the same to Caesar in Rome, along with his private report, writing thus:

To the most potent, august, divine and awful Augustus Caesar, Pilate, the administrator of the Eastern Province:

I have received information, most excellent one, in consequence of which I am seized with fear and trembling. For in this province which I administer, one of whose cities is called Jerusalem, the whole multitude of Jews delivered unto me a certain man called Jesus, and brought many accusations against him, which they were unable to establish by consistent evidence. But they charged him with one heresy in particular, namely,

That Jesus said the Sabbath was not a rest, nor to be observed by them. For he performed many cures on that day, and made the blind see, and the lame walk, raised the dead, cleansed lepers, healed the paralytic who were wholly unable to move their body or brace their nerves, but could only speak and discourse, and he gave them power to walk and run, removing their infirmity by his word alone.

There is another very mighty deed which is strange to the gods we have: he raised up a man who had been four days dead, summoning him by his word alone, when the dead man had begun to decay, and his body was corrupted by the worms which had been bred, and had the stench of a dog; but, seeing him lying in the tomb be commanded him to run, nor did the dead man at all delay, but as a bridegroom out of his chamber, so did he go forth from his tomb, filled with abundant perfume. Moreover, even such as were strangers, and clearly demoniacs, who had their dwelling in deserts, and devoured their own flesh, and wandered about like cattle and creeping things, he turned into inhabiters of cities and by a word rendered them rational, and prepared them to become wise and powerful, and illustrious, taking their food with all the enemies of the unclean spirits which were destructive in them, and which he cast into the depth of the sea.

And, again, there was another who had a withered hand, and not only the hand but rather the half of the body of the man was like a stone, and be had neither the shape of a man nor the symmetry of a body: even him He healed with a word and rendered whole.

And a woman also, who had an issue of blood for a long time, and whose veins and arteries were exhausted, and who did not bear a human body, being like one dead, and daily speechless, so that all the physicians of the district were unable to cure her, for there remained unto her not a hope of life; but as Jesus passed by she mysteriously received strength by his shadow falling on her, from behind she touched the hem of his garment, and immediately, in that very hour, strength filled her exhausted limbs, and as if she had never suffered anything, she began to run along towards Capernaum, her own city, so that she reached it in a six days' journey.

And I have made known these things which I have recently been informed of, and which Jesus did on the Sabbath. And he did other miracles greater than these, so that I have observed greater works of wonder done by him than by the gods whom we worship.

But Herod and Archelaus and Philip, Annas and Caiaphas, with all the people, deivered him to me, making a great tumult against me in order that I might try him.

Therefore, I commanded him to be crucified, when I had first scourged him, though I found no cause in him for evil accusations or dealings.

Now when he was crucified, there was darkness over all the world and the sun was obscured for half a day, and the stars appeared, but no lustre was seen in them; and the moon lost its brightness, as though tinged with blood; and the world of the departed was swallowed up;so that the very sanctuary of the temple, as they call it, did not appear to the Jews themselves at their fall, but they perceived a chasm in the earth, and the rolling of successive thunders.

And amid this terror the dead appeared rising again, as the Jews themselves bore witness, and said that it was Abraham, and Isaac, and Jacob, and the twelve patriarchs, and Moses, and Job, who had died before, as they say, some three thousand five hundred years.

And there were very many whom I myself saw appearing in the body, and they made lamentation over the Jews, because of the transgression which was committed by them, and because of the destruction of the Jews and of their law.

And the terror of the earthquake continued from the sixth hour of the preparation until the ninth hour; and when it was evening on the first day of the week, there came a sound from heaven, and the heaven became seven times more luminous than on all other days.

And at the third hour of the night the sun appeared more luminous than it had ever shone, lighting up the whole hemisphere. And as lightning - flashes suddenly come forth in a storm, so there were seen men, lofty in stature, and surpassing in glory, a countless host, crying out, and their voice was heard as that of exceedingly loud thunder, Jesus that was crucified is risen again: come up from Hades ye that were enslaved in the subterraneous recesses of Hades.

And the chasm in the earth was as if it had no bottom; but it was so that the very foundations of the eaith appeared, with those that shouted in heaven, and walked in the body among the dead that were raised. And He that raised up all the dead and bound Hades said, Say to my disciples,

He goeth before you into Galilee, there shall ye see Him.

And all that night the light ceased not shining. And many of the Jews died in the chasm of the earth, being swallowed up, so that on the morrow most of those who had been against Jesus were not to be found. Others saw the apparition of men rising again whom none of us had ever seen. One synagogue of the Jews was alone left in Jerusalem itself, for they all disappeared in that ruin.

Therefore being astounded by that terror, and being possessed with the most dreadful trembling, I have written what I saw at that time and sent it to thine excellency; and I have inserted what was done against Jesus by the Jews, and sent it to thy divinity, my lord.

The Report of Pontius Pilate, Governor of Judea

Which was sent to Tiberius Caesar in Rome

To the most potent, august, dreadful, and divine Augustus, Pontius Pilate, administrator of the Eastern Province.

I have undertaken to communicate to thy goodness by this my writing, though possessed with much fear and trembling, most excellent king, the present state of affairs, as the result hath shown. For as I administered this province, my lord, according to the command of thy serenity, which is one of the eastern cities called Jerusalem, wherein the temple of the nation of the Jews is erected, all the multitude of the Jews, being assembled, delivered up to me a certain man called Jesus, bringing many and endless accusations against him; but they could not convict him in anything.

But they had one heresy against him, that he said the sabbath was not their proper rest. Now that man wrought many cures and good works: he caused the blind to see, he cleansed lepers, he raised the dead, he healed paralytics, who could not move at all, but had only voice, and all their bones in their places; and he gave them strength to walk and run, enjoining it by his word alone.

And he did another yet more mighty work, which had been strange even among our gods, he raised from the dead one Lazarus, who had been dead four days, commanding by a word alone that the dead man should be raised, when his body was already corrupted by worms which bred in his wounds. And he commanded the fetid body, which lay in the grave, to run, and as bridegroom from his chamber so he went forth from his grave, full of sweet perfume.

And some that were grievously afflicted by demons, and had their dwellings in desert places, and devoured the flesh of their own limbs, and went up and down among creeping things and wild beasts, he caused to dwell in cities in their own houses, and by a word made them reasonable, and caused to become wise and honorable those that were vexed by unclean spirits, and the demons that were in them he sent out into a herd of swine into the sea and drowned them. Again, another who had a withered hand, and lived in suffering, and had not even the half of his body sound, he made whole by a word alone. And a woman who had an issue of blood for a long time, so that because of the discharge all the joints of her bones were seen and shone through like glass, for all the physicians had dismissed her without hope, and had not cleansed her, for there was in her no hope of health at all; but once, as Jesus was passing by she touched from behind the hem of his garments, and in that very hour the strength of her body was restored, and she was made whole, as if she had no affliction, and began to run fast towards her own city of Paneas. And these things happened thus: but the Jews reported that Jesus did these things on the sabbath. And I saw that greater marvels had been wrought by him than by the gods whom we worship.

Him then Herod and Archelaus and Philip, and Annas and Caiaphas, with all the people, delivered up to me, to put him on his trial. And because many raised a tumult against me, I commanded that he should be crucified.

Now when he was crucified darkness came over all the world; the sun was altogether hidden, and the sky appeared dark while it was yet day, so that the stars were seen, though still they had their lustre obscured, wherefore, I suppose your excellency is not unaware that in all the world they lighted their lamps from the sixth hour until evening. And the moon, which was like blood, did not shine all night long, although it was at the full, and the stars and Orion made lamentation over the Jews, because of the transgression committed by them.

And on the first day of the week, about the third hour of the night, the sun appeared as it never shone before, and the whole heaven became bright.

And as lightnings come in a storm, so certain men of lofty stature, in beautiful array, and of indescribable glory, appeared in the air, and a countless host of angels, crying out and saying,

Glory to God in the highest, and on earth peace, good will among men: Come up from Hades, ye who are in bondage in the depths of Hades.

And at their voice all the mountains and hills were moved, and the rocks were rent, and great chasms were made in the earth, so that the very places of the abyss were visible. And amid the terror dead men were seen rising again, so that the Jews who saw it said.

We beheld Abraham and Isaac, and Jacob, and the twelve patriarchs, who died some two thousand five hundred years before, and we beheld Noah clearly in the body.

And all the multitude walked about and sang hymns to God with a loud voice, saying, The Lord our God, who hath risen from the dead, hath made alive all the dead, and Hades he hath spoiled and slain.

Therefore, my lord king, all that night the light ceased not. But many of the Jews died, and were sunk and swallowed up in the chasms that night, so that not even their bodies were to be seen. Now I mean, that those of the Jews suffered who spake against Jesus. And but one synagogue remained in Jerusalem, for all the synagogues which had been against Jesus were overwhelmed.

Through that terror, therefore, being amazed and being seized with great trembling, in that very hour, I ordered what had been done by them all to be written, and I have sent it to thy mightiness.

The Trial and Condemnation of Pilate

Now when the letters came to the city of the Romans, and were read to Caesar with no few standing there, they were all terrified, because, through the transgression of Pilate, the darkness and the earthquake had happened to all the world. And Caesar, being filled with anger, sent soldiers and commanded that Pilate should be brought as a prisoner.

And when he was brought to the city of the Romans, and Caesar heard that he was come, he sat in the temple of the gods, above all the senate, and with all the army, and with all the multitude of his power, and commanded that Pilate should stand in the entrance. And Caesar said to him, Most impious one, when thou sawest so great signs done by that man, why didst thou dare to do thus?

By daring to do an evil deed thou hast ruined all the world.

And Pilate said, King and Autocrat, I am not guilty of these things, but it is the multitude of the Jews who are precipitate and guilty. And Caesar said, And who are they? Pilate saith, Herod, Archelaus, Philip, Annas and

Caiaphas, and all the multitude of the Jews.

Caesar saith, For what cause didst thou execute their purpose?

And Pilate said, Their nation is seditious and insubordinate, and not submissive to thy power.

And Caesar said, When they delivered him to thee thou oughtest to have made him secure and sent him to me, and not consented to them to crucify such a man, who was just and wrought such great and good miracles, as thou saidst in thy report. For by such miracles Jesus was manifested to be the Christ, the King of the Jews.

And when Caesar said this and himself named the name of Christ, all the multitude of the gods fell down together, and became like dust where Caesar sat with the senate.

And all the people that stood near Caesar were filled with trembling because of the utterance of the word and the fall of their gods, and being seized with fear they all went away, every man to his house, wondering at what had happened.

And Caesar commanded Pilate to be safely kept, that he might know the truth about Jesus. And on the morrow when Caesar sat in the capitol with all the senate, he undertook to question Pilate again. And Caesar said, Say the truth, most impious one, for through thy impious deed which thou didst commit against Jesus, even here the doing of thy evil works were manifested, in that the gods were brought to ruin.

Say then, who is he that was crucified, for his name hath destroyed all the gods?

Pilate said, And verily his records are true; for even I myself was convinced by his works that he was greater than all the gods whom we venerate.

And Caesar said, For what cause then didst thou perpetrate against him such daring and doing, not being ignorant of him, or assuredly designing some mischief to my government?

And Pilate said, I did it because of the transgression and sedition of the lawless and ungodly Jews.

And Caesar was filled with anger, and held a council with all his senate and officers, and ordered a decree to be written against the Jews thus:-

To Licianus who holdeth the first place in the East Country. Greeting:

I have been informed of the audacity perpetrated very recently by the Jews inhabiting Jerusalem and the cities round about, and their lawless doing, how they compelled Pilate to crucify a certain god called Jesus, through which great transgression of theirs the world was darkened and drawn into ruin.

Determine therefore, with a body of soldiers, to go to them there at once and proclaim their subjection to bondage by this decree.

By obeying and proceeding against them, and scattering them abroad in all nations, enslave them, and by driving their nation from all Judea as soon as possible show, wherever this hath not yet appeared, that they are full of evil.

And when this decree came into the East Country, Licianus obeyed, through fear of the decree, and laid waste all the nation of the Jews, and caused those that were left in Judea to go into slavery with them that were scattered among the Gentiles, that it might be known by Caesar that these things had been done by Licianus against the Jews in the East Country, and to please him.

And again Caesar resolved to have Pilate questioned, and commanded a captain, Albius by name, to cut off Pilate's head, saying,

As he laid hands upon the just man, that is called Christ, he also shall fall in like manner, and find no deliverance.

And when Pilate came to the place he prayed in silence saying,

O Lord, destroy not me with the wicked Hebrews, for I should not have laid hands upon thee, but for the nation of lawless Jews, because they provoked sedition gainst me: but thou knowest that I did it in ignorance. Destroy me not, therefore, for this my sin, nor be mindful of the evil that is in me, O Lord, and in thy servant Procla who standeth with me in this the hour of my death, whom thou taughtest to prophecy that thou must be nailed to the cross. Do not punish her too in my sin, but forgive us, and number us in the portion of thy just ones. And behold, when Pilate had finished his prayer, there came a voice from heaven, saying, All generations and the families of the Gentiles shall call thee blessed, because under thee were fulfilled all these things that were spoken by the prophets concerning me; and thou thyself must appear as my witness at my second coming, when I shall judge the twelve tribes of Israel, and them that have not confessed my name. And the Prefect cut off the head of Pilate, and behold an angel of the Lord received it. And when his wife Procla saw the angel coming and receiving his head, she also, being filled with joy, forthwith gave up the ghost, and was buried with her husband.

[The Synaxaria of the Greeks, under Oct. 28th, intimate the commemoration of Procla, the wife of Pilate. The AEthiopic calendar inserts 'Pilate and his wife Procla' under June 25th. The reason for putting these names among the saints is, that Pilate by washing his hands attested the innocence of Jesus, while Procla sought to dissuade her husband from complying with the Jews.

The above story makes of Pilate almost a martyr; and Tertullian makes him almost a saint in Apol. c. Gentes, cap. 21.]

The Death of Pilate, who condemned Jesus

ow whereas Tiberius Caesar emperor of the Romans was suffering from a grievous sickness, and hearing that there was at Jerusalem a certain physician, Jesus by name, who healed all diseases by his word alone; not knowing that the Jews and Pilate had put him to death, he thus bade one of his attendants, Volusianus by name, saying, Go as quickly as thou canst across the sea, and tell Pilate, my servant and friend, to send me this physician to restore me to my original health. And Volusianus, having heard the order of the emperor, immediately departed, and came to Pilate, as it was commanded him.

And he told the same Pilate what had been committed to him by Tiberius Caesar, saying, Tiberius Caesar, emperor of the Romans, thy Lord, having heard that in this city there is a physician who healeth diseases by his word alone, earnestly entreateth thee to send him to him to heal his disease. And Pilate was greatly terrified on hearing this, knowing that through envy he had caused him to be slain. Pilate answered the messenger, saying thus, This man was a malefactor, and a man who drew after himself all the people; so, after counsel taken of the wise men of the city, I caused him to be crucified. And as the messenger returned to his lodgings he met a certain woman named Veronica, who had been acquainted with Jesus, and he said, O woman, there was a certain physician in this city, who healed the sick by his word alone, why have the Jews slain him? And she began to weep, saying, Ah, me, my lord, it was my God and my Lord whom Pilate through envy delivered up, condemned, and commanded to be crucified. Then he, grieving greatly, said, I am exceedingly sorry that I cannot fulfil that for which my lord hath sent me.

Veronica said to him, When my Lord went about preaching, and I was very unwillingly deprived of his presence, I desired to have his picture painted for me, that while I was deprived of his presence, at least the figure of his likeness might give me consolation. And when I was taking the canvas to the painter to be painted, my Lord met me and asked whither I was going. And when I had made known to him the cause of my journey, He asked me for the canvas, and gave it back to me printed with the likeness of his venerable face. Therefore, if thy lord will devoutly look upon the sight of this, he will straightway enjoy the benefit of health.

Is a likeness of this kind to be procured with gold or silver? he asked. No, said she, but with a pious sentiment of devotion. Therefore, I will go with thee, and carry the likeness to Caesar to look upon, and will return.

So Volusianus came with Veronica to Rome, and said to Tiberius the emperor, Jesus, whom thou hast long desired, Pilate and the Jews have surrendered to an unjust death, and through envy fastened to the wood of the cross. Therefore, a certain matron hath come with me bringing the likeness of the same Jesus, and if thou wilt devoutly gaze upon it, thou wilt presently obtain the benefit of thy health. So Caesar caused the way to be spread with cloths of silk, and ordered the portrait to be presented to him; and as soon as he had looked upon it he regained his original health.

Then Pontius Pilate was apprehended by command of Caesar and brought to Rome.

Caesar, hearing that Pilate had come to Rome, was filled with exceeding wrath against him, and caused him to be brought to him. Now Pilate brought with him the seamless coat of Jesus, and wore it when before the emperor. As soon as the emperor saw him he laid aside all his wrath, and forthwith rose to him, and was unable to speak harshly to him in anything: and he who in his absence seemed so terrible and fierce now in his presence is found comparatively gentle.

And when he had dismissed him, he soon became terribly inflamed against him, declaring himself wretched, because he had not expressed to him the anger of his bosom.

And immediately he had him recalled, swearing and protesting that he was a child of death, and unfitted to live upon earth. And when he saw him he instantly greeted him, and laid aside all the fury of his mind.

All were astonished, and he was astonished himself, that he was so enraged against Pilate while absent, and could say nothing to him sharply while he was present. At length, by Divine suggestion, or perhaps by the persuasion of some Christian, he had him stripped of the coat, and soon resumed against him his original fury of mind.

And when the emperor was wondering very much about this, they told him it had been the coat of the Lord Jesus. Then the emperor commanded him to be kept in prison till he should take counsel with the wise men what ought to be done with him.

And after a few days sentence was given against Pilate that he should be condemned to the most ignominious death. When Pilate heard this he slew himself with his own dagger, and by such a death put an end to his life.

When Pilate's death was made known Caesar said, Truly he has died a most ignominious death, whose own hand has not spared him. He was therefore fastened to a great block of stone and sunk in the river Tiber. But wicked and unclean spirits, rejoicing in his wicked and unclean body, all moved about in the water, and caused in the air dreadful lightning and tempests, thunder and hail, so that all were seized with horrible fear. On which account the Romans dragged him out of the river Tiber, bore him away in derision to Vienne, and sunk him in the river Rhone. For Vienne means, as it were, Way of Gehenna, because it was then a place of cursing. And evil spirits were there and did the same things.

Those men, therefore, not enduring to be so harassed by demons, removed the vessel of cursing from them and sent it to be buried in the territory of Losania. But when they were troubled exceedingly by the aforesaid vexations, they put it away from them and sunk it in a certain pool surrounded by mountains, where even yet, according to the account of some, sundry diabolical contrivances are said to Issue forth.

The Lost Gospel According to Peter

n the valley of the Upper Nile, on the right bank of the river, is the myste ous town of Akhmim.

It was called Panopolis in ancient times when it was the capital af the district. The remnants of monasteries and the ruins of temples mark the intellectual life of a former day.

In 1816, the French Achseological Mission excavating in the grave of a monk, came upon a parchment codex. Six years later a translation of this was published in the Memoirs of the French Archaological Mission at Cairo. Scholars realized for the first time that a striking discovery, possibly of overwhelming importance, had been made. A portion of The Gospel According to Peter appeared to have been restored to the Christian Community after having been lost for ages. But until now, this document has never been made available to the general public.

Centuries rolled over that remote tomb at Akhmim, while nations rose and fell, wars blasted civilization, science metamorphosed the world, Shakespeares and Miltons wrote their names and passed on, the American nation was born and grew up -all the while the ink on the parchment in that Egyptian tomb was scarcely changing and the beautiful words of this Scripture were preserving for us this version of the most tragic and momentous event in history. That briefly is the romance of The Lost Gospel According to Peter.

Such a gospel was referred to by Serapion, Bishop of Antioch, In 190 A.u.; Origen, historian, in 253 A.D.; Eusebius, Bishop of Caesarea in 300 A.D.; Theodoret in 455 in his Religious History said that the Nazarenes used The Gospel According to Peter; and Justin Martyr includes the Memoirs of Peter in his "Apostolic Memoirs." Thus scholars have always recognized that such a document existed long ago, although its whereabouts and fate were a mystery until the discovery at Akhmim.

BUT of the Jews none washed his hands, neither Herod nor any one of his judges. And when they had refused to wash them, Pilate rose up. And then Herod the king commandeth that the Lord be taken saying to them, What things soever I commanded you to do unto him, do.

2. And there was standing there Joseph the friend of Pilate and of the Lord; and, knowing that they were about to crucify him, he came to Pilate and asked the body of the Lord for burial. And Pilate sent to Herod and asked his body. And Herod said, Brother Pilate, even if no one has asked for him, we purposed to bury him, especially as the sabbath draweth on: for it is written in the law, that the sun set not upon one that hath been put to death.

3. And he delivered him to the people on the day before the unleavened bread, their feast.

And they took the Lord and pushed him as they ran, and said, Let us drag away the Son of God, having obtained power over him. And they clothed him with purple, and set him on the seat of judgment, saying, Judge righteously, 0 king of Israel. And one of them brought a crown of thorns and put it on the head of the Lord. And others stood and spat in his eyes, and others smote his cheeks: others pricked him with a reed; and some scourged him, saying, With this honor let us honor the Son of God.

4. And they brought two malefactors, and they crucified the Lord between them.

But he held his peace, as though having no pain. And when they had raised the cross, they wrote the title: This is the king of Israel .

And having set his garments before him they parted them among them, and cast lots for them.

And one of those malefactors reproached them, saying, We for the evils that we have done have suffered thus, but this man, who hath become the Saviour of men, what wrong hath he done to you? And they, being angered at him, commanded that his legs should not be broken, that he might die in torment.

5. And it was noon, and darkness came over all Judaea: and they were troubled and distressed, lest the sun had set, whilst he was yet alive: [for] it is written for them, that the sun set not on him that hath been put to death.

And one of them said, Give him to drink gall with vinegar. And they mixed and gave him to drink, and fulfilled all things, and accomplished their sins against their own head.

And many went about with lamps, supposing that it was night, and fell down. And the Lord cried out, saying,

My power, my power, thou hast forsaken me. And when he had said it he was taken up.

And in that hour the vail of the temple of Jerusalem was rent in twain.

6. And then they drew out the nails from the hands of the Lord, and laid him upon the earth, and the whole earth quaked, and great fear arose.

Then the sun shone, and it was found the ninth hour: and the Jews rejoiced, and gave his body to Joseph that he might bury it, since he had seen what good things he had done.

And he took the Lord, and washed him, and rolled him in a linen cloth, and brought him to his own tomb, which was called the Garden of Joseph.

7. Then the Jews and the elders and the priests, perceiving what evil they had done to themselves, began to lament and to say, Woe for our sins: the judgment hath drawn nigh, and the end of Jerusalem.

And I with my companions was grieved; and being wounded in mind we hid ourselves: for we were being sought for by them as malefactors, and as wishing to set fire to the temple.

And upon all these things we fasted and sat mourning and weeping night and day until the sabbath.

8. But the scribes and Pharisees and elders being gathered together one with another, when they heard that all the people murmured and beat their breasts saying, If by his death these most mighty signs have come to pass, see how righteous he is, -the elders were afraid and came to Pilate beseeching him and saying,

Give us soldiers, that we may guard his sepulchre for three days, lest his disciples come and steal him away, and the people suppose that he is risen from the dead and do us evil.

And Pilate gave them Petronius the centurion with soldiers to guard the tomb.

And with them came elders and scribes to the sepulchre, and having rolled a great stone together with the centurion and the soldiers, they all together who were there set it at the door of the sepulchre; and they affixed seven seals, and they pitched a tent there and guarded it.

And early in the morning as the sabbath was drawing on, there came a multitude from Jerusalem and the region round about, that they might see the sepulchre that was sealed.

9. And in the night in which the Lord's day was drawing on, as the soldiers kept guard two by two in a watch, there was a great voice in the heaven; and they saw the heavens opened, and two men descend from thence with great light and approach the tomb.

And that stone which was put at the door rolled of itself and made way in part; and the tomb was opened, and both the young men entered in.

10. When therefore those soldiers saw it, they awakened the centurion

and the elders; for they too were hard by keeping guard.

And as they declared what things they had seen, again they see three men come forth from the tomb, and two of them supporting one, and a cross following them: and of the two the head reached unto the heaven, but the head of him who was lead by them overpassed the heavens. And they heard a voice from the heavens, saying, Thou hast preached to them that sleep.

And a response was heard from the cross, Yea.

11. They therefore considered one with another whether to go away and shew these things to Pilate. And while they yet thought thereon, the heavens again are seen to open, and a certain man to descend and enter into the sepulchre.

When the centurion and they that were with him saw these things, they hastened in the night to Pilate, leaving the tomb which they were watching, and declared all things which they had seen, being greatly distressed and saying, Truly he was the Son of God. Pilate answered and said, I am pure from the blood of the Son of God: but it was ye who determined this. Then they all drew near and besought him and entreated him to command the centurion and the soldiers to say nothing of the things which they had seen:

For it is better, say they, for us to be guilty of the greatest sin before God, and not to fall into the hands of the people of the Jews and to be stoned. Pilate therefore commanded the centurion and the soldiers to say nothing.

12. And at dawn upon the Lord's day Mary Magdalene, a disciple of the Lord, fearing because of the Jews, since they were burning with wrath, had not done at the Lord's sepulchre the things which women are wont to do for those that die and for those that are beloved by them -- she took her friends with her and came to the sepulchre where he was laid. And they feared lest the Jews should see them, and they said,

Although on that day on which he was crucified we could not weep and lament, yet now let us do these things at his sepulchre.

But who shall roll away for us the stone that was laid at the door of the sepulchre, that we may enter in and sit by him and do the things that are due?

For the stone was great, and we fear lest some one see us.

And if we cannot, yet if we but set at the door the things which we bring as a memorial of him, we will weep and lament, until we come unto our home.

13. And, they went and found the tomb opened, and coming near they looked in there; and they see there a certain young man sitting in the midst of the tomb, beautiful and clothed in a robe exceeding bright; who said to them, Wherefore are ye come? Whom seek ye? Him that was crucified?

He is risen and gone. But if ye believe not, look in and see the place where he lay, that he is not [here]; for he is risen and gone thither, whence he was sent. Then the women feared and fled.

14. Now it was the last day of the unleavened bread, and many were going forth, returning to their homes, as the feast was ended.

But we, the twelve disciples of the Lord, wept and were grieved: and each one, being grieved for that which was come to pass, departed to his home. But I Simon Peter and Andrew my brother took our nets and went to the sea; and there was with us Levi the son of Alphaeus, whom the Lord ...

The Martyrdom of Ignatius

CHAPTER 1
Desire Of Ignatius For Martyrdom

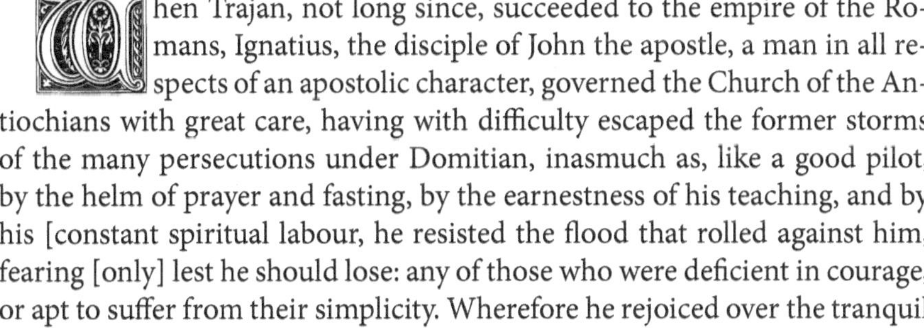hen Trajan, not long since, succeeded to the empire of the Romans, Ignatius, the disciple of John the apostle, a man in all respects of an apostolic character, governed the Church of the Antiochians with great care, having with difficulty escaped the former storms of the many persecutions under Domitian, inasmuch as, like a good pilot, by the helm of prayer and fasting, by the earnestness of his teaching, and by his [constant spiritual labour, he resisted the flood that rolled against him, fearing [only] lest he should lose: any of those who were deficient in courage, or apt to suffer from their simplicity. Wherefore he rejoiced over the tranquil state of the Church, when the persecution ceased for a little time, but was grieved as to himself, that he had not yet attained to a true love to Christ, nor reached the perfect rank of a disciple. For he inwardly reflected, that the confession which is made by martyrdom, would bring him into a yet more intimate relation to the Lord. Wherefore, continuing a few years longer with the Church, and, like a divine lamp, enlightening every one's understanding by his expositions of the [Holy] Scriptures, he [at length] attained the object of his desire.

CHAPTER 2
Ignatius Is Condemned By Trajan

For Trajan, in the ninth year of his reign, being lifted up [with pride], after the victory he had gained over the Scythians and Dacians, and many other nations, and thinking that the religious body of the Christians were yet wanting to complete the subjugation of all things to himself, and [thereupon] threatening them with persecution unless they should agree to worship daemons, as did all other nations, thus compelled all who were living godly lives either to sacrifice [to idols] or die. Wherefore the noble soldier of Christ [Ignatius], being in fear for the Church of the Antiochians, was, in accordance with his own desire, brought before Trajan, who was at that time staying at Antioch, but was in haste [to set forth] against Armenia and the Parthians. And when he was set before the emperor Trajan, [that prince] said unto him, "Who art thou, eked wretch, who settest thyself to transgress our commands, and persuadest others to do the same, so that they should miserably perish?" Ignatius replied, "No one ought to call Theophorus wicked; for all evil spirits have departed from the servants of God. But if, because I am an enemy to these [spirits], you call me wicked in respect to them, I quite agree with you; for inasmuch as I have Christ the King of heaven [within me], I destroy all the devices of these [evil spirits]." Trajan answered, "And who is Theophorus?" Ignatius replied, "He who has Christ within his breast." Trajan said, "Do we not then seem to you to have the gods in our mind, whose assistance we enjoy in fighting against our enemies?" Ignatius answered, "Thou art in error when thou callest the daemons of the nations gods. For there is but one God, who made heaven, and earth, and the sea, and all that are in them; and one Jesus Christ, the only-begotten Son of God, whose kingdom may I enjoy." Trajan said, "Do you mean Him who was crucified under Pontius Pilate?" Ignatius replied, "I mean Him who crucified my sin, with him who was the inventor of it, and who has condemned [and cast down] all the deceit and malice of the devil under the feet of those who carry Him in their heart." Trajan said, "Dost thou then carry within thee Him that was crucified?" Ignatius replied, "Truly so; for it is written, 'I will dwell in them, and walk in them.'" Then Trajan pronounced sentence as follows: "We command that Ignatius, who affirms that he carries about within him Him that was crucified, be bound by soldiers, and carried to the great [city] Rome, there to be devoured by the beasts, for the gratification of the people." When the holy martyr heard this sentence, he cried out with joy, "I thank thee, O Lord, that Thou hast vouchsafed to honour me with a perfect love towards Thee, and hast made me to be bound with iron chains, like Thy Apostle Paul." Having spoken thus, he then, with delight, clasped the chains about him; and when he had first prayed for the Church, and commended it with tears to the Lord, he was hurried away by the savage cruelty of the soldiers, like a distinguished ram the leader of a goodly flock, that he might be carried to Rome, there to furnish food to the bloodthirsty beasts.

CHAPTER 3
Ignatius Sails To Smyrna

Wherefore, with great alacrity and joy, through his desire to suffer, he came down from Antioch to Seleucia, from which place he set sail. And after a great deal of suffering he came to Smyrna, where he disembarked with great joy, and hastened to see the holy Polycarp, [formerly] his fellow-disciple, and [now] bishop of Smyrna. For they had both, in old times, been disciples of St. John the Apostle. Being then brought to him, and having communicated to him some spiritual gifts, and glorying in his bonds, he entreated of him to labour along with him for the fulfilment of his desire; earnestly indeed asking this of the whole Church (for the cities and Churches of Asia had welcomed the holy man through their bishops, and presbyters, and deacons, all hastening to meet him, if by any means they might receive from him some spiritual gift), but above all, the holy Polycarp, that, by means of the wild beasts, he soon disappearing from this world, might be manifested before the face of Christ.

CHAPTER 4
Ignatius Writes To The Churches

And these things he thus spake, and thus testified, extending his love to Christ so far as one who was about to secure heaven through his good confession, and the earnestness of those who joined their prayers to his in regard to his [approaching] conflict; and to give a recompense to the Churches, who came to meet him through their rulers, sending letters of thanksgiving to them, which dropped spiritual grace, along with prayer and exhortation. Wherefore, seeing all men so kindly affected towards him, and fearing lest the love of the brotherhood should hinder his zeal towards the Lord, while a fair door of suffering martyrdom was opened to him, he wrote to the Church of the Romans the Epistle which is here subjoined.

CHAPTER 5
Ignatius Is Brought To Rome

Having therefore, by means of this Epistle, settled, as he wished, those of the brethren at Rome who were unwilling [for his martyrdom]; and setting sail from Smyrna (for Christophorus was pressed by the soldiers to hasten to the public spectacles in the mighty [city] Rome, that, being given up to the wild beasts in the sight of the Roman people, he might attain to the crown for which he strove), he [next] landed at Troas. Then, going on from that place to Neapolis, he went [on foot] by Philippi through Macedonia, and on to that part of Epirus which is near Epidamnus; and finding a ship in one of the sea-ports, he sailed over the Adriatic Sea, and entering from it on the Tyrrhene, he passed by the various islands and cities, until, when Puteoli came in sight, he was eager there to disembark, having a desire to tread in the footsteps of the Apostle Paul. But a violent wind arising did not suffer him to do so, the ship being driven rapidly forwards; and, simply expressing his delight over the love of the brethren in that place, he sailed by. Wherefore, continuing to enjoy fair winds, we were reluctantly hurried on in one day and a night, mourning [as we did] over the coming departure from us of this righteous man. But to him this happened just as he wished, since he was in haste as soon as possible to leave this world, that he might attain to the Lord whom he loved. Sailing then into the Roman harbour, and the unhallowed sports being just about to close, the soldiers began to be annoyed at our slowness, but the bishop rejoicingly yielded to their urgency.

CHAPTER 6
Ignatius Is Devoured By The Beasts At Rome

They pushed forth therefore from the place which is called Portus; and (the fame of all relating to the holy martyr being already spread abroad) we met the brethren full of fear and joy; rejoicing indeed because they were thought worthy to meet with Theophorus, but struck with fear because so eminent a man was being led to death. Now he enjoined some to keep silence who, in their fervent zeal, were saying that they would appease the people, so that they should not demand the destruction of this just one. He being immediately aware of this through the Spirit, and having saluted them all, and begged of them to show a true affection towards him, and having dwelt [on this point] at greater length than in his Epistle, and having persuaded them not to envy him hastening to the Lord, he then, after he had, with all the brethren kneeling [beside him], entreated the Son of God in behalf of the Churches, that a stop might be put to the persecution, and that mutual love might continue among the brethren, was led with all haste into the amphitheatre. Then, being immediately thrown in, according to the command of Caesar given some time ago, the public spectacles being just about to close (for it was then a solemn day, as they deemed it, being that which is called the thirteenth in the Roman tongue, on which the people were wont to assemble in more than ordinary numbers), he was thus cast to the wild beasts close, beside the temple, that so by them the desire of the holy martyr

Ignatius should be fulfilled, according to that which is written, "The desire of the righteous is acceptable [to God]," to the effect that he might not be troublesome to any of the brethren by the gathering of his remains, even as he had in his Epistle expressed a wish beforehand that so his end might be. For only the harder portions of his holy remains were left, which were conveyed to Antioch and wrapped in linen, as an inestimable treasure left to the holy Church by the grace which was in the martyr.

CHAPTER 7
Ignatius Appears In A Vision After His Death

Now these things took place on the thirteenth day before the Kalends of January, that is, on the twentieth of December, Sun and Senecio being then the consuls of the Romans for the second time. Having ourselves been eye-witnesses of these things, and having spent the whole night in tears within the house, and having entreated the Lord, with bended knees and much prayer, that He would give us weak men full assurance respecting the things which were done, it came to pass, on our filling into a brief slumber, that some of us saw the blessed Ignatius suddenly standing by us and embracing us, while others beheld him again praying for us, and others still saw him dropping with sweat, as if he had just come from his great labour, and standing by the Lord. When, therefore, we had with great joy witnessed these things, and had compared our several visions together, we sang praise to God, the giver of all good things, and expressed our sense of the happiness of the holy [martyr]; and now we have made known to you both the day and the time [when these things happened], that, assembling ourselves together according to the time of his martyrdom, we may have fellowship with the champion and noble martyr of Christ, who trode under foot the devil, and perfected the course which, out of love to Christ, he had desired, in Christ Jesus our Lord; by whom, and with whom, be glory and power to the Father, with the Holy Spirit, for evermore! Amen.

The Encyclical Epistle Of The Church At Smyrna Concerning The Martyrdom Of The Holy Polycarp

CHAPTER 1
Subject Of Which We Write

We have written to you, brethren, as to what relates to the martyrs, and especially to the blessed Polycarp, who put an end to the persecution, having, as it were, set a seal upon it by his martyrdom. For almost all the events that happened previously [to this one], took place that the Lord might show us from above a martyrdom becoming the Gospel. For he waited to be delivered up, even as the Lord had done, that we also might become his followers, while we look not merely at what concerns ourselves but have regard also to our neighbours. For it is the part of a true and well-founded love, not only to wish one's self to be saved, but also all the brethren.

CHAPTER 2
The Wonderful Constancy Of The Martyrs

All the martyrdoms, then, were blessed and noble which took place according to the will of God. For it becomes us who profess greater piety than others, to ascribe the authority over all things to God. And truly, who can fail to admire their nobleness of mind, and their patience, with that love towards their Lord which they displayed?--who, when they were so torn with scourges, that the frame of their bodies, even to the very inward veins and arteries, was laid open, still patiently endured, while even those that stood by pitied and bewailed them. But they reached such a pitch of magnanimity, that not one of them let a sigh or a groan escape them; thus proving to us all that those holy martyrs of Christ, at the very time when they suffered such torments, were absent from the body, or rather, that the Lord then stood by them, and communed with them. And, looking to the grace of Christ, they despised all the torments of this world, redeeming themselves from eternal punishment by [the suffering of] a single hour. For this reason the fire of their savage executioners appeared cool to them. For they kept before their view escape from that fire which is eternal and never shall be quenched, and looked forward with the eyes of their heart to those good things which are laid up for such as endure; things "which ear hath not heard, nor eye seen, neither have entered into the heart of man," but were revealed by the Lord to them, inasmuch as they were no longer men, but had already become angels. And, in like manner, those who were condemned to the wild beasts endured dreadful tortures, being stretched out upon beds full of spikes, and subjected to various other kinds of torments, in order that, if it were possible, the tyrant might, by their lingering tortures, lead them to a denial [of Christ].

CHAPTER 3
The Constancy Of Germanicus; The Death Of Polycarp Is Demanded

For the devil did indeed invent many things against them; but thanks be to God, he could not prevail over all. For the most noble Germanicus strengthened the timidity of others by his own patience, and fought heroically with the wild beasts. For, when the proconsul sought to persuade him, and urged him to take pity upon his age, he attracted the wild beast towards himself, and provoked it, being desirous to escape all the more quickly from an unrighteous and impious world. But upon this the whole multitude, marvelling at the nobility of mind displayed by the devout and godly race of Christians, cried out, "Away with the Atheists; let Polycarp be sought out!"

CHAPTER 4
Quintus The Apostate

Now one named Quintus, a Phrygian, who was but lately come from Phrygia, when he saw the wild beasts, became afraid. This was the man who forced himself and some others to come forward voluntarily [for trial]. Him the proconsul, after many entreaties, persuaded to swear and to offer sacrifice. Wherefore, brethren, we do not commend those who give themselves up [to suffering], seeing the Gospel does not teach so to do.

CHAPTER 5
The Departure And Vision Of Polycarp

But the most admirable Polycarp, when he first heard [that he was sought for], was in no measure disturbed, but resolved to continue in the city. However, in deference to the wish of many, he was persuaded to leave it. He departed, therefore, to a country house not far distant from the city. There he stayed with a few [friends], engaged in nothing else night and day than praying for all men, and for the Churches throughout the world, according to his usual custom. And while he was praying, a vision presented itself to him three days before he was taken; and, behold, the pillow under his head seemed to him on fire. Upon this, turning to those that were with him, he said to them prophetically," I must be burnt alive."

CHAPTER 6
Polycarp Is Betrayed By A Servant

And when those who sought for him were at hand, he departed to another dwelling, whither his pursuers immediately came after him. And when they found him not, they seized upon two youths [that were there], one of whom, being subjected to torture, confessed. It was thus impossible that he should continue hid, since those that betrayed him were of his own household. The Irenarch then (whose office is the same as that of the Cleronomus), by name Herod, hastened to bring him into the stadium. [This all happened] that he might fulfil his special lot, being made a partaker of Christ, and that they who betrayed him might undergo the punishment of Judas himself.

CHAPTER 7
Polycarp Is Found By His Pursuers

His pursuers then, along with horsemen, and taking the youth with them, went forth at supper-time on the day of the preparation? with their usual weapons, as if going out against a robber. And being come about evening [to the place where he was], they found him lying down in the upper room of a certain little house, from which he might have escaped into another place;

but he refused, saying, "The will of God be done." So when he heard that they were come, he went down and spake with them. And as those that were present marvelled at his age and constancy, some of them said. "Was so much effort made to capture such a venerable man? Immediately then, in that very hour, he ordered that something to eat and drink should be set before them, as much indeed as they cared for, while he besought them to allow him an hour to pray without disturbance.

And on their giving him leave, he stood and prayed, being full of the grace of God, so that he could not cease for two full hours, to the astonishment of them that heard him, insomuch that many began to repent that they had come forth against so godly and venerable an old man.

CHAPTER 8
Polycarp Is Brought Into The City

Now, as soon as he had ceased praying, having made mention of all that had at any time come in contact with him, both small and great, illustrious and obscure, as well as the whole Catholic Church throughout the world, the time of his departure having arrived, they set him upon an ass, and conducted him into the city, the day being that of the great Sabbath. And the Irenarch Herod, accompanied by his father Nicetes (both riding in a chariot), met him, and taking him up into the chariot, they seated themselves beside him, and endeavoured to persuade him, saying, "What harm is there in saying, Lord Caesar, and in sacrificing, with the other ceremonies observed on such occasions, and so make sure of safety?" But he at first gave them no answer; and when they continued to urge him, he said, "I shall not do as you advise me." So they, having no hope of persuading him, began to speak bitter words unto him, and cast him with violence out of the chariot,   insomuch that, in getting down from the carriage, he dislocated his leg [by the fall]. But without being disturbed, and as if suffering nothing, he went eagerly forward with all haste, and was conducted to the stadium, where the tumult was so great, that there was no possibility of being heard.

CHAPTER 9
Polycarp Refuses To Revile Christ

Now, as Polycarp was entering into the stadium, there came to him a voice from heaven, saying, "Be strong, and show thyself a man, O Polycarp!" No one saw who it was that spoke to him; but those of our brethren who were present heard the voice. And as he was brought forward, the tumult became great when they heard that Polycarp was taken. And when he came near, the proconsul asked him whether he was Polycarp. On his confessing that he was, [the proconsul] sought to persuade him to deny [Christ], saying, "Have respect to thy old age," and other similar things, according to their custom, [such as], "Swear by the fortune of Caesar; repent, and say, Away with the Atheists." But Polycarp, gazing with a stern countenance on all the multitude of the wicked heathen then in the stadium, and waving his hand towards them, while with groans he looked up to heaven, said, "Away with the Atheists." Then, the proconsul urging him, and saying, "Swear, and I will set thee at liberty, reproach Christ;" Polycarp declared, "Eighty and six years have I served Him, and He never did me any injury: how then can I blaspheme my King and my Saviour?"

CHAPTER 10
Polycarp Confesses Himself A Christian

And when the proconsul yet again pressed him, and said, "Swear by the fortune of Caesar," he answered, "Since thou art vainly urgent that, as thou sayest, I should swear by the fortune of Caesar, and pretendest not to know who and what I am, hear me declare with boldness, I am a Christian. And if you wish to learn what the doctrines of Christianity are, appoint me a day, and thou shalt hear them." The proconsul replied, "Persuade the people." But Polycarp said, "To thee I have thought it right to offer an account [of my faith]; for we are taught to give all due honour (which entails no injury upon ourselves) to the powers and authorities which are ordained of God. But as for these, I do not deem them worthy of receiving any account from me."

CHAPTER 11
No Threats Have Any Effect On Polycarp

The proconsul then said to him, "I have wild beasts at hand ; to these will I cast thee, except thou repent." But he answered, "Call them then, for we are not accustomed to repent of what is good in order to adopt that which is evil; and it is well for me to be changed from what is evil to what is righteous." But again the proconsul said to him, "I will cause thee to be consumed by fire, seeing thou despisest the wild beasts, if thou wilt not repent." But Polycarp said, "Thou threatenest me with fire which burneth for an hour, and after a little is extinguished, but art ignorant of the fire of the coming judgment and of eternal punishment, reserved for the ungodly. But why tarriest thou? Bring forth what thou wilt."

CHAPTER 12
Polycarp Is Sentenced To Be Burned

While he spoke these and many other like things, he was filled with confidence and joy, and his countenance was full of grace, so that not merely did it not fall as if troubled by the things said to him, but, on the contrary, the proconsul was astonished, and sent his herald to proclaim in the midst of the stadium thrice, "Polycarp has confessed that he is a Christian." This proclamation having been made by the herald, the whole multitude both of the heathen and Jews, who dwelt at Smyrna, cried out with uncontrollable fury, and in a loud voice, "This is the teacher of Asia, the father of the Christians, and the overthrower of our gods, he who has been teaching many not to sacrifice, or to worship the gods." Speaking thus, they cried out, and besought Philip the Asiarch to let loose a lion upon Polycarp. But Philip answered that it was not lawful for him to do so, seeing the shows of wild beasts were already finished. Then it seemed good to them to cry out with one consent, that Polycarp should be burnt alive. For thus it behooved the vision which was revealed to him in regard to his pillow to be fulfilled, when, seeing it on fire as he was praying, he turned about and said prophetically to the faithful that were with him," I must be burnt alive."

CHAPTER 13
The Funeral Pile Is Erected

This, then, was carried into effect with greater speed than it was spoken, the multitudes immediately gathering together wood and fagots out of the shops and baths; the Jews especially, according to custom, eagerly assisting them in it. And when the funeral pile was ready, Polycarp, laying aside all his garments, and loosing his girdle, sought also to take off his sandals,--a thing he was not accustomed to do, inasmuch as every one of the faithful was always eager who should first touch his skin. For, on account of his holy life, he was, even before his martyrdom, adorned with every kind of good. Immediately then they surrounded him with those substances which had been prepared for the funeral pile. But when they were about also to fix him with nails, he said, "Leave me as I am; for He that giveth me strength to endure the fire, will also enable me, without your securing me by nails, to remain without moving in the pile."

CHAPTER 14
The Prayer Of Polycarp

They did not nail him then, but simply bound him. And he, placing his hands behind him, and being bound like a distinguished ram [taken] out of a great flock for sacrifice, and prepared to be an acceptable burnt-offering unto God, looked up to heaven, and said, "O Lord God Almighty, the Father of thy beloved and blessed Son Jesus Christ, by whom we have received the knowledge of Thee, the God of angels and powers, and of every creature, and of the whole race of the righteous who live before thee, I give Thee thanks that Thou hast counted me, worthy of this day and this hour, that I should have a part in the number of Thy martyrs, in the cup of thy Christ, to the resurrection of eternal life, both of soul and body, through the incorruption [imparted] by the Holy Ghost. Among whom may I be accepted this day before Thee as a fat and acceptable sacrifice, according as Thou, the ever-truthful God, hast fore-ordained, hast revealed beforehand to me, and now hast fulfilled. Wherefore also I praise Thee for all things, I bless Thee, I glorify Thee, along with the everlasting and heavenly Jesus Christ, Thy beloved Son, with whom, to Thee, and the Holy Ghost, be glory both now and to all coming ages. Amen."

CHAPTER 15
Polycarp Is Not Injured By The Fire

When he had pronounced this amen, and so finished his prayer, those who were appointed for the purpose kindled the fire. And as the flame blazed forth in great fury, we, to whom it was given to witness it, beheld a great miracle, and have been preserved that we might report to others what then took place. For the fire, shaping itself into the form of an arch, like the sail of a ship when filled with the wind, encompassed as by a circle the body of the martyr. And he appeared within not like flesh which is burnt, but as bread that is baked, or as gold and silver glowing in a furnace. Moreover, we perceived such a sweet odour [coming from the pile], as if frankincense or some such precious spices had been smoking there.

CHAPTER 16
Polycarp Is Pierced By A Dagger

At length, when those wicked men perceived that his body could not be consumed by the fire, they commanded an executioner to go near and pierce him through with a dagger. And on his doing this, there came forth a dove, and a great quantity of blood, so that the fire was extinguished; and all the people wondered that there should be such a difference between the unbelievers and the elect, of whom this most admirable Polycarp was one, having in our own times been an apostolic and prophetic teacher, and bishop of the Catholic Church which is in Smyrna. For every word that went out of his mouth either has been or shall yet be accomplished.

CHAPTER 17
The Christians Are Refused Polycarp's Body

But when the adversary of the race of the righteous, the envious, malicious, and wicked one, perceived the impressive nature of his martyrdom, and [considered] the blameless life he had led from the beginning, and how he was now crowned with the wreath of immortality, having beyond dispute received his reward, he did his utmost that not the least memorial of him should be taken away by us, although many desired to do this, and to become possessors of his holy flesh. For this end he suggested it to Nicetes, the father of Herod and brother of Alce, to go and entreat the governor not to give up his body to be buried, "lest," said he, "forsaking Him that was crucified, they begin to worship this one. "This he said at the suggestion and urgent persuasion of the Jews, who also watched us, as we sought to take him out of the fire, being ignorant of this, that it is neither possible for us ever to forsake Christ, who suffered for the salvation of such as shall be saved throughout the whole world (the blameless one for sinners), nor to worship any other. For Him indeed, as being the Son of God, we adore; but the martyrs, as disciples and followers of the Lord, we worthily love on account of their extraordinary affection towards their own King and Master, of whom may we also be made companions and fellow-disciples!

CHAPTER 18
The Body Of Polycarp Is Burned

The centurion then, seeing the strife excited by the Jews, placed the body in the midst of the fire, and consumed it. Accordingly, we afterwards took up his bones, as being more precious than the most exquisite jewels, and more purified than gold, and deposited them in a fitting place, whither, being gathered together, as opportunity is allowed us, with joy and rejoicing, the Lord shall grant us to celebrate the anniversary of his martyrdom, both in memory of those who have already finished their course, and for the exercising and preparation of those yet to walk in their steps.

CHAPTER 19
Praise Of The Martyr Polycarp

This, then, is the account of the blessed Polycarp, who, being the twelfth that was martyred in Smyrna (reckoning those also of Philadelphia), yet occupies a place of his own in the memory of all men, insomuch that he is everywhere spoken of by the heathen themselves. He was not merely an illustrious teacher, but also a pre-eminent martyr, whose martyrdom all desire to imitate, as having been altogether consistent with the Gospel of Christ. For, having through patience overcome the unjust governor, and thus acquired the crown of immortality, he now, with the apostles and all the righteous[in heaven], rejoicingly glorifies God, even the Father, and blesses our Lord Jesus Christ, the Saviour of our souls, the Governor of our bodies, and the Shepherd of the Catholic Church throughout the world.

CHAPTER 20
This Epistle Is To Be Transmitted To The Brethren

Since, then, ye requested that we would at large make you acquainted with what really took place, we have for the present sent you this summary account through our brother Marcus. When, therefore, ye have yourselves read this Epistle, be pleased to send it to the brethren at a greater distance, that they also may glorify the Lord, who makes such choice of His own servants. To Him who is able to bring us all by His grace and goodness into his everlasting kingdom, through His only-begotten Son Jesus Christ, to Him be glory, and honour, and power, and majesty, for ever. Amen. Salute all the saints. They that are with us salute you, and Evarestus, who wrote this Epistle, with all his house.

CHAPTER 21
The Date Of The Martyrdom

Now, the blessed Polycarp suffered martyrdom on the second day of the month Xanthicus just begun, the seventh day before the Kalends of May, on the great Sabbath, at the eighth hour. He was taken by Herod, Philip the Trallian being high priest, Statius Quadratus being proconsul, but Jesus Christ being King for ever, to whom be glory, honour, majesty, and an everlasting throne, from generation to generation. Amen.

CHAPTER 22
Salutation

We wish you, brethren, all happiness, while you walk according to the doctrine of the Gospel of Jesus Christ; with whom be glory to God the Father and the Holy Spirit, for the salvation of His holy elect, after whose example the blessed Polycarp suffered, following in whose steps may we too be found in the kingdom of Jesus Christ!

These things Caius transcribed from the copy of Irenaeus (who was a disciple of Polycarp), having himself been intimate with Irenaeus. And I Socrates transcribed them at Corinth from the copy of Caius. Grace be with you all.

And I again, Pionius, wrote them from the previously written copy, having carefully searched into them, and the blessed Polycarp having manifested them to me through a revelation, even as I shall show in what follows. I have collected these things, when they had almost faded away through the lapse of time, that the Lord Jesus Christ may also gather me along with His elect into His heavenly kingdom, to whom, with the Father and the Holy Spirit, be glory for ever and ever. Amen.

The Narrative of Joseph of Arimathaea

CHAPTER 1

I am Joseph of Arimathaea, who begged from Pilate the body of the Lord Jesus for burial, and who for this cause was kept close in prison by the murderous and God-fighting Jews, who also, keeping to the law, have by Moses himself become partakers in tribulation and having provoked their Lawgiver to anger, and not knowing that He was God, crucified Him and made Him manifest to those that knew God. in those days in which they condemned the Son of God to be crucified, seven days before Christ suffered, two condemned robbers were sent from Jericho to the procurator Pilate; and their case was as follows:--

The first, his name Gestas, put travellers to death, murdering them with the sword, and others he exposed naked. And he hung up women by the heels, head down, and cut off their breasts, and drank the blood of infants limbs, never having known God, not obeying the laws, being violent from the beginning, and doing such deeds.

And the case of the other was as follows: He was called Demas, and was by birth a Galilaean, and kept an inn. He made attacks upon the rich, but was good to the poor--a thief like Tobit, for he buried the bodies of the poor. And he set his hand to robbing the multitude of the Jews, and stole the law itself in Jerusalem, and stripped naked the daughter of Caiaphas, who was priestess of the sanctuary, and took away from its place the mysterious deposit itself placed there by Solomon. Such were his doings.

And Jesus also was taken on the third day before the passover, in the evening. And to Caiaphas and the multitude of the Jews it was not a passover, but it was a great mourning to them, on account of the plundering of the sanctuary by the robber. And they summoned Judas Iscariot, and spoke to him, for he was son of the brother of Caiaphas the priest. He was not a disciple before the face of Jesus; but all the multitude of the Jews craftily supported him, that he might follow Jesus, not that he might be obedient to the miracles done by Him, nor that he might confess Him, but that he might betray Him to them, wishing to catch up some lying word of Him, giving him gifts for such brave, honest conduct to the amount of a half shekel, of gold each day. And he did this for two years with Jesus, as says one of His disciples called John.

And on the third day, before Jesus was laid hold of, Judas says to the Jews: Come, let us hold a council; for perhaps it was not the robber that stole the law, but Jesus himself, and I accuse him. And when these words had been spoken, Nicodemus, who kept the keys of the sanctuary, came in to us, and said to all: Do not do such a deed. For Nicodemus was true, more than all the multitude of the Jews. And the daughter of Caiaphas, Sarah by name, cried out, and said: He himself said before all against this holy place, I am able to destroy this temple, and in three days to raise it. The Jews say to her: Thou hast credit with all of us. For they regarded her as a prophetess. And assuredly, after the council had been held, Jesus was laid hold of.

CHAPTER 2

And on the following day, the fourth day of the week, they brought Him at the ninth hour into the hall of Caiaphas. And Annas and Caiaphas say to Him: Tell us, why hast thou stolen our law, and renounced the ordinances of Moses and the prophets? And Jesus answered nothing. And again a second time, the multitude also being present, they say to Him: The sanctuary which Solomon built in forty and six years, why dost thou wish to destroy in one moment? And to these things Jesus answered nothing. For the sanctuary of the synagogue had been plundered by the robber.

And the evening of the fourth day being ended, all the multitude sought to burn the daughter of Caiaphas, on account of the loss of the law; for they did not know how they were to keep the passover. And she said to them: Wait, my children, and let us destroy this Jesus, and the law will be found, and the holy feast will be fully accomplished. And secretly Annas and Caiaphas gave considerable money to Judas Iscariot, saying: Say as thou saidst to us before, I know that the law has been stolen by Jesus, that the accusation may be turned against him, and not against this maiden, who is free from blame. And Judas having received this command, said to them: Let not all the multitude know that I have been instructed by you to do this against Jesus; but release Jesus, and I persuade the multitude that it is so. And craftily they released Jesus.

And Judas, going into the sanctuary at the dawn of the fifth day, says to all the people: What will you give me, and I will give up to you the over-thrower of the law, and the plunderer of the prophets? The Jews say to him: If thou wilt give him up to us, we will give thee thirty pieces of gold. And the people did not know that Judas was speaking about Jesus, for many of them confessed that he was the Son of God. And Judas received the thirty pieces of gold.

And going out at the fourth hour, and at the fifth, he finds Jesus walking in the street. And as evening was coming on, Judas says to the Jews: Give me the aid of soldiers with swords and staves, and I will give him up to you. They therefore gave him officers for the purpose of seizing Him. And as they were going along, Judas says to them: Lay hold of the man whom I shall kiss, for he has stolen the law and the prophets. Going up to Jesus, therefore, he kissed Him, saying: Hail, Rabbi! it being the evening of the fifth day. And having laid hold of Him, they gave Him up to Caiaphas and the chief priests, Judas saying: This is he who stole the law and the prophets. And the Jews gave Jesus an unjust trial, saying: Why hast thou done these things? And be answered nothing.

And Nicodemus and I Joseph, seeing the seat of the plagues, stood off from them, not wishing to perish along with the counsel of the ungodly.

CHAPTER 3

Having therefore done many and dreadful things against Jesus that night, they gave Him up to Pilate the procurator at the dawn of the preparation, that he might crucify Him; and for this purpose they all came together. After a trial, therefore, Pilate the procurator ordered Him to be nailed to the cross, along with the two robbers. And they were nailed up along with Jesus, Gestas on the left. and Demas on the right.

And he that was on the left began to cry out, saying to Jesus: See how many evil deeds I have done in the earth; and if I had known that thou wast the king, I should have cut off thee also. And why dost thou call thyself Son of God, and canst not help thyself in necessity? how canst thou afford it to another one praying for help? If thou art the Christ, come down from the cross, that I may believe in thee. But now I see thee perishing along with me, not like a man, but like a wild beast. And many other things he began to say against Jesus, blaspheming and gnashing his teeth upon Him. For the robber was taken alive in the snare of the devil.

But the robber on the right hand, whose name was Demas, seeing the Godlike grace of Jesus, thus cried out: I know Thee, Jesus Christ, that Thou art the Son of God. I see Thee, Christ, adored by myriads of myriads of angels. Pardon me my sins which I have done. Do not in my trial make the stars come against me, or the moon, when Thou shall judge all the world; because in the night I have accomplished my wicked purposes. Do not urge the sun, which is now darkened on account of Thee, to tell the evils of my heart, for no gift can I give Thee for the remission of my sins. Already death is coming upon me because of my sins; but Thine is the propitiation. Deliver me, O Lord of all, from Thy fearful judgment. Do not give the enemy power to swallow me up, and to become heir of my soul, as of that of him who is hanging on the left; for I see how the devil joyfully takes his soul, and his body disappears. Do not even order me to go away into the portion of the Jews; for I see Moses and the patriarchs in great weeping, and the devil rejoicing over them. Before, then, O Lord, my spirit departs, order my sins to be washed away, and remember me the sinner in Thy kingdom, when upon the great most lofty throne thou shalt judge the twelve tribes of Israel. For Thou hast prepared great punishment for Thy world on account of Thyself.

And the robber having thus spoken, Jesus says to him: Amen, amen; I say to thee, Demas, that to-day thou shalt be with me in paradise. And the sons of the kingdom, the children of Abraham, and Isaac, and Jacob, and Moses, shall be cast out into outer darkness; there shall be weeping and gnashing of teeth. And thou alone shalt dwell in paradise until my second appearing, when I am to judge those who do not confess my name. And He said to the robber: Go away, and tell the cherubim and the powers, that turn the flaming sword, that guard paradise from the time that Adam, the first created, was in paradise, and sinned, and kept not my commandments, and I cast him out thence. And none of the first shall see paradise until I am to come the second time to judge living and dead. And He wrote thus: Jesus Christ the Son of God, who have come down from the heights of the heavens, who have come forth out of the bosom of the invisible Father without being separated from Him, and who have come down into the world to be made flesh, and to be nailed to a cross, in order that I might save Adam, whom I fashioned,--to my archangelic powers, the gatekeepers of paradise, to the officers of my Father: I will and order that he who has been crucified along with me should go in, should receive remission of sins through me; and that he, having put on an incorruptible body, should go in to paradise, and dwell where no one has ever been able to dwell.

And, behold, after He had said this, Jesus gave up the ghost, on the day of the preparation, at the ninth hour. And there was darkness over all the earth; and from a great earthquake that happened, the sanctuary fell down, and the wing of the temple.

CHAPTER 4

And I Joseph begged the body of Jesus, and put it in a new tomb, where no one had been put. And of the robber on the right the body was not found; but of him on the left, as the form of a dragon, so was his body.

And after I had begged the body of Jesus to bury, the Jews, carried away by hatred and rage, shut me up in prison, where evil-doers were kept under restraint. And this happened to me on the evening of the Sabbath, whereby our nation transgressed the law. And, behold, that same nation of ours endured fearful tribulations on the Sabbath.

And now, on the evening of the first of the week, at the fifth hour of the night, Jesus comes to me in the prison, along with the robber who had been crucified with Him on the right, whom He sent into paradise. And there was a great light in the building. And the house was hung up by the four corners, and the place was opened, and I came out. Then I first recognised Jesus, and again the robber, bringing a letter to Jesus. And as we were going into Galilee, there shone a great light, which the creation did not produce. And there was also with the robber a great fragrance out of paradise.

And Jesus, having sat down in a certain place, thus read: We, the cherubim and the six-winged, who have been ordered by Thy Godhead to watch the garden of paradise, make the following statement through the robber who was crucified along with Thee, by Thy arrangement: When we saw the print of the nails of the robber crucified along with Thee, and the shining light of the letter of Thy Godhead, the fire indeed was extinguished, not being able to bear the splendour of the print; and we crouched down, being in great fear. For we heard that the Maker of heaven and earth, and of the whole creation, had come down from on high to dwell in the lower parts of the earth, on account of Adam, the first created. And when we beheld the undefiled cross shining like lightning from the robber, gleaming with sevenfold the light of the sun, trembling fell upon us. We felt a violent shaking of the world below; and with a loud voice, the ministers of Hades said, along with us: Holy, holy, holy is He who in the beginning was in the highest. And the powers sent up a cry: O Lord, Thou hast been made manifest in heaven and in earth, bringing joy to the world; and, a greater gift than this, Thou hast freed Thine own image from death by the invisible purpose of the ages.

CHAPTER 5

After I had beheld these things, as I was going into Galilee with Jesus and the robber, Jesus was transfigured, and was not as formerly, before He was crucified, but was altogether light; and angels always ministered to Him, and Jesus spoke with them. And I remained with Him three days. And no one of His disciples was with Him, except the robber alone.

And in the middle of the feast of unleavened bread, His disciple John comes, and we no longer beheld the robber as to what took place. And John asked Jesus: Who is this, that Thou hast not made me to be seen by him? But Jesus answered him nothing. And falling down before Him, he said: Lord, I know that Thou hast loved me from the beginning, and why dost Thou not reveal to me that man? Jesus says to him: Why dost thou seek what is hidden? Art thou still without understanding? Dost thou not perceive the fragrance of paradise filling the place? Dost thou not know who it is? The robber on the cross has become heir of paradise. Amen, amen; I say to thee, that it shall belong to him alone until that the great day shall come. And John said: Make me worthy to behold him.

And while John was yet speaking, the robber suddenly appeared; and John, struck with astonishment, fell to the earth. And the robber was not in his first form, as before John came; but he was like a king in great power, having on him the cross. And the voice of a great multitude was sent forth: Thou hast come to the place prepared for thee in paradise. We have been commanded by Him that has sent thee, to serve thee until the great day. And after this voice, both the robber and I Joseph vanished, and I was found in my own house; and I no longer saw Jesus.

And I, having seen these things, have written them down, in order that all may believe in the crucified Jesus Christ our Lord, and may no longer obey the law of Moses, but may believe in the signs and wonders that have happened through Him, and in order that we who have believed may inherit eternal life, and be found in the kingdom of the heavens. For to Him are due glory, strength, praise, and majesty for ever and ever. Amen.

The Correspondence of Paul and Seneca

1. SENECA TO PAUL

I believe, Paul, that you have been informed of the talk which I had yesterday with my Lucilius about the apocrypha (or possibly the secret mysteries) and other things; for certain sharers in your teaching were with me. For we had retired to the gardens of Sallust, where, because of us, those whom I speak of, going in another direction, saw and joined us. Certainly we wished for your presence, and I would have you know it. We were much refreshed by the reading of your book, by which I mean some of the many letters which you have addressed to some city or capital of a province, and which inculcate the moral life with admirable precepts. These thoughts, I take it, are not uttered by you but through you, but surely sometimes both by you and through you: for such is the greatness of them and they are instinct (warm) with such nobility, that I think whole generations (ages) of men could hardly suffice for the instilling and perfecting of them. I desire your good health, brother.

2. PAUL TO SENECA

I received your letter yesterday with delight, and should have been able to answer it at once, had I had by me the youth I meant to send to you. For you know when, and by whom, and at what moment, and to whom things ought to be given and entrusted. I beg, therefore, that you will not think yourself neglected, when I am respecting the dignity of your person. Now in that you somewhere write that you are pleased with my letter (or, write that you are pleased with part of my letter) I think myself happy in the good opinion of such a man: for you would not say it, you, a critic, a sophist, the teacher of a great prince, and indeed of all -unless you spoke truth. I trust you may long be in health.

3. SENECA TO PAUL

I have arranged some writings in a volume, and given them their proper divisions: I am also resolved to read them to Caesar, if only fortune be kind, that he may bring a new (an interested) ear to the hearing. Perhaps you, too, will be there. If not, I will at another time fix you a day, that we may look over the work together: indeed, I could not produce this writing to him, without first conferring with you, if only that could be done without risk: that you may know that you are not being neglected. Farewell, dearest Paul.

4. PAUL TO ANNAEUS SENECA

Whenever I hear your letters read, I think of you as present, and imagine nothing else but that you are always with us. As soon, then, as you begin to come, we shall see each other at close quarters. I desire your good health.

5. SENECA TO PAUL

We are much pained by your retirement. What is it? what causes keep you away? if it be the anger of the lady (Poppaea) because you have left the old rite and sect, and have converted others, there will be a possibility of pleading with her, that she may consider it as done on due reflection and not lightly.

6. PAUL TO SENECA AND LUCILIUS

Of the subject on which you have written I must not speak with pen and ink, of which the former marks out and draws somewhat, and the latter shows it clearly, especially as I know that among you -that is, in your homes and in you- there are those who understand me. Honour is to be paid to all, and so much the more because men catch at opportunities of being offended. If we are patient with them, we shall certainly over-come them at every point, provided they be men who can be sorry for their actions. Farewell.

7. ANNAEUS SENECA TO PAUL AND THEOPHILUS

I profess myself well content with the reading of your letters which you sent to the Galatians, Corinthians, and Achaeans; and may we so live together as you show yourself to be inspired with the divine frenzy (horror). For it is the holy spirit which is in you and high above you which expresses these exalted and adorable thoughts. I would therefore have you careful of other points, that the polish of the style may not be wanting to the majesty of the thought. And, brother, not to conceal anything from you, and have it on my conscience, I confess to you that the Augustus was moved by your views. When I read to him the beginning of the power (virtue) that is in you (perhaps he meant your exordium about virtue) his words were these: that he could wonder that a man not regularly educated could think thus. I replied that the gods often speak by the mouths of the simple (innocent), not of those who try deceitfully to show what they can do by their learning. And when I cited him the example of Vatienus the rustic, to whom two men appeared in the territory of Reate, who afterwards were recognized as Castor and Pollux, he appeared fully convinced. Farewell.

8. PAUL TO SENECA

Though I am aware that Caesar, even if he sometimes lapses, is a lover of our wonders, you will suffer yourself to be, not wounded but admonished. For I think that you took a very serious step in bringing to his notice a matter alien to his religion and training. For since he is a worshipper of the gods of the nations, I do not see why you thought you would wish him to know this matter, unless I am to think that you did it out of excessive attachment to me. I beg you not to do so in future; For you must be careful not to offend the empress in your love for me: yet her anger will not hurt us if it lasts, nor do good if it does not [this is nonsense]. As a queen, she will not be angry: as a woman, she will be offended. Farewell.

9. SENECA TO PAUL

I know that you are not so much disturbed on your own account by my letter to you on the showing of your letters to Caesar, as by the nature of things, which so calls away the minds of men from all right learning and conduct -so that I am not surprised, for I have learnt this for certain by many examples. Let us then act differently, and if in the past anything has been done carelessly, you will pardon it. I have sent you a book on elegance of expression (store of words). Farewell, dearest Paul.

10. TO SENECA, PAUL

Whenever I write to you and do not place my name after yours (see the heading) I do a serious thing and one unbefitting my persuasion (sect). For I ought, as I have often declared, to be all things to all men, and to observe in your person that which the Roman law has granted to the honour of the senate, and choose the last place in writing (text, reading) a letter, not striving to do as I please in a confused and disgraceful way. Farewell, most devoted of masters. Given on the 5th of the kalends of July; Nero the fourth time, and Messala, consuls (A. D. 58).

11. SENECA TO PAUL

Hail, my dearest Paul. If you, so great a man, so beloved in all ways, be -I say not joined- but intimately associated with me and my name, it will indeed be well with your Seneca. Since then, you are the summit and topmost peak of all people, would you not have me glad that I am so near you as to be counted a second self of yours ? Do not, then, think that you are unworthy to be named first on the heading of letters, lest you make me think you are testing me rather than playing with me -especially as you know yourself to be a Roman citizen. For the rank that is mine, I would it were yours, and yours I would were mine. Farewell, dearest Paul. Given on the 10th of the kalends of April; Apronianus and Capito consuls.

12. SENECA TO PAUL

Hail, my dearest Paul. Think you that I am not in sadness and grief, that your innocent people are so often condemned to suffer? And next, that the whole people thinks you so callous and so prone to crime, that you are supposed to be the authors of every misfortune in the city? Yet let us bear it patiently and content ourselves with what fortune brings, until supreme happiness puts an end to our troubles. Former ages had to bear the Macedonian, Philip's son, and, after Darius, Dionysius, and our own times endured Gaius Caesar: to all of whom their will was law. The source of the many fires which Rome suffers plain. But if humble men could speak out what the reason is, and if it were possible to speak without risk in this dark time, all would be plain to all. Christians and Jews are commonly executed as contrivers of the fire. Whoever the criminal is whose pleasure is that of a butcher, and who veils himself with a lie, he is reserved for his due season: and as the best of men is sacrificed, the one for the many, so he, vowed to death for all, will be burned with fire. A hundred and thirty-two houses and four blocks have been burnt in six days, the seventh brought a pause. I pray you may be well, brother. Given the 5th of the kalends of April; Frugi and Bassus consuls.

13. SENECA TO PAUL

Much in every part of your works is enclosed in allegory and enigma, and therefore the great force that is given you of matter and talent (?) should be beautified, I do not say with elegance of words, but with a certain care. Nor should you fear what I remember you have often said; that many who affect such things vitiate the thought and emasculate the strength of the matter. But I wish you would yield to me and humour the genius of Latin, and give beauty to your noble words, that the great gift that has been granted you may be worthily treated by you. Farewell.

Given on the day before the nones of June; Leo and Sabinus consuls (non-existent).

14. PAUL TO SENECA

To your meditations have been revealed those things which the Godhead has granted to few. With confidence, therefore, I sow in a field already fertile a most prolific seed, not such matter as is liable to corruption, but the abiding word, an emanation from God who grows and abides for ever. This your wisdom has attained and you will see that it is unfailing -so as to judge that the laws of heathens and Israelites are to be shunned. You may become a new author, by showing forth with the graces of rhetoric the unblameable wisdom of Jesus Christ, which you, having well nigh attained it, will instil into the temporal monarch, his servants, and his intimate friends, yet the persuading of them will be a rough and difficult task, for many of them will hardly incline to your admonitions. Yet the word of God, if it be instilled into them, will be a vital gain, producing a new man, incorrupt, and an everlasting soul that shall hasten from hence to God. Farewell, Seneca, most dear to me.

Given on the kalends of August; Leo and Sabinus consuls.

The Report of Pontius Pilate, Procurator of Judaea Sent to Rome to Tiberius Caesar.

Second Greek Form

To the most mighty, venerable, awful, most divine, the august,--Pilatus Pontius, the governor of the East: I have to report to thy reverence, through this writing of mine, being seized with great trembling and fear, O most mighty emperor, the conjuncture of the present times, as the end of these things has shown. For while I, my lord, according to the commandment of thy clemency, was discharging the duties of my government, which is one of the cities of the East, Jerusalem by name, in which is built the temple of the Jewish nation, all the multitude of the Jews came together, and delivered to me a certain man named Jesus, bringing against him many and groundless charges; and they were not able to convict him in anything.

And one heresy of theirs against him was, that he said that the Sabbath was not their right rest. And that man wrought many cures, in addition to good works. He made the blind see; he cleansed lepers; he raised the dead; he healed paralytics who could not move at all, except that they only had their voice, and the joining of their bones; and he gave them the power of walking about and running, commanding them by a single word. And another mightier work he did, which was strange even with our gods: he raised up a dead man, Lazarus, who had been dead four days, by a single word ordering the dead man to be raised, although his body was already corrupted by the worms that grow in wounds; and that ill-smelling body lying in the tomb he ordered to run; and as a bridegroom from the bridal chamber, so he came forth out of the tomb, filled with exceeding fragrance.

And some that were cruelly vexed by demons, and had their dwellings in deserts, and ate the flesh of their own limbs, and lived along with reptiles and wild beasts, he made to be dwellers in cities in their own houses, and by a word he rendered them sound-minded; and he made those that were troubled by unclean spirits to be intelligent and reputable; and sending away the demons in them into a herd of swine, he suffocated them in the sea. Another man, again, who had a withered hand, and lived in sorrow, and had not even the half of his body sound, he rendered sound by a single word.

And a woman that had a flow of blood for many years, so that, in consequence of the flowing of her blood, all the joinings of her bones appeared, and were transparent like glass; and assuredly all the physicians had left her without hope, and had not cleansed her, for there was not in her a single hope of health: once, then, as Jesus was passing by, she took hold of the fringe of his clothes behind, and that same hour the power of her body was completely restored, and she became whole, as if nothing were the matter with her, and she began to run swiftly to her own city Paneas.

And these things indeed were so. And the Jews gave information that Jesus did these things on the Sabbath. And I also ascertained that the miracles done by him were greater than any which the gods whom we worship could do.

Him then Herod and Archelaus and Philip, and Annas and Caiaphas, with all the people, delivered to me to try him. And as many were exciting an insurrection against me, I ordered him to be crucified.

And when he had been crucified, there was darkness over the whole earth, the sun having been completely hidden, and the heaven appearing dark though it was day, so that the stars appeared, but had at the same time their brightness darkened, as I suppose your reverence is not ignorant of, because in all the world they lighted lamps from the sixth hour until evening. And the moon, being like blood, did not shine the whole night, and yet she happened to be at the full. And the stars also, and Orion, made a lament about the Jews, on account of the wickedness that had been done by them.

And on the first of the week, about the third hour of the night, the sun was seen such as it had never at any time shone, and all the heaven was lighted up. And as lightnings come on in winter, so majestic men of indescribable splendour of dress and of glory appeared in the air, and an innumerable multitude of angels crying out, and saying: Glory in the highest to God, and on earth peace, among men goodwill: come up out of Hades, ye who have been kept in slavery in the underground regions of Hades. And at their voice all the mountains and hills were shaken, and the rocks were burst asunder; and great chasms were made in the earth, so that also what was in the abyss appeared. And there were seen in that terror dead men raised up, as the Jews that saw them said: We have seen Abraham, and Isaac, and Jacob, and the twelve patriarchs, that died two thousand five hundred years ago; and we have seen Noah manifestly in the body. And all the multitude walked about, and sang praises to God with a loud voice, saying: The Lord our God that has risen from the dead has brought to life all the dead, and has plundered Hades, and put him to death.

All that night therefore, my lord, O king, the light ceased not. And many of the Jews died, and were engulphed and swallowed up in the chasms in that night, so that not even their bodies appeared. Those, I say, of the Jews suffered that had spoken against Jesus. And one synagogue was left in Jerusalem, since all those synagogues that had been against Jesus were engulphed.

From that fear, then, being in perplexity, and seized with much trembling, at that same hour I ordered what had been done by them all to be written; and I have reported it to thy mightiness.

The Secret Gospel of Mark

The Secret Gospel of Mark, the text here, is only a portion of a scripture the author (said to be Clement of Alexandria) claims to be in the custody of the Headquarters of the Church in Alexandria, but whose existence is publicly refuted, so as to battle the copies circulated by the infamous sect of the Carpocrations. This letter was found by Morton Smith in the Mar Saba monastery, southeast of Jerusalem, in 1958. Translation by Morton Smith.

You did well in silencing the unspeakable teachings of the Carpocrations. For these are the "wandering stars" referred to in the prophecy, who wander from the narrow road of the commandments into a boundless abyss of the carnal and bodily sins. For, priding themselves in knowledge, as they say, "of the deep things of Satan", they do not know that they are casting themselves away into "the nether world of the darkness" of falsity, and boasting that they are free, they have become slaves of servile desires. Such men are to be opposed in all ways and altogether. For, even if they should say something true, one who loves the truth should not, even so, agree with them. For not all true things are the truth, nor should that truth which merely seems true according to human opinions be preferred to the true truth, that according to the faith.

Now of the things they keep saying about the divinely inspired Gospel according to Mark, some are altogether falsifications, and others, even if they do contain some true elements, nevertheless are not reported truly. For the true things, being mixed with inventions, are falsified, so that, as the saying goes, even the salt loses its savor.

As for Mark, then, during Peter's stay in Rome he wrote an account of the Lord's doings, not, however, declaring all of them, nor yet hinting at the secret ones, but selecting what he thought most useful for increasing the faith of those who were being instructed. But when Peter died a martyr, Mark came over to Alexandria, bringing both his own notes and those of Peter, from which he transferred to his former book the things suitable to whatever makes for progress toward knowledge. Thus he composed a more spiritual Gospel for the use of those who were being perfected. Nevertheless, he yet did not divulge the things not to be uttered, nor did he write down the hierophantic teaching of the Lord, but to the stories already written he added yet others and, moreover, brought in certain sayings of which he knew the interpretation would, as a mystagogue, lead the hearers into the innermost sanctuary of that truth hidden by seven veils. Thus, in sum, he prepared matters, neither grudgingly nor incautiously, in my opinion, and, dying, he left his composition to the church in 1, verso Alexandria, where it even yet is most carefully guarded, being read only to those who are being initiated into the great mysteries.

But since the foul demons are always devising destruction for the race of men, Carpocrates, instructed by them and using deceitful arts, so enslaved a certain presbyter of the church in Alexandria that he got from him a copy of the secret Gospel, which he both interpreted according to his blasphemous and carnal doctrine and, moreover, polluted, mixing with the spotless and holy words utterly shameless lies. From this mixture is drawn off the teaching of the Carpocratians.

To them, therefore, as I said above, one must never give way; nor, when they put forward their falsifications, should one concede that the secret Gospel is by Mark, but should even deny it on oath. For, "Not all true things are to be said to all men". For this reason the Wisdom of God, through Solomon, advises, "Answer the fool from his folly", teaching that the light of the truth should be hidden from those who are mentally blind. Again it says, "From him who has not shall be taken away", and "Let the fool walk in darkness" . But we are "children of Light", having been illuminated by "the dayspring" of the spirit of the Lord "from on high", and "Where the Spirit of the Lord is" , it says, "there is liberty", for "All things are pure to the pure".

To you, therefore, I shall not hesitate to answer the questions you have asked, refuting the falsifications by the very words of the Gospel. For example, after "And they were in the road going up to Jerusalem" and what follows, until "After three days he shall arise", the secret Gospel brings the following material word for word:

"And they come into Bethany. And a certain woman whose brother had died was there. And, coming, she prostrated herself before Jesus and says to him, 'Son of David, have mercy on me.' But the disciples rebuked her. And Jesus, being angered, went off with her into the garden where the tomb was, and straightway a great cry was heard from the tomb. And going near, Jesus rolled away the stone from the door of the tomb. And straightaway, going in where the youth was, he stretched forth his hand and raised him, seizing his hand. But the youth, looking upon him, loved him and began to beseech him that he might be with him. And going out of the tomb, they came into the house of the youth, for he was rich. And after six days Jesus told him what to do, and in the evening the youth comes to him, wearing a linen cloth over his naked body. And he remained with him that night, for Jesus taught him the mystery of the Kingdom of God. And thence, arising, he returned to the other side of the Jordan."

After these words follows the text, "And James and John come to him", and all that section. But "naked man with naked man," and the other things about which you wrote, are not found.

And after the words, "And he comes into Jericho," the secret Gospel adds only, "And the sister of the youth whom Jesus loved and his mother and Salome were there, and Jesus did not receive them." But the many other things about which you wrote both seem to be, and are, falsifications.

Now the true explanation, and that which accords with the true philosophy ...
phy ...

 Patience

by Tertullian

CHAPTER 1

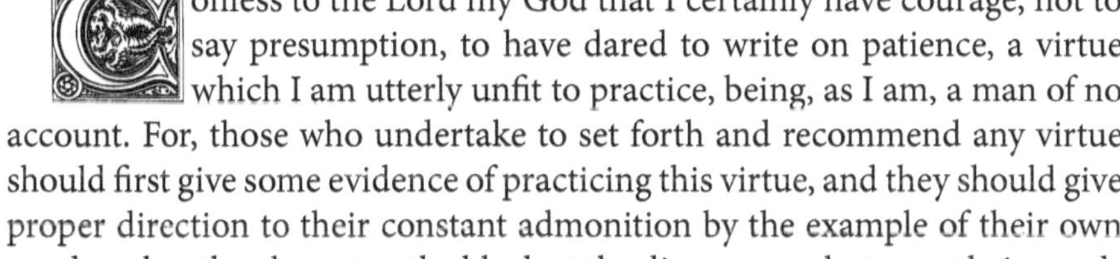onfess to the Lord my God that I certainly have courage, not to say presumption, to have dared to write on patience, a virtue which I am utterly unfit to practice, being, as I am, a man of no account. For, those who undertake to set forth and recommend any virtue should first give some evidence of practicing this virtue, and they should give proper direction to their constant admonition by the example of their own conduct, lest they be put to the blush at the discrepancy between their words and deeds.

And would that the blushing brought an improvement, that the shame (we feel) at not doing what we have suggested to others would teach us to do it! But, of course, it is with certain virtues as with certain vices: their greatness is so overwhelming that only the grace of divine inspiration can help us to attain and practice them.

For, that which is in the highest sense good belongs in the highest degree to God, and no one dispenses it save He who possesses it, to each one as He sees fit.

It will be, then, a comfort to discuss that which it is not granted us to enjoy, somewhat in the manner of the sick, who, when deprived of health, cannot refrain from proclaiming its blessings.

Thus, in my pitiable state, ever suffering from the fever of impatience, I must sigh after the health of patience which I do not possess, and I must beg and beseech it, remembering and reflecting, as I consider my weakness, that one does not easily attain the good health of faith and the soundness of the discipline of the Lord unless patience lends assistance thereto.

Patience has been given such pre-eminence in matters pertaining to God that no one can fulfill any precept or perform any work pleasing to the Lord without patience.

Even those who do not possess it pay recognition to its excellence by giving it the honorable title of 'the highest virtue.' In fact, the philosophers, who are regarded as creatures possessing some degree of wisdom, attribute such value to it that, while there are disagreements among them because of the various inclinations of the schools and their opposing tenets, they are, nevertheless, of one mind with regard to patience alone, and in this alone of their interests they enter into agreement. With regard to this they are in accord: for this they band together, with one mind they apply themselves to it in their efforts to attain virtue; every display of wisdom they usher in with a show of patience.

A great compliment it is to this virtue to be the moving force behind even the vain pursuits of the world to their praise and renown! Or is it rather an insult that divine things are involved in the doings of the world?

Let them see to it who will one day be ashamed of their wisdom when it is destroyed and brought to disgrace along with this world!

CHAPTER 2

There has been given to us as a model in the practice of patience no (merely) human product fashioned of the dullness of Cynic indifference, but the divine ordinance of a life-giving and heavenly way of life which points out as an exemplar of patience God Himself.

Long has He been scattering the brilliance of this light (of the sun) upon the just and unjust alike and has allowed the deserving as well as the undeserving to enjoy the benefits of the seasons, the services of the elements, and the gifts of all creation.

He endures ungrateful peoples who worship the trifles fashioned by their skill and the works of their hands, who persecute His name and His children, and who, in their lewdness, their greed, their godlessness and depravity, grow worse from day to day; by His patience He hopes to draw them to Himself. There are many, you see, who do not believe in the Lord because for so long a time they have no experience of His wrath (directed) against the world.

CHAPTER 3

This is, indeed, a picture of the divine patience which exists, so to speak, far away from us, the patience, we might say, which prevails on high. But what about that patience which exists openly among men on earth, which is, as it were, within our reach?

God allows Himself to become incarnate: in His mother's womb He awaits (the time of birth) and after His birth suffers Himself to grow into manhood, and, when an adult, shows no eagerness to become known, but bears reproaches and is baptized by His own servant and by His words alone repels the attacks of the Tempter.

When He, (begotten) of the Lord, becomes a master teaching man how to avoid death, He teaches him for his own good how to offer reparation to outraged patience.

He did not wrangle or cry aloud; neither did anyone hear His voice in the streets; a bruised reed He did not break, a smoking wick He did not quench. (Now, the Prophet--or, rather, the testimony of God Himself, placing His own spirit in His Son with all patience--has not lied!)

He did not force one who was unwilling to stay close to Him; He scorned no one's table or dwelling; in fact, He ministered personally to His disciples by washing their feet.

He did not despise sinners or publicans, He showed no anger even toward that city which refused to receive Him, even when the disciples wished fire from heaven to fall upon such a shameful town; He healed the ungrateful, yielded to His persecutors.

More than this, He even kept in His company the one who would betray Him and did not firmly denounce him. Why, even when He is betrayed, when He is led like a beast to the slaughter--for thus (is it written): 'He does not open His mouth any more than does a lamb in the power of its shearer'-- He who could have had if He wished, at a single word, legions of angels from heaven to assist Him did not approve of an avenging sword on the part of even one of His disciples.

It was the forbearance of the Lord that was wounded in (the person of) Malchus. And so, He actually cursed for all time the works of the sword and by healing him whom He had not Himself struck, He made satisfaction by forbearance, which is the mother of mercy.

I say nothing about His crucifixion; it was for this that He had come. Still, did there have to be such insults attending the death He must undergo? No; but as He went forward to His death, He willed to have His fill of joy in suffering: He is spat upon, beaten, mocked, disgracefully clothed, and even more disgracefully crowned.

Marvel at the constancy of His meekness: He who had proposed to escape notice in the guise of man has in no degree imitated man's impatience. For this reason particularly, you Pharisees, you should have recognized the Lord! Patience such as this no mere man had ever practiced!

Such were the manifestations (of His patience), the very magnitude of which is the reason why pagan nations reject the faith; for us they are its rational foundation. For those to whom there has been granted the gift of faith they suffice to make it very clear, not only by the words our Lord used in His precepts, but also by the sufferings which He endured, that patience is the very nature of God, the effect and manifestation of a certain connatural property (of His being).

CHAPTER 4

Now, if we see that all servants of righteous character and good disposition live according to the mind of their lord--obedience, as you know, is a facility in rendering service, but the principle of obedience is compliant submission--how much more does it behoove us to be found modeled upon our Lord! Servants indeed we are of the living God whose sway over His (creatures) consists not in manacles or the granting of the slave's cap, but in allotting everlasting punishment or salvation.

To escape His severity or to invite His liberality one needs diligence in obeying which is proportionate to the threats uttered by His severity or the promises made by His liberality.

Yet, we ourselves exact obedience not only from men who are bound to us by the bonds of slavery or who, because of some other legal bond, are under obligation to us, but also from our flocks and even from the wild animals. We understand that they have been provided and granted by the Lord for our purposes.

I ask you: in the practice of obedience, shall those creatures which God has made subject to us surpass us? In a word, creatures which obey (their masters) acknowledge (their condition as creatures): do we hesitate to heed Him to whom alone we are subject, namely, the Lord? Why, how unjust it would be, and in addition how ungrateful, for you not to make a return of what you have obtained from others through the kindness of a third party, to him through whom you obtained it!

But, no more about the manifestation of the obedience which we owe to the Lord our God. For, in the act of recognition of God one understands sufficiently what is incumbent upon him. However, lest we seem to have inserted something irrelevant to this discussion of obedience, (let me remark that) obedience itself also stems from patience: never does one who is impatient obey nor does a patient man ever refuse obedience.

Who, then, could deal adequately with the value of that patience which the Lord our God, the model and patron of all that is good, has displayed in Himself? Who would doubt that those who belong to God have an obligation to strive with their whole soul for every good, since it has reference to God? By these considerations our recommendation and exhortation on the subject of patience is briefly established in a summary, as it were, of the prescribed rule.

CHAPTER 5

Now, to thrash out a question about essential points of faith is not wearisome, since it is not without profit. Verboseness, though a fault at times, is no fault when it tends to edification.

Therefore, if some good is being discussed, the matter demands that we examine also the evil which is its opposite. You will throw a better light upon what one should strive for if you discuss in connection with it what should be avoided.

Let us, then, with regard to impatience, consider whether, as patience (exists) in God, its opposite was born and discovered in our adversary. From this it will appear how impatience, more than anything else, is opposed to faith.

For, that which is conceived by God's rival is certainly not a friend to the things of God. There is the same hostility in the things as there is in their authors. Furthermore, since God is infinitely good, and the Devil, on the other hand, is superlatively evil, by their very difference they bear witness that neither one effects anything for the other; it can no more seem to us that some good is produced from evil than some evil from good.

Now, I find the origin of impatience in the Devil himself. Even when the Lord God subjected to His own image, that is, to man, all the works He had made, the Devil bore it with impatience.

For, he would not have grieved, had he endured it, nor would he have envied man, had he not grieved; he deceived man because he envied him; he envied him because he grieved; he grieved because he certainly had not borne it with patience.

What the angel of perdition was first--I mean, whether he was first evil or impatient--I do not bother to inquire; it is clear that, whether impatience had its beginning in evil or evil in impatience, they entered into combination and grew as one in the bosom of one father.

For, as soon as he perceived that it was through his impatience that he had committed the first sin, having learned from his own experience what would assist in wrong-doing, he availed himself of this same impatience to lead men into sin.

Without delay, and would say not without forethought, he contrived a meeting with the woman, and simply and solely through their conversation she was touched by his breath, already infected with impatience. But never would she have sinned at all had she preserved her patience according to the divine command!

And what of the fact that she could not endure having met (the Devil) alone but, being unable to remain silent about it in the presence of Adam--he was not yet her husband, nor as yet under any obligation to lend her his ear-- she makes him the carrier of that which she had imbibed from the Evil One?

Thus, a second member, too, of the human race falls through the impatience of the first; and his fall, too, results from his own impatience committed in two ways: with regard to the forewarning of God, and with regard to the deceit of the Devil; for he was unable to observe the former or to oppose the latter.

Condemnation began with him in whom sin originated; God's anger began with him by whom man was induced to offend Him. God's patience began with him who had aroused His indignation; for at that time He was content with simply cursing him and He refrained from inflicting punishment upon the Devil.

What sin previous to this sin of impatience can be imputed to man? He was innocent and a close friend of God and a tenant dwelling in paradise. But, when once he yielded to impatience, he ceased to relish God and could no longer endure the things of heaven.

From that time on, as a man delivered up to the earth and cast away from the eyes of God, he began to serve as an easy instrument for impatience to use for everything that would offend God.

For, immediately, that impatience which was conceived by the seed of the Devil with the fecundity of evil gave birth to a child of wrath and instructed its offspring in its own arts. Since it had plunged Adam and Eve into death, it taught their son, also, to commit the first murder.

Vain were it for me to ascribe this sin to impatience, had Cain, the first homicide and the first fratricide, accepted it with equanimity and without impatience when his offerings were refused by the Lord; if he had not been angry with his brother; if, in fine, he had killed no one.

Therefore, since he could not commit murder unless he were angry, and could not be angry unless he were impatient, it proves that what he did in anger is to be referred to that which prompted the anger.

Such was the cradle of impatience which was then, so to speak, in its infancy. But to what proportions it soon grew! And no wonder: if it was the prime source of sin, it follows that, being the prime source, it was therefore also the sole fashioner of all sin, pouring forth from its own abundant resources the varied channels of crimes.

Homicide has already been mentioned. It sprang originally from anger, and whatever causes it finds for itself afterwards, it ascribes them to impatience at its origin. For, whether one commits this crime through enmity or for some gain, the original cause is that one is overwhelmed by hatred or greed.

Whatever is the motivating force, a crime could not be perpetrated unless one lacks patience. Who has ever attempted adultery save one who was unable to withstand his lustful desires? Even the fact that (disgrace) is forced upon (some) women for a price, that sale of one's honor is certainly set in order by an inability to set at naught despicable gain.

Impatience is, as it were, the original sin in the eyes of the Lord. For, to put it in a nutshell, every sin is to be traced back to impatience. Evil cannot endure good. No unchaste person but is intolerant of chastity; no scoundrel but is irked by righteousness; no negligent person but resents his obligations; no agitator but is impatient of peace. Although anyone may become evil, not everyone can persevere in good.

Why, then, should not this hydra-like generator of sins offend the Lord, who condemns all wickedness? Is it not clear that Israel itself, through its impatience, was ever sinning against God?

Forgetting the heavenly arm whereby it had been rescued from the afflictions of the Egyptians, it demanded of Aaron gods to be its leaders, while it poured its contributions into an idol of its own gold. For, it had borne without patience the delay necessitated by Moses' meeting with the Lord.

After the rain of manna as food, after the water that followed and flowed from the rock, they gave up hope in the Lord, unable to endure a three-days' thirst. For this, too, they were charged with impatience by the Lord.

But, not to range over individual instances: never would they have been destroyed had they not fallen into sin by impatience. Why did they lay hands on the Prophets, except that they could not bear to listen to them? And more than that: they laid hands upon the Lord Himself, being unable to endure even the sight of Him. But had they acquired patience, they would now be free.

CHAPTER 6

Such is the patience which is both subsequent to and antecedent to faith. Accordingly, Abraham believed in God and it was credited to him by God as justice. Now, he proved his faith by patience, when he was commanded to offer in sacrifice his son--I do not say for a trial, but rather for a typical attestation, of his faith.

But God knew the man whom He had reputed for his justice. This severe command, which the Lord did not intend should be carried out, Abraham heard with patience and, had God so willed, he would have fulfilled it. Rightly, then, is he blessed because he was faithful; and rightly was he faithful because he was patient.

Thus faith was illuminated by patience, since it was sown among the heathens by the seed of Abraham which is Christ and added grace to the Law, and it has made patience its helpmate in amplifying and fulfilling the Law, because in times past this was the only thing lacking to the teaching of justice.

Heretofore, men demanded an eye for an eye and a tooth for a tooth and they returned evil for evil. As yet, patience was not found upon the earth, for as yet, you see, there was not faith. Meanwhile, impatience was enjoying the opportunities occasioned by the Law. It was easy when the Lord and Teacher of patience was not on hand.

But after He came and united the grace of faith with patience, no longer was one permitted to do injury with so much as a word, or even say 'Thou fool!' without being in danger of the judgment. Wrath was forbidden, passions were kept in check, unruly hands were restrained, the poison of the tongue was removed.

The Law acquired more than it lost when Christ said: 'Love your enemies and bless those who curse you and pray for those who persecute you, so that you may be children of your Father in heaven.' Just see what a Father patience acquires for us!

CHAPTER 7

The entire practice of patience is compressed within this fundamental precept whereby not even a lawful injury is permitted. But now, as we run through the causes of impatience, all the other precepts, too, will correspond in their own context.

Is the mind disturbed by the loss of property? In practically every passage of the holy Scriptures one is admonished to despise the world, and no greater exhortation is there to an indifference toward money than that our Lord Himself is without it.

He always justifies the poor and condemns the rich. Thus He has set disdain for wealth ahead of the endurance of losses, pointing out through His rejection of riches that one should make no account of the loss of them.

Hence, we need not seek wealth, since our Lord did not seek it; and we ought to bear the deprivation of even the theft of it without regret.

The Spirit of the Lord, through the Apostle, has called the desire of money the root of all evils. We may infer that this consists not only in the desire for that which belongs to another; even that which seems to be our own belongs to another; for nothing is our own, since all things belong to God to whom we, too, belong.

Therefore, if we feel impatient when we suffer some loss, we will be found to possess a desire for money, since we grieve over the loss of that which is not our own. We are seeking what belongs to another when we are unwilling to bear the loss of that which belongs to another.

The man who is upset and unable to bear his loss sins, you might say, against God Himself by preferring the things of earth to those of heaven. For, the soul which he has received from the Lord is upset by the attractiveness of worldly goods.

Let us, then, with glad hearts, relinquish earthly goods that we may preserve those of heaven! Let the whole world fall in ruins provided I gain the patience to endure it! In all probability, a man who has not resolved to bear with fortitude a slight loss occasioned by theft or violence or even by his own stupidity will not readily or willingly touch what he owns for the sake of charity.

For, what man who refuses to undergo any operation at all at the hands of another puts a knife to his own body? Patience to endure, shown on occasions of loss, is a training in giving and sharing. He who does not fear loss is not reluctant to give.

Otherwise, how would one who has two tunics give one of them to him who is destitute, unless the same is one who can offer his cloak as well to the one going off with his tunic? How will we make friends for ourselves with mammon if we love him only to the extent that we do not share in his loss? We shall be damned together with the damned.

What do we find here where we have (only something) to lose? It is for pagans to be unable to sustain all loss; they would set worldly goods before their life perhaps.

And they do this when, in their eager desire for wealth, they engage in lucrative but dangerous commerce on the sea; when, for money's sake, they unhesitatingly engage in transactions also in the forum, even though there be reason to fear loss; they do it, in fine, when they hire themselves out for the games and military service or when, in desolate regions, they commit robbery regardless of the wild beasts.

On the other hand, in view of the difference between them and ourselves, it befits us to give up not our life for money but money for our life, either by voluntary charity or by the patient endurance of loss.

CHAPTER 8

Our very life and our very body we have exposed in this world as a target for all manner of injury and we endure this injury with patience; shall we, then, be vexed by the deprivation of lesser things? Far be such shame from the servant of Christ, that his patience, trained by greater trials, should fail in trifling ones!

If one tries to provoke you to a fight, there is at hand the admonition of the Lord: 'If someone strike thee,' He says, ' on the right cheek, turn to him the other also.' Let wrong-doing grow weary from your patience; whoever be struck, the one who strikes, weighed down by pain and shame, will suffer more severely from the Lord; by your meekness you will strike a more severe blow to the wrong-doer; for he will suffer at the hands of Him by whose grace you practice meekness.

If a spiteful tongue bursts out in cursing or wrangling, recall the saying: 'When men reproach you, rejoice.' The Lord Himself was accursed before the Law, yet He alone is blessed. Let us, then, His servants, follow our Lord and patiently submit to maledictions that we may be blessed!

If, with slight forbearance, I hear some bitter or evil remark directed against me, I may return it, and then I shall inevitably be bitter myself. Either that, or I shall be tormented by unexpressed resentment.

If, then, I retaliate when cursed, how shall I be found to have followed the teaching of our Lord? For it has been handed down that a man is not defiled by unclean dishes, but by the words which proceed from his mouth; and, what is more, that it remains for us to render an account for every vain and idle word.

It follows, then, that our Lord forbids us to do certain acts, but at the same time admonishes us to endure with meekness the same treatment at the hands of another.

(We shall speak) now of the joy which comes from patience. For every injury, whether occasioned by the tongue or the hand, coming in contact with patience, will meet the same end as a weapon which is flung and dashed upon a hard, unyielding rock. An ineffectual and fruitless action will lose its force immediately and will sometimes vent its passion and strike with the force of a boomerang upon him who sent it forth.

This is true, of course, since one insults you with the intention of causing you pain, because the one who inflicts the injury reaps his reward in the pain of the one injured. Consequently, if you cheat him of his reward by not showing any pain, he will himself inevitably feel pain because he has lost his reward.

Then you will go off, not only uninjured (which of itself should suffice for you) but over and above that you will have the pleasure of seeing your enemy frustrated while you yourself are preserved from pain. Herein lies the advantage of patience and the joy which derives from it

CHAPTER 9

Not even that form of impatience which results from the loss of our dear ones is excused, although in this case a sort of rightful claim to grieve justifies it. Observance of the precept of the Apostle must be put first: 'Grieve not,' he says,' over one who has fallen asleep even as the gentiles who have no hope.'

And rightly so. For, if we believe in the resurrection of Christ, we believe in our own, also, since it was for us that He died and rose again. Therefore, since there is sure ground for faith in the resurrection of the dead, there is no grief associated with death, and no inability to bear grief.

Why should you grieve if you believe that (the loved one) has not perished utterly? Why should you show impatience that one has been taken away for the time being if you believe he will return? That which you think of as death is merely the beginning of a journey. He who has gone ahead is not to be mourned, though certainly he will be missed. But this lonesomeness must be alleviated by patience. Why should you be inconsolable over the departure of one whom you are soon to follow?

Moreover, impatience in such things is a sad indication of our own hope and gives the lie to our faith. Likewise, we injure Christ when we fail to accept with resignation (the death of) those whom He has called, as though they were to be pitied.

'I desire,' says the Apostle, 'to be welcomed home now and to be with the Lord.' How much better a prayer he holds forth! As for the Christians' prayer, then, if we bear it with impatience and grief that others have attained their goal, we ourselves do not want to attain our goal!

CHAPTER 10

There is another, and very strong, motive which gives rise to impatience, namely, the desire for revenge, which busies itself in the interest of either reputation or wrong-doing. Now, reputation is everywhere empty, and evil never fails to be hateful to the Lord, especially in this situation when, occasioned by wrong-doing on the part of another, it takes the upper hand in executing vengeance and, in paying back the evil, does twice as much as was done in the first place.

Revenge mistakenly appears to be a soothing of one's pain, but in the light of truth it is seen to be only evil contending with evil. What difference is there between the one who provokes and the one provoked except that the one is caught doing wrong sooner than the other? Nevertheless, before the Lord each is guilty of having injured a fellow man and the Lord forbids and condemns every act of wrong-doing.

There is no hierarchical arrangement in wrong-doing, nor does position make any distinction in that which similarity makes one. Therefore, the precept is unequivocally laid down: evil is not to be rendered for evil. Like deed merits like treatment.

But how shall we observe this precept if, in loathing (evil), we have no loathing for revenge? What tribute of honor shall we offer to the Lord our God if we assume to ourselves the right to inflict punishment?

We who are matter subject to decay, vessels of clay, are grievously offended when our servants take it upon themselves to seek revenge from their fellow slaves; as for those who show us patience, we not only praise them as slaves who are conscious of their lowly position, men attentive to the respect they owe their lord, but we recompense them even more than they had themselves anticipated. Is there any risk for us in such a course when we have a Lord so just in His judgments, so powerful in His deeds?

Why, then, do we believe Him a judge, but not also an avenger? Of this He assures us when He says: 'Revenge is mine and I will repay them,' that is: 'Have patience with Me and I will reward your patience.'

When He says: 'Do not judge, that you may not be judged,' is He not demanding patience? What man will refrain from judging another except one who will forego (the right) of self-defense? What man judges with the intention of forgiving? And if he does forgive, he has but shied away from the impatience of a man who judges and has usurped the honor of the true Judge, that is, God!

What misfortunes has such impatience, as a rule, brought upon itself! How often has it regretted its self-defense! How often has its obstinacy become worse than the occasions which provoked it! Now, nothing undertaken through impatience can be transacted without violence, and everything done with violence has either met with no success or has collapsed or has plunged to its own destruction.

If you are too mild in your self-defense, you will be acting like a madman; if your defense is excessive, you will be depressed. Why should I be concerned about revenge when I cannot regulate its extent because of my inability to endure pain? Whereas, if I yield and suffer the injury, I shall have no pain; and if I have no pain, I shall have no desire for revenge.

CHAPTER 11

Now that we have, to the best of our ability, set forth these principal provocations to impatience in the order of their intensity, with which of the rest that (we encounter) at home and in public life should we concern ourselves? Widespread and extensive are the workings of the Evil One who extends innumerable incentives to impatience which, at times, are slight, at times very great.

The slight ones you should ignore for their insignificance; to the great you should yield in view of their invincible power. When the injury is not very important, there is no need for impatience, but when the injury is more serious, then there is greater need for a remedy against the injury, namely, patience.

Let us strive, then, to bear the injuries that are inflicted by the Evil One, that the struggle to maintain our self-control may put to shame the enemy's efforts. If, however, through imprudence or even of our own free will we draw down upon ourselves some misfortune, we should submit with equal patience to that which we impute to ourselves.

But if we believe some blow of misfortune is struck by God, to whom would it be better that we manifest patience than to our Lord? In fact, more than this, it befits us to rejoice at being deemed worthy of divine chastisement: 'As for me,' He says, 'those whom I love I chastise.' Blessed is that servant upon whose amendment the Lord insists, at whom He deigns to be angry, whom He does not deceive by omitting His admonition!

From every angle, then, we are obliged to practice patience, because we meet up with our own mistakes or the wiles of the Evil One or the warnings of the Lord alike. Great is the recompense for practicing it, namely, happiness.

Whom has the Lord declared happy? Those who are patient; for He said: 'Blessed are the poor in spirit, for theirs is the kingdom of heaven.' Assuredly, no one but the humble man is poor in spirit. And who is humble but the man who is patient? No one can take a position of subjection without patience, the prime factor in subjection.

'Blessed,' He says, 'are those who weep and mourn.' Who can endure such things without patience? To such, then, is consolation and joy promised.

'Blessed are the meek.' Certainly, in this word one cannot by any means include the impatient. Likewise, when He applies this same title of happiness to the peace-makers and calls them the children of God, I ask you: Do the impatient share in this peace? Only a fool would think so!

And when He says: 'Rejoice and exult when men reproach you and persecute you because your reward is great in heaven,' certainly this promise of great joy is not made to the impatient, for no one will rejoice in adversity unless he has first come to despise it; no one will despise it unless he possesses patience.

CHAPTER 12

As for what pertains to the practice of this peace so pleasing to God (I ask you): What man, completely given over to impatience, will forgive his brother, I will not say seven times and seventy times seven times, but even once?

What man, taking his case with his adversary to a judge, will settle his trouble to the accommodation of the other party, unless he first puts an end to his wrath, his resentment, his harshness and bitterness, that is, his impatient disposition?

How will you forgive and experience forgiveness if you cling to your injury through a total lack of patience? No one whose mind is violently disturbed against his brother will complete his offering at the altar unless first he has been reconciled to his brother through patience.

If the sun goes down upon our anger, we are in danger. We may not live a single day without patience. Yet, since patience governs every aspect of a salutary way of life, what wonder that it also paves the way for repentance which, as a rule, comes to the assistance of those who have fallen?

What benefits it produces in both parties when, in spite of their forbearance from their marriage rights--provided it be only for that reason which makes it lawful for a man or woman to persist in their separation--it waits for, hopes for, wins by its prayers repentance for those who will eventually be saved. It purifies the one without causing the other to become an adulterer!

So, too, in those examples in our Lord's parables there is a breath of patience: it is the patience of the shepherd that seeks and finds the straying sheep (for impatience would readily take no account of a single sheep, whereas patience undertakes the wearisome search) and he carries it on his shoulders, a patient bearer of a forsaken sinner.

In the case of the prodigal son, too, it is the patience of his father that welcomes him and clothes him and feeds him and finds an excuse for him in the face of the impatience of his angry brother. The one who had perished is rescued, therefore, because he embraced repentance; repentance is not wasted because it meets up with patience!

Consider now charity, the great bond of faith, the treasure of the Christian religion, which the Apostle extols with all the power of the Holy Spirit: how is it learned except by the exercise of patience?

'Charity,' he says, 'is magnanimous.' It derives this from patience. 'It is kind.' Patience works no evil. 'It does not envy.' Envy is certainly a characteristic of impatience. 'It is not pretentious.' It has derived its contentment from patience. 'It is not puffed up, is not ambitious,' for that does not befit patience. 'It is not self-seeking.' It suffers (the loss of) its own goods provided that it be to another's advantage. 'It is not provoked.' What, then, would it have left to impatience? Therefore, he says, 'charity bears with all things, endures all things.' Of course it does, because it is itself patient.

He is correct, then, in stating that it will never fall away. Everything else will pass away and come to an end. Tongues, knowledge, prophecies are made void, but there persist faith, hope, and charity: faith, which the patience of Christ has instilled; hope, to which the patience of man looks forward; charity, which patience accompanies, according to the teaching of God.

CHAPTER 13

Thus far (we have been speaking), however, of a patience which constitutes simply and uniformly and solely an operation of the soul, whereas in various ways we should strive for this same patience also in the body in order to attain the good pleasure of the Lord, inasmuch as it was practiced by the Lord Himself as a virtue also of the body; for the soul, as the directing agent, readily shares the inspirations of the Spirit with that wherein it dwells.

What, then, is the operation of patience in the body? Primarily, mortification of the flesh as a sacrifice acceptable to the Lord. This is an offering of (one's) humility, since it offers to the Lord a sacrifice of mourning dress along with meager rations, contenting itself with plain food and a drink of clear water, joining fast with fast and persevering in sackcloth and ashes.

This patience on the part of the body contributes to the value of our petitions and strengthens our prayers for deliverance. It opens the ears of Christ our God, dispels His severity, elicits His mercy.

Thus, after offending the Lord, the King of Babylon lived for seven years in squalor and filth, an exile from human society. By this offering of the patient endurance of bodily (discomfort) not only did he regain his kingdom, but--and this is even more desirable in a man--he made satisfaction to God.

Now, if we go on to consider the higher and more blessed degrees of bodily patience, (we see that) it turns continence, too, into an opportunity for sanctity: this it is which preserves the widow (in her state), places its seal upon the virgin, and raises to the kingdom of heaven one who of his own free will embraces a life of celibacy.

That which derives from the power of the soul finds its fulfillment in the flesh. In persecutions the endurance of the flesh engages in battle. If flight besets one, the flesh surmounts the hardships of flight. If imprisonment precludes flight, it is the flesh which submits to the chains, the block of wood, and the bare ground. It is the flesh which endures both the scanty light (of the dungeon) and the deprivation of worldly comforts.

But, when one is led forth to the ordeal that will prove his happiness, to the opportunity to renew one's baptism, to the very ascent to the throne of divinity, there is nothing (which avails) more in that situation than endurance on the part of the body. If the spirit is willing but the flesh--without patience--weak, where is there salvation for the spirit as well as for the flesh itself?

On the other hand, when the Lord speaks thus of the flesh and declares it weak, He points out what is needed for strengthening it, namely, patience in the face of everything that is ready to overthrow our faith and impose a penalty for it, that one may bear with constancy stripes, and fire, the cross, wild beasts, or the sword as the Prophets and Apostles bore them and won the victory.

CHAPTER 14

In virtue of his power of endurance, Isaias, though cut in pieces, does not refrain from speaking of the Lord. Stephen, as he is stoned, prays for pardon for his enemies.

Happy, too, was that man who displayed every manner of patience against every vicious attack of the Devil! His flocks were driven away, his wealth in cattle destroyed by lightning, his children killed at a single stroke when his house collapsed, his own body, finally, was tortured by painful sores --yet, by none of these was he lured from his patience and the trust he owed the Lord. Though the Devil struck him with all his strength, he struck in vain!

Far from being turned away by so many misfortunes from the reverence which he owed to God, he set for us an example and proof of how we must practice patience in the spirit as well as in the flesh, in soul as well as in body, that we may not succumb under the loss of worldly goods, the death of our dear ones, or any bodily afflictions.

What a trophy over the Devil God erected in the case of that man! What a banner of His glory He raised above His enemy when that man let fall from his lips no other word than 'Thanks be to God!' as each bitter message reached him; when he severely rebuked his wife who, weary by now of misfortunes, was urging him to improper remedies.

How God laughed, and how the Evil One was split asunder, when Job, with perfect calm, would wipe away the discharge oozing from his ulcer and, with a jesting remark, would call back to the cavity and sustenance of his open flesh the tiny creatures that were trying to make their way out!

Thus did that hero who brought about a victory for his God beat back all the darts of temptation and with the breastplate and shield of patience soon after recover from God complete health of body and the possession of twice as much as he had lost.

Had he wanted his sons to be restored, too, he would once again have heard himself called 'father.' But he preferred that they be restored to him on the last day; placing all his trust in the Lord, he deferred that great joy; for the prevent, he was willing to endure the loss of his children that he might not live without something to suffer!

CHAPTER 15

God is fully capable of being the trustee of our patience: if you place in His hands an injustice you have suffered, He will see that justice is done; if a loss, He will see that you receive compensation; if a pain, He acts as healer; if death, He restores life. How much is granted to patience that it should have God for a debtor!

And not without reason. For it pays attention to all His prescriptions, it becomes surety for all His commands: it strengthens faith, governs peace, sustains love, instructs humility, awaits repentance, places its seal upon the discipline of penance, controls the flesh, preserves the spirit, puts restraint upon the tongue, holds back the (violent) hand, treads under foot temptations, pushes scandal aside, consummates martyrdom.

In poverty it supplies consolation; upon wealth it imposes moderation; the sick it does not destroy, nor does it, for the man in health, prolong his life; for the man of faith it is a source of delight. It attracts the heathen, recommends the slave to his master, the master to God. It adorns a woman, perfects a man. It is loved in a child, praised in a youth, esteemed in the aged. In both man and woman, at every age of life, it is exceedingly attractive.

Now, then! If you will, let us try to grasp the features and appearance of patience. Its countenance is peaceful and untroubled. Its brow is clear, unruffled by any lines of melancholy or anger. The eyebrows are relaxed, giving an impression of joyousness. The eyes are lowered, in an attitude rather of humility than moroseness.

The mouth is closed in becoming silence. Its complexion is that of the serene and blameless. It shakes its head frequently in the direction of the Devil, and its laughter conveys a threat to him. The upper part of its garment is white and close-fitting so that it is not blown about or disturbed (by the wind).

It sits on the throne of its spirit which is extremely mild and gentle and is not whipped into a knot by the whirlwind, is not made livid by a cloud, but is a breeze of soft light, clear and simple, such as Elias saw the third time. For where God is, there, too, is the child of His nurturing, namely, patience.

When the Spirit of God descends, patience is His inseparable companion. If we fail to welcome it along with the Spirit, will the latter remain within us at all times? As a matter of fact, I rather think the Spirit would not remain at all. Without its companion and assistant it would feel very uncomfortable anywhere and at any time. It could not endure, all by itself, the blows which its enemy inflicts, if stripped of the means which helps it to endure.

CHAPTER 16

This is the theory, this the practice, this the operation of the patience which is divine and true, namely, Christian; a patience not like the patience practiced by the peoples of the earth, which is false and disgraceful.

For, that the Devil might rival the Lord in this respect, also, and be really on an equal footing with Him as it were (except that good and evil are extremes of equal magnitude) the Devil also taught his own a special brand of patience.

It is a patience, I say, which renders subject to the power of their wives husbands who are purchased by a dowry or who negotiate with panderers; a patience in virtue of which (a wife) bears, with feigned affection, all the irritation resulting from a forced association so that, as a childless widow, she may lay hands upon her husband's estate; a patience which sentences gormandizers to sacrifice their freedom and become disgraceful slaves to their gluttony.

Such are the goals of patience as the heathens know it and by such despicable efforts they appropriate the name of so noble a virtue; they live in patient endurance of their rivals, the wealthy, and their hosts; it is only God alone whom they cannot endure. But let their patience and the patience of their chief take care: there is fire beneath the earth awaiting this kind of patience.

Let us, then, love the patience that is of God, the patience of Christ; let us return to Him that which He expended for us; let us who believe in the resurrection of the flesh and of the spirit offer Him both the patience of the spirit and the patience of the flesh.

Prayer

by Tertullian

CHAPTER 1

Jesus Christ our Lord the Spirit of God and the Word of God and the Reason of God--the Word (which expresses) the Reason, and the Reason (which possesses) the Word, and the Spirit of both--has prescribed for His new disciples of the New Testament a new form of prayer. For in this matter, also, it was fitting that new wine be stored in new wine skins and that a new patch be sewed upon a new garment. Whatever had prevailed in days gone by was either abolished, like circumcision, or completed, like the rest of the Law, or fulfilled, like the prophecies, or brought to its perfection, like faith itself.

Everything has been changed from carnal to spiritual by the new grace of God which, with the coming of the Gospel, has wiped out the old completely; and in this grace it has been proved there is the Spirit of God and the Word of God and the Reason of God, Jesus Christ our Lord; as the Spirit wherein He prevailed, the Word whereby He taught, and the Reason or which He came. Consequently, the prayer formulated by Christ consists of three elements: the spirit whereby it can have such power, the word by which it is expressed, and the reason why it produces reconciliation.

John, too, had taught his disciples to pray, but everything that John did was a preparation for Christ, until He would increase--even as John himself announced that He (Christ) must increase, but he himself must decrease--and the entire work of the servant would pass over, along with the spirit itself, to the Master. Hence it is that the words in which John taught men to offer their prayer are not extant, for the earthly have given place to the heavenly. 'He who is from the earth,' He says, 'of the earth speaks, and he who comes from heaven bears witness to that which he has seen.' And what that is of Christ the Lord is not of heaven, as is also this instruction concerning prayer?

Let us then, my blessed ones, consider His heavenly wisdom, in the first place with regard to the admonition to pray in secret. By this, He demanded of man the faith to believe that he is seen and heard by Almighty God even when he is within the house and out of sight; and He desired a modest reserve in the manifestation of his faith so that he would offer his homage to God alone who he believed was listening and observing everywhere.

The next recommendation in the following precept would, then, pertain to faith and the proper display of faith; we should not think that the Lord is to be approached with a barrage of words since we are certain that of His own accord He has regard for His creatures.

Yet, that concise phrase which forms the third point of His teaching rests for support upon a profound and effective figure of speech: the thought compressed within such few words carries a flood of meaning to the mind. For not only does it embrace the proper duties of prayer, namely, worship of God and man's act of supplication, but practically every word of the Lord, the whole content of His teaching, so that, really, in (the Lord's) Prayer, there is contained an abridgment of the entire Gospel.

CHAPTER 2

It begins with a proof of (our belief in) God and a meritorious act of faith when we say, 'Father, who art in heaven.' For we adore God and prove our faith, of which this form of address is the result. It is written: 'To them that believe in God He gave the power to be called the sons of God.'

Our Lord very frequently spoke to us of God as a Father; in fact, He even taught us to call none on earth 'father,' but only the one we have in heaven. Therefore, when we pray like this we are observing this precept, too.

Happy they who know the Father! This is the reproach made against Israel, when the Spirit calls heaven and earth to witness saying: 'I have begotten sons and they have not known me.'

Moreover, when we say 'Father,' we also add a title to God's name. This form of address is one of filial love and at the same time one of power.

In the Father, the Son is also addressed. For Christ said, 'I and the Father are one.'

Nor is Mother Church passed over without mention, for in the Son and the Father the Mother is recognized, since upon her the terms 'Father' and 'Son' depend for their meaning. With this one form, then, or word, we honor God with His own, we heed His precept, and we reproach those who are unmindful of the Father.

CHAPTER 3

The title 'God the Father' had not been revealed to anyone. Even Moses who had inquired about God's name had heard a different one. It has been revealed to us in His Son. For, before the Son (came) the name of the Father did not exist. 'I have come,' said Christ, 'in the name of my Father.' And again: 'Father, glorify thy name.' And, more explicitly: 'I have manifested thy name to men.'

We ask that this name be hallowed; not that it would be the proper thing for men to wish God well as if He were (just) another man and we could express some wish in his regard; or as if it would hurt Him if we did not express the wish. Certainly it is right that God should be blessed in all places and at all times because it is every man's duty to be ever mindful of His benefits, but this wish takes the form of a benediction.

Moreover, when is the name of God not holy and blessed in itself, when of itself it makes others holy? To Him the attending hosts of angels cease not to say: 'Holy, holy, holy!' Therefore, we, too--the future comrades of the angels, if we earn this reward--become familiar even while here on this earth with that heavenly cry of praise to God and the duty of our future glory.

So much for the glory we give to God. Over and above that, there is reference to our own petition when we say 'Hallowed be thy name.' We are asking that it be sanctified in us who are in Him, as well as in all other men for whom the grace of God is still waiting. In this, too, we obey the precept by praying for all men, even our enemies. And thus, by an ellipsis, we say, not: 'May Thy name be hallowed among us,' but, we say: 'Among all men.'

CHAPTER 4

Next, we add this phrase: 'Thy will be done in heaven and on earth.' Not that anyone could prevent the fulfillment of God's will and we should pray that His will be successfully accomplished, but we pray that in everything His will may be done. For, by a figure of speech, under the symbol of flesh and spirit we represent heaven and earth.

But, even if this is to be understood literally, the sense of the petition is the same, namely, that the will of God be done in us on earth, in order that it may be done (by us) also in heaven. Now, what does God will but that we walk according to His teaching? We ask, therefore, that He grant us the substance and riches of His will, for our salvation both in heaven and on earth, since the sum total of His will is the salvation of those whom He has adopted as His children.

This is the will of God which our Lord accomplished by His teaching, His works, and His sufferings. For, if He Himself said that He did not His own will, but the will of His Father, without a doubt what He did was the will of His Father, to which we are now summoned as to a model, that we, too, may teach and work and suffer even unto death. That we may accomplish this there is need of God's will.

Likewise, when we say: 'Thy will be done,' we thereby wish well to ourselves because there is no evil in God's will, even if some adversity be inflicted upon one according to his deserts.

Now, by this phrase we forearm ourselves for patient endurance since our Lord, too, willed to point out in His own flesh under the intensity of His Passion the weakness of the flesh. 'Father,' He said, 'remove this cup from Me,' and then, after reflection, He added: 'Yet not my will but thine be done.' He Himself was the will and power of the Father, yet He surrendered Himself to the will of His Father to indicate the patient endurance which is rightly due.

CHAPTER 5

The phrase, 'Thy kingdom come,' also refers to the same end as 'Thy will be done,' namely, (May Thy kingdom come) in ourselves. For, when does God not reign, 'in whose hand is the heart of every king'? But, whatever we wish for ourselves, we direct our hope toward Him, and we attribute to Him what we expect from Him. Well, then, if the realization of our Lord's kingdom has reference to the will of God and to our uncertain condition, how is it that some ask for an extension of time, as it were, for this world, since the kingdom of God--for the coming of which we pray--tends toward the consummation of the world? Our hope is that we may sooner reign, and not be slaves any longer.

Even if it were not prescribed to ask in prayer for the coming of His kingdom, we would, of our own accord, have expressed this desire in our eagerness to embrace the object of our hope.

With indignation the souls of the martyrs beneath the altar cry aloud to the Lord: 'How long, O Lord, dost thou refrain from avenging our blood on those who dwell on the earth?' For, at least from the end of the world vengeance for them is ordained.

Indeed, as quickly as possible, O Lord, may Thy kingdom come! This is the prayer of Christians; this shall bring shame to the heathens; this shall bring joy to the angels; it is for the coming of this kingdom that we are harassed now, or rather, it is for this coming that we pray.

CHAPTER 6

With what exquisite choice has divine Wisdom arranged the order of this prayer that, after the matters which pertain to heaven--that is, after the name of God, the will of God, and the kingdom of God--it should make a place for a petition for our earthly needs, too! For our Lord has taught us: 'Seek first the kingdom, and then these things shall be given you besides.'

However, we should rather understand 'Give us this day our daily bread' in a spiritual sense. For Christ is 'our bread,' because Christ is Life and the Life is Bread. 'I am,' said He, 'the bread of life.' And shortly before: 'The bread is the word of the living God who hath come down from heaven.' Then, because His Body is considered to be in the bread: 'This is my body.' Therefore, when we ask for our daily bread, we are asking to live forever in Christ and to be inseparably united with His Body.

But, since there is admitted also an interpretation of this phrase according to the flesh, it cannot be devoid of religious sense and spiritual instruction. Christ commands that we ask for bread, which, for the faithful, is the only thing necessary, for the pagans seek all other things. Thus, too, He impresses His teaching by examples and He instructs by parables, saying, for example: 'Does a father take bread from his children and cast it to the dogs?' And again: 'If his son asks him for a loaf, will he hand him a stone?' He indicates what children expect from their father. That caller, too, who knocked upon the door in the night was asking for bread.

Moreover, He has rightly added: 'Give us this day' in view of what He had previously said: 'Do not be anxious about tomorrow, what you shall eat.' To this idea He also referred in the parable of that man who, when his crops were plentiful, laid plans for an addition to his barns and a long-range program of security--though he was destined to die that very night.

CHAPTER 7

Having considered God's generosity, we pray next for His indulgence. For, of what benefit is food if, in reality, we are bent on it like a bull on his victim? Our Lord knew that He alone was without sin. Therefore, He taught us to say in prayer: 'Forgive us our trespasses.' A prayer for pardon is an acknowledgment of sin, since one who asks for pardon confesses his guilt. Thus, too, repentance is shown to be acceptable to God, because God wills this rather than the death of the sinner.

Now, in Scripture, 'debt' is used figuratively to mean sin, because of this analogy: When a man owes something to a judge and payment is exacted from him, he does not escape the just demand unless excused from the payment of the debt, just as the master forgave the debt to that servant. Now, this is the point of the whole parable: Just as the servant was freed by his lord, but failed in turn to be merciful to his debtor and therefore, when brought before his lord, was handed over to the torturer until he paid the last penny, that is, the least and last of his faults, (Christ) intended by this parable to get us, also, to forgive our debtors.

This is expressed elsewhere under this aspect of prayer; 'Forgive,' He said, 'and you shall be forgiven.' And when Peter asked if one should forgive his brother seven times, our Lord said, 'Rather, seventy times seven times,' that He might improve upon the Law, for in Genesis vengeance was demanded of Cain seven times, of Lamech seventy times seven.

CHAPTER 8

To complete the prayer which was so well arranged, Christ added that we should pray not only that our sins be forgiven, but that they be shunned completely: 'Lead us not into temptation,' that is, do not allow us to be led by the Tempter.

God forbid that our Lord should seem to be the tempter, as if He were not aware of one's faith or were eager to upset it!

That weakness and spitefulness belongs to the Devil. For, even in the case of Abraham, God had ordered the sacrifice of his son not to tempt his faith, but to prove it, that in him He-might set forth an example for His precept whereby He was later to teach that no one should hold his loved ones dearer than God.

Christ Himself was tempted by the Devil and pointed out the subtle director of the temptation.

This passage He confirms (by His words to His Apostles) later when He says: 'Pray that you may not enter into temptation.' They were so tempted to desert their Lord because they had indulged in sleep instead of prayer.

Therefore, the phrase which balances and interprets 'Lead us not into temptation' is 'But deliver us from evil.'

CHAPTER 9

How many utterances of the Prophets, Evangelists, and Apostles; how many of our Lord's sermons, parables, examples, and precepts are touched in the brief compass of a few little words! How many duties are fulfilled!

The honor due to God in the word 'Father'; a testimony of faith in the very title used; the offering of obedience in the mention of God's will; the remembrance of hope in the mention of His kingdom; a petition for life in the mention of bread; the confession of sins in asking for pardon; solicitude regarding temptation in the request for protection.

Yet, why be surprised? God alone could teach us how He would have us pray. The homage of prayer, then, as arranged by Him and animated by His Spirit at the very moment it went forth from His divine lips, because of the prerogative granted to Him, ascends to heaven, recommending to the Father what the Son has taught.

CHAPTER 10

Since, however, our Lord, who saw the needs of men, after giving them the method of prayer, said: 'Ask and you shall receive,' and since every man has petitions to make according to his own circumstances, everyone first sends ahead the prescribed and customary prayer which will, so to speak, lay the ground work for his additional desires. He then has the right to heap upon this (substructure) petitions, over and above--ever keeping in mind, however, the prescribed conditions, that we may be no farther from the ears of God than from His teachings.

CHAPTER 11

The remembrance of these teachings paves the way for our prayers to reach heaven, and the first of these is not to approach the altar of God without settling any controversy or quarrel we may have contracted with our brethren. For, how can one approach the peace of God without peace, or the forgiveness of sin when he nurses a grudge? How will he please his Father if he be angry with his brother, when all anger has been forbidden us from the beginning?

For Joseph, sending his brothers home to bring their father, said: 'Do not quarrel on the way!' He was, in fact, admonishing us--for elsewhere our manner of life is called our 'way'--that on the way of prayer that has been set up we must not approach the Father if we are angry.

Furthermore, our Lord, clearly enlarging upon the Law, adds anger with one's brother to the sin of murder. He does not permit even an evil word to be expressed; even if one must experience anger, it should not outlast the setting of the sun, as the Apostle reminds us. How foolhardy it is, moreover, either to pass a day without prayer, while you fail to give satisfaction to your brother, or to pray to no avail since your anger persists!

CHAPTER 12

Since the attention of our prayer is bestowed by and directed to the same Spirit, it should be free not only from anger, but from any and every disturbance of the mind. For the Holy Spirit does not acknowledge an impure spirit, neither is a sad spirit recognized by the Spirit of Joy, nor a spirit that is bound by one that is free. No one extends a welcoming hand to an opponent; no one admits another unless he is a kindred spirit.

CHAPTER 13

Furthermore, what is the sense of approaching prayer with hands that have been cleansed but with a spirit that is stained? Why, even the hands themselves need a spiritual cleansing that they may be raised to heaven cleansed of falsehood, murder, cruelty, poisoning, idolatry, and all other stains which, conceived in the spirit, are accomplished by the operation of the hands. This is the real cleansing, not the kind which many, in superstitious anxiety, attend to, taking water at every prayer, even when they come after a complete bath!

When I pondered this in detail and sought an explanation, I found it told of Pilate that he washed his hands in the act of surrendering Christ. We adore Christ, we do not surrender Him. Surely, we ought rather to follow a course of conduct different from that of the traitor and for that very reason not wash our hands; except to wash them because of some stain resulting from our dealings with men, for our conscience's sake; but the hands are sufficiently clean which we have washed once and for all, together with the whole body, in Christ.

CHAPTER 14

Though Israel may wash all its members every day, it is never clean. Its hands, at least, are always stained, forever red with the blood of the Prophets and of our Lord Himself. Conscious, therefore, of this hereditary stain of their fathers, they do not dare to raise their hands to the Lord, lest some Isaias cry out, lest Christ abominate them. In our case, not only do we raise them, we even spread them out, and, imitating the Passion of our Lord, we confess Christ as we pray.

CHAPTER 15

Now, since we have mentioned one detail of religious observance that is foolish, we shall not be loathe to censure the others, too, in which vanity deserves to be reproved, inasmuch as they are without the authority of any precept, either on the part of our Lord or any of the Apostles. Practices such as this are to be considered superstition rather than devout homage; affected and forced and indicative of scrupulosity rather than of a rational service; at any rate, constrained to match those of the pagans.

Take, for example, the practice some have of laying aside their cloaks when they pray. This is the way pagans approach their idols. Now certainly, if this were necessary, the Apostles would have included it in their instructions about the dress for prayer; unless there are some who think that it was during his prayer that Paul left his cloak with Carpus! I suppose that the God who heeded the prayer of the three holy youths in the furnace of the Babylonian king when they prayed in their wide oriental trousers and turbans would not listen to those who wear their cloaks during prayer!

CHAPTER 16

Similarly, regarding the custom some have of sitting down when their prayer is ended: I see no reason for it except that they are acting like children. What do I mean? If that Hermas, whose writings generally bear the title 'The Shepherd,' had not sat upon his bed when his prayer was finished, but had done something else, would we adopt this practice, too? Certainly not!

For the phrase, 'When I had offered my prayer and had seated myself on the bed,' was set down simply and solely in the course of the narrative, not as a point of discipline.

Otherwise, we would not be obliged to offer prayers anywhere except where there was a bed! On the other hand, it would be violating his directions to sit upon a chair or bench!

Furthermore, since this is what the pagans do--sit down before the images of the gods which they adore--it is on this score that what is done before idols deserves to be reproved in us.

For this reason it is set down as a charge of irreverence, and would be so understood, even by those pagans, if they had any understanding. For, if it is disrespectful to sit down in the presence and sight of one whom you hold in very high esteem and honor, how much more is it the height of disrespect to do so in the presence of the living God with the angel of prayer standing beside Him? Unless we are offering a reproach to God because our prayer has wearied us!

CHAPTER 17

On the other hand, when we offer our prayer with modesty and humility, we commend our petitions to God all the more, even though our hands have not been raised very high in the air, but only slightly and to a proper position, and even though our gaze has not been lifted up in presumption.

For, even the publican who, not only in his words but in his countenance as well, was humble and prayed with downcast eyes went away justified rather than the haughty Pharisee.

The tone of voice, too, should be lowered; otherwise, what lungs we will need, if being heard depended upon the noise we make! But God is not one who heeds the voice; rather, it is the heart which He hears and beholds.

'Even the speechless I hear, and the silent petition I answer.' So runs an oracle of the Pythian demon. Do the ears of God await a sound? If they did, how could Jonas' prayer from the depths of the whale's belly have made its way to heaven, up through the organs of such a great beast from the very bottom of the sea, up through such a vast amount of water?

As for those who pray in such a loud voice, what else will they attain but the annoyance of their neighbors?

Let us say, rather, when they thus publicize their petitions, what else are they doing but praying in public?

CHAPTER 18

There is another custom which has now become established: when those who are fasting have finished their prayer with their brethren, they withhold the kiss of peace; yet this is the seal of prayer.

But, when is the kiss of peace to be given to our brethren if not when our prayer ascends to heaven, made more worthy of praise because of our charity? So that they themselves may share in our charity, who have contributed to it by passing on their peace to their brother.

What prayer is complete without the bond of a holy kiss?

With whom does the kiss of peace interfere in his service of the Lord?

What kind of sacrifice is it from which one departs without giving the kiss of peace?

Whatever the reason may be, it will not outweigh the observance of the precept whereby we are bidden to conceal our fasting. For, when we refrain from the kiss, it is recognized that we are fasting. But, even if there is some reason for it, still, that you may not be guilty of transgressing this precept, you may, if you wish, dispense with the kiss of peace at home, since there you are among those from whom it is not entirely possible to conceal your fasting. But, wherever else you can conceal your acts of mortification, you ought to remember this precept; in this way you will satisfactorily comply with religious discipline in public, and with ordinary usage at home.

Thus, too, on Good Friday, when the fasting is a general and, as it were, a public religious obligation, we rightly omit the kiss of peace, having no anxiety about concealing that which we are doing along with everyone else.

CHAPTER 19

Similarly, with regard to the station days, many do not think that there should be any attendance at the prayers of sacrifice, because the station should be ended when the Lord's Body is received.

Has the Eucharist, then, dispensed with a duty vowed to God, or does it place upon us a greater obligation to God?

Will not your station be more solemn if you stand at the altar of God?

When the Body of our Lord is received and reserved, both are preserved: the participation in the sacrifice and the fulfillment of a duty.

Since 'station' has taken its name from military procedure (for we are God's militia), certainly no joy nor sadness which befalls the camp releases the soldiers on guard duty. For, in joy one will perform his duty more readily, and, in sadness, more conscientiously.

CHAPTER 20

As regards dress--I refer only to that of women--the difference of custom since the time of the holy Apostle has caused me, though a man of no rank (in the Church), to deal with this matter, which is a daring thing to do; except that it is not so daring if we deal with it as did the Apostle.

As for the modesty of their attire and adornment, the admonition of Peter, too, is clearly expressed. Using the same words as Paul, because inspired by the same Spirit, he imposes restraint regarding ostentation in their dress, the proud display of gold, and the overcareful, meretricious arrangement of their hair.

CHAPTER 21

A point which must be treated, since in general, throughout the Church, it is regarded as a matter of dispute, is the question of whether or not virgins should be veiled.

Those who grant to virgins the right of having their heads uncovered seem to support their position by the fact that the Apostle designated specifically, not that virgins, but that women, are to be veiled; that is, he referred not to the sex, using the generic term 'females,' but to one group within the sex, saying 'women.'

For, if he had specified the (entire) sex by the term 'females' he would have laid down an absolute law relating to every woman; but since he designates one group within the sex, he sets it apart by his silence regarding another group.

For, they say, he could have included them in the general term 'females.'

CHAPTER 22

Those who take this stand ought to give some thought to the basic meaning of this word. What does 'woman' mean right from the first pages of holy Scripture? They will discover that it is the term used to designate the sex, not a group within the sex; for God called Eve, although she had not yet known man, both woman and female: female, as an over-all term for the sex; woman, with special reference to a stage of life within the sex. Thus, since Eve, who up to that time was still unmarried, was designated by the term 'woman,' this term came to be commonly applied to a virgin, also. No wonder, then, if the Apostle, actuated by the same Spirit which has inspired all the sacred Scriptures as well as that Book of Genesis, used this same word, 'woman,' which, because of its application to the unmarried Eve, means also a virgin.

Everything else, then, is in agreement. For, by the very fact that he has not named virgins, just as is the case in another passage, where he is teaching about marriage, he makes it clear that he is speaking about all women and the entire sex and that there is no distinction between a woman and a virgin since he does not mention the latter at all. For, since he did not forget to make a distinction in another passage where the difference demands it (he distinguishes both classes by designating each with its proper term), in a passage where he does not distinguish, since he does not name each, he does not intend any distinction.

But what of the fact that in the Greek, in which the Apostle wrote his epistles, the ordinary usage is to speak of 'women' rather than 'females,' that is, y~*va;KaS rather than ~as? Well, if this word is the one commonly used to designate the sex, then the Apostle, in saying yuvalKa, referred to the (entire) sex (by using) a word which, in translation, means 'females.' But in the (entire) sex the virgin, too, is included.

The form of expression is unmistakable: 'Every woman,' he says, 'praying or prophesying with her head uncovered disgraces her head.' What is the meaning of the expression 'every woman' except women of every age, every rank, and every circumstance? In saying 'every,' he excepts no member of the female sex, even as he does not command that men should have their heads covered. For then he would say 'every man.' Therefore, as in the reference to the male sex, under the term 'man' he forbids that even unmarried men should have their heads covered, similarly, in reference to the female sex, under the term 'woman' he commands that even a virgin should have her head covered. Without discrimination, in the case of both sexes, the younger should follow the rule for the elder; or else unmarried men should have their heads covered, too, if unmarried women should not have their heads covered; for the former are not specifically named in the regulation; let the (married) man be different from the unmarried if the woman is different from the virgin.

Of course, it is on account of the angels, he says, that the woman's head is to be covered, because the angels revolted from God on account of the daughters of men. Who, then, would contend that it is only women, that is, married women no longer virgins, that are a source of temptation?

Unless, of course, unmarried women may not present an attractive appearance and find their lovers? Rather, let us see whether it was virgins alone whom they desired when Scripture speaks of the 'daughters of men'; for it could have used the terms 'men's wives' or 'women' indifferently.

But, since it says: 'And they took to themselves wives,' it does so because they took as their wives those without husbands. Scripture would have used a different expression for those who had husbands. Now, they could be without husbands either because they were widows or virgins. So, in naming the sex in general by the term 'daughters,' he embraced species in genus.

Likewise, when he says that nature itself teaches that women should cover their heads because it has bestowed hair on woman both as a covering and an adornment, has not this same covering and this same adornment for the head been bestowed upon virgins as well? If it is a disgrace for a woman to have her hair shorn, it is for a virgin then, also.

Since, then, one and the same condition is attributed to each in regard to the head, then one and the same regulation regarding the head is imposed upon them--even upon those virgins whom their tender age protects. For, right from the start she is included in the term 'woman.' Finally, Israel has the same regulation. But even if it did not, our law, amplified and supplemented, would demand an addition, imposing a veil upon virgins, also. Granted that at the moment that period of life which is unaware of its own sex should be excused. (Granted that it should retain the privilege of its innocence; for both Eve and Adam, when realization came to them, immediately covered what they had come to know.) At any rate, in the case of those who have left childhood, their age ought to confer much both by way of nature and of discipline. For women are revealed by their members and their duties. No one is a virgin from the time she is of marriageable age, since the age now in her has become the bride of its own partner, that is, time.

'But (suppose that) someone has consecrated herself to God.' Nevertheless, from this time on, she rearranges her hair and changes her whole appearance to that of a woman. Therefore, let her be earnest about the whole business and present the complete appearance of a virgin; what she conceals for God's sake let her keep completely out of sight. It is to our interest to entrust to the knowledge of God alone what is done for the sake of God, lest we bargain with men for what we hope to receive from God. Why do you expose before the eyes of God what you cover in the presence of men? Will you be more modest in the public street than in church? If it is a gift from God and 'thou hast received it, why dost thou boast,' says the Apostle, 'as if thou hadst not received it?' Why do you condemn other women by this exhibition of yourself? Or are you inviting others to good by your vanity? Yet you are in danger of losing it yourself if you boast of it, and you force others to the same dangers. That is easily destroyed which is assumed with an inclination to vanity. Virgin, cover your head if you are a virgin, for you ought to blush for shame! If you are a virgin, avoid the gaze of many eyes. Let no one look in admiration upon your face. Let no one realize your deceit. It is praiseworthy for you to create the false impression that you are married by covering your head. Rather, it will not be a false impression you are creating; for you are the bride of Christ. To Him you have surrendered your body; act according to the instructions of your Spouse. If He bids other men's brides to cover their heads, how much more His own!

'But (suppose that) someone thinks the arrangement of his predecessor should not be changed.' Many apply their own ideas and persistence in the same to the custom established by another. Granted that virgins should not be forced to cover their heads; at any rate, those who are willing to do so should not be prevented. If some cannot deny that they are virgins, they should be content, for the sake of preserving their conscience before God, to risk their reputation. However, in regard to those who are betrothed, I can declare and avow this with more than my usual firmness: their heads should be covered from the day when they first trembled at the kiss and handclasp of their future husband. For, in these symbols they have pledged every bit of themselves--their life throughout its full development, their flesh throughout their lifetime, their spirit through their understanding (of the contract), their modesty through the exchange of a kiss, their hope through their expectation, and their mind through their willingness. For us, Rebecca stands as sufficient example; when her future husband had been pointed out to her, she covered her head with her veil merely because she knew she was to marry him.

CHAPTER 23

With regard to kneeling, too, prayer allows a difference in custom because of certain ones--a very few--who stay off their knees on the Sabbath, an opposing point of view which is just now strongly defending itself in the churches.

The Lord will give His grace so that either they will yield, or else maintain their own opinion without giving scandal to others. As for ourselves, according to our tradition, only on the day (which commemorates) our Lord's Resurrection should we refrain from this custom; and not only from this, but from every sign that bespeaks solicitude and every ceremony arising therefrom. This includes deferring business, lest we give any opportunity to the Devil. The same holds for the season of Pentecost, which is marked by the same joyous celebration.

But who would hesitate every day to prostrate himself before God for at least the first prayer with which we approach the light of day?

Moreover, during the periods of fasting and on the station days no prayer should be said except on the knees and with every other sign of a humble spirit. For we are not merely praying, but beseeching and offering satisfaction to God our Lord.

CHAPTER 24

Regarding the time for prayer there has been no regulation at all, except that we are to pray at all times and everywhere. But how can we pray everywhere when we are forbidden to pray in public? 'In every place,' He said, which circumstance or even necessity provides. For it is not considered that when the Apostles, within the hearing of their guards, prayed in prison and sang to God they were acting contrary to the precept any more was Paul when, aboard ship, in the sight of all, he gave thanks to God.

CHAPTER 25

With regard to the time, the outward observance of certain hours will not be without profit. I refer to those hours of community prayer which mark the main divisions of the day, namely, Terce, Sext, and None. These, it can be found, are mentioned in holy Scripture as being more deserving of note.

It was at the third hour--Terce--when the disciples were assembled, that the Holy Spirit was infused into them for the first time.

It was at the sixth hour--Sext-- on the day when he had the vision of all creatures in the sheet that Peter had climbed to a higher spot in order to pray.

Similarly, it was at the ninth hour--None--that he went into the Temple with John where he restored the paralytic to health.

Although these incidents simply happen without any precept of observing (these hours), it would be good to establish some precedent which would make the admonition to pray a binding force to wrest us violently at times, as by a law, from our business to such an obligation so that we may offer adoration no less than three times a day at least, being debtors to the three divine Persons, Father, Son and Holy Spirit. And this, too, we read was observed by Daniel according to the rites of Israel. Of course, we are excepting the appropriate prayers which are due without any admonition at the approach of dawn and evening.

It is befitting for the faithful not to take food and not to bathe before saying a prayer. For the refreshment and food of the spirit are to be put before (the needs) of the flesh, because the things of heaven are to be put before those of the earth.

CHAPTER 26

When a brother has entered your home, do not let him go away without a prayer. ('You have seen,' He said, 'a brother; you have seen your Lord'). Particularly should this be observed in the case of a stranger, lest he should happen to be an angel.

But, even after one has been welcomed by his brethren, you should not attend to earthly refreshment before the heavenly. For immediately will your faith be revealed. Or how can you say, according to the precept, 'Peace to this house,' unless you exchange the kiss of peace with those who are in the house?

CHAPTER 27

Those who are more exact about prayer are in the habit of adding to their prayers an 'Alleluia' and psalms of such a character that those who are present may respond with the final phrases. Assuredly, the practice is excellent in every respect which by its high praise and reverence of God is competent to offer Him, as a rich victim, a prayer that has been filled out in every detail.

CHAPTER 28

Now, this is the spiritual victim which has set aside the earlier sacrifice. 'To what purpose do you offer me the multitude of your victims,' saith the Lord? 'I am full, I desire not holocausts of rams, and fat of fatlings, and blood of calves and goats. For who required these things at your hands?'

The Gospel teaches what God demands. 'The hour is coming,' He says, 'when the true worshipers will worship the Father in spirit and in truth. For God is spirit,' and therefore He requires that His worshipers be of the same nature.

We are the true worshipers and true priests who, offering our prayer in the spirit, offer sacrifice in the spirit--that is, prayer--as a victim that is appropriate and acceptable to God; this is what He has demanded and what He has foreordained for Himself.

This prayer, consecrated to Him with our whole heart, nurtured by faith, prepared with truth--a prayer that is without blemish because of our innocence, clean because of our chastity--a prayer that has received the victor's crown because of our love for one another--this prayer we should bring to the altar of God with a display of good works amid the singing of psalms and hymns and it will obtain for us from God all that we ask.

CHAPTER 29

For what will God refuse to the prayer that comes to Him from the spirit and in truth, since this is the prayer He has exacted? What proofs of its efficacy do we read of an hear of and believe! To be sure, the prayer of old would save one from fires and wild beasts and starvation; yet, had not received its form from Christ. But how much more wrought by Christian prayer! It does not cause an angel (dew to appear in the midst of fire, nor does it stop the mouth of lions nor take the breakfast of country folk to the hungry it does not destroy all sense of pain by the grace that is conferred; but by patient endurance it teaches those who suffer, those who are sensitive, and those who have sorrow; by virtue it increases grace that our faith may know what comes from the Lord and understand what it suffers for the name of God.

Then, too, in the past, prayer would impose stripes, set loose the armies of the enemy, and prevent the beneficent effects of rain. But now, the prayer of justice averts the wrath of God, is on the alert for enemies, and intercedes for persecutors. What wonder if it could wrest water from the heavens, when it could even ask for fire and obtain it! Prayer alone overcomes God; but Christ has willed that it work no evil, upon it He has conferred all power for good. Therefore, it has no power except to recall the souls of the dead from the very path of death, to make the weak recover, to heal the sick, to exorcise demons, to open prison doors, to loosen the chains of the innocent. It likewise remits sins, repels temptations, stamps out persecution, consoles the fainthearted, delights the courageous, brings travelers safely home, calms the waves, stuns robbers, feeds the poor, directs the rich, raises up the fallen, sustains the falling, and supports those who are on their feet.

Prayer is the wall of faith, our shield and weapons against the foe who studies us from all sides. Hence, let us never set forth unarmed. Let us be mindful of our guard-duty by day and our vigil by night. Beneath the arms of prayer let us guard the standard of our general, and let us pray as we await the bugle call of the angel.

All the angels pray, too; every creature prays; the beasts, domestic and wild, bend their knees, and as they go forth from their stables and caves they look up to heaven with no idle gaze. Even the birds, upon rising in the morning, mount into the sky and stretch out their wings as a cross in place of hands and say something which might seem to be a prayer. What need, then, is there of further discussion of the duty of prayer? Even our Lord Himself prayed, to whom be honor and power forever and ever.

Spectacles

by Tertullian

CHAPTER 1

Learn, O you servants of God who are just now entering upon His service, and you who have already solemnly sworn allegiance to Him recall what principle of faith, what reason inherent in truth, what rule in our way of life forbid, along with the other errors of the world, also the pleasures of the spectacles, lest by ignorance or self-deception anyone fall into sin.

For so strong is the appeal of pleasure that it can bring about a prolongation of ignorance with a resulting facility for sin, or a perversion of conscience leading to self-deception.

In addition, some may perhaps be allured to either error by the opinions of the heathens who commonly use the following arguments against us in this matter: such comforting and merely external pleasures of the eyes and ears are not opposed to religion which is founded in man's mind and conscience; neither is God offended by a man's enjoying himself, nor is taking delight in such enjoyment in its proper time and place a sin as long as the fear of God and God's honor remain unimpaired.

But this is precisely what we intend to prove: that these things are not compatible with true religion and true obedience to the true God.

There are some who think that the Christians, a sort of people ever ready to die, are trained in that stubbornness of theirs that they more easily despise life, once its ties have been cut, as it were, and lose their craving for that which, as far as they themselves are concerned, they have already made empty of everything desirable; and thus it is considered a rule laid down by human design and forethought rather than by divine command.

It would, indeed, be loathsome for people continuing in the enjoyment of such delightful pleasures to die for God. On the other hand, if what they say were true, stubbornness in a rule of life so strict as ours might well submit to a plan so apt.

CHAPTER 2

Moreover, there is no one of our adversaries who will not offer this excuse, too: that all things have been created by God and handed over to man--just as we Christians teach--and that they are undoubtedly good, as coming from a good Creator; and among them we must count all the various components that make up the spectacles, the horse, for instance, and the lion, the strength of body and the sweetness of voice. Accordingly, they say that a thing which exists by God's creation cannot be considered either foreign or opposed to God, nor must a thing which is not opposed to God, because it is not foreign to Him, be considered opposed to God's worshipers.

Obviously, they continue, the very structures of the places--the squared stones, unhewn stones, marble slabs and columns--also are all the handi-work of God who gave them to furnish the earth; indeed, the performances themselves take place under God's heaven. How clever in adducing proofs does human ignorance think itself, especially when it is afraid of losing some of these delights and enjoyments of the world!

Accordingly, you will find more people turned away from our religion by the danger to their pleasures than by the danger to their lives. For of death even a fool is not particularly afraid, feeling that it is a debt he owes to nature; but pleasure, inasmuch as it is born with man, even a sage does not despise, since both fool and sage have no other gratification in life but pleasure.

No one denies-- because everyone knows what nature of its own accord tells us--that God is the Creator of the universe, and that this universe is good and has been made over to man by its Creator.

But because they have no real knowledge of God--knowing Him only by natural law and not by right of friendship, knowing Him only from afar and not from intimate association--it is inevitable that they prove ignorant of His commands regarding the use of His creation. Likewise, must they be un-aware of the rival power that by its hostile actions seeks to pervert to wrong uses the things of divine creation. For with such defective knowledge of God one cannot know either His will or His adversary.

We must, then, consider not only by whom all things were created, but also by whom they were perverted. For in this way it will become clear for what use they were created, once it is evident for what use they were not.

The state of corruption differs vastly from that of innocence, because there is an enormous difference between the Creator and the perverter. Why, every form of evil-doing--misdeeds which also the heathens forbid and punish as such--comes from things created by God.

You see murder committed by iron dagger, poison, or magic incantation:

but iron, poisonous herbs, demons are all equally creatures of God. Yet, did the Creator design those creatures of His for man's destruction? Certainly not. He forbids man-slaying by the one summary commandment: 'Thou shalt not kill.'

In like manner, gold, brass, silver, ivory, wood, and any other material used in the manufacture of idols--who has brought them into the world if, not God, the Maker of the world? Yet, has He done this that they may be made into objects of worship set up in opposition to Himself? Certainly not. For the most grievous sin in His eyes is idolatry. What is there that offends God and is not His own? But, when it offends God, it has ceased to be His; and when it has ceased to be His, it offends Him.

Man himself, the perpetrator of every kind of villainy, is not only the work of God, but also His likeness--yet, both in body and spirit he has fallen away from his Creator. For we did not receive the eyes for gratifying carnal appetite, the tongue for speaking evil, the ears for listening to slander, the gullet for indulging in the sin of gluttony, the belly to be the gullet's partner, the organs of sex for immodest excesses, the hands for committing acts of violence, and the feet to lead a roving life; nor was the spirit implanted in the body that it might become a workshop for contriving acts of treachery and fraud and injustice. I think not.

For if God, who demands innocence of us, hates all wickedness, even if it be only in thought, then it is certain beyond all doubt that it was never His intention in creation that whatever He created should lead to acts He condemns, even if those acts are done through the medium of His handiwork. The whole reason for condemnation is, rather, the misuse of God's creation by God's creatures.

We, therefore, in coming to know the Lord, have also looked upon His rival, and in learning the Creator, we have likewise detected the perverter; we ought, then, to feel neither surprise nor doubt. For man himself, God's handiwork and image, the lord of the whole universe, was hurled down in the very beginning from his state of innocence by the power of that angel, perverter of God's creation and His rival, at the same time, that same perverter corrupted along with man the whole material world, man's possession, created like man for innocence, and turned it against the Creator. And in his anger that God had given it to man and not to him he intended to make man in this very possession guilty before God as well as establish his own power in it.

CHAPTER 3

Armed with this knowledge against heathen opinion, let us now turn, instead, to the same excuses put forward by people in our own ranks. For there are some brethren who, being either too naive or overparticular in their faith, demand a testimony from holy Scripture, when faced with giving up the spectacles, and declare the matter an open question, because such a renunciation is neither specifically nor in so many words enjoined upon the servants of God.

Now, to be sure, nowhere do we find it laid down with the same precision as 'Thou shalt not kill', 'Thou shalt not worship an idol', 'Thou shalt not commit adultery', 'Thou shalt not commit fraud'--nowhere do we find it thus clearly declared: 'Thou shalt not go to the circus', 'Thou shalt not go to the theater', 'Thou shalt not watch a contest or show of gladiators'.

But we do find that to this special case there can be applied that first verse of David, where he says: 'Happy is the man who has not gone to the gathering of the ungodly, nor stood in the ways of sinners, nor sat in the chair of pestilence'.

For, even though David seems to have praised that well-known just man, because he took no part in the gathering and meeting of the Jews deliberating on the killing of the Lord, divine Scripture admits always a broader interpretation wherever a passage, after its actual sense has been exhausted, serves to strengthen discipline. So, in this case, too, the verse of David is not inapplicable to the prohibition of spectacles.

For, if then he called a mere handful of Jews 'a gathering of the ungodly', how much more such a vast crowd of heathen people? Are the heathens less ungodly, less sinners, less the enemies of Christ that the Jews were then?

Moreover, the other details also fit in well. For at the spectacles there is both sitting 'in the chair' (in cathedra) and standing 'in the way' (in via). For 'ways' (viae) they term both the gangways that run round the girding walls and the aisles that slope down the incline and divide the seats of the populace; in like manner is the very place for chairs in the curving gallery called 'chair' (cathedra).

And so, to take the converse of the verse of David, 'he is unhappy who has gone to any gathering whatsoever of the ungodly, stood in any way at all of sinners, and sat in any chair of pestilence'. Let us take, then, the general application, even when, besides the general, a special interpretation is conceded. For some things that are said with special intent have also a general meaning.

When God reminds the Israelites of discipline and upbraids them, His words apply undoubtedly to all men; and when He threatens destruction to Egypt and Ethiopia, He certainly cautions every sinful nation against judgment to come. Thus, if we reason from a special case to the general type that every sinful nation is an Egypt and Ethiopia, in the same manner we reason from the general class to a special case that every spectacle is a gathering of the ungodly.

CHAPTER 4

Lest anyone think that I am avoiding the point in question, I shall now appeal to the prime and principal authority of our 'seal' itself. When we step into the water and profess the Christian faith in the terms prescribed by its law, we bear public witness that we have renounced the Devil and his pomp and his angels.

What, however, shall we call the chief and foremost manifestation by which the Devil and his pomp and his angels are recognized, if not idolatry? From this source, in a few words--because I will not dwell any longer on this subject--comes every unclean and evil spirit.

So, if it shall be proved true that the entire apparatus of the spectacles originates from idolatry, we will have reached a decision in advance that our profession of faith in baptism refers also to the spectacles, since they belong to the Devil and his pomp and his angels because of the idolatry involved.

We shall, therefore, set forth the origins of the various spectacles, explaining in what nurseries they grew up; next in order, the titles of some of them, that is, the names by which they are called; then their equipment and the superstitions observed in them; thereafter the places and the presiding spirits to whom they are dedicated; and finally the arts employed in them and the authors to whom they are ascribed. If, among these, we find anything that is not related to an idol, we shall declare it to be free from the stain of idolatry and, as a result, to have no connection with our renunciation.

CHAPTER 5

Concerning the origins of the spectacles, which are somewhat obscure and, therefore, unknown among most of our people, we had to make a rather thorough investigation, our authority being none other than the works of pagan literature.

There are many authors who have published treatises on the subject. They give the following report on the origin of the games. The Lydians migrated from Asia and settled in Etruria, according to the account of Timaeus, under the leadership of Tyrrhenus, who, in the struggle for the kingship, had succumbed to his brother. In Etruria, then, they also introduced, along with their other superstitious customs, the spectacles in the name of religion. From that place, in turn, the Romans invited the performers, borrowing also the name, so that the 'performers' (ludii) were so called from the 'Lydians' (Lydii).

And though Varro derives "ludii" from "ludus," that is, from "lusus" ('the play'), as they used to call also the Luperci "ludii," because, as "ludendo" ('in play') indicates, they ran to and fro, this play of the youths belongs in his view to festal days, temples, and religious ceremonies.

But it is, after all, not the name that matters; the real issue is idolatry. For, since the games also went under the general name of Liberalia, they clearly proclaimed the honor of Father Liber. They were first held in honor of Liber by the country folk because of the blessing which they say he bestowed upon them by making known to them the delicious taste of wine.

Then came the games called Consualia, which originally were celebrated in honor of Neptune, because he is also called Consus. After that, Romulus consecrated the Ecurria, derived from "equi" (horses), to Mars, though they claim the Consualia as well for Romulus on the ground that he consecrated them to Consus, the god, as they will have it, of counsel, to wit, of that very counsel by which he arrived at the scheme of carrying off the Sabine girls to be wives for his soldiers.

A noble counsel, indeed, even now considered just and lawful among the Romans themselves, not to say in the eyes of a god! For, also, this tends to stain their origin, lest you think something good that, had its origin in evil, in shamelessness, violence and hatred, in a founder who was a fratricide and the son of Mars.

Even now, at the first goal posts in the Circus, there is an underground altar dedicated to that Consus with an inscription that reads as follows: CONSUS MIGHTY IN COUNSEL, MARS IN WAR, THE LARES AT THE CROSSROAD. Sacrifice in offered on this altar on the seventh day of July by the priests of the state, and on the twenty-first of August by the Flamen of Quirinus and the Vestal Virgins.

On a later date, the same Romulus instituted games in honor of Jupiter Feretrius at the Tarpeian Rock, which, according to the tradition handed down by Piso, were called Tarpeian and Capitoline Games. After him, Numa Pompilius initiated games in honor of Mars and Robigo--for they invented also a goddess of "robigo" (mildew). Later still came Tullus Hostilius, then Ancus Martius and, in their order, the other founders of games. As to the idols in whose honor they bistituted these games, information is found in Tranquillus Suetonius or in his sources. But this will suffice to prove the guilty origin of the games in idolatry.

CHAPTER 6

The testimony of antiquity is confirmed by that of the succeeding generations. For the titles by which the games still go today betray the nature of their origin. In these titles there is clearly expressed for what idol and for what superstition of one kind or other they were designed.

For instance, the games of the Great Mother and Apollo, and also those of Ceres, Neptune, Jupiter Latiaris, and Flora are general festivals; the remaining trace their superstitious origin back to birthdays and commemorative celebrations of the emperors, to happy political events, and municipal feasts.

Among them are also the funeral games, established by bequests to render honor to the memory of private persons. This, too, is in accordance with ancient custom. For from the very beginning two kinds of games were distinguished: sacred and funereal; that is, games in honor of pagan deities and those in honor of dead persons.

But in the question of idolatry, it makes no difference to us under what name and title they are exhibited, as long as the matter concerns the same spirits that we renounce. Whether they exhibit these games in honor of their dead or in honor of their gods, they render the very same honor to their dead as to their gods. On either side you have one and the same situation: it is one and the same idolatry on their part, and one and the same renunciation of idolatry on our part.

CHAPTER 7

Both kinds of games, then, have a common origin; common, too, are their names, inasmuch as the reasons for their being held are the same. Therefore, also, their equipment must be the same because of the common guilt of idolatry which founded them.

Somewhat greater pomp, however, is displayed in the spectacles in the circus to which the term is properly applied. The "pompa"'procession'--which comes first, proves in itself to whom it belongs, with the long line of idols, the unbroken train of images, the cars and chariots and conveyances for carrying them, the portable thrones and garlands and the attributes of the gods.

Moreover, how many sacred rites are observed, how many sacrifices offered at the beginning, in the course, and at the end of the procession, how many religious corporations, furthermore, how many priesthoods, how many bodies of magistrates are called upon to march in it--each is known to the inhabitants of that city where all the demons have gathered and taken up their abode.

And if in the provinces less care is given to management of the games because of less ample funds, all the spectacles in the circus everywhere must be considered as belonging to the model from which they are copied, and are contaminated by the source from which they are drawn. For also, the small brook from its spring, and the tiny shoot from its stem, contain in them the nature of their origin.

Let splendor and frugality look to it where they come from. The pomp of the circus, whatever its nature, offends God. Even if there be carried but a few idols in procession, it takes only one to have idolatry; even if there be driven but one chariot, it is Jupiter's car; every kind of idolatry, even one meanly or moderately equipped, is still rich and splendid because of its sinful origin.

CHAPTER 8

In accordance with my plan, I shall deal next with the places. The circus is primarily consecrated to the Sun. His temple stands in the middle of it, and his image shines forth from the pediment of the temple. For they did not think it proper to worship beneath a roof a god whom they see above them in the open.

Those who maintain that the first circus show was exhibited by Circe in honor of the Sun, her father, as they will have it, conclude also that the name is derived from her. Plainly, the sorceress undoubtedly transacted the business in behalf of those whose priestess she was, namely, the demons and evil spirits. How many evidences of idol worship do you recognize accordingly in the decoration of the place?

Every ornament of the circus is a temple by itself. The eggs are regarded as sacred to Castor and Pollux by people who do not feel ashamed to believe the story of their origin from the egg made fertile by the swan, Jupiter. The dolphins spout water in honor of Neptune; the columns bear aloft images of Seia, so called from "sementatio" ('sowing'); of Messia, so called as deity of "messis" ('reaping'); and of Tutulina, so called as 'tutelary spirit' of the crops.

In front of these are seen three altars for the triple gods: the Great, the Potent, the Prevailing. They think these deities are Samothracean.

The huge obelisk, as Hermateles maintains, has been set up in honor of the Sun. Its inscription which, like its origin, is Egyptian, contains a superstition. The gathering of the demons would be dull without their Great Mother, so she presides there over the ditch.

Consus, as we have mentioned, keeps in hiding underground at the Murcian Goals. The latter are also the work of an idol. For Murcia, as they will have it, is a goddess of love to whom they have dedicated a temple in that part (of the valley).

Take note, O Christian, how many unclean deities have taken possession of the circus. You have nothing to do with a place which so many diabolic spirits have made their own. Speaking of places, this is the appropriate occasion for throwing more light on the subject in order to anticipate a question that some may raise.

What will happen, you say, if I enter the circus at some other time? Shall I be then, too, in danger of contamination? There is no law laid down with regard to places as such. For not only these places where people gather for the spectacles but also the temples may be entered by the servant of God without peril to his rule of life, provided that he do so for an urgent and honest reason which has no connection with the business and function proper of the place.

Moreover, there is no place--whether streets or marketplace or baths or taverns or even our own homes--that is completely free of idols: Satan and his angels have filled the whole world.

Yet, it is not by our being in the world that we fall away from God, but by taking part in some sins of the world. Therefore, if I enter the temple of Jupiter on the Capitol or that of Serapis as a sacrificer or worshiper, I shall fall away from God, just as I do if I enter the circus theater as a spectator. It is not the places in themselves the defile us, but the things done in them, by which the places themselves, as we have contended, are defiled; it is by defiled that we are defiled.

It is for this reason that we remind you who those to whom places of this kind are dedicated to prove what takes place in them is the work of those to whom very places are sacred.

CHAPTER 9

Next let us consider the arts displayed in the circus games. In times past, equestrian skill was simply a matter riding on horseback, and certainly no guilt was involved the ordinary use of the horse. But when this skill was pressed into the service of the games, it was changed from a gift God into an instrument of the demons.

Accordingly, t kind of exhibition is regarded as sacred to Castor and Pollux to whom horses were allotted by Mercury, as Stesichorus tells us. Also, Neptune is an equestrian deity, since the Greeks call him "Hippios" ('Lord of Steeds').

Moreover, concerning the chariot, the four-horse team was consecrated to the Sun; the two horse team, to the Moon. But we also read: "Erichthonius first dared to yoke four steeds to the car And to ride upon its wheels with victorious swiftness." This Erichthonius, a son of Minerva and Vulcan, fruit of lust, in truth, that fell to earth, is a demon-monster, or, rather, the Devil himself, not a mere snake.

If, however, the Argive Trochilus is the inventor of the chariot, he dedicated this work of his in the first place to Juno. And if, at Rome, Romulus was the first to display a four-horse chariot, he, too, in my view, has been enrolled among the idols himself, provided that he is identical with Quirinus.

The chariots having been produced by such inventors, it was only fitting that they clad their drivers in the colors of idolatry. For at first there were only two colors: white and red. White was sacred to Winter because of the whiteness of its snow; red, to Summer because of the redness of its sun. But afterwards, when both love of pleasure and superstition had grown apace, some dedicated the red to Mars, others the white to the Zephyrs, the green to Mother Earth or Spring, the blue to Sky and Sea or Autumn.

Since, however, every kind of idolatry is condemned by God, this condemnation certainly applies also to that kind which is impiously offered to the elements of nature.

CHAPTER 10

Let us pass on to the exhibitions on the stage. We have already shown that they have a common origin with those in the circus, that they bear identical titles, inasmuch as they were called "ludi" ('games') and were exhibited together with equestrian displays.

The pageantry is likewise the same, inasmuch as a procession is held to the theater from the temples and altars, with that whole wretched business of incense and blood, to the tune of flutes and trumpets, under the direction of the two most polluted masters of ceremonies at funerals and sacrifices: the undertaker and soothsayer.

And so, as we passed from the origins of the games to the spectacles in the circus, now we will turn to the performances on the stage. Because of the evil character of the place, the theater is, strictly speaking, a shrine of Venus. It was in that capacity, after all, that this type of structure gained influence in the world.

For many a time the censors would tear down theaters at the very moment they began to rise. In their solicitude for public morals, they foresaw, no doubt, the great danger arising from the theater's lasciviousness. In this occurrence already, then, the heathens have their own opinion coinciding with ours as evidence, and we have the foreboding situation of a merely human code of morality giving additional strength to our way of life.

So, when Pompey the Great, a man who was surpassed only by his theater in greatness, had erected that citadel of all vile practices, he was afraid that some day the censors would condemn his memory. He therefore built on top of it a shrine of Venus, and when he summoned the people by edict to its dedication, he termed it not a theater, but a temple of Venus, 'under which,' he said, 'we have put tiers of seats for viewing the shows.'

In this way he misrepresented the character of a building, condemned and worthy of condemnation, with a temple's name, and employed superstition to make sport of morality. Venus and Liber (Bacchus), however, are close companions. The two demons of lust and drunkenness have banded together in sworn confederacy.

Therefore, the temple of Venus is also the house of Liber. For they appropriately gave the name of Liberalia also to other stage performances which, besides being dedicated to Liber (and called Dionysia among the Greeks), were also instituted by him.

And, quite obviously, the arts of the stage are under the patronage of Liber and Venus. Those features which are peculiar to, and characteristic of, the stage, that wantonness in gesture and posture, they dedicate to Venus and Liber, deities both dissolute: the former by sex perversion, the latter by effeminate dress.

And all else that is performed with voice and melodies, instruments and script, belongs to the Apollos and the Muses, the Minervas and Mercuries. You will hate, O Christian, the things whose authors you cannot help but hate.

At this point we intend to make a few remarks concerning the arts and things whose authors we utterly detest in their very names. We know that the names of dead men are nothing, even as their images are nothing. But we are not unaware of the identity of those who are at work behind those displayed names and images, who exult in the homage paid to them and pretend to be divine, namely, the evil spirits, the demons.

We see then, also, that the arts are consecrated to the honor of those who appropriate the names of the inventors of those arts, and that they are not free from the taint of idolatry when their inventors for that very reason are considered gods.

Even more, as far as the arts are concerned, we ought to have gone further back and take exception to all further arguments, on the ground that the demons, from the very beginning looking out for themselves contrived, along with the other foul practices of idolatry, also those of the shows in order to turn man from the Lord and bind him to their glorification, and gave inspiration to men of genius in these particular arts.

For no one else but the demons would have contrived what was going to redound to their advantage, nor would they have produced the arts at that time through the agency of anyone except those very men in whose names and images and fables they accomplished the fraud of consecration which would work out to their advantage. To follow our plan, let us now begin the treatment of the contests (agones).

CHAPTER 11

Their origin is akin to that of the games. As a result, they, too, are instituted either as sacred or as funereal, and are performed in honor either of the gods of the Gentiles or of the dead. Accordingly, you have such titles as the Olympian contests in honor of Jupiter (these are called the Capitoline at Rome), the Nemean in honor of Hercules, the Isthmian in honor of Neptune; the rest are various contests to honor the dead.

What wonder is it, then, if the whole paraphernalia of these contests are tainted with idolatry--with unholy crowns, priestly superintendents, assistants from the sacred colleges, and last, but not least, with the blood of bulls?

To add a supplementary remark concerning the place: as you may expect from a place where the arts of the Muses, of Minerva, of Apollo, and even of Mars meet in common, with contest and sound of trumpet they endeavor to equal the circus in the stadium, which is no doubt a temple, too--I mean of the very idol whose festival is celebrated there.

The gymnastic arts also had their origin in the teaching of the Castors and Herculeses and Mercuries.

CHAPTER 12

It still remains to examine the most prominent an most popular spectacle of all. It is called "munus" ('a obligatory service') from being an "officium" ('a duty'). For "munus" and "officium" are synonyms. The ancients thought they were performing a duty to the dead by this sort of spectacle after they had tempered its character by a more refined form of cruelty.

For in time long past, in accordance with the belief that the souls of the-dead are propitiated by human blood, they used to purchase captives or slaves of inferior ability and to sacrifice them at funerals.

Afterwards, they preferred to disguise this ungodly usage by making it a pleasure. So, after the persons thus procured had been trained--for the sole purpose of learning how to be killed!-- in the use of such arms as they then had and as best as they could wield, they then exposed them to death at the tombs on the day appointed for sacrifices in honor of the dead. Thus they found consolation for death in murder.

Such is the origin of the gladiatorial contest. But gradually their refinement progressed in the same proportion as their cruelty. For the pleasure of these beasts in human shape was not satisfied unless human bodies were torn to pieces also by wild beasts. What was then a sacrifice offered for the appeasement of the dead was no doubt considered a rite in honor of the dead. This sort of thing is, therefore, idolatry, because idolatry, too, is a kind of rite in honor of the dead: the one and the other is a service rendered to dead persons.

It is, furthermore, in the images of the dead that the demons have their abode. To come to the consideration of the titles also: though this type of exhibition has been changed from being an act in honor of the dead to being one in honor of the living--I mean those entering upon quaestorships, magistracies, flaminates, and priesthoods--still, since the guilt of idolatry cleaves the dignity of the title, whatever is carried out in the name this dignity shares necessarily in the taint of its origin.

In the same way we must interpret the paraphernal which are considered as belonging to the ceremonies of the very offices. For the purple robes, the fasces, the fillets, and crowns--finally, also, the announcements made in meeting and on posters, and the pottage dinners given on the eve of exhibitions--do not lack the pomp of the Devil and the invocation of demons.

In conclusion, what shall I say about that horrible place which not even perjurers can bear? For the amphitheater is consecrated to names more numerous and more dreadful than the Capitol, temple of all demons as it is. There, as many unclean spirits have their abode as the place can seat men. And to say a final word about the arts concerned, we know that Mars and Diana are the patrons of both types of games.

CHAPTER 13

I have, I think, adequately carried out my plan by showing in how many and in what ways the spectacles involve idolatry. I discussed their origins, their names, their equipment, their locations, and their arts--all that we may be certain that the spectacles in no way become us who twice renounce idols.

'Not that an idol is anything,' as the Apostle says, 'but because what they do, they do in honor of demons' who take up their abode there at the consecration of idols, whether of the dead, or, as they think, of gods.

It is for this reason, therefore, since both kinds of idols belong to one and the same category (the dead and the gods being the same thing) that we refrain from both types of idolatry.

Temples and tombs, we detest both equally; we know neither kind of altar, we adore neither kind of image, we offer no sacrifice, we celebrate no funeral rites. Nor do we eat of what is sacrificed, or offered at funeral rites, because 'we cannot share the Lord's supper and the supper of demons.'

If we keep, then, our palate and stomach free from defilement, how much more should we guard our nobler organs, our ears and eyes, from pleasures connected with sacrifices to idols and sacrificers to the dead--pleasures which do not pass through the bowels, but are digested in the very spirit and so with whose purity God is more concerned than with that of the bowels.

CHAPTER 14

Having established the charge of idolatry, which itself should be reason enough for our giving up the spectacles, let us now treat the matter fully from another point of view, chiefly for the benefit of those who delude themselves with the thought that such abstention is not expressly enjoined.

The latter excuse sounds as if judgment enough were not pronounced on spectacles, when the lusts of the world are condemned. For, just as there is a lust for money, a lust for high station in life, for gluttony, for sensual gratification, for fame, so there is a lust for pleasure. The spectacles, however are a sort of pleasure.

In my opinion, under the general heading of lust, there are also included pleasures; similarly, under the general idea of pleasures, spectacles are treated as a special class.

CHAPTER 15

Dealing with the matter of the places, we have already mentioned above that they do not contaminate us of themselves, but on account of what is done in them, that is, once these places have imbibed contamination by such actions, they spit it out again to the same degree on others. So much, then, as we have said, for the main charge: idolatry. Now let us also point out that the other characteristics of the things which are going on at the spectacles are all opposed to God.

God has given us the command both to deal with the Holy Spirit in tranquillity, gentleness, quiet, and peace, inasmuch as, in accordance with the goodness of His nature, He is tender and sensitive, and also not to vex Him by frenzy, bitterness of feeling, anger, and grief.

How, then, can the Holy Spirit have anything to do with spectacles? There is no spectacle without violent agitation of the soul. For, where you have pleasure, there also is desire which gives pleasure its savor; where you have desire, there is rivalry which gives desire its savor.

And where, in turn, you have rivalry, there also are frenzy and bitterness of feeling and anger and grief and the other effects that spring from them, and, moreover, are incompatible with our moral discipline.

For, even if a man enjoys spectacles modestly and soberly, as befits his rank, age, and natural disposition, he cannot go to them without his mind being roused and his soul being stirred by some unspoken agitation.

No one ever approaches a pleasure such as this without passion; no one experiences this passion without its damaging effects. These very effects are incitements to passion. On the other hand, if the passion ceases, there is no pleasure, and he who goes where he gains nothing is convicted of foolishness.

But I think that foolishness also is foreign to us. Is it, further, not true that a man really condemns himself when he has taken his place among those whose company he does not want and whom, at any rate, he confesses to detest?

It is not enough to refrain from such acts, unless we also shun those who commit them. 'If thou didst see a thief,' says holy Scripture, 'thou didst run with him.' Would that we did not live in the world with them! Still, we are separated from them in the things of the world. For the world is God's, but the things of the world are the Devil's.

CHAPTER 16

Since, then, frenzy is forbidden us, we are debarred from every type of spectacle, including the circus, where frenzy rules supreme. Look at the populace, frenzied even as it comes to the show, already in violent commotion, blind, wildly excited over its wagers.

The praetor is too slow for them; all the time their eyes are rolling as though in rhythm with the lots he shakes up in his urn. Then they await the signal with bated breath, one outcry voices the common madness.

Recognize the madness from their foolish behavior. 'He has thrown it!' they shout; everyone tells everybody else what all of them have seen just that moment. This I take as a proof of their blindness: they do not see what has been thrown--a signal cloth, they think--but it is the symbol of the Devil hurled headlong from on high.

Accordingly, from such beginnings the affair progresses to outbursts of fury and passion and discord and to everything forbidden to the priests of peace. Next come curses, insults without any justified reason for the hatred, and rounds of applause without the reward of affection.

What are the partakers in all this --no longer their own masters--likely to achieve for themselves? At best, the loss of their self-control. They are saddened by another's bad luck; they rejoice in another's success. What they hope for and what they dread has nothing to do with themselves, and so their affection is to no purpose and their hatred is unjust.

Or are we, perhaps, permitted love without cause any more than to hate without cause? God who bids us to love our enemies certainly forbids us to hate even with cause; God who commands us to bless those who curse us does not permit us to curse even with cause.

But what is more merciless than the circus, where they do not even spare their rulers or their fellow citizens? If any of these frenzies of the circus become the faithful elsewhere, then it will be lawful also in the circus; but, if nowhere, then neither in the circus.

CHAPTER 17

In like manner we are commanded to steer clear of every kind of impurity. By this command, therefore, we are precluded also from the theater, which is impurity's own peculiar home, where nothing wins approval but what elsewhere finds approval.

And so, the theater's greatest charm is above all produced by its filth--filth which the actor of the Atellan farces conveys by gestures; filth which the mimic actor even exhibits by womanish apparel, banishing all reverence for sex and sense of shame so that they blush more readily at home than on the stage; filth, finally, which the pantomime experiences in his own body from boyhood in order to become an artist.

Even the very prostitutes, the victims of public lust, are brought upon the stage, creatures feeling yet more wretched in the presence of women, the only members in the community who were unaware of their existence; now they are exhibited in public before the eyes of persons of every age and rank; their address, their price, their record are publicly announced, even to those who do not need the information, and (to say nothing of the rest) things which ought to remain hidden in the darkness of their dens so as not to contaminate the daylight.

Let the senate blush, let all the orders blush, let even those very women who have committed murder on their own shame blush once a year when, by their own gestures, they betray their fear of the light of the day and the gaze of the people.

Now, if we must detest every kind of impurity, why should we be allowed to hear what we are not allowed to speak, when we know that vile jocularity and every idle word are judged by God? Why, in like manner, should we be permitted to see that which is sinful to do? Why should things which, spoken by the mouth, defile a man not be regarded as defiling a man when allowed access by the ears and eyes, since the ears and eyes are the servants of the spirit, and he whose servants are filthy cannot claim to be clean himself?

You have, therefore, the theater prohibited in the prohibition of uncleanness. Again, if we reject the learning of the world's literature as convicted of foolishness before God, we have a sufficiently clear rule also concerning those types of spectacles which, in profane literature, are classified as belonging to the comic or tragic stage.

Now, if tragedies and comedies are bloody and wanton, impious and prodigal inventors of outrage and lust, the recounting of what is atrocious or base is no better; neither is what is objectionable in deed acceptable in word.

CHAPTER 18

Now, if you maintain that the stadium is mentioned in the Scriptures, I will admit at once that you have a point. But as for what is done in the stadium, you cannot deny that it is unfit for you to see--punches and kicks and blows and all the reckless use of the fist and every disfiguration of the human face, that is, of God's image.

Never can you approve the foolish racing and throwing feats and the more foolish jumping contests ; never can you be pleased with either harmful or foolish exhibitions of strength nor with the cultivation of an unnatural body, outdoing the craftsmanship of God; you will hate men bred to amuse the idleness of Greece.

Also, the art of wrestling belongs to the Devil's trade: it was the Devil who first crushed men. The very movements of the wrestler have a snakelike quality: the grip that takes hold of the opponent, the twist that binds him, the sleekness with which he slips away from him. Crowns are of no use to you; why do you seek pleasure from crowns?

CHAPTER 19

Are we now to wait for a scriptural repudiation of the amphitheater, also? If we can claim that cruelty, impiety, and brutality are permitted us, let us by all means go to the amphi-theater. If we are what people say we are, let us take delight in human blood.

It is a good thing when the guilty are punished. Who will deny this but the guilty? Yet it is not becoming for the guiltless to take pleasure in the punishment of another; rather, it befits the guiltless to grieve that a man like himself, has become so guilty that he is treated with such cruelty.

And who is my voucher that it is the guilty always who are condemned to the beasts, or whatever punishment, and that it is never inflicted on innocence, too, through the vindictiveness of the judge or the weakness of the defense or the intensity of the torture? How much better it is, then, not to know when the wicked are punished, lest I come to know also when the good are destroyed, provided, of course, that there is savor of good in them.

Certain it is that innocent men are sold as gladiators to serve as victims of public pleasure. Even in the case of those who are condemned to the games, what a preposterous idea is it that, in atonement for a smaller offense, they should be driven to the extreme of murder!

This reply I have addressed to Gentiles. Heaven forbid that a Christian should need any further instruction about the detestableness of this kind of spectacle. No one, however, is able to describe all the details at full length except one who is still in the habit of going to the spectacles. I myself prefer to leave the picture incomplete rather than to recall it.

CHAPTER 20

How foolish, then--rather, how desperate--is the reasoning of those who, obviously as a subterfuge to avoid the loss of pleasure, plead as their excuse that no regulation concerning such an abstinence is laid down in Scripture, precise terms or in a definite passage, forbidding the servant of God to enter gatherings of this kind.

Only recently heard a novel defense offered by one of these devotees of games. 'The sun,' he said, 'nay, even God Himself, looks from heaven and is not defiled.' Why, the sun also sends rays into the sewer and is not soiled!

Would that God looked on at no sins of men that we might all escape judgment! But He looks on at robberies, He looks on at falsehood and adulteries and frauds and acts of idolatry and at the very spectacles. And it is for that reason that we will not look at them, lest we be seen by Him who looks on at everything.

My man, you are putting the defendant on the same footing as the judge: the defendant who is a defendant because he is seen, and the judge who, because he sees, is judge.

Do we, perhaps, indulge in frenzy also outside the confines of the circus, outside the gates of the theater give free play to lewdness, outside the stadium to haughty deportment, outside the amphitheater to cruelty, just because

God has eyes also outside the covered seats and the tiers and the stage? We are wrong: nowhere and never is there any exemption from what God condemns; nowhere and never is there any permission for what is forbidden always and everywhere.

It is the freedom from the change of opinion and from the mutability of judgment that constitutes the fullness of truth and--what is due to truth--perfect morality, unvarying reverence, and faithful obedience. What is intrinsically good or evil cannot be anything else.

CHAPTER 21

All things, we maintain, are firmly defined by the truth of God. The heathens who do not possess the fullness of truth, since their teacher of truth is not God, form their judgment of good and evil in accordance with their own opinion and inclination, making what is good in one place evil in another, and what is evil in one place good in another.

Thus it happens that the same man who in public will scarcely raise the tunic to ease nature will put it off in the circus in such a way as to expose himself completely to the gaze of all; and the man who protects the ears of his maiden daughter from every foul word will take her himself to the theater to hear such words and see the gestures which accompany them.

The same man who tries to break up or denounces a quarrel in the streets which has come to fisticuffs will in the stadium applaud fights far more dangerous; and the same man who shudders at the sight of the body of a man who died in accordance with nature's law common to all will in the amphitheater look down with tolerant eyes upon bodies mangled, rent asunder, and smeared with their own blood.

What is more, the same man who allegedly comes to the spectacle to show his approval of the punishment   for murder will have a reluctant gladiator driven on with lashes and with rods to commit murder; and the same man who wants every more notorious murderer to be cast before the lion will have the staff and cap of liberty granted as a reward to a savage gladiator, while he will demand that the other man who has been slain be dragged back to feast his eyes upon him, taking delight in scrutinizing close at hand the man he wished killed at a distance--and, if that was not his wish, so much more heartless he!

CHAPTER 22

What wonder! Such are the inconsistencies of men who confuse and confound the nature of good and evil through their fickleness of feeling and instability in judgment.

Take the treatment the very providers and managers of the spectacles accord to those idolized charioteers, actors, athletes, and gladiators, to whom men surrender their souls and women even their bodies, on whose account they commit the sins they censure: for the very same skill for which they glorify them, they debase and degrade them; worse, they publicly condemn them to dishonor and deprivation of civil rights, excluding them from the council chamber, the orator's platform, the senatorial and equestrian orders, from all other offices and certain distinctions.

What perversity! They love whom they penalize; they bring into disrepute whom they applaud; they extol the art and brand the artist with disgrace.

What sort of judgment is this--that a man should be vilified for the things that win him a reputation? Yes, what an admission that these things are evil, when their authors, at the very peak of their popularity, are marked with disgrace!

CHAPTER 23

Since, then, man reflecting on these matters, even over against the protest and appeal of pleasure, comes to the conclusion that these people should be deprived of the benefits of posts of honor and exiled to some island of infamy, how much more will divine justice inflict punishment on those who follow such professions?

Or will God take pleasure in the charioteer, the disturber of so many souls, the minister to many outbursts of frenzy, flaunting his rostral crown as a priest wears his wreath, dressed up in gay colors like a pimp, attired by the Devil as a ludicrous counterpart of Elias to be swept away in his chariot?

Will God be pleased with the man who alters his features with a razor, belying his own countenance and, not content with making it resemble that of Saturn or Isis or Liber, on top of that submits it to the indignity of being slapped, as if in mockery of the Lord's commandment?

The Devil, to be sure, also teaches that one should meekly offer his cheek to be struck. In the same way, he also makes the tragic actors taller by means of their high shoes, because 'no one can add a single cubit to his stature.' He wishes to make Christ a liar.

Again, I ask whether this whole business of masks is pleasing to God, who forbids the likeness of anything to be made--how much more of His own image? The Author of truth does not love anything deceitful; all that is counterfeit is a kind of adultery in His eyes.

Accordingly, He will not approve the man who feigns voice, sex, or age, or who pretends love, anger, groans, or tears, for He condemns all hypocrisy. Moreover, since in His law He brands the man as accursed who dresses in woman's clothes, what will be His judgment upon the pantomime who is trained to play the woman?

No doubt, also, the artist in punching will go unpunished. For those scars and wales, marks left by boxing gloves and blows, and those growths upon his ears he got from God when his body was being fashioned; God gave him eyes to have them blinded in fighting!

I say nothing of the man who pushes another to the lion lest he seem less a murderer than the fellow who afterwards cuts the same victim's throat.

CHAPTER 24

In how many ways are we expected to prove that none of the things connected with the spectacles is pleasing to God? Or, because it is not pleasing to God, befits His servant?

If we have shown that all these things have been instituted for the Devil's sake, and furnished from the Devil's stores (for everything which is not God's or which displeases God is the Devil's), then this represents the pomp of the Devil which we renounce in the 'seal' of faith.

No share, however, ought we to have, whether in deed or word, whether by beholding or watching, in what we renounce. Moreover, if we ourselves renounce and rescind the 'seal' by making void our testimony to it, does it remain, then, for us to seek an answer from the heathen? Yes, let them tell us whether it be permitted for Christians to attend a spectacle. Why, for them this is the principal sign of a man's conversion to the Christian faith, that he renounces the spectacles.

A man, therefore, who removes the mark by which he is recognized, openly denies his faith. What hope is there left for such a man? No one deserts to the camp of the enemy without first throwing away weapons, deserting his standards, renouncing his oath of allegiance to his leader, and without pledging himself to die with the enemy.

CHAPTER 25

Will the man, seated where there is nothing of God, at that moment think of God? He will have peace in his soul, I suppose, as he cheers for the charioteer; he will learn purity as he gazes with fascination at the mimic actors.

No, indeed, in every kind of spectacle he will meet with no greater temptation than that over careful attire of women and men. That sharing of feelings and that agreement or disagreement over favorites fan the sparks of lust from their fellowship.

Finally, no one going to a spectacle has any other thought but to see and be seen. But, while the tragic actor is ranting, our good friend will probably recall the outcries of some prophet! Amid the strains of the effeminate flute-player, he will no doubt meditate on a psalm! And while the athletes are engaged in combat, he is sure to say that a blow must not be struck in return for a blow!

He will, therefore, also be in a position to let himself be stirred by pity, with his eyes fixed on the bears as they bite, and the net-fighters as they roll up their nets. May God avert from His own such a passion for murderous delight!

What sort of behavior is it to go from the assembly of God to the assembly of the Devil, from sky to sty, as the saying goes? Those hands which you have lifted up to God, to tire them out afterwards applauding an actor? To cheer a gladiator with the same lips with which you have said 'Amen' over the Most Holy? To call out 'for ever and ever' to anyone else but to God and Christ?

CHAPTER 26

Why, then, should such people not also be susceptible to demoniac possession? For we have the case of that woman--the Lord is witness--who went to the theater and returned home having a demon.

So, when in the course of exorcism the unclean spirit was hard pressed with the accusation that he had dared to seize a woman who believed, he answered boldly: 'I was fully justified in doing so, for I found her in my own domain.'

It is well known, too, that to another woman, during the night following the very day on which she had listened to a tragic actor, a shroud was shown in a dream, and a rebuke called out to her, mentioning the tragic actor by name; nor was that woman still alive after five days.

Indeed, how many other proofs can be drawn from those who, by consorting with the Devil at the spectacles, have fallen away from the Lord. For 'no man can serve two masters. ' 'What fellowship has light with darkness?' What has life to do with death?

CHAPTER 27

We ought to hate those gatherings and meetings of the heathen, seeing that there the name of God is blasphemed, there the cry to set the lions upon us is raised every day, there persecutions have their source, thence temptations are let loose.

What will you do when you are caught in that surging tide of wicked applause? Not that you are likely to suffer anything there at the hands of men (no one recognizes you as a Christian), but consider how you would fare in heaven.

Do you doubt that at the very moment when the Devil is raging in his assembly, all the angels look forth from heaven and note down every individual who has uttered blasphemy, who has listened to it, who has lent his tongue, who has lent his ears to the service of the Devil against God?

Will you, therefore, not shun the seats of Christ's enemies, that 'chair of pestilences', and the very air that hangs over it and is polluted with sinful cries? I grant you that you have there some things that are sweet, pleasant, harmless, and even honorable. No one flavors poison with gall and hellebore; it is into spicy, well-flavored, and mostly sweet dishes that he instills that noxious stuff. So, too, the Devil pours into the deadly draught he prepares the most agreeable and most welcome gifts of God.

Everything, then, you find there, whether manly or honorable or sonorous or melodious or tender, take it for drippings of honey from a poisoned cake, and do not consider your appetite for the pleasure worth the danger you run from its sweetness.

CHAPTER 28

Let the Devil's own guests stuff themselves with sweets of that sort: the places, the times, and the host who invites are theirs. Our banquet, or marriage feast, has not yet come. We cannot recline with them at table, as they cannot with us. Things in this matter run their course in succession. Now they rejoice, and we are afflicted.

'The world,' holy Scripture says, 'will rejoice, you will be sad.' Let us mourn therefore while the heathen rejoice, that, when they have begun to mourn, we may rejoice: lest sharing their joy now, then we may be sharing their mourning too.

You are too dainty, O Christian, if you desire pleasure also in this world; nay, more, you are a fool altogether if you deem this pleasure.

The philosophers at least have given the name 'pleasure' to quiet and tranquillity; in it they rejoice, they find their diversion in it, they even glory in it. But you—why, I find you sighing for goal posts, the stage, dust, the arena.

I wish you would say plainly: 'We cannot live without pleasure!' Whereas we ought to die with pleasure. For what other prayer have we but that of the Apostle--'to leave the world and find our place with the Lord'? Our pleasure is where our prayer is.

CHAPTER 29

And finally, if you think that you are to pass this span of life in delights, why are you so ungrateful as not to be satisfied with so many and so exquisite pleasures given you by God, and not to recognize them? For what is more delightful than reconciliation with God, our Father and Lord, than the revelation of truth, the recognition of errors, and pardon for such grievous sins of the past?

What greater pleasure is there than distaste of pleasure itself, than contempt of all the world can give, than true liberty, than a pure conscience, than a contented life, than freedom from fear of death?

To trample under foot the gods of the heathen, to drive out demons, to effect cures, to seek revelations, to live unto God --these are the pleasures, these are the spectacles of the Christians, holy, everlasting, and free of charge. In these find your circus games: behold the course of the world, count the generations slipping by, bear in mind the goal of the final consummation, defend the bonds of unity among the local churches, awake at the signal of God, arise at the angel trumpet, glory in the palms of martyrdom.

If the literary accomplishments of the stage delight you, we have sufficient literature of our own, enough verses and maxims, also enough songs and melodies; and ours are not fables, but truths, not artful devices, but plain realities.

Do you want contests in boxing and wrestling? Here they are --contests of no slight account, and plenty of them. Behold impurity overthrown by chastity, faithlessness slain by faith, cruelty crushed by mercy, impudence put in the shade by modesty. Such are the contests among us, and in these we win our crowns. Do you have desire for blood, too? You have the blood of Christ.

CHAPTER 30

Moreover, what a spectacle is already at hand--the second coming of the Lord, now no object of doubt, now exalted, now triumphant! What exultation will that be of the angels, what glory of the saints as they rise again! What a kingdom, the kingdom of the just thereafter! What a city, the new Jerusalem!

But there are yet other spectacles to come--that day of the Last Judgment with its everlasting issues, unlooked for by the heathen, the object of their derision, when the hoary age of the world and all its generations will be consumed in one file.

What a panorama of spectacle on that day! Which sight shall excite my wonder? Which, my laughter? Where shall I rejoice, where exult--as I see so many and so mighty kings, whose ascent to heaven used to be made known by public announcement, now along with Jupiter himself, along with the very witnesses of their ascent, groaning in the depths of darkness? Governors of provinces, too, who persecuted the name of the Lord, melting in flames fiercer than those they themselves kindled in their rage against the Christians braving them with contempt?

Whom else shall I behold? Those wise philosophers blushing before their followers as they burn together, the followers whom they taught that the world is no concern of God's whom they assured that either they had no souls at all or that what souls they had would never return to their former bodies? The poets also, trembling, not before the judgment seat of Rhadamanthus or of Minos, but of Christ whom they did not expect to meet.

Then will the tragic actors be worth hearing, more vocal in their own catastrophe; then the comic actors will be worth watching, more lither of limb in the fire; then the charioteer will be worth seeing, red all over on his fiery wheel; then the athletes will be worth observing, not in their gymnasiums, but thrown about by fire--unless I might not wish to look at them even then but would prefer to turn an insatiable gaze on those who vented their rage on the Lord.

'This is He,' I will say, 'the son of the carpenter and the harlot, the sabbath-breaker, the Samaritan who had a devil. This is He whom you purchased from Judas, this is He who was struck with reed and fist, defiled with spittle, given gall and vinegar to drink. This is He whom the disciples secretly stole away to spread the story of His resurrection, or whom the gardener removed lest his lettuces be trampled by the throng of curious idlers.'

What praetor or consul or quaestor or priest with all his munificence will ever bestow on you the favor of beholding and exulting in such sights? Yet, such scenes as these are in a measure already ours by faith in the vision of the spirit. But what are those things which 'eye has not seen nor ear heard and which have not entered into the heart of man'? Things of greater delight, I believe, than circus, both kinds of theater, and any stadium.

To the Martyrs

by Tertullian

CHAPTER 1

Blessed martyrs elect, along with the nourishment for the body which our Lady Mother the Church from her breast, as well as individual brethren from their private resources, furnish you in prison, accept also from me some offering that will contribute to the sustenance of the spirit. For it is not good that the flesh be feasted while the spirit goes hungry. Indeed, if care is bestowed on that which is weak, there is all the more reason not to neglect that which is still weaker.

Not that I am specially entitled to exhort you. Yet, even the most accomplished gladiators are spurred on not only by their trainers and managers but also from afar by people inexperienced in this art and by all who choose, without the slightest need for it, with the result that hints issuing from the crowd have often proved profitable for them.

In the first place, then, O blessed, 'do not grieve the Holy Spirit who has entered prison with you. For, if He had not accompanied you there in your present trial, you would not be there today. See to it, therefore, that He remain with you there and so lead you out of that place to the Lord.

Indeed, the prison is the Devil's house too, where he keeps his household. But you have come to the prison for the very purpose of trampling upon him right in his own house. For you have engaged him in battle already outside the prison and trampled him underfoot.

Let him, therefore, not say: 'Now that they are in my domain, I will tempt them with base hatreds, with defections or dissensions among themselves.' Let him flee from your presence, and let him, coiled and numb, like a snake that is driven out by charms or smoke, hide away in the depths of his den. Do not allow him the good fortune in his own kingdom of setting you against one another, but let him find you fortified by the arms of peace among yourselves, because peace among yourselves means war with him.

Some, not able to find this peace in the Church, are accustomed to seek it from the martyrs in prison. For this reason, too, then, you ought to possess, cherish and preserve it among yourselves that you may perhaps be able to bestow it upon others also.

CHAPTER 2

Other attachments, equally burdensome to the spirit, may have accompanied you to the prison gate; so far your relatives, too, may have escorted you. From that very moment on you have been separated from the very world. How much more, then, from its spirit and its ways and doings? Nor let this separation from the world trouble you. For, if we reflect that it is the very world that is more truly a prison, we shall realize that you have left a prison rather than entered one.

The world holds the greater darkness, blinding men's hearts. The world puts on the heavier chains, fettering the very souls of men. The world breathes forth the fouler impurities--human lusts.

Finally, the world contains the larger number of criminals, namely, the entire human race. In fact, it awaits sentence not from the proconsul but from God.

Wherefore, O blessed consider yourselves as having been transferred from prison to what we may call a place of safety. Darkness is there, but you are light; fetters are there, but you are free before God. It breathes forth a foul smell, but you are an odor of sweetness. There the judge is expected at every moment, but you are going to pass sentence upon the judges themselves.

There sadness may come upon the man who sighs for the pleasures of the world The Christian, however even when he is outside the prison, has re-nounced the world and, when in prison, even prison itself. It does not matter what part of the world you are in, you who are apart from the world.

And if you have missed some of the enjoyments of life, remember that it is the way of business to suffer one losses in order to make larger profits. I say nothing yet about the reward to which God invites the martyrs. Meanwhile, let us compare the life in the world with that in prison to see if the spirit does not gain more in prison than the flesh loses there.

In fact, owing to the solicitude of the Church and the charity of the breth-ren, the flesh does not miss there what it ought to have, while, in addition, the spirit obtains what is always beneficial to the faith: you do not look at strange gods; you do not chance upon their images; you do not, even by mere physical contact, participate in heathen holidays; you are not plagued by the foul fumes of the sacrificial banquets, not tormented by the noise of the spectacles, nor by the atrocity or frenzy or shamelessness of those taking part in the celebrations; your eyes do not fall on houses of lewdness; you are free from inducements to sin, from temptations, from unholy reminiscences, free, indeed, even from persecution.

The prison now offers to the Christian what the desert once gave to the Prophets. Our Lord Himself quite often spent time in solitude to pray there more freely, to be there away from the world. In fact, it was in a secluded place that He manifested His glory to His disciples. Let us drop the name 'prison' and call it a place of seclusion.

Though the body is confined, though the flesh is detained, there is nothing that is not open to the spirit. In spirit wander about, in spirit take a walk, setting before yourselves not shady promenades and long porticoes but that path which leads to God. As often as you walk that path, you will not be in prison.

The leg does not feel the fetter when the spirit is in heaven. The spirit carries about the whole man and brings him wherever he wishes. And where your heart is, there will your treasure be also. There, then, let our heart be where we would have our treasure.

CHAPTER 3

Granted now, O blessed, that even to Christians the prison is unpleasant--yet, we were called to the service in the army of the living God in the very moment when we gave response to the words of the sacramental oath. No soldier goes out to war encumbered with luxuries, nor does he march to the line of battle from the sleeping chamber, but from light and cramped tents where every kind of austerity, discomfort, and inconvenience is experienced.

Even in time of peace soldiers are toughened to warfare by toils and hardships: by marching in arms, by practicing swift maneuvers in the field, by digging a trench, by joining closely together to form a tortoise-shield. Everything is set in sweating toil, lest bodies and minds be frightened at having to pass from shade to sunshine, from sunshine to icy cold, from the tunic to the breastplate, from hushed silence to the warcry, from rest to the din of battle.

In like manner, O blessed, consider whatever is hard in your present situation as an exercise of your powers of mind and body. You are about to enter a noble contest in which the living God acts the part of superintendent and the Holy Spirit is your trainer, a contest whose crown is eternity, whose prize is angelic nature, citizenship in heaven and glory for ever and ever.

And so your Master, Jesus Christ, who has anointed you with His Spirit and has brought you to this training ground, has resolved, before the day of the contest, to take you from a softer way of life to a harsher treatment that your strength may be increased. For athletes, too, are set apart for more rigid training that they may apply themselves to the building up of their physical strength. They are kept from lavish living, from more tempting dishes, from more pleasurable drinks. They are urged on, they are subjected to torturing toils, they are worn out: the more strenuously they have exerted themselves, the greater is their hope of victory.

And they do this, says the Apostle, to win a perishable crown. We who are about to win an eternal one recognize in the prison our training ground, that we may be led forth to the actual contest before the seat of the presiding judge well practiced in all hardships, because strength is built up by austerity, but destroyed by softness.

CHAPTER 4

We know from our Lord's teaching that, while the spirit is willing, the flesh is weak. Let us, however, not derive delusive gratification from the Lord's acknowledgment of the weakness of the flesh. For it was on purpose that He first declared the spirit willing: He wanted to show which of the two ought to be subject to the other, that is to say, that the flesh should be submissive to the spirit, the weaker to the stronger, so that the former may draw strength from the latter.

Let the spirit converse with the flesh on their common salvation, no longer thinking about the hardships of prison but, rather, about the struggle of the actual contest. The flesh will perhaps fear the heavy sword and the lofty cross and the wild beasts mad with rage and the most terrible punishment of all--death by fire--and, finally, all the executioner's cunning during the torture.

But let the spirit present to both itself and the flesh the other side of the picture: granted, these sufferings are grievous, yet many have borne them patiently nay, have even sought them on their own accord for the sake of fame and glory; and this is true not only of men but also of women so that you, too, O blessed women may be worthy of your sex.

It would lead me too far were I to enumerate each one of those who, led by the impulse of their own mind put an end to their lives by the sword. Among women there is the well-known instance of Lucretia. A victim of violence, she stabbed herself in the presence of her kinsfolk to gain glory for her chastity. Mucius burnt his right hand on the altar that his fair fame might include this deed.

Nor did the philosophers act less courageously: Heraclitus, for instance, who put an end to his life by smearing himself with cow dung ; Empedocles, too, who leaped down into the fires of Mt. Etna; and Peregrinus who not long ago threw himself upon a funeral pile. Why, even women have despised the flames:

Dido did so in order not to be forced to marry after the departure of the man she had loved most dearly; the wife of Hasdrubal, too, with Carthage in flames, cast herself along with her children into the fire that was destroying her native city, that she might not see her husband a suppliant at Scipio's feet.

Regulus, a Roman general, was taken prisoner by the Carthaginians, but refused to be the only Roman exchanged for a large number of Carthaginian captives. He preferred to be returned to the enemy, and, crammed into a kind of chest, suffered as many crucifixions as nails were driven in from the outside in all directions to pierce him. A woman voluntarily sought out wild beasts, namely, vipers, serpents more horrible than either bull or bear, which Cleopatra let loose upon herself as not to fall into the hands of the enemy.

You may object: 'But the fear of death is not so great as the fear of torture.' Did the Athenian courtesan yield on that account to the executioner? For, being privy to a conspiracy, she was subjected to torture by the tyrant. But she did not betray her fellow conspirators, and at last bit off her own tongue and spat it into the tyrant's face to let him know that torments, however prolonged, could achieve nothing against her.

Everybody knows that to this day the most important festival of the Lacedaemonians is the "diamastigosis," that is, The Whipping. In this sacred rite all the noble youth are scourged with whips before the altar, while their parents and kinsfolk stand by and exhort them to perseverance. For they regard it as a mark of greater distinction and glory if the soul rather than the body has submitted to the stripes.

Therefore, if earthly glory accruing from strength of body and soul is valued so highly that one despises sword, fire, piercing with nails, wild beasts and tortures for the reward of human praise, then I may say the sufferings you endure are but trifling in comparison with the heavenly glory and divine reward. If the bead made of glass is rated so highly, how much must the true pearl be worth? Who, therefore, does not most gladly spend as much for the true as others spend for the false?

CHAPTER 5

I omit here an account of the motive of glory. For inordinate ambition among men as well as a certain morbidity of mind have already set at naught all the cruel and torturing contests mentioned above. How many of the leisure class are urged by an excessive love of arms to become gladiators? Surely it is from vanity that they descend to the wild beasts in the very arena, and think themselves more handsome because of the bites and scars. Some have even hired themselves out to tests by fire, with the result that they ran a certain distance in a burning tunic. Others have pranced up and down amid the bullwhips of the animal-baiters, unflinchingly exposing their shoulders.

All this, O blessed, the Lord tolerates in the world for good reason, that is, for the sake of encouraging us in the present moment and of confounding us on that final day, if we have recoiled from suffering for the truth unto salvation what others have pursued out of vanity unto perdition.

CHAPTER 6

Let us, however, no longer talk about those examples of perseverance proceeding from inordinate ambition. Let us, rather, turn to a simple contemplation of man's ordinary lot so that, if we ever have to undergo such trials with fortitude, we may also learn from those misfortunes which sometimes even befall unwilling victims. For how often have people been burned to death in conflagrations! How often have wild beasts devoured men either in the forests or in the heart of cities after escaping from their cages! How many have been slain by the sword of robbers! How many have even suffered the death of the cross at the hands of enemies, after having been tortured first and, indeed, treated with every kind of insult!

Furthermore, many a man is able to suffer in the cause of a mere human being what he hesitates to suffer in the cause of God. To this fact, indeed, our present days may bear witness. How many prominent persons have met with death in the cause of a man, though such a fate seemed most unlikely in view of their birth and their rank, their physical condition and their age! Death came to them either from him, if they had opposed him, or from his enemies, if they had sided with him.